Evictions
in Scotland

This edition is dedicated to the memory of my mother,
Jean-Anne Stalker

Evictions in Scotland

Second edition

Adrian Stalker
Advocate

EDINBURGH
University Press

Edinburgh University Press is one of the leading university presses in the UK. We publish academic books and journals in our selected subject areas across the humanities and social sciences, combining cutting-edge scholarship with high editorial and production values to produce academic works of lasting importance. For more information visit our website: edinburghuniversitypress.com

First edition published 2007 by Avizandum Publishing Ltd

Edinburgh University Press Ltd
The Tun – Holyrood Road
12 (2f) Jackson's Entry
Edinburgh EH8 8PJ
www.euppublishing.com

Typeset in 10/11 Plantin by
Servis Filmsetting Ltd, Stockport, Cheshire
and printed and bound by CPI Group (UK) Ltd,
Croydon, CR0 4YY

A CIP record for this book is available from the British Library

ISBN 978 1 4744 8216 5 (paperback)
ISBN 978 1 4744 8271 4 (webready PDF)
ISBN 978 1 4744 8270 7 (epub)

Contents

Preface

It has been 13 years since the publication of the first edition – a longer period than I had originally envisaged. A draft of the second edition was completed in January 2015, which took into account various important changes in the law since 2007, including the introduction of pre-action requirements in rent arrears cases in the social rented sector, the human rights jurisprudence following *Manchester City Council v Pinnock*, and the changes to be made by the Housing (Scotland) Act 2014. However, that draft was shelved when it became apparent that the Scottish Government was shortly to introduce a wholly new form of tenancy in the private rented sector, under what became the Private Housing (Tenancies) (Scotland) Act 2016.

This now seems as good a time as any to publish a new edition, though that is not to say that the dust has settled. In due course, the summary cause procedure in the sheriff court will finally be abolished, and eviction proceedings in that forum will be conducted under the new Simple Procedure (Special Claims) Rules. It is also to be hoped that some of the questions raised in the chapters dealing with private-sector cases in the First-tier Tribunal will be resolved by the Upper Tribunal in the coming years. In April 2020, schedule 1 of the Coronavirus (Scotland) Act 2020 came into force. This affords additional protection to tenants in eviction proceedings. The relevant measures are intended to be temporary. They are discussed in the appendix. Subsequently, further changes were made by primary and secondary legislation (with effect from the beginning of October 2020), which came too late to be included in the text. An update on all legislative changes made up to the date of publication is available to readers on the EUP website, at https://edinburghuniversitypress.com/book-evictions-in-scotland.html

I would like to thank Aileen Devanny, Neil Kinnear, David Anderson, Rory Cowan, Jim Bauld, Claire Mullen, David Bartos and Chris Ryan, all of whom were kind enough to comment on draft chapters. I am especially indebted to Fiona McPhail, my most recent successor as Principal Solicitor at Shelter Housing Law Service, not only for commenting on draft chapters, but for keeping me abreast of what is happening on the ground now that I am no longer involved in the day-to-day practice of litigating eviction proceedings in the sheriff court. I am grateful also to Margaret Cherry and Laura Williamson of EUP for their patience and support, and to EUP for agreeing to publish the second edition. Finally, I thank my wife, Tiziana, the *sine qua non* of this and all my other endeavours.

All errors are mine. I have sought to state the law as at 31 May 2020.

Table of Statutes

Table of Statutory Instruments

Table of European Legislation

Table of Cases

[Note: Citations in the form: "EV/19/0001, 1/1/20" are decisions made by the First-tier Tribunal Housing and Property Chamber. The full decision can be found on the Chamber's website.]

Introduction

Any owner[1] wishing to recover possession of heritable property from its occupier, or any occupier wishing to remain in possession, will have to consider one or more of the following questions:

1. Is it possible to evict the occupier without legal proceedings?
2. If legal proceedings are necessary, what steps must be taken before those proceedings are raised?
3. In those proceedings, what must be established before an eviction order can be granted, and on what basis may the granting of the order be resisted?

The purpose of this book to consider how those questions should be answered.

There are basically three types of lease in Scotland: agricultural, residential and commercial. Both agricultural leases and residential leases are heavily regulated by statute, while commercial leases are, on the whole, unregulated.[2] This book is concerned with residential property, and particularly issues relating to, or arising from, termination of leases of residential property, and the eviction proceedings that follow. That is because the vast majority of actions for recovery of possession of residential property are against tenants; and the legal protection from eviction given to tenants is much more extensive, and thus stands in need of lengthier consideration.

In **Chapter 1**, some historical context is given, which, it is hoped, will be of assistance to the reader in understanding the discussion in later chapters. In particular, an outline is given of two main themes: the development of Scots law in relation to evictions, and statutory security of tenure. Also, certain important concepts are considered. Much of the legislation analysed in this book extends protection to tenants and other occupiers on the basis that they have some relationship, variously described as "occupying", or "residing in", with a "home", "house", "dwelling" or "residence". These terms are fundamental to the subject, and are therefore considered at the outset.

Chapter 2 then discusses the first of the three questions above by way of an analysis of unlawful eviction and, in particular, Part III of the Rent (Scotland)

1 Throughout this book, unless otherwise indicated, the term "owner" is used in the same sense as in s 23(3) of the Rent (Scotland) Act 1984, denoting the person who, in relation to premises, is entitled, as against the occupier, to possession thereof.

2 The distinction made in the older authorities was between "rural" and "urban" leases. A rural lease is one where the main subject let is the use of the *solum* or ground and what is naturally on it or below it. An urban lease is one where the main subject is what has been put on the ground artificially, such as buildings. With the introduction of the Rent Acts in the early twentieth century, "urban" leases of residential property became subject to different legal rules.

Act 1984: "Protection against harassment and eviction without due process of law."

Chapter 3 begins the answer to the second of the three questions. It serves as an introduction to the issue of pre-action notices. For readers new to the subject, the first part of this chapter should be useful, in outlining the notices that it is necessary to serve in relation to the various forms of statutory and non-statutory tenancies. The chapter then goes on to examine the difficult issue of termination of tenancy contracts. In many cases, such termination is a necessary preliminary to an action for recovery of possession. Particular attention is given to notices to quit, and termination prior to the natural term of the lease, especially by irritancy or rescission.

Apart from termination of the tenancy, other procedural steps may have to be taken before the action is raised, because the tenancy in question is subject to one of the statutory schemes that give security of tenure to tenants. In particular, two issues arise: whether the tenancy in question is a tenancy covered by the relevant legislation and, if it is, what steps are prescribed.

Chapter 4 looks at the requirements of the Housing (Scotland) Act 2001, which applies to tenancies in the social rented sector, by analysing the qualifying conditions for the creation of Scottish secure tenancies under that Act, and the notice that must be given to the tenant before eviction proceedings may be raised. Consideration is also given to the "pre-action" requirements introduced by the Housing (Scotland) Act 2010, which apply to actions in which the ground for possession (or one of the grounds) is rent arrears. Chapter 4 also looks at the procedure under sections 17–19 of the 2001 Act, by which a social landlord may recover possession of tenancy property without court proceedings, where it appears to have been abandoned by the tenant and is no longer occupied.

Chapter 5 considers the last of the three questions, in relation to Scottish secure tenancies under the 2001 Act, by examining the statutory grounds for recovery of possession together with any additional requirement that the Act lays down in respect of those grounds.[3]

Chapter 6 analyses the statutory code applying to short Scottish secure tenancies ("SSST"s) in sections 34–37 of the 2001 Act. The SSST is a special type of statutory tenancy granted by social landlords, in circumstances in which it is considered inappropriate to offer full security of tenure to the tenant.

Chapters 7 and 8 look at assured and short assured tenancies under the Housing (Scotland) Act 1988. **Chapter 7** analyses the qualifying conditions which existed for the creation of those tenancies, and the notices that must be given to the tenant in terms of the Act, before eviction proceedings may be raised. It also considers the various steps that must be taken in making an application to the First-tier Tribunal (Housing and Property Chamber) for an order for possession. At the end of the chapter, the statutory arrangements for the transition from the assured tenancy regime to the private residential tenancy under the Private Housing (Tenancies) (Scotland) Act 2016 are

3 In actions for recovery of possession of Scottish secure tenancies under s 16 of the 2001 Act, the additional requirement for grounds 1–7 is that the court must be satisfied that "it is reasonable to make the order". For grounds 8–14, the court must be satisfied that: "other suitable accommodation will be available for the tenant when the order takes effect".

analysed. **Chapter 8** examines the statutory grounds for recovery of possession of assured tenancies.

Chapters 9 and 10 consider the process of obtaining an eviction order in relation to a private residential tenancy under the 2016 Act. **Chapter 9** analyses the qualifying conditions for the creation of that tenancy, the "notice to leave" that must be given to the tenant, and various steps that must be taken in making an application to the tribunal. **Chapter 10** examines the statutory grounds for granting an eviction order.

Chapter 11 concerns a special type of defence that may be pled in eviction proceedings, in which the defender may argue that, in terminating his tenancy (or right of occupation), or raising eviction proceedings, or pursuing those proceedings, the pursuer/owner is acting unlawfully, or that it would be an unlawful violation of his rights for an order for possession to be granted. In particular, he may rely on "public law" arguments of the type that would usually feature in judicial review proceedings, or on the Human Rights Act 1998 or the Equality Act 2010.

Chapter 12 considers the rights of various classes of occupier, apart from tenants: (1) sub-tenants; (2) putative successors to tenancies under the 1988, 2001 and 2016 Acts; (3) non-entitled spouses under the Matrimonial Homes (Family Protection) (Scotland) Act 1981; (4) qualifying occupiers under the 2001 Act; (5) occupiers under contracts that are not tenancies, such as occupancy agreements, licences, service occupancies (tied tenancies) and tenancies where services are rendered in lieu of rent; and (6) hostel dwellers.

Chapter 13 is concerned with proceedings in the sheriff court, in particular the summary cause rules that are of particular importance to eviction proceedings.[4]

Chapter 14 is concerned with applications to the First-tier Tribunal (Housing and Property Chamber), in particular the provisions of the tribunal's Procedure Rules that are of importance to eviction cases.

Chapter 15 first considers certain issues that can arise in eviction proceedings, being: title of the pursuer or applicant; the mode of service of notices, and proof of their content; and violent profits, payment in respect of occupation, and caution for pecuniary claims. This chapter goes on discuss what happens after the decree or order is granted, in particular as regards the law applicable to the enforcement of decrees and orders in eviction cases.

The appendix is a briefing note prepared by the author, at the beginning of April 2020, for legal members of the First-tier Tribunal, on the changes temporarily made to eviction proceedings by the Coronavirus (Scotland) Act 2020. As these changes are time limited and expected to expire, at the latest, on 30 September 2021, they are considered in the appendix rather than in the main text, which makes no reference to the 2020 Act.

4 Under the Sheriff Courts (Scotland) Act 1971, s 35(1)(c), actions for recovery of possession of heritable property must be raised as summary causes. That rule and the exceptions to it are discussed at the beginning of Chapter 13.

GENERAL COMMENTS AS TO CONTENT

The content of this book is a reflection of the author's practice as the principal solicitor of Shelter's Housing Law Service between 1999 and 2006, and his subsequent practice at the Bar. Issues that have arisen frequently in that practice are examined in detail, whereas other questions that have seldom or never arisen are given more cursory consideration.

The major casualty of this approach is the statutory regime for regulated tenancies under the Rent (Scotland) Act 1984, about which a great deal has already been written. Given that only a small number of these tenancies now remain,[5] it was considered reasonable to refer readers to other works that deal with regulated tenancies.[6] That said, a general overview of the Rent Acts is given in Chapter 1.[7]

As this book concerns recovery of possession of residential property, there is no coverage of agricultural or commercial tenancies, though cases involving such tenancies are discussed in so far as they are relevant to residential tenancies. There is also no discussion of legal proceedings that might ultimately result in the eviction of the owner of residential property, such as in the case of mortgage repossession, bankruptcy, civil recovery under the Proceeds of Crime legislation, and so on.

REFERENCES

In various parts of the text, the following Acts are referred to as "the 1984 Act", "the 1988 Act" and so on:

- Rent (Scotland) Act 1984;
- Housing (Scotland) Act 1987;
- Housing (Scotland) Act 1988;
- Housing (Scotland) Act 2001;
- Housing (Scotland) Act 2014; and
- Private Housing (Tenancies) (Scotland) Act 2016.

A "PRT" is a private residential tenancy, under the 2016 Act. An "SSST" is a short Scottish secure tenancy, under sections 34–37 of the 2001 Act.

"RSL" means "registered social landlord", being a body that is included in the register of social landlords kept by the Scottish Housing Regulator, under section 20 of the Housing (Scotland) Act 2010. Most RSLs are housing associations.

5 The 1988 Act provided for the phasing out of regulated tenancies: since 2 January 1989, it has been possible to create a new tenancy covered by the 1984 Act only in the very limited circumstances set out in the 1988 Act, ss 42–46. See the discussion of the transition from the 1984 Act to the 1988 Act, and from the 1988 Act to the 2016 Act regimes at the end of Chapter 7.

6 Such as Megarry, *The Rent Acts* (11th edn); A G M Duncan and J A D Hope QC:,*The Rent (Scotland) Act 1984*; Robson and Combe, *Residential Tenancies* (4th edn) particularly at appendix 3); and McAllister, *Scottish Law of Leases* (4th edn, 2013) 428–447.

7 At the end of Chapter 7, consideration is also given to the effect of the parties to a regulated tenancy bringing it to an end and replacing it with a short assured tenancy.

FTT means "First-tier Tribunal". A reference to the "Procedure Rules" denotes the rules contained in the schedule to the First-tier Tribunal for Scotland Housing and Property Chamber (Procedure) Regulations 2017, as amended.[8]

Many important provisions in this legislation, particularly the older Acts, have equivalent provisions, which are the same or very similar, in the housing legislation that applies to England and Wales.[9] Where appropriate, reference is made to legislation and case law from that jurisdiction. With apologies to Welsh readers, the text refers to the "English" legislation, for the sake of brevity.

"The Convention" or "ECHR" denotes the European Convention on Human Rights, and "ECtHR" the European Court of Human Rights.

For much of this book, an approach has been adopted of setting out the text of a section from a statute and then analysing it detail.[10] As to the status of that commentary, readers are reminded of Lord Diplock's observation: "The persuasive effect of learned commentaries, like the arguments of counsel in . . . court, will depend on the cogency of their reasoning."[11] The complexity of housing legislation, and its interaction with Scots common law, gives rise to some thorny problems, with which the author has attempted to grapple. No doubt readers will critically examine his reasoning, and come to their own views.

8 SSI 2017/328.

9 In particular, the Housing Acts of 1985, 1988 and 1996.

10 In some cases, however, where the provisions are very lengthy, a summary is given.

11 *Fothergill v Monarch Airlines Ltd* [1981] AC 251, 284.

Chapter 1

Historical Context and Important Concepts

The purpose of this chapter is twofold: to aid understanding by enabling the reader to view subsequent material in a historical context; and to consider the scope of concepts, such as "occupation" and "home", that are fundamental to the statutory regimes for security of tenure.

HISTORY

Two themes are considered in this section: the development of Scots law in relation to evictions:[1] and statutory security of tenure.

Scots law in relation to evictions

Pre-1900

Statutory regulation of evictions in Scotland began with the Act of 1555 (c 39), which was passed, as Rankine put it, "in order to rid the country of the violence which was a usual accompaniment of the older removings[2] (often of the most wholesale kind) on verbal warning only".[3] The Act required that lawful warning should be made to the tenant in the form of a precept from the landlord, which was served at any time in the year up to forty days before Whitsunday[4] and published within the local parish church. If the tenant did not remove at the term, the landlord had to obtain a decree for removing in the Court of Session. Thereafter, upon executing and registering a charge on that decree, the landlord had to apply directly to the local sheriff for a warrant of ejection.[5]

1 For readers interested in the historical development of eviction proceedings, the Scottish Law Commission's *Discussion Paper on Aspects of Leases: Termination* (Scot Law Com No 165, 2018) is recommended, particularly ch 3. It is available on the SLC's website: https://www.scotlawcom.gov.uk/law-reform/law-reform-projects/proprietary-aspect-of-leases/. The discussion paper focuses on commercial leases, but its account of the history leading up to the Sheriff Courts (Scotland) Act 1907 is equally applicable to urban leases of residential property.

2 In Scots law, "removing" is the technical term for the giving up of possession by a tenant, whether voluntarily or enforced at the instance of the landlord.

3 Rankine, *Leases* (3rd edn, 1916) 550. See also the quotation from Stair's *Institutions* at the end of Chapter 2.

4 I.e. 15 May, after the Acts of 1690 (c 39) and 1693 (c 24).

5 Rankine, *Leases* 552, where the author also describes an alternative and no less cumbersome procedure that was available to the landlord under the Act, in terms of which he proceeded by letters of removing obtained on a bill presented in the Bill Chamber.

Two features of this process are notable, because they were to become important characteristics of the procedure for evictions under Scots law. First, the purpose of giving adequate notice to the tenant is achieved by a stipulation that warning is given on a period of notice of forty days before the date on which the tenancy is to end. Secondly, the landlord's notice has two effects: it will not only prevent tacit relocation from taking place; it will also initiate the process of removing under the Act. As will be seen, this creates a distinction between (a) notice that merely has the effect of preventing tacit relocation,[6] which may be served by a tenant as well as a landlord, and (b) a notice that, in addition to preventing tacit relocation, also forms the first step in a process of removing outlined in a particular piece of legislation.

Between 1555 and 1900, the rules were modified in piecemeal fashion. Because the notice procedure under the 1555 Act was cumbersome, a simpler process was introduced by an Act of Sederunt of 1756, which was held to be limited to the jurisdiction of the Judge Ordinary (a sheriff).[7] As a result, the Act of 1555 fell into desuetude.[8]

The 1555 Act and the 1756 Act of Sederunt applied only to tenancies of agricultural land. At common law the rules as to removings from urban subjects depended on the custom of the locality in which the buildings were situated. In the case of subjects in a burgh, the practice was for the burgh officer to chalk the most patent door of the building in the presence of one witness forty days before the term of removing, which was normally Whitsunday.[9] Thereafter, in the event that the tenant failed to remove, the landlord proceeded to raise an action in the local sheriff court, which was described as a "summary removing".[10]

The 1907 Act

These various procedures were considered to be overly elaborate and slow. Sections 34–38 of the Sheriff Courts (Scotland) Act 1907 were designed to address this problem by allowing for the eviction process to be truncated. In particular, the purpose of sections 36–38 of the Act was to enable the landlord, following service of the requisite notice of removal, to utilise a form of action in which the decree for removing and the warrant for ejection could be obtained in a single process. The 1907 Act continued the pattern initiated by the Act of 1555, by allowing for a period of notice of forty days, and providing for a form of notice that both prevented tacit relocation and commenced the removal process.

Unfortunately, the 1907 Act's new scheme for removings caused as many problems as it solved. The first important case in which it was discussed

6 Tacit relocation is considered in the introduction to the Termination of Leases, at p 51.

7 *Cameron v McDonald* (1804) Mor 13875.

8 It was subsequently repealed by the Statute Law Revision (Scotland) Act 1964.

9 Rankine (n 5) 559.

10 As Rankine points out at 558, the term "summary" in this context did not indicate a truncated procedure, but was simply used to distinguish between "solemn" removings under the 1555 Act or the 1756 Act of Sederunt and all other removings; where the necessity for an action of removing existed, all such actions initiated in the sheriff court were treated in the same fashion.

was *Campbell's Trustees v O'Neill.*[11] Lord Johnston's opinion begins with the statement:[12]

> "The Sheriff Courts Act 1907, in sections 34–38, makes provision for removings which, whether intended as a complete code or not, is manifestly very incomplete. . . . The result has been, I am persuaded, to throw the whole matter, which was by no means devoid of confusion at any rate, into still greater confusion."[13]

Law reform; "removing" and "ejection"

Among the first tasks entrusted to the Law Reform Committee for Scotland appointed in 1954 was the consideration of the procedural law relating to evictions.[14] At that time, the principal problem in this area was considered to be the difficulty surrounding the distinction between actions of removing and actions of ejection, and the circumstances in which such actions should be raised. The term "removing" refers, in a wider sense, to the relinquishing of possession of subjects, either voluntarily or compulsorily, by a person who has, or had, a right of occupation. In a narrower sense, it refers to the process (an action for removing) by means of which an occupier whose right of occupation has expired is judicially warned to remove from the subjects occupied by him, and the right that he formerly possessed is judicially cut down.[15] "Ejection" denotes the process by means of which a person is ejected from the subjects by officers of the court, either where he had a title but it has already been judicially cut down, or where he never had any title to occupy at all.[16] However, there are situations in which it is difficult to judge which action is appropriate to the circumstances. In particular, there had been instances in which an action for ejection was competent, although the occupier had previously possessed a right to occupy, such as a service occupier;[17] a licensee;[18] or the previous owner of property where a disposition had been delivered to the purchaser.[19]

As the remedies of ejection and removing cannot be pled as alternatives in the one action, this led to situations in which the wrong alternative was chosen, leading to the action being dismissed as incompetent, irrespective of its other merits.[20] Accordingly, the first and most important proposal of the

11 1911 SC 188; also reported as *Watson's Trustees v O'Neill* at 1910 2 SLT 392.

12 At 192.

13 In *Brown Ltd v Collier* 1954 SLT (Sh Ct) 98, Sheriff Substitute Murray expressed the view that the drafter of s 37 "certainly did not deserve a pass in the Scottish Leaving Certificate Examination". See also the discussion in *Lormor Ltd v Glasgow City Council* 2014 SLT 1055.

14 The Committee's report is published as Cmnd 114 (1957).

15 See the *Encyclopaedia of the Laws of Scotland* vol 6, para 265; as discussed in *Bradford and Bingley Building Society v Roddy* 1987 SLT (Sh Ct) 109. For the distinction between "ordinary removing" and "extraordinary removing", see Chapter 3, p 52.

16 Thus "ejection" can refer to two different processes: (1) the purely accessory proceedings by means of which a decree of removing, or other process equivalent to a decree of removing, is carried into effect where the occupant refuses or delays to quit possession of the subjects; or (2) an independent action by means of which a person possessing no right or title to occupy is put out without the necessity of any previous process of removing.

17 *Cairns v Innes* 1942 SC 164, 1942 SLT 129.

18 *Asher v Macleod* 1948 SC 55; 1948 SLT 227; *Wallace v Simmers* 1960 SC 255, 1961 SLT 34.

19 *Scottish Property Investment Co Building Society v Horne* (1881) 8 R 737.

20 A leading example is *Lowe v Gardiner* 1921 SC 211, (1921) 1 SLT 44, in which an action of ejection was raised against the purchaser of subjects under missives for sale, on the basis that he was said to be in precarious possession due to his failure to make payment of the purchase

Law Reform Committee's report was the recommendation that one form of action should be provided for all cases where recovery of possession of heritable property from an occupier was sought. This proposal was subsequently endorsed by the Grant Committee on Sheriff Court Procedure[21] and eventually received effect in the Sheriff Courts (Scotland) Act 1971, the Act that created the summary cause as a form of process. Under section 35(1)(c) of the 1971 Act, "actions for the recovery of possession . . . of heritable property" were to be raised as summary causes.[22] The rules provided that a decree for the recovery of possession in a summary cause was to have the same force and effect as a decree of removing or a decree of ejection.[23]

However, certain other important recommendations of the Committee went unimplemented, in particular as to: (a) the period, form and content of notices terminating tenancies; (b) the right or title of parties to give notice and initiate proceedings; and (c) the effect of decree in those proceedings.

These and other issues were revisited by the Law Commission in the 1980s, leading to its report *Recovery of Possession of Heritable Property.*[24] The report's opening remarks under the heading "Background" are worth quoting:

> "The general law relating to recovery of possession of heritable property . . . is in an unsatisfactory state. The problems associated with this branch of the law arise from statute, from the common law and from case law. Statute law is unquestionably the main source of difficulty, in particular the Sheriff Courts (Scotland) Act 1907. The provisions in the 1907 Act are unnecessarily complicated and can lead to confusion, particularly in regard to the statutory forms of notice to quit, the number and variety of periods of such notice and the processes by which questions relating to removing and ejection are brought before the court."

The report recommended the repeal of sections 34–38A of the 1907 Act, and included a draft Removing From Heritable Property (Scotland) Bill. However, the Bill was never enacted.[25]

price. With some considerable reluctance, the Inner House ultimately sustained the defender's plea to the competency of the action; Lord President Clyde called for the legislature to consider changes to the law at the earliest opportunity.

21 Cmnd 3248 (1967).

22 Except where the pursuer sought, in addition to an order for recovery of possession, decree for payment of money exceeding £1,500 (subsequently raised to £5,000). This provision gave rise to some difficulty in relation to cases in which a party wished to raise an action seeking an order for recovery of possession together with another order that cannot be sought in summary cause proceedings, such as declarator or interdict. This issue will be discussed in Chapter 13.

23 Under r 69 of the original Summary Cause Rules (Act of Sederunt (Summary Cause Rules, Sheriff Court) 1976 (SI 1976/476)). The Rules were substantially overhauled by the Act of Sederunt (Summary Cause Rules) 2002 (SSI 2002/132). The provision equivalent to r 69 is r 30.3 in the 2002 Rules, which provides that the decree is to have the same force and effect as a summary warrant of ejection, a warrant for summary ejection in common form or a decree pronounced in a summary application for removing under ss 36, 37 and 38 respectively of the 1907 Act.

24 (Scot Law Com No 118, 1989, preceded in 1984 by A G M Duncan, *Research Paper on Actions of Ejection and Removing* , and the Commission's Consultative Memorandum No 59.

25 More recently, the SLC's *Discussion Paper on Aspects of Leases: Termination* (n 1) has sought views on proposals for reform of the law on tacit relocation and notices to quit, in relation to commercial leases.

STATUTORY SECURITY OF TENURE[26]

The Rent Acts

Rent control was introduced in Great Britain by the Increase of Rent and Mortgage Interest (War Restrictions) Act 1915. Some measure of security of tenure was then added by the Increase of Rent, &c Act 1919, and by the Increase of Rent and Mortgage Interest (Restrictions) Act 1920.

Over the next 70 years further legislation, known collectively as "the Rent Acts", was enacted, ending with the Rent (Scotland) Act 1984, which consolidated all the existing legislation that applied to Scotland.[27] Two principal features of the protection afforded to tenants have evolved under the Acts. First, the tenant may apply for a "fair rent" to be registered. Secondly, the tenant is entitled to remain in the tenancy after his lease has been terminated. At the point of termination, the tenant ceases to occupy by virtue of his rights under that contract, and thereafter occupies under a statutory tenancy, the terms of which are, subject to a few exceptions, the same as the parties' original contract. These points were neatly summed up by Lord Justice Scrutton in one of the earliest Rent Acts cases:

> "The object of the various Rent Restrictions Acts is clear. It was intended to prevent the tenant from having his rent raised against him, or from being turned out, though his tenancy by agreement had expired, so long as he was willing to pay the rent authorised by statute."[28]

The landlord cannot recover possession of a tenancy subject to the Rent Acts protection (described by the 1984 Act as a "regulated" tenancy), except by an order from the court, which cannot be made until the requirements of the legislation are met. The 1984 Act requires the landlord to establish one of the grounds for recovery of possession listed in schedule 2. In addition, in relation to some of those grounds he must also establish that granting the order would be *reasonable*. As will be seen, this latter test is of considerable importance.[29]

It has been said of the Rent Acts that they had "not been framed with any scientific accuracy of language",[30] and that it is essential "that, wherever possible, [they] should be construed in a broad, practical, common-sense manner so as to give effect to the intention of the Legislature".[31] The Acts have also long held a reputation for difficulty and complexity.[32]

26 What follows is a short history of security of tenure in relation to residential property. A more comprehensive account is given in Robson and Combe, *Residential Tenancies* (4th edn, 2019) ch 1.

27 In Scotland, the Rent Acts had previously been consolidated by the Rent (Scotland) Act 1971, which was updated by the 1984 Act.

28 *Remon v City of London Real Property Co Ltd* [1921] 1 KB 49, 57.

29 The requirement that the order must be reasonable was introduced by the Rent and Mortgage Interest (Restrictions) Act 1933.

30 Sargant LJ in *Roe v Russell* [1928] 2 KB 117, 138.

31 McCardie J in *Read v Goater* [1921] 1 KB 611, 615. This purposive approach to the Rent Acts was re-emphasised by the House of Lords in *Cadogan Estates Ltd v McMahon* [2001] 1 AC 378; see, in particular, the opinions of Lord Hoffmann and Lord Hutton.

32 In his great work on the Rent Acts, Sir Robert Megarry said: "latterly they have been recognised as forming a more enduring part of the present social structure, deplorable in their complexity, yet affecting the lives of millions . . . the increasing prolixity of the Acts . . . bear

The Rent Acts came to encompass aims other than the regulation of rent and security of tenure. For example, unlawful eviction was proscribed for the first time by the Rent Act 1965, and further legislation in this area was enacted in 1984 and 1988.[33] Another important step was the introduction, by section 16 of the Rent Act 1957, of certain requirements for notices to quit, including a minimum period of notice of four weeks. This provision, which is now section 112 of the 1984 Act, is considered in Chapter 3.

Housing (Scotland) Act 1988

With the Housing (Scotland) Act 1988 the Conservative Government of the day replaced the Rent Acts system with a new "assured" tenancy, which, being more favourable to the landlord, was intended to have the effect of stimulating the market in private-sector letting. The general scheme of the previous legislation was preserved,[34] subject to several important changes. First, rather than a "fair rent", assured tenants were entitled to seek a "market rent",[35] which would be higher. Secondly, the Act introduced provisions that made it easier for the landlord to obtain an eviction order. In particular, new grounds for eviction were introduced, which were easier to establish.[36] Thirdly, the Act provided for a special type of assured tenancy called a "short assured tenancy", in respect of which the court could order recovery of possession after termination of the tenancy at the ish, on being satisfied that the landlord had met certain procedural requirements. This meant that the landlord of a short assured tenancy would not be required to establish that he had any particular ground for recovery of possession, or that it would be reasonable to grant the order.[37]

However, the Act also set up a new hurdle for landlords. Under section 19, the landlord is required to serve a notice of proceedings for possession, which warns the tenant of his intention to raise an action, states the statutory ground on which the order will be sought, and advises the tenant of the date after which proceedings will be raised. This new notice was modelled on the notice of proceedings for recovery of possession that local authority landlords were required to serve on their tenants, which is discussed below.[38]

The 1988 Act provided for the phasing out of regulated tenancies: since 2 January 1989 it has been possible to create a new tenancy subject to the 1984

witness to the manifold difficulties of achieving substantial justice without undue elaboration and complication" (*The Rent Acts* (11th edn) 12).

33 Unlawful eviction will be discussed in Chapter 2.

34 For that reason, it is submitted that the purposive approach to interpreting the Rent Acts, described above, is also appropriate in relation to the 1988 Act.

35 Unlike "fair rent", "market rent" is not a term that appears in the legislation; it has been used as a shorthand way of describing the way in which rent is assessed under the 1988 Act.

36 Robson and Combe (n 26) contains, in appendix 4, a table that compares the various grounds for eviction under the 1984, 1988, 2001 and 2016 Acts.

37 The short assured tenancy was not entirely novel: the Tenants' Rights, Etc (Scotland) Act 1980, ss 34–36 (subsequently the 1984 Act, ss 9, 13 and 14) provided for a "short tenancy", in relation to which the landlord could recover possession after the ish without demonstrating a ground for eviction, or that it would be reasonable to grant the order. However, the minimum period for the tenancy was one year, and a fair rent for the property had to be registered at the outset. As a result of these requirements the short tenancy failed to achieve popularity.

38 The s 19 notice is not required for actions raised under s 33 of the Act: see the discussion of the latter section in Chapter 7.

Act only in very limited circumstances.[39] As a result, it is increasingly rare to encounter regulated tenancies in practice. A similar process is now taking place with assured tenancies, following the coming into force of the Private Housing (Tenancies) (Scotland) Act 2016.[40]

As is described in the following paragraphs, the 2001 Act effected a transfer of tenancies[41] to the new Scottish secure tenancy regime. Sections 12–35 of the 1988 Act thereafter applied only to private-sector landlords, who, almost without exception, opted to create the more advantageous short assured tenancy. This meant that assured tenancies (which were not short assured tenancies) were much less common.[42]

Housing (Scotland) Act 2001

Security of tenure in the public rented sector was introduced to Scotland by Part II of the Tenants' Rights, Etc (Scotland) Act 1980.[43] "Secure" tenancies afforded to tenants protection that bore strong similarities to that enjoyed by tenants under the Rent Acts. In particular, it was necessary for the landlord in eviction proceedings to establish one of the Act's grounds for recovery of possession and, in relation to some of those grounds, that it was reasonable to grant the order. The remaining grounds required the court to be satisfied that "suitable alternative accommodation" would be offered to the tenant if the eviction order was granted.[44]

However, under the 1980 Act, the relationship between the tenancy contract and the statute was fundamentally different. Under the Rent Acts and the 1988 Act, the "statutory" tenancy begins when the parties' contract ends; but the 1980 Act provided that the "secure tenancy" under the statute was to apply throughout the course of the tenancy, such that the tenant's contractual and statutory rights co-existed. Eviction actions were to be preceded by service on the tenant of a "notice of proceedings for recovery of possession". The tenancy was not terminated until the order for eviction was granted. This difference is of significant practical importance: as termination of the tenancy is not necessary before the eviction action is commenced, landlords were, for the most part, not subject to the procedural problems in relation to termination of tenancies that continued to bedevil landlords in the private sector.

The secure tenancy regime was re-enacted as Part III of the Housing (Scotland) Act 1987, which consolidated the existing legislation in relation to housing functions duties of local authorities and other public bodies. Part III of the Act continued to apply to public-sector tenancies, the vast majority of which were local authority tenancies, until 30 September 2002, when the

39 These are outlined in the 1988 Act, ss 42–46.

40 The various transitional arrangements, as between the three regimes in the private sector (the 1984, 1988 and 2016 Acts), will be examined at the end of Chapter 7.

41 "Registered social landlord": see Introduction, p 4.

42 Prior to the 2001 Act, the vast majority of housing associations had assured tenancies; short assured tenancies in this sector were unusual.

43 Prior to the 1980 Act a local authority tenant was liable to be evicted following termination of her tenancy by notice to quit. See the discussion in Chapter 11, p 370.

44 These are generally referred to as the "management grounds", as their use involves a landlord moving a tenant from one house in its stock to another.

relevant sections of the 2001 Act came into force. Subject to certain important modifications, the provisions of Part II of the 2001 Act represent a further re-enactment of the security of tenure provisions of the 1980 Act.

One of the principal aims of the 2001 Act was to achieve uniformity of tenure in what is now described as the "social rented sector". Between 1989 and 2002, most tenants of housing associations had assured tenancies under the 1988 Act. In its consultation paper "Better Homes for Scotland's Communities: The Executive's proposals for the Housing Bill", the Scottish Executive argued that this created anomalous situations in which tenants of different "social" landlords, perhaps living in close proximity to one another in houses of identical design, were subject to different forms of tenancy, as a result of which one tenant's rights were significantly better.[45] This was to be addressed by creating one form of tenancy: the "Scottish secure tenancy", which would apply both to the tenants of local authorities and to registered social landlords. In a radical step, the new form of tenancy was to apply not only to new tenancies created after the relevant provisions of the Act came into force, but to all existing tenancies of those landlords. Thus, on 30 September 2002, thousands of secure and assured tenancies became Scottish secure tenancies under the 2001 Act regime.

The provisions of Part II of the 2001 Act, at least in relation to recovery of possession by the landlord, are similar to the original scheme of the 1980 Act. Thus, the landlord is required to serve a "notice of proceedings for recovery of possession" before commencement of the action and thereafter establish that one of the grounds for eviction set out in schedule 2 to the Act is satisfied. However, there are certain important differences, which are discussed in Chapters 4 and 5.

The short Scottish secure tenancy ("SSST") was a major innovation of the 2001 Act. It is a hybrid of the Scottish secure tenancy and the short assured tenancy of the 1988 Act. It can only be offered to the classes of prospective tenant listed in schedule 6 to the 2001 Act. In addition to new tenancies, a short Scottish secure tenancy may be created under section 35 of the 2001 Act, by conversion from a standard Scottish secure tenancy. The landlord may serve notice on the tenant of an SSST, indicating that it requires possession of the tenancy subjects. If the tenant fails to remove, the landlord may then raise proceedings. As with the short assured tenancy, the landlord does not require to establish that it has any ground for recovery of possession, or that it would be reasonable to grant the order.

Certain important amendments were made to the statutory scheme for short Scottish secure tenancies by the Housing (Scotland) Act 2014.[46] As is explained in Chapter 6, there are two categories of short Scottish secure tenancy. In the first, an SSST is granted, or created by conversion under section 35, because of previous antisocial behaviour. Within the second category are

45 The more cynical view is that uniformity of tenure was designed to facilitate stock transfer: the process by which, following a vote by tenants, the housing stock of local authorities is transferred to housing associations, which, unlike local authorities, are not exclusively reliant on public money. Without the 2001 Act, local authority tenants could be warned off voting for stock transfer because it would entail relinquishing some of their statutory rights as tenants, moving from a secure tenancy to the less favourable assured tenancy. Uniformity of tenure removed this objection.

46 With effect from 1 May 2019.

new short Scottish secure tenancies created under section 34, because one of the paragraphs 3–7A of schedule 6 to the 2001 Act applies. Broadly speaking, those paragraphs describe various circumstances, other than previous anti-social behaviour, in which it is considered appropriate for a social landlord to offer a tenancy that is temporary. Under the amended statutory scheme, tenancies in the first category are subject to a fixed term of twelve months, which may be extended by a further six months. On expiry of that term, if the landlord has not served a notice of proceedings, the tenancy will convert to a full Scottish secure tenancy under section 37. Tenancies in the second category have no fixed term, though must be for a period of at least six months. Such tenancies do not convert under section 37, and therefore may remain short Scottish secure tenancies indefinitely.[47]

LEGISLATIVE DEVELOPMENTS SINCE THE FIRST EDITION

Housing is one of the most important matters within the legislative competence of the Scottish Parliament, and it has shown a particular enthusiasm for making law in this area. The period since 1999 has seen the passing of four major Housing Acts (2001, 2006, 2010 and 2014); a new form of private-sector tenancy under the Private Housing (Tenancies) (Scotland) Act 2016; the creation of the First-tier Tribunal (Housing and Property Chamber) ("FTT"), to which the jurisdiction for cases arising under the 1984 and 1988 Acts has been transferred; the Homelessness etc. (Scotland) Act 2003; the Private Rented Sector (Scotland) Act 2011; and significant provisions relating to housing and evictions in the Antisocial Behaviour (Scotland) Act 2004[48] and part 15 of the Bankruptcy and Diligence etc. (Scotland) Act 2007. Furthermore, the summary cause procedure, under which the vast majority of eviction actions are currently raised in the sheriff court, is due to be replaced with the simple procedure for heritable cases, under the Courts Reform (Scotland) Act 2014.[49]

For residential letting in the private sector, 1 December 2017 was a particularly significant day: the 2016 Act came into force, and the jurisdiction for proceedings arising from 1984 and 1988 Act tenancies, including eviction cases, was transferred to the FTT.

Private Housing (Tenancies) (Scotland) Act 2016

In September 2013, the Scottish Government set up the Private Rented Sector Tenancy Review Group, which produced a report for the Scottish Ministers on 9 May 2014. It had one main recommendation: "that the current tenancy for the Private Rented Sector, the Short Assured Tenancy and the Assured Tenancy, be replaced by a new private tenancy that covers all future PRS lets".[50]

47 Other differences between the two categories are described in Chapter 6, at p 177.

48 Part 8 of which introduces a system for the registration of landlords in the private rented sector.

49 See Chapter 13.

50 The Government consulted on "A New Tenancy for the Private Sector" at the end of 2014.

The key policy aim of the 2016 Act is to abolish the short assured tenancy as a form of tenure. The private residential tenancy ("PRT") is the only form of tenancy under the Act. It is analogous to an assured tenancy (which is not a short assured tenancy) under the 1988 Act. In order for the FTT to grant an "eviction order", it must find "that one of the eviction grounds in schedule 3 applies".[51] There is no equivalent to sections 32 and 33 of the 1988 Act, which allow the parties to create a special form of the statutory tenancy under which the landlord can insist on repossession on the basis that the term of the tenancy has expired. This change, which is favourable to tenants, is balanced by the extension of the grounds for eviction available to the landlord. In comparison with the grounds in schedule 5 to the 1988 Act, there are new grounds for eviction, and the threshold for obtaining an order is generally lower.[52]

The 2016 Act also effects a major break with the legislative scheme for security of tenure that has operated in respect of private-sector tenancies in Scotland since the first Rent Acts. Under the Rent Acts (and the 1988 Act), the statutory tenancy, with its attendant rent control and security of tenure, comes into effect once the tenancy contract has been terminated. Thus, under the 1988 Act, the termination of the tenancy contract (which is not controlled by the legislation) results in a *statutory* assured tenancy under section 16, which *is* subject to statutory control. There is no equivalent to section 16 in the 2016 Act. Instead, the fundamental provision is section 44, which succinctly says:

> "**44 No termination by parties except in accordance with this Part**
> A tenancy which is a private residential tenancy may not be brought to an end by the landlord, the tenant, nor by any agreement between them, except in accordance with this Part."[53]

Significantly, this section begins chapter 1 ("Security of tenure") of part 5 ("Termination") in the Act. It confirms that the fundamental way in which the statute confers security on the tenant is by bringing termination of the tenancy entirely under statutory regulation. Under the 1988 Act, it may be critical, for the purposes of eviction proceedings (and for other purposes) to identify whether the tenancy: (a) is a contractual assured tenancy or has become a statutory assured tenancy under section 16; and (b) is a short assured tenancy under section 32. Under the 2016 Act there are no such distinctions. There is no "contractual", "statutory" or "short" PRT. The PRT exists in only one form.

Among other things, this means that it is not necessary for either party to terminate the tenancy contract by a notice to quit. Instead, a landlord wishing to terminate a PRT will simply serve the appropriate statutory "notice to leave".[54]

A second consultation paper was issued in March 2015. This can be found on the Scottish Government's website, under "Second Consultation on a New Tenancy for the Private Sector".

51 Section 51(1).

52 In sch 3 to the 2016 Act, which is discussed in Chapter 10.

53 Section 44 is effectively incorporated into every tenancy agreement that is subject to the 2016 Act, by para 9 of the schedule to the Private Residential Tenancies (Statutory Terms) (Scotland) Regulations 2017 (SSI 2017/408).

54 As is the case with a Scottish secure tenancy under the Housing (Scotland) Act 2001, in which the landlord begins the eviction process by serving a notice of proceedings for recovery of possession under s 14.

Also, the 2016 Act departs from the common law (and the Leases Act 1449), in dispensing with the requirement that a tenancy must have an ish.[55] This is another reason why a notice to quit is inept in relation to a PRT. The effect of this change on the overall statutory scheme is significant. For example, the landlord does not have to wait for any particular period (in terms of the tenancy or otherwise) before increasing the rent (see section 22). The tenant does not have to wait out any particular period before terminating the tenancy under sections 49 and 50. Nor is the landlord prevented from making an application to the FTT, for an eviction order under section 51, by the fact that any agreed term for the tenancy has not expired.

Transfer of jurisdiction to First-tier Tribunal (Housing and Property Chamber)

Section 16 of the 2014 Act provides that the "functions and jurisdiction" of the sheriff in relation to actions "arising from" tenancies under the 1984 and 1988 Acts are transferred to the FTT. Under section 16(3) of and schedule 1 to the 2014 Act, references to the "court" in those Acts are replaced with references to the FTT. The 2016 Act confers jurisdiction for matters arising under that Act to the FTT. An application for an eviction order in relation to a PRT is made to the tribunal, under chapter 3 of part 5 of the Act.[56]

Consequently, since 1 December 2017, eviction proceedings in relation to tenancies subject to the 1984, 1988 and 2016 Acts have been raised at the tribunal. Where a tenancy in the private sector is not subject to those Acts, or does not "arise from" a regulated, assured or private residential tenancy, or the owner of the property maintains that occupation is not under a tenancy, eviction proceedings will continue to be raised in the sheriff court.[57]

TENANCIES EXCEPTED FROM STATUTORY CONTROL: OCCUPATION OTHER THAN UNDER A TENANCY

All four of the statutory schemes currently in force (being the Acts of 1984, 1988, 2001 and 2016) contain provisions to the effect that certain types of tenancies are excepted from the scheme of that Act.[58] Generally speaking, these exceptions relate to:

(1) the character of what is let – for example, agricultural tenancies;
(2) the status of the tenant – for example, asylum seekers;
(3) the status of the landlord – for example, where the landlord is also resident in the building of which the tenancy subjects form part; or

55 By s 4(a) of the Act. Notably, under the Model PRT Agreement produced by the Scottish Government, cl 6 requires the parties to state the "start date" of the tenancy, but there is no reference in the agreement to any duration or termination date.

56 Under s 71 of the 2016 Act, the FTT also has jurisdiction in relation to "all civil proceedings" arising from a PRT.

57 The transfer of jurisdiction is discussed in greater detail in Chapter 2 (in the discussion of s 23(1) of the 1984 Act, at p 36) and Chapter 14 (p 477).

58 In the 1984 Act, excepted tenancies are listed in s 2; in the 1988 Act in sch 4; in the 2001 Act in sch 1; and in the 2016 Act in sch 1.

(4) some combination of these factors, such as temporary accommodation for homeless persons, or tenancies granted by educational institutions to students.

However, in all such cases the legal effect is the same: as the tenant has no statutory right of occupation, his entitlement to retain possession ends when the tenancy contract ends. That being the case, he has no defence to proceedings for recovery of possession, provided that the parties' lease has been terminated.

Because they do not enjoy statutory security of tenure, excepted tenancies are often referred to as "common law" tenancies. However, this description is perhaps misleading, in that certain important statutory protections are still enjoyed by a tenant. In particular, he has the protection of the Leases Act 1449, under which his rights held under the lease, including the right to remain in occupation, are valid against the singular successors of the landlord.[59] He is also subject to the protection of the statutory provisions regarding notices to quit, in particular section 112 of the 1984 Act.[60] To that extent, he is in a better position than a person occupying subjects other than under a tenancy contract.

Moreover, it is generally not lawful to evict a person occupying a property as a "dwelling", without obtaining a court order, even if they do not occupy under a tenancy.[61] Furthermore, despite having no right of occupation under the statute or common law, such a person might nevertheless seek to defend eviction proceedings on the basis that they are contrary to the Human Rights Act 1998 or the Equality Act 2010, or on public law grounds.[62]

SECURITY OF TENURE: SUMMARY

If one attempts to bring the histories of eviction proceedings and statutory control of residential tenancies together, a picture emerges that is, in several respects, difficult to bring into clear focus. Areas of doubt arise, usually because statutory provisions, the drafting of which has often been less than ideal, have been superimposed on to an already confused background. The various problematic issues are discussed in the succeeding chapters.

In this book, six types of tenancy are considered:[63]

(1) tenancies excepted from the statutory regimes;
(2) assured tenancies under the 1988 Act;
(3) short assured tenancies under the 1988 Act;
(4) Scottish secure tenancies under the 2001 Act;
(5) short Scottish secure tenancies under the 2001 Act; and
(6) private residential tenancies under the 2016 Act.

59 I.e. if the landlord's title is transferred to another person, by sale or otherwise, this does not have the effect of terminating the tenancy. See Rennie and others, *Leases* (SULI 2015) para 1-10 and ch 5.

60 This provision will be discussed in greater detail in Chapter 3.

61 Subject to certain exceptions. See the discussion of s 23 of the 1984 Act in Chapter 2.

62 For which, see Chapter 11.

63 Regulated tenancies under the 1984 Act, a number of which are still in existence, are not given particular coverage, for the reasons stated in the Introduction.

IMPORTANT CONCEPTS[64]

Much of the legislation analysed in this book extends protection to "tenants" and other "occupiers" on the basis that they are "occupying" or "retaining possession of" premises that are variously described as a "house", "dwelling", "residence" or "property".[65] In some instances, the protection is extended only if the house in question is "occupied" as a person's "only or principal home".

There follows a discussion of meaning of certain terms: (1) "house", "home", etc; (2) "tenancy"; and (3) "retains possession", "occupies" and "only or principal home".

"House", "home", "dwelling", "residence", "premises", "property" and "house let as a separate dwelling"

Over the last century, a great deal of judicial ink has been spilt on discussing what terms such as "house" mean.[66] That a question as to the meaning of words such as "dwelling" and "residence" is still capable of giving rise to a sharp divergence of opinion at a high level is apparent from the decision of the Supreme Court in *R (N) v Lewisham LBC*.[67]

Part of the problem is that the discussion is capable of taking in several different dimensions, such as: (a) the physical features of the entity under discussion, and whether it was built, designed or adapted to be used as a residence; (b) the use that was envisaged by the parties when they entered into the arrangement under which a person is in occupation; (c) the use to which it is actually being put, at the time when the question arises for determination; (d) the temporal aspect of the arrangement under which occupation takes place, and whether one or both of the parties envisaged that it was merely temporary; (e) whether a building was built (or adapted) for more than one purpose, or is actually being used for more than one purpose, and which of the purposes takes primacy; (f) the extent to which the particular statutory context in which the relevant term appears, and the apparent policy behind the statute, informs the interpretation of that term.

Moreover, the term in question may be defined, or defined only for certain purposes, in the statute in question, whereas in other legislation no definition is given.[68] Thus, for example, the 1988 Act uses the term "house" without

64 The remainder of this chapter introduces certain concepts in housing law that are considered to be of particular importance to security of tenure and evictions. For a more comprehensive analysis of these, and other concepts, see the "Key Issues" section in the *Encyclopedia of Housing Law and Practice* vol 1.

65 To take one example, in Chapter 2 it will be seen that statutory criminal and civil sanctions may be imposed on the unlawful eviction from premises of a "residential occupier", who is "a person *occupying* the premises as a *residence*".

66 Not only judicial ink, as is evidenced by articles in the legal journals with titles such as: "What is a house?" (2017) 21(5) Landlord and Tenant Review ; "When is a house not a house?" (2016) 25 Nov Local Government Lawyer; and "What is a flat?" [2013] 157 Solicitors Journal 24 Supp (Property Focus) 11, 13.

67 [2015] AC 1259. This case concerned the issue of whether the statutory requirement to raise proceedings in court before evicting an occupier applied to homeless persons in temporary accommodation in England. It is more fully considered in Chapter 2.

68 Bennion opines: "It is notoriously difficult to say what is and what is not a 'house', particularly

defining it, other than to say that it "includes part of a house";[69] however, it makes provision to the effect that certain types of accommodation are to be regarded as a house for the purposes of the Act.[70] Section 111 of the 2001 Act provides that "house" includes: (a) any part of a building, being a part which is occupied or intended to be occupied as a separate dwelling, and in particular includes a flat, and (b) any yard, garden, outhouses and pertinents belonging to the house or usually enjoyed with it.[71]

It is evident that, in *R (N) v Lewisham LBC*, the Justices of the Supreme Court were treated to an extensive discussion of the authorities bearing upon the meaning of "dwelling", the term under examination in that case.[72] However, it is also clear that the Justices found earlier authorities to be of limited assistance, particularly where the statutory context was different. Thus, at paragraph 45, Lord Hodge said:

> "Pulling together the threads of the case law, in my view the following can be stated: (i) the words 'live at', 'reside' and 'dwell' are ordinary words of the English language and do not have technical meanings, (ii) those words must be interpreted in the statutes in which they appear having regard to the purpose of those enactments . . .".[73]

The same may be said of all the concepts discussed in this chapter. Some caution must be exercised in taking a statement as to the meaning of a term in one case and applying it another, particularly where the cases involve different statutory provisions.[74] However, in order to provide readers with some orientation, the following comments may be usefully made.

In the first edition of this work, the author hazarded the view that the terms "dwelling", "home" and "residence" may usually be regarded as referring to the same thing, at least in the context of the housing legislation. That is now doubtful, standing *R (N) v Lewisham LBC*. In that case, the majority were of the view that "as a matter of nuance, 'dwelling' as a general rule suggests a more settled occupation than 'residence' and can be equated with one's home, although 'residence' itself can in certain contexts (such as the two-home cases)

since it and other terms (such as 'dwelling') have often been artificially extended by statute": *Statutory Interpretation* (6th edn, 2013) 1093, in a section entitled: "Meaningless Terms" (not reproduced in subsequent editions).

69 Section 55(1).

70 Most importantly in terms of s 14, the purpose of which is described under the heading "House let as a separate dwelling". See also Chapter 7 at p 222.

71 This is almost identical to the definition used in s 338 of the Housing (Scotland) Act 1987. The 2016 Act eschews "house" in favour of "property".

72 See the authorities referred to in the judgments, listed in the Appeal Cases report, 1550–1551.

73 *R (N) v Lewisham LBC* (n 67) was a majority (5–2) decision. Four of the other Justices agreed with Lord Hodge, and his judgment therefore states the view of the majority, though some additional points were made by Lord Carnwath. It is evident from Lord Neuberger's dissenting judgment that he also found some of the previous authorities to be of little or no assistance: see the discussion at paras 104–115.

74 In *Quiltotex Co v Minister of Housing and Local Government* [1966] 1 QB 704 (a case that concerned the meaning of the word "house" in s 42 of the Housing Act 1957), Salmon LJ said (at 712): "I have had the advantage of a number of cases being cited to me on both sides relating to the construction which the courts have placed upon the word 'house' where it has appeared in other statutes . . . no real help can be gained as to the meaning of a word in Statute A by reference to its meaning in Statute B, C or D. All one can derive from the cases are the relevant principles of construction to be applied. These are not in doubt. What is the ordinary natural meaning of the word within the context of the section in which it appears?"

require such an equation".[75] Thus, "dwelling" and "home" should normally be regarded as synonymous,[76] however these words denote a more settled occupation than "residence", subject to statutory context.

It is suggested that to describe a building as a "house" normally connotes that it has been designed, adapted or built for use as a residence, and is actually being used in that manner.[77] This may be contrasted with the terms "premises" and "property", which carry no such connotation. Therefore, it is suggested that the use of "premises" in sections 22 and 23 of the 1984 Act, and of "property" in section 1 of the 2016 Act, is significant, because it indicates that the statutory protection extends to persons using any building as a dwelling, even if it is not intended for that purpose.[78]

The position of caravans, houseboats and mobile homes depends on the extent to which the subjects have become attached to the land, or are still mobile. In *Chelsea Yacht and Boat Co Ltd v Pope*,[79] a houseboat that had been moored by ropes to pontoons on the Thames was let to the defendant. It was held by a chain and anchor, and it periodically rested on the river bed below it. The Court of Appeal decided that no assured tenancy existed; the houseboat was not immobile, and the fact that it could not move under its own power was not to the point.[80] In *Gordon v Kirkcaldy District Council*[81] the court decided that static caravans were dwellinghouses, although in a different statutory context. These were large holiday caravans, which could not be towed

75 At para 45 (Lord Hodge), with whom the other Justices in the majority agreed. For a cogent view as to why it is problematic to make a distinction between "dwelling" and "residence", see Lord Neuberger's dissenting judgment, especially at para 120. It seems that the view of the majority was strongly influenced by the legal context in which temporary accommodation, which is usually in short supply, is made available to homeless persons, and the policy issues that arise: see paras 33–37. One wonders whether the notion that "dwelling" means something more settled than "residence" would be sustainable in another statutory context.

76 That is also apparent from the passage quoted (at p 22 below) from Lord Millett's judgment in *Uratemp Ventures Ltd v Collins*, [2002] 1 AC 301.

77 Section 2(1) of the Leasehold Reform Act 1967 defines a "house" as including "any building designed or adapted for living in and reasonably so called, notwithstanding that the building is not structurally detached, or was or is not solely designed or adapted for living in, or is divided horizontally into flats or maisonettes . . .". Although the 1967 Act does not apply in Scotland, this definition is helpful, and the cases decided under s 2 are of interest. In *Tandon v Trustees of Spurgeons Homes* [1982] AC 755, which concerned a property in mixed commercial and residential use, the House of Lords decided that as long as such a building could reasonably be called a "house" it was within the meaning of "house" for the purposes of the Act, even though it might also reasonably be called something else; if a building was designed or adapted for living in, i.e. for occupation as a residence, only exceptional circumstances (such that nobody could reasonably call it a "house") would justify a holding that it could not reasonably be so called. In *Day v Hosebay Ltd* [2012] 1 WLR 2884, the Supreme Court held that in order for a property to be a "house . . . reasonably so called" under the 1967 Act, the determinative factor was the use of the building rather than its physical appearance. See also: *Grosvenor (Mayfair) Estate v Merix* [2017] EWCA Civ 190; [2017] L & TR 18.

78 Sections 22 and 23 of the 1984 Act are discussed in Chapter 2. For s 1 of the 2016 Act, see Chapter 9.

79 [2000] 1 WLR 1941, (2001) 33 HLR 245.

80 On the question of whether the boat was attached to the land, Tucky LJ observed (at 1945): "One is bound to ask 'which land?'. There is in my judgment no satisfactory answer to this question." In the analogous case *Elitestone Ltd v Morris* [1997] 1 WLR 687, (1998) 30 HLR 266, particular emphasis was placed on whether the subjects in question could be removed without being destroyed. See also *Mew v Tristmire Ltd* [2012] 1 WLR 852, [2011] HLR 47.

81 1990 SC 107; 1990 SLT 644.

on public roads and, accordingly, would require to have been transported on a lorry. The caravans had each remained for several years on their respective pitches. The court could see no reason in principle why a structure that rested by its own weight upon a hard base could not be regarded as a "house".[82] A structure that was capable under certain conditions of being transported to another base might be a "house", provided that it had in its existing location a sufficient degree of permanence and immobility.[83]

"House let as a separate dwelling"

The phrase "house *let as a separate dwelling*" has a long and distinguished history under the Rent Acts, and it appears again in section 12 of the 1988 Act and section 11 of the 2001 Act. Section 1(1)(a) of the 2016 Act uses the phrase "property . . . *let as a separate dwelling*". The following observations are made, on the basis of the reported cases.

A flat,[84] or premises which have combined business and residential use,[85] may be a "house let as a separate dwelling". The building has to be looked at as a whole to ascertain whether, as a question of degree, it can properly be described as a "house".[86] However, the house cannot be let as *a* separate dwelling if the subjects comprise two or more separate units of accommodation.[87]

Under the Rent Acts, a significant body of case law examined the requirement that the premises be let as a "separate" dwelling. In these cases, the use of a room or rooms was shared between the tenant and others, and the question was whether the shared part was of such a character or of such significance as to preclude description of the tenancy subjects as a "separate" dwelling. In this context, distinctions were drawn between "living" rooms (i.e. rooms in which one "lives"), such as bedrooms and kitchens, and other rooms, such as bathrooms and lavatories, which one uses from time to time. Common enjoyment of "living" rooms tended to weigh against recognition of the premises let as a separate dwelling, whereas common enjoyment of bathrooms and lavatories did not affect the status of the rooms let as a "separate dwelling".[88]

In private-sector letting, it is very common to have bedsits and HMOs[89] in which there is shared use of "living" rooms, especially the kitchen. Given the cases described, that would remove bedsit tenants from the protection of any legislation that relates to accommodation let as a separate dwelling. Therefore, for some time the legislation has contained a provision, such as section 14 of

82 I.e. it did not require to have foundations.

83 At 125 (Lord Justice-Clerk Ross).

84 *Langford Property Co Ltd v Goldrich* [1949] 1 KB 511; *Assessor for Lothian Region v Viewpoint Housing Association Ltd* 1983 SLT 479.

85 *Ashbridge Investments Ltd v Minister of Housing and Local Government* [1965] 1 WLR 1320; *British Land Co v Herbert Silver (Menswear)* [1958] 1 QB 530; *Tan and Anr v Sitkowski* [2007] 1 WLR 1628.

86 *Annicola Investments v Minister of Housing and Local Government* [1968] 1 QB 631.

87 *Horford Investments Ltd v Lambert* [1976] Ch 39; *St Catherine's College v Dorling* [1980] 1 WLR 66; *Kavanagh v Lyroudias* [1985] 1 All ER 560. On the other hand, two or more dwellings may be let together for use as a single house: *Langford Property Co Ltd v Goldrich* (n 84).

88 These authorities were discussed by Lord Millett in his judgment in *Uratemp Ventures Ltd v Collins* (n 76), considered at p 22.

89 Houses in multiple occupation.

the 1988 Act, or section 2(4) of the 2016 Act,[90] which has the effect of deeming the tenant's accommodation to be "let as separate dwelling", even though some of that accommodation is shared.[91]

Even a single room may be a "house" for the purposes of the legislation, provided that it is let as a "separate dwelling", and all the normal activities of living can be carried on there.[92] The leading authority is the House of Lords' decision in *Uratemp Ventures Ltd v Collins*.[93] Prior to that case, it had been thought that a "separate dwelling" must provide the necessary facilities for living, sleeping and cooking, and thus in a number of cases the courts were required to consider, for example, whether the tenant in question had what could be described as "cooking facilities".[94] *Uratemp*, at least initially, was a case of exactly this type. From 1985, Mr Collins was a resident in the Viscount Hotel, Kensington. During the course of his time there, he changed rooms on several occasions. When the owners sought to bring his occupation to an end in 1998, he was living in a room containing a single bed, some furniture, a shower and a washbasin. Initially, breakfast was included in the rent, but this ceased in 1988. No cooking facilities were provided in any of the rooms occupied by Mr Collins, although each contained at least one power point. He brought in some furniture of his own and electrical equipment to enable him to prepare simple meals: a pizza warmer, a warming plate, a kettle and an underlight. He also regularly ate ready-cooked take-away meals in his room.

The judge at first instance held that the room was let as a separate dwelling. The Court of Appeal disagreed, considering itself to be bound by earlier decisions to the effect that the presence of cooking facilities was an essential characteristic of a dwelling. That decision was reversed by the House of Lords, which took the view that a less restrictive approach was appropriate, the gist of which may be gathered from the following passage in Lord Millett's judgment:

> "In both ordinary and literal usage, residential accommodation is 'a dwelling' if it is the occupier's home (or one of his homes). It is the place where he lives and to which he returns and which forms the centre of his existence. Just what use he makes of it when living there, however, depends on his mode of life. No doubt he will sleep there and usually eat there; he will often prepare at least some of his meals there. But his home is not the less his home because he does not cook there but prefers to eat out or bring in ready-cooked meals. It has never been a legislative requirement that cooking facilities must be available for premises to qualify as a dwelling. Nor is it at all evident what policy considerations dictate that a tenant who prepares his meals

90 Section 2(4) appears to have been overlooked in the Upper Tribunal's decision in *Affleck v Bronsdon* [2019] UT 49, specifically at para [18]. That decision was subsequently quashed by the Inner House on an appeal that was not opposed.

91 There is no equivalent provision in the 2001 Act in relation to accommodation let by social landlords. That is also the case in England. See *Parkins v Westminster City Council* (1998) 30 HLR 894, which concerned a teacher whose employers, the council, gave him a licence to occupy what was, in effect, a bedsit, with a shared living room and kitchen. The court held that, on a true construction of the licence agreement, it did not confer exclusive possession on the plaintiff; premises occupied under such a right could not be occupied "as a separate dwelling".

92 *Cole v Harris* [1945] KB 474. As indicted above, s 55 of the 1988 Act defines "house" as "includes part of house", and s 111 of the 2001 Act defines "house" as "includes any part of a building . . . occupied or intended to be occupied as a separate dwelling". Section 1(1)(b) of the 2016 Act refers to the tenant occupying "the property (or any part of it)".

93 (n 76).

94 See, e.g., *Westminster City Council v Clarke* [1992] 2 AC 288.

at home should enjoy security of tenure while a tenant who brings in all his meals ready-cooked should not."

This judgment suggests that, in considering whether the house is let as a separate dwelling, one should not primarily consider the physical features or facilities of the accommodation itself, but rather the manner in which it is used by the tenant.[95]

The use of words such as "dwelling" does not necessarily require use as an only home or principal home, unless the relevant provision so states.[96]

"Tenancy" and "let"

Under section 12 of the 1988 Act, section 11 of the 2001 Act and section 1 of the 2016 Act,[97] the protection of the legislation is, subject to certain conditions, conferred on a "tenancy" under which a house[98] is "let". Thus, there is no "assured tenancy"[99] under the 1988 Act, or "Scottish secure tenancy" under the 2001 Act, or "private residential tenancy" under the 2016 Act, unless there is, in the first place, a "tenancy". Where a person occupies on some other basis or some other arrangement, that occupation is not protected under the legislation. However, under these three Acts, the term "tenancy" has somewhat different meanings.

Lease at common law

A lease is a contract whereby one party who owns heritable property cedes the right of possession to another for a set period in exchange for a return. However, there are many situations where the owner of heritable property grants some sort of subsidiary right in that property to another, but these are not necessarily leases.[100]

In Scots law, the term "licence" has often been used to denote an agreement under which a person is entitled to use heritable subjects, but which is not a lease, and therefore does not attract the rights and obligations associated with a lease.[101] This type of agreement may also be called an "occupancy agreement", or given some other similar title.

95 This is consistent with the decision in *Day v Hosebay Ltd* (n 76). For a Scottish case that came to a similar conclusion, albeit in a different context, see *Assessor for Lothian Region v Viewpoint Housing Association Ltd* (n 84).

96 *Phillips v Francis* [2010] L & TR 28, [2010] 2 EGLR 31. This case concerned the imposition of service charges for chalets, many of which were used by the tenants as second homes. As the court observed, such tenants were every bit as deserving of being protected from unscrupulous landlords as are tenants of accommodation that is their primary home. Similarly, in *JLK Ltd v Ezekwe* [2017] UKUT 277 (LC), [2017] L & TR 29 the Upper Tribunal decided that student "pods", most of which were single bedrooms with en-suite shower and toilet facilities, were "dwellings" for the purposes of s 38 of the Landlord and Tenant Act 1985, even though they were not the students' homes. However, they were not "separate dwellings", because the kitchens and lounges for the pods were communal, and there was no equivalent, in the 1985 Act, to the deeming provisions described above (such as s 14 of the 1988 Act).

97 These sections are quoted in Chapters 7 and 9.

98 Or, under the 2016 Act, a "property . . . let . . . as a . . . dwelling".

99 Or short assured tenancy; under the 1988 Act, such a tenancy is a form of assured tenancy.

100 See Rennie (n 61) ch 1.

101 The rights of licensees are summarised in Chapter 12, at p 432.

In England, the distinction between leases and licences has been discussed in numerous cases, because of the many and various attempts made by private landlords to defeat security of tenure by creating licences rather than leases. The main point that may be derived from the relevant authorities is that the court will be astute to shams,[102] pretences and collusive devices the purpose of which is to enable one or both of the parties to contract out of the protections afforded by the Housing Acts or to evade their own contractual obligations; the presence of such devices may rebut the presumption that the parties' intentions expressed in the agreement should be given effect. Where there is such a rebuttal, and the essential elements of a lease are present, a lease may have been created as a matter of law, notwithstanding any expressed intention to the contrary.[103] Conversely, in a case in which parties' agreement uses language appropriate to a tenancy, the court may find that the agreement does not have that status, particularly where its terms are inconsistent with a grant of exclusive possession.[104]

There is comparatively little authority in Scots law on the lease/licence distinction. For that reason, Sheriff Collins' examination of the subject in *St Andrews Forest Lodges Ltd v Grieve*[105] is welcome. There, he explains that the "four cardinal elements in a lease", being the parties, the subjects, the rent and the duration, may nowadays be regarded as being supplemented by a fifth element: the grant of exclusive possession.[106] This is consistent with the analysis of the lease/licence distinction in *Leases*,[107] in which the authors describe certain key factors that, although not conclusive, are indicative of whether a contract may be regarded as a lease or a licence. These include, in particular, whether the occupant does not have exclusive possession, such that the other party can take access at will.[108] After discussing the relevant English authorities, Sheriff Collins concluded:[109]

102 There is a discussion of the English authorities on "sham" agreements in *Dickson v MacGregor* 1992 SLT (Land Ct) 83 and in *MacFarlane v Falfield Investments Ltd* 1997 SLT 518, and 1998 SC 14, 1998 SLT 145, both of which were cases involving agricultural tenancies.

103 See, in particular, *Street v Mountford* [1985] AC 809; *AG Securities v Vaughan* [1990] 1 AC 417.

104 See, for example: *Watts v Stewart* [2018] Ch 423, [2017] HLR 8.

105 [2017] SC DUN 25, 2017 GWD 14-224, [24]–[44]. The case is discussed in M Skilling, *St Andrew's Forest Lodges Ltd v Grieve: the lease's Fifth Element in action* (2018) 2 Juridical Review 122–127 . In his decision, Sheriff Collins analyses the older cases *Scottish Residential Estates Development Co Ltd v Henderson* 1991 SLT 490; and *Brador Properties Ltd v British Telecommunications plc* 1992 SLT 490.

106 For a case in which the existence of exclusive possession was in issue, see *Conway v Glasgow City Council* 1999 Hous LR 67, in which the pursuer occupied a room in a hostel for homeless people. It is discussed in Chapter 12.

107 (n 100) paras 2-10 to 2-18.

108 Other factors are whether one of the cardinal elements of a lease (in particular, rent) is missing; and whether occupation is tied to the provision of other services. These elements all point to a licence, rather than a lease. There is also a short but informative discussion of the lease/licence distinction in A G M Duncan and J A D Hope's commentary to s 1 of the Rent (Scotland) Act 1984 in *Current Law Statutes*. This refers in particular, to English authorities to the effect that a licence may be more readily inferred where the advantage given to the suggested tenant is obviously intended to be personal to him and where there has been something in the circumstances, such as a family arrangement, an act of friendship or generosity, or such like, to negative any intention to create a tenancy: *Facchini v Bryson* [1952] 1 TLR 1386, 1389 (Denning LJ); *Heslop v Burns* [1974] 1 WLR 1241, 1248–1249 (Roskill LJ).

109 At para [35].

> "I would readily hold that in Scotland too, where it has been established that there is *consensus in idem* as to parties, premises, rent, duration and exclusive possession, and that possession is not referable, exceptionally, to another legal contract (such as in the case of a lodger or service occupier) then the agreement will as a matter of law be a lease and not a licence, and this will be so even if the parties did not intend it to have that legal characterisation."

"Tenancy" under the 1988, 2001 and 2016 Acts

Section 55(1) of the 1988 Act tells us that a "tenancy" includes a "sub-tenancy", and that "tenant" "includes a sub-tenant, and any person deriving title from the original tenant" such as an assignee of the tenancy. Otherwise, the term "tenancy" is not defined in the 1988 Act.[110] Therefore, "tenancy" in the 1988 Act means a tenancy, including a sub-tenancy, at common law.[111]

Likewise, by section 78(1) of the 2016 Act, a "tenancy" includes a "sub-tenancy". However, as is explained in Chapter 9, section 4 of the 2016 Act extends the meaning of "tenancy", by providing that, for the purposes of the Act, an agreement that would give rise to a tenancy but for the fact that it does not specify an ish is to be regarded as giving rise to a tenancy.[112]

By contrast, under section 41 of the 2001 Act, "tenancy" means an agreement under which a house is made available for human habitation, and "lease" and related expressions are to be construed accordingly. This provision is of some significance, because it precludes any attempt by a landlord in the social rented sector to avoid the Act by creating a licence or an "occupancy agreement" instead of a lease. Provided that the agreement in question makes a house available for human habitation, and it meets the other requirements of section 11, it will constitute a Scottish secure tenancy or short Scottish secure tenancy, even though it may not amount to a lease at common law.

"Retaining possession", "only or principal home" and "occupies"

"Retains possession"

The Rent Acts did not originally impose any specific requirement that, in order to have the protection of the legislation, the tenant must actually be in occupation of the house. However, in a series of cases the courts had developed a rule to that effect, based on the consideration that the policy of the Acts was protection of the tenant's home.[113]

110 This is the same approach as was adopted under the Rent Acts: see s 115(1) of the 1984 Act.

111 Hence, in *St Andrew's Forest Lodges Ltd v Grieve* (n 105), having decided that the parties' agreement was a lease, rather than a licence, and that it was not a "holiday let" under para 8 of sch 4 to the 1988 Act, the sheriff concluded that the tenancy was an assured tenancy under s 12 of the Act.

112 As to the requirement for a duration in a lease, at common law, see the discussion of duration of tenancies in Chapter 3, at n 14.

113 See, in particular: *Menzies v Mackay* 1938 SC 74, in which Lord Justice-Clerk Aitchison concluded (at 78) that: "It is . . . not open to reasonable doubt that the benefit of the statutory tenancy was a privilege given to the occupying tenant. It depended on the premises being in the personal occupation of the tenant and continuing to be in his personal occupation". Another useful summary of the policy of the Rent Acts was given by Lord President Cooper

In Scotland, section 3(1) of the consolidating Rent (Scotland) Act 1971 effectively codified this rule, by providing that, after termination of the parties' protected tenancy, the tenancy would be the statutory tenant "so long as he *retains possession* of the dwelling-house without being entitled to do so under a contractual tenancy". This wording was repeated in section 3(1) of the 1984 Act, which updated the 1971 Act, and the formula was again repeated, subject to the necessary modifications, in section 16 of the 1988 Act.[114]

The annotations to the 1984 Act in *Scottish Current Law Statutes*[115] indicate that section 3(1) is to be understood in light of the aforementioned cases.[116] It is submitted that this must be correct, even though the gist of those cases is better conveyed by the words "*occupies . . . as his residence*"[117] than "*retains possession*"; clearly it is possible to retain possession of subjects, in the sense of having the sole right to use them, without actually being in occupation, or using the subjects as a residence or home.[118] The intention of the 1971 Act was to consolidate and codify the existing law, and there seems to be no reason why the protection of the legislation should have been extended to persons possessing but not using tenancy subjects. Therefore, it is submitted that the obligation to "retain possession" under section 16(1) of the 1988 Act should be read as requiring occupation.[119]

"Occupies", "only or principal home" and "occupies . . . as only or principal home"

In the early 1980s, the legislation that introduced the secure tenancy regime for local authority tenants stipulated certain conditions for the creation of a secure tenancy, one of which was that the house must be the tenant's "only or principal home".[120] This has been carried through to section 11(1)(c) of the 2001 Act. When the tenancy is created, it cannot be a Scottish secure tenancy, unless it is the tenant's "only or principal home".[121] However, there is, in section 11, no requirement that the tenant is actually going to be in occupation

in *Stewart v Mackay* 1947 SC 287 (at 293): "The keynote of the Acts is domesticity and the protection of the home, and their purposes is to keep a roof over the occupier's head."

114 Under s 16, the termination of the parties' contractual assured tenancy, say by notice to quit, has the effect that a statutory assured tenancy then exists, so long as the tenant "retains possession of the house without being entitled to do so under a contractual tenancy".

115 Duncan and Hope (n 108).

116 The annotation states: "Since the whole policy of the Act is to protect the home, a tenant who ceases to reside in the premises to any substantial extent loses protection."

117 This is the wording that was used in s 3(1) of the Rent Act 1968, which was the consolidating legislation in England.

118 In short, it is possible to possess a thing without using it.

119 As is indicated below, the 1988 Act also uses the "occupies . . . as his only or principal home" test in s 12. It is one of the quirks of the 1988 Act that it contains two different standards in respect of possession/residence, whereas in other equivalent legislation only one standard applies.

120 In Scotland, the Tenants' Rights, Etc (Scotland) Act 1980, s 10(1)(b), which later became s 44(1)(b) of the 1987 Act.

121 As the property cannot be the tenant's home until she has moved in, presumably what is intended is that the prospective tenancy cannot be a Scottish secure tenancy unless it *will be* the tenant's only or principal home. The purpose of introducing the "only or principal home" test in the 1980 Act was apparently to avoid a situation in which the tenant could have more than one secure tenancy at the same time because, in that case, it would be possible to exercise the right to buy two or more houses.

of the tenancy. Moreover, under section 11(8), the tenancy continues to be a Scottish secure tenancy, even if the property ceases to be the tenant's only or principal home.[122] Nevertheless, occupation is an important part of the application of other provisions in the 2001 Act, such as the status "qualifying occupier" under section 14, or the operation of the abandonment procedure under sections 17–21.[123]

Under section 12 of the 1988 Act, and section 1(1)(b) of the 2016 Act, the combined test "occupies . . . as only or principal home" forms an important part of determining whether the parties have created an assured tenancy or a PRT. However, as will be explained in Chapters 7 and 9, in relation to assured tenancies, the test continues to apply throughout the tenancy. The protection of the 1988 Act will be lost if the property is no longer the tenant's only or principal home.[124] By contrast, a tenancy remains a PRT even if the tenant ceases to occupy it as his only or principal home.[125]

As with terms such as "house", the question of whether a person "occupies" accommodation or it is his "only or principal home" may be affected by the context in which the test is being applied. In Scotland, a key decision was *Beggs v Kilmarnock and Loudoun District Council*,[126] in which the court confirmed that a tenant serving a period of imprisonment was entitled to exercise the right to buy. This was on the basis that, although he had no physical presence in the house, occupation could nevertheless be established by there being a *corpus possessionis* (that is, physical signs of occupation)[127] together with an *animus revertendi* (that is, an intention to return that could be established by some visible state of affairs).[128] Likewise, in *Roxburgh District Council v Collins*,[129] Sheriff Principal Nicholson held that regular or habitual residence was not a prerequisite for qualification as a successor to a secure tenancy,

122 Though, in that case, there would be a ground for recovery of possession: ground 5 in sch 2, considered in Chapter 5. In relation to whether the term "occupation" implies physical presence, note that ground 5 is established where the tenant has "been absent from the house without reasonable cause for a continuous period exceeding 6 months" *or* has "ceased to occupy the house as [his] principal home". If the term "absent from the house" entails a lack of physical presence, then it may be said that this ground makes a distinction between that lack, and ceasing to occupy the tenancy as a home, which are treated in the ground as distinct and separate circumstances. This is consistent with the decision in *Beggs v Kilmarnock and Loudon District Council* 1995 SC 333, 1996 SLT 461. Reference is also made to *Crawley Borough Council v Sawyer* (1988) 20 HLR 98, in which Parker LJ observed: "It is quite plain that it is possible to occupy as a home two places at the same time, and indeed it is inherent in [the words 'only or principal home']. It is therefore plain that, if you occupy two houses at the same time as a home, actual physical occupation cannot be necessary, because one cannot be physically in two places at the same time."

123 Discussed at the end of Chapter 4.

124 Because of the phrase: "if and so long as" in s 12.

125 Section 1(2) of the 2016 Act.

126 (n 122).

127 Such as belongings being left at the property.

128 This argument was based on several English cases in which the court had considered the requirement of occupation in relation to analogous provisions: in particular, *Brown v Brash and Ambrose* [1948] 2 KB 247. See also *Kalas v Farmer* [2010] HLR 25, in which the landlord defended an action for damages of unlawful eviction at the instance of the tenant, arguing that the tenant (who had been in prison at the time), was no longer in occupation. This was unsuccessful, as it was apparent that the tenant was still keeping his belongings there.

129 1991 SLT (Sh Ct) 49.

and that the question that had to be asked, in cases where such residence was lacking, was whether, on the facts of the case, the person concerned had such a real, tangible and substantial connection with the house that it, rather than any other place of residence, could properly be described as having been his only or principal home during the relevant period.

This may be contrasted with the Court of Appeal's decision in *Sumeghova v McMahon*,[130] in which the defendant argued that he was entitled to evict the claimant without a court order, because the statutory protection against such eviction did not apply where the parties shared accommodation, and the landlord occupied, as his only or principal home, premises of which the whole or part of the shared accommodation formed part.[131] In that case, Longmore LJ said: "It seems to me that a place where a person sleeps is of the most enormous importance in determining whether that is his only or principal home. Circumstances might arise where that might not be decisive, but on any view it is a matter which is going to influence a court very considerably."[132]

Islington LBC v Boyle[133]

This decision of the Court of Appeal is now the leading English authority, on the application of the "occupies" and "only or principal home" tests, where the tenant is absent from the property and living elsewhere, but intends to return. As to occupation, Lord Justice Etherton set out the relevant principles as follows:

> "55 . . . First, absence by the tenant from the dwelling may be sufficiently continuous or lengthy or combined with other circumstances as to compel the inference that, on the face of it, the tenant has ceased to occupy the dwelling as his or her home. In every case, the question is one of fact and degree. Secondly, assuming the circumstances of absence are such as to give rise to that inference:
>
> (1) the onus is on the tenant to rebut the presumption that his or her occupation of the dwelling as a home has ceased;
> (2) in order to rebut the presumption the tenant must have an intention to return;
> (3) while there is no set limit to the length of absence and no requirement that the intention must be to return by a specific date or within a finite period, the tenant must be able to demonstrate a 'practical possibility' or 'a real possibility' of the fulfilment of the intention to return within a reasonable time;
> (4) the tenant must also show that his or her inward intention is accompanied by some formal, outward and visible sign of the intention to return, which sign must be sufficiently substantial and permanent and otherwise such that in all the circumstances it is adequate to rebut the presumption that the tenant, by being physically absent from the premises, has ceased to be in occupation of it.
>
> Thirdly, two homes cases, that is to say where the tenant has another property in which he or she voluntarily takes up full-time residence, must be viewed with

130 [2003] HLR 26.
131 The equivalent Scottish provision is s 23A(1) of the 1984 Act. See Chapter 2.
132 In that case, the landlord was sleeping at one property, but spent most of his time in another. So, perhaps *Sumeghova* (n 130) may be regarded as important authority in that type of situation, as opposed to circumstances, such as those in *Beggs* (n 122), where the person is temporarily absent.
133 [2011] EWCA Civ 1450, [2012] HLR 18.

particular care in order to assess whether the tenant has ceased to occupy as a home the place where he or she formerly lived.

Fourthly, whether or not a tenant has ceased to occupy premises as his or her home is a question of fact. In the absence of an error of law, the trial judge's findings of primary fact cannot be overturned on appeal unless they were perverse, in the sense that they exceeded the generous ambit within which reasonable disagreement about the conclusions to be drawn from the evidence is possible; but the appeal court may in an appropriate case substitute its own inferences drawn from those primary facts."

As to whether the property was still then the tenant's "only or principal home", he said:

"65 . . . First, the length or other circumstances of the tenant's absence may raise the inference that the dwelling which is the subject of the proceedings ceased to be the tenant's principal home so as to cast on the tenant the burden of proving the contrary. Secondly, in order to rebut that presumption, it is not sufficient for the tenant to prove that at the material time it was his or her subjective intention and belief that the dwelling remained the principal home. The objective facts must bear out the reality of that belief and intention both in the sense that the intention and belief are or were genuinely held and also that the intention and belief themselves reflect reality. The reason for the absence, the length and other circumstances of the absence and (where relevant) the anticipated future duration of the absence, as well as statements and conduct of the tenant, will all be relevant to that objective assessment. Thirdly, the court's focus is on the enduring intention of the tenant, which, depending on the circumstances, may not be displaced by fleeting changes of mind. Fourthly, the issue is one of fact to be determined in the light of the evidence as a whole . . ."

These principles have been applied in subsequent cases.[134]

Sub-letting

Where the tenant has sub-let the whole the subjects, that will tend to indicate that he is no longer occupying them as his only or principal home. In *Ujima Housing Association v Ansah*,[135] the defendant was an assured tenant who sub-let his flat on an assured shorthold tenancy.[136] He left furniture in the flat, but no personal possessions. However, he was unable to return to the flat unless his sub-tenant voluntarily surrendered the property to him, and therefore he could not show that it was his intention to preserve his occupation of the flat as his principal residence. Therefore, there was no longer an assured tenancy under the 1988 Act, and accordingly the court found in favour of the landlords.[137]

134 *Dove v Havering BC* [2017] EWCA Civ 156, [2017] HLR 19; and *Southwark LBC v Ibidun* [2017] EWHC 2775 (QB), [2018] HLR 5.

135 (1998) 30 HLR 831.

136 This is broadly the equivalent of a short assured tenancy in the English legislation.

137 This case is not authority for a general proposition that a tenant who grants a sub-let will thereby forfeit his assured tenancy. Each case would depend on its own circumstances. For example, standing the decision in *Beggs* (n 122), it may be possible for a prisoner to sub-let for the duration of his sentence and still maintain that he occupied the tenancy subjects as his only or principal home.

Chapter 2

Unlawful Eviction and Harassment

INTRODUCTION

Protection for "residential occupiers" is found in Part III of the Rent (Scotland) Act 1984,[1] which has the title "Protection Against Harassment and Eviction Without Due Process of Law", and sections 36 and 37 of the Housing (Scotland) Act 1988, headed "Protection from Eviction".[2] In essence, these provisions set out criminal and civil sanctions for anyone who evicts an occupier before carrying out the necessary preliminary steps. At common law, a landlord could not evict a tenant *brevi manu*.[3] Unlawful eviction is also a delict at common law and may give rise to an action for damages, as will be discussed below.[4] Harassment of a residential occupier may also give rise to proceedings under the Protection from Harassment Act 1997 or the Equality Act 2010.[5] These various statutory provisions are discussed in this chapter.

Some further points are made at the end of the chapter in relation to the issue of eviction *brevi manu* and, in particular, why eviction without a court order may be inadvisable, even in cases in which it would appear to be lawful.

UNLAWFUL EVICTION AND HARASSMENT: s 22

Section 22 states:

> "**22.— Unlawful eviction and harassment of occupier.**
>
> (1) If any person unlawfully deprives the residential occupier of any premises of his occupation of the premises or any part thereof or attempts to do so he shall be

1 The 1984 Act was a consolidating Act; ss 22 and 23 were derived from the Rent Act 1965, ss 30 and 32, which were enacted as a response to public concern over "Rachmanism", one of the features of which was the ejection of tenants without due process of law (after Peter Rachman, who achieved notoriety in the 1960s as a landlord who threatened and exploited his tenants). The history (including Rachman's connection to the Profumo scandal) is recounted in Robson and Combe, *Residential Tenancies* (4th edn, 2019) ch 13.

2 The 1988 Act, ss 39 and 40 respectively amended the 1984 Act, s 23 and added a new s 23A. Those sections are discussed below.

3 "*brevi manu*": "summarily, without a legal warrant" (J Traynor, *Latin Maxims and Phrases*), i.e. without obtaining a court order. In *Ali v Serco Ltd* 2020 SC 182, 2019 SLT 1335 the Inner House rejected an argument that the common law protection extended beyond tenancies to any contract under which a person has a right to occupy heritable subjects. See p 39.

4 At p 42. Interdict may also be sought to prevent an unlawful eviction.

5 However, the definitions of "harassment" are different in the 1984, 1997 and 2010 Acts respectively.

guilty of an offence unless he proves that he believed, and had reasonable cause to believe, that the residential occupier had ceased to reside in the premises.

(2) If any person with intent to cause the residential occupier of any premises—
(a) to give up the occupation of the premises or any part thereof: or
(b) to refrain from exercising any right or pursuing any remedy in respect of the premises or part thereof;

does acts likely to interfere with the peace or comfort of the residential occupier or members of his household, or persistently withdraws or withholds services reasonably required for the occupation of the premises as a residence, he shall be guilty of an offence.

(2A) Subject to subsection (2B) below the landlord of any premises or an agent of the landlord shall be guilty of an offence if—
(a) he does acts likely to interfere with the peace or comfort of the residential occupier or members of his household; or
(b) he persistently withdraws or withholds services reasonably required for the occupation of the premises in question as a residence,

and (in either case) he knows, or has reasonable cause to believe, that that conduct is likely to cause the residential occupier to give up the occupation of the whole or part of the premises or to refrain from exercising any right or pursuing any remedy in respect of the whole or part of the premises.

(2B) A person shall not be guilty of an offence under subsection (2A) above if he proves that he had reasonable grounds for doing the acts or withdrawing or withholding the services in question.

(3) A person guilty of an offence under this section shall be liable—
(a) on summary conviction, to a fine not exceeding the statutory maximum or to imprisonment for a term not exceeding six months or to both; and
(b) on conviction on indictment, to a fine or to imprisonment for a term not exceeding two years or to both.

(4) Nothing in this section shall be taken to prejudice any liability or remedy to which a person guilty of an offence thereunder may be subject in civil proceedings.

(5) In this section 'residential occupier', in relation to any premises, means a person occupying the premises as a residence, whether under a contract or by virtue of any enactment or rule of law giving him the right to remain in occupation or restricting the right of any other person to recover possession of the premises."

In Scotland, prosecutions under this provision have been very rare. For case law, one has to look to proceedings taken under section 1 of the Protection from Eviction Act 1977, the equivalent provision that applies in England. There it is possible for local authorities to bring criminal prosecutions and, perhaps as a result, convictions are more common.[6]

The meaning of the term "occupier" is discussed at the end of Chapter 1. The meanings of other terms used in section 22 are as follows.

"Any person"

An offence under section 22(1) or (2) may be committed by "any person", not just the owner of the premises. The owner or landlord has not committed an

6 Occasionally, prosecutions in England have led to sentences of imprisonment. An example is *R v Allen (Jay)* [2013] EWCA Crim 676, in which the defendant was sentenced to nine months' imprisonment and ordered to pay £5,575 towards prosecution costs.

offence if the relevant acts are done by other persons, even if they are apparently done on his behalf.[7]

"Unlawfully"

It is suggested that the meaning of the word "unlawfully" must be considered with reference to section 22(5), which defines the term "residential occupier" as meaning "in relation to any premises . . . a person occupying the premises as a residence, whether under a contract or by virtue of any enactment or rule of law giving him the right to remain in occupation or restricting the right of any other person to recover possession of the premises". It is the eviction of a "residential occupier", so defined, that is "unlawful". That definition is not restricted to persons occupying under a tenancy.[8] It includes persons occupying:

- under a contract;[9] or
- by virtue of any enactment or rule of law.

Thus, one has to look beyond section 22 to find whether there is such a contract, enactment or rule of law, in order to determine whether a person is a "residential occupier" having the protection of section 22.[10]

We will shortly go on to consider section 23, the purpose of which is to protect occupiers who *had* a right to occupy the subjects as a dwelling, by providing that legal proceedings are necessary before such an occupier can be evicted, even though that right of occupation has come to an end. It is important to understand the relationship between sections 22 and 23. This is apt to be confusing because of the manner in which the provisions in the 1984 Act are laid out, and the fact that the heading of section 23 ("Prohibition of eviction without due process of law") tends to suggest the purpose of outlining all the cases in which such eviction will be unlawful.

For the purposes of section 22(5), section 23 is, strictly speaking, simply one enactment that restricts the right of a person (i.e. the owner) to recover possession of the premises; the class of occupiers protected by section 23 of the 1984 Act is thus only part of the wider class of "residential occupiers" protected by section 22, and a person who is not subject to section 23[11] may nevertheless have the protection of section 22.

7 In other words, there is no vicarious liability. However, the owner or landlord might be convicted if there was evidence of his instructing or inciting another person to evict an occupier unlawfully: *R v Qureshi (Mohammed)* [2012] 1 WLR 694, [2011] HLR 34. By contrast, a landlord is liable to pay statutory damages, under s 36 of the 1988 Act, where an unlawful eviction is effected by any person "acting on his behalf".

8 Rennie, *Leases* (SULI 2015) para 21-105.

9 Where a person is a residential occupier under a contract, he has the protection of the legislation even if the contract is not a tenancy: *R v H* [2008] EWCA Crim 483.

10 In *Ali v Serco Ltd* 2019 SLT 463 (Outer House), Lord Tyre said (at [27]) of s 22: "I am not persuaded that this provision created any new civil right in favour of the residential occupier . . . One is . . . directed elsewhere to identify a basis upon which the person unlawfully deprived of possession may seek a remedy in the civil courts. That is unsurprising when one bears in mind that the offence consists of *unlawful* deprivation of occupation; the section does not purport to determine what is or is not unlawful in this context."

11 As will be outlined below, the 1984 Act s 23A lists categories of occupation that are excepted from s 23.

At the end of Chapter 1 it was submitted that the use of the word "premises" in sections 22(5) and 23 of the 1984 Act, as opposed to a word such as "house", is significant, because it indicates that the intention of the legislature was to extend the protection of these provisions to persons occupying any sort of building as a residence – not just buildings designed or adapted for that purpose.[12]

"Deprives"

The offence does not require violence, or the threat of violence. Unlawful evictions are often effected simply by changing the locks while the tenant is out or away.[13]

Deprivation of occupation need not be permanent. It could include a period of weeks or months, such that the occupier has to find alternative accommodation. However, not allowing entry to an occupier on one or even more than one isolated occasion, constitutes harassment, rather than eviction.[14] In a case in which the landlord had purported to give notice to quit, and the tenant then received threatening phone calls from the landlord and his son, and decided to leave, this was said to amount to a "constructive eviction", because the tenant could not reasonably be expected to remain.[15]

It has been suggested that unlawful eviction could be committed by sending a notice to quit that the sender knows to be invalid, or by sending a solicitor's letter that, without any justification, denies the existence of a tenancy or other right to occupy.[16]

"Believes, and had reasonable cause to believe"

In a prosecution under section 22(1), the accused is not guilty of the offence if he is able to prove that he both believed, *and* had reasonable cause to believe, that the residential occupier had ceased to reside in the premises. This

12 The term "occupying" was also discussed in Chapter 1.

13 As was done in *Mackay v Leask* 1996 Hous LR 94, a civil action under s 36 of the 1988 Act (see below), in which the tenant was awarded damages of £15,750.

14 *R v Yuthiwattana* (1985) 80 Cr App R 55, (1984) 16 HLR 49, in which exclusion for one night was held not to constitute deprivation. For an unusual instance of deprivation, see *Osei-Bonsu v Wandsworth LBC* [1999] 1 WLR 1011, in which the plaintiff was forced to leave the property when his wife obtained an "ouster injunction" (the Scottish equivalent would be an exclusion order). His wife then left the property and the injunction was discharged. However, the local authority landlord refused to allow the plaintiff to be readmitted to the property, because it had been offered to another person. This was found to be an unlawful eviction giving rise to a claim for statutory damages.

15 *Abbott v Bayley* (2000) 32 HLR 72. There is some tension between this conclusion and the decision in *Yuthiwattana* (n 14), in which the court said that "deprivation" was committed "only if the act complained of had the character of an eviction". Note that *Abbott v Bayley* was an action for statutory damages, whereas *Yuthiwattana* involved a criminal prosecution. See also *Costelloe v Camden LBC* [1986] Crim LR 249.

16 Rennie (n 8) para 21-104. Presumably the letter or notice would have to cause the occupier to leave. As to whether this constitutes deprivation, see n 15. If the occupier stays put, such notices or letters might constitute harassment. On the sending of correspondence threatening eviction proceedings, see the discussion of the Protection from Harassment Act 1997 below.

indicates both a subjective and an objective standard. The same defence is available in an action for statutory damages for unlawful eviction.[17]

"Under a contract"

The leading example of a contract by which the owner of premises may allow another person to occupy heritable subjects is a lease. A contract that allows for such occupation, but which falls short of being a lease, is generally described as a "licence". Licences do not attract any of the statutory rights available to tenants under the legislation considered in Chapters 4–10.[18] However, a licensee of premises does have the protection of section 22, as long as the contract under which he occupies continues.[19] When the contract comes to an end, it will still be necessary to raise proceedings in order to recover possession, because the licensee has the protection of section 23(2A) unless his occupation comes under one of the excepted categories listed in section 23A. Those provisions are discussed below.

"By virtue of any enactment or rule of law"

As was broadly described in Chapter 1, the 1984, 1988, 2001 and 2016 Acts confer security of tenure on certain residential occupiers, such that they cannot be dispossessed unless the requirements of the relevant Act are met. In the cases of the 1984 Act and the 1988 Act, a residential occupier may have a continuing right of occupation, after the termination of the contract under which he originally occupied.[20] The following is intended to be a non-exhaustive list of other enactments or rules of law that give a residential occupier the right to remain in occupation or restrict the right of any other person to recover possession:

- Section 23 of the 1984 Act, which will be discussed below.
- At common law, where a person occupies under a tenancy and the tenancy comes to an end, he cannot be evicted except by order of the court.[21]
- Occupancy rights conferred by the Matrimonial Homes (Family Protection) (Scotland) Act 1981.
- It also seems reasonable to proceed on the basis that there is a common law rule that a contract for residential occupation contains an implied term that it may be terminated only on reasonable notice.[22]

17 Under s 36(7)(a) of the 1988 Act. See *Kalas v Farmer* [2010] HLR 25 and *Mackay v Leask* (n 13).

18 For this reason, landlords have often sought to avoid security of tenure by creating licences instead of leases. See Chapter 1, p 23 and Chapter 12, p 432.

19 *R v H* (n 9), though note that the offence under s 22(2A) appears to be restricted to cases in which there is a relationship of landlord and tenant.

20 Under the 2016 Act, termination of a PRT only takes place under the Act. See Chapter 9.

21 This rule is codified by s 23(1) of the 1984 Act. However, the operation of s 23 is excluded in certain cases: s 23A. In those cases, the common law rule continues to apply: see the discussion of s 23(5) of the 1984 Act below.

22 This appears to have been the basis for the pursuer's ultimate success in *Conway v Glasgow City Council* 2001 SLT 1472 (Note). See Chapter 12, p 434.

Harassment

Section 22(2) sets out a further offence, applying if any person "does acts" likely to interfere with the peace or comfort of the residential occupier or members of his household, or the persistent withdrawal or withholding of services reasonably required for the occupation of premises as a residence, if this is done with intent to cause the residential occupier to give up occupation of the premises or any part thereof, or to refrain from exercising any right or pursuing any remedy in respect of the premises.[23]

Subsections (2A) and (2B) were inserted by section 38 of the 1988 Act. Evidently, subsection (2A) is directed at the same sort of conduct as subsection (2). The purpose of the newer provisions is apparently to lower the threshold for the offence in respect of conduct by a landlord or his agent.[24] In that case, it is not necessary to prove intent to cause the specified result to occur, but merely that the accused knew, or had reasonable cause to believe, that the result was likely.

In order to constitute harassment, the acts in question need not be actionable civil wrongs, or be in breach of the contract between the owner and the residential occupier.[25]

DUE PROCESS OF LAW: ss 23, 23A

Prohibition of eviction: s 23

Section 23 states:

"**Prohibition of eviction without due process of law**

(1) Where any premises have been let as a dwelling under a tenancy which is not a statutorily protected tenancy within the meaning of this Part of this Act or a right of a kind to which Part VII of this Act applies to use a dwelling-house has been granted before or after the commencement of this Act and—
  (a) the tenancy or, as the case may be, the right to use (in this Part of this Act referred to as the former tenancy) has come to an end; but
  (b) the occupier continues to reside in the premises or part of them;
subject to section 23A, it shall not be lawful for the owner to enforce against the occupier, otherwise than by proceedings in the [court or First-tier Tribunal], his right to recover possession of the premises.

(2) For the purposes of this Part of this Act a person who, under the terms of his employment, had exclusive possession of any premises otherwise than as a tenant shall be deemed to have been a tenant and the expressions 'let' and 'tenancy' shall be construed accordingly.

(2A) Subsections (1) and (2) above apply in relation to any premises occupied (whether exclusively or not) as a dwelling other than under a tenancy as they

23 The necessary intent must be proved. Where services were cut off due to the incompetence or indifference of the landlord, that was insufficient: *McCall v Abelesz* [1976] QB 585, 598.

24 Whereas, under subss (1) and (2), the offence might be committed by any person carrying out the proscribed acts, against a residential occupier. Note that, under s 115(1) of the 1984 Act, the definition of "landlord" includes any person from time to time deriving title under the original landlord.

25 *R v Burke* [1991] 1 AC 135.

apply in relation to premises let as a dwelling under a tenancy, and in those subsections the expressions 'let' and 'tenancy' shall be construed accordingly.

(3) In this Part of this Act 'the owner', in relation to any premises, means the person who, as against the occupier, is entitled to possession thereof; and in this section 'the occupier' means any person lawfully residing in the premises or part of them at the termination of the former tenancy.

(4) The preceding provisions of this section shall, with the necessary modifications, apply where the owner's right to recover possession arises on the death of the tenant under a statutory tenancy.

(5) Nothing in this section shall be taken to affect any rule of law prohibiting the securing of possession otherwise than by due process of law."

Section 23(1)

It is clearly "unlawful" to evict, without legal proceedings, a person who has an ongoing right to occupy subjects, whether under a contract or otherwise. The purpose of section 23 is to require that proceedings are also necessary to evict certain occupiers who *had* such a right, where that right is said to have ended.

Section 23(1) applies where premises have been let as a dwelling under a non-statutory tenancy that has come to an end, provided that the former tenant "continues to reside in the premises or part of them".

The placing of the words "court or First-tier Tribunal" in square brackets needs explanation. As originally enacted, section 23(1) required proceedings to be raised "in the court". However, as a result of section 16 of the Housing (Scotland) Act 2014, and part 5 of the 2016 Act, eviction proceedings in relation to tenancies under the 1984, 1988 and 2016 Acts are now raised in the First-tier Tribunal ("FTT").[26]

That change was thought to require an amendment to section 23, with the result that paragraph 7 of part 1 of schedule 1 to the 2014 Act deletes "court" in section 23(1) as set out above, and replaces it with "First-tier Tribunal".[27] However, the commencement order for section 16[28] states that schedule 1 to the 2014 Act, so far as it relates to paragraph 7, comes into force only "For the purpose of proceedings in relation to a regulated tenancy . . . and an assured tenancy".[29] Hence, "court" in section 23(1) is not deleted and replaced in relation to any other proceedings.[30]

26 See the discussion of the transfer of jurisdiction at Chapter 14, p 477.

27 Section 16(3) of the 2014 Act states that pt 1 of sch 1 "makes minor and consequential amendments".

28 Being the Housing (Scotland) Act 2014 (Commencement No. 7, Amendment and Saving Provision) Order 2017 (SSI 2017/330).

29 This is confirmed by the explanatory note to the commencement order.It is suggested that, in this context, "in relation to" should be understood as meaning "*arising from*", because the transfer of jurisdiction, under s 16 of the 2014 Act, is in relation to actions "arising from" tenancies under the 1984 and 1988 Act; likewise, the FTT has jurisdiction in relation to civil proceedings "arising from" a PRT under s 71 of the 2016 Act. As to the meaning of "arising from", see Chapter 14, p 477.

30 This seems a rather unsatisfactory way of achieving the desired end. One suspects that there was a drafting error in the amending provision; instead of deleting "court", it ought to have inserted "or First-tier Tribunal" in s 23(1), after "court". Perhaps this was spotted between the passing of the 2014 Act and the making of the commencement order.

This means that the sheriff court retains jurisdiction for eviction proceedings, other than those arising from regulated or assured tenancies, or private residential tenancies ("PRTs").[31] This was confirmed by the decision of Sheriff Jamieson in *Reid v Redfern (No 3)*.[32] The sheriff observed that the print of section 23 in the *Parliament House Book* appeared to be in error in stating otherwise. That is why, in setting out section 23(1) above, the words "court or First-tier Tribunal" appear in square brackets.[33]

Section 23(2), (3) and (4)

Subsection (2) extends the same protection to service occupiers; subsection (3) confirms that the protection is not restricted to landlords and tenants; and subsection (4) provides that the protection also applies where the right to recover possession arose on the death of a tenant of a statutory tenancy under the 1984 Act. These subsections are rendered somewhat superfluous by the significant extension of section 23 by subsection (2A).

Section 23(2A)

The scope of section 23 was altered by amendments made by sections 39 and 40 of the 1988 Act, which added section 23(2A) and section 23A. The first of these provisions appears to compel the owner to raise legal proceedings to recover possession of any premises occupied as a dwelling. However, the extent of this requirement is limited by section 23A and the other provisions of section 23. Thus, section 23(3) makes it clear that the protection does not apply to squatters, as the "occupier" must be a person who is lawfully residing at the premises. When subsection (2A) is read with subsections (1) and (3), it is apparent that protection is extended only where:

- the premises are occupied as a "dwelling";[34]
- the occupation was originally lawful;
- the occupier was resident in the premises at the point of termination of that right, and continues to reside there; and
- the occupation is not covered by any of the section 23A provisions.

Notwithstanding those restrictions, section 23(2A) is capable of applying in a manner that might seem surprising. Say, for example, that the owner of premises grants permission to a friend or relative in distressed circumstances to occupy those premises for an indefinite period, free of charge. In due course, the owner decides that this person has outstayed his welcome, and withdraws the permission. In this case, a court order will be necessary before possession

31 The FTT has jurisdiction to grant eviction orders in relation to PRTs, under s 51 of the 2016 Act.

32 2019 SLT (Sh Ct) 281.

33 At [23] the sheriff observed: "The irony is that s.23 is in reality only needed for those few types of tenancies of dwellinghouses [or other agreements under which premises are occupied as a dwelling] where there is no other statutory form of protection and which are outwith the jurisdiction of the First-tier Tribunal in the first place."

34 The meaning of "dwelling" is discussed below. As for the meaning of "occupied", see Chapter 1.

may be recovered, provided that the section 23A exclusions, in particular subsection (1), do not apply.

"Dwelling" and the decision in Lewisham

As indicated above, section 23(2A) requires occupation as a "dwelling". The meaning of that term in the equivalent English legislation – section 3 of the Protection from Eviction Act 1977 – was considered by the Supreme Court in *R (N) v Lewisham LBC*.[35] The issue in that case was whether the statutory requirement to raise proceedings in court applied as regards homeless persons in temporary accommodation provided by a local authority, under its duties in terms of the homelessness legislation. By a majority, the court decided that it did not, because the accommodation was not "premises occupied as a dwelling under a licence" under section 3(2B) of the 1977 Act (the equivalent of section 23(2A) in the 1984 Act): such accommodation was not a "dwelling".[36]

It is suggested that this decision has limited significance for practice in Scotland, for two reasons. First, where local authorities in Scotland provide interim accommodation for homeless persons under section 29 of the 1987 Act,[37] they invariably do so under a tenancy agreement.[38] For the reasons explained in the discussion of section 23(5) below, under Scots law tenants and former tenants cannot be evicted without a court order, and therefore do not stand in need of the protection of section 23: they are protected at common law.

Secondly, even in the case of a person accommodated under section 29 by an agreement that is correctly regarded as a licence rather than a lease, it is doubtful that the decision in *R(N) v Lewisham LBC* would apply. That is because there is a significant difference between section 23(2A) and the equivalent English provision.[39] The latter addresses the purpose of the licence, rather than the use of the premises by the occupier. Therefore, under English law the issue of whether the statutory protection applies is determined by interpreting the parties' contract. The Scottish provision addresses the use of the premises by the occupier, and makes no reference to the purpose of any agreement or permission under which the occupation was taken up. Thus, under the Scottish legislation, the issue in each case appears to be a simple

35 [2015] AC 1259. See also the discussion of the case in Chapter 1.

36 The reasons for the majority so finding were: (1) temporary accommodation for homeless persons was not a home, and the applicant remained "homeless" under the legislation; (2) the licences used by the local authority were from day to day or nightly; and (3) the imposition of a requirement to obtain a court order would significantly hamper the operation by the authorities of the statutory scheme under the homelessness legislation. This is a broad summary of paras 33–35 of the judgment. Note that this case was distinguished by the Court of Appeal in *Dacorum BC v Bucknall (formerly Acheampong)* [2017] EWHC 2094 (QB), [2017] HLR 40. In that case the defendant's application for assistance under the homelessness accommodation had been successful, and she had accepted an offer from the council to reside in her temporary accommodation indefinitely, pending an offer of accommodation in the private sector.

37 The statutory scheme for provision of assistance and accommodation for homeless persons under pt II of the 1987 Act is described in Chapter 5, p 151.

38 Or an agreement that, although it is described as an "occupancy agreement" or similar, is a tenancy at common law.

39 Section 3(2B) of the 1977 Act applies the extended protection from eviction without due process in to "any premises *occupied as a dwelling under a licence*".

question of fact: "Are the premises occupied as a dwelling?". If they are, the section 23 protection applies, subject to section 23A.[40]

Section 23(5): preservation of the common law

Section 23(5) preserves any rule of law that prohibited the securing of possession otherwise than by court proceedings. The significant point here is that, prior to the introduction of the statutory protection from unlawful eviction in 1965, it was already the case in Scots law that a former tenant could not be evicted without a court order.[41] Proceedings are therefore required to evict tenants and former tenants, even where the tenancy is an occupancy falling under one of the categories described by section 23A.

In the appeal to the Inner House in *Ali v Serco Ltd*,[42] the Court rejected an argument that the prohibition of *brevi manu* evictions extended beyond tenancies, and applied to any contract under which a person had a right to occupy heritable subjects.[43] At common law, therefore, the owner of the property is entitled to recover possession by means of summary ejection in any case where a contractual right to occupy, which does not amount to a lease, has come to an end.[44]

It is also follows from the decisions in *R (N) v Lewisham LBC* and *Ali v Serco Ltd* that article 8 of the European Convention on Human Rights ("ECHR") is not a rule of law that prohibits the securing of possession by a public authority, otherwise than by due process of law, where there are adequate procedural safeguards that enable the proportionality of eviction to be assessed.[45]

Excluded tenancies: s 23A

Section 23A counterbalances the extension of section 23 that was effected by subsection (2A) by listing a series of cases in which section 23 will not apply. Further cases have been added by subsequent amending legislation.[46] The various categories excepted from section 23 may be summarised as follows.

Any tenancy or right of occupancy is excepted from section 23:

- if, under its terms, the occupier has the use of any accommodation in common with the owner or a member of his family and, immediately before the tenancy or right was granted and at all times since then, the owner

40 And, in particular, s 23A(5), which would exclude the protection of s 23 in the case of hostel accommodation for homeless persons.

41 Rankine, *Law of Leases in Scotland* (3rd edn, 1916) 512, 592; Paton and Cameron, *The Law of Landlord and Tenant in Scotland* (1967) 248. This is the case even if the lease is said to be voidable because it was obtained by fraud: *Brash v Munro and Hall* (1903) 5 F 1102.

42 2020 SC 182, 2019 SLT 1335.

43 In *Ali*, the pursuer argued, at first instance, that the contract under which she occupied her accommodation was a lease. This was rejected on the basis that no rent was payable: *Ali* (n 42) [43] and [44]. Reliance on the common law was necessary because, as an asylum seeker, the pursuer was excluded from the statutory protection in s 23, in terms of s 23A(5A).

44 *Ali* (n 3) [46].

45 See *R (N) v Lewisham LBC* (n 35) [64]–[76]; and paras [34]–[42] in the Lord Ordinary's decision in *Ali v Serco Ltd* 2019 SLT 463. His conclusion was endorsed on appeal: (n 3), [49].

46 Subsections (4A), (5A) and (5B).

occupied as his only or principal home premises of which the whole or part of the accommodation formed part;[47]

- if it was granted as a temporary expedient to a person who entered the premises in question or any other premises without right or title, whether or not before the beginning of that tenancy or grant of that right another tenancy or right to occupy the premises or any other premises had been granted to him;[48]
- if it confers on the tenant or occupier the right to occupy the premises for a holiday only;[49]
- if it was granted, for a term of less than six months, to a person who is under supervision in pursuance of the functions of a local authority under certain provisions of the Social Work (Scotland) Act 1968, or who has requested the provision of advice, guidance or assistance by a local authority in pursuance of the authority's functions under those provisions;[50]
- which confers rights of occupation in a hostel, which is provided by certain bodies, in particular local authorities or registered housing associations;[51] or
- if it is granted in order to provide accommodation under section 4 or part VI of the Immigration and Asylum Act 1999, or under the Displaced Persons (Temporary Protection) Regulations 2005.[52]

As indicated above, section 23A only excludes the protection of section 23, which is just one example of an "enactment or rule of law" that gives a residential occupier the right to remain in occupation, or restricts the right of any other person to recover possession. Therefore, where the occupier has a right of occupation other than that provided by section 23, it will still be necessary to obtain a court order to evict him, even if he falls into one of the section 23A categories.[53]

47 Section 23A(1). For the purposes of this exception, s 23A(2) provides that "accommodation" includes neither an area used for storage nor a staircase, passage, corridor or other means of access; "owner" means, in relation to a tenancy, the landlord and, in relation to a right to occupy, the person granting it and, in any case where there are joint landlords or grantors any one of them shall be regarded as the "owner"; and "occupier" means, in relation to a tenancy, the tenant and, in relation to a right to occupy, its grantee. Section 83 of the 1987 Act is to apply for the purposes of determining whether a person is a member of another's family. As to whether the accommodation is the owner's "only or principal home", see the discussion in Chapter 1. Note that, in *Sumeghova v McMahon* [2003] HLR 26, it was said that the fact that the owner sleeps at the accommodation is of "the utmost importance".

48 Section 23A(3).

49 Section 23A(4).

50 Section 23A(4A).

51 SI 2005/1379. See s 23A(5). The eviction of hostel dwellers is discussed in Chapter 12.

52 Section 23A(5A) and (5B). It was under s 23A(5A) that the pursuer in *Ali v Serco* (n 3) was excluded from the protection of s 23. She relied, *inter alia*, on the argument that she was protected by the common law, which was preserved by s 23(5). That argument was rejected; see the discussion of s 23(5) above.

53 And the occupier will also have the protection of s 22, even if the occupation is under a licence and the owner is resident in the property: *R v H* (n 9).

CLAIMS FOR DAMAGES

Statutory damages: 1988 Act ss 36, 37[54]

The statutory protection against unlawful eviction was strengthened by the introduction, by sections 36 and 37 of the 1988 Act, of a scheme for statutory damages, which applies where a landlord[55] or any person acting on his behalf[56] "unlawfully deprives the residential occupier"[57] of any premises of his occupation or attempts to do so.[58]

Unlawful eviction may found an action for damages at common law[59] but, as is noted below, damages cannot be awarded on both statutory and common law bases. Unlawful eviction may also be prevented by interdict.

Where an unlawful eviction takes place under section 36, the landlord is liable to pay to the former residential occupier damages assessed on the basis set out in section 37.[60] This entails taking two figures, being the value of the landlord's interest in the property with, and without, a residential occupier with the same right[61] of occupation.[62] The award is the difference between those figures, which may be a substantial sum.[63]

54 The equivalent provisions in the English legislation are ss 27 and 28 of the Housing Act 1988. As with criminal prosecutions for unlawful eviction, actions for statutory damages have been more common in England.

55 Section 55 of the 1988 Act provides that "'*landlord*' includes any person from time to time deriving title from the original landlord". Thus, ss 36 and 37 appear to be limited to unlawful eviction by landlords and their agents, rather than persons in general, as is also the case with subsections (2A) and (2B) of s 22 (see p 35 above), which were added by the 1988 Act. This is more restrictive than the definition of "landlord" in the English legislation: the Housing Act 1988, s 27(9) states that "'landlord', in relation to a residential occupier, means the person who, but for the occupier's right to occupy, would be entitled to occupation of the premises".

56 In *Scott v Thomson* 2003 SLT 99, 2002 Hous LR 114, the Inner House held that the expression "acting on his behalf" encompassed anyone who was acting either as direct agent of the landlord or as someone employed to do a particular act, or to undertake the management of the property with no particular fetter on that management. The pursuer is not required to prove that the landlord instigated or connived at his agent's illegitimate activities.

57 For the terms "unlawfully", "deprives" and "residential occupier", see the discussion of s 22 of the 1984 Act, above.

58 Section 36(2) provides that the right to statutory damages also applies where the residential occupier gives up her occupation as a result of attempted unlawful eviction, or the harassment described in s 36(2)(b): see *Anderson v Cluny Investment Service Ltd* 2004 SLT (Sh Ct) 37. Where harassment takes place, but the occupier remains in occupation, she may have a remedy under the Protection from Harassment Act 1997, as indicated at p 45.

59 Unlawful eviction is a delict. It may also give rise to a claim for damages for breach of contract, if the eviction was effected before the contract by virtue of which occupation took place was terminated.

60 Section 36(3).

61 The words "the same right" in s 37(1)(a) are significant: the assessment of the level of statutory damages may depend on the nature of the right of occupation that was terminated.

62 Section 37(1). In some cases, this is not a straightforward exercise, given the nature of the tenanted property and the type of tenancy. See *Tagro v Cafane* [1991] 1 WLR 378; *Melville v Bruton* (1997) 29 HLR 319; *Osei-Bonsu v Wandsworth LBC* (n 14); *Lambeth LBC v Loveridge* [2014] 1 WLR 4516. The decision of the Supreme Court in the last of these cases makes it clear that statutory damages can be awarded against a local authority, although the court was somewhat uncomfortable with that conclusion (see para 30 of the judgment). The possibility of damages being awarded against a social landlord is implicitly recognised by s 36(4A), which will be discussed below.

63 See, e.g.: *Scott v Thomson* (n 56) (£33,000); *Kalas v Farmer* (n 17) (£49,500); *Lambeth LBC v Loveridge* (n 62) (£90,500).

No liability arises if, before the date on which the proceedings to enforce the liability are finally decided, the former residential occupier is reinstated in the premises in question in such circumstances that he becomes again the residential occupier of them;[64] or, at the request of the former residential occupier, the sheriff or the FTT makes an order as a result of which he is reinstated.[65] Accordingly, a residential occupier can ultimately obtain either statutory damages or reinstatement to the property, but is not entitled to both.[66] There is English authority to the effect that the right to elect between those remedies may be exercised at trial.[67]

In addition, proceedings may be defended on the basis that the defender believed, and had reasonable cause to believe, that the residential occupier had ceased to reside in the premises at the time when he was deprived of occupation[68] or, as the case may be, when the attempt was made or the acts were done as a result of which he gave up his occupation of those premises.[69] Furthermore, the court or the FTT may reduce statutory damages if the conduct of the residential occupier or any person living with him was such that it is reasonable to mitigate the damages, or where the residential occupier refused an offer of reinstatement made by the landlord before the proceedings commenced.[70]

Damages at common law

Under section 36(4) and (5), the liability to statutory damages is in the nature of a liability in delict, and is in addition to any liability arising apart from that section, whether in delict, contract or otherwise. However, the court (or the FTT) cannot award statutory damages and damages in respect of liability that arises apart from section 36 on account of the same loss, being the loss of the right to occupy the premises in question as a residence. Therefore, the claimant must elect to seek either statutory or common law damages, or both, in the alternative.[71]

In some cases, for example those involving bedsit accommodation, it may not be possible to calculate statutory damages because the "dwelling" in question, which might include exclusive occupation of one room and shared use of other parts of a building, cannot be given a value in terms of section

64 As to what constitutes "reinstatement", see *Tagro v Cafane* (n 62).

65 Section 36(6). Subsection (6A) clarifies the meaning of the words "finally decided" in relation to any appeal that might be made in the case.

66 Note that reinstatement would not preclude a claim for common law damages.

67 *Osei Bonsu v Wandsworth LBC* (n 14). There seems to be no reason why the same approach would not be applicable in Scotland, such that the election could be made at proof or, in an FTT case, at the hearing.

68 As was indicated above, this is also a defence to a criminal prosecution under s 22(1) of the 1984 Act. Examples of the defence being relied upon (unsuccessfully) in statutory damages cases are: *Kalas v Farmer* (n 17), *Mackay v Leask* (n 13), and *Baral v Arif* 2020 Hous LR 11.

69 Or, where the liability would otherwise arise by virtue only of the doing of acts or the withdrawal or withholding of services, he had reasonable grounds for doing the acts or withdrawing or withholding the services in question.

70 Section 36(6B). In *Regalgrand Ltd v Dickerson* (1997) 29 HLR 620, the Court of Appeal confirmed that for the purposes of this provision "conduct" could include the previous non-payment of rent.

71 In the FTT, seeking statutory and common law damages in the alternative would have to be done in separate applications. See the discussion of FTT cases below.

37. Also, in a case in which the tenant's security of tenure is limited, such as where he occupies under a short assured tenancy, the difference between the two figures in section 37(1)(a) is likely to be low, because an eviction order could easily be obtained by the landlord, and so the existence of the right of occupation does not significantly affect the value of his interest in the property.[72] In that case, the aggrieved former occupier can elect to seek damages at common law.[73]

As unlawful eviction[74] is a delict, common law damages should, as nearly as possible, amount to the sum of money which will put the injured party in the position which he would have occupied if he had not sustained the wrong.

There is a dearth of Scottish authority on the assessment of common law damages.[75] A good, and recent, example of the approach of the English courts to assessment of such damages is the decision of the Court of Appeal in *Smith v Khan*.[76] There, the date of unlawful eviction was found to be 15 April 2015, but the tenancy would have ended, in any event, on 30 June, 76 days later. It was accepted that a "daily rate" ought to be applied to this period, which, in the view of the court, should be set at £130 per night, leading to a figure of £9,880.[77] The court viewed unlawful eviction as being a form of trespass.[78] It remains to be seen whether a Scottish court (or the FTT) would take the same approach.

Sheriff court and tribunal proceedings

Reference has already been made to some of the difficulties caused by the transfer of jurisdiction from the sheriff court to the FTT, in relation to section 23 of the 1984 Act. As regards statutory damages, the following subsection was added to section 36 of the 1988 Act:

> "(4A) Any action to enforce liability arising from this section must be raised in the First-tier Tribunal unless the residential occupant's claim is founded on the premises in question being subject to a Scottish secure tenancy or to a short Scottish secure tenancy (within the meaning of the Housing (Scotland) Act 2001."

72 This may also be the case with a PRT under the 2016 Act where there is a mandatory ground for eviction, such as where the landlord intends to sell the property.

73 As was done, e.g., in *Conway v City of Glasgow Council* (n 22). See also *Baral v Arif* (n 68). In that case, the applicant originally sought common law damages, on the basis that the tenancy was short assured. However, the FTT decided that the tenancy was assured, but not short assured. Subsequently, the applicant amended the application to seek damages under ss 36 and 37, which were awarded in the sum of £18,000.

74 Or "wrongous ejection", as it is called in the older Scottish cases.

75 Most of the cases on "wrongous ejection" are of some vintage, and deal with the issue of whether the pursuer was entitled to damages at all, given his status as, say, an employee or a servant of the defender.

76 [2018] HLR 31.

77 To this was added a further £4,200 made up of awards of aggravated and exemplary damages (totalling £2,700) and awards of damages for harassment and special damages (being £1,500, £1,000 of which was in respect of the lost possessions), which were not in issue in the appeal. Aggravated and exemplary damages are not awarded in Scotland.

78 See paras 37 and 45 of the judgment.

Again, the drafting of this provision is problematic. Given the terms of section 16 of the 2014 Act, and section 71 of the 2016 Act, it is to be expected that claims for statutory damages "arising from" regulated tenancies, assured tenancies or PRTs would go to the FTT, whereas other claims under section 36, such as those arising from common law tenancies, licences, and tenancies under the 2001 Act, would stay in the sheriff court. Instead, section 36(4A) indicates that *any* action for statutory damages has to go to the FTT, unless the claim is founded on the premises being a short Scottish secure tenancy (an "SSST") or a Scottish secure tenancy under the 2001 Act.

Let us say that a claim under section 36 is made against a local authority, by a person who was provided with accommodation under the homelessness legislation, under a tenancy excepted from the 2001 Act under paragraph 5 of schedule 1.[79] Given the terms of section 36(4A), the claim would have to be made in the FTT. However, a claim for common law damages would have to be raised in the sheriff court, because such a claim would not "arise from" section 36, or from a regulated tenancy, an assured tenancy or a PRT.

Rule 69 of the FTT's Procedure Rules[80] ("Application for damages for unlawful eviction") applies "Where a former residential occupier makes an application under section 36(3) (damages for unlawful eviction) of the 1988 Act".[81] Rule 69 is in chapter 6 of part 3 of the Rules. This chapter is headed "Procedure in respect of assured tenancy applications". However, given the terms of section 36(4A), it is suggested that an application under rule 69 may also be made where the claim arises from, say, a PRT.

A claim for common law damages would be made under rule 70 in a case arising from an assured tenancy, or under rule 111 if arising from a PRT. Thus, where the applicant seeks statutory and common law damages in the alternative, two separate applications require to be made, which presumably could be conjoined.[82]

Claims for lost or damaged property

A common feature of unlawful eviction cases is that the defender or respondent is said to have disposed of the tenant's belongings and personal effects, or that the tenant's property has been damaged or lost, in the process of the eviction being carried out, or that tenant has incurred some cost, in the way of storage charges or otherwise, as a result of the eviction. Such losses may be added as an additional head of damages, whether the principal claim is for statutory or common law damages.

79 For tenancies granted by social landlords, but excluded from coverage by the 2001 Act, see Chapter 4.

80 First-tier Tribunal for Scotland Housing and Property Chamber (Procedure) Regulations 2017 (SSI 2017/328).

81 The rule requires that the application must state: (i) the name and address of the former residential occupier; (ii) the name, address and profession of any representative of the former residential occupier; (iii) the name, address and registration number (if any) of the landlord; and (iv) the details of the amount of damages sought based on s 37 of the 1988 Act in respect of the loss of the right to occupy the premises.

82 Section 36(5) precludes statutory and common law damages being awarded in respect of the loss of the right to occupy the accommodation, but there seems to be no reason why they could not be sought, in the alternative, in the FTT, as has happened in the sheriff court.

PROTECTION FROM HARASSMENT ACT 1997

A course of conduct that amounts to harassment may give rise to proceedings under the 1997 Act, under which interdict and damages may be sought.[83]

In *Worthington v Metropolitan Housing Trust Ltd*,[84] damages were awarded to two tenants against a housing association, in respect of a course of conduct, being the sending of correspondence threatening eviction proceedings, which was found to amount to harassment under section 1 of the 1997 Act.[85] The court characterised the correspondence as "exceptional and not the kind that would usually be sent by social landlords to their tenants". It included "totally unjustified threats to commence proceedings without taking basic steps to ensure that there was a proper foundation for taking action".[86]

HARASSMENT UNDER THE EQUALITY ACT 2010

Under 35(2) of the 2010 Act, a person who manages premises must not, in relation to their management, harass a person who occupies them.[87] The concept of harassment under section 26 of the Act is explained, in some detail, in chapter 8 of the Equality and Human Rights Commission's ("EHRC's") Statutory Code of Practice on Services, Public Functions and Associations,[88] to which readers are referred. The definition of harassment contained in section 26 covers different forms of harassment including sexual harassment[89] and applies, in particular, where "unwanted conduct" has the purpose or effect of creating an intimidating, hostile, degrading, humiliating or offensive environment for the person said to have been harassed.[90]

EVICTION *BREVI MANU*

From the preceding discussion it will be apparent that eviction of a "residential occupier" *brevi manu* may incur criminal and civil liability if there is a contract, or an enactment or rule of law, giving him the right to remain in occupation or restricting the right of any other person to recover possession of the premises. In any other case, eviction *brevi manu* is permissible. Nevertheless, proceedings are very often raised in such circumstances, so that a court order for recovery of possession may be obtained. There are several reasons for this approach.

83 As already described, statutory damages may also be sought under s 36 of the 1988 Act, but only in the circumstances described in subsection (2). This is restricted to cases in which the residential occupier gives up occupation.

84 [2018] HLR 32.

85 The equivalent provision for Scotland is s 8 of the 1997 Act.

86 The two claimants were awarded £4,750 and £4,160 respectively.

87 Section 35 of the 2010 Act is discussed in detail in chs 2 and 3 of the author's *Housing and Equality Law in Scotland* (Shelter Scotland 2018).

88 This is available on the EHRC's website.

89 Being unwanted conduct of a sexual nature (s 26(2)) or that is related to gender reassignment or sex (s 26(3)).

90 Under s 26(3), A also sexually harasses B if, because of B's rejection of or submission to the conduct (of A or another person), A treats B less favourably.

First, where there is any doubt whatsoever as to the status of an occupier, eviction *brevi manu* entails a risk. If the owner has misapprehended that status, he may be committing a criminal offence under section 22 of the 1984 Act, and may also expose himself to an action for damages by the evictee.[91] A person unlawfully evicted *brevi manu* may also raise proceedings under section 46 of the Court of Session Act 1988, seeking an order from the court to reinstate him in his possessory right, and ordaining the defender to perform such act or acts as shall be necessary to enable him to resume occupation. Under section 47(2), an interim order to that effect may be made.[92]

Secondly, against persons who do not have, and have never had, a right to be in occupation of the subjects, a court order can be obtained fairly easily in most cases, and without much delay. There is no legal requirement for the owner to take any particular steps before such proceedings are raised,[93] and normally there will be no defence to the action.[94] Accordingly, it should be possible to obtain decree at the first calling of the case. Moreover, it should be possible to obtain an order quickly: this is facilitated by special rules of court that apply to eviction proceedings of this type.[95] For these reasons, where an occupier without right or title seeks legal advice in respect of the threat of proceedings, he may well be advised that he should leave by agreement as soon as possible, so as to avoid incurring legal expenses.

Thirdly, the availability of a court order, enforced by officers of court, is desirable in any case in which eviction may be resisted by the occupier. This was the principal reason for the origination of judicial procedures for recovery of possession of heritable property in the sixteenth century; in former times, evictions carried out *brevi manu* often led to violence and public disorder:

> "39. The order of removing of old was thus: The master of the ground did only verbally intimate to the tenant to remove at the next Whitsunday; and the only solemnity requisite was, that before the said term, he appeared before the door of the tenant, and broke a lance there, as a symbol of his breaking of the tacit relocation betwixt them; whereupon, the second day after Whitsunday, he came *brevi manu*, and expelled the tenant; or at least laid out some of his goods to complete the solemnity of his removing. Hence arose many quarrels, violences and breaches of the public peace; as when the tenant had any defence, reason or pretence, for which he could not be removed, or otherwise was unwilling, and not compelled by law or public authority, but by private force."[96]

91 For example, see *Kalas v Farmer* (n 17).

92 An interim order under s 88(1)(a)(i) of the Courts Reform (Scotland) Act 2014 could also have the effect of reinstating the evictee, while proceedings (say for declarator of a tenancy) were ongoing. Note that successfully enforcing a right to reinstatement would preclude a claim for statutory damages, given the terms of s 36(6) of the 1988 Act.

93 Though it may well be appropriate to give some form of warning to the occupier if the owner intends to seek the expenses of the proceedings.

94 Assuming that the defender is correctly understood not to have any right to remain in occupation.

95 In particular, the Act of Sederunt (Summary Cause Rules) 2002 (SI 2002/132) (Summary Cause Rules), r 30.2 deals with actions "against persons in possession of heritable property without right or title". This rule is considered in Chapter 13.

96 Stair *Institutions* II, 9, 39.

Nowadays, eviction following an order granted by the court or the FTT is carried out by officers of the court, who may seek the assistance of the police if they meet with resistance.[97]

97 See Chapter 15 for further discussion of the procedure involved in carrying out an eviction.

Chapter 3

Terminating the Lease

This chapter begins by returning, in the context of tenancies, to the second of the three questions that began the Introduction:

WHAT STEPS MUST BE TAKEN BY THE LANDLORD BEFORE PROCEEDINGS ARE RAISED?

It will be apparent from the historical and legal context outlined in Chapter 1 that notice or notices must be given by the landlord to the tenant under the rules that are applicable to the tenancy in question. Those rules may be divided into two categories:

(1) the particular rules for notices under the 1988, 2001 and 2016 Acts, which apply to the forms of tenancy created by each Act;
(2) all other rules, being the statutory and common law rules that apply to residential tenancies in general.

Taking these in turn:

Where a tenancy is subject to the *1988, 2001 or 2016 Acts*, notice must be served in terms of the relevant provisions of the Act, as a necessary preliminary to an action for eviction. If the landlord fails to serve the right notice in the right way, subsequent eviction proceedings are liable to fail. This is because an order cannot be granted for possession of subjects let under those Acts unless the correct statutory procedures are followed.[1]

As regards the *other rules*, we may begin by saying that, at common law, the tenancy has to be terminated before proceedings are raised by the landlord. If the tenant has an ongoing contractual right to remain in possession of the subjects, the landlord has no right to recover possession, and subsequent eviction proceedings are thus liable to fail.

For that reason, termination of the parties' contract is necessary in relation to some of the types of tenancy discussed in this book, being:

(a) tenancies excepted from the statutory regimes;[2]

1 For the purposes of the different types of statutory tenancy considered in this work, these are: for Scottish secure tenancies, the notice required by the 2001 Act, s 14(2); for short Scottish secure tenancies, the notice required by the 2001 Act, s 36(2); for assured tenancies, the AT6 notice in terms of the 1988 Act, s 19; for short assured tenancies, notice in terms of the 1988 Act, s 33(1)(d); and for private residential tenancies, the notice to leave required by s 53(2) and described in s 62 of the 2016 Act.

2 As is explained in Chapter 1 (p 16), all the Acts contain provisions under which certain

(b) assured tenancies under the 1988 Act, subject to an important exception under section 18(6), being (d) below;[3] and
(c) short assured tenancies under the 1988 Act.[4]

Where the tenancy contract must be terminated, it may then be said that there are further statutory and common law rules that require notice to be given in order to effect that termination and specify how such notice is to be given. As described in Chapter 1, some of these rules have been inextricably linked with particular judicial procedures.

It will be clear from the outline so far that *two* notices will be required in cases (b) and (c) above, because the landlord must serve notice under the relevant Act *and* also terminate the contract before proceedings are raised. In case (a), only a notice to terminate the contract is necessary, because the tenancy has no statutory protection.

Termination of the parties' contract prior to raising proceedings, by notice to quit or otherwise, is *not* necessary in relation to:

(d) assured tenancies if section 18(6) of the 1988 Act applies;
(e) Scottish secure tenancies under the 2001 Act; and
(f) private residential tenancies ("PRTs") under the 2016 Act.

In these cases, only the relevant statutory notice is required.

It is not necessary (or possible) to terminate a Scottish secure tenancy as a preliminary to an action for recovery of possession for reasons that are outlined in Chapters 1 and 4.[5] In the event that the action succeeds, termination takes place when the order for recovery of possession is made or, in the case of an action in which the ground (or one of the grounds) is rent arrears, when the order is enforced.[6]

Similarly, a PRT cannot be terminated by either party except in accordance with part 5 of the 2016 Act.[7] Where the landlord successfully applies to the First-tier Tribunal ("FTT") for an eviction order, that brings the tenancy

residential tenancies are excluded from protection; such contracts are usually called "common law" tenancies.

3 Hence an application to the FTT for an order for possession under s 18 of the 1988 Act must be accompanied by "a copy of the notice to quit served by the landlord on the tenant (if applicable)" (r 65(b)(iii) of the First-tier Tribunal for Scotland Housing and Property Chamber (Procedure) Regulations 2017 (SSI 2017/328) (Procedure Rules)). Section 18(6) of the 1988 Act allows the court to grant a decree for recovery of possession of a house in relation to which the contractual tenancy is still ongoing. Where it applies, termination of the contract, by notice to quit or otherwise, is not necessary, as preliminary to an application for recovery of possession under s 18 of the Act. Section 18(6) is discussed in detail in Chapter 7.

4 Termination of the contract is necessary if the landlord is seeking an order under the 1988 Act, s 33: see the discussion of that section in Chapter 7. Accordingly, an application to the FTT for an order under s 33 must be accompanied by a copy of the notice to quit served by the landlord on the tenant: r 66(b)(iv). The landlord of a short assured tenancy can also seek an order under s 18 of the Act. In that case, termination of the contract is not a necessary preliminary to an application, if s 18(6) applies.

5 As is explained in Chapter 1, at p 10: under the 1988 Act, as with older Rent Acts, there is a distinction between the "contractual" tenancy and the "statutory" tenancy. Under s 16 of the 1988 Act, the statutory tenancy begins when the contractual tenancy ends. See Chapter 7, p 229. There is no such distinction in relation to Scottish secure tenancies or PRTs.

6 Under s 16(5)(a), and s 16(5A)(b).

7 2016 Act, s 44.

to an end on the day specified by the tribunal in the order.[8] Consequently, where the tenancy is a PRT, it is not necessary to serve a notice to quit before making an application to the tribunal for an eviction order.

The notice requirements in respect of short Scottish secure tenancies ("SSSTs") under the 2001 Act are considered in Chapter 6. As is explained in that chapter, there are two types of SSST, which may be termed the ASB SSST (antisocial behaviour) and the non-ASB SSST. In the case of a non-ASB SSST, termination of the parties' contract by notice to quit, and service of the statutory notice, is necessary. That is also the case as regards ASB SSSTs created before 1 May 2019. For ASB SSSTs created after that date, only the statutory notice under section 36 is necessary.

It follows from this discussion that, in order to serve the right notice(s) in the right way, three issues must be clarified:

(1) What is the statutory status of the tenancy?[9]
(2) If it is necessary to give notice in terms of the statutory provisions applicable to the tenancy, how is this done?
(3) If it is necessary to terminate the parties' contract, how is that done?

The first two of these issues are addressed in Chapter 4 (for Scottish secure tenancies), in Chapter 6 (for SSSTs), Chapter 7 (for assured and short assured tenancies) and Chapter 9 (for PRTs).

The remainder of this chapter deals with the third issue by considering how the tenancy contract may be terminated.[10]

Included in this chapter is a discussion of some difficulties that arise from the historical narrative in Chapter 1. The structure is as follows:

- termination of the tenancy contract: introduction;
- termination at the natural term: notices to quit;
- errors in notices to quit;
- termination of the contract before the natural term;
- irritancy and rescission.

Issues as to the mode of service of notices to quit and other notices, and as to proof of service, are considered in Chapter 15.

Notice by public authority of the reasons for seeking possession

Finally, in the case of an action by a "public authority" for the purposes of section 6 of the Human Rights Act 1998, notice will have to be given to the occupier or tenant of the reasons for recovery of possession being sought.[11] This makes no difference to actions in relation to Scottish secure tenancies

8 ibid s 51(4).

9 I.e. is it an assured or a short assured tenancy under the 1988 Act; or a PRT under the 2016 Act; or a Scottish secure tenancy or an SSST under the 2001 Act; or a tenancy that is not subject to any of the statutory regimes?

10 This means that the rest of this chapter is relevant to tenancies excepted from the statutory regimes, assured tenancies (where s 18(6) of the 1988 Act does not apply), short assured tenancies, non-ASB SSSTs, and ASB SSSTs created before 1 May 2019. It is not relevant to assured tenancies in cases in which s 18(6) applies, Scottish secure tenancies, PRTs or ASB SSSTs created on or after 1 May 2019.

11 See the discussion in Chapter 11, at p 395.

under the 2001 Act, because the statutory notice of proceedings under section 14 already requires that the grounds for eviction be stated. In terms of an amendment to section 36 of the 2001 Act made by the 2014 Act, the notice of proceedings in relation to SSSTs also requires the landlord to state the reasons for seeking recovery of possession.[12] However, in the case of other actions by public authorities, in relation to tenancies excepted from security of tenure,[13] or for the eviction of persons who have never had a contractual relationship with the public authority but have made the subjects their home, the public authority will have to give notice to the prospective defender of the reasons for recovery of possession being sought.

TERMINATING THE LEASE: INTRODUCTION

It is best to begin by making a fundamental distinction between termination of a lease at its natural term and termination prior to the natural term.

Most leases have a duration of a specified period of time, called the "ish", which ends on the ish or termination date.[14] In cases in which the parties do not agree any particular duration, the court may imply a term of one year if the circumstances of the case allow such an implication to be made.[15]

The expiry of the agreed duration does not bring the lease to an end. Subject to express contrary stipulation, a lease contains an implied agreement that its duration may be extended by the tacit consent of the parties.[16]

If either party wishes to avoid the tenancy being prolonged in this way, he must give notice to the other party of his desire to terminate the lease at the next ish. If neither party gives notice, the lease continues by tacit relocation for the same period as the original term, except where the lease is for more

12 Under s 36(3)(aa), added by s 11 of the 2014 Act, with effect from 1 May 2019.

13 Schedule 1 to the 2001 Act sets out categories of tenancies that are excepted from Scottish secure tenancy status under the 2001 Act. It is discussed in Chapter 4.

14 However, it is possible for parties to agree that the lease has an indeterminate duration, ending perhaps on the occurrence of some event in the future, the date of which is not yet known: Paton and Cameron, *Landlord and Tenant* 7. See, e.g., *Glasgow City Council v Torrance* 2000 SLT (Sh Ct) 32, in which Sheriff Principal Bowen decided that the lease in question was properly to be regarded as ending one month after the cessation of the defender's employment. For termination of leases of this type, reference must be made to the terms of the contract. It is also quite common, particularly in the case of verbal agreements, for there to be no agreement as to duration, or at least a degree of uncertainty as to what parties agreed. Lack of an agreed duration does not preclude the creation of a lease, but it does deprive the tenant of the protection of the Leases Act 1449. This means that the contract will bind the landlord and his heirs, but not his singular successors. See the instructive discussion in Lord Hope's judgment in *Mexfield Housing Co-operative Ltd v Berrisford* [2012] 1 AC 955, [2012] HLR 15.

15 *Gibson v Adams* (1875) 3 R 144; *Gray v University of Edinburgh* 1962 SC 157, 1962 SLT 173. In *Poole v Poole* EV/19/2191, 13/9/19 and *Walker v Evans* EV/19/1639, 21/11/19 the FTT implied a duration of one year, where there was no written tenancy and no agreement as to duration.

16 There is authority to suggest that the doctrine of tacit relocation does not apply to certain types of lease, including the lease of a furnished house for less than one year, and, on that basis, notice to quit is not required, as the lease simply terminates at the ish: Paton and Cameron (n 14) 223; *Gloag on Contract* 733. This view is doubted however, on apparently strong grounds, by C B Burns and E S Young in their article "Security of Tenure in Furnished Lettings" 1970 SLT (News) 101.

than one year, in which case it relocates annually from the original ish.[17] At common law, the party seeking to end the tenancy by preventing the operation of tacit relocation had to give reasonable notice to the other party. The accepted basic minimum period appears to have been forty days[18] prior to the ish date and this was adopted in the earliest statutory provisions in relation to removing.

The notice given by either party to terminate a lease at its next ish is a notice to quit.[19] The effect of this notice is to rebut the presumption in favour of the occurrence of tacit relocation, with the result that the parties' contract terminates at the ish.

A lease may terminate prematurely in a variety of circumstances. However, as this chapter is concerned with the termination of the lease as a preliminary to an action of eviction by the landlord, we will be particularly interested in the means by which the landlord may terminate the lease prematurely in response to a breach of contract by the tenant, such as the non-payment of rent. Traditionally, the landlord's primary weapon in this instance has been his power to terminate the lease by invoking an irritancy clause.[20] In cases in which there is no such clause, the landlord may wish to rescind. Both these remedies raise particular issues in the context of residential tenancies, for reasons outlined below.

In Scots law, "removing" is the technical term for the relinquishing of possession by a tenant. It may be during the lease or at termination, and may be voluntary from the tenant's perspective or may be instigated by the landlord.[21] Historically, the landlord's remedy against a tenant who refused to vacate the subjects following termination of the lease was described as an *action of removing*.[22] The term "ordinary removing", be it voluntary or compulsory, applies to instances in which the tenant leaves, or is compelled to leave, after termination at the ish. The term "extraordinary removing" applies to the voluntary or

17 For a more detailed consideration of tacit relocation, see: Rennie and others, *Leases* (SULI 2015) ch 11; McAllister, *Scottish Law of Leases* (4th edn) ch 10; and chs 2 and 3 of the Scottish Law Commission's Discussion Paper *Aspects of Leases: Termination* (Scot Law Com No 165, 2018), which is available on the SLC's website, Tacit relocation has been held to be excluded if the parties' lease states that it is not to apply: *MacDougall v Guidi* 1992 SCLR 167; *Mexfield Housing Co-operative v Berrisford* (n 14) [78] (Lord Hope). Note also that the operation of tacit relocation is excluded where the tenant does not retain possession after the ish: *Dundee City Council v Dundee Valuation Appeal Committee* 2012 SC 463.

18 Rankine, *Leases* (3rd edn, 1916) 556; Stair *Institutions* II, 9, 38; Erskine *Institute* II, 6, 47. This rule was reaffirmed in *Signet Group plc v C & J Clark Retail Properties Ltd* 1996 SC 444, 1996 SLT 1325.

19 Particularly in the older authorities, the term "notice of removing" is also used. Unless the context indicates otherwise, the terms "notice to quit" and "notice of removing/removal" are interchangeable. However, sometimes "notice of removing/removal" refers to a notice that is not only intended to prevent tacit relocation, but serves as the first step in some specific statutory procedure for removing: for example, s 38 of the Sheriff Courts (Scotland) Act 1907. It is suggested that the requirements of these procedures (for example, in relation to service of the notice) do not apply to a notice that is served simply for the purpose of preventing tacit relocation. See the discussion of service in Chapter 15.

20 Although some irritancy clauses allow for termination in circumstances that do not amount to a breach of contract, such as the bankruptcy of the tenant.

21 Rankine (n 18) 511; Paton and Cameron (n 14) 245.

22 As opposed to an action for ejection, which was appropriate where defender had a title but it has already been judicially cut down, or where he never had any title to occupy the subjects at all.

compulsory removal of the tenant prior to the term of the lease. Thus, the invoking of an irritancy clause is a "compulsory extraordinary removing".[23] In the context of residential leases, this terminology was largely superseded by the creation of the summary cause "action for recovery of possession of heritable property" under section 35 of the Sheriff Courts (Scotland) Act 1971, as was discussed in Chapter 1.[24]

TERMINATION AT THE NATURAL TERM: NOTICES TO QUIT

Termination at the natural term is achieved by the service of a valid notice to quit. As to the requirements for validity of such notice, the law has developed over time, adding to the formalities required in respect of the notice and, in relation to lets of dwellinghouses, these can now be listed under the six numbered headings below.[25] If the party giving notice fails to adhere to any of these requirements, the notice is ineffective, and therefore tacit relocation takes place and the parties' contract continues. A defective notice to quit may therefore be fatal to any action for recovery of possession where termination of the parties' contract is a necessary preliminary to obtaining decree against the tenant.

Rent (Scotland) Act 1984, s 112

Section 16 of the Rent Act 1957 made provision for certain minimum requirements in relation to "notice by a landlord or a tenant to quit any premises let . . . as a dwelling-house"; in particular, that the minimum period for such a notice is four weeks, and that the notice must contain certain information prescribed by statutory instrument. Section 16 was replaced by section 112 of the Rent (Scotland) Act 1984.[26] This provision does not, of itself, create any requirement for the service of such a notice where it would not otherwise be necessary. There is no prescribed form for the notice to be given in terms of section 112. Unlike the notices required by previous statutory provisions applying in Scotland, such as sections 37 and 38 of the Sheriff Courts (Scotland) Act 1907, it is not related to any particular form of court process.

23 *Stair Memorial Encyclopaedia* vol 13 paras 463–466.

24 At p 9. The term "removing" is used by pt 15 of the Bankruptcy and Diligence etc. (Scotland) Act 2007, which creates a new code for the enforcement of evictions (discussed in Chapter 15). Under s 214, the term "decree for removing from heritable property" is given a very wide scope, in order to cover the various types of procedure (listed at s 214(2)) leading to an order under which a person may be evicted from heritable subjects. In this context, the words "decree for removing" have a much wider meaning than they had at common law. In particular, the phrase includes decrees for ejection, which is distinct from removing at common law: see Chapter 1 p 8.

25 The law as regards the mode of service of notices to quit, and the statutory notices discussed in other chapters, is considered in Chapter 15.

26 The 1984 Act consolidated the existing Rent Acts applicable to Scotland, and those parts of UK-wide Rent Acts that applied to Scotland.

Section 112(1) states:

> "No notice by a landlord or a tenant to quit any premises let (whether before or after the commencement of this Act) as a dwelling-house shall be valid unless it is in writing and contains such information as may be prescribed and is given not less than four weeks before the date on which it is to take effect."

It is not possible to contract out of this provision and, accordingly, its protection cannot be waived by the party on whom notice requires to be served.[27]

The landlord is not required to give, in the notice to quit or elsewhere, any explanation or ground for terminating the tenancy at the natural term. To do so (if there is an explanation) is misplaced, because it may suggest that termination arises from some cause, such as a breach of contract by the tenant, which the landlord is under no obligation to establish.

Requirements for valid notice to quit

An application to the FTT for an order for possession under section 18 of the 1988 Act must be accompanied by "a copy of the notice to quit served by the landlord on the tenant (if applicable)".[28] An application for an order under section 33 must be accompanied by a copy of the notice to quit served by the landlord on the tenant.[29]

With the benefit of the decisions now available on the First-tier Tribunal Housing and Property Chamber website,[30] it is now possible to say that many applications for eviction orders under sections 18 and 33 of the 1988 Act fail because they are accompanied by defective notices to quit.[31] Of the six requirements listed below, it is the fourth (the notice specifies a date that is not an ish) which seems to be most commonly breached, followed by the third requirement (requisite period of notice).[32]

27 Contracting out is generally not permissible in relation to provisions of the Rent Acts that are designed to protect the tenant: *Smith v Barclay* 1920 1 SLT 13, 18 (Lord McKenzie); *Baxter v Eckersley* [1950] 1 KB 480, 485 (Somervell LJ); *AG Securities v Vaughan* [1990] 1 AC 417, 459 (Lord Templeman).

28 Rule 65(b)(iii) of the Procedure Rules (n 3). A notice to quit is not necessary if s 18(6) of the Act applies, for which see Chapter 7. Also, a notice to quit is not applicable if the parties' contract has been terminated in another way, such as by irritancy.

29 Rule 66(b)(iv).

30 The website has a section in which the tribunal's decisions are published. It is possible to search for decisions by the rule under which an application was made, so that one can see, for example, the decisions made in applications under r 66, for an order under s 33 of the 1988 Act.

31 Or where there is inadequate evidence of service of the notice, or where there is simply no notice at all. As is explained in Chapter 14, the tribunal sifts applications. An application under r 65 or r 66 is apt to be rejected if it is not accompanied by a valid notice to quit.

32 Tribunal decisions in which applications have been rejected, due to the failure to produce a valid notice to quit, are too numerous to cite here. On 4 February 2020, the author looked at the 150 most recent decisions in r 65 applications. Of those, thirty-six were rejected at the sift, or dismissed at the case management discussion ("CMD"), because there was some problem with the notice to quit. In twenty-nine of those cases, the wrong date had been stated in the notice.

(1) *Notice to quit must be in writing*

At common law, formal notice in relation to "urban subjects" was not required, and verbal notice was permissible.[33] Tacit relocation could be prevented in any given year by any overt intimation by either party that he did not consent to the prolongation of the lease.[34] In relation to lets of dwellinghouses, written notice is required by section 112.

(2) *Where applicable, notice must contain prescribed information*

Section 112 does not prescribe a form for the notice as such, but requires that the notice must contain any prescribed information. In relation to assured tenancies, that information is stipulated by the Assured Tenancies (Notices to Quit Prescribed Information) (Scotland) Regulations 1988.[35] It is as follows:

> "1. Even after the Notice to Quit has run out, before the tenant can lawfully be evicted, the landlord must get an order for possession from the First-tier Tribunal.[36]
> 2. If a landlord issues a Notice to Quit but does not seek to gain possession of the house in question the contractual assured tenancy which has been terminated will be replaced by a statutory assured tenancy. In such circumstances the landlord may propose new terms for the tenancy and may seek an adjustment in rent at annual intervals thereafter.
> 3. If a tenant does not know what kind of tenancy he has or is otherwise unsure of his rights he can obtain advice from a solicitor. Help with all or part of the cost of legal advice and assistance may be available under the Legal Aid legislation. A tenant can also seek help from a Citizens Advice Bureau or Housing Advisory Centre."

There is English authority to suggest that the notice may be regarded as sufficient even if the prescribed information is not stated *verbatim*; especially if the recipient is not left in any doubt as to the meaning of the notice.[37]

(3) *Requisite period of notice must be given*

Under section 112 of the 1984 Act, the notice must be "given not less than four weeks before the date on which it is to take effect". However, that provision does not have the effect of setting the correct notice period at four weeks in all cases; it sets an irreducible minimum. This means that any previous rule of law

33 See the quotation from Stair's *Institutions* at the end of Chapter 2, and *Craighall Cast Stone Co v Wood Bros* 1931 SC 66, 1931 SLT 67. Verbal notice is still permissible in commercial leases, unless written notice is required by the parties' contract. See *Brucefield Estate Trustee Co Ltd v Computacenter (UK) Ltd* 2017 Hous LR 66.

34 *Signet Group plc v C & J Clark Retail Properties Ltd* (n 18); *McDonald v O'Donnell* 2008 SC 189, 2007 SLT 1227.

35 SI 1988/2067. The equivalent provision in relation to protected tenancies under the 1984 Act is to be found in reg 4 of and sch 2 to the Rent Regulation (Forms and Information etc.) (Scotland) Regulations 1991 (SI 1991/1521).

36 The original reference to "court" was replaced, someone belatedly, by "First-tier Tribunal", with effect from 6 March 2019, under the First-tier Tribunal for Scotland Housing and Property Chamber (Incidental Provisions) Regulations (SSI 2019/51) reg 3(2).

37 *Swansea City Council v Hearn* (1991) 23 HLR 284. Reference is also made to the discussion of errors in notices (below); and in relation to AT5 notices under the 1988 Act s 32 (Chapter 7).

or any contractual stipulation, in terms of which a notice to quit a dwelling-house given on a period of *less* than four weeks would be valid, is overridden.[38] The minimum period of four weeks cannot be reduced. However, section 112 does not affect any previous rule of law or any contractual stipulation in terms of which the period of notice is *more* than four weeks.

In particular, section 112 does not affect the common law rule requiring forty days' clear notice, in the absence of any contrary stipulation. That rule was emphatically restated in *Signet Group v C J Clark Retail Properties*,[39] in which the court said: "In our opinion, the law has long been settled that 40 clear days' notice is required so as to prevent the operation of tacit relocation in a lease."[40]

This statement is subject to the qualification that in the case of a lease "not exceeding four calendar months", notice "shall, in the absence of express stipulation, be given as many days before the date of ish as shall be equivalent to at least one third of the full period of duration of the lease". This rule comes from section 5 of the Removal Terms (Scotland) Act 1886, which is still in force. However, that provision was amended by section 135(2) of the Rent (Scotland) Act 1971 to provide for the minimum of twenty-eight days for notices in relation to dwellinghouses now found in section 112 of the 1984 Act. This has the effect that section 5 of the 1886 will serve to allow a longer period than four weeks only in the case of tenancies with an ish of between twelve weeks and four calendar months – a somewhat unusual duration – and then only in the absence of a contrary stipulation in the lease.

As regards leases of longer than four months, the common law rule requiring forty days' clear notice applies, in the absence of contrary stipulation. There does not appear to be authoritative support for any shorter period, in the case of leases between four months and one year.

Periods of notice in respect of the termination of tenancies, and "summary removings", are provided for in sections 37 and 38 of the Sheriff Courts (Scotland) Act 1907. However, there is a preponderance of authority to the effect that the requirements of sections 37 and 38 do not apply to tenancies in general, and operate only where the landlord chooses to use the specific procedure set out in each section.[41] Those procedures were largely rendered

38 In particular, s 112 overrides any "no warning" clause, of the type occasionally seen in residential leases, e.g: "the tenants bind and oblige themselves to flit and remove themselves from the premises at the expiry of the lease, and that without any previous warning or process of removing to be used against them".

39 n 18.

40 At 448B. See also *Lambert v Smith* (1864) 3 M 43, 48 per the Lord Justice-Clerk: "This is a question of considerable importance, and not a question merely of form, but of substance, affecting the interests of the poorer classes of the community. Our law has provided that no person can be removed from an heritable subject, however small, without forty days warning – a rule, especially regarding leases of dwelling-houses, of the greatest importance, the reason of the rule being that forty days are regarded as the shortest period that should be given to enable a man to look out for a new dwelling-house." The development of the law in relation to periods of notice is described in the SLC Discussion Paper *Aspects of Leases: Termination* (n 16) ch 3.

41 That was emphatically the view taken by the Inner House in *Craighall Cast-Stone Co Ltd v Wood Brothers* (n 33), and confirmed in *Lormor Ltd v Glasgow City Council* 2015 SC 213, 2014 SLT 1055. See also McAllister (n 17) para 10.32, and the SLC Discussion Paper (n 16) paras 3.21–3.26. In any event, the periods of notice provided under ss 37 and 38 are the same as required by common law, and s 5 of the 1886 Act.

obsolete by the introduction of the summary cause under section 35 of the Sheriff Courts (Scotland) Act 1971.[42]

For practical purposes, in relation to residential tenancies, it is submitted that the following conclusions may be drawn:

(1) In all cases, the irreducible minimum period is four weeks, under section 112 of the 1984 Act.
(2) Given (1), section 5 of the 1886 Act applies only to leases of between twelve weeks and four calendar months in duration. In that case, the period of notice is one third of the duration.
(3) For leases of more than four months in duration the minimum period of notice at common law is forty clear days.
(4) Rules (2) and (3) apply only in the absence of any express contrary provision, by which the period of notice may be reduced, subject to (1).
(5) Rules (1)–(3) set minimum periods. Parties may contractually stipulate a longer period of notice and, if they do so, that longer period of notice must be given.[43]

As the period allowed by section 112 is "not less than" four weeks, it does not include the day on which notice is served on the tenant, or the ish date, being the date on which the notice is to take effect. Therefore, if the ish date is, for example, 30 June, notice must be effected on or before 1 June, the four-week period under the Act commencing at midnight beginning 2 June and concluding at midnight ending 29 June.[44] In so far as there is a requirement to give forty days' notice, the same principle applies. This is illustrated by the case of *Signet Group v C J Clark Retail Properties*,[45] in which the court determined that a notice served by sub-tenants on 5 April to terminate a commercial lease on 15 May was invalid, as forty days' clear notice had not been given. Where a longer notice period is stipulated by the contract, the issue of whether the date of service and the ish date are to be excluded from the period should be considered with reference to the wording of the contract. However, to assume that these days are excluded is the safest course.[46]

As mentioned above, many applications to the FTT have been refused because the period of notice given in the notice to quit is inadequate.

42 Under r 30.3 of the Summary Cause Rules 2002 (Act of Sederunt Summary Cause Rules) 2002 (SSI 2002/132), "when decree for the recovery of possession is granted in a summary cause, it has the same force and effect as: (a) a decree of removing; (b) a decree of ejection; (c) a summary warrant of ejection; (d) a warrant for summary ejection in common form; or (e) a decree pronounced in a summary application for removing, in terms of sections 36, 37 and 38 respectively of the 1907 Act". Thus, the summary cause replaces these older forms of process. See the SLC Discussion Paper (n 16) para 3.18.

43 It is quite common for short assured tenancies to stipulate two months, to tie in with the period required by the 1988 Act s 33(1)(d).

44 Note that this is different from the position under English law; the leading case on the statutory provision equivalent to s 112 is *Schnabel v Allard* [1967] 1 QB 627, in which the court decided that notice given on 4 March to take effect on 1 April was valid; only one of the two days (being the date of service and the date of effect) required to be excluded.

45 (n 18).

46 This issue is discussed in *Stair Memorial Encyclopaedia* vol 13, para 480. Questions as to the calculation of time can also arise in relation to the duration of tenancies, which is important for certain purposes. This is considered at note 50 below, and more fully in Chapter 7, in the discussion of the 1988 Act, s 32.

(4) Notice must specify date on which it is to take effect, being an ish date

The notice must specify the term and date at which the tenant is required to remove.[47] As the purpose of the notice is to avoid tacit relocation taking place at the ish, it follows that the date stated in the notice should be the ish date. That is "the date on which it is to take effect", under section 112, and in relation to which the requisite period of notice is calculated.[48]

Example. Say that the lease runs from 1 March to 1 September. The landlord decides in April that he wishes to end the tenancy as soon as possible. He may, if he wishes, serve a notice to quit immediately, but the effective date stated in the notice should be 1 September, which is the next ish. If, for some reason, he serves a notice before 1 September that does not meet the various requirements for validity, the notice will be ineffective, and he will have to put up with his tenant until 1 March in the following year.[49]

If the lease runs for a period expressed in months, or one or more years, without specifying the date on which the let ends, it is submitted that the prudent course is to take it that the termination date is the corresponding date in the calendar. For example, if the lease runs "for six months from 1 March", the ish is 1 September; if it runs "for one year from 1 March", the ish is 1 March in the following year. This issue is further considered in Chapter 7, in the discussion of section 32(1)(a) of the 1988 Act.[50] In the absence of clear agreement as to when the duration begins, the lease may be held to run from the date on which the contract was completed, the date when the tenant took possession, or the date from which the rent was payable or paid.[51]

Date stated in notice is not an ish

This appears to be the single most common basis on which the validity of a notice to quit is called into question. That is confirmed by the database of decisions of the FTT, which provides numerous examples of applications for

47 Paton and Cameron (n 14) 276.

48 As in *Signet Group v C J Clark Retail Properties* (n 18), the circumstances of which are described above.

49 Unless he becomes aware of the invalidity of the notice in sufficient time to serve a valid notice that is effective to end the tenancy on 1 September. Obviously, this example assumes that there is no basis on which the landlord could end the tenancy early, by irritancy, break clause or otherwise.

50 *Stair Memorial Encyclopaedia* vol 30, para 386. This is a surprisingly difficult question. In *Morrison's Exrs v Rendall* 1989 SLT (Land Ct) 89, the Land Court decided that, in respect of a lease running from year to year from 1 March, a notice to quit that took effect on 28 February was valid, as that was the correct termination date. That conclusion is open to question. However, in any event, the Land Court took the view that a notice to quit served on 1 March would also have been valid. Therefore, it would appear that a notice that bears to take effect on 1 March is the safer course, as its validity has the support of *Morrison's Exrs* and the other authorities discussed in Chapter 7, whereas 28 February has only partial support. For a discussion of this issue, and of the problems posed by the decision in *Morrison's Exrs*, see D J Coull, "Termination Date in a Notice to Quit" 1989 SLT (News) 431.

51 *Christie v Fife Coal Co* (1899) 2 F 192; *Watters v Hunter* 1927 SC 310; Rankine (n 18) 338. That said, there may be circumstances where, due to the passage of time, it becomes very difficult to ascertain any of the relevant dates. This tends to be an issue in the case of verbal leases where there has been no agreement as to duration, such that a duration of one year can be implied (see p 51 above).

evictions orders being rejected because the landlord has served a notice to quit that calls upon the tenant to leave on a date that is not an ish.[52]

It is thought that this usually arises from a misunderstanding, on the part of the landlord or his agents, as to the effect of tacit relocation;[53] or confusion between the form of notice that is appropriate to terminate a tenancy at its ish, and one that is intended to terminate the tenancy during its term, usually as a result of some breach of contract on the part of the tenant.

Where the landlord calls upon the tenant to leave before the ish, that requires some indication, in the notice, as to the basis on which that call is being made.[54] By contrast, a notice to quit that calls upon the tenant to leave at the next ish requires no explanation.

It follows that if the date stated on the notice to quit is earlier than the ish, but without any indication of why the tenant is being asked to leave early, the notice is ineffective; the landlord cannot call on the tenant to leave before the tenant is contractually obliged to do so.[55]

What if the notice states a date that is later than the ish? It is suggested that a notice to quit is not necessarily invalid if it calls upon the tenant to leave the day after the ish.[56] The point is that, in the absence of any stipulation to the contrary, the tenant has the right to stay on until the last minute of the last day. Let us say that the ish is 1 April. A notice that calls upon him to leave on that date is effectively asking him to be out by the expiry of the last minute of that day. A notice that takes effect on 2 April is effectively calling upon the tenant to be out at the instant that day commences. That, it is suggested, is not objectionable. That is particularly so if the notice calls upon him to leave "by" 2 April. However, it is submitted that a notice calling upon him to quit "on" 2 April is also valid.

Notices that call upon the tenant to leave at a later date are more problematic. There have been cases in which the court has upheld the validity of a notice that called upon the tenant to leave later than the ish, because there was said to be no prejudice to him. However, a major factor in the court's decision appears to have been the fact that the correct termination date was ruled by a statutory provision, knowledge of which was imputed to the tenant. Therefore, the tenant could not be confused by an error as to the ish date in the notice, because he already knew the true ish.[57]

That was not, however, the position in the most recent authority that bears upon this issue: the decision of the Inner House in *McDonald v O'Donnell*.[58] In that case, the parties were principally at odds on the question of whether the

52 See note 32 above.

53 The SLC Discussion Paper *Aspects of Leases: Termination* (n 16) suggests, at para 2.40, that there is widespread ignorance as to the effect of tacit relocation.

54 This is may be done by stating the contractual basis (say, an irritancy or break clause) on which the tenant is being asked to leave early. See p 70 below.

55 *Earl of March v Dowie* (1754) Mor 13843; *Macdonald v Cameron* (1916) 32 Sh Ct Rep 261; *Anderson v Scott* 1939 SLT (Sh Ct) 28; *James Grant & Co Ltd v Moran* 1948 SLT (Sh Ct) 8; *Hamilton District Council v Maguire* 1983 SLT (Sh Ct) 76; *Urquhart v Hamilton* 1996 GWD 37-2171.

56 That also appears to be the position in England: see the discussion of the relevant cases in *Fernandez v McDonald* [2004] 1 WLR 1027, [2004] HLR 13.

57 See: *Campbell's Trustees v O'Neill* 1911 SC 188, 1910 2 SLT 392; *Callander v Watherston* 1970 SLT (Land Ct) 13; *Austin v Gibson* 1979 SLT (Land Ct) 12.

58 (n 34).

tenancy was an agricultural holding. There had also been a dispute, before the sheriff at an earlier stage of the case, as to whether the ish had been changed from 5 February to 31 March by virtue of an offer made on behalf of the landlord to enter into a new lease from 1 April 1990. The sheriff had held that offer to be of no effect, with the result that the original ish operated. Thus, the landlord's notice to quit, which bore to take effect on 31 March, was called into question. On this point Lord Justice-Clerk Gill, with whom the other two judges agreed, said:

> "32. If this had been a tenancy of an agricultural holding, the pursuer's notice to quit would have been invalid. But since the lease in this case was, in my opinion, a commercial lease running from year to year, relocation could be prevented in any given year by any overt intimation by either party that he did not consent to the prolongation of the lease (*Signet Group plc v C & J Clark Retail Properties Ltd*).
>
> 33. The pursuer's notice to quit constituted such an intimation. Whatever the specified date of ish, it notified the defender that the pursuer would not consent to a prolongation for a further year. It was not suggested by counsel for the defender that the period of notice was insufficient; and since the notice specified a date of removal that was later than the true anniversary date, the defender was not prejudiced in any way by the error."

Accordingly, the court decided that the notice to quit had the effect of preventing tacit relocation. Clearly this offers some comfort for the landlord who has served a notice that gives a date later than the ish. It is arguable, in light of the above passage, that any such notice will nevertheless constitute an overt intimation that operates to prevent tacit relocation, because the statement of a later date does not prejudice the tenant.

However, one might question whether the Lord Justice-Clerk intended to set out a general principle to that effect. In the case before the court, there was no ambiguity in the notice. It would have been clear to the tenant that the notice presupposed the landlord's view that the tenancy ended on 31 March, and that was why he was being called upon to leave on that date. In other words, the notice did not offend against the requirement, described below, that the notice should be definite and unconditional; it did not leave the tenant in doubt as to where he stood.

Let us say, however, that L and T entered into a lease that ran from 21 March 2017 to 21 March 2018, and relocated on 21 March 2018, 2019 and 2020. Before the end of January 2021, L's agent serves a notice to quit on T, which calls upon him to quit on 21 April 2021. What is T to make of this notice? Has L or his agent made a mistake? Or does L intend to let T stay on for an extra month? If it is suggested that the notice has the effect of avoiding tacit relocation and ending the existing tenancy on 21 March, what is the status of T's occupation between 21 March and 21 April? In these circumstances, it is suggested that the notice *does* offend against the requirement that it should leave the recipient in no doubt as to where he stands, and therefore its validity is in question. If it is invalid, it does not operate to prevent tacit relocation.[59]

59 Or, to put this another way, T *does* suffer prejudice (in contrast to the tenant in *McDonald v O'Donnell* (n 16)) because the notice leaves him in doubt as to the date on which he is should leave, and he cannot arrange his affairs accordingly. Against that, it may be suggested that he

(5) *Notice must be definite and unconditional*

It has been said that the essence of a notice to quit, whether given by the landlord or the tenant, "is that it must be a definite and unconditional intimation enabling the other party to know exactly his position"; and in the case of a notice given by the landlord it "must explicitly require the tenant to remove".[60]

(6) *Notice served by a person having title to do so, on person on whom it should be served*

Generally speaking, any person who has title to sue in an action for removing has title to serve a notice to quit.[61] Problems may arise where title in the property has passed during the course of the tenancy. In the case of a sale, the purchaser does not require to complete title,[62] but the date of entry must have passed before he may serve notice to quit.[63] A notice served by the seller may be assigned to the purchaser, but the assignation must be express; a general assignation of writs will not suffice.[64]

Notice should be served on all the other parties to the lease, including all joint tenants.[65] Notice should also be given to assignees of the tenant, and sub-tenants where the assignation or sub-tenancy is lawful.[66]

In cases involving joint landlords, the law is unclear. There is certainly authority for the proposition that notice by one of two or more joint tenants is sufficient to terminate the lease at the ish. That is because tacit relocation requires the silent consent of all parties.[67] On that basis, it might be thought that the notice served by one of two or more joint landlords would also have the effect of avoiding tacit relocation. However, that is subject to the objection that a single joint owner would not have title to sue in an action against a tenant, and cannot have title to serve a notice to quit.[68] Accordingly, it is not clear that a notice to quit by one joint landlord is valid; in practice, notice should be given by all of them.

could easily contact L to clarify the position. But, if such clarification is necessary, is the notice itself not inadequate? This example is further discussed at p 63 below.

60 Paton and Cameron (n 14) 276–278, citing: Bell's *Principles* para 1271 *Craighall Cast Stone Co v Wood Brothers* (n 33); *Murray v Grieve* (1920) 36 Sh Ct Rep 126; and *Ritchie v Lyon* (1940) 56 Sh Ct Rep 39. The rule was reaffirmed in *City of Glasgow Council v Torrance* 2000 SLT (Sh Ct) 32. See also *Brucefield Estate Trustee Company Limited v Computacenter (UK) Ltd* (n 33).

61 For a discussion of title to raise an action, at common law, see Chapter 15, p 492. The term "removing" is discussed at p 52 in this chapter.

62 *Stair Memorial Encyclopaedia* vol 13 para 495; *Walker v Hendry* 1925 SC 855, 1925 SLT 592.

63 *Grandison v Mackay* 1919 1 SLT 95; *James Grant & Co Ltd v Moran* (n 55).

64 *George M Brown Ltd v Collier* 1954 SLT (Sh Ct) 98; *Life Association of Scotland Ltd v Black's Leisure Group plc* 1989 SC 166, 1989 SLT 674, 1989 SCLR 459. The latter case concerned a notice of irritancy; the same principle was said to apply to notices of removing.

65 On the basis that all joint tenants would have to be evicted, if the action is a summary cause for recovery of possession of heritable property.

66 *Stair Memorial Encyclopaedia* vol 13 paras 459 and 502; Rankine (n 18) 521 and 599.

67 *Smith v Grayton Estates Ltd* 1960 SC 349, 1961 SLT 38, 1960 SLT (Notes) 81.

68 "The leading rule is that common property being a right of ownership vested *pro indiviso* in two or more persons, all of whom are equally entitled to enjoyment, the consent of all is requisite in the management or disposal of the subject. . . . All must concur in the granting of a lease . . . and in removings. Thus a removing could not go on without the consent of all the proprietors . . ." (Rankine, *Leases* (n 18) 82).

ERRORS IN NOTICES TO QUIT

Under Scots law, a fairly rigorous view has tended to be taken of the requirement for accuracy in giving notice to quit. This is typified by the opinion of the court in *Signet Group v C J Clark Retail Properties*, in which it was said:[69]

> "Considerations of equity do not arise in this field of law where precision is required."

The same rigour has been applied to the requirement that notices are given in a statutory form, or contain information prescribed by statute. The reason for that approach was described by Lord Justice-Clerk Thomson as follows:

> "The consistent policy of the Legislature as to notices has been to say what must be in them. The theory is that, if the form is properly defined, then, so long as the statutory instructions are obeyed, there can be no room for doubt. There may, of course, be occasions where disputes arise as to whether the instructions are obeyed, but the theory is that the troubles so arising are fewer and simpler than those which might be expected to arise if the thing were left at large to the discretion of the author."[70]

The older English authorities showed the courts in that jurisdiction taking a similarly firm line.[71] However, those were reconsidered by the House of Lords in *Mannai Investment Co Ltd v Eagle Star Life Assurance Co Ltd*.[72] In that case, the court applied the so-called "reasonable recipient" test, under which notices are open to interpretation, the standard of reference being that of the reasonable man exercising his common sense in the context and in the circumstances of the particular case. If there is an error in the notice, the test is "Is the notice [notwithstanding the error] quite clear to a reasonable tenant reading it? Is it plain that he cannot be misled by it?"[73]

The decision in *Mannai* has given rise to a substantial body of case law, in Scotland as well as England, and it is beyond the scope of this work to consider it in detail. Nevertheless, the following observations may assist.

Mannai, and most of the cases following thereon, concern notices given under contractual provisions, in a commercial context. Where the validity of the notice is challenged, the court interprets the relevant contractual provisions as to the circumstances in which the notice may be given, and construes the terms of the notice in order to decide whether it supplies the information required in terms of the contractual provision.[74] The issue is whether the party giving notice has met the contractual requirements.

By contrast, where the validity of a notice to quit is called into question, that is invariably by reference to the statutory provisions and common law

69 (n 18) 449D.

70 *Rae v Davidson* 1954 SC 361, 366, 1955 SLT 25. On this theme, reference might also be made to *Scott v Livingstone* 1919 SC 1, 1918 2 SLT 225, in which Lord Dundas said: "I believe that in the main justice is done by enforcing fairly strict compliance with the statutory provisions in a matter of this sort, and not by any undue relaxation of them by accepting alleged equivalents or otherwise."

71 For example: *Cadby v Martinez* (1840) 11 A&E 720 and *Hankey v Clavering* [1942] 2 KB 326.

72 [1997] AC 749.

73 This was the test adopted Goulding J in *Carradine Properties Ltd v Aslam* [1976] 1 WLR 442, which was approved by the House of Lords in *Mannai* (n 72).

74 See *HOE International Ltd v Andersen* 2017 SC 313. This is the most important recent Scottish authority.

principles already described rather than to the parties' contract.[75] It will be apparent that *Mannai* does not assist the giver of notice who fails, through error or otherwise, to comply with the first and third requirements described at pp 55–57 above. The "reasonable recipient" test has no application where there is no written notice, or where the requisite period of notice has not been given. No question of interpretation or construction arises here. What about the other requirements described above?

Information prescribed by statute

The Court of Appeal has been willing to apply the "reasonable recipient" test to the inclusion in the notice of information prescribed by the relevant legislation,[76] provided that the notice actually given is "substantially to the same effect" as that which is required by the statute. However, this approach would appear to be at odds with the older Scottish authorities mentioned above.[77] It remains to be seen whether acceptance of the *Mannai* test will extend to reconsideration of those authorities.[78]

Notice must specify the date on which it is to take effect, being an ish date

Mannai was a case in which the error was the misstatement of a date. In the context of notices to quit, a paradigm example is *Carradine Properties Ltd v Aslam.*[79] In that case the parties' lease contained a provision allowing either party to determine the lease by giving twelve months' notice in writing. On 6 September 1974 Carradine served a notice to quit on Aslam, which stated: "we hereby give you notice that we intend to determine the term created by the lease on September 27, 1973, and that we require you to quit and deliver up possession . . . on that date". The court held that it was clear that the date in the notice to quit was erroneous and that the corresponding date in 1975 was intended. One wonders whether Carradine would have succeeded had the notice said "August 27, 1975" or "October 27, 1975".

Returning to the example given at p 60 above, if, as a result of other circumstances in the case, such as prior communications between the parties, it

75 Though, of course, where there are applicable contractual provisions as to termination of the contract by written notice, the parties may join issue on whether the party giving notice has complied with those provisions.

76 See, in particular, *York v Casey* (1999) 31 HLR 209 and *Ravenseft Properties Ltd v Hall* [2002] HLR 33. The application of *Mannai* (n 72) to notices under the Housing Act 1988 has recently been re-examined in *Pease v Carter* [2020] 1 WLR 1459, discussed in Chapter 7. Those cases concerned notices under the Housing Act 1988, but it would seem likely that a similar approach would be applied by the English courts to the requirement for prescribed information in a notice to quit. In *Swansea City Council v Hearn* (n 37), which pre-dated *Mannai*, something very similar to a "reasonable recipient" approach was adopted.

77 Being *Rae v Davidson* (n 70) and *Scott v Livingstone* (n 70).

78 In *Scott v Muir* 2012 SLT (Sh Ct) 179, Sheriff Principal Stephen was of the view that the "reasonable recipient" test set out in *Mannai* (n 72)was not the apposite test where the question was whether the statutory requirements of notice had been satisfied. In any event, it seems that the notice under consideration in that case did not contain information that was "substantially to the same effect" as that required by the legislation. See also the similar cases of *Wing v Henry Tse & Co Ltd* 2009 GWD 11-175 and *Tawne Overseas Holdings Ltd v Firm of Newmiln Farm* 2008 Hous LR 18.

79 (n 73).

would have been evident to a reasonable recipient in the position of T that L intended to call upon him to leave on 21 March, it being clear that "21 April" was an error, the reasoning in *Mannai* would apply. However, if the tenant was left with the doubts described in the discussion above, the "reasonable recipient" test ought to lead to the conclusion that the notice is invalid.

Notice must be definite and unconditional, enabling other party to know his position exactly

If the effect of an error in the notice is that it leaves the tenant in doubt as to where he stands, it fails the "reasonable recipient" test.

Notice must be given by a person having title to do so . . .

There have been cases in which the notice was given in the name of the wrong person. However, the attempt to invoke *Mannai* in support of the validity of the notice was not successful.[80]

. . . on the person on whom notice should be served

A notice that is not served on the correct person is simply invalid. This problem cannot be cured by an exercise of construction or interpretation by the court, and therefore *Mannai* has no application.[81]

Does a defective notice nevertheless prevent tacit relocation?

In the past, a question has arisen as to whether a notice in the prescribed form, which has the dual purpose of terminating the tenancy and initiating the statutory removal procedure, might, if not in the prescribed form, be valid for the purposes of preventing tacit relocation, though invalid for the purposes of raising an eviction action under the relevant act.[82]

In particular, this question might arise in relation to notices of removing under sections 37 and 38 of the Sheriff Courts (Scotland) Act 1907, because those sections provide for a specific form of action that is initiated by the relevant notice, which also terminates the parties' contract at the ish date. As the notice has two purposes, there may be an issue as to whether the notice that fails to fulfil both of its purposes can nevertheless fulfil one of them. There appears to be no clear answer to this question.

80 *Lemmerbell Ltd v Britannia LAS Direct Ltd* [1999] L&TR 102, [1998] 3 EGLR 67; *Procter & Gamble Technical Centres Ltd v Brixton Estates Plc* [2002] EWHC 2835 (Ch), [2003] 2 EGLR 24. These were cases such as *Mannai* (n 72), in which the tenant sought to terminate the lease under a break clause. The latter case was a decision of Lord Neuberger. He said (at para 35): "[*Mannai*] did not give a green light to inaccurate and sloppily drafted notices. The test, even in relation to the construction of notices, is relatively strict."

81 *Batt Cables plc v Spencer Business Parks Ltd* 2010 SLT 860. In that case, however, Lord Hodge decided that the notice had been sent to a person who had authority to act as the defenders' agent, and who, on the pleadings and agreed documents, had authority to receive the notice, and thus it was valid.

82 Paton and Cameron (n 14) 225. In *Recovery of Possession of Heritable Property*, the Scottish Law Commission indicated that this was a matter about which there was some doubt.

However, it is difficult to see how this issue arises in relation to any notice the sole purpose of which is to terminate the tenancy at the ish date. If the notice is invalid because it fails to comply with one of the requirements 1–6 stated above, it does not fulfil that purpose.

Let us take what is a common example in the context of residential leasing. The landlord serves a notice to quit on the tenant of a short assured tenancy, which is intended to terminate the contractual assured tenancy at the next ish date, so that, thereafter, the landlord may raise proceedings under section 33 of the 1988 Act. The sole purpose of the notice is prevent tacit relocation from operating, so that the landlord may thereby satisfy section 33(1)(b) of the 1988 Act.

A defective notice cannot fulfill that purpose, because it is invalid. It may be argued that a communication by one party that he wishes to terminate the lease at the ish date is sufficient to rebut the presumption in favour of *tacit* relocation. However, the law has evolved certain rules as to how such a communication may be effected. If those rules are not followed, silence is deemed to have been maintained.

TERMINATION PRIOR TO THE NATURAL TERM

There are various ways in which a lease might terminate early:

- by destruction of the subjects;
- by renunciation;[83]
- by the operation of a break clause;[84]
- on resumption by the landlord;[85]
- by *rei interitus*;[86] or
- by reduction.[87]

For a discussion of these matters, which rarely arise in the context of residential leases, readers are referred to the standard works.[88]

83 The term "renunciation" refers to circumstances in which the parties to the lease agree to discharge each other from their respective obligations. This may be express or implied. A common instance of implied renunciation occurs when, during the currency of the lease, the parties enter into a new lease that materially differs from their existing agreement. In such a case, the old lease is impliedly renounced. The relevant law is expounded by Rankine (n 18) ch XX; see also Rennie *I* and others (n 17).

84 A break clause gives one or both of the parties the right to terminate the lease, usually at one or more stipulated dates. Normally, the clause would also specify that notice in a certain form requires to be given by one party to the other, on or before a certain date, in order to utilise the clause.

85 The landlord may reserve a contractual right to resume possession of the subjects. Again, one would expect that a resumption clause would contain some provision as to notice by the landlord to the tenant. However, in *Kininmonth v British Aluminium Co* 1915 SC 271, 1915 1 SLT 13, there was no provision for notice to be given prior to resumption, and the court held that notice on the tenant was accordingly unnecessary.

86 I.e. destruction of the subjects: see Rennie and others (n 17) paras 20-08 to 20-17.

87 Reduction is a judicial remedy that may be granted on equitable grounds, where the lease is void or voidable – for example, due to fraud. For an example of reduction of a residential tenancy, see *Govanhill Housing Association Ltd v Palmer* 1998 SLT 887.

88 Rankine and others (n 18) ch XX; Paton and Cameron (n 14) ch XVI; McAllister (n 17) ch 10; Rennie and others (n 17) ch 20.

In this chapter, particular attention is given to two ways by which a tenancy may be terminated before its natural term: irritancy and rescission. In practice, these are most likely to give rise to eviction proceedings. However, it is necessary to note in passing three further circumstances that might give rise to termination of the parties' contract.

First, a transfer of the landlord's title to another person does not terminate the lease, given the terms of the Leases Act 1449, provided that the requirements of the Act are fulfilled. These are that: (a) the lease relates to land; (b) the lease is in writing, if it is for more than one year; (c) it has a definite ish; (d) it has a specific rent; and (e) the tenant is in possession.[89]

Secondly, the death of the tenant may have the effect of terminating the lease. Succession to assured tenancies, Scottish secure tenancies and private residential tenancies is discussed elsewhere.[90] In relation to tenancies excepted from the 1988, 2001 and 2016 Acts, the position depends on the terms of the lease. The death of the tenant will terminate the lease if there is a contractual provision to that effect. In any other case, the interest of the tenant may vest in the deceased's executor.[91]

Thirdly, the bankruptcy of the tenant does not in itself have the effect of terminating the lease, although, as will be seen in the following paragraphs, it may have the effect of triggering an irritancy clause. Under section 79(3) of the Bankruptcy (Scotland) Act 2016 the "whole estate of the debtor" that vests in the trustee in the sequestration at the date of sequestration does not include any interest of the debtor in a protected tenancy under the 1984 Act, an assured tenancy,[92] a Scottish secure tenancy or a private residential tenancy. In other cases, where the tenancy interest does vest in the trustee, he has the discretion to adopt the lease or reject it. If he elects not to adopt it, the tenancy will be at an end.[93]

IRRITANCY AND RESCISSION

Introduction

A full consideration of the remedies of rescission and irritancy is given in the standard works.[94] The following paragraphs summarise the points that are relevant for present purposes.

89 However, in a case in which those requirements are not fulfilled, the contract will bind the landlord and his heirs, but not his singular successors (for discussion of this issue, see Lord Hope's judgment in *Mexfield Housing Co-operative v Berrisford* (n 14)). Transfer of the landlord's interest to a singular successor will therefore terminate the tenancy, and service of a notice to quit for that purpose will be unnecessary. For a more detailed discussion of the 1449 Act, see Rennie and others (n 17) ch 5.

90 In Chapter 12. There are no succession rights to SSTs which accordingly terminate on the death of the tenant.

91 Under ss 14 and 16 of the Succession (Scotland) Act 1964. See Rennie and others (n 17) ch 19 and McAllister(n 17) ch 9.

92 This includes a short assured tenancy, which is an assured tenancy in terms of the 1988 Act s 32.

93 Rennie and others (n 17) para 20-18.

94 McBryde, *The Law of Contract in Scotland* (3rd edn) ch 20 (pt 10); Rankine (n 18) ch XX; Paton and Cameron (n 14) ch XV; Rennie and others (n 17) ch 17; McAllister(n 17) ch 5.

Rescission is a non-judicial remedy in relation to a breach of contract, whereby the aggrieved party brings the contract to an end.[95] The right to rescind arises where there is a material breach of a contract, or a refusal to perform, by the other party. However, not every breach of a contract will justify rescission. Termination of the contract is a drastic remedy that requires a breach which, in the circumstances, is material. As well as the issue of materiality of the breach, a question has often arisen as to whether the breach on which the aggrieved party relies is remediable, and whether the aggrieved party should, or should not, be entitled to rescind without giving the party in breach an opportunity to remedy the situation.

An irritancy is a contractually stipulated remedy. The parties to the lease agree that if a particular event occurs the landlord will be entitled to terminate the lease. In the case of a "legal" irritancy the agreement of the parties is implied by law; in that of a "conventional" irritancy, the agreement is express. The event stipulated as triggering the landlord's right to irritate the lease will often constitute a breach of a term of the lease. However, this need not be the case. The right to irritate may arise upon a change in the status of the tenant – for example, if the tenant becomes bankrupt. It is therefore inaccurate to describe a landlord's right to irritate the lease as being, like rescission, a remedy in response to a tenant's breach of the term of the lease, though a breach of the term of the lease will often trigger the right to irritate.[96]

Irritancy should be much the easier remedy to deploy. This is because any question as to whether the event that triggers the remedy is sufficiently material to justify termination does not arise, as this is already predetermined by the contract. The same is true of any question as to whether a breach of contract is remediable. In the case of rescission, this may be open to doubt. Where irritancy is triggered by a breach of contract, the remediability of the breach, or the ability to "purge" the irritancy is determined by the contract and the relevant common law rules, which are discussed below.

For this reason, the possibility of rescission by the landlord leading to eviction is a relatively unexplored area; this is no doubt due to the prevalence of irritancy clauses in tenancy contracts, which (if properly drafted) obviate the need to resort to rescission.[97] However, rescission is worth considering in the context of leases of residential property, which are very often characterised by the greatest degree of informality. Verbal leases are quite commonplace, as are contracts, perhaps drawn up by the landlord without legal advice, which have no irritancy clause, or in which the irritancy clause has been poorly drafted, and presents some difficulty in application. Often these tenancies are for periods of six months or more, in an effort to achieve short assured tenancy status

Also helpful is the Scottish Law Commission's Discussion Paper *Remedies for Breach of Contract* (Scot Law Com No 109, 1999).

95 The other non-judicial remedy is suspension of performance. The judicial remedies are, first, those that enforce performance, being specific implement, interdict and decree for payment of a sum stipulated by the contract; and secondly those remedies that are given in substitution of performance, being damages and interest. This classification is taken from the SLC's Discussion Paper (n 94).

96 The discussion of the nature of irritancy in this paragraph is taken from pt 2 of the SLC Discussion Paper *Irritancy in Leases of Land* (Scot Law Com No 117, 2001).

97 Prior to *Crieff Highland Gathering Ltd v Perth and Kinross Council* 2011 SLT 992, considered below, the last reported case to give a detailed discussion of rescission in leases dated from 1948. The last Inner House case to consider the issue was *Edmond v Reid* (1871) 9 M 782.

under section 32 of the 1988 Act. This leads to problems, in particular where the tenant stops paying the rent and the landlord wishes to recover possession during the currency of the lease.

Irritancy

Various issues arise in relation to the application of irritancy in eviction proceedings, which are discussed under the following headings:

- legal irritancy;
- conventional irritancy;
- irritancy and recovery of possession of residential tenancies;
- notice;
- effect of irritancy;
- what type of action?;
- irritancy and eviction proceedings: assured tenancies;
- defences;
- unfair terms.

Legal irritancy

At common law, there was only one implied legal irritancy: where the tenant had failed to pay rent for two successive years, when the rent was due for the third. This was confirmed by the Act of Sederunt of 14 December 1756, which, however, applied only to agricultural leases. This was in turn modified and extended by the Hypothec Abolition (Scotland) Act 1880. However, these provisions, in relation to agricultural holdings, were rendered obsolete by the introduction of a legal irritancy in respect of non-payment of the rent for a period of six months, which is now contained in section 20 of the Agricultural Holdings (Scotland) Act 1991.

Under section 5 of the House Letting and Rating (Scotland) Act 1911 there was a statutory irritancy for non-payment of rent of no less than seven days in relation to "small dwelling-houses". However, this provision was subsequently repealed.[98] Thus, the only irritancy implied by law in relation to urban subjects is the non-payment of rent for two years.[99] As exercise of such a right must be considered impractical in present-day circumstances, it might be said that there is, effectively, no common law right of irritancy for the landlord of urban dwellinghouses except as provided in the parties' contract. However, as will be seen, the existence of the common law legal irritancy does have some relevance to the issue of whether it is possible for the landlord to rescind.

There is a general principle in relation to legal irritancies at common law that the irritancy may be purged[100] by payment of the arrears of rent before decree is extracted in the action taken to enforce it.[101]

98 By the Local Government (Scotland) Act 1973, s 237 and sch 29.

99 It would appear that this still applies to the leases of dwellinghouses: see Rankine (n 18) 532; Gloag and Henderson, *The Law of Scotland* (14th edn, 2017) para 35.26.

100 I.e. cleared off by payment or by remedying the failure by which the irritancy was incurred.

101 Under the Agricultural Holdings (Scotland) Act 1991, s 20(2), the tenant can retain possession by paying or finding caution for the arrears. This is why the legal irritancy in terms of

Conventional irritancy

Traditionally, contractual irritancy clauses gave the option of termination to the landlord in the event of non-payment of rent, prohibited assignation or sub-letting, the insolvency of the tenant, or failure to reside at the subjects; however, any lawful condition of the contract may be fenced with an irritancy clause,[102] and many modern leases adopt this approach.

A conventional irritancy cannot be purged at common law, unless it is simply the expression of a recognised legal irritancy.[103] In particular, where a conventional irritancy is incurred by the non-payment of rent, it cannot be purged by payment of the arrears in full before the raising of proceedings.

Because any clause may be fenced with an irritancy clause, which may then be rigorously enforced by the landlord, it is possible for irritancies to be incurred in a manner that might be characterised as oppressive. In theory, the tenant may defend eviction proceedings following the operation of an irritancy clause on the grounds of oppression by the landlord. However, a series of important cases, all relating to commercial leases, made it clear that this is so difficult as to be practically impossible.[104]

Irritancy and recovery of possession of residential tenancies

Statutory security of tenure substantially defuses the landlord's remedy of irritancy, because the grounds for termination of the tenant's right to remain in occupation are predicated by the relevant Act, rather than by any irritancy clause contained in the parties' contract. In effect, in the case of a tenancy subject to the Rent Acts (or an assured tenancy under the 1988 Act) the only advantage of an irritancy clause is that it may enable the landlord to terminate the tenancy at an earlier date than the tenancy's natural term, so that eviction proceedings under the relevant Act may be initiated as soon as possible.[105] However, in proceedings under these Acts, it makes no difference whether the tenancy was terminated at the ish date, or before its natural term by way of irritancy or otherwise. This is in contrast to the position that existed in relation to proceedings before statutory security of tenure, in which there was a distinction between the process of "ordinary removing" (applicable to tenancies terminated at the ish date) and "extraordinary removing"[106] (applicable

s 20 is not often used; where there is a lease it will usually contain a conventional irritancy for non-payment of rent that cannot be purged.

102 Or, as Rankine put it: "There is, of course, no limit to the number of conventional irritancies with which the caprice of a landlord and the necessities of a tenant may encumber a lease" (n 18) 532.

103 *Stewart v Watson* (1864) 2 M 1414.

104 ibid; *McDouall's Trs v MacLeod* 1949 SC 593; *Lucas's Exrs v Demarco* 1968 SLT 89; *Dorchester Studios (Glasgow) Ltd v Stone* 1975 SC (HL) 56; and *CIN Properties Ltd v Dollar Land (Cumbernauld) Ltd* 1992 SC (HL) 104. Sections 4–7 of the Law Reform (Miscellaneous Provisions) (Scotland) Act 1985 introduced certain limitations to the use of the remedy of irritancy. These provisions do not apply to residential lets or agricultural tenancies, but have considerable importance in commercial leases.

105 In the case of a tenancy that is a PRT under the 2016 Act, an irritancy clause would be of no effect: under s 44, the tenancy can be terminated only in accordance with the provisions of the Act.

106 The term "removing" is discussed earlier in this chapter, at p 52.

to tenancies that the landlord sought to terminate during the currency of the lease). The effect of this progression is that, for practitioners in the field of residential leasing, the distinction between termination at the ish date and premature termination by irritancy or otherwise, which is still clear to practitioners in agricultural and commercial leasing, has become blurred.[107]

Notice

In the case of a conventional irritancy, the landlord must take overt steps to exercise his option, and an irritancy clause does not dispense with the necessity to give notice of intention to invoke it.[108] Termination under a term of the parties' contract, be it by irritancy or otherwise, requires the landlord to comply with the stipulations of the relevant clause, including any rules as to the manner of giving notice.[109] In the case of irritancy, subject to any such stipulation as to form, content or otherwise, it will be sufficient for the notice given to the tenant to refer to the irritancy clause in the contract and the circumstances that triggered the clause, and indicate that the landlord is exercising his option to terminate.

It is not clear whether section 112 of the 1984 Act applies to such a notice. There are authorities to the effect that a "notice to quit" is neither necessary nor appropriate in the case of an irritancy. However, those authorities are based on the view that a notice of removing under section 37 of the Sheriff Courts (Scotland) Act 1907 is not a necessary preliminary to an action for extraordinary removing.[110] These cases do not determine whether a notice stating the intention to invoke an irritancy clause, and calling upon the tenant to give up possession as a certain date, is a "notice to quit" for the purposes of section 112(1). Arguably, the term "notice to quit" is capable of encompassing such a notice.[111] Therefore it is suggested that the prudent course is to assume that section 112(1) applies. If that is correct, a clear twenty-eight days will be required before the date on which the notice is to take effect. In the

107 As is described at p 59 above, it is not uncommon to see actions founder because the process has been initiated by a notice to quit, when the landlord clearly intended to bring the tenancy to an end prematurely on the basis of a breach of contract by the tenant, as occurred in *Royal Bank of Scotland v Boyle* 1999 Hous LR 43 and 63, which is discussed in detail in Chapter 7.

108 Paton and Cameron (n 14) 228; *Waugh v More Nisbett* (1882) 19 SLR 427; *Life Association of Scotland Ltd v Black's Leisure Group plc* (n 64).

109 Subject to the view that s 112(1) applies, in which case a minimum applies. If the party giving notice fails to comply with contractual conditions due to error, the "reasonable recipient" test may apply: see p 62 above.

110 I.e. an action intended to compel the tenant to remove, before the natural term of the lease, usually enforcing an irritancy clause. See p 53 above. The authorities are: *Pickard v Reid* 1953 SLT (Sh Ct) 5, followed in *Simpson v Goswami* 1976 SLT (Sh Ct) 94.

111 "A notice to quit may be given to prevent tacit relocation, or as a foundation for an action of removing, or both. A notice to quit is sometimes referred to as a 'notice of removing', and if instigated by the tenant as a 'letter of removal'. Removing is the technical term for the giving up of possession by a tenant. It may be during the lease or at termination, and may be voluntary from the tenant's perspective or may be instigated by the landlord." (SLC Discussion Paper *Aspects of Leases: Termination* (n 16), citing Rankine (n 18) 511, and Paton and Cameron (n 14) 245).

case of an assured or a regulated tenancy, the prescribed information ought to be stated.[112]

As is the position in relation to notices to quit,[113] it is thought that, in the case of joint landlords, the prudent course is that all the joint landlords should exercise the option to irritate the lease.[114]

Effect of irritancy

As regards tenancies excepted from the statutory regimes, the effect of irritancy at common law is as described above.

As regards assured or short assured tenancies under the 1988 Act, termination by irritancy triggers section 16, in terms of which the tenant continues to have a statutory assured tenancy of the house on substantially the same terms. He is accordingly obliged to continue meeting his obligations under the lease, including the requirement to pay rent.[115] In relation to short assured tenancies, the landlord may terminate the contract by invoking an irritancy clause and proceed to an action under section 33 of the Act. However, given the terms of section 33(1)(a) this can be done only after the tenancy has reached its ish. Sections 16 and 33 of the 1988 Act are more fully discussed in Chapter 7.

What type of action?: Sheriff court cases[116]

The traditional position is that an action for eviction following the termination by irritancy is an action of extraordinary removing. Conventional irritancies do not become effective without such an action, unless the tenant agrees to remove. The facts constituting the breach must be admitted or proved and, at common law, the court exercises a discretion as to the time of removal.[117] The pursuer raises an ordinary action seeking a declarator of irritancy, with a further crave or conclusion for decree of removing.[118] That said, there is authority that indicates that a declaratory crave is not necessary, where the facts on which the irritancy depends are admitted or are instantly verifiable.[119]

The status of actions for declarator of irritancy and removing in the sheriff court has been rendered problematic by section 35 of the Sheriff Courts (Scotland) Act 1971. Because section 35 stipulates that all actions for recovery

112 See points 2 and 3 at p 55 above.
113 For which see p 61 above.
114 This was the view expressed by A G M Duncan in his *Research Paper on Actions of Ejection and Removing* (SLC 1984) para 2.25.
115 This point is further discussed in Chapter 7.
116 This section does not apply to assured tenancies, in relation to which eviction proceedings are raised in the FTT. See below.
117 *Stair Memorial Encyclopaedia* vol 13 para 436; *Macniven v Murray* (1847) 9 D 1138; *Williamson v Johnstone* (1848) 11 D 332; *Stewart v Watson* (n 103); *Lyon v Irvine* (1874) 1 R 512.
118 A style is given in *Greens Litigation Styles* para B04-01. Actions for declarator of irritancy and removing are often raised in the Court of Session in relation to commercial lets. Under s 38(2)(f) of the Courts Reform (Scotland) Act 2014 the sheriff court also has jurisdiction in regard to such actions.
119 *Duke of Argyll v Campbeltown Coal Co Ltd* 1924 SC 844, 1924 SLT 514; Rankine (n 18) 546–547; Dobie, *Sheriff Court Practice* (1948) 416. See also *Hart v Kitchen* 1989 SC 391, 1990 SLT 54.

of possession must be raised as summary causes, except where there is an additional crave for a sum of money exceeding £5,000, it appears to exclude the possibility of actions with other additional craves, such as declarator or interdict. This issue is further discussed at the beginning of Chapter 13.

Given this difficulty, and given further that there is authority to suggest that in many cases a declaratory crave is unnecessary, it would seem that, practically speaking, the best course might be to raise a summary cause action, and thereafter ask for the action to be remitted to the ordinary cause roll[120] in the event that it becomes apparent that a declaratory crave is going to be necessary,[121] which could thereafter be added by amendment. If the application to remit the cause is opposed, the pursuer may argue that his only alternative course of action would have been to raise the actions of declarator and recovery of possession separately, which would have caused unnecessary delay and expense.

Irritancy and eviction proceedings: assured tenancies

Under section 18(6) of the 1988 Act, which is discussed in detail in Chapter 7, the FTT may make an order for possession of a house that is let on an assured tenancy, notwithstanding the fact that the tenancy contract has never been terminated. This is subject to two conditions:

(1) the ground for possession is one of the grounds specified in section 18(6)(a);[122] and

(2) the terms of the tenancy make provision for it to be brought to an end on the ground in question (i.e. there is an irritancy clause that reproduces the relevant statutory ground(s)).

In cases in which the landlord is able to utilise this provision, there is no necessity to terminate the tenancy contract. Therefore, there is no requirement to serve notice with that purpose, or to seek a declarator of irritancy from the court. In that case, she may simply serve the form AT6 in terms of section 19 of the Act, and make an application to the tribunal seeking recovery of possession.

In cases to which section 18(6) does not apply, the landlord may nevertheless maintain that she has terminated the parties' contract by irritancy, such as to bring a statutory assured tenancy into being, under section 16. There seems to be no reason why she could not then ask the FTT to make a determination to that effect, in the context of an application for an order under section 18 or section 33 of the 1988 Act.

Defences

In cases of irritancy of a common law tenancy of a dwellinghouse the possibilities for defending the action may be fairly limited. Apart from denying that he

120 Under the Sheriff Courts (Scotland) Act 1971, s 37.

121 This would depend on the basis on which the action was defended. Possible defences are discussed below. In *Hart v Kitchen* (n 119), the court expressed the view (at 394) that if the defender raised the issue of competency of the action, it would have expected him to move under s 37 of the 1971 Act, that the cause should be treated as an ordinary cause.

122 Being grounds 2 or 8 in pt I of sch 5 to the Act or any of the grounds in part II thereof, other than grounds 9, 10, 15 or 17.

is in breach of contract, the defender may aver that the landlord is personally barred from relying on the irritancy; that he has waived the right to rely on the irritancy clause;[123] or that he is not entitled to rely on the irritancy clause due to his breaching his own obligations under the contract.[124]

Unfair terms: Part 2 of the Consumer Rights Act 2015

Part 2 of the 2015 Act replaces the Unfair Terms in Consumer Contract Regulations 1999, in implementing EC Directive 93/13 on unfair terms in consumer contracts.[125]

Part 2 of the Act applies to leases. In *Asbeek Brusse and de Man Garabito v Jahani BV*,[126] the European Court of Justice confirmed that where a tenancy agreement relating to residential premises was concluded between a landlord acting for purposes relating to his trade, business or profession and a tenant acting for purposes that did not so relate, that came within the scope of the Directive. The court held that the protection of the Directive was particularly important in the case of a residential tenancy agreement concluded between an individual acting on a non-commercial basis and a real estate professional. The consequences of the inequality existing between the parties were aggravated by the fact that, from an economic perspective, such a contract related to an essential need of the consumer (namely, to obtain lodging) and involved sums that most frequently represented one of the most significant items in the tenant's budget, while, from a legal perspective, it was a contract that, as a general rule, was covered by complex national rules about which individuals were often poorly informed. However, contractual terms that reflected mandatory statutory or regulatory provisions of national law were not subject to the provisions of the Directive.

Part 2 of the 2015 Act applies to a contract between a trader and a consumer.[127] Under section 62(1), an unfair contract term is not binding on a

123 The question of whether the subsequent acceptance of rent would amount to a waiver of the right to terminate the lease is one of fact, which must be answered in light of the surrounding circumstances: *HMV Fields Properties Ltd v Bracken Self Selection Fabrics* 1991 SLT 31, 1990 SCLR 677. Note that no such question arises in relation to assured tenancies, because the tenant is obliged to continue paying rent under the statutory tenancy that arises on termination of the contract, under the 1988 Act, s 16. On waiver of irritancy, see McAllister(n 17) paras 5.8–5.12.

124 See, e.g., *Macnab v Willison* 1960 SLT (Notes) 25; *British Transport Commission v Forsyth* 1963 SLT (Sh Ct) 32.

125 Council Directive (EC) 93/13 on unfair terms in consumer contracts [1993] OJ L93/29. The original implementation was by the Unfair Terms in Consumer Contract Regulations 1994 (SI 1994/3159), which came into force on 1 July 1995. These were replaced by the 1999 Regulations (SI 1999/2083), which came into force on 1 October 1999. Part 2 of the 2015 Regulations also replaces the Unfair Contract Terms Act 1977, so far as applicable to consumers.

126 [2013] HLR 38. For earlier examples of the application of the 1999 regulations to leases, see *R (Khatun and others) v Newham London Borough Council* [2005] QB 37, [2004] HLR 29; *UK Housing Alliance (North West) Ltd v Francis* [2010] EWCA Civ 117, [2010] 3 All ER 519, [2010] HLR 28; *Rochdale BC v Dixon* [2011] EWCA Civ 1173, [2012] HLR 6. For further aspects of the application of Consumer protection law to residential letting, see Chapter 5 (at n 51) and Chapter 8, at p 283.

127 Section 61(1). Under s 2(2), a "trader" means "a person acting for purposes relating to that person's trade, business, craft or profession, whether acting personally or through another person acting in the trader's name or on the trader's behalf". Under s 2(3), a "consumer"

consumer. A term is "unfair" if, contrary to the requirement of good faith, it causes a significant imbalance in the rights and obligations of the parties under the contract, to the detriment of the consumer.[128]

Part 1 of schedule 2 to the Act contains "an indicative and non-exhaustive list of terms of consumer contracts that may be regarded as unfair for the purposes of this Part".[129] Two entries in this list may be regarded as being of particular interest. Those are:

> "7. A term which has the object or effect of authorising the trader to dissolve the contract on a discretionary basis where the same facility is not granted to the consumer . . .
> 8. A term which has the object or effect of enabling the trader to terminate a contract of indeterminate duration[130] without reasonable notice except where there are serious grounds for doing so."

In 2005, the Office of Fair Trading issued "Guidance on Unfair Terms in Tenancy Agreements", which included the following paragraphs:

> "3.62 . . . we object to forfeiture clauses[131] that are not in plain language and that do not make the legal position with regard to eviction completely clear to the tenant, i.e. that a landlord is obliged to seek a court order to recover possession if the tenant remains in occupation.
> 4.49: The ultimate sanction for breach of a term of a tenancy is termination of the agreement and eviction of the tenant. There should be no possibility within the contract, however remote, of any attempt by the landlord to terminate the agreement and evict the tenant for a default that poses no real threat to the landlord's legitimate interests."

That guidance has now been withdrawn, and replaced by the Competition and Markets Authority's "Unfair Contract Terms Guidance", which does not specifically address tenancy agreements.[132] Nevertheless, it is suggested that the 2005 Guidance is still of interest, in giving some indication of contractual terms that may be regarded as unfair.[133]

means "an individual acting for purposes that are wholly or mainly outside that individual's trade, business, craft or profession". See paras 3.6–3.11 of the Competition and Market Authority's (CMA's) "Guidance for Lettings Professionals on Consumer Protection Law".

128 Schedule 2 to the Regulations provides an "indicative and non-exhaustive" list of terms that may be unfair (generally referred to as the "grey list", as opposed to the "black list" of automatically ineffective terms given by the Unfair Contract Terms Act 1977).

129 This is known as the "grey list", because what is listed is under suspicion of unfairness, but not necessarily unfair. See the CMA's "Unfair Contract Terms Guidance".

130 As the "grey list" is "indicative and non-exhaustive", there seems little doubt that a clause allowing termination without reasonable notice or on trivial grounds would also be objectionable in a contract of determinate duration.

131 Under English law, a forfeiture clause is similar to an irritancy clause. Forfeiture clauses were considered at p 105 of the Guidance.

132 Though para 5.32.2 states: "Rights of entry. An example is a term which purports to give the right of entry without consent to private property, whether to repossess goods for which consumers have not paid on time, to evict the consumer, or for any other purpose. Such a term seeks to permit direct resort to a sanction that can normally and properly only be authorised by court order."

133 The CMA Guidance contains a "Historic Annex A to unfair contract terms guidance", which preserves examples of fair and unfair terms, considered by the Office of Fair Trading.

Rescission

As indicated above, the neglected issue of rescission in leases may be of some importance in the context of residential leasing, particularly in relation to leases that do not have an irritancy clause.[134]

The "non-judicial" remedy of rescission in respect of a material breach of contract was not established in Scots law until the second half of the nineteenth century.[135] Prior to this development, a court declarator was needed to terminate a contract or, as has been seen, there could be a contractual provision for termination, such as an irritancy clause. But otherwise Scots law did not originally recognise a non-judicial remedy in the form of a unilateral termination by one of the parties to the contract as a response to a material breach by the other party. Rescission became established as a remedy in a series of cases in the second half of the nineteenth century.[136]

It can be said, as a matter of general principle, that, excepting the special rules applicable to tenancy contracts at statute and common law, the general law of contract applies to leases.[137] Therefore, it might be anticipated that a right of rescission is available to either party to a lease contract, in response to any material breach of contract by the other party.

In particular, one might expect that the remedy of rescission would be available to a landlord in respect of a breach of contract by the tenant, such as the non-payment of rent, in cases where, for whatever reason, the landlord cannot rely on an irritancy clause.

In "To Irritate or Rescind: Two Paths for the Landlord?"[138] Martin Hogg analysed all the cases in which the landlord sought to terminate a lease on the basis of a material breach.[139] He concluded that the authorities make clear that the landlord may rescind, but only under certain conditions. That conclusion subsequently received judicial approval in the decision of Lord Pentland in the case of *Crieff Highland Gathering Ltd v Perth and Kinross Council*.[140] He said:

> "Having regard to the views expressed in the authorities I have cited, it seems to me that a landlord may only rescind a lease where a number of conditions are satisfied. These are: (1) that the tenant has committed a material breach of the contract of lease; (2) that the landlord has given the tenant a fair and reasonable opportunity to fulfil its contractual obligations and (3) that the tenant has demonstrated that it is unwilling or unable to perform in the future. It is clear from this analysis that the court must take into account the conduct and attitude of the tenant right up to the time when decree is sought. In the present case, I have already held that the defender has not committed a material breach of the lease. In addition, I consider that the pursuer has not proved that the defender is unable or unwilling to fulfil its contractual obligations in the future. In my view, the right conclusion to draw from

134 Apart from the authorities mentioned below, readers are referred to the discussion of rescission in McAllister (n 17) ch 4.

135 In particular by the case of *Turnbull v McLean & Co* (1874) 1 R 730.

136 See McBryde (n 94) ch 20 pt 10.

137 *Edmond v Reid* (n 97).

138 1999 SLT (News) 1.

139 Being, in particular, *Hamilton v Hamilton* (1845) 8 D 308; *Edmond v Reid* (n 97); *Kilmacolm Hydropathic Co Ltd v Hall* (1922) 38 Sh Ct Rep 233; *Blair Trust Co v Gilbert* 1940 SLT 322; *O'Brien v O'Brien* (1945) 61 Sh Ct Rep 158; and *Couper v McGuiness* (1948) 64 Sh Ct Rep 249.

140 n 97.

the evidence is that the defender is indeed committed to ensuring that it adheres to its contractual responsibilities in the future. So the pursuer has, in my judgment, failed to satisfy conditions (1) and (3)."[141]

Given the dearth of recent authority in this area, this decision is welcome. However, it still leaves an important question unanswered: is rescission possible where the breach in question is the non-payment of rent?[142]

In the 1967 edition of Paton and Cameron, under the heading "Remedies of Landlord",[143] the authors describe the various possible remedies available to the landlord for recovery of rent, such as an action for payment of the rent as a debt; and various forms of diligence such as arrestment, summary diligence, sequestration for rent and so on. They then state:

"In respect of breach by the tenant of any of the other obligations of the lease – that is, *those other than payment of rent* – the landlord may be entitled to rescind the lease and claim damages against the tenant."

In the 1929 edition of *Gloag on Contract*, the author states:

"In leases, mere non-payment of rent does not entitle the landlord to bring the lease to an end; and even if a legal irritancy has been incurred by failure in payment for two years, it may be purged by payment before decree of removing."[144]

These authors do not explain why the non-payment of rent is an exceptional case. It is suggested that the answer probably lies in the existence of legal irritancies in respect of non-payment of rent at common law.[145] Although these are, in practical terms, virtually obsolete, they may be said to comprise the rules of law that provide for the landlord having an implied right to terminate a lease on the basis of non-payment of rent. If the requirements of those rules are not met, for example where the rent arrears are for less than two years in relation to a lease that is not an agricultural lease, the landlord has no implied right to terminate the contract.

That said, it is submitted that although *Crieff Highland Gathering*[146] does not deal with rescission on the ground of non-payment of rent, Lord Pentland's analysis of the authorities nevertheless supports the view that rescission on that basis is possible. As he describes, the development of the law in this area may be traced back to the dissenting opinion of Lord Fullarton in *Hamilton v Hamilton*.[147] He thought that a lease was similar to any other mutual contract when it came to termination on the ground of material breach of its terms. However, the right to rescind a lease would apply only where the tenant was

141 At para [54].

142 In *Crieff Highland Gathering* (n 97) the obligations said to have been breached by the tenants related to repair and maintenance of the subjects.

143 (n 14) 144–145. Rankine (n 18), writing in 1916, barely makes reference to the remedy of rescission. At the beginning of his ch XX, "Termination During Currency", he simply states: "Leases come to end sooner than at the most remote ish contemplated, in three ways – by renunciation; in pursuance of a break; and by virtue of an irritancy."

144 (n 16)618, in the chapter "Rights arising from Breach of Contract", in which the remedy of rescission is discussed.

145 As described above. Note the connection made by Gloag between termination on the ground of rent arrears, and the rules regarding legal irritancies.

146 n 97.

147 n 139.

refusing to undertake performance of its obligations in the future. Thus he said:

> "the landlord is entitled to make the tenant say whether he will implement (the lease) or not; and if he will not, to have the contract of lease set aside".

As Lord Pentland explains, the court was prepared, in subsequent cases, to declare that a tenant had forfeited her right to possession, where she had failed to confirm that she was willing and able to fulfil the conditions of the lease in the future.[148] There does not appear to be any reason why that approach is not applicable to non-payment of rent. The basis of termination is not, as Gloag describes it, "mere non-payment of rent". Rather, termination is founded on the existence of all three of the elements identified by the quotation from Lord Pentland's judgment, above. That includes, in particular, the judgment that the tenant is unwilling or unable to comply with her obligation under the lease to pay rent as it falls due in the future.

Conclusion: a practical example

Let us say that, in 2017, parties entered into an assured tenancy with an ish of one year, from 1 October. The landlord draws up a rudimentary lease himself. It has no irritancy clause. The tenancy continues by tacit relocation on 1 October 2018, 2019 and 2020. However, the tenant fails to make payment of the rent for October, November and December 2020. The landlord contacts the tenant by telephone and letter, asking for payment. He receives assurances that the arrears will be paid, but no money is forthcoming. The landlord does not wish to wait until October 2021 to terminate the lease.

It is suggested that the landlord may reasonably regard this set of circumstances as constituting a material breach of contract; thus the first of Lord Pentland's three conditions is satisfied. The landlord could give notice to the tenant in writing, calling upon him to pay the outstanding rent arrears within a reasonable period, say twenty-eight days, failing which he will take it that the tenant is unwilling or unable to comply with his obligation to pay rent. The notice would also state that in that in the event of non-payment, following the expiry of the twenty-eight-day period, the landlord may terminate the contract, serve notice of proceedings under section 19 of the 1988 Act, and thereafter make an application to the FTT on grounds 8, 11 and 12 of schedule 5 to the Act.

The tenant may respond in various ways. He may make partial payment. He may offer to pay off the arrears in instalments. In that case, it will be for the landlord to decide, subject to advice, whether at the end of the ultimatum period he has a sufficiently strong argument that Lord Pentland's three conditions are established.

If the landlord decides that he wishes to press on with the application, it is submitted that he ought to notify the tenant in writing that he is terminating the lease, in accordance with his previous letter, and that he intends to raise proceedings under section 18 of the 1988 Act. A form AT6 can be served at the same time. After the expiry of the period of notice specified in the AT6, he may then make an application to the FTT under grounds 8, 11 and 12.

148 *Edmond v Reid* (n 97); *Blair Trust Co v Gilbert* (n 139).

That application might be opposed by the tenant on the basis that, as the landlord was not entitled to rescind, the lease has not been terminated, and, as section 18(6) of the 1988 Act does not apply, decree for recovery of possession cannot be granted. Those issues could then be determined by the tribunal.

Chapter 4

Scottish Secure Tenancies

INTRODUCTION

The 2001 Act introduced two new forms of tenancy for the "social rented sector": the Scottish secure tenancy and the short Scottish secure tenancy ("SSST"). The background to the 2001 Act, and some outline of the nature of these tenancies, is given in Chapter 1. In essence, the Scottish secure tenancy is an updated form of the secure tenancy that was introduced in 1980. The SSST, however, was an innovation of the 2001 Act. It is a hybrid of the secure tenancy and the short assured tenancy under the 1988 Act, which is designed to give landlords in the social rented sector the option of granting a tenancy without security of tenure, in certain specified circumstances.

In relation to Scottish secure tenancies, the service of a notice of proceedings for recovery of possession under section 14 of the 2001 Act is an essential prerequisite to raising proceedings under section 16.[1] In order to succeed in those proceedings, the landlord must establish (a) one or more of the statutory grounds for recovery of possession set out in schedule 2; and (b) the "additional requirement" appropriate to that ground.[2] Thus, the tenant may join issue with the landlord on the procedural question of whether the landlord has served a valid notice under section 14, and/or the substantive question of whether the landlord is able to establish the ground and the additional requirement.

In 2012, certain amendments were made to the 2001 Act by section 155 of the Housing (Scotland) Act 2010. These had the effect of creating a new "pre-action" procedure in relation to rent arrears cases.[3] The older section

1 The landlord is also required, under s 14(5A), to give notice of the raising of the proceedings to the local authority in whose area the house in question is situated, unless the landlord is that local authority. That provision is discussed below.

2 For grounds 1, 3, 4, 5, 6 and 7, the court must be satisfied that it would be reasonable to grant the order. The landlord does not need to establish the additional requirement in relation to ground 2, provided that it fulfils the conditions of s 16(2)(aa), introduced by the 2014 Act: see the discussion of this provision in Chapter 5. For grounds 8–14, the court must be satisfied that other suitable accommodation will be available for the tenant when the order takes effect. For ground 15, the court must be satisfied that both of these additional requirements have been established. The grounds and additional requirements are discussed in Chapter 5.

3 For the purposes of this chapter and the succeeding ones, a "rent arrears case" under the 2001 Act is an action for recovery of possession under that Act in which the ground, or one of the grounds, for eviction is that the tenant is in arrears of rent. Section 153 of the 2010 Act also makes important amendments to s 16 of the 2001 Act, which change the nature of the decree that is granted in proceedings under that section, in rent arrears cases. Those changes are discussed in Chapter 15.

14 procedure, which is more straightforward, continues to apply to all other cases.

The procedure for rent arrears cases requires the landlord first to comply with the "pre-action requirements" that are set out in section 14A.[4] The form of notice of proceedings in such cases must then specify the steps taken by the landlord that it considers to constitute compliance with the pre-action requirements.[5] On raising proceedings under section 16, the landlords' statement of claim must include an averment confirming to the court that the pre-action requirements have been complied with.[6] As in the case of actions to which the old procedure applies, the landlord must establish the statutory ground(s) upon which it relies, together with the applicable "additional requirement".[7] As well as the procedural and substantive matters described above, the tenant in a rent arrears case may join issue with the landlord on the question of whether it has complied with these various requirements.

The purpose of this chapter is to consider the basis on which tenancies are subject to the 2001 Act regime and, further, certain procedural issues in relation to actions for recovery of possession under the Act:

- creation and termination of Scottish secure tenancies under sections 11 and 12 of the Act;
- the "pre-action requirements" for rent arrears cases under section 14A;
- the service of the requisite notice under section 14.

This chapter also considers the abandonment procedure, in terms of sections 17–19 of the Act, under which the landlord may recover possession without obtaining a court order, if the property has been abandoned by the tenant.

The statutory code in relation to SSSTs under sections 34–37 of the Act is considered in Chapter 6.

4 There are no "pre-action requirements" in relation to an action that is not a rent arrears action. However, under s 16(3)(d), in deciding whether it is reasonable to grant an order under any of grounds 1–7, the court should "have regard . . . to . . . any action taken by the landlord, before raising the proceedings, with a view to securing the cessation of [the conduct which is said to give rise to the ground]". Section 16(3) is discussed in Chapter 5.

5 Section 14(4)(c). The two forms of s 14 notice, for rent arrears cases and other cases, may be found in the Scottish Secure Tenancies (Proceedings for Possession) (Form of Notice) Regulations 2012 (SSI 2012/92), as amended by the Scottish Secure Tenancies (Proceedings for Possession) (Form of Notice) Amendment Regulations (SSI 2018/156) (Form of Notice Regulations). See below, at p 107.

6 Scottish Secure Tenancies (Proceedings for Possession) (Confirmation of Compliance with Pre-Action Requirements) Regulations (SSI 2012/93). However, in *Aberdeen City Council v Beattie* (unreported decision of Sheriff Lewis, Aberdeen Sheriff Court, 21 October 2014), the sheriff held that it was competent to add the necessary averment by amendment, during the course of the action.

7 The sole ground, or one of the grounds, will be "Rent lawfully due from the tenant has not been paid, or any other obligation of the tenancy has been broken." under para 1 of sch 2. The additional requirement applicable to that ground is that it would be reasonable to grant the order.

CREATION AND TERMINATION

Section 11

For present purposes, the relevant provisions of section 11 are as follows:

"**Scottish secure tenancy**

(1) A tenancy of a house is a Scottish secure tenancy if–

(a) the house is let as a separate dwelling,

(b) the landlord is–

(i) a local authority landlord, or

(ii) a registered social landlord,[8]

specified, or of a description specified, in an order made by the Scottish Ministers, or is Scottish Water,

(c) the tenant is an individual and the house is the tenant's only or principal home,

(d) where the landlord is a registered social landlord which is a co-operative housing association, the tenant is a member of the association, and

(e) the tenancy–

(i) was created on or after such date as the order may specify in relation to the landlord, or

(ii) was created before that date and is of a description specified in the order in relation to the landlord.

. . .

(3) In this Act, 'local authority landlord' means a landlord which is a local authority, a joint board or joint committee of two or more local authorities, or the common good of a local authority, or any trust under the control of a local authority.

(4) A tenancy is not a Scottish secure tenancy if it is a tenancy of a kind mentioned in schedule 1.

. . .[9]

(7) It is a term of every Scottish secure tenancy that the tenant complies with paragraphs (c) and (d) of subsection (1).

(8) Without prejudice to sections 14 and 16 and schedule 2, a tenancy which is a Scottish secure tenancy continues to be a Scottish secure tenancy even if subsection (1)(b), (c) or (d) is no longer satisfied,

. . ."

What qualifies as a Scottish secure tenancy?: s 11(1)

The terms "house", "let as a separate dwelling" and "only or principal home" are discussed in Chapter 1. The order referred to in section 11(1)(b) and (e) is the Housing (Scotland) Act 2001 (Scottish Secure Tenancy etc.) Order 2002,[10] which provided that all local authorities, all registered social landlords

8 The Housing (Scotland) Act 2010 makes provision for the regulation and registration of registered social landlords ("RSLs"), most of which are housing associations. Under s 111 of the 2001 Act, "registered social landlord" now means a body registered in the register of RSLs maintained under s 20(1) of the 2010 Act.

9 Subsections (5), (6), (6A) and (6B) apply where one or more individuals apply to the landlord to be included with the tenant as joint tenants under the tenancy.

10 SSI 2002/318, as amended by the Housing (Scotland) Act 2001 (Scottish Secure Tenancy etc.) Amendment Order 2002 (SSI 2002/415).

and all water or sewage authorities were specified.[11] In terms of that order, the effective date for the purposes of section 11(1)(e)(i) was 30 September 2002, and on that date all secure tenancies under the 1987 Act, and all assured tenancies[12] under the 1988 Act, held by the landlords specified, became Scottish secure tenancies.

As was described in Chapter 1, under section 41 of the 2001 Act, "tenancy" means an agreement under which a house is made available for human habitation, and "lease" and related expressions are to be construed accordingly. Provided that the agreement in question makes a house available for human habitation, and it meets the other requirements of section 11, it will constitute a Scottish secure tenancy or an SSST, even though it may not amount to a lease at common law.

Prior to the 2001 Act, when housing associations were subject to the 1988 Act regime, some landlords sought to create an "occupancy agreement" with the purpose, *inter alia*, of affording some form of support or treatment to the occupant, such as long-term drug or alcohol rehabilitation. In such cases, the accommodation provider typically wished to give exclusive occupation to a room in return for payment of a "rent" (met by housing benefit) and continued co-operation with the support offered. Naturally, the accommodation provider did not wish this arrangement to attract security of tenure, as it wished the occupant to move on where the treatment or support was at an end, or had broken down, in order that those facilities could be offered to another person.

Under the 2001 Act, this type of arrangement is possible only if the agreement in question would not be a Scottish secure tenancy in any event, because it does not meet the other requirements of section 11.[13] Otherwise, occupancy agreements of the type described will be Scottish secure tenancies, given the terms of section 41, or SSSTs under section 34(2) and paragraph 6 of schedule 6[14] to the Act, provided that the landlord meets the requirements for constitution of an SSST under section 34(1).

Tenancy agreements: s 23

Under section 23(1), the landlord must draw up a tenancy agreement stating the terms of the tenancy, and ensure that , before the commencement of the tenancy, it is subscribed or authenticated by the landlord and the tenant in accordance with the Requirements of Writing (Scotland) Act 1995. It must also supply a copy to the tenant. However, failure to comply with these requirements does not affect the existence or validity of the tenancy, or the tenant's status as a Scottish secure tenant.[15]

11 The Amendment Order also provides that "all registered social landlords which are co-operative housing associations" are specified for the purposes of s 11(1)(b).

12 The Order makes a specific exception in respect of short assured tenancies, which did not convert to the new regime. In addition, there is authority to suggest that statutory assured tenancies under the 1988 Act, s 16 did not convert either. See *Grampian Housing Association v Pyper* 2004 Hous LR 22.

13 For example, if the accommodation is not provided to the occupier as "separate dwelling", or if it falls within one of the excepted categories under sch 1.

14 Schedule 6 para 6 (Accommodation for person requiring housing support services).

15 *MacDonald v Strathclyde RC* 1990 SLT (Lands Tr) 10.

Tenancies excepted under schedule 1: s 11(4)

The classes of excepted tenancies may be summarised as follows:

(1) Service occupancies: where the tenant, or any one of the joint tenants, is an employee of the landlord, or of any local authority, and the contract of employment requires that he occupy the house for the better performance of his duties.
(2) Police and fire service accommodation.[16]
(3) Lettings to students: where the tenancy is granted to a person who is pursuing, or intends to pursue, a course of study provided by a specified educational institution and is granted either by that institution or by another specified institution or body.[17]
(4) Decant accommodation: where the house is occupied by the tenant while work is being carried out on the house that the tenant normally occupies as the tenant's home, and the tenant is, by agreement, or by virtue of an order of the sheriff under section 16(6), entitled to return there after the work is completed.
(5) Homeless accommodation: where the house is being let to the tenant expressly on a temporary basis, for a term of less than six months, in fulfilment of a duty imposed on a local authority by part II of the 1987 Act (homeless persons).
(6) Accommodation for offenders: where the tenancy is granted, for a term of less than six months, to a person who is under supervision by a local authority in terms of certain provisions of the Social Work (Scotland) Act 1968,[18] or who has requested the provision of advice, guidance or assistance by a local authority in pursuance of its functions under the relevant parts of that Act.
(7) Shared ownership agreements: these are defined in terms of section 83(3) of Act.
(8) Agricultural and business premises: where the house: (a) is let together with agricultural land exceeding two acres in extent; (b) consists of or includes premises that are used as a shop or an office for business, trade or professional purposes; (c) consists of or includes premises licensed

16 This paragraph was subject to substantial amendment by s 154 of the 2010 Act, following conflicting decisions of the Lands Tribunal on the question of whether police officers were entitled to exercise the right to buy accommodation provided to them in connection with their employment (*Robb v Tayside Joint Police Board* 2009 SLT (Lands Tr) 23; *Cochrane v Grampian Joint Police Board* 2010 SLT (Lands Tr) 19, 2010 Hous LR 57). It was further modified by the Police and Fire Reform (Scotland) Act 2012 sch 8(2) para 1, and the Police and Fire Reform (Scotland) Act 2012 (Consequential Modifications and Savings) Order (SSI 2013/119) sch 1 para 18. It has consequently become quite complex, and readers are referred to its terms. It should be noted that this category does not only apply to cases in which the tenant is employed by a police force or fire authority, but can also apply where the house is let expressly on a temporary basis, to any person, pending its being required for the purposes of a police force or fire authority.

17 The educational institutions for the purpose of this paragraph are specified by the Scottish Secure Tenancies (Exceptions) Regulations 2002 (SSI 2002/314), as amended by SSI 2002/434.

18 In particular, under para (b)(i), (ii) or (vi) of s 27(1), relating to the supervision and care of persons on probation, released from prison etc.

for the sale of alcohol, or (d) is let in conjunction with any purpose mentioned in either (b) or (c).

(9) Houses part of, or within curtilage of, certain other buildings: the house forms part of, or is within the curtilage of, a building that: (a) is held by the landlord mainly for purposes other than the provision of housing accommodation; and (b) mainly consists of accommodation other than housing accommodation.

(10) Accommodation in property not owned by the landlord: where the house is leased by the landlord from another body and the terms of the lease preclude the letting of the house by the landlord under a Scottish secure tenancy.

(11) Accommodation for persons with temporary protection: where the tenancy is granted in order to provide accommodation under the Displaced Persons (Temporary Protection) Regulations 2005.[19]

In relation to excepted tenancies, the following points may usefully be made.

Paragraphs 1 and 9 have been the subject of numerous decisions in the Lands Tribunal, in cases in which the landlord refused to allow the tenant to exercise the right to buy under section 61 of the 1987 Act, on the basis that the tenancy was not a Scottish secure tenancy.[20]

For paragraph 5 to apply, the tenant must have made an application as a homeless person under part II of the 1987 Act, which is being considered by the local authority, and the tenancy must be let expressly on a temporary basis, for that purpose, and expressly for a period of less than six months. Particular care is therefore required in the drafting of contract in terms of which homeless persons are provided with temporary accommodation: if the requirements of paragraph 5 are not met, it is likely that the agreement will be a Scottish secure tenancy under section 11.[21] In *Nisala v Glasgow City Council*,[22] the landlords' eviction action failed because the tenancy did not expressly state that it was for a period of less than six months. The court found that the tenancy was not excepted under paragraph 5. The Inner House came to the same conclusion in *Falkirk Council v Gillies*.[23] In that case the relevant clause of the agreement provided that it "will take effect from 9 December 2009 and will continue

19 SI 2005/1379, made pursuant to the EC Temporary Protection Directive (Council Directive (EC) 2001/55 of 20 July 2001 on minimum standards for giving temporary protection in the event of a mass influx of displaced persons).

20 In his commentary to the 1987 Act, Paul Watchman gives a detailed discussion of the older cases, to which the reader is referred: Watchman, *Annotated Housing (Scotland) Act 1987* (1991). Important cases under the 2001 Act are: *McAuslane v Highland Council* 2004 Hous LR 30, in respect of para 1; *Fee v East Renfrewshire Council* 2006 Hous LR 99; *Taylor v Renfrewshire Council* 2010 SLT (Lands Tr) 2; and *Hopwood v West Lothian Council* 2017 GWD 22-380 in respect of para 9.

21 Note also that some local authorities have operated a policy in terms of which a person who applies for assistance as a homeless person on the basis that he is fleeing violence from neighbours or other persons is given a tenancy in temporary accommodation pending a management transfer, rather than being treated as a homeless person in terms of s 24(2A) of the 1987 Act. However, this type of tenancy does not appear to be covered by any of the exceptions in sch 1 to the 2001 Act, and therefore there is a danger, at least from the local authority's point of view, that a Scottish secure tenancy may be created in respect of the temporary accommodation.

22 2006 Hous LR 66.

23 2017 SC 230.

on a fortnightly basis . . .". The court held that a reference to an agreement continuing fortnightly was not the same as an express agreement that it was to last for a fortnight.

As well as the exceptions listed at schedule 1, the Housing (Scotland) Act 2001 (Accommodation for Asylum-Seekers) Order 2002[24] provides that a tenancy shall not be a Scottish secure tenancy if it is granted in order to provide accommodation under part VI of the Immigration and Asylum Act 1999 (support for asylum-seekers).[25]

Changes in circumstances: s 11(4), (7) and (8)

It is a feature of legislation that confers security of tenure that the relevant Act contains provisions that set out which type of tenancy is covered by the statutory regime, and which types are specifically excepted.[26] As we have seen, in the 2001 Act, those provisions are section 11, which defines a Scottish secure tenancy, and schedule 1, which lists the tenancies that are not covered by the Act. In the 1988 Act, the equivalent provisions are section 12 and schedule 4, and in the 2016 Act, section 1 and schedule 1.

Where an Act contains provisions of this nature, a question can arise as to the legal effect of any change of circumstances during the course of the tenancy. If the tenancy does not fulfil the conditions for coverage by the Act at the outset, but fulfils those conditions at some later date, does it then become protected under the legislation? Conversely, if it is initially protected, can it lose that status if circumstances change?

In the 2001 Act, the effect of section 11(8) is that where a tenancy is a Scottish secure tenancy at its inception, it will *retain* that status so long as it is still let as a separate dwelling in terms of section 11(1)(a). That is the case, even if the interest of the landlord is transferred to a person that is not a local authority or a registered social landlord (an RSL).

The tenancy will also continue to be a Scottish secure tenancy even if the tenant no longer occupies it as his only or principal home.[27] Where the tenant has ceased occupation, the appropriate remedy for the landlord seeking recovery of possession is (a) the abandonment procedure, if the tenancy is unoccupied by any person,;[28] or (b) an action for recovery of possession against the tenant under ground 5 of schedule 2, and ground 1, where a person or persons other than the tenant is in occupation. An action under ground 1 is appropriate because, given the terms of section 11(7), the tenant's failure to occupy the tenancy as his only or principal home constitutes a breach of contract.[29]

24 SI 2002/2367.

25 ibid. The 2002 Order is made under powers granted under ss 104 and 112 of the Scotland Act 1998, including the power to amend Acts of the Scottish Parliament by subordinate legislation of the Westminster Parliament.

26 Excepted tenancies, not being subject to statutory control, are sometimes called "common law tenancies". See Chapter 1, p 16.

27 Or, where the Scottish secure tenancy was granted, a member of a co-operative housing association under s 11(1)(d), and the tenant subsequently ceases to be a member of the association.

28 The abandonment procedure is analysed at the end of this chapter.

29 Grounds 1 and 5 of sch 2 to the 2001 Act are further discussed in Chapter 6.

However, it is submitted that there is no indication in the 2001 Act, in section 11 or elsewhere, that there was an intention on the part of the legislature to allow tenancies to *lose* or *gain* Scottish secure tenancy status, on there being a change in circumstances.[30]

Under the 1988 Act (and the older Rent Acts), the statutory tenancy, with its attendant rent control and security of tenure, comes into effect once the tenancy contract between the parties has been terminated. Thus, under the 1988 Act, the termination of the tenancy triggers the statutory assured tenancy under section 16(1).[31] Under the 2001 Act,[32] the status of the tenancy as a statutory "Scottish secure tenancy", controlled by the legislation, applies from the very beginning of the tenancy, and throughout its existence, such that the tenant's contractual and statutory rights co-exist. They begin and end at the same time. The termination of the tenancy can take place only under section 12. Under the legislative provisions, there is no "contractual" Scottish secure tenancy as distinct from the statutory tenancy[33] and, for that reason, the tenancy contract between a landlord and the tenant does not have to be terminated before the landlord raises proceedings under section 16 of the 2001 Act. That is why the landlord of a Scottish secure tenancy does not have to serve a notice to quit before raising proceedings under sections 14 and 16 of the Act.

Thus, chapter 1 of part 2 of the 2001 Act is headed: "*Creation and termination of tenancy*". The "creation" part of this heading applies to section 11; sections 12–21 relate to termination of a Scottish secure tenancy, in particular by eviction proceedings or abandonment. A Scottish secure tenancy comes into being when a "tenancy" is "created",[34] to which the conditions in section 11 apply. The tenancy then remains a Scottish secure tenancy until termination takes place under one of the circumstances listed in section 12(1) of the Act.

Therefore, it is suggested that where an RSL purchases a property that is let under a tenancy that is not a Scottish secure tenancy, because the landlord is not one of the bodies specified in section 11(1)(b), that tenancy does not become a Scottish secure tenancy, because it did not have that status when it was created. Likewise, a tenancy that is excepted under, say, paragraph 1 of schedule 1 does not become a Scottish secure tenancy if the tenant's employment with the landlord is terminated. In both these cases, the creation of a Scottish secure tenancy would require a new tenancy agreement that meets the requirements of section 11.

30 This may be contrasted with the position in relation to assured tenancies, because of the words "if and so long as" in s 12 of the 1988 Act. See Chapter 7, p 223. Likewise, under the English legislation (Housing Act 1985, s 79(1)) a tenancy has statutory secure status "at any time when" the relevant conditions, as regards the landlord and tenant, are fulfilled.

31 Discussed at p 229.

32 And its predecessors the Housing (Scotland) Act 1987 and the Tenants' Rights, Etc (Scotland) Act 1980.

33 That is also the case, under the 2016 Act; that is one reason why the 2016 Act represents a major departure from the previous legislation applicable to private-sector tenancies.

34 I.e. when parties enter into a contract that is a "tenancy" for the purposes of the 2001 Act. The term "tenancy" is given a fairly wide definition in s 41 of the Act.

Section 12

Section 12 provides:

> "**Restriction on termination of tenancy**
> (1) Despite anything in the tenancy agreement, a Scottish secure tenancy may not be brought to an end except–
> (a) by an order for recovery of possession under section 16(2),
> (b) by operation of section 18(2),
> (c) by operation of section 22,
> (d) by operation of section 35,
> (e) by written agreement between the landlord and the tenant, or
> (f) by 4 weeks' notice given by the tenant to the landlord.
> . . ."

Section 12(1)

As described above, there is no requirement to serve a notice to quit in relation to a Scottish secure tenancy. The process of recovery of possession by the landlord is governed by the statute, which provides for a single notice: the notice of proceedings for recovery of possession in terms of section 14, the service of which is an essential prerequisite to an eviction action under section 16(2).[35]

The purpose of section 12 is to limit the ways in which a Scottish secure tenancy may be ended. Over the years, various unsuccessful attempts have been made to bypass this provision[36] – for example, by an action to irritate the tenancy due to rent arrears,[37] and an action for declarator that the tenancy was null and void in terms of a contractual provision.[38] However, it has been said that where a tenancy contract is void, perhaps due to essential error, it would not be necessary to terminate it, because it never existed.[39]

Taking the six cases listed in section 12(1) in turn: sections 16(2), 18(2), 22 and 35 are discussed elsewhere.[40] Termination by written agreement and by four weeks' notice from the tenant are considered in the following paragraphs. In those latter two cases, in the event that the tenant refuses to leave after termination, the landlord will require to raise an action for recovery of possession, on the basis that the Scottish secure tenancy has come to an end, and the tenant therefore has no right or title to remain in occupation. Proceedings must be raised, and order for ejection must be obtained; eviction *brevi manu* would not be permissible, given the terms of section 23 of the 1984 Act.[41] However, it will not be necessary to serve a section 14 notice, as the action is not proceeding under section 16(2). The same type of action may be required against a person who remains in occupation of the subjects following the death

35 However, a notice to quit may be required to recover possession of an SSST, for reasons that will be discussed in Chapter 6.

36 Or its statutory predecessors.

37 *Glasgow City Council v Everson* 1998 Hous LR 56.

38 *Monklands District Council v Johnstone* 1987 SCLR 480.

39 *Clydebank District Council v Sweeney* 1998 Hous LR 84, 88 (Sheriff Principal Prosser).

40 Section 16(2) in Chapter 5; s 18 later in this chapter; and s 22 in Chapter 12. Conversion under s 35 is discussed in Chapter 6.

41 See Chapter 2.

of the tenant. In such cases the occupant may defend the action by asserting a right to succeed to the tenancy under section 22. This issue is discussed in Chapter 12.[42]

Section 12(1)(e) and (f)

In practice, the "written agreement" referred to in section 12(1)(e) is often a new tenancy agreement in relation to the existing tenancy subjects, or other subjects where those have been allocated to the tenant. Some social landlords periodically review and change their standard form tenancy agreements, and then ask their tenants to sign the new standard form. Tenants may also be asked to sign new agreements in other circumstances.[43] In relation to a tenancy at common law, completion of a new lease may constitute an implied renunciation, and therefore termination, of the existing tenancy agreement. The same effect could be achieved in relation to Scottish secure tenancies by virtue of section 12(1)(e). However, in certain circumstances it may not be clear whether it is parties' intention to create a new tenancy, or simply to assign or vary the existing tenancy.[44]

Although section 12(1)(f) does not require that the notice given by the tenant be in writing, this almost always occurs in practice; most local authorities and registered social landlords have standard form termination notices that they will require the tenant to sign.

There are occasionally cases in which the tenant changes his mind, and seeks to withdraw the notice given under section 12(1)(f), at some point during the four-week period. The Act does not indicate whether this is possible. At common law the notice cannot be withdrawn where: (a) it has been expressly accepted by the recipient;[45] or (b) the recipient has acted in reliance on the notice.[46] Generally speaking, notices of termination of a Scottish secure tenancy could be said to be expressly accepted by the landlord, in so far as the tenant is usually asked to complete and sign the appropriate standard form, and is then given a date on which the obligation to pay rent will end. Also, it would appear that, in practice, local authorities and registered social landlords act in reliance of the tenant's termination notice fairly quickly, by

42 The remaining paragraphs of s 12(1) will not give rise to eviction proceedings. The termination of the tenancy under s 16 follows such proceedings. Section 18 allows the landlord to recover possession without proceedings. Section 35 converts the Scottish secure tenancy into an SSST.

43 For example, where a new joint tenant is added under s 11(5), or a joint tenant terminates his interest under s 13.

44 The relevant law is expounded by Rankine, *Leases* from 522. As the author explains at 524, the issue in cases of implied renunciation is often as to whether there is any material difference between the old and new contracts. He states: "everything turns on the intention of the parties as set out in the new lease". In discussing the same issue, Paton and Cameron, *Landlord and Tenant* 239 state: "a renunciation may be inferred from conduct of the parties plainly implying that it is their final intention that the lease should be terminated . . . Renunciation may also be inferred from fact and circumstances inconsistent with the continued existence of the lease in question, such as the granting of a new lease differing materially from the old".

45 *Gilmour v Cook* 1975 SLT (Land Ct) 10.

46 This issue was discussed in the Scottish Law Commission's report *Recovery of Possession of Heritable Property*, with a recommendation that there should be a statutory provision to the effect that a notice of termination of tenancy cannot be withdrawn without the consent of the other party.

making arrangements to offer the tenancy to a person on their waiting list. Where either of these circumstances pertains, or the notice has been otherwise expressly accepted or acted upon, it is suggested that the notice under section 12(1)(f) cannot be withdrawn, without the consent of the landlord.

There is authority to the effect that section 12(1)(f) should be read as subject to the qualification that a landlord is entitled to agree the termination of a tenancy without notice, where there is no prejudice to the tenant, and no merit in insisting on compliance with the four-week period.[47]

PRE-ACTION REQUIREMENTS FOR RENT ARREARS CASES

Introduction

By section 14(2) of the 2001 Act, it is stipulated that the landlord cannot raise proceedings for recovery of possession of a house let on a Scottish secure tenancy unless it has served the notice of proceedings under that section. Subsection (2A) then states:

> "(2A) Where such proceedings are to include the ground that rent lawfully due from the tenant has not been paid (as set out in paragraph 1 of schedule 2)—
> (a) the notice under subsection (2) must not be served unless the landlord has complied with the pre-action requirements in section 14A, and
> (b) the proceedings may not be raised unless the landlord has confirmed to the court in such form as the Scottish Ministers may prescribe by regulations that those requirements have been complied with."[48]

The first part of this provision is not as straightforward as it appears. That is because paragraph 1 of schedule 2 effectively contains two distinct grounds, in that it states: "Rent lawfully due from the tenant has not been paid, *or any other obligation of the tenancy has been broken.*"[49] It is only in respect of the first part of this ground that sections 14(2A) and 14A have application. Thus, the breach of an obligation under the rental agreement to pay money that is not "rent" has the effect that ground 1 is established, but it does not trigger the application of the pre-action requirements.

Section 14A

Section 14A of the 2001 Act states:

> "14A Pre-action requirements where grounds for possession include rent arrears
> (1) The pre-action requirements referred to in section 14(2A) are set out in subsections (2) to (7) below.
> (2) The landlord must provide the tenant with clear information about—
> (a) the terms of the tenancy agreement, and

47 *Ireland v Dundee City Council* 2015 GWD 40-635.

48 Under reg. 2 of the Scottish Secure Tenancies (Proceedings for Possession) (Confirmation of Compliance with Pre-Action Requirements) Regulations 2012 (SSI 2012/93) this is achieved by the inclusion of an averment in the statement of claim to the effect that the landlord has complied with the pre-action requirements. However, see Chapter 13, at p 444.

49 See the discussion of ground 1 in Chapter 5, and in particular the term "rent".

(b) outstanding rent and any other outstanding financial obligation of the tenancy.

(3) The landlord must make reasonable efforts to provide the tenant with advice and assistance on the tenant's eligibility to receive—

(a) housing benefit, and

(b) other types of financial assistance (for example, other benefits or grants).

(4) The landlord must provide the tenant with information about sources of advice and assistance in relation to management of debt.

(5) The landlord must make reasonable efforts to agree with the tenant a reasonable plan for future payments to the landlord, such plan to include proposals in respect of—

(a) future payments of rent, and

(b) outstanding rent and any other outstanding financial obligation of the tenancy.

(6) The landlord must not serve a notice under section 14(2) if—

(a) an application for housing benefit for the tenant—

(i) has been made but has not yet been determined, and

(ii) is, in the opinion of the landlord, likely to result in the benefit being paid at a level allowing the tenant to pay, or reduce by an amount acceptable to the landlord, the outstanding rent and any other outstanding financial obligation of the tenancy,

(b) the tenant is taking other steps which, in the opinion of the landlord, are likely to result in the payment to the landlord within a reasonable time of—

(i) the outstanding rent, and

(ii) any other outstanding financial obligation of the tenancy, or

(c) the tenant is complying with the terms of a plan agreed to in accordance with subsection (5).

(7) The landlord, unless it is a local authority landlord, must encourage the tenant to contact the local authority in whose area the house is situated.

(8) In complying with the pre-action requirements the landlord must have regard to any guidance issued by the Scottish Ministers.

(9) The Scottish Ministers may by order make further provision about the preaction requirements, including provision—

(a) specifying particular steps to be taken, or not to be taken, by a landlord in complying with any requirement;

(b) modifying or removing any requirement.

(10) In this section, 'housing benefit' has the same meaning as in section 123 of the Social Security Contributions and Benefits Act 1992 (c.4)."[50]

This section was inserted by section 155 of the 2010 Act, which, with section 153, effectively introduced a new legal code for evictions on the ground of rent arrears under the 2001 Act.[51] It came into force on 1 August 2012.[52]

50 Note that, at the time of writing, no amendment has been made to this section, or the Pre-Action Requirements Order discussed below, to reflect the replacement of housing benefit by universal credit. This may be contrasted with the amendments made to s 18 of the 1988 Act, by reg 4 of the Welfare Reform (Consequential Amendments) (Scotland) (No. 2) Regulations 2013 (SSI 2013/137). In any event, universal credit would presumably count as one of the "other types of financial assistance" under subs 3(b).

51 Section 153, which amends s 16 of the 2001 Act, concerns the effect of an eviction decree in rent arrears cases. It is discussed in Chapter 15.

52 Housing (Scotland) Act 2010 (Commencement No. 7 and Transitional Provision) Order 2012 (SSI 2012/91).

Section 14A is clearly inspired by section 24A of the Conveyancing and Feudal Reform (Scotland) Act 1970,[53] to which it bears a strong similarity. Its introduction may be regarded as the continuation of a trend that began with the amendments made to the 1970 Act by part 1 of the Home Owner and Debtor Protection (Scotland) Act 2010. One of the aims behind that legislation was to afford additional protection to borrowers against repossession of their homes, by making proceedings under the 1970 Act more like actions for the eviction of tenants.[54] The effect of section 14A is to harmonise the processes from the opposite direction, by making rent arrears cases more like the new form of mortgage repossession case under the 1970 Act, as amended.

Subject to differences in terminology, much of section 14A is similar to section 24A of the 1970 Act. Both are supplemented by a statutory instrument and guidance. These are again similar as between the two forms of action (mortgage repossessions and rent arrears evictions). It is possible that there could be cross-fertilisation in the development of the case law in relation to these two different processes, with authorities in respect of section 24A being cited in section 14A cases, and vice versa.[55] In the discussion that follows, cases under section 24A of the 1970 Act are cited, where relevant.

The Scottish Secure Tenancies (Proceedings for Possession) (Pre-Action Requirements) Order 2012 (commonly referred to as "the PAR Order"),[56] is the "further provision" made under section 14A(9). The guidance issued under section 14A(8) is entitled "Housing (Scotland) Act 2001 and 2010 Guidance for Social Landlords on Pre-Action Requirements and Seeking Repossession of Social Housing" ("the Guidance").[57]

Like the requirements set out in section 14A, the provisions of the PAR Order are expressed in mandatory terms. The effect of failure to comply is that the landlord will not have met the relevant pre-action requirement in section 14A. In that event, the notice of proceedings served under section 14 will be invalid: under subsection (2A)(a) of that section, "the notice . . . must not be served unless the landlord has complied with the pre-action requirements in section 14A". It follows that anything done after the service of the section 14 notice cannot count as fulfilment of the pre-action requirements.[58]

As regards the Guidance, the lenders' obligation is "to have regard" to it. In so far as the Guidance makes suggestions or recommendations, it is suggested

53 Section 24A, along with various other provisions affecting mortgage repossession actions, was inserted into the 1970 Act with effect from 30 September 2010. Section 24A was in turn inspired by the "pre-action" protocol used by the English courts in relation to mortgage repossession proceedings.

54 By measures such as ensuring that all such actions call in court, and introducing a requirement that the repossession is "reasonable in the circumstances of the case" (1970 Act s 24(5)(b)).

55 However, that has not happened so far: at the time of writing, there are a number of reported cases under s 24A of the 1970 Act, but none under s 14A of the 2001 Act. The decision of Appeal Sheriff MacFadyen in *Glasgow West Housing Association v Silva* (GLA-SD422-18, 12 July 2019), to which reference is made below, is unreported at the time of writing. In any event, that decision did not determine the defender's argument that the pursuers had carried out the pre-action requirements, because he was taken to have abandoned the point.

56 SSI 2012/127.

57 Issued in June 2012.

58 In cases under s 24A of the 1970 Act, the court has held that the pre-action requirements have to be fulfilled during a certain stage in the process (in those cases, as soon as reasonably practicable after the expiry of the calling-up notice). See, in particular: *Northern Rock (Asset Management) Plc v Millar* 2012 SLT (Sh Ct) 58, 2012 Hous LR 2.

that a failure to follow such a recommendation would not, in itself, constitute a basis for holding that the pre-action requirement had not been met. However, the failure to follow the guidance would usually call for an explanation from the landlord. If a satisfactory reason were not forthcoming, the court might well be inclined to determine the issue of compliance in favour of the tenant.[59]

It is submitted that describing the requirements as "pre-action" is somewhat misleading. If the landlord were to wait until the point when it was considering raising an action before carrying out the requirements, it would already be too late. That is not only because the requirements would be more accurately called "pre-notice of proceedings" rather than "pre-action". The point is that, taken together, section 14A, the PAR Order and the Guidance constitute a code of good practice on the management of rent arrears. That is why certain of the articles contained in the PAR Order require, either explicitly or implicitly, early intervention, which might take place some time before an action is raised, and long before court proceedings are contemplated. Rather than suggesting good practice and then inviting landlords to follow it, the Government and the legislature have imposed upon the landlords what is considered to be good practice, by means of the primary and secondary legislation, supported by the Guidance.

Effect of sections 14(2A) and 14A on eviction proceedings

What is clear is that the assertion "the landlord has not complied with the pre-action requirements" forms a basis on which an action for possession on the ground of rent arrears may be defended.[60] An assertion that the pre-action requirements have not been fulfilled amounts, in effect, to an argument that service of the notice of proceedings was incompetent and ineffective, and therefore, the action could not be raised under section 16.[61] If that is correct, then the action falls to be dismissed.[62] That has the obvious consequence that the parties to such an action will have to give careful consideration to the question of whether the steps taken by the landlord constitute compliance.

Three further points, perhaps less obvious, may be usefully made.

First, the pre-action requirements may be regarded, for the purposes of section 16(3)(d) of the Act, as action taken by the landlord, before the service of notice of proceedings, with a view to securing the cessation of the conduct

59 The obligation to "have regard" to guidance is discussed in more detail, with reference to authority, in Chapter 6, at p 192.

60 See para 37 of the decision in *Glasgow West Housing Association v Silva* (n 55).

61 In the legislative scheme, termination of the tenancy by an order for recovery of possession can only be done under s 16(2), given the terms of s 12. An order under s 16(2) can only be obtained in an action under s 14, subs (1) of which gives the landlord the right to raise proceedings. Under s 14(2), those proceedings cannot be raised unless the notice of proceedings is served. Under 14(2A)(a) that must not be done unless the landlord has complied with the pre-action requirements. Therefore, where the landlord has not so complied, the court has no power to grant a decree under s 16(2).

62 That has been the outcome, in cases under the 1970 Act, in which the court concluded that the lender had failed to comply with the pre-action requirements under section 24A. See, for example: *Northern Rock (Asset Management) Plc v Millar* (n 58) and *Outlook Finance Ltd v Lindsay's Executor Nominate* 2016 Hous LR 75.

that gives rise to the ground, i.e. failure to pay rent.[63] The Guidance tells us[64] that the pre-action requirements are aimed at "making sure that landlords and tenants explore other ways of resolving the arrears, and making sure that eviction for rent arrears is a last resort". Thus, by the time a case calls in court for its first hearing, the landlord may point out that measures required to assist the tenant have been taken (some time ago, before the section 14 notice was served), other ways of resolving the arrears have been explored, the proceedings are indeed a last resort, and yet the arrears have still not been addressed by the tenant. That being so, and having regard to section 16(3)(d), it may be argued that the court ought to decide in favour of the landlord.[65]

Secondly, the pre-action requirements potentially increase the scope for disputed issues of fact in arrears cases.[66] As will be explained in Chapter 13, there is some doubt, and difference in practice between courts, as to whether it is necessary to fix a diet of proof in arrears cases, given that there is rarely any dispute of fact, parties being at issue only on the question of whether it is reasonable to grant the order.[67] In light of section 14A, a proof may be necessary if an argument concerning compliance with the pre-action requirements gives rise to a disputed issue of fact.[68]

Thirdly, it is submitted that the statutory provisions lack flexibility as to how the court deals with a failure to meet the requirements of section 14A. In this respect, it is useful to make a comparison with the position in England. There has been a Protocol for Possession Claims based on Rent Arrears in that jurisdiction since 2006.[69] It contains a series of requirements that are similar to those set out in section 14A. However, the effect of non-compliance is that the court may impose sanctions in the form of costs and/or adjournment of

63 Section 16(3) sets out four factors to which the court is to have regard in deciding whether it is reasonable to grant an order for recovery of possession on any one of grounds 1–7 under sch 2 to the 2001 Act. It is discussed in Chapter 5.

64 At para 3.

65 Note, however, that s 16(3)(d) contemplates steps taken up to the raising of proceedings, and, in deciding whether it is reasonable to grant the order, the court might also take into account steps that have been taken (or not taken) up to the date of the hearing, or could be taken in the future. There is no reason why the landlord cannot, or should not, adopt any of the measures described in the pre-action requirements, after service of the s 14 notice.

66 In *Glasgow West Housing Association v Silva* (n 55) the defender had argued that the pre-action requirements had not been met, because the pursuer had failed to make reasonable efforts to enter into a payment arrangement with the defender. On appeal, Sheriff MacFadyen said of that argument, at para 37: "If insisted upon, that would have required the exercise of a judgment by the sheriff, probably after hearing evidence."

67 Under the Summary Cause Rules 2002 (Act of Sederunt (Summary Cause Rules) 2002 (SSI 2002/132). The position may be different under the Simple Procedure Rules for eviction cases, when they come into force.

68 On this point, it is worthwhile noting that the notice of proceedings applicable to rent arrears cases (see points 3 and 7 in the next section) requires the landlord to state (albeit briefly) the steps that it has taken to comply with the pre-action requirements, after which it is said "if you are the tenant and you disagree we have taken the steps set out above, you should contact us to discuss your concerns". Therefore, the landlord might rely on a failure to make contact, or otherwise dispute the terms of the notice of proceedings, if the recorded steps are disputed for the first time during the course of the proceedings. Realistically, however, it may only be when the tenant seeks advice, on the raising of proceedings, that the notice of proceedings is critically examined.

69 That comparison is apt: as is explained above, the s 14A requirements have been largely adapted from the pre-action requirements amended into the 1970 Act by s 24A. Those, in turn, were inspired by pre-action protocols for proceedings in England.

the proceedings or may strike out or dismiss the claim. Also, the conduct of the landlord in relation to the pre-action requirements may inform the court's decision as to whether it is reasonable to grant the order. Thus, the court in England has a range of options where non-compliance by the landlord is shown.[70] One might therefore expect that, in a similar way, a sheriff would have the option of dealing with non-compliance by, say, awarding expenses against the landlord, or by adjourning or sisting the proceedings until such time as the requirement has been met. However, as was outlined above, the only option for the Scottish court is to determine that decree for recovery of possession cannot be granted under section 16(2) of the Act.[71] That may impact on the sheriff's willingness to sustain arguments as to non-compliance that are debatable, such as: whether information provided under subsection (2) is "clear", or whether efforts made under subsection (3) or (5) are "reasonable", or whether the landlord has failed to "have regard" to the Guidance.

It is suggested that the pre-action requirements contained in section 14A may be broken down in a way that corresponds with articles 2–7 of the 2012 Pre-Action Requirements Order. Under those articles is found further detail on the mode of compliance with, respectively, subsections (2), (3), (5) and (6) (a), (b) and (c) of section 14A.[72] They are as follows:

- requirement to provide information (article 2);
- requirement to make reasonable efforts to provide advice and assistance (article 3);
- requirement to make reasonable efforts to agree a plan (article 4);
- applications for housing benefit (article 5);
- steps that are likely to result in a payment within a reasonable time (article 6);
- compliance with agreed repayment plan (article 7).

Articles 4 and 7 are considered together: they both concern agreed repayment plans.

As well as carrying out the requirements, the landlord must also record the steps that it has taken to achieve compliance, and the dates on which those steps were taken. That is because the tenant must be informed of those steps, and the relevant dates, in the notice of proceedings.[73]

70 The latest version of the protocol (Pre-Action Protocol for Possession Claims by Social Landlords) came into effect on 13 January 2020. There is an informative discussion of the previous version of the protocol, and the court's powers in relation to it, in the Legal Action Group's Luba and others, *Defending Possession Proceedings,* (8th edn) 121.

71 If that were the only order sought by the pursuers, it would be appropriate to dismiss the action.

72 The requirements under subs (4) (to provide the tenant with information about sources of advice and assistance in relation to management of debt) and subs (7) (to encourage the tenant to contact the local authority, unless the landlord is the local authority) do not apparently require further elaboration, at least in the Order. However, paras 44 and 45 of the Guidance give some advice to landlords in relation to s 14A(4), including the important point that tenants should only be referred to sources of advice and information that are "free and independent".

73 See point 7 in the next section, at p 111 below.

Requirement to give the tenant information (article 2 and section 14A(2))

Article 2 states:

> "**2.— Requirement to provide information**
>
> (1) In providing the tenant with clear information for the purposes of section 14A(2) (requirement to provide information) of the 2001 Act the landlord must include—
>
> (a) a description of the rent and any other financial obligations of the tenant under the tenancy agreement; and
>
> (b) information about the amount due to the landlord under the tenancy agreement, which must be broken down so as to show—
>
> (i) the total amount of outstanding rent and of any other outstanding financial obligations of the tenancy; and
>
> (ii) a description of any charges which the landlord anticipates will be incurred if the arrears of rent or any other financial obligation of the tenancy are not paid.
>
> (2) In (1)(b)(ii), *'charges'* means any future charges detailed in the tenancy agreement resulting from arrears of rent and any other outstanding financial obligation of the tenancy, and any illustrative indication of legal expenses which may be incurred in relation to such obligations.
>
> (3) The landlord must provide the information required by section 14A(2) of the 2001 Act and this article as soon as the landlord considers reasonably practicable after the tenant enters into arrears."

The information must be "clear". In the Guidance,[74] it is said that landlords:

> "must make sure that the information they give to tenants is clear, not misleading and easily understandable. Landlords should aim to give tenants the information they need in plain language and in a format that is accessible".

The Guidance also points out that not all tenants will have English as a first language, which may make it difficult for them to access information in standard formats. Some tenants may have literacy problems, visual impairments or learning difficulties.

Where landlords know that tenants have particular needs in relation to communication they should take account of them. The aim is to make sure that, as far as possible, tenants understand their financial position.[75]

Where the tenant is a disabled person, she might request that reasonable adjustments are made to the manner in which the landlord provides information under the Equality Act 2010.[76] Also, it is suggested that, in complying with the pre-action requirements in relation to disabled persons, or any persons having a relevant protected characteristic under the 2010 Act, the landlord would be required to comply with the public sector equality duty under s 149 of the 2010 Act, which will be described at the end of Chapter 11.

As the landlord will usually have a standard form Scottish secure tenancy agreement, it is to be expected that the information in paragraph (1)(a) could be provided in standard form.[77] As regards paragraph (1)(b)(i), the Guidance

74 At para 27.

75 Paras 27 and 28.

76 See Chapter 11, p 406.

77 However, the requirement is not fulfilled by the fact that the tenant was given a copy of the agreement at the beginning of the tenancy. The obligation to provide information before

requires that the statement of the amount of unpaid rent and other financial obligations of the tenancy must give the tenant a total figure for the amount that is owed.[78] It also suggests[79] that:

> "it would be helpful if, wherever possible, landlords can provide tenants with a breakdown of the total figure so that they can clearly understand how the arrears have accumulated. This breakdown should include the amount housing benefit covers wherever practicable. It would also be helpful if landlords explained to tenants how much they need to pay towards their rent, and when, over and above any housing benefit entitlement."

Paragraph 22 of the Guidance indicates that effect of the reference to an "illustrative indication of legal expenses" in article 2(2) is that landlords "*may* choose to give tenants illustrative information about costs that tenants have had to pay in similar cases, where that information is available. The intention is for the tenant to receive an indication of the likely legal expenses they may incur if court action as a result of rent arrears becomes necessary."[80]

Paragraph (3) of article 2 seems ill considered. Although the information mentioned in paragraph (1)(a) might to be useful to the tenant at the point when he first falls into arrears, the information described in paragraphs (1)(b) and (2) would be more usefully given when significant arrears have accumulated, and the landlord is considering raising the proceedings that are described in the Guidance as a "last resort".

Making reasonable efforts to provide advice and assistance (article 3 and section 14A(3))

This is further described by article 3:

> "**3. Requirement to make reasonable efforts to provide advice and assistance**
> In complying with the pre-action requirement contained in section 14A(3) (requirement to make reasonable efforts to provide advice and assistance) of the 2001 Act the landlord must—
> (a) make reasonable efforts to contact the tenant in order to identify whether the tenant requires advice and assistance on the tenant's eligibility to receive housing benefit and other types of financial assistance;
> (b) provide the tenant with details of persons or bodies who may be able to provide the tenant with such advice and assistance; and
> (c) provide the tenant with reasonable assistance with claiming housing benefit, if requested to do so by the tenant."

raising proceedings, under s 14A(2)(a) is distinct from that to provide a copy of the tenancy agreement under s 23.

78 At para 25. Article 2(1)(b) is very similar to art 2(2)(b) of the PAR Order in relation to mortgage repossession cases: Applications by Creditors (Pre-Action Requirements) (Scotland) Order 2010 (SSI 2010/317). See: *Outlook Finance Ltd v Lindsay's Executor Nominate* (n 62) for a case in which the court concluded that the pursuers had failed to comply with art 2(2)(b).

79 At para 26.

80 This suggests that the provision of the "illustrative indication of legal expenses" is optional. That said, the wording of para 22 is confusing. It is suggested that judicial expenses, awarded at the end of legal proceedings, are not an "amount due to the landlord under the tenancy agreement" under art 2(2)(b). Therefore, the provision of a pre-estimate of such expenses should be regarded as optional.

It appears to be the effect of the Act and the PAR Order, taken together, that where the landlord fails to do anything set out in article 3(a)–(c), it has not made reasonable efforts, for the purposes of section 14A(3). In other words, whereas in some cases the issue of whether the landlord has made "reasonable efforts" will be one for the judgment of the court, in a case in which some part of article 3 has not been complied with, the court is effectively directed to come to the conclusion that reasonable efforts have not been made.[81]

The Guidance suggests that a "single unsuccessful attempt" is unlikely to be enough for landlords to show that they have made reasonable efforts to provide tenants with help and advice. It also reminds landlords that they will have to give tenants information on the reasonable efforts they have made, in the notice of proceedings, and may have to subsequently prove those efforts. Therefore, even where the landlord's efforts meet with no response from the tenant, the recording of certain details is necessary, including the dates, and the method of contact (or attempted contact) used.[82]

At paragraphs 34–36 of the Guidance, advice is given to landlords as to the methods they might use in seeking to contact tenants. Particular advice is given in relation to tenants who are vulnerable or have special needs, or who are under 18. The reader is referred to their detailed terms.

The Guidance also makes the important point that the obligation of the landlord is not merely to give advice to tenants; it must also help them.[83] Thus, it is suggested that the landlord cannot discharge the obligation simply by preparing standard form leaflets or information sheets and doling them out to tenants whenever they fall into arrears. This is recognised by the many landlords in the social rented sector that employ in-house money advice specialists, welfare rights officers and the like. Where that is not the case, tenants may be assisted by referral to an advice agency, under article 3(b).[84]

Article 3(c) requires landlords to provide reasonable assistance with claiming housing benefit, if asked to do so by the tenant. This may include helping the tenant to fill in necessary forms, helping them to gather the information necessary for the application to be made, or referring them to a person specialising in such claims.[85] Thus the legislation envisages a role for landlords in relation to the tenant's application for housing benefit, which is further specified by article 5 of the PAR Order, which will be discussed below.

From housing benefit to universal credit; discretionary housing payments

At the time of writing, there has been no amendment to section 14A, or the articles of the PAR Order, to accommodate the phasing out of housing benefit by universal credit, which includes an element to cover "housing costs".[86] This seems particularly unfortunate, given the well-publicised difficulties

81 By the words "the landlord must" in art 3(1).

82 Para 38.

83 Para 39.

84 At para 42, it is said that "Referral is where a landlord contacts the appropriate person or body for the tenant . . . It would be good practice to also get the tenants' consent to find out the outcome of the referral".

85 Para 43.

86 See Chapter 5, pp 124 and 154.

experienced by universal credit claimants. It is suggested that this problem might be overcome in two ways.

First, it is arguable that the Act ought to be given an updating construction: in construing an ongoing Act, the interpreter is to presume that Parliament intended the Act to be applied at any future time in such a way as to give effect to the true original intention, making allowances for any relevant changes that have occurred since the Act's passing.[87]

Given that, in respect of many tenants, universal credit has replaced housing benefit, an updating construction is necessary to give effect to the true original intention of section 14A.[88] If that is correct, then section 14(3)(a) could be read as though the words "or universal credit" appeared after "housing benefit".

If that is not persuasive, universal credit would therefore fall under the reference to "other types of financial assistance (for example, other benefits or grants)" in section 14A(3)(b). The obligation then, under the primary legislation, is for the landlord to "make reasonable efforts to provide the tenant with . . . assistance on the tenant's eligibility to receive" universal credit. The issue of whether the landlord has made "reasonable efforts" is ultimately for the judgment of the court, having regard to the circumstances of the case. Under section 14A(3)(a) and article 3(3)(c), reasonable efforts to provide the tenant with assistance on the tenant's eligibility to receive housing benefit includes providing the tenant "with reasonable assistance with claiming housing benefit, if requested to do so by the tenant". Therefore it is arguable that, where the tenant's rental liability is apt to be paid by universal credit, rather than housing benefit, the court ought to judge that reasonable efforts under section 14A(3)(b) include providing the tenant with reasonable assistance in claiming universal credit, if requested to do so by the tenant.

Reasonable efforts under section 14A(3)(b) ought also to take into account the possibility of discretionary housing payments ("DHPs") being made by the local authority.[89]

Making reasonable efforts to agree a repayment plan (article 4; section 14A(5)); compliance with an agreed payment plan (article 7; section 14A(6)(c))

Article 4 of the PAR Order states:

> "**4.— Requirement to make reasonable efforts to agree a plan**
> (1) In complying with the pre-action requirement contained in section 14A(5) (requirement to make reasonable efforts to agree a reasonable plan including

87 Bennion, *Statutory Interpretation* (7th edn) ch 14, "Updating Construction" 409.

88 That intention is expressed in the Introduction in the Guidance, in particular para 3: "Pre-action requirements are aimed at providing further protection for tenants facing eviction for rent arrears by . . . making sure that landlords and tenants explore other ways of resolving the arrears; and making sure that eviction for rent arrears is a last resort."

89 Under the Discretionary Financial Assistance Regulations 2001 (SI 2001/1167). It is Scottish Government policy to mitigate the effect of the under-occupancy charge (bedroom tax) https://www.gov.scot/policies/social-security/support-with-housing-costs/ by way of funding DHPs made by local authorities. Therefore, it is suggested that where tenants are known to be "under-occupying", landlords ought to be making reasonable efforts to provide the tenant with advice and assistance on making a DHP application.

proposals for future payments of rent and outstanding debt) of the 2001 Act the landlord must—

(a) make prompt and reasonable attempts to contact the tenant to discuss the arrears with a view to agreeing a plan for future payments of rent and repayment of the arrears and any other outstanding financial obligation of the tenancy;

(b) encourage the tenant to provide the landlord with all relevant information on the tenant's financial circumstances;

(c) advise the tenant to seek assistance from an appropriate debt advice agency where the tenant makes the landlord aware that they have debts in addition to those related to the tenancy;[90]

(d) provide the tenant with details of any plan proposed by the landlord for the purposes of that section, set out in such a way as to allow the tenant to consider the proposal;

(e) allow the tenant time to consider any such plan proposed by the landlord;

(f) consider the affordability of any such plan for the tenant taking into account, where known to the landlord, the tenant's personal and financial circumstances; and

(g) provide the tenant with a copy of any such plan agreed for the purposes of that section.

(2) Where a plan is proposed by the tenant for the purposes of section 14A(5) of the 2001 Act which the landlord rejects, the landlord must provide reasons for rejecting the plan in writing."

As with article 3, it appears to be the effect of the Act and the PAR Order, taken together, that, where the landlord fails to do anything set out in article 4, the court is directed[91] to come to the conclusion that reasonable efforts have not been made for the purposes of section 14A(5).

The Guidance states that: "The aim is to arrive at a payment plan which is affordable and sustainable for tenants." Consequently, "Where a payment plan would be affordable and sustainable for tenants, but landlords do not consider it reasonable, landlords may have to explain their reasons for this to the court."[92] Furthermore: "Where tenants receive welfare benefits and their rent is being met by housing benefit, an example of an affordable and sustainable plan for tenants may be on-going direct deductions towards the rent arrears from welfare benefits."[93]

These points tend to reinforce the requirement for "prompt" action in article 4(1)(a). Lower repayments will obviously be more affordable, and probably more sustainable. However, lower repayments will be less palatable for the landlord if the arrears are high – hence the need for early intervention.

At paragraphs 51–56, the Guidance makes various suggestions as to the approach that might be adopted by landlords, particularly where the tenant has a housing benefit claim outstanding. However, it recognises that "The approach taken by landlords may depend on the circumstances of each case".

Where the landlord rejects the proposed repayment plan, the tenant ought to be strongly advised nevertheless to make payments in terms of the proposal, the better to argue her position when the case calls in court. This is a fairly

90 Landlords should tell tenants that any debt agency they contact about their debts should be one that offers free and independent advice: Guidance para 50.

91 By the words "the landlord must" in art 4(1) and (2).

92 Presumably these would be the same reasons given to the tenant under art 4(2).

93 Paragraphs 51–53.

obvious point, but it tends to be overlooked by tenants having other financial commitments who, on rejection of their proposal, simply pay nothing towards the arrears. In the absence of agreement, the landlord is enjoined by the Guidance to make all reasonable efforts to resolve the problem before serving the notice of proceedings.[94]

Under section 14A(6)(c) the landlord must not serve a notice of proceedings if the tenant is complying with an agreed repayment plan. Article 7 states:

> "**7. Compliance with agreed repayment plan**
> In complying with the requirement contained in section 14A(6)(c) (compliance with agreed plan) of the 2001 Act the landlord must—
> (a) promptly take reasonable steps to establish the reason for any default or shortfall in respect of an agreed payment;
> (b) consider whether the plan agreed for the purposes of section 14A(5) of that Act ('the agreed plan') continues to be affordable to the tenant taking into account any information of the tenant's personal and financial circumstances known to the landlord;
> (c) review the agreed plan where the landlord considers it is no longer affordable for the tenant; and
> (d) allow the tenant reasonable time to—
> (i) make repayments within the terms of the agreed plan, including repayment of any shortfall or missed payment; or
> (ii) enter into a new plan agreed for the purposes of section 14A(5) of that Act."

In practice, the landlord will need some degree of co-operation from the tenant in order for this article to achieve its purpose. In effect, it requires the landlord to try to contact the tenant in order to find out whether the default is due to a change in her circumstances. If it is, the landlord then needs to look again at the repayment arrangement. If it is not, or the landlord considers the existing plan to be appropriate, notwithstanding the change in circumstances, the tenant should be given a reasonable time to comply with the agreement by making good any missed payment.[95] If, instead, a new plan is agreed, it is suggested that the landlord should again comply with article 4(1)(g) by providing the tenant with a copy of the new plan.

Housing benefit applications (article 5; section 14A(6)(a))

> "**5.— Applications for housing benefit**
> (1) In complying with the requirement contained in section 14A(6)(a) (applications for housing benefit) of the 2001 Act the landlord must encourage a tenant who has made a housing benefit application to provide written authority to allow the landlord to discuss that housing benefit application with the relevant housing benefit staff.
> (2) If the landlord has written authority from the tenant to discuss a housing benefit application made by the tenant with the relevant housing benefit staff the landlord must take such steps as are reasonable to—
> (a) confirm that a housing benefit application has been made;
> (b) establish when a determination on the application is likely to be made;
> (c) establish whether the tenant has provided all of the necessary evidence and

94 Paragraph 58.
95 Paragraphs 77–79.

verification to support the application, or is within the permitted period for providing such evidence or verification; and

(d) establish the likely outcome of the housing benefit application.

(3) If the tenant does not provide the landlord with such written authority the landlord must take such steps as it can to establish the likely outcome of the housing benefit application.

(4) The landlord must consider the results of the steps taken under paragraphs (2) or (3) in arriving at a decision as to the effect that the decision on the housing benefit claim will have on the outstanding rent and any other outstanding financial obligation of the tenancy.

(5) Where a landlord has made reasonable efforts to comply with the steps set out in this article and is unable to arrive at a decision as to the likely outcome of a housing benefit application the landlord must make reasonable efforts to agree a plan in accordance with section 14A(5) of the 2001 Act and article 4."

As was indicated in the discussion of article 3, there has been no amendment to section 14A, or the articles of the PAR Order, to accommodate the phasing out of housing benefit by universal credit. Arguably, therefore, an updating construction of the Act is appropriate.

In complying with article 5(1), the Guidance suggests that landlords: explain to tenants the need for information on their housing benefit claim; ask them for written authority; and make clear that they will use this authority to try to get information on the likely outcome of the housing benefit claim.[96] Where the tenant does not give written authority, it is not appropriate for the landlord to contact housing benefit staff at the local authority.[97]

In contrast with article 3(c), the various steps in article 5 do not impose upon the landlord the obligation of assisting the tenant with the application for housing benefit. Rather, it is keeping itself informed as to the progress of the tenant's application for housing benefit, and ascertaining any difficulties that have arisen.[98] That is because article 5 relates to section 14A(6)(a), in terms of which the landlord must not serve a notice of proceedings if: (i) the tenant has made an application for housing benefit that has not been determined; and (ii) that application is, in the opinion of the landlord, likely to result in the benefit being paid at a level allowing the tenant to pay, or reduce by an amount acceptable to the landlord, the outstanding rent and any other outstanding financial obligation of the tenancy. The information-gathering exercise set out in article 5 is done in order to facilitate the landlord's decision under section 14A(6)(a)(ii), as is made clear by article 5(4). It is important to appreciate that this decision must be made, irrespective of whether the landlord has the co-operation of the tenant under article 5(1).[99] If the landlord finds itself unable

96 Paragraph 61. Para 62 points out that the "Guidance for local authorities on the use of social security data" published by the DWP includes an example of a customer consent form in Annex A.

97 Paragraph 66.

98 That said, the Guidance suggests that landlords "could do what they can to help tenants progress their . . . application, where appropriate": para 65.

99 Thus the Guidance points out that, irrespective of co-operation from the tenant, the landlord may: seek advice from housing benefit officers, and other benefits specialists and advisers, as well as using online housing benefit calculators. With such co-operation, the landlord may, in addition, receive electronic transfer of information from housing benefit officers. See paras 64 and 66.

to make the decision under section 14A(6)(a)(ii), it is directed by article 5(5) to go back to article 4, and try to reach a repayment arrangement.

The relationship between articles 4 and 5 is further explained in paragraph 68 of the Guidance:

> "Landlords must consider whether the likely amount to be paid would cut the arrears to an amount acceptable to them.[100] In making that decision landlords should consider the remaining amount of arrears and the sums affordable to tenants for future payment towards those arrears. If the amount of arrears remaining after taking into account the housing benefit application is not acceptable to the landlord, the landlord must be able to explain that decision to the tenant. Landlords should also bear in mind that they may have to justify their opinion to the court."

The Guidance notes that when considering the likely outcome of the housing benefit application, landlords may discover that the Department for Work and Pensions ("DWP") will reduce the tenant's housing benefit entitlement due to earlier housing benefit overpayments. In such cases, landlords could assist the tenant's effort to minimise the reduction made by the DWP.[101]

It must be noted that the prescriptive effect of section 14A(6)(a) is somewhat diluted by the fact that it relies on it being "the opinion of the landlord" that the payment of the benefit is likely to result in the arrears being paid, "or reduce[d] by an amount acceptable to the landlord".[102] If that is not the case, section 14A(6)(a) does not apply, and the landlord may raise proceedings, provided that the other requirements are met. It remains to be seen whether the court would be willing to entertain arguments that challenge the position of the landlord on these issues.[103] As has already been pointed out, the court may be reluctant to decide such debatable issues against the landlord, if the only sanction is dismissal of the action. If the court doubts the judgment of the landlord on these issues, perhaps it may decide that the pre-action requirements are met, but that it favours the tenant's position on the question of whether it is ultimately reasonable to grant an eviction order under section 16(2)(a)(ii) of the Act.

100 I.e. as a result of the housing benefit application. When such an application is made, the applicant may ask for the payment of benefit to be backdated to the point when he became eligible for the benefit, where there has been a delay in making the application. With or without a backdate, a successful application may result in a lump-sum payment that reduces the arrears significantly.

101 Paragraph 69. For further information on overpayments, see Chapter 5, p 125. Note that this may be more difficult in universal credit cases because, in practice, landlords seem to receive less information on the reasons for benefit shortfalls, as was the case under the housing benefit system.

102 That could also be said of art 2(3), which requires the provision of information to the tenant "as soon as the landlord considers reasonably practicable".

103 Perhaps it is enough for the landlord to show that it formed the opinion, or that it found the relevant amount not to be acceptable, and to argue that the court cannot look behind these judgments. The tenant might argue that no reasonable landlord would have reached such a view, and that the court is not precluded from considered this type of argument (which would normally be made in judicial review proceedings) in an eviction action at the instance of the landlord. See Chapter 11.

Steps likely to result in payment within a reasonable period of time (article 6; section 14A(6)(b))

Under section 14A(6)(b), the landlord cannot serve a notice of proceedings if the tenant is taking steps that, in the opinion of the landlord, are likely to result in the payment to the landlord within a reasonable time of the outstanding rent, and any other outstanding financial obligation of the tenancy.[104] Article 6 provides:

> "**6. Steps which are likely to result in a payment within a reasonable time**
> In determining if steps taken by the tenant are steps with the meaning of section 14A(6)(b) (payment within a reasonable time) the landlord must—
> (a) attempt to establish whether the tenant is taking other steps to pay the outstanding rent and any other outstanding financial obligation of the tenancy, in addition to meeting their ongoing rental obligations;
> (b) consider all evidence available to the landlord of steps taken by the tenant to pay the outstanding rent and any other outstanding financial obligations of the tenancy, including evidence of a claim for benefits, grants, or lump sum payments due; and
> (c) assess whether any of the steps that the landlord ascertains are being taken by the tenant in paragraphs (a) and (b) are likely to result in payment within a reasonable time of the outstanding rent and any other outstanding financial obligation of the tenancy."

As with article 6, this requires a degree of co-operation from the tenant: the Guidance recognises that that the landlord can only reach a view based on the information that the tenant gives it. The tenant should be encouraged to give such information.[105] Where the tenant is relying on money from other sources, the landlord may seek evidence: that the tenant has given all the necessary information and evidence needed to process the claim, application or payment; that the tenant can reasonably expect payment; and as to whether the claim, application or payment has been refused. The landlord may also take into account the expected source of the payment, and any evidence that the sum is actually due to the tenant. Finally, in reaching a judgement as to whether payment will be made within a reasonable period of time, the landlord is reminded that it ought to explain any adverse decision to the tenant, and it may be required to justify such a decision before the court.[106]

NOTICE OF PROCEEDINGS FOR RECOVERY OF POSSESSION

Section 14 of the 2001 Act provides:

> "**Proceedings for possession**
> (1) The landlord under a Scottish secure tenancy may raise proceedings by way of summary cause for recovery of possession of the house.
> (2) Such proceedings may not be raised unless—

104 Again, this involves an element of judgement on the part of the landlord: see the preceding section.
105 Paragraph 72.
106 Paragraphs 73 and 74.

(a) the landlord has served on the tenant and any qualifying occupier a notice complying with subsection (4),
(b) the proceedings are raised on or after the date specified in the notice, and
(c) the notice is in force at the time when the proceedings are raised.

(2A) [Pre-action requirements: see preceding part of this chapter]

. . .[107]

(3) [Concerns qualifying occupiers: see below]

(4) A notice under subsection (2) must be in such form as the Scottish Ministers may prescribe by regulations, and must specify—
(a) the ground, being a ground set out in Part 1 of schedule 2, on which proceedings for recovery of possession are to be raised,
(b) a date, not earlier than—
(i) 4 weeks from the date of service of the notice, or
(ii) the date on which the tenancy could have been brought to an end by a notice to quit had it not been a Scottish secure tenancy,

whichever is later, on or after which the landlord may raise proceedings for recovery of possession.
(c) where subsection (2A) applies, the steps taken by the landlord which the landlord considers to constitute compliance with the pre-action requirements in section 14A.

(5) A notice under subsection (2) ceases to be in force 6 months after the date specified in it in accordance with subsection (4)(b) or when it is withdrawn by the landlord, whichever is earlier.

(5A) Where a landlord raises proceedings under this section, the landlord must give notice of the raising of the proceedings to the local authority in whose area the house in question is situated, unless the landlord is that local authority.

(5B) Notice under subsection (5A) is to be given in the form and manner prescribed under section 11(3) of the Homelessness etc. (Scotland) Act 2003 (asp 10).

(6) [Concerns qualifying occupiers: see below.]"

As originally enacted, section 14 was a restatement of section 47 of the 1987 Act, with one significant addition: the provisions in relation to "qualifying occupiers" at subsections (2)(a), (3) and (6). Subsections (2A) and (4)(c) were then added by section 155 of the 2010 Act. Along with the new section 14A, they created the new procedure for rent arrears cases. Subsections (5A) and (5B) were added by the Homelessness etc. (Scotland) Act 2003.

The purpose of the notice of proceedings is to serve as a warning to the tenant that an action may be raised on the grounds specified. It is not a notice to quit; and it does not end the tenancy.[108]

The requirements of section 14 may be summarised as follows:[109]

(1) In a rent arrears case, the landlord must comply with the pre-action requirements under section 14A of the Act, before serving the notice.[110]
(2) The notice must be served on the tenant and any qualifying occupier.[111]

107 Section 14 of the 2014 Act adds new subss (2B) and (2C) to s 14 of the 2001 Act. These new provisions concern actions under ground 2 of sch 2 to the Act, and are considered inChapter 5.

108 The tenancy may be ended only in terms of s 12.

109 Apart from the nine requirements listed, it is arguable that, in addition, s 14(1) ought to be understood as stipulating that proceedings following the notice must be raised as a summary cause. This issue is discussed in Chapter 13.

110 Section 14(2A)(a).

111 Section 14(2)(a).

(3) The notice must be in the form prescribed by the Scottish Ministers under the relevant regulations.[112]
(4) The notice must specify the ground(s) under which proceedings will be raised.[113]
(5) The notice must inform the tenant of the basis on which it is said that the ground has arisen (the particulars of the ground).
(6) The notice must specify a date after which proceedings may be raised. This must be a date that is not earlier than four weeks from the date of service or, alternatively, the date on which the tenancy could have been brought to an end by a notice to quit had it not been a Scottish secure tenancy. The date specified must be the later of those two dates.[114]
(7) In a rent arrears case, the notice must describe how the landlord has met the pre-action requirements.
(8) The proceedings must be raised while the notice is in force.[115]
(9) The landlord must give notice of the proceedings to the local authority in the form and manner prescribed, unless the landlord is that local authority.[116]

These requirements are considered in greater detail below. A failure on the part of the landlord to comply with section 14 may be fatal to subsequent proceedings. The court has no power to dispense with the requirement for service of a notice of proceedings, where it considers it to be reasonable to do so.[117] This is to be contrasted with the AT6 notice in terms of the 1988 Act, in relation to which the tribunal's power to dispense with the notice may be relied upon by the landlord where a defective notice has been served.[118] Accordingly, landlords and their agents must take care to ensure that all the above tests are met. For agents instructed by the defender in eviction proceedings, it is essential to obtain copies of the notices as soon as possible, so as to ascertain whether any point can be taken as to the competency of the action.[119]

(1) Pre-action requirements for rent arrears cases

These are considered in the preceding section of this chapter.

112 Section 14(4). The regulations are the Scottish Secure Tenancies (Proceedings for Possession) (Form of Notice) Regulations 2012 (n 5), as amended.
113 Section 14(4)(a).
114 Section 14(4)(b).
115 Section 14(2)(c).
116 Section 14(5A) and (5B).
117 Interestingly, the equivalent section in relation to secure tenancies in England (the Housing Act 1985, s 83) contains a provision to the effect that the court can dispense with the requirement to serve a notice of proceedings for recovery of possession where it considers it to be "just and equitable" to do so.
118 1988 Act, s 19(1)(b), discussed in Chapter 7.
119 The importance of this point cannot be overstated. Defective s 14 notices are common, especially in relation to the date to be specified for the purposes of s 14(4)(b). Objection to the competency of summary cause proceedings ought to be taken at the first calling of the case, or a continuation thereof. See Chapter 13.

(2) Service of the notice on the tenant and qualifying occupier

Section 14 is subject to section 40 of the Act, by which notice may be given: (a) by delivering it to that person, (b) by leaving it at that person's proper address, being, in terms of section 40(2), the person's last known address, or (c) by sending it by recorded delivery letter to that person at that address. Service of notices is discussed in Chapter 15.

Qualifying occupiers: ss 14(3) and (6) and 15

In terms of section 14(2)(a), service of the notice of proceedings for recovery of possession must be effected on the tenant and any "qualifying occupier". The Act makes further provision in relation to qualifying occupiers, as follows:

> "(3) Before serving a notice under subsection (2) the landlord must make such inquiries as may be necessary to establish so far as is reasonably practicable whether there are any qualifying occupiers of the house and, if so, their identities.
>
> . . .
>
> (6) In this section and section 15, 'qualifying occupier' means a person who occupies the house as that person's only or principal home and who is—
> (a) a member of the tenant's family[120] aged at least 16 years,
> (b) a person to whom the tenant has, with the landlord's consent under section 32(1), assigned, sublet or otherwise given up possession of the house or any part of it, or
> (c) a person whom the tenant has, with such consent, taken in as a lodger.
>
> **15. Rights of qualifying occupiers in possession proceedings**
> Where a qualifying occupier applies to the court to be sisted as a party to proceedings under section 14, the court must grant the application."

These provisions were new to the 2001 Act, there being no such provision in the 1987 Act. Clearly there is a logical relationship between section 15 and the requirement to serve notice on the qualifying occupier in terms of section 14(2)(a), it being appropriate that service be effected on anyone who may insist on entering the proceedings as a party.

The requirement for service on a qualifying occupier under section 14(2)(a) should not be too onerous in respect of persons in categories (b) and (c) of section 14(6), as in those cases the landlord will be aware of the qualifying occupier's presence at the tenancy subjects. However, the requirement for service on persons in category (a) places the landlord in the position of having to establish which members of the tenant's family are occupying the tenancy as their only or principal home, at the time when the section 14 notice is served.

In practice, there are various ways in which the landlord may keep track of the composition of the tenant's household. Information to that effect will normally be obtained from the tenant prior to the inception of the tenancy. The lease may contain a provision requiring the tenant to inform the landlord of any changes to the household. Where the tenant is in receipt of housing benefit, the application form by which he makes or renews his claim will require him to list the persons resident at his home.[121]

120 The term "family" is defined in s 108.

121 Note also that, on 1 November 2019, important amendments were made to s 32 (assignation

However, any landlord relying on that information alone takes the risk that the tenancy property may have become the only or principal home of a member of the tenant's family at some point after the information was obtained. Therefore, it is suggested that a prudent landlord will do more than simply check its most recent information as to the composition of the household. It will also make an inquiry as to that composition, at the point when it intends to serve the notice. That would be done by inquiring with the tenant directly, or at least attempting to do so.

Section 15 of the Act allows the qualifying occupier to be sisted as a party to proceedings, which would be done by way of an application under chapter 14 of the Summary Cause Rules,[122] seeking the court's leave to allow the qualifying occupier to be sisted as an additional defender. The issues that may arise after such an application is granted are discussed in Chapter 12.[123]

(3) Notice must be in the prescribed form: s 14(4)

There are two forms of notice, which are set out in the Scottish Secure Tenancies (Proceedings for Possession) (Form of Notice) Regulations 2012.[124] The form of notice for a case that is not a rent arrears case is found in schedule 1 to the regulations. The form of notice for a rent arrears case is at schedule 2.

The schedule 1 form is in two parts. In the first, the landlord informs the tenant or qualifying occupier that, at any time during a period of six months commencing on a given date (see point (8) below), it may raise proceedings against the tenant under one or more specified grounds (see point (4)). The particulars of how the ground(s) arose are then also given (see point (5)). The second part of the notice contains certain guidance notes, the nature of which depends on the ground, and whether the intended recipient is the tenant or the qualifying occupier. The drafter of the notice is required to delete sections of the guidance note, as appropriate.

The form of notice for a rent arrears case is at schedule 2 to the regulations. Its first part is similar to that of the schedule 1 notice. There then follows a checklist of eight paragraphs, corresponding to the various requirements of section 14A. The completion of this part of the form is discussed at point (7) below. The last part of the notice is the guidance notes, sections of which are deleted as appropriate.

Where the notice is not in the prescribed form, it will be ineffective. Accordingly, it is important that the notice served on the tenant or any qualifying occupier is checked against the prescribed form. This applies not only

and sub-letting) of and sch 3 (succession) to of the 2001 Act, by ss 12 and 13 of the 2014 Act, which had the effect of encouraging tenants to notify landlords of the identity of persons who occupy the tenancy was their only or principal home. See Chapter 12, at p 424.

122 Summary Cause Rules (n 67).

123 See also Chapter 13 for a discussion of the cases in which a qualifying occupier has sought to recall a decree, under Summary Cause Rules (n 67) r 24.1.

124 SSI 2012/92 (n 5). These regulations were amended by SSI 2018/156 (Form of Notice Regulations) (n 5), with effect from 1 May 2019. This amendment took account of the introduction of the "streamlined" procedure for ground 2 cases, by s 16(2)(aa) of the Act, for which see Chapter 5, p 164.

to the information for tenants and qualifying occupiers, but also the headings, the references to statute and the guidance notes.[125]

Where it is argued by the defender that the notice departs from the prescribed form, the landlord may rely on section 21 of the Interpretation and Legislative Reform (Scotland) 2010, which states:

> **"21 Forms**
> Where a form is prescribed in or under an Act of the Scottish Parliament, a form that differs from the prescribed form is not invalid unless the difference materially affects the effect of the form or is misleading."[126]

(4) Ground must be specified: s 14(4)(a)

Section 14(4) provides that the notice must state the ground "on which proceedings for recovery of possession are to be raised". The prescribed form of the notice provides a space on which the ground can be entered. It is suggested that the notice should, at least, narrate the terms of the ground or grounds[127] rather than simply stating, for example, "Schedule 2 Ground 1".[128]

Given that notice need be given only of the grounds on which proceedings *are to be raised*, it might be thought that the landlord could add additional grounds by amendment during the course of the proceedings. However, that is precluded by section 16(2), under which decree can be granted only on the grounds stated in the notice.[129]

(5) Notice must inform tenant of basis on which ground is said to have arisen (particulars of ground)

Section 14(4) itself contains no express requirement that particulars of the ground be given.[130] However, it requires that the notice be in the prescribed form, being that provided in either schedule 1 or schedule 2 of the Form of

125 As indicated above, the drafter of the notice is required to delete sections of the guidance note, as appropriate.

126 At the time of writing, there are no reported decisions on s 21. As to the meaning of the phrase "materially affects the effect", see the discussion of s 73 of the 2016 Act, in Chapter 9, at p 326.

127 The word "ground" means "ground or grounds" for these purposes. Under s 22 of the Interpretation and Legislative Reform (Scotland) 2010: "In an Act of the Scottish Parliament . . . (a) words in the singular include the plural and (b) words in the plural include the singular."

128 In *Mountain v Hastings* (1993) 25 HLR 427, Ralph Gibson LJ said, at 434: "I would add that [the requirement] is also not merely to identify the ground. If the ground is specified in the notice in terms which set out all the necessary information, i.e. the substance of the ground, it seems to me that the requirement that the ground be specified would be met. I would add that it is difficult to think of any good reason why a person, given the task of settling a form of notice, should choose to use words different from those in which the ground is stated in the schedule."

129 In *Midlothian Council v Tweedie* 1993 GWD 16-1068 Sheriff Principal Nicholson allowed an appeal by the tenant against a decree for recovery of possession on the basis that the action had been incompetent, because the ground stated in the notice was ground 1 of sch 3 to the 1987 Act, whereas it had been clear that the landlords were founding on ground 7.

130 In contrast to s 19(2) of the 1988 Act: "The First-tier Tribunal shall not make an order for possession on any of the grounds in Schedule 5 to this Act unless that ground and particulars of it are specified in the notice under this section . . .".

Notice Regulations.[131] The schedule 1 form contains a blank section headed "We also inform you that we are seeking possession under the above ground(s) for the following reasons:". After the space allowed by the form, the following words appear in italics, apparently as a direction to the landlord: "*(state particulars of the ground(s) arose: continue on additional sheets if required)*". The fourth paragraph of the guidance notes for the recipient states: "The landlord has explained in the notice the reason or reasons why they are considering taking court action."[132]

The schedule 2 notice is slightly different: the corresponding blank section is headed "We also inform you that we are seeking possession under the above ground(s) for rent arrears of (insert amount) and for the following additional reasons (if any)". As with the schedule 1 form, the words "*(state particulars of the ground(s) arose . . .*" appear after the blank space, as well as the same statement in the fourth paragraph of the guidance notes. This tends to suggest that, in a case in which the sole ground is rent arrears, it will be sufficient to state the amount outstanding at the date of service of the notice; whereas, if there are additional grounds, it is intended that the particulars of those grounds will be given, as in the schedule 1 form.

The need to state particulars was considered in *Glasgow Housing Association v Du*,[133] in which the landlords raised proceedings against the defender on various grounds, including rent arrears and overcrowding. Objection was taken to the competency of those proceedings on the basis that the notice of proceedings merely stated the schedule 2 grounds verbatim, and did not give any detail as the basis on which it was said that the ground was established in this case. The sheriff agreed with the defender's submission on this point, and dismissed the action. The pursuers appealed to the sheriff principal.

At the appeal, the pursuers argued that, under section 14(4), they were required to do no more than state the grounds, as they were set out in schedule 2 to the Act. The respondent argued that the sheriff had been correct to reject a narrow and technical interpretation of the word "ground", as it appeared in section 14(4)(a). That word had to be given the wider sense that it would have in common usage, which would encompass not only a statement of the relevant paragraph under schedule 2, but also the basis on which, in any particular case, that paragraph was said to be established. That interpretation was supported by the statutory instrument that set out the prescribed form for the notice. It was clear that the statutory instrument envisaged that particulars would be given in the notice. The sheriff principal agreed with the respondent's argument, and dismissed the appeal. On the basis of this authority, it is insufficient merely to state the statutory ground in the notice; the particulars of the ground must also be given.[134]

In order to fulfil the requirement to give particulars of the ground, the notice must give the tenant sufficient details of the circumstances upon which

131 (n 5) For which, see point (3) above.

132 The same material appears in both the sch 1 and sch 2 notices set out in SSI 2012/92, and appeared in the original form of notice, given in the schedule to the Scottish Secure Tenancies (Proceedings for Possession) Regulations 2002 (SSI 2002/320).

133 2009 Hous LR 91.

134 Subject to the proviso, stated above, that where the sch 2 form is being used, and the only ground for eviction is rent arrears, it appears that only the amount outstanding need be stated.

the landlord relies in asserting that a ground is made out; the purpose of the notice is to tell the tenant what complaint is made against him such that the tenant knows what he has to do in order to put matters right.[135] The landlord should state in summary form the facts that he intends to prove in support of the stated ground.[136] For example, if the ground for eviction is rent arrears, the amount of the arrears should be stated or the notice must contain sufficient information so as to enable the tenant to calculate the amount that is due.[137]

There are numerous English authorities on particulars that have been held to be insufficient, examples being: "The reasons for taking this action are non-payment of rent";[138] "various acts of nuisance";[139] "instances of dilapidation";[140] "the tenant frequently disturbs his neighbour, and on one occasion has threatened his neighbour with physical violence";[141] and "major refurbishment scheme".[142]

(6) Date specified in the notice: s 14(4)(b)

Section 14(4)(b) was originally section 14(3)(b) of the Tenants' Rights, Etc. (Scotland) Act 1980 and thereafter, section 47(3)(b) of the Housing (Scotland) Act 1987. It requires the landlord to specify a date on or after which proceedings may be raised, thereby giving a period of notice to tenant.

This provision presents some difficulty in interpretation and explanation. In effect, the landlord is required to hypothesise that the tenancy is not a Scottish secure tenancy, and then work out the date on which the tenancy could be brought to an end, in that case by a notice to quit.

The words "whichever is later" appear to envisage that the application of section 14(4)(b)(i) and (ii) could lead to two different dates, in which case the landlord must apply the later of those two dates. However, although the hypothetical tenancy would not be a Scottish secure tenancy, it would presumably still be subject to section 112 of the 1984 Act. If that is the case, it apparently has the effect of rendering section 14(4)(b)(i) superfluous. In order for the section 14(4)(b)(i) date to be the later of the two dates, one would have to hypothesise that the tenancy could be brought to an end by a notice to quit less than twenty-eight days from the date of service of the notice. However, section 112 of the 1984 Act makes that impossible. The date referred to in section 14(4)(b)(ii) could never be less than twenty-eight days from service of the notice and, accordingly, the date given in section 14(4)(b)(i) can never be the later of the two dates.[143]

That being so, the following rule may be tentatively stated: the date stated in the notice of proceedings for the purposes of section 14(4)(b) must be no

135 *Torridge District Council v Jones* (1986) 18 HLR 107, [1985] 2 EGLR 54.
136 *Dudley Metropolitan Borough Council v Bailey* (1990) 22 HLR 424, [1991] 1 EGLR 53.
137 *Marath v MacGillivray* (1996) 28 HLR 486; *Torridge District Council v Jones* (n 135).
138 *Torridge District Council v Jones* (n 135).
139 *South Buckinghamshire District Council v Francis* (1985) 11 CL 152.
140 *Slough Borough Council v Robbins* December 1996 *Legal Action* 13.
141 *Camden London Borough Council v Oppong* (1996) 28 HLR 701.
142 *Waltham Forest London Borough Council v England* March 1994 *Legal Action* 11.
143 The s 14(4)(b)(i) date might be applicable if it was impossible to calculate "the date on which the tenancy could have been brought to an end by a notice to quit" for the purposes of s 14(4)(b)(ii), say where the tenancy agreement does not have a determinate duration.

earlier than the first ish date that occurs more than twenty-eight clear days after the date of service of the notice. In relation to that rule, the following points should be noted:

- The date stated in the notice need not be an ish date of the tenancy. Section 14(4)(b) simply requires that the stated date is "not earlier than" the date calculated in terms of that provision.
- In cases in which section 14(4)(b)(ii) applies, it is feasible that a period of longer that twenty-eight clear days would be required (say, forty days). Reference is made to the discussion of periods of notice in Chapter 3. In practice, a longer period would be unusual, as the vast majority of Scottish secure tenancies have a duration of one month or less.[144]
- If for any other reason it is impossible to calculate the date in terms of section 14(4)(b)(ii), the date specified in the notice should, under section 14(4)(b)(i), be no earlier than the twenty-ninth day after the date of service of the notice. In that case, if service of the notice is effected on, say, 1 March, the date specified should not be earlier than 30 March, thus allowing twenty-eight clear days' notice.

It is perhaps appropriate to illustrate some of the above points with an example:

Example 1. The tenancy begins on Monday, 7 March 2022. The term is two weeks. Accordingly, every second Monday thereafter is an ish. Towards the end of August 2022, the landlord decides to serve a notice under section 14. The ish dates are 5 and 19 September, and 3 and 17 October. If the notice is served on, say, 8 September, the date stated for the purposes of section 14(4)(b) must be no earlier than 17 October, as this is the first ish date that occurs more than twenty-eight clear days after service. If, however, the notice is served on, say, 2 September, the stated date could be on or after 3 October.

Where the tenancy is an SSST,[145] section 36(8) of the Act provides that the date to be specified is a date not earlier than four weeks from the date of service of the notice.[146]

(7) In rent arrears cases, landlord must describe how it has met pre-action requirements

As was described in relation to point (3) above, the prescribed form of notice for a rent arrears case is found at schedule 2 to the Form of Notice Regulations.[147] Its first part is similar to that of the schedule 1 notice, appropriate for use in other actions.

There then follows a checklist of eight paragraphs, corresponding to the various requirements of section 14A. Each of those paragraphs is followed by two boxes.[148] Beside the first box, the word "completed" appears. This will be ticked to indicate completion of the requirement. In each case the second

144 So, the common law and statutory rules that require a period of notice of forty days would not apply.

145 Where the tenancy is an SSST, eviction proceedings are invariably raised under s 36. However, s 36(7) provides that the landlord may also raise proceedings under ss 14 and 16. See p 214.

146 I.e. s 36(8) effectively deletes s 14(4)(b)(ii) where the tenancy is an SSST.

147 n 5.

148 Except number 7, which has a third ("not applicable") box.

box is provided for the purposes of indicating when and how the pre-action requirement has been met. It is by the completion of the second boxes that the landlord will comply with the stipulation in section 14(4)(c), to: "specify . . . the steps taken by the landlord which the landlord considers to constitute compliance with the pre-action requirements in section 14A". Each of those second boxes has an italicised text, which indicates the information that should be provided. In each case, that text directs the landlord to "note briefly" or similar.

These eight paragraphs are followed by a statement to the effect that "if you are the tenant and you disagree we have taken the steps set out above, you should contact us to discuss your concerns". Thus, it is suggested that although the measures taken by the landlord towards compliance may be summarised, the tenant should be given enough detail to enable her to decide whether she accepts the relevant step has actually been carried out.

It is suggested that the purpose of this part of the schedule 2 form is to notify the tenant that his case has moved from one stage of the process (where the landlord attempts to address the arrears by performing the pre-action requirements) to the next (where those attempts have ended, and the landlord resorts to eviction proceedings). The form gives the tenant a brief summary of the steps taken by the landlord, which, in its view, enable it to assert that it has completed the pre-action requirements.

This is not to say that the landlord cannot, or should not, adopt any of the measures described in the pre-action requirements, after service of the section 14 notice. It is just that those steps would not be steps taken under section 14A, which have to be taken before the notice is served. If such steps were taken after service of the notice, but before proceedings were raised, they might be regarded, for the purposes of section 16(3)(d) as "action taken by the landlord, before raising proceedings, with a view to securing the cessation of [non-payment of rent]".[149]

(8) Proceedings must be raised while notice is in force

Under section 14(5), the notice ceases to be in force six months after the date specified in accordance with section 14(4)(b). If the landlord has not served the proceedings on the tenant by the time that the six-month period expires, the notice falls. Lodging the summons and obtaining a warrant for service within the six-month period is insufficient; service must be effected on the tenant.[150] In calculating the six-month period, the date stated in the notice would be included, because it would be possible for the landlord to raise the action on that date. Therefore, if the date on or after which proceedings may be raised is 22 April, proceedings must be served on the tenant on or before 21 October.[151]

(9) Notice must be served on local authority

The notice under section 14(5A) is the same as the notice under section 19A of the 1988 Act. Both of these provisions arise from section 11 of the

149 See the discussion of s 16(3) in Chapter 5, at p 146.
150 *Edinburgh District Council v Davis* 1987 SLT (Sh Ct) 33.
151 Reference is made to the discussion of calculation of time in Chapter 7.

Homelessness etc. (Scotland) Act 2003. The reader is referred to the discussion of section 19A of the 1988 Act in Chapter 7.

ABANDONMENT: 2001 ACT, ss 17–19

The landlord of a Scottish secure tenancy or an SSST[152] may recover possession without a court order under the abandonment procedure outlined in sections 17 and 18 of the 2001 Act.[153] The procedure is widely used by landlords in the social rented sector, and accordingly these provisions are of some importance. Under section 19, a tenant who is aggrieved by termination of the tenancy under the abandonment procedure may raise proceedings by summary application, the possible outcome of which is considered below.

Sections 17 and 18

"**17 Abandoned tenancies**

(1) This section applies where a landlord under a Scottish secure tenancy has reasonable grounds for believing that—
   (a) the house is unoccupied, and
   (b) the tenant does not intend to occupy it as the tenant's home.

(2) The landlord may enter the house at any time for the purpose of securing the house and any fittings, fixtures or furniture against vandalism.

(3) For the purposes of subsection (2), the landlord and its servants or agents may open, by force if necessary, doors and lockfast places.

(4) The landlord may take possession of the house in accordance with section 18.

18 Repossession

(1) A landlord wishing to take possession of a house under section 17(4) must serve on the tenant a notice—
   (a) stating that the landlord has reason to believe that the house is unoccupied and that the tenant does not intend to occupy it as the tenant's home,
   (b) requiring the tenant to inform the landlord in writing within 4 weeks of service of the notice if the tenant intends to occupy the house as the tenant's home, and
   (c) informing the tenant that, if it appears to the landlord at the end of that period that the tenant does not intend so to occupy the house, the tenancy will be terminated with immediate effect.

(2) Where—
   (a) the landlord has—
      (i) served on the tenant a notice complying with subsection (1), and
      (ii) made such inquiries as may be necessary to satisfy the landlord that the house is unoccupied and that the tenant does not intend to occupy it as the tenant's home, and

152 Under s 34(6), the provisions of pt 2 ch 1 of the 2001 Act are applied to SSSTs, with certain exceptions (such as the right to succeed to the tenancy). The abandonment procedure under ss 17–19 is not one of the exceptions, and therefore it follows that the procedure is available for SSSTs.

153 Sections 20 and 21 of the Act set out a procedure for abandonment by a joint tenant, where the other joint tenant or tenants remain in occupation, at the end of which the "abandoning tenant" ceases to be a joint tenant. These sections are not discussed because they do not entail recovery of possession by the landlords.

(b) at the end of the period mentioned in subsection (1)(b) the landlord is so satisfied,

the landlord may serve a further notice on the tenant bringing the tenancy to an end with immediate effect.

(3) Where a tenancy has been terminated in accordance with this section the landlord is entitled to take possession of the house without any further proceedings.

(4) The Scottish Ministers may by order make provision for the landlord, in taking possession of the house, to secure the safe custody and delivery to the tenant of any property which is found in a house to which this section applies and, in particular—

(a) for requiring charges to be paid in respect of such property before it is delivered to the tenant, and

(b) for authorising the disposal of such property, if the tenant has not arranged for its delivery to the tenant before the expiry of such period as the order may specify, and the application of any proceeds towards any costs incurred by the landlord and any rent due but unpaid by the tenant to the landlord."

The crux of the abandonment provisions lies in section 18(3). Their purpose is to enable landlords in the social rented sector to recover tenancies that have been abandoned, without the necessity of court proceedings, in order that they may be allocated to a tenant on the landlords' waiting list, with the minimum delay and administrative cost.

In order to obtain that benefit, the landlord must meet the various requirements of sections 17 and 18, which may be categorised under three general headings:

- the points on which the landlord must be satisfied, under section 17(1) and section 18(2)(a)(ii);
- the stipulations as to notice to the tenant, at section 18(1) and (2); and
- the safe custody of the tenant's property under section 18(4).

Section 17(1)(a) does not specifically refer to the tenant, and therefore it is submitted that it means unoccupied by *any* person, not simply unoccupied by the tenant. If the landlord has reason to believe that the tenant is no longer in occupation, but someone else is living at the tenancy instead, the abandonment procedure cannot be used.[154] In those circumstances the landlord should take steps to raise proceedings under ground 1 or ground 5 of schedule 2 to the Act.[155]

Points on which the landlord must be satisfied: ss 17(1) and 18(2)(a)(ii) and (b)

The abandonment procedure runs in three stages. In the first, the landlord has reasonable grounds for believing that: (a) the house is unoccupied; and (b) the tenant does not intend to occupy it as his home.

In the second stage the landlord serves the notice under section 18(1). There then follows a period of four weeks, during which the landlord makes such enquiries as may be necessary to satisfy it that points (a) and (b) above are indeed the case.[156]

154 Or else, by using the abandonment procedure, the landlord might be effecting an unlawful eviction of the occupiers.

155 See the commentary on the second leg of ground 1 and on ground 5 in Chapter 5.

156 However, there is no requirement, as such, that enquiries are delayed until the period

At the end of that period, the landlord being so satisfied, the third stage is the service of the notice under section 18(2), which terminates the tenancy. That notice has immediate effect, and the landlord may then recover possession of the property. This is usually done by clearing it of any goods or personal effects left by the tenant, and changing the locks.

In most abandonment cases, there is no contact between the landlord and the tenant from the beginning to the end of the process, and therefore the landlord cannot ascertain from the tenant directly whether he is still in occupation, or intends to return to the tenancy.[157] Also, landlords do not often deploy their right, under section 17(2), to enter the house for the purposes of securing it, before finally entering into possession under section 18(3), at the end of the process.[158] This means that, in practice, the landlord tends to have quite limited information on the basis of which to draw conclusions (a) and (b) above, which must be a matter of inference from the evidence that it does have available, including, in particular, the knowledge that the tenant has failed to respond to the notice served under section 18(1). Typically, stage one of the process will be triggered by the tenant's failure to respond to the landlord's attempts to communicate with him; in particular letters or notes delivered to the tenant by housing officers or other employees, asking him to contact the local housing office as soon as possible. Very often, further enquiries may take the form of information obtained from the tenant's neighbours, to the effect that there are no signs of occupation.[159] However, it is clear that an impression that the tenant has abandoned the tenancy may be erroneous, and it is for this reason that the tenant's "recourse to the court" in terms of section 19 of the Act, may proceed on the basis that the landlord's view that the tenant did not intend to occupy the subjects was formed in error.[160]

The relationship between section 18(1)(b) and section 18(2)(b) is not entirely clear. The section does not stipulate what consequence follows when the tenant does or does not comply with the request to inform the landlord, in writing, that he intends to occupy the tenancy as his home. It is submitted

between service of the notices under s 18(1) and (2). It may be the case that the landlord has made all reasonable enquiries, and has all the information to satisfy it as to points (a) and (b), before the notice under s 18(1) is served, in which case further enquiries would not be necessary. On the other hand, s 18(2)(b) seems to preclude the possibility of termination of the tenancy on the basis of enquiries that have been made *after* the expiry of the four-week period. If further information comes to light after that period has elapsed, it appears that a further s 18(1) notice will be necessary: *Lech v Highland Council* 2010 Hous LR 52.

157 In cases in which the tenant contacts the landlord to indicate that he does *not* wish the tenancy to continue, it is suggested that the landlord should arrange, if possible, to have the tenancy terminated under s 12(1)(f) of the Act, by four weeks' notice given by the tenant to the landlord. It is suggested that this is a better option than the abandonment procedure, because the landlord does not then incur the s 18(4) duty for the safe custody and delivery of the tenant's belongings, and there is also no possibility of an action under s 19 by the tenant at some later stage.

158 Though it is apparently quite common for housing officers or other employees, when delivering notices or letters to the tenant, to look in the windows of the house, to see whether there are any signs of occupation.

159 In practice, of course, these events may be reversed: the landlord may in the first place receive information from neighbours to the effect that the subjects are empty, after which housing officers or other employees of the landlord may be sent out to deliver a note or letter, asking the tenant to get in touch.

160 In terms of s 19(2)(c), discussed below.

that if the tenant does not so respond, that is not sufficient, in itself, to enable the landlord to proceed to serve notice under section 18(2)(b). The basis for proceeding to the final stage of the process is that the landlord is satisfied that points (a) and (b) above are the case – not that the tenant has failed to respond in writing. Accordingly, if the landlord has information that tends to suggest otherwise, including information from the tenant given in the course of a telephone call or a visit to the housing office, it would be wrong for the landlord to proceed to section 18(2)(b) simply on the basis that the tenant has failed to provide a written response. In those circumstances, it is submitted that the landlord ought to assess all the information available to it, including the fact that the tenant has responded, but not in writing, before deciding whether it is satisfied that points (a) and (b) are the case.

One would have thought that perhaps the converse should apply: i.e. if the tenant sends a letter to the landlord, within four weeks of service of the section 18(1) notice, stating that he intends to occupy the house as his home, the landlord is not precluded, by virtue of that letter, from serving the notice under section 18(2). If that were correct, it would be open to the landlord to be satisfied, on the basis of all the evidence before it, that the tenant's letter is not a true statement of his intentions. This was the position adopted by the landlords in *Smith v Dundee City Council.*[161]

In that case the sheriff observed:

> "Ultimately the respondents appear to have made their decision on the basis that they did not believe the applicant as to his future intentions. Such a position would be best explored in the context of a summary action for recovery of possession of heritable property rather than under the short cut statutory procedure which is best deployed in clear cut cases."

However, he went on to remark:

> "It is equally apparent that mere expressions of intent to occupy frequently repeated cannot frustrate the statutory procedure. In exercising its discretion the local authority ought to be able to list a number of these instances over a reasonably prolonged period coupled with other facts and circumstances tending towards non-occupation before proceeding in this vein."[162]

The sheriff accordingly found in favour of the applicant, because the period in question was a relatively short one, enquiries by the council were limited, and there were other circumstances that pointed to his intention to occupy.

If the landlord is satisfied that the tenant does intend to occupy the subjects, its view may subsequently change, on the basis of further information. In that case, there is no time limit that must expire before a further section 18(1) notice may be served.[163]

161 2003 Hous LR 55. See also *Lech v Highland Council* (n 156).

162 At 61.

163 Accordingly, a further notice may be served within days, as was the case in *Tannoch v Glasgow City Council* 2000 Hous LR 64.

Stipulations as to notice to tenant: s 18(1) and (2)(b)

The notice must contain the three points listed at section 18(1)(a), (b) and (c). At various points in this book,[164] there is a discussion of the effect of notices that contain errors. It is not clear whether the same considerations would apply to notices under section 18(1). It is submitted that, given the drastic effect of the notice, which is the unilateral termination of the tenancy without a court order, the margin for error must be small; in particular, it is submitted that the omission of any of the three points, or any element of them, would render the notice invalid.

Given the terms of section 18(1)(b) and (2)(b), a clear four-week period should be allowed before notice is served under section 18(2). For example, if the notice is served by delivering at the tenant's "proper address" in terms of section 40(1)(b) of the Act, on 27 May, the four-week period would commence at the end of that day, and finish at the end of 24 June. The section 18(2) notice could then be served on 25 June.[165]

Safe custody of tenant's property: s 18(4)

The order referred to in section 18(4) is the Scottish Secure Tenancies (Abandoned Property) Order 2002.[166] It provides that where property is found in a house to which section 18(1) of the Act applies, the landlord must immediately serve a notice on the tenant that the property is available for delivery into the hands of the tenant or his agent at a place specified in the notice, on payment of any costs incurred by the landlord in complying with the order or such lesser amount (including a nil amount) as the landlord may think. The tenant must also be notified that if the property is not collected by the date specified in the notice (being a date not fewer than twenty-eight days from the date of service) it may be disposed of in accordance with the order.

Where the property is not collected by that date, it must be stored by the landlord for a period of six months from the date on which the landlord took possession of the dwellinghouse, unless the value of the property would not exceed the amount of any costs incurred by the landlord in complying with the order and the amount of any arrears of rent owed by the tenant. In that case, it may be disposed of by the landlord on expiry of the date specified in the notice to the tenant. After the expiry of the six-month period, the landlord may sell any item remaining in its custody and deduct from the proceeds any costs or rent arrears.

Where at any time prior to the sale or disposal of property under the order the tenant, or any other person who appears to the landlord to have a right of ownership or of possession in the property, arranges for delivery to the tenant or such other person of any item the landlord is obliged to relinquish custody

164 See, in particular, the discussion of effect of an error in a notice to quit in Chapter 3, and the treatment of AT5 notices in Chapter 7.

165 This is on the basis that a weekly period would be calculated *civilis computatio*, as further described in Chapter 7, in analysis of s 32(1)(a) of the 1988 Act. For agents advising the tenant, this point is always worth checking: in their eagerness to serve the s 18(2) notice, landlords have been known to serve the second notice too early, four weeks after the day of service.

166 SSI 2002/313.

of that item upon receipt of a payment equal to the amount of any costs incurred by the landlord in complying with the order in relation to that item or such lesser amount as the landlord may think fit.

The Order also provides that landlords of Scottish secure tenancies are obliged to maintain a register of houses in which property has been found on the exercise of their powers under section 18 of the Act, which must be made available for inspection by members of the public at all reasonable times.

If the landlord fails to comply with these requirements, the tenant may seek compensation for his lost property and, in practice, disputes of this type commonly arise.

Section 19

A tenant under a Scottish secure tenancy who is aggrieved by termination of the tenancy by the landlord under section 18(2) may raise proceedings by summary application within six months after the date of the termination.[167] The tenant must satisfy the court that the landlord:

> "(a) has failed to comply with any provision of section 18,
> (b) did not have reasonable grounds for finding—
>   (i) that the house was unoccupied, or
>   (ii) that the tenant did not intend to occupy it as the tenant's home, or
> (c) was in error in finding that the tenant did not intend to occupy the house as the tenant's home, and the tenant had reasonable cause, by reason of illness or otherwise, for failing to notify the landlord of the tenant's intention so to occupy it."[168]

If he succeeds in doing so, the court must make one of two orders. If the house has not been let to a new tenant, it must grant a declarator that the notice under section 18(2) is of no effect, and may make such further order in relation to the Scottish secure tenancy as it thinks fit.[169] In that case, the tenancy will begin again, and the landlords will be obliged to allow the tenant to resume occupation. In any other case, the court will direct the landlord to make other suitable accommodation available to the tenant.[170]

Applications under section 19, and its predecessor (section 51 of the 1987 Act) have been fairly rare. If the landlords have met all the requirements of sections 17 and 18, the application will have to proceed on the basis of paragraph (c) above. Such cases will turn on their own facts and, given what the former tenant requires to prove, the court's assessment of his credibility is liable to be of some importance. Thus, in *Tannoch v Glasgow City Council*,[171] the application appears to have failed because the sheriff strongly preferred the evidence of the council's witnesses to that of the former tenant.[172]

167 2001 Act, s 19(1).
168 ibid s 19(2).
169 ibid s 19(3)(a) and (4).
170 ibid s 19(3)(b). Under s 19(5), part 2 of sch 2 to the Act, which is discussed at the end of Chapter 5, has effect to determine whether accommodation is suitable for the purposes of subsection (3)(b).
171 (n 163).
172 *Fallens v Stirling Council* 1996 SCLR 1058 is another example of an application that failed, on the basis that the tenant was unable to show reasonable cause for not having advised the

ABANDONMENT AND UNLAWFUL EVICTION

If the landlord repossesses the tenancy subjects without meeting all the requirements of the Act, it might be argued that it has carried out an unlawful eviction, and could face an action by the aggrieved tenant for statutory or common law damages.[173]

In *Wylie v Argyll Community Housing Association Ltd*,[174] Sheriff Principal Kerr held that a claim for damages for unlawful eviction could not be made by the pursuer, because he had not made an application under section 19. That is necessary, because it is the only procedure by which a notice under section 18(2) may be challenged. That notice terminates the tenancy and allows the landlord to repossess. Absent an action under section 19, the section 18(2) notice must be taken to be valid, and the eviction is not unlawful.

That does, however, leave some doubt as to the circumstances in which an action for damages could be pursued by a tenant who *has* utilised the section 19 procedure. As indicated above, the sheriff has two options in any case in which he finds that the former tenant's challenge to the abandonment procedure is well founded. If the tenancy subjects have not been let to a new tenant, he may grant a declarator that the notice under section 18(2) is of no effect. That would result in the tenancy being resurrected (because its purported termination has no effect), and the tenant could then be reinstated. Presumably the door to an action of damages would then be open, though only to damages at common law: statutory damages are not available to a tenant reinstated in the subjects, under section 36(6) of the 1988 Act. However, in a case under section 19 in which the landlord has let the tenancy subjects to another tenant, the sheriff only has the power to direct the landlord to make other suitable accommodation available to the tenant. In that case, no order can be made to the effect that the section 18(2) notice is of no effect, given the existence of a new tenancy under the 2001 Act.

It is nevertheless possible to envisage a case in which damages, including statutory damages, could still be sought. If the sheriff has found, under section 19(2)(a), that the landlord has failed to comply with any provision of section 18, in carrying out the abandonment procedure, the eviction could still be characterised as unlawful, even though it is impossible, given the letting of the property to another tenant, to secure a declarator that the section 18(2) notice is of no effect. However, in this scenario, the parties to the section 19 application would have to go to proof, and the court would have to make the necessary findings. Let us say that the defending landlord agrees to settle by providing suitable alternative accommodation without the necessity of a proof. It seems that the tenant would be obliged to accept that offer, otherwise he

landlord of her intention to occupy the property as her home. However, the s 19 application was successful in *Smith v Dundee Council* (n 161) and *Lech v Highland Council* (n 156).

173 Or, in the case of a failure to meet the requirements of s 18(4), an action for compensation for the loss of the tenant's property. It is clear from the decision of the Supreme Court in *Lambeth LBC v Loveridge* [2014] 1 WLR 4516 that statutory damages can be awarded against a local authority, though the court was somewhat uncomfortable with that conclusion (see para 30 of the judgment).

174 Unreported, decision of the Sheriff Principal of North Strathclyde, April 2011, in action number A46/08 at Oban Sheriff Court.

could not continue with the section 19 application.[175] That being the case, his application under section 19 would effectively be at an end. The court would not then make any finding under section 19(2), and the legitimacy of the procedure under sections 17 and 18 would not be challenged.

For these reasons, it is suggested that although, in theory, it is possible for a tenant subject to the abandonment procedure to have a claim for damages for unlawful eviction, in practice the availability of the remedy under section 19 will tend to preclude such an action.

175 In a case in which the original tenancy has been let to another person, the only remedy that can be sought in a s 19 application is that the defenders be directed to make other suitable accommodation available to the tenant. It is difficult to see how the pursuer could insist on that remedy if other suitable accommodation is being offered by the defenders.

Chapter 5

Scottish Secure Tenancies: Recovery of Possession

INTRODUCTION

An order for recovery of possession of a Scottish secure tenancy is granted in accordance with section 16 of the 2001 Act, which is set out below. Before such an order may be granted, the court must first be satisfied that the landlord has a ground for recovery of possession.[1] There are fifteen grounds, set out in numbered paragraphs in part 1 of schedule 2 to the Act. The onus is on the landlord to show that the ground on which it relies has been established. The landlord's action may proceed on more than one ground, but only one need be established. The ground on which the order is made must be a ground set out in the section 14 notice, the service of which preceded the action.[2]

The landlord must then establish that the "additional requirement" has been met. The nature of the additional requirement depends on the ground. For grounds 1–7 the court must be satisfied that "it is reasonable to make the order". For grounds 8–14, the court must be satisfied that "other suitable accommodation will be available for the tenant when the order takes effect". For ground 15, the court must be satisfied that both of these additional requirements have been established.

Where the landlord relies on ground 2 (criminal conviction), amendments made by section 14 of the 2014 Act have the effect that it is no longer necessary to establish the additional requirement of reasonableness, provided that the landlord served the notice of proceedings for recovery of possession within twelve months of the conviction for the offence that forms the basis for the action.[3]

The purpose of this chapter is to consider the grounds, the corresponding additional requirement, and the new rules in relation to ground 2 cases. It will be clear that the analysis is weighted heavily in favour of the grounds that most commonly arise, such as rent arrears and antisocial behaviour. The structure is as follows:

1 Section 16(2). Note that the jurisdiction of the First-tier Tribunal ("FTT") applies only to proceedings arising from tenancies under the 1984, 1988 and 2016 Acts. Otherwise, eviction proceedings (including proceedings under ss16 and 36 of the 2001 Act) are still raised in the sheriff court.

2 This follows from the terms of s 16(2)(a)(i) and (b)(i). That is in contrast to actions for recovery of possession under s 18 of the 1988 Act, or s 51 of the 2016 Act, in which the FTT may allow additional grounds to be added to those specified in the statutory notice (s 19(2) of the 1988 Act; s 52(5)(b) of the 2016 Act).

3 This is known as the "streamlined eviction process". It is discussed at p 164 below.

- Grounds 1–7.
- The additional requirement in relation to those grounds: that it is reasonable to grant the order.
- Streamlined eviction process for ground 2 cases.
- Grounds 8–15.
- The additional requirement in relation to those grounds: that suitable alternative accommodation is made available to the tenant.

Many of the statutory grounds for eviction are similar, or identical, to the grounds under the equivalent English legislation; authorities from that jurisdiction are extensively quoted in this chapter.

Section 16

Section 16 provides:

> "**Powers of court in possession proceedings**
>
> (1) The court may, as it thinks fit, adjourn proceedings under section 14 on a ground set out in any of paragraphs 1 to 7 and 15 of schedule 2 for a period or periods, with or without imposing conditions as to payment of outstanding rent or otherwise.
>
> (2) Subject to subsection (1), in proceedings under section 14 the court must make an order for recovery of possession if it appears to the court–
>
> (a) that–
>
> (i) the landlord has a ground for recovery of possession set out in any of paragraphs 1 to 7 of that schedule and specified in the notice required by section 14, and
>
> (ii) it is reasonable to make the order,
>
> (aa) [New rules in relation to ground 2 cases: see p 164 below]
>
> (b) that–
>
> (i) the landlord has a ground for recovery of possession set out in any of paragraphs 8 to 14 of that schedule and so specified, and
>
> (ii) other suitable accommodation will be available for the tenant when the order takes effect, or
>
> (c) that–
>
> (i) the landlord has a ground for recovery of possession set out in paragraph 15 of that schedule and so specified,
>
> (ii) it is reasonable to make the order, and
>
> (iii) other suitable accommodation will be available for the tenant when the order takes effect.
>
> (3) For the purposes of subsection (2)(a)(ii) the court is to have regard, in particular, to–
>
> (a) the nature, frequency and duration of–
>
> (i) where the ground for recovery of possession is one set out in any of paragraphs 1 and 3 to 7 of schedule 2, the conduct taken into account by the court in concluding that the ground is established,
>
> (ii) where the ground for recovery of possession is that set out in paragraph 2 of that schedule, the conduct in respect of which the person in question was convicted,
>
> (b) the extent to which that conduct is or was conduct of, or a consequence of acts or omissions of, persons other than the tenant,
>
> (c) the effect which that conduct has had, is having and is likely to have on any person other than the tenant, and
>
> (d) any action taken by the landlord, before raising the proceedings, with a view to securing the cessation of that conduct.

(3A) Subsection (2) does not affect any other rights that the tenant may have by virtue of any other enactment or rule of law.

(4) Part 2 of schedule 2 has effect to determine whether accommodation is suitable for the purposes of subsection (2)(b) or (c).

(5) An order under subsection (2) must appoint a date for recovery of possession and has the effect of–
   (a) terminating the tenancy, and
   (b) giving the landlord the right to recover possession of the house,
   at that date.

(5A) Where an order is made under subsection (2) in proceedings under section 14 on the ground that rent lawfully due from the tenant has not been paid (as set out in paragraph 1 of schedule 2) or on grounds including that ground—
   (a) subsection (5)(a) does not apply,
   (b) the tenancy is terminated only if the landlord recovers possession of the house in pursuance of the order,
   (c) the order must specify the period for which the landlord's right to recover possession of the house is to have effect (being no longer than any maximum period which the Scottish Ministers by order prescribe), and
   (d) the landlord must have regard to any guidance issued by the Scottish Ministers about recovery of possession in pursuance of the order.

. . ."[4]

Power to adjourn cases: s 16(1)

In relation to actions relying on grounds 1–7 and 15, the court has an unfettered power to adjourn proceedings at any time, with or without imposing conditions on the adjournment. This power overlaps, to some extent, with the court's power to continue cases under the Summary Cause Rules. This issue is discussed in Chapter 13.

The effect of decree: s 16(5) and 16(5A)

Under the original section 16, an order granted under section 16(2) had the effect of immediately terminating the tenancy in all cases. Under the new section 16(5A), this is no longer the case in relation to rent arrears actions. These provisions are also linked to the rules of court in relation to decrees, extract and so on, and the statutory scheme for the enforcement of such decrees set out in part 15 of the Bankruptcy and Diligence (Scotland) Act 2007. Those matters are discussed in Chapter 15.

The remaining parts of section 16, being subsections (2), (3) and (4), are the focus of this chapter.

Other enactments or rules of law: section 16(3A)

This provision was inserted by section 14(3) of the 2014 Act. It is thought that it is intended to recognise to the rights of the tenant under the Human Rights Act 1998 and the Equality Act 2010, which are discussed in Chapter 11.[5]

4 Section 16(6), which relates to decants, is discussed in relation to ground 10, at p 169 below.

5 See the Scottish Government's "Streamlined Eviction Process – Criminal or Antisocial Behaviour Statutory Guidance for Social Landlords" para 2.7. The Guidance is discussed at p 165 below.

GROUNDS 1–7 ("CONDUCT GROUNDS"): s 16(2)(a)(i)

Ground 1 is:

> "Rent lawfully due from the tenant has not been paid, or any other obligation of the tenancy has been broken."

In effect, ground 1 comprises two separate grounds: rent arrears and breach of some other condition of the tenancy.

Ground 1 (part 1): rent arrears

In most cases the figure for arrears should be readily ascertainable. The amount of arrears at the date when the summons was prepared, and perhaps also at the date of service of the section 14 notice, is invariably given in the statement of claim attached to the summons served on the tenant at the beginning of the case. By the time that the action calls in court, that figure will usually have changed. It is to be anticipated that the landlord's representative will be in a position to advise the court of the current figure, if asked to do so by the court, at the first calling or at any subsequent calling. Where a proof is fixed in the case, the rent account is usually lodged by the landlord as a production.[6]

As regards the first "branch" of ground 1, the analysis is broken down as follows:

- "rent";
- "lawfully due";
- "from the tenant";
- "has not been paid".

It will be apparent in what follows that any analysis of eviction proceedings on the ground of rent arrears must take into account the housing benefit system. However, the aim of the Welfare Reform Act 2012 is to phase out housing benefit and certain other welfare benefits, and to replace them with a single "universal credit" that is paid monthly.[7] At the time of writing, that change is gradually being introduced. At the end of 2018, the roll-out of universal credit in Scotland was extended to all new claimants. Existing claimants are undergoing a process of "migration".

It has become apparent that this change has led to increased rent arrears, due to delays and difficulties in payment of universal credit, and the challenges faced by claimants in budgeting, under a system in which claimants receive their benefits monthly.[8] The UK Government has issued guidance for land-

6 However, in practice it is usually possible for the tenant's agent to obtain a copy from the landlords by request, at an earlier stage. The rent account shows: the payments that have been made; periods when the arrears were increasing; backdated payments of housing benefit, which may appear as lump-sum credits; deductions from benefits, and so on. Many tenants are vague about the history of their arrears. For example, where the rent has usually been paid by benefits, the tenant may not know when or why the benefit was stopped, causing the arrears to build up. The rent account almost always assists in clarifying these issues.

7 Under the 2012 Act and the Universal Credit Regulations 2013 (SI 2013/376), universal credit has a "housing costs" element "in respect of any liability of a claimant to make payments in respect of the accommodation they occupy as their home" (s 11(1) of the Welfare Reform Act 2012).

8 For example, a BBC *Panorama* report aired in November 2018 showed that, in Flintshire in

lords in the private and social rented sectors, which provides information "to help them understand what they can do to help their tenants prepare" for the move to universal credit.[9]

"Rent"

The rent is the gross rent payable in respect of the tenant's occupation of the property, in terms of the tenancy agreement.[10] Unless the contract makes specific provision to the contrary,[11] it does not include service charges, water rates, heating charges, other amenity payments, insurance premiums and the like,[12] although non-payment of those charges may constitute a breach of the tenancy contract for the purposes of the second leg of ground 1, provided that payment is a condition of the lease.

Debiting legal expenses and housing benefit overpayments

An examination of the rent account may show significant debits that have not been made in respect of the liability to pay rent. The two leading examples of such debits are legal expenses and housing benefit overpayments. Agents advising the tenant should therefore be alert to the possibility of such debits being made, and should check the rent account accordingly.

The ongoing legal expenses of the eviction proceedings should not be debited to the rent account, although this practice is not uncommon.[13] Liability to pay legal expenses does not establish ground 1, and attributing such expenses to the rent account may lead the authority to misrepresent the true level of rent arrears.

north Wales, one of the first areas in the UK to roll out universal credit, council tenants on the new benefit owed six times as much rent as those using the old benefits system, with evictions in the county up by 55% compared with the same time in the previous year.

9 "Universal Credit and Rented Housing: Guide for Landlords" (Updated December 2019), available on the gov.uk site.

10 The original gross rent is subject to increase from time to time. Most local authorities and registered social landlords ("RSLs") increase their rents at the beginning of April. The issue of rent increases is further discussed at p 127 below.

11 Parties may agree that a service charge or other payment is deemed to be "rent" and recoverable as such: *Escalus Properties v Robinson* [1996] QB 231. However, it is suggested that payment of the charge would have to be an obligation of the tenancy, which is incidental to the tenant's occupation of the property.

12 This distinction between rent and other payments is apt to be obscured: some social landlords use the rent payment system to collect a variety of charges.

13 This tends to happen at the point when the decree for eviction is granted. It is not unusual to encounter cases in which an action has been raised against a tenant in respect of rent arrears of a sum in the order of, say, £200–£300, where the consequent legal expenses, added to the rent account, have the effect of substantially increasing the tenant's indebtedness, sometimes more than doubling the original amount. Thereafter, the landlords will often make payment of the entire rent arrears and the legal expenses, or a substantial proportion thereof, a condition of their refraining from enforcing the decree. The effect of a minute for recall under chapter 24 of the Summary Cause Rules in such a case should be that the "rent arrears" are substantially reduced, because the decree for expenses is also recalled, along with the decree for eviction. However, in some cases no reduction is made by the landlord: the legal expenses remain on the rent account, notwithstanding recall of decree.

Overpayment of housing benefit is a rather more complex issue.[14] Overpayments may occur for a variety of different reasons. However, a leading cause is the failure of the tenant to advise the housing benefit authority of a change in his or her financial circumstances, which, if known to the authority, would have caused the benefit to be reduced.

Where the benefit is paid by a local authority that is also the landlord, the applicable legislation allows the local authority to recover the overpayment by deducting an amount, at source, from the housing benefit payable to the tenant, before it is credited to his rent account.[15]

Example. The tenant has a gross rent of £75 per week, which would normally be paid fully by housing benefit, such that she does not have to pay anything towards her rent. She is in arrears by the sum of £500. She is repaying the arrears at the rate of £5 per week. The authority decides to recover a previous overpayment of £215 at the rate of £8.60 per week. This means that the benefit credited to the rent account will be £66.40 per week for 25 weeks. For that period, the tenant must pay £13.60 per week to the authority, if she wants her arrears to continue decreasing at the rate of £5 per week. If she simply continues to pay £5 per week as she did before, the arrears will increase at the rate of £3.60 per week.

The decision that the overpayment is payable and the fixing of the rate of the deduction are challengeable by the tenant. However, it is a legitimate exercise of the authority's powers to deduct benefit at source in this manner, provided that it is done before the benefit is credited to the rent account.[16]

In some cases, however, the authority simply debits the whole overpayment to the rent account. In the example given above, this would have the effect of increasing the tenant's rent arrears from £500 to £715. This practice is not authorised by the relevant legislation, and is therefore *ultra vires* of the authority.[17] Furthermore, it may lead the authority to misrepresent the true level of rent arrears to the tenant, and further to the court, if eviction proceedings have been raised.[18]

By contrast, where housing benefit payment has been made to a housing association or private landlord, such deductions are effectively lawful. Section 75 of the Social Security Administration Act 1992[19] enables the Secretary of

14 For that reason, tenants are well advised to obtain specialist welfare rights advice. Local authorities often make decisions to recover overpayments, which could be subject to challenge.

15 Housing Benefit Regulations 2006 (SI 2006/213), reg 102. An amendment to the regulation made in 2009 (which inserts reg 102(1ZA)) allows a local authority to recover the overpayment by deduction from any housing benefit payable to the claimant's partner, where he or she "has one or more partners". An overpayment is also a civil debt, recoverable by the local authority that paid the benefit, by means of the usual remedies.

16 *Aberdeen City Council v McCarthy* 2004 Hous LR 53.

17 If the landlord is the benefit authority, payment of the benefit is made in the form of a rebate of the rent. It appears to follow from the forms of "payment" listed in the Social Security Administration Act 1992, s 134(2), that the tenant's liability to pay the rent is discharged by the rebate, notwithstanding any subsequent decision that there was an overpayment of housing benefit.

18 The practice of local authorities debiting an overpayment of housing benefit to the rent account, so that it appears to be rent arrears, was repeatedly held to be maladministration by the Commissioner for Local Administration in England: see, e.g., *Wychavon District Council*, Complaint 90/B/2514 and *Hackney London Borough Council*, Complaint 91/A/0730.

19 As amended by s 16 of the Social Security Administration (Fraud) Act 1997, following the decision in *R v London Borough of Haringey, ex p Ayub* (1993) 25 HLR 566.

State, or the authority that paid the benefit, to recover it from the person to whom it was paid. It is typical for a housing benefit authority to make large lump-sum payments to landlords in respect of the housing benefit entitlement of a number of tenants, at the same time. In doing so, section 75 authorises the authority to claw back the total overpayment due in respect of tenant A from benefits payable to the landlord in respect of tenants B–Z. However, section 75(6) has the effect that the rent payable by tenants B–Z, which would have been discharged by payment of the housing benefit, is deemed to have been discharged in any event, notwithstanding the recovery of A's overpayment from that housing benefit. Thus the recovery of the overpayment from the housing benefit payable in respect of the rental liabilities of tenants B–Z does not prejudice them. Instead, under regulation 95(2) of the Housing Benefit Regulations 2006, the rental payments due by tenant A, which were previously discharged by the overpaid housing benefit, are effectively "undischarged" when the overpayment is clawed by the authority. As a result, after the claw-back, A is in arrears of those rental payments, and the landlord is entitled to debit his rent account by the relevant sum, and to proceed on the basis that his total arrears have increased by that amount.

In successive editions of the Child Poverty Action Group's *Housing Benefit and Council Tax Benefit Legislation*, the authors have argued that regulation 95(2) is *ultra vires*, because it purports to affect the substantive obligations and rights, under the general law of landlord and tenant, of the claimant and the landlord *inter se*, in a manner not authorised by power to make the regulations, in terms of section 5(1)(p) of the 1992 Act. However, regulation 95(2)[20] has been in effect for many years without this point having been authoritatively decided. Therefore, as the law stands, the rule under regulation 95(2) applies.

"Lawfully due"

In practice, there are two situations in which the tenant asserts that the rent is not lawfully due to the landlord.

Rent increases

The tenant may argue that the rent has been increased unlawfully, in a manner that exceeds the powers of the landlord under the tenancy contract and the relevant legislation.[21] The tenant may be withholding that part of the rent that he maintains is not due, causing "arrears" to accumulate over time.

The landlord of a Scottish secure tenancy has the power to increase rent or charges under section 25 of the 2001 Act. Although that section imposes certain procedural requirements on the landlord in raising the rent,[22] the power is otherwise unfettered. To that extent, rent increases affecting a large number of tenants tend to be an issue of local politics, rather than a matter

20 And its predecessor regulation: Housing Benefit (General) Regulations 1987 (SI 1987/1971), reg 93(2).

21 See, example.g.: *Riverside Housing Association v White* [2007] HLR 31.

22 In particular, to give the tenants four weeks' notice of the increase. Where the landlord proposes to increase the rents or any other charges payable by all, or any class of, its tenants, it must, before giving the four weeks' notice: (a) consult those of its tenants who would be affected by the proposal, and (b) have regard to the views expressed by those consulted.

that might give rise to a legal challenge. That said, there will be instances in which the procedure adopted by the landlord may be questionable, or the increase may be challengeable on the standard judicial review grounds, which may be pled by the tenant in defending an action for possession on the ground of rent arrears.[23]

Breach of tenancy contract by landlord: withholding rent, abatement and damages

Various important repairing and maintaining obligations are imposed on the landlord of a Scottish secure tenancy by the 2001 Act, section 27 and schedule 4, and further by the common law.[24] In the vast majority of Scottish secure tenancies, the schedule 4 and common law obligations are incorporated into the tenancy contract.[25]

The tenant may assert that the rent is not lawfully due because the landlord is in breach of those obligations, in that it has failed to repair and maintain the tenancy subjects properly. In particular, the tenant may contend that: (a) he has been exercising his right to withhold (retain) his rent; (b) he is entitled to an abatement of the whole, or part, of the rent over the period during which the landlords were in breach of their obligations (i.e. he invites the court to find that in respect of that period he should pay less than the gross rent in terms of the lease); or (c) he is seeking damages in respect of the losses he has suffered in consequence of the landlords' breach, which he proposes to set off against any liability for rent arrears.

Confusion can arise as to which of these remedies the defender is exercising, particularly as it is possible to maintain all three positions at the same time.[26]

Withholding or retention of rent is a remedy open to the defender if the landlord is in breach of its obligations.[27] The remedy of retention has two purposes. It may be used as a means of compelling the landlord to fulfil its

23 The deployment of "public law" arguments in eviction proceedings is discussed in Chapter 11.

24 Rankine, *Leases* (3rd edn) 241: "The rule of the common law, as applied to urban tenements, is that they shall be put into tenantable and habitable condition by the landlord at entry . . . The landlord of an urban tenement is further bound at common law, and unless it be otherwise stipulated, to uphold it in a tenantable and habitable condition during the course of the lease."

25 For a discussion of statutory and common law repairing obligations in residential tenancies, see the author's article "*Todd v Clapperton*: the evolving law on repairing obligations and claims against landlords of residential property" 2010 SLT (News) 31.

26 This text gives a summary of these remedies in the context of eviction proceedings. For a more detailed discussion, see Paton and Cameron:,*The Law of Landlord and Tenant* 141–142; Rennie, *Leases* (2015) paras 4-20 to 4-23 and 17-52 to 17-56; McAllister, *Scottish Law of Leases* (4th edn) paras 4.37–4.49; Robson and Combe, *Residential Tenancies* (4th edn) para 4.23. There is also comprehensive discussion of the older cases in Rankine (n 24) 327–335.

27 As Rankine (n 24) explains (at 329), it is long established that a tenant is entitled to retain his rent if and so long as the landlord fails to put or maintain him in possession of a material part of the subjects let. At 331, he further notes: "The principle extends to the enforcement of conditions of the lease, which are so material as to stand on the same level with stipulations relating to the quantum of the subject let." It is apparent from the older authorities such as *McDonald v Kydd* (1901) 3 F 923 and *Earl of Galloway v McConnell* 1911 SC 846, that the tenant is entitled to retain rent in response to a failure by the landlord to put subjects in tenantable and habitable condition, and to plead retention as a defence to action for payment of the rent.

obligations, and it also provides the tenant with security for a claim for damages.[28] If the retention is only for the first purpose then, in theory, the tenant would pay the whole amount of the rent retained as soon as the obligation was fulfilled.[29] However, that is unlikely to happen in practice, because the tenant will invariably wish to assert a right to have some of the retained rent abated,[30] or will seek damages to be paid from the amount retained.[31] The right to retention is not a term or condition of the parties' contract; rather it is an equitable remedy, the exercise of which is regulated by the courts. Thus, in *Stobbs v Hislop*, Lord Russell said, in a case concerning a residential tenancy:[32]

> "It was, in my judgment, an implied condition of the contract that the landlord should, during the tenancy, maintain the house in tenantable condition, *i.e.*, reasonably fit for habitation and wind and water tight. On a breach by the landlord of that implied condition the tenant might resort to an equitable remedy recognised by the general law – for the purpose of compelling the landlord to make the house habitable and as a security for satisfaction of any claims for damages to be proffered by the tenant – by withholding payment of the rent and continuing the occupation. Such a right of retention is one of the equitable remedies available generally in respect of mutual contracts containing reciprocal obligations, wherever circumstances permit of resort to it (see Gloag on Contract, (2nd ed.) pp. 623 *et seq.*). Its exercise is, however, always controlled by the Court and regulated by reference to equitable considerations in the light of the circumstances of each case. It is not, therefore, a right which is peculiar to a lessee. I do not doubt that, as between the parties to the present case during the currency of the original contract, the contractual tenant was entitled to exercise his right to retain the rent whenever the house ceased to be reasonably fit for habitation (see, *e.g. Fingland & Mitchell v. Howie*). But I am unable to agree that that right was in any sense a term or condition of the original contract. It was and is an equitable remedy sanctioned by the general law and regulated by the Courts under appropriate safeguards."

Because the tenant's retention of rent is an *equitable* remedy, which is controlled by the court, it has to be satisfied that the remedy is being exercised in good faith. In the older cases, it was common for the tenant, pending the outcome of the action, to consign the full amount of the rental payment with the court, either by the court's order or voluntarily. This demonstrated that the tenant was in good faith and had not withheld the rent because of financial difficulty.[33] Although consignation is not compulsory,[34] it is suggested that the court still has to be satisfied that the tenant is exercising the remedy in good

28 Rennie (n 26) paras 17-53 and 17-54.

29 The right of retention also ends on termination of the parties' contract: *Pacitti v Manganiello* 1995 SCLR 557; *J H & W Lamont of Heathfield Farm v Chattisham Ltd* 2018 SC 440.

30 "In certain circumstances the tenant's obligation to pay rent may be suspended and he will be entitled to retain the rent until an abatement of rent has been allowed and its amount fixed" (Paton and Cameron (n 26) 141).

31 "The aspect of retention of rent which predominates is not its value as a means of enforcing compliance by the landlord, but its value as security for a claim by the tenant for damages . . . It is thus in my view quite fallacious to take this case on the footing that the whole retained rent would be available to the landlord the moment he completes the repairs. Unless the tenant is a philanthropist this will not be so." (*Stobbs & Sons v Hislop* (n 32) 226 (Lord President Cooper)).

32 1948 SC 216, 228.

33 McAllister (n 26) para 4.42.

34 Rankine (n 24) 330–331. In *City of Edinburgh Council v Robbin* 1994 SCLR 43, Sheriff Principal Nicholson indicated that consignation was incompetent in any case in which the

faith. This may be difficult where (as is commonly the case) the tenant does not say that he is exercising the remedy until after eviction proceedings on the ground of rent arrears are raised.

It is suggested that, in order to demonstrate good faith, it would be advisable for the tenant to warn the landlord that he is about to cease paying rent, unless the necessary repairs are effected.[35] Furthermore, "retention" entails that the tenant puts the rent to one side; once the repairs have been effected, his obligation to pay rent, including the withheld rent, revives, subject to any claim that he may have for an abatement over the period during which the repairs were delayed, or damages. If he cannot demonstrate that he has kept the rent for this purpose, the court may form the view that he is not acting in good faith. Also, if a decision is made at the end of the case that there are arrears due to the landlord, this may lead the court to decide that it would be reasonable to grant the order for eviction.[36] Where the tenant has put the rent aside, he will be in a position to advise the court that full payment will be made, from the retained monies, in respect of any period in relation to which the court decides that the landlords were not in breach of their obligations. In that case, it is clearly less likely that the court will decide that it would be reasonable to make the eviction order.[37]

Where the tenant seeks an *abatement* of the rent, he asserts that the rent sought by the landlord is not lawfully due; the landlord is not entitled to be paid rent in respect of a period during which it failed to meet its contractual obligations to the tenant. This may constitute a complete defence to an action on the ground of rent arrears, as the court may ultimately find that the landlord's failure to meet its obligations is sufficiently serious to merit a finding that no rent is payable in respect of the relevant period, and therefore that ground 1 is not established. In that case, the issue of whether it would be reasonable to grant the order would not arise, and the defender would not be prejudiced by his failure actually to retain the rent, if he had not in fact done so. Alternatively, the court may find that only part of the rent is payable, in which case the abatement has the effect of reducing the rent arrears payable to the landlord; then the ground would be established, and the court could proceed to consider whether it would be reasonable to grant the order for eviction. Clearly there will be cases in which it will be appropriate for the defender to combine the withholding of rent with a claim for abatement in respect of the

pursuer did not seek payment of a sum of money as well as an order for eviction, and was in any event an undesirable practice.

35 It is to be assumed that the tenant has already brought the disrepair to the landlord's attention; there is no breach of contract by the landlord until notice is given by the tenant that there is some problem that requires to be remedied.

36 This is in essence what happened in the English case *Haringey London Borough Council v Stewart* (1991) 23 HLR 557, [1991] 2 EGLR 252, in which the court decided that the tenant's claim that the landlords had breached their repairing obligations was ill founded, and subsequently granted an order for eviction on the ground of rent arrears. Mr Stewart was memorably described (by his own counsel) as "like a shorn lamb suddenly exposed to the wind when his counterclaim fell to the ground".

37 It is therefore suggested that the tenant is well advised to open a separate bank account into which the rent money can be deposited, so that a copy of the bank statement, or something equivalent, can be produced to the court. That said, any decision to withhold rent entails a degree of risk, and the tenant contemplating using the remedy should also receive advice to that effect.

period during which it was withheld, presumably due to a delay in the repairs being carried out. If the court finds in his favour, the rent is not lawfully due, and the tenant will be allowed to keep the retained payments.

These principles are well illustrated by *Renfrew District Council v Gray*.[38] In that case, it was a matter of agreement that the condition of the defenders' tenancy had been such as to make it uninhabitable over the period during which the outstanding rent was payable, but they had, nonetheless, continued to reside there. In stating his reasons for granting decree for payment in favour of the pursuers the sheriff accepted that the defenders were entitled to retain rent during such time as the premises were in a state of disrepair. However, he took the view that, after the landlord fulfils his obligations by repairing the premises, the tenant must pay over the rent: where there is no counterclaim by the tenant, the obligation to pay rent is merely postponed but not extinguished by the landlord's failure in his obligations. He observed that the tenants should have rejected the contract and moved out of the subjects. Thereafter they could have claimed damages, but they could not reject the contract and still continue to use the subjects. That decision was reversed on appeal by Sheriff Principal Caplan, who stated:

> "On my reading of the authorities there are three remedies open to a tenant who does not get full or effective possession of the subjects leased. In the first place he can retain the rent. However this measure is to secure performance or secure against the rent such rights as may ultimately be established and does not by itself govern the eventual obligation to pay rent. Secondly, the tenant may be able to claim damages if loss is incurred due to the landlord's breach of contract. Thirdly, the tenant may claim an abatement of the rent on the basis that he has not enjoyed what he contracted to pay rent for. Rights to abatement of rent and damages for loss due to breach of the lease may in many cases be equivalent in practical terms but they are different concepts. It is a prerequisite of damages that there has been a breach of contract and the quantification is based on established loss flowing from the breach. Abatement of rent as illustrated by the authorities is an equitable right and is essentially based on partial failure of consideration. That is to say, if the tenant does not get what he bargained to pay rent for it is inequitable that he should be contractually bound to pay such rent."[39]

A claim for *damages* by the tenant in respect of the landlord's breach of repairing obligations would normally be made in an action raised by the tenant, but

38 1987 SLT (Sh Ct) 70. This was an action for payment of rent arrears only, which was raised by the council after the tenants had been decanted, repairs had been carried out, and the tenants had resumed occupancy. A previous action for eviction on the ground of rent arrears had been unsuccessful.

39 At 72. The sheriff principal placed particular reliance on *Muir v McIntyres* (1887) 14 R 470; *Sivright v Lightbourne* (1890) 17 R 917; *Munro v McGeoghs* (1888) 16 R 92; and *Stewart v Campbell* (1889) 16 R 346. Notably, he also expressed the view that the right to an abatement arises even if the inability to enjoy the subjects is through accident rather than breach of contract by the landlord. An abatement of rent was also successfully sought in *MacLeod v Alexander* 2000 Hous LR 136. In neither of these cases (*Gray* (n 38) and *MacLeod*) was the court referred to the decision of the Inner House in *Stobbs & Son v Hislop* (n 32), which is considered in the discussion of grounds 8, 11 and 12 of sch 5 to the 1988 Act, in Chapter 8. The decision in that case was to the effect that the right to retain rent does not apply to a statutory tenancy under the Rent Acts. In essence, the equitable remedy of retention terminates with the contract. In *Gray*, that reasoning did not apply, because in a secure tenancy, the contract continues until it is terminated under the provisions of the Act. In *MacLeod*, the parties' contract does not appear to have been terminated.

it can also be pled as a counterclaim in an action by the landlord for recovery of possession on the ground of rent arrears. The tenant's damages usually comprise: (a) inconvenience, including perhaps loss of amenity and enjoyment of the subjects suffered by the tenant; and (b) patrimonial loss, normally in respect of personal possessions of the tenant damaged or lost as a result of, for example, dampness or flooding at the subjects.[40]

"From the tenant"

The ground is not established by rent owed by anyone other than the tenant. For example, where the tenancy is transferred to a non-entitled spouse in terms of section 13 of the Matrimonial Homes (Family Protection) (Scotland) Act 1981, the new tenant does not become liable to pay the rent arrears of the former entitled spouse.[41] Likewise it is thought that a tenant who succeeds to a Scottish secure tenancy in terms of the Act does not become liable to pay the rent arrears that were owed by the deceased former tenant.[42]

"Has not been paid"

Entitlement to housing benefit, or the housing element of universal credit, that has not yet been paid to the landlord does not prevent the ground from being established, although it will of course be a factor in the court's consideration of whether to adjourn the case, or whether it is reasonable to grant decree. Once money is paid to the landlord towards rent or arrears, whether in the form of benefit or otherwise, it is submitted that the liability to pay the relative rent is satisfied, even if the money has not yet been credited to the tenant's rent account.[43]

It is perhaps not entirely clear from the wording of the ground whether it could still be established if full payment of the arrears was made at some point during the course of the proceedings. It appears from the relevant English

40 It may also be possible for the tenant, and other persons residing in the tenancy, to make a claim for *solatium* where, for example, it is said that the condition of the subjects has caused or exacerbated some medical condition. A claim by another person residing in the tenancy, not being a tenant, would have to be raised as a separate action (probably under the Occupiers' Liability (Scotland) Act 1960, ss 2 and 3.) However, it could not form part of a counterclaim by the tenant against the landlord, since there is no contractual relationship between that person and the landlord. In Robson and Combe(n 26) para 7-69, there is a useful discussion of claims for solatium, including a list of cases.

41 In *Notting Hill Housing Trust v Jones* [1999] L&TR 397, this was the decision made by the Court of Appeal in relation to the analogous English legislation.

42 Outstanding rent arrears, along with the deceased's other debts, would fall to be paid by the deceased's executors, in the administration of his estate. The Scottish secure tenancy does not form part of that estate, because it either passes by operation of law to a qualified person or terminates, in accordance with the rules under the 2001 Act, s 22 and sch 3. There is no provision in the Act to the effect that liability for rent arrears is also transferred to the qualified person. For the relationship between the right of the qualified person and the rights of the deceased's representatives, see: *Cooper's Executors v Edinburgh District Council* 1991 SC (HL) 5, 15 (Lord Hope) and 21 (Lord Keith).

43 From time to time, large payments are made to housing associations by a local authority in respect of the total entitlement of the housing association's tenants in receipt of housing benefit. The appropriate sums are then credited to the relevant rent accounts. For a variety of reasons, this process may become problematic and therefore subject to delay.

cases that if payment is made before the proceedings are raised, ground 1 would not be established; but where full payment is made during the course of the proceedings, the ground may still be made out.[44] Certainly, there is no equivalent in the 2001 Act to ground 11 under the 1988 Act, that the tenant "has persistently delayed paying rent", which may be established "whether or not any rent is in arrears on the date on which proceedings for possession are begun". In any event, the point is probably academic, because it is unlikely that the court would consider it reasonable to grant an order in terms of ground 1 where there was no outstanding liability for arrears.[45]

Ground 1 (part 2): other breach of the tenancy agreement

The possibility of raising proceedings on the basis of a breach of contract is of some importance, because it enables landlords, in effect, to supplement the statutory grounds for recovery of possession by imposing obligations on the tenant under the contract, the breach of which establishes ground 1. The landlords may also restate the statutory grounds with certain alterations, which would make the ground easier to establish.

For the purposes of ground 1 part 2, contractual terms may be usefully categorised as follows:

- express terms of the contract that are related to the existing grounds;
- express terms of the contract that are not related to the existing grounds;
- terms implied in the contract by the Act, and at common law.

In any case where breach of the express terms of the tenancy is alleged, the tenant's adviser should obtain a copy of the agreement so as to check the clause relied upon by the landlord, bearing in mind that the original tenancy agreement may have been renewed. Any breach of the old agreement cannot establish the ground, though it may be relevant to the issue of whether it would be reasonable to grant an eviction order where the conduct in question has continued under the new agreement. The relevant agreement is the last one entered into by the tenant, subject to the procedure for variation in terms of section 26 of the Act; a variation cannot be achieved simply by sending the tenant a new lease, even if, after receiving it, he remains in occupation and continues to pay the rent.[46] The obligation that is relied upon must arise from an express or implied term of the tenancy agreement, and not from some collateral agreement.[47]

44 *Bird v Hildage* [1948] 1 KB 91; *Dellenty v Pellow* [1951] 2 KB 858; *Haringey London Borough Council v Stewart* (1991) (n 36).

45 *Dellenty v Pellow* (n 44); *Haringey LBC v Stewart* (n 36); *Moray District Council v Lyon* 1992 GWD 14-824; June 1992 SCOLAG Journal 91, in which the tenant had a history of repeatedly building up the arrears before paying them off with a lump-sum payment, just before the court was due to consider whether an eviction order should be granted. Notwithstanding this background, the sheriff stated: "I did not consider it reasonable to make an order with such drastic consequences when the tenant is not currently in default." Contrast this with *GHA v Li* 2010 Hous LR 31 (at [33]) in which the defender's record of payment was so bad that the sheriff would have been minded to grant decree even if the arrears had been cleared before the proof.

46 *Palmer v Sandwell Metropolitan Borough Council* (1988) 20 HLR 74.

47 Such as the separate renting of a garage, or an undertaking by the tenant to pay arrears due under another tenancy: *Notting Hill Housing Trust v Jones* (n 41).

The term relied upon by the landlord must also be "fair" for the purposes of the Consumer Rights Act 2015.[48] If it is unfair, the tenant may object to it being relied upon, in eviction proceedings.

Express terms of contract related to existing grounds

As indicated above, where the lease includes an obligation to pay service charges, heating payments and so on, non-payment will establish ground 1, even though those payments are not "rent".[49]

It is not uncommon for landlords in the social rented sector to have a standard form tenancy agreement that imposes on the tenant an obligation to desist from various forms of criminal activity at, or in the vicinity of, the tenancy subjects, particularly drug dealing.[50] This raises the possibility that an action could be initiated under ground 1 where the authority has evidence that such activity has occurred, even though it did not lead to a conviction, such as to found an action on ground 2. It is also common for the contract to impose on the tenant an obligation to desist from antisocial behaviour. This means that antisocial behaviour may lead to an action under ground 1 and ground 7 together. However, in order to establish ground 7, the landlord must satisfy the court that "it is not reasonable in all the circumstances that the landlord should be required to make other accommodation available to the tenant". This would not be a requirement in relation to an action under ground 1, because the landlord would only have to show that antisocial behaviour had occurred in breach of the tenancy agreement. Therefore, it would appear that it may be possible for the landlord to circumvent the requirement to satisfy the court that it would not be reasonable to make other accommodation available to the tenant by raising the action under ground 1 in addition to, or instead of, ground 7.[51]

48 See Chapter 3, p 73. The Court of Appeal's decision in *R (Khatun and others) v Newham London Borough Council* [2005] QB 37, [2004] HLR 29 confirmed that the legislation in relation to unfair contract terms (derived from EU law) applies to tenancy contracts, including lets granted by public authorities. A potential application of the 2015 Act is described at note 51 below.

49 Unless parties expressly agree that these payments are deemed to be "rent" and recoverable as such. See p 125. If the payments in arrears are not "rent", the pre-action requirements under s 14A of the 2001 Act do not apply.

50 E.g. the Scottish Executive's Model Scottish Secure Tenancy Agreement contains, at cl 3.3, a prohibition against, *inter alia*, using or selling unlawful drugs, using or carrying offensive weapons, and harassing or assaulting any person in the house, or neighbourhood, for whatever reason.

51 There is, however, a possible objection. One may conceive of the statutory grounds as a protection for the tenant, in that he may be evicted only if the circumstances set out in those grounds are established. For example, he cannot be evicted on the grounds of antisocial behaviour unless alternative accommodation is provided (ground 8), or if the landlord satisfies the court that it is not reasonable to make such accommodation available (ground 7). Can clauses of the type described be objected to on the basis that they represent an attempt to contract out of the protection afforded to the tenant under the Act? It is submitted that this would be a statable argument. It is notable that the Competition and Markets Authority ("CMA") Unfair Contract Terms Guidance states, at para 5.35.1: "Any contract wording which could have the effect of depriving consumers of protection normally afforded to them under the law is liable to be considered unfair as well as being potentially blacklisted under Part 1 of the Act."

Express terms of contract not related to existing grounds

Scottish secure tenancy contracts invariably contain obligations in relation to the use of the subjects, such as, in particular, the keeping of pets, and the unauthorised erection of structures such as sheds and pigeon huts. In many instances the breach may be regarded as less serious by the landlords and to that extent, they may be more amenable to settlement.[52]

In order to establish ground 1, the obligation that has been breached must be an obligation *of* the *tenancy*. Not everything written in a lease agreement will create such an obligation. It must be binding on the tenant as a tenant, and not merely something binding on him as an individual. To give an example,[53] a clause to the effect that the tenant "will be in breach of the lease if he is convicted of any offence related to or constituted in whole or in part by racial harassment" may be unenforceable in terms of the tenancy because it involves no connection between the prohibited conduct and the occupation of the house.[54]

Terms implied in the contract by the Act and at common law

Section 11(7) of the 2001 Act provides that it is a term of every Scottish secure tenancy that the tenant complies with paragraphs (c) and (d) of section 11(1),[55] which outline two of the prerequisites for the tenancy being a Scottish secure tenancy at the outset.[56]

Sections 32 and 33 of the Act provide that it is a term of the tenancy that the tenant may assign, sub-let, exchange or otherwise give to another person possession of the house or any part of it or take in a lodger only with the consent in writing of the landlord.[57] Unauthorised sub-lets and assignations therefore constitute a breach of a condition of the tenancy, which may found an action under ground 1.

Various obligations upon the tenant are implied at common law,[58] the breach of which would also establish ground 1.

52 Thus, it is to be presumed that in many cases the landlord will agree to drop the case if the tenant desists from the breach by, e.g., taking his shed down again, although one might expect that an order for expenses would be sought.

53 Taken from Collins and O'Carroll, *Anti-Social Behaviour and Housing: The Law*.

54 Other examples: an obligation to participate in counselling, treatment or resettlement programmes: *Paddington Churches Housing Association v Boateng* January 1999 Legal Action 27; and an obligation to pay outstanding debts to the landlord, such as arrears from a previous tenancy.

55 Section 11(1)(c): the tenant is an individual and the house is the tenant's only or principal home; s 11(1)(d) where the landlord is an RSL that is a co-operative housing association and the tenant is a member of the association.

56 This means, for example, that where the tenancy ceases to be the tenant's only or principal home, he is in breach of the tenancy conditions, and may therefore be subject to an action under ground 1. This stipulation was added by the 2001 Act, and appears to overlap to some extent with ground 5. The phrase "only or principal home" is discussed in Chapter 1.

57 Sub-lets are further discussed in Chapter 12.

58 Such as the obligation to take reasonable care in the use and management of the subjects. The various implied obligations are discussed in Paton and Cameron (n 26) ch IX and Rennie and others (n 26) ch 14.

Ground 2: convicted of offence

"2. The tenant (or any one of joint tenants), a person residing or lodging in the house with, or subtenant of, the tenant, or a person visiting the house has been convicted of–
(a) using the house or allowing it to be used for immoral or illegal purposes, or
(b) an offence punishable by imprisonment committed in, or in the locality of, the house."

This ground may be seen as an augmentation of the equivalent ground under the Rent Acts, to which has been added clause (b) and the words "or a person visiting the house".

The first and obvious point is that ground 2 requires a conviction.[59] Mere arrest is not sufficient. Also clear is that the tenant effectively bears the responsibility for acts committed by other persons. The effect of the ground is analogous to strict liability: it may be satisfied where the tenant was not aware that an offence was being committed, or in cases in which he would have been powerless to prevent the conduct in question, even if he had been aware of it.[60]

As regards offences by persons other than the tenant, it is submitted that the references to "residing", "lodging" or "visiting" must be capable of referring to the state of affairs that existed at the time when the offence was committed, such that continuing residence, lodging or visiting, at the time of the conviction, or at the time when the court determines the matter, is not necessary to establish the ground. If it were otherwise, it would be very easy for the ground to be avoided, by the simple expedient of the offending person moving out of the subjects until after the proceedings had been determined. That would tend to defeat the purpose of the legislation. Also, the fact that the ground is capable of being established by the conduct of a "visitor" to the subjects strongly indicates that the relevant date may be the date of commission of the offence. The status of "visitor" is transient. There is no reason to expect that a person visiting on the date of the offence would still be visiting at some later date.[61] Notably, in the case of *Raglan Housing Association v Fairclough*[62] the ground was held to be established in respect of conduct that had taken place before the tenancy commenced.[63]

59 The Scottish Government's "Streamlined Eviction Process – Criminal or Antisocial Behaviour Statutory Guidance for Social Landlords" (paras 4.3–4.6) suggests that landlords consider obtaining an extract conviction from the relevant court and lodging it as a production when proceedings are raised, but it notes that an extract may not be available, until any appeal proceedings are determined. This advice is equally applicable to ground 2 cases in which the new procedure is not being used. The Guidance is considered at p 165.

60 *Portsmouth City Council v Bryant* (2000) 32 HLR 906; though in such a case the tenant might rely on these circumstances in any question as to whether it would be reasonable to grant the order.

61 There have been cases in which the court has granted decree under ground 2, where the offending person was no longer resident in the subjects. See, e.g.: *Glasgow City Council v McAlinden* 2001 Hous LR 110; *East Ayrshire Council v Tait* 1999 SCLR 566. The use of the present tense in legislative provisions may indicate that the relevant time is not the point at which the court is considering the matter, but when the relevant action was initiated or took place: *Armour v Anderson* 1994 SLT 1127; *Re M* [1994] 2 AC 424; Bennion, *Statutory Interpretation* (7th edn) section 22.1, 528. This would appear to be the appropriate interpretation in respect of grounds 2 and 7.

62 [2008] HLR 21.

63 The defendant had surrendered a tenancy with Raglan, and was granted another tenancy

The addition of the words "or a person visiting the house" to the ground also avoids the necessity of showing that the convicted person was actually residing or lodging with the tenant; it is presumably sufficient that he was present at the subjects at the apparent invitation of the tenant. It is suggested that the term "visiting" entails that the person in question has been invited or permitted by the tenant to be at the subjects. In cases under grounds 2 and 7, this issue may not be straightforward.

There are cases in which the tenant operates an "open house", exercising no real control over the persons who are permitted entry, or where people are coming and going while the tenant is incapable or insensible through drink or drugs. It is suggested that such persons can be categorised as visitors, in so far as the tenant, by his conduct, has effectively acquiesced in their presence at the subjects. Also common are instances in which the tenant tries to address the problem by refusing entry to persons who have caused trouble in the past, who then respond by creating a disturbance outside. In that situation, it is suggested that the persons in question are not visitors: they have been refused permission to visit, and therefore such incidents do not establish ground 2 or ground 7.

The first leg of ground 2 ("using the house or allowing it to be used for immoral or illegal purposes") is now of much less importance given the second leg ("an offence punishable by imprisonment committed in, or in the locality of, the house"). Under the first leg, the old Rent Acts ground, it is necessary for the landlord to show that the conviction involves the *use* of the premises for some illegal or immoral purpose, i.e. "putting the house to an improper use to carry out an unlawful purpose",[64] such as keeping stolen goods,[65] having unlawful carnal knowledge of young girls thereon,[66] and so on. Ground 2(a) is not established if the premises have nothing to do with the offence beyond being merely the scene of its commission.[67] Thus it is apparent that the vast majority of convictions that are sufficiently serious to prompt an action for eviction to be raised by the landlords will be covered by part (b) of the ground, though they may not be covered by part (a).[68]

It is submitted that the words "offence punishable by imprisonment" mean all offences, with the exception of those statutory offences in respect of which a sentence of imprisonment is a disposal that is not available to the court in terms of the relevant statute.[69] In practice, actions under ground 2 invariably involve quite serious offences, particularly those under the Misuse of Drugs Act 1971, all of which are punishable by imprisonment.

The word "locality" is not defined in the Act, but apparently has a wider scope than "vicinity", the term that was used, for example, in the "nuisance"

in the same street. Later, he was convicted of a number of offences of possessing indecent photographs of children, which were committed at his previous tenancy. Note that the judges disagreed on the question of whether the same result would have followed if both the offence *and* the conviction had preceded the granting of the tenancy.

64 *Waller & Son Ltd v Thomas* [1921] 1 KB 541, 550 (Lush J).

65 *S Schneiders & Sons Ltd v Abrahams* [1925] 1 KB 301; *Abrahams v Wilson* [1971] 2 QB 88.

66 *A and B v C* 1930 SLT (Sh Ct) 30.

67 *S Schneiders & Sons Ltd v Abrahams* (n 65) and *Abrahams v Wilson* (n 65).

68 E.g. an assault by the tenant on one of the neighbours at the tenancy subjects would be covered by (b), but not by (a).

69 I.e. the ground does not require that a sentence of imprisonment was actually imposed.

statutory grounds in previous legislation. On this point, it is notable that a circular issued by the Department of the Environment in relation to the augmentation of ground 2 stated that it "may be particularly useful for a local authority which is concerned about drug dealing where the trafficking is taking place in the common parts of the estate rather than a house or flat".[70] Any issue as to whether the offence was committed within the "locality" of the subjects will be resolved as a question of fact on all the evidence in the case.[71]

As will be described below, the 2014 Act introduces a "streamlined eviction process" where ground 2 is established by conviction within the previous twelve months. Should the landlord choose to use that process, it is relieved of the burden of showing that it would be reasonable to grant the order.

Grounds 3 and 4: condition of premises and furniture

Grounds 3 and 4 relate to the condition of the tenancy subjects and any included furniture. They are as follows:

> "3. (1) The condition of the house or of any of the common parts has deteriorated owing to acts of waste by, or the neglect or default of, the tenant (or any one of joint tenants) or any person residing or lodging with, or any subtenant of, the tenant; and in the case of acts of waste by, or the neglect or default of, a person residing or lodging with, or subtenant of, a tenant, the tenant has not, before the making of the order in question, taken such steps as the tenant ought reasonably to have taken for the removal of that person.
>
> (2) In sub-paragraph (1), 'the common parts' means any part of a building containing the house and any other premises which the tenant is entitled under the terms of the tenancy to use in common with the occupiers of other houses.
>
> 4. The condition of any furniture provided for use under the tenancy, or for use in any of the common parts (within the meaning given in paragraph 3(2)), has deteriorated owing to ill-treatment by the tenant (or any one of joint tenants) or any person residing or lodging with, or any subtenant of, the tenant; and in the case of ill-treatment by a person residing or lodging with, or subtenant of, a tenant, the tenant has not, before the making of the order in question, taken such steps as the tenant ought reasonably to have taken for the removal of that person."

Again, both of these grounds were derived from grounds under the Rent Acts. However, they have not been subject to the changes that have been made to ground 2. In particular, there is no reference to persons visiting the house and, in addition, the court must consider whether the tenant has taken such steps as he ought reasonably to have taken for the removal of the person causing the damage.[72]

To establish that the condition of the house or common parts has deteriorated it is necessary to show that there has been at least some physical damage

70 DofE Circ 2/97 para 28(iii).

71 *Manchester City Council v Lawler* (1999) 31 HLR 119. In *Knowsley Housing Trust v Prescott* [2009] L&TR 24, the ground was established where there was no suggestion that there had been any drug-related activity at the tenancy property, but the tenant had been involved in the operation of a "drugs factory" based in a house about half a mile away.

72 Under the older Rent Acts (pre-1968) this additional requirement was applied to the "nuisance" and "using for illegal and immoral conduct" grounds.

to the structure or fabric of the building. The fact that the tenant has a lack of housekeeping skills will be insufficient if there is no evidence of any actual deterioration.[73] The onus will be on the tenant to show, if he can, that the deterioration or dilapidation was due to "fair wear and tear" and nothing else.[74] There must be a causal connection between the deterioration and the waste, neglect or ill treatment.[75]

It is submitted that the word "default" in this context means a failure to do something that the tenant ought to have done. There is an implied obligation on the part of the tenant to use reasonable care in his management of the subjects. For that reason, he is liable to make good any damage attributable to his failure to do so.[76] It is also suggested that the tenant's implied obligation to use reasonable care in his management of the subjects would entail bringing to the attention of the landlord any disrepair or defect in the subjects that would be liable to cause a deterioration in its condition. To do so is clearly in the interests of both the tenant and the landlord. It enables the landlord to take steps to protect and preserve its property, and to in doing so to improve the tenant's living conditions.

Examples of conduct that established ground 3 (or its equivalent in older legislation) are: causing the floor of the house to sag by using a room for storing heavy bales of cloth,[77] allowing a substantial deterioration in the house to be caused by damp due to the tenant's failure to occupy the house during the winter,[78] doing nothing to prevent the garden from becoming overgrown,[79] Merely permitting the premises to become dirty, without causing them to deteriorate, is not sufficient.[80]

As regards ground 4, the question of what constitutes "furniture" has been considered by the English courts. It has been held that the word has a statutory meaning regardless of the terms of the lease and does not include items so fixed to the fabric of the building that appreciable damage would be caused in removing them.[81] It has, however, been held to include fitted cupboards or

73 *MacIver v Struthers* 1924 SLT (Sh Ct) 15.

74 *Brown v Davies* [1958] 1 QB 117(CA), 127 (Lord Evershed MR).

75 *MacIver v Struthers* (n 73).

76 Paton and Cameron (n 26) 138. Erskine states that the tenant is "bound to use a reasonable degree of diligence in preserving [the subjects] from harm" (Erskine, II, vi, 43). At p 50 of *Scottish Law of Leases* (3rd edn), McAllister indicates: "Irrespective of whether repairs are the landlord's or the tenant's responsibility under a lease, the tenant will be liable for damage caused by his own negligence." Often cited in this context is *Mickel v M'Coard* 1913 SC 896; 1913 SLT 463, in which it was held that the tenant of a villa, who left it unoccupied for a month in winter without having either turned off the water and emptied the cisterns or informed the landlord of her intended absence, was liable to the landlord for damage caused by the bursting of the water pipes owing to frost.

77 *Thomson v Ford* (1945) 62 Sh Ct Rep 60.

78 *Robertson v Wilson* 1922 SLT (Sh Ct) 21.

79 *Holloway v Povey* (1984) 15 HLR 104.

80 *MacIver v Struthers* (n 75). For a more recent example of an action based on ground 3, see *Paragon Housing Association v Manclark* 2013 Hous LR 28. In that case, the floorboards and internal doors were damaged, windows had been smashed and boarded up and the garden was contaminated with rubbish. The sheriff granted decree, notwithstanding the defender's history of mental illness. There was no suggestion of a defence under ss 15 and 35 of the Equality Act 2010 (see Chapter 11). However, in the circumstances, the sheriff is likely to have been satisfied that it was proportionate to grant the order.

81 *Palser v Grinling, Property Holding Co Ltd v Mischeff* [1948] AC 291 (HL).

wardrobes,[82] crockery and kitchen utensils,[83] linoleum[84] and the cooker,[85] but not water heaters or panel fires.[86]

Ground 5: absence from premises

"The tenant and–

(a) the tenant's spouse or civil partner, or

(b) any person with whom the tenant has, for a period of at least 6 months immediately prior to the commencement of the period referred to below, been living in the house as husband and wife or in a relationship which has the characteristics of the relationship between civil partners, have been absent from the house without reasonable cause for a continuous period exceeding 6 months or have ceased to occupy the house as their principal home."

This ground would probably be used only where there is still some person in occupation, such as an unauthorised sub-tenant. If the house is not occupied by anyone, the landlord can use the abandonment procedure in sections 17 and 18 of the Act.[87]

Ground 5 may be established in one of two ways: (a) where the tenant (and partner/spouse) have "been absent from the house without reasonable cause for a continuous period exceeding 6 months"; or (b) have "ceased to occupy the house as their principal home".

The terms "occupy" and "principal home" are discussed in Chapter 1. In summary: the term "occupy" does not necessarily imply physical presence, and occupation may be established by there being a *corpus possessionis* (that is, physical signs of occupation) together with an *animus revertendi* (that is, an intention to return that could be established by some visible state of affairs).[88]

However, the phrase "absent from the house" does appear to entail a lack of physical presence, although in order to establish the ground that absence must be for a continuous period of six months, and "without reasonable cause". It is suggested that the ground will be made out where the tenant/spouse/civil partner has moved back into the tenancy by the time that the case is determined, although in that situation the court may not find it reasonable to grant the order.

In *Fife Council v Grenville*,[89] the tenant had been sentenced to a period of imprisonment in March 2001, and was due to be released in August 2001. In the meantime, the subjects had been occupied by his father, who was paying the rent on his behalf. In finding that the ground had been established, the sheriff took the view that although imprisonment was a "cause" for absence, it was not a reasonable cause.[90]

82 *Gray v Fidler* [1943] KB 694.
83 *Maddox Properties v Klass* [1946] 1 All ER 487.
84 *Wilkes v Goodwin* [1923] 2 KB 86.
85 *New London Properties v Barabas* [1945] EGD 256; *Roppel v Bennett* [1949] 1 KB 115.
86 *Blackpool Rent Tribunal, ex p Ashton* [1948] 2 KB 277. Although see *R v Hampstead and St Pancras Furnished Houses Rent Tribunal, ex p Ascot Lodge Ltd* [1947] KB 973.
87 This is described in Chapter 4.
88 *Beggs v Kilmarnock and Loudoun District Council* 1995 SC 333, 1996 SLT 461.
89 2003 Hous LR 38.
90 An action based on ground 5 was also successful in *East Lothian Council v Duffy* 2012 SLT (Sh Ct) 113, 2012 Hous LR 73. In that case the tenants had sub-let, and had no intention of

Ground 6: misrepresentation

Ground 6 is:

> The tenant is the person, or one of the persons, to whom the tenancy was granted and the landlord was induced to grant the tenancy by a false statement made knowingly or recklessly by the tenant.

This ground is intended to deal with a particular situation: where the landlord finds that the tenant, when applying to the landlords for housing, misrepresented his circumstances, with the result that he achieved a more favourable position in respect of his application[91] than would otherwise have been the case. In practice, this is often a misrepresentation as to the applicant's housing position, involving a failure to disclose that he owns a home, or has an existing tenancy. However, the ground could also be established by, for example, a misrepresentation that the applicant had some medical condition, with a view to achieving higher priority in terms of the landlord's allocation policy.[92]

Where a person completes an application form for housing on the basis that he will inform the council of any changes in his circumstances that might affect his need for housing, the subsequent failure to disclose new information may amount to a false statement that induces the grant of the tenancy.[93]

The landlord must prove not only a false statement, but also that the statement induced it to grant the tenancy. In *Waltham Forest London Borough Council v Roberts*,[94] the Court of Appeal held that the correct approach was to ask whether the misstatement was material to the council's discharge of its public functions. Once this materiality was established, it was a "fair inference" of fact that the decision maker had been influenced by it, and thereby induced to grant the tenancy. This was confirmed in *Windsor & District Housing Association v Hewitt*,[95] in which the tenant had applied for a transfer from a one-bedroomed property, stating in her application that she needed two bedrooms so that her son, who was her carer, could live with her. She was offered a two-bedroomed flat, which she subsequently occupied on her own. In deciding in favour of the landlords, the court held that the tenant should be regarded as having made a statement of an existing and continuing intention, rather than a mere prediction.[96]

returning. The action was defended by the sub-tenants as qualifying occupiers under s 14 of the Act.

91 E.g. being accorded a higher degree of priority, or a more favourable position on the waiting list.

92 The obtaining of tenancies by alleged deception appears to be much more common in England; there are numerous reported cases on the equivalent ground in the Housing Act 1985 (ground 5 of sch 2). In November 2009, the Department for Communities and Local Government published "*Tackling unlawful subletting and occupancy: Good practice guidance for social landlords*". This includes advice on evidence gathering and case preparation for cases under this ground.

93 *North Herts District Council v Carthy* [2003] EWCA Civ 20. Note also that a misrepresentation in an earlier application form may be considered material to the grant of a later tenancy. See *Oshin v Greenwich RBC* [2020] EWCA Civ 388.

94 [2005] HLR 2.

95 [2011] HLR 39: another decision of the Court of Appeal.

96 Note, however, that the court appeared to leave open the possibility of a defence to the effect: "at the point when I entered into the tenancy agreement, I did not remember the statement that I had previously made, and did not appreciate that it was no longer true".

It appears that, in order to establish the ground, the false statements in question must have been made by the tenant, rather than any other person.[97]

Ground 7:[98] antisocial behaviour

"(1) The tenant (or any one of joint tenants), a person residing or lodging in the house with, or any subtenant of, the tenant, or a person visiting the house has–
(a) acted in an anti-social manner in relation to a person residing in, visiting or otherwise engaged in lawful activity in the locality, or
(b) pursued a course of conduct amounting to harassment of such a person, or a course of conduct which is otherwise anti-social conduct in relation to such a person,
and it is not reasonable in all the circumstances that the landlord should be required to make other accommodation available to the tenant.
(2) In sub-paragraph (1)–
'anti-social', in relation to an action or course of conduct, means causing or likely to cause alarm, distress, nuisance or annoyance,
'conduct' includes speech, and a course of conduct must involve conduct on at least two occasions,
'harassment' is to be construed in accordance with section 8 of the Protection from Harassment Act 1997 (c 40)."

The opening words of this ground ("The tenant" to "visiting the house"), and the term "locality", are discussed in relation to ground 2.

Ground 7 is the latest incarnation of the statutory ground that was originally stated as: "The tenant has been guilty of conduct which is a nuisance or annoyance to adjoining occupiers." Over time, the net has been cast wider by extending the ground to: (a) conduct on the part of persons other than the tenant, (b) a wider class of potential victims, from adjoining occupiers to persons not only residing in the locality,[99] but who might happen to be in the locality, (c) conduct, including "speech", which causes alarm or distress, as well as conduct which causes nuisance or annoyance, and further harassment,[100] and (d) situations in which the conduct in question "is likely to cause" the requisite result in the victim. This final change is of particular significance, because it means that the landlord does not need to lead evidence from persons who can speak to the fact that they were alarmed, distressed, annoyed or caused nuisance by the conduct. It may, for example, rely entirely on the evidence of police officers, or its own employees, as to the nature of

97 This is to be contrasted with the position under the equivalent ground 5 of sch 2 to the Housing Act 1985, in terms of which the ground may be established if the false statements were made by "a person acting at the tenant's instigation". This provision was considered by the Court of Appeal in *Merton London Borough Council v Richards* [2005] HLR 44, a case in which the tenant had obtained a tenancy due to certain false statements made by her mother, who was one of the council's housing officers.

98 For a more detailed and comprehensive analysis of antisocial behaviour in the field of housing law, see Collins and O'Carroll (n 53) and the Scottish Executive Central Research Unit's Paper "The Use of Civil Remedies for Neighbour Nuisance in Scotland" (2000), which is available online.

99 As opposed to the "vicinity", a more restricted term that was used in the older legislation.

100 That said, it is difficult to see why harassment is included as a separate mode of establishing the ground, as any conduct that establishes ground 7(b) would also establish ground 7(a). "Harassment of a person" is not defined by the Protection from Harassment Act 1997, s 8; s 8(3) simply states that it "includes causing the person alarm or distress".

the conduct, and invite the court to draw the inference that such conduct would be likely to cause the required effect on anyone within the wide class of potential victims. There seems to be no reason why the ground could not be established purely by hearsay evidence, provided that the sheriff is prepared to give it sufficient weight.[101]

These changes have several important consequences. First, the threshold is now set so low that, in practice, the landlord will almost always be able to establish the ground.[102] Secondly, landlords can rely on the evidence of "professional witnesses", being persons who are employed by the landlords to be on call, in response to telephone complaints by neighbours of the tenant, to attend the subjects in order to witness the conduct. It is not the role of these employees to take any direct action to stop the conduct from continuing by, for example, banging on the tenant's door and asking him to desist. Their job is to witness the conduct in order to increase the body of evidence against the tenant, and so that the neighbours making complaints can remain anonymous, and need not be required to attend court to give evidence.[103] Thirdly, the scope of the ground and the process of evidence gathering has the effect that there may be a very large number of incidents by the time that the summons is prepared. This is in turn liable to result in a lengthy proof.[104]

It must be emphasised that in order for ground 7 to be established, the court must be satisfied that it is not reasonable in all the circumstances that the landlord should be required to make other accommodation available to the tenant.[105]

As is discussed in Chapter 6, amendments made to section 35 of the 2001 Act by the 2014 Act have the effect that the landlord will be able to convert the tenancy to a short Scottish secure tenancy ("SSST"), under section 35(2)(b), in circumstances that are the same as those set out in ground 7. This change

101 In England there is now a well-established practice, approved by the Court of Appeal, of admitting anonymous hearsay evidence in cases of this type: *Moat Housing Group-South Ltd v Harris* [2006] QB 606; *Solon South West Housing Association Ltd v James* [2005] HLR 24; and *Boyd v Incommunities Ltd* [2013] HLR 44.

102 Subject to satisfying the court that it is not reasonable in all the circumstances that the landlord should be required to make other accommodation available to the tenant.

103 However, evidence given by long-suffering neighbours might be expected to have a greater impact, and is therefore likely to assist the pursuers in persuading the court that it would be reasonable to grant the order for eviction. Accordingly, one may see evidence given by a combination of police officers, the landlords' employees and neighbours.

104 In the author's experience, the longest statement of claim ran to 180 paragraphs. A number of ground 7 proofs have run to several weeks, spread over a lengthy period. Although it is understandable that the landlords might wish to afford themselves the best chance of success by showing a large volume of incidents, this may conflict with the need to have the proceedings determined as quickly as possible.

105 Reference is made in particular to the comments of Sheriff Principal Bowen in *City of Glasgow Council v McAlinden* (n 61) at 113: "It appears clear to me that where a situation of nuisance or annoyance arises a landlord must make a decision as to whether to require the tenant to move to other accommodation [i.e. to proceed under ground 8, rather than ground 7]. If it is decided not to make that requirement but to proceed to seek recovery of possession that particular decision becomes the subject of scrutiny before ground 7 can be established. . . . In the present case it does not appear to have been addressed in evidence and consequently in the sheriff's findings as a distinct issue and as a consequence in my opinion ground 7 should not have been held to be established." The failure to meet this requirement also proved fatal to the pursuers' case in *City of Glasgow District Council v Brown* 1988 SCLR 433.

may reduce the number of actions raised under ground 7. Before raising such an action, the landlord would usually wait until there was enough evidence of antisocial behaviour to afford a reasonable prospect of success in proceedings that might be lengthy and expensive. Now, the landlord may convert the tenancy at an earlier stage, and thereafter raise proceedings under section 36. The drawback with conversion is that, under the changes made by the 2014 Act, the SSST thereby created is for a period of twelve months. The delay created by conversion may be inappropriate, where the behaviour in question is considered so extreme as to warrant proceedings being raised as soon as possible.

ADDITIONAL REQUIREMENT OF REASONABLENESS: s 16(2)(a)(ii)

The delegation to the court of the function of deciding whether it would be "reasonable" to grant an order for eviction was a feature of the earliest statutes providing for security of tenure, and provisions of this type have featured in all of the subsequent statutory schemes. In respect of Scottish secure tenancies, the additional requirement to satisfy the court that the eviction order would be reasonable is restated in section 16(2)(a)(ii), in relation to grounds 1–7 of schedule 2.[106] However, the 2001 Act contained a significant innovation in relation to that requirement: section 16(3) provides that the court is to have regard, in particular, to four matters in exercising its judgment as to whether it would be reasonable to grant the order.

Analysis of the "reasonableness" requirement is divided into the following sections:

(1) General outline of the additional requirement of reasonableness.
(2) The statutory provisions: section 16(3) of the 2001 Act.
(3) Other considerations in relation to the "reasonableness" test.
(4) Reasonableness in relation to particular grounds.

(1) General outline of additional requirement of reasonableness

The leading Scottish authority is still *Barclay v Hannah*.[107] The importance of this case is such that it is worth considering in detail.

The landlord, Mrs Barclay, brought an action against her tenant, Mr Hannah, for recovery of possession of a dwellinghouse to which the Rent and Mortgage Interest Restrictions (Amendment) Act 1933 applied, section 3(1) of which stated: "No order or judgment for the recovery of possession of any dwelling-house . . . shall be made or given unless the court considers it reasonable to make such an order".

Mrs Barclay sought an order under the ground specified in paragraph (g) of the first schedule to the Act: "The dwelling-house is reasonably required by the landlord for occupation as a residence for some person engaged in . . . the whole-time employment of some tenant from him . . . and . . . the court is satisfied by a certificate . . . of the Department of Agriculture for Scotland

106 Subject to the new procedure in relation to ground 2 cases, which is discussed below.
107 1947 SC 245, 1947 SLT 235.

that the person for whose occupation the dwelling-house is required by the landlord is, or is to be, employed on work necessary for the proper working of an agricultural holding." She had produced a certificate in those terms.

The defender averred that it would not be reasonable for the court to grant decree of ejection. The house had eight apartments, and he had two sons, four daughters and the husband of one of the daughters residing with him. Another son was due to be demobilised shortly and would come to live in the house. He had been unable to obtain other suitable accommodation.

The sheriff-substitute found those defences to be irrelevant, and granted decree in favour of the pursuer; the sheriff, on appeal, adhered to that interlocutor. They appear to have based their decision on the view that the certificate provided by the Department of Agriculture was conclusive of the matter. The defender appealed to the Inner House. His appeal was successful. Lord President Cooper said:

> "The Act of 1933 . . . section 3, begins with a primary prohibition addressed to the Court to the effect that no order for the recovery of possession shall be made unless the Court considers it reasonable to make such an order. Although couched in negative form, that is an imperative direction to the Court to exercise a judicial function on the question of reasonableness, and I can find nothing in what follows to take that duty away from the Court."[108]

Lord Moncrieff said:

> "It is expressly enacted in . . . the Act of 1933 . . . that an order for the ejection of a tenant such as is here applied for is not to be made unless the Court considers it reasonable to make such an order. That enactment thus charges the Court with a judicial duty to consider the whole of the circumstances in which the application is made. The power of the Court to pronounce any such order is thus only a discretionary, and is moreover only a limited, power."[109]

It followed from these considerations that the case had to be remitted back to the sheriff-substitute. The Lord President's judgment ended thus:

> "In these circumstances, I consider that the Sheriff's judgment cannot stand, and that the case must go back to the Court below for proof of the averments bearing upon the reasonableness of making the order, unless the parties, who do not seem to be very far apart, are able to agree on a minute of admission and renunciation of probation."[110]

It is submitted that two important points follow from this case.

First, the assertion that it would not be reasonable to grant the order, supported by averments as to the basis for that assertion, constitutes a relevant defence to any action for recovery of possession in relation to which the court must be satisfied, in terms of a statutory provision, that it would be reasonable to grant the order.

Secondly, as the court has a duty, in such cases, to consider the whole of the circumstances in which the application is made, it follows that anything that might dispose the court to grant decree or decline to grant decree will be

108 At 248.
109 At 249.
110 ibid.

relevant. This is confirmed by one of the leading English cases, *Cumming v Danson*, in which Lord Greene MR said, in an oft-quoted passage:

> "[I]n considering reasonableness . . . it is, in my opinion, perfectly clear that the duty of the Judge is to take into account all relevant circumstances as they exist at the date of the hearing. That he must do in what I venture to call a broad commonsense way as a man of the world, and come to his conclusion giving such weight as he thinks right to the various factors in the situation. Some factors may have little or no weight, others may be decisive, but it is quite wrong for him to exclude from his consideration matters which he ought to take into account."[111]

It has been said that "a time inevitably comes when all that the judge can say is 'I have weighed the pros and cons which I have stated and I now give judgment for so and so . . .' The important thing is that it is of the essence of the judicial process that pros and cons should be first weighed."[112]

The judicial duty to determine whether an eviction order would be reasonable applies in all cases, even in those in which the tenant consents to decree. In several cases, the courts in England have held that a decree granted by way of a consent order is open to challenge, if the court has not satisfied itself that all the statutory requirements have been met.[113]

In the paragraphs that follow, some general guidance is given as to the issues that might be relevant for the court in coming to a decision, and the various arguments that are often made. All that said, however, the reader will appreciate that although many cases are similar, no two cases are identical. The court's discretion is wide, and the extent to which any argument is persuasive will depend on the particular circumstances of each case.

(2) The statutory provisions: 2001 Act, s 16(3)

As regards the circumstances that are to be taken into account, it is now possible, following the changes made by the 2001 Act, to make a distinction between the matters outlined in section 16(3) and the other factors that have been raised in the various cases, which are naturally very diverse. Section 16(3) provides:

> "For the purposes of subsection (2)(a)(ii) the court is to have regard, in particular, to–
>
> (a) the nature, frequency and duration of–
>
> (i) where the ground for recovery of possession is one set out in any of paragraphs 1 and 3 to 7 of schedule 2, the conduct taken into account by the court in concluding that the ground is established,

111 [1942] 2 All ER 653 at 655. In *Manchester City Council v Pinnock* [2011] 2 AC 104, at [56], the Supreme Court referred to this passage in summarising the approach to be taken by the court in deciding whether it was reasonable to grant an order for eviction.

112 Sir Rupert Cross:, *Precedent in English Law* (3rd edn, 1977) 196–197. This quote appears in an interesting discussion in Bennion, *Statutory Interpretation* (6th edn) 92–93 (not reproduced in subsequent editions) on statutory provisions that require an exercise of judgment in relation to abstract concepts such as "justice" or "reasonableness" (as opposed to provisions that confer a discretion, which require a determination at any point within a given range).

113 See, e.g., *Hounslow London Borough Council v McBride* (1999) 31 HLR 143; and *Wandsworth London Borough Council v Fadayomi* [1987] 1 WLR 1473, in which the Court of Appeal stated that "consent orders" have no place in public-sector proceedings.

(ii) where the ground for recovery of possession is that set out in paragraph 2 of that schedule, the conduct in respect of which the person in question was convicted,

(b) the extent to which that conduct is or was conduct of, or a consequence of acts or omissions of, persons other than the tenant,

(c) the effect which that conduct has had, is having and is likely to have on any person other than the tenant, and

(d) any action taken by the landlord, before raising the proceedings, with a view to securing the cessation of that conduct."

Initially, the courts were slow to embrace the change made by the introduction of section 16(3). The first reported case that gave the factors (a)–(d) any considered discussion was *Fife Council v Buchan*,[114] a decision of Sheriff Holligan at Kirkcaldy in a ground 2 case in which the defender had been convicted of firearms offences.[115] The key points of the sheriff's analysis are as follows:

(1) The starting point in determining reasonableness is the identification of the statutory factors set out in section 16(3).
(2) The effect of that provision is that the court is directed to consider whether those factors exist in the case and, further, to look closely at issues such as the gravity of the offence, the degree of culpability of the tenant and the effect on others, which are factors relevant in determining whether it is reasonable that the conviction should lead to the making of an order.
(3) That does not mean that other considerations are irrelevant. There may be other factors that the court considers should be taken into account in deciding whether it is reasonable to grant the order.
(4) It is also not the case that the statutory factors are matters to which the court must attach specific weight, or weight to the exclusion of all other factors. That is because each case will turn on its own facts and there may be other factors which, in reaching a judgement as to reasonableness, weigh more heavily than the statutory factors.

Having thus directed himself, the sheriff considered the significance of each of the statutory factors in the case.

It is respectfully suggested that this is the correct approach. It must be borne in mind by practitioners that the statutory factors *must* be considered in all cases in which they exist. They should, as the sheriff said, be taken as the starting point. This applies not only to illegal conduct or antisocial behaviour cases, but to any case under grounds 1–7. Thus, tenants' advisers should check whether, for example, it is possible to make a submission that, with regard to factor (d), more ought to have been done by the landlords to secure the cessation of the conduct in question. Where the court is considering granting an order under section 16(2)(a)(ii), whether at a first calling (or a continuation thereof) in the heritable court, or at a proof, the sheriff ought to be addressed on the statutory factors that exist. It also seems at least arguable that the sheriff ought to enquire as to whether each of the statutory factors exists, even if he is not addressed on the particular factor in question. That

114 2008 SLT (Sh Ct) 79; 2008 Hous LR 74.

115 For more recent cases in which specific reference was made to the s 16(3) factors, see: *South Lanarkshire Council v Gillespie* 2012 Hous LR 45; *Shetland Islands Council v Hassan and Anr* 2012 Hous LR 107; *Glasgow Housing Association Ltd v Stuart* 2015 GWD 1-30; and *Glasgow Housing Association Ltd v Lilley* 2015 Hous LR 68.

appears to follow from the direction made by section 16(3), which has effect irrespective of the position adopted by the parties.[116]

That said, it is open to the court to decide that the section 16(3) factors are not applicable to the circumstances of the case, or that they simply have little or no weight when set against other relevant matters. Thus in *East Lothian Council v Duffy*,[117] Sheriff Braid said:

> "Parties devoted considerable time and effort to trying to fit the facts of this case into those four factors. While this is a conduct case, in that the tenants have chosen to stop living in the subjects, the nature of that conduct is such that the factors set out in (b) to (d) of section 16(3) have no meaningful application here. I do not think that the court must always strain to apply all the factors, where it is clear that they have no application."

This, it is respectfully suggested, is also correct. *Prima facie*, the factors (a)–(d) in section 16(3) must always be regarded as relevant to the exercise of the court's judgment: the effect of that provision is to preclude their being left out of the account. However, in many cases, one or more of the factors will have no application to the circumstances in which eviction is sought. Also, section 16(3) does not require that the factors (a)–(d) are to be given any more weight than any other matters that are relevant. Rather, they must be taken into account, if applicable, and given such weight as the sheriff considers appropriate.

Nature, frequency and duration of conduct: s 16(3)(a)

The nature of conduct is necessarily apparent to the sheriff, as she will require to be satisfied that the ground for eviction is established, before she can consider whether it would be reasonable to grant the order. However, it could be said that section 16(3)(a) brings the questions "How long?" and "How often?" more sharply into focus. The following considerations may enable the court to distinguish between a problem that is, to use the medical terminology, "acute" as opposed to "chronic":

- whether the conduct has occurred from time to time or whether it has taken place over a single period;
- the times at which the conduct has occurred, in relation to the duration of the tenancy, i.e. whether it has occurred since soon after the tenancy commenced, or whether it has recently arisen for the first time; and
- whether the conduct has persisted and, in particular, whether it has occurred in contravention of an agreement made with the landlords, in terms of which the proceedings were continued, adjourned, or sisted.[118]

116 This point is further discussed in Chapter 13.
117 (n 90). This was a ground 5 case.
118 As one might expect, at adjourned or continued hearings of the case, the court tends to place significance on what has happened since the case last called and, in particular, whether the tenant has failed to avail himself of an opportunity to improve his position, for example by adhering to a payment arrangement with the landlords. This factor may weigh more heavily than any other, such that, for example, increased rent arrears or further antisocial behaviour since the action first called in court may prove fatal to the defender's case.

Acts or omissions of persons other than the tenant: s 16(3)(b)

As has already been seen, it is a feature of certain of the grounds that they may be established by the conduct of persons other than the tenant. This is usually the tenant's spouse or cohabitee, or a member of his family. For example, it is not unusual to see antisocial behaviour cases in which the conduct giving rise to the action was entirely on the part of one or more of the tenant's children. Clearly section 16(3)(b) is a provision that will usually be pled in favour of the tenant, and this may be particularly effective where, for example, the conduct is on the part of someone who no longer resides at or visits the tenancy. However, an issue may arise as to the extent to which the tenant has acquiesced in the acts or omissions in question.[119]

Section 16(3)(b) has other possible applications. The wording of the provision could arguably encompass conduct on the part of the tenant that was provoked, because it occurred in consequence of the acts or omissions of other persons, such as neighbours. In addition, as with section 16(3)(c), there appears to be no reason why the description "person[s] other than the tenant" could not include the landlords.

Effect of the conduct: s 16(3)(c)

In contrast to section 16(3)(b), this factor will be relied upon by the landlord. The persons affected by the tenant's conduct may include the landlord. It may also include the landlord's other tenants, and prospective tenants.

However, section 16(3)(c) will most clearly apply in cases under grounds 2 and 7, where neighbours, for example, have suffered as a result of the conduct of the tenant. This issue arises in various contexts, and is discussed below under the reasonableness requirement in relation to particular grounds.

Steps taken by the landlord: s 16(3)(d)

Unlike the previous two factors, section 16(3)(d) may be relied on by either party: by the landlord in terms of steps that have been taken, and by the tenant in terms of steps that might usefully have been taken by the landlord, but were not. The tenant may also seek to rely on steps that have been taken and are still in progress, and argue that they should be allowed to continue.

The "action taken by the landlord . . . with a view to securing the cessation of . . . conduct" may usefully be divided into three categories.

(1) Steps specific to rent arrears cases. These will include, in particular, the action taken by the landlord to fulfil the pre-action requirements set out in section 14A of the 2001 Act.[120]
(2) Steps that might be taken by the landlord with a view to supporting the tenant in bringing the conduct to an end, and thus retaining his tenancy. In cases involving tenants with drug or alcohol abuse issues, or mental

119 See, e.g., *East Ayrshire Council v Tait* 1999 SCLR 566; *City of Glasgow Council v McAlinden* (n 61); *Glasgow Housing Association v Gourlay* 2006 Hous LR 52.

120 The relationship between s 14A and s 16(3)(d) is considered in Chapter 4, at p 92. See also the discussion of the "reasonableness" requirement in the context of rent arrears cases, below.

health problems, it is common to find that the tenant is receiving support and assistance of some kind through the social work department of a local authority, either directly or indirectly by referral to another agency. This may lead to a situation in which the housing department of the authority is proceeding with an action to have the tenant evicted, while at the same time the social work department is trying to support the tenant in maintaining his tenancy. It is perhaps not so surprising that such a case can arise, given the separate functions of the departments involved, but it may leave the authority open to criticism where some co-ordination in approach between the departments might appear to be appropriate, but has not been attempted.

Where there is a basis on which to suggest that some co-ordination between local authority departments may have been (or may still be) useful, the defender could argue that it would not be reasonable to grant the order, and perhaps seek an adjournment of the case under section 16(1) of the Act, so that the possibility of further assistance, different forms of support, or even rehousing can be investigated.

(3) Other approaches, such as mediation, regular communication with the tenant, or rehousing through management transfer. In this respect, it may be useful to consider the approaches adopted by other landlords in the social rented sector for comparative purposes.[121] Some landlords have highly organised and generally effective procedures for communicating with tenants by various means. This may not be simply to warn the tenant of the consequences of his conduct, but so as to offer support and assistance, often by referral to other agencies. In cases where numerous efforts have previously been made to communicate with the tenant, to no avail, the defence will be more difficult, as the court is more likely to sympathise with the landlord's position.

(3) Other considerations in relation to "reasonableness" test

Because the court must take into account anything that is relevant to the issue of whether the order should be granted, the circumstances that might be brought to its attention are diverse. However, there are some issues that arise very frequently. From the landlord's side, the circumstances put to the sheriff in relation to certain grounds may be very similar from one case to another. Thus in arrears cases, the court would always expect to hear of the level of the arrears, and be apprised of at least a general history of failures in payment.

From the tenant's side, the relevant issues usually arise from personal circumstances, and are accordingly more variable. Thus, the defender will often apprise the court of various personal problems such as loss of employment, relationship breakdown or bereavement, the details of which will be particular and specific. Other issues, however, occur in a number of cases, and these are discussed in greater detail in the following paragraphs.

121 E.g., various approaches to antisocial behaviour are discussed in the Scottish Executive Central Research Unit's Paper "The Use of Civil Remedies for Neighbour Nuisance in Scotland" (n 98).

Ill health, disability, old age, infirmity

The tenant's health may be relevant in two ways: in explaining the conduct giving rise to the ground, and in persuading the court that eviction would cause particular hardship to the tenant or members of his household.

There has been an increasing focus in recent years on the extent to which the behaviour giving rise to grounds for eviction may be attributable to mental health problems suffered by persons who are disabled for the purposes of the Equality Act 2010.[122] This may have a bearing on whether it is reasonable to grant an order, particularly in antisocial behaviour cases. This issue is discussed in Chapter 11.

Mood disorders, and in particular depression, seem to be especially prevalent among defenders in rent arrears cases; difficulty in coping with paperwork, benefit applications and financial matters are common characteristics of that condition. This may be a relevant factor, even if the defender's condition does not meet the test for "disability" under the 2010 Act.

In cases in which a medical condition is thought to be relevant, a report is usually obtained from the defender's GP or any specialist to whom the defender has been referred for treatment.[123] Proofs in eviction cases often feature medical evidence, or the production of medical reports, the terms of which have been agreed.

Proposals by the tenant as to future conduct

In most cases, the court will look to the tenant for some proposal to the effect that he will desist from the conduct giving rise to the ground and, if appropriate, take steps to put right the effects of previous failures. This is the principal basis on which the court may decline to grant an order for eviction, but instead continue or adjourn the case so that the tenant's future conduct can be monitored. The extent to which the tenant's proposals will be persuasive depends on the circumstances of the case and, in particular, whether the tenant has failed in previous arrangements made directly with the landlord.

Effect of eviction on the tenant and other members of the household; homelessness

The court ought to take into account the effect of granting, or refusing to grant, the order on both the landlord and the tenant.[124] However, the specific contention that an order for eviction will result in homelessness, which is often made on behalf of tenants, is more problematic.

122 Or, previously, the Disability Discrimination Act 1995.

123 In cases under the 2010 Act, it is usually necessary to obtain an expert report as to whether the statutory test for the protected characteristic of disability is met, unless that is a matter of agreement.

124 *Cresswell v Hodgson* [1951] 2 KB 92, 95 (Somervell LJ): "I think the words of the section themselves indicate that the county court judge must look at the effect of the order on each party to it. I do not see how it is possible to consider whether it is reasonable to make an order unless you consider its effect on landlord and tenant, firstly, if you make it, and secondly, if you do not." This approach was reiterated in the Court of Appeal's decision in *Whitehouse v Lee* [2010] HLR 11.

On or before the eviction takes place, the tenant is entitled to make an application to a local authority, as a homeless person, for assistance and accommodation under part II of the 1987 Act.[125] The authority has a duty to provide him with interim accommodation while investigating his claim, if it is satisfied that he may be homeless,[126] together with any person that might reasonably be expected to reside with him.[127] The quality of temporary accommodation is variable, and single applicants have often been offered B&B or hostel accommodation, especially applicants to the larger authorities in urban areas.[128]

The authority must then investigate and determine the application.[129] In order to succeed, the applicant must usually overcome three hurdles:[130] the authority must be satisfied: (a) that he is homeless;[131] (b) that he is not intentionally homeless (i.e. that he did not become homeless as a result of an act or omission which caused him to lose accommodation which it would have been reasonable for him to continue to occupy);[132] and (c) that he has a local connection with the authority to which the application is made.[133]

As one might anticipate, an application made by a person who has been evicted on any of the "conduct" grounds in terms of schedule 2 to the 2001 Act is liable to result in a determination that the applicant is intentionally homeless, having caused the eviction by his own acts or omissions. This is not by any means a foregone conclusion.[134] However, it is the likely outcome in practice.

It is important to appreciate that the applicant's having dependent children has no bearing on the issue of intentional homelessness.[135]

125 In discharging their statutory duties to homeless persons, authorities are bound to have regard to the Code of Guidance on Homelessness (s 37 of the 1987 Act) the most recent edition of which was published in May 2005. It is available on the Scottish Government's website.

126 1987 Act, s 29.

127 ibid s 40.

128 Under the Homeless Persons (Unsuitable Accommodation) (Scotland) Order 2014 (SSI 2014/243) certain limitations are placed on the types of temporary accommodation that may be made available to applicants.

129 1987Act, ss 28 and 30.

130 Until 2012 there were four: under s 25 of the Act, the applicant had to show that he had a "priority need" for accommodation. This was repealed at the end of 2012.

131 As defined in s 24 of the Act.

132 Section 26. Note that, with effect from 7 November 2019, local authorities are no longer obliged to consider intentional homelessness. Under the amended s 28(2) of the 1987 Act, they "may, if they think fit, make . . . further inquiries . . . to satisfy themselves as to whether [the applicant] became homeless . . . intentionally".

133 Section 27. By s 30, the authority determines the issues of homelessness, intentional homelessness and local connection in that order. If it finds against the applicant on the first or second issue, it is not required to determine the subsequent issues.

134 E.g., the Code of Guidance (at para 7.17) provides that, in relation to cases where the applicant has been evicted on the ground of rent arrears: "It should not be assumed automatically that an applicant is intentionally homeless where they have lost their accommodation because of rent or mortgage arrears. Reasons should be fully explored and decisions made as to whether arrears resulted from deliberate acts or omissions."

135 It is necessary to emphasise this point because there appears to be an urban myth that local authorities are always bound to rehouse homeless persons if they have dependent children. There is also a misapprehension (often on the part of tenants) that, for this reason, local authorities do not evict families. In fact, the eviction of families by social landlords in Scotland is commonplace, and local authorities are under no obligation to rehouse families permanently, unless the hurdles imposed by the homelessness legislation are overcome.

Where the local authority decides that the applicant is intentionally homeless,[136] the authority then has a further limited obligation to provide temporary accommodation to him "for such period as they consider will give him a reasonable opportunity of himself securing accommodation".[137] During that period, the authority is obliged to furnish the applicant with advice and assistance.[138] This means that the applicant (and those residing with him) will remain in temporary accommodation from the point when he makes his application to the point (following a negative decision on the application) when the authority decides that he has had a reasonable opportunity of securing his own accommodation. The prospects for the applicant "himself securing accommodation" may be hampered by external factors (such as lack of availability of housing) and factors particular to the applicant (such as mental health or substance abuse issues). The length of the period allowed by the authority may be as little as two weeks, but in some cases is substantially longer.[139] Once the authority considers that the applicant has had a reasonable opportunity, it will treat its obligations under the 1987 Act as discharged, and the applicant's temporary accommodation is terminated.

There is conflicting authority as to the extent to which the court should consider the tenant's homelessness as a consequence of a possession order. For example, in *Bristol City Council v Mousah*,[140] the view was taken that although the court could consider the effect that an order for possession would have on the defendant tenant, it was not entitled to speculate on the outcome of any application that the tenant might make to the local authority as a homeless person, after the order took effect. However, in the later case of *Croydon London Borough Council v Moody*,[141] Evans LJ said: "I . . . remain unconvinced that the judge should, as a matter of law, disregard the fact that the tenant, if he is evicted, will be liable to be treated as intentionally homeless and, secondly, what his fate in fact will be." Accordingly this point appears to be unresolved.

Eviction would be disproportionate

In *Manchester City Council v Pinnock*,[142] the Supreme Court said that the conclusion that article 8 might found a defence to eviction proceedings by a public authority would not affect cases in which the reasonableness of granting

136 The applicant may ask the local authority to review this decision in terms of s 35A of the 1987 Act. There is no right of appeal thereafter, though a decision may be challenged by judicial review, on the usual grounds.

137 1987 Act, s 31(3)(a).

138 ibid s 31(3)(b).

139 This is a rather fraught issue. The Code of Guidance (at paras 9.30–9.36) indicates that the accommodation should continue until such time as other accommodation is identified. However, some authorities have difficulty in following this guidance, because the demand for temporary accommodation may put pressure on the authority to move existing applicants on, in order to make room for new cases. In addition, the standard of advice and assistance provided by local authorities is variable. Many applicants receive a basic period of four weeks to find accommodation from the date of a finding of intentional homelessness, and are simply given a list of private landlords in the locale.

140 (1998) 30 HLR 32.

141 (1999) 31 HLR 738, 745.

142 (n 111) paras [55]–[57]. This decision is discussed in Chapter 11.

an order has to be established. In short, the concept of "reasonableness" was already sufficiently wide to encompass any question of whether an order would be proportionate. However, the court also thought it "highly unlikely" that it could be reasonable for a court to make an order for possession in circumstances in which it would be disproportionate to do so under article 8. Thus it is clear that the defender might challenge the reasonableness of granting an order on the basis that eviction would be disproportionate. See Chapter 11 for a discussion of the "proportionality" test.

Length of time living in the premises

Where the tenant has been resident in the subjects for many years, this may weigh against an order being granted.[143]

(4) Reasonableness considerations in relation to particular grounds

Ground 1 (part 1): the "reasonableness" test in rent arrears cases

As indicated above, all relevant matters ought to be considered and weighed by the court in the exercise of its judgment, and it will generally be appropriate to look at the matters outlined in section 16(3) first, before going on to any other issues that are before the court. In relation to section 16(3)(a), one would generally expect that the pursuers' agent will be in a position to apprise the court of the nature, frequency and duration of non-payment.[144] The following issues of importance frequently arise in arrears cases, some of which now fall to be considered under the relevant section 16(3) factors:

- section 16(3)(b): non-payment of housing benefit or universal credit;
- section 16(3)(c): the "effect" of non-payment;
- section 16(3)(d): action taken by the landlord before raising proceedings;
- payment arrangements and rent arrears direct;
- sequestration cases.

Non-payment of housing benefit or universal credit: s 16(3)(b)

The court will often be advised that some or all of the arrears are due to non-payment of housing benefit, or of universal credit.[145] In some housing benefit cases, that non-payment will be on the part of the local authority that is the pursuer in the action. The benefits system is very complex, and there are numerous possible ways in which claims can run into difficulties.[146]

143 *Minchburn Ltd v Fernandez (No 2)* (1987) 19 HLR 29; *Castle Vale Housing Action Trust v Gallagher* [2001] EWCA Civ 944, (2001) 33 HLR 72..

144 In *Midlothian Council v Drummond* 1991 SLT (Sh Ct) 67, it was said that the landlord should show whether the court is "dealing with a bad tenant who was persistently in arrears with rent, or a tenant with a good record who had only recently fallen into arrears through misfortune". For a rent arrears case in which various arguments in relation to reasonableness were canvassed, see: *GHA v Li* (n 45).

145 Universal credit includes a "housing costs" element, in respect of any liability of the claimant to make payments in respect of his occupation of accommodation.

146 It is usually possible to identify, on the rent account, periods during which housing benefit or universal credit was not being paid. Because of the complexity of the system, the tenant may

However, it is perhaps useful at this point to summarise the most common issues:

(1) The defender, for whatever reason, has not applied for benefits for which he was financially eligible. In such cases an application may be made late, with a request that payment of the benefit is backdated to the point at which the applicant became eligible. However, the maximum backdating period has now been reduced to only one month.[147] That application will be granted by the authority if it was satisfied that there was "continuous good cause" for the application being made late.[148]
(2) There is a dispute between the applicant and the benefit authority as to whether he is eligible for the relevant benefit. This may arise at the point of application, or the authority may have suspended an ongoing claim, where it decides that the applicant is no longer eligible.
(3) The authority has reduced the benefit paid to the applicant, generally on the basis of information that it has about the applicant's circumstances, or the composition of his household, which is in dispute.
(4) The defender may assert that he has made an application for universal credit, but there is a delay in payment, or that the correct amount is not being paid. There is a standard five-week wait for the first payment of universal credit, although advance payments can be requested. There have also been well-publicised issues with the administration of the benefit.[149] Delay can also occur because a dispute has arisen between the applicant and the benefit authority as to whether the applicant has supplied the information that is necessary to enable the authority to make a determination.

All these situations occur very frequently, and may result in an appeal. Under the Tribunals, Courts and Enforcement Act 2007, appeals are now made to the FTT, Social Entitlement Chamber, thereafter to the Upper Tribunal, and then to the Inner House of the Court of Session, although this is rare.

The important point to appreciate is that in cases in which a benefit issue is resolved in favour of the tenant, a credit will be made to the rent account, which consists of the payments that he ought to have been receiving over the relevant period. This may be a substantial sum of money that has the effect of reducing, or even clearing, the balance of arrears. It is therefore quite common for the court to be advised at the first calling, or a continuation thereof, that the arrears are partly or wholly due to an issue with the payment of benefits,

not understand why this has happened. If possible, tenants should be referred to specialist welfare rights advisers. In some cases, requests for late reviews, or appeals against decisions, can be submitted within thirteen months.

147 In terms of reg 83(12) of the Housing Benefit Regulations 2006 (SI 2006/213) and the Universal Credit and Miscellaneous Amendments Regulations 2015 (SI 2015/1754), with effect from 1 April 2016. Previously the maximum period was six months and, before that, it was one year.

148 The rules are different if the applicant is over the qualifying age for pension credit and is not claiming income support or income-based jobseeker's allowance. In that case, it is not necessary to have a good reason for making a backdated claim, but the maximum period for backdating is three months.

149 These are described in Shelter Scotland's: *The Impact of Social Security on Housing in Scotland* (July 2019). The National Audit Office's: *Rolling Out Universal Credit* (2018) reported that more than 20% of claimants were not paid the correct amount of universal credit on time.

and to be moved by the defender to adjourn, continue or sist the case for the matter to be resolved. In the past, such motions have usually been granted on the basis that the court is not in a position properly to exercise its judgment as to whether it would be reasonable to grant the order until the true arrears figure is known.[150]

In some cases, however, the court may ask the defender or his agent to indicate the amount of the arrears that will still be outstanding, assuming that the benefit issue is resolved in his favour. Alternatively, where the pursuer is also the benefit authority, its agent will be in a position to advise the court of the authority's understanding as to the figures involved. The possibility of this approach should be anticipated by the defender in any case in which the arrears are substantial. Where the court is satisfied that a successful resolution of the benefit issue will not have the effect of significantly reducing the arrears, the sheriff may be inclined to proceed on the basis of a "notional" figure, being the amount of the arrears under deduction of any housing benefit that might be payable to the defender, once his outstanding claims are resolved.

The pre-action requirements imposed upon the landlord by section 14A of the 2001 Act, together with the subordinate legislation and Guidance,[151] include an obligation on the part of the landlord to provide the tenant with reasonable assistance in claiming housing benefit, if requested to do so by the tenant.[152] The Guidance suggests that landlords "could do what they can to help tenants progress their . . . application, where appropriate".[153] If such assistance has been offered and rejected, that may make it more difficult for the tenant to persuade the court that the case ought to be adjourned or continued for an application now to be made.

The "effect" of non-payment: s 16(3)(c)

As suggested above, for the purposes of section 16(3)(c) the landlord should be taken to be one of the persons affected by the conduct of the defender.

In rent arrears cases, the landlord occasionally asserts that the non-payment of rent by tenants prevents the landlord from carrying out repair and maintenance work or effecting improvements to the stock, and increases administrative work or otherwise disrupts housing provision.[154] This point is not as obvious as it might seem and, from the defender's point of view, it may be

150 For an example, see *Renfrewshire Council v Hainey* 2008 Hous LR 43.

151 Discussed in Chapter 4. As indicated there, no amendment has been made to s 14A, or the subordinate legislation and guidance, which addresses the replacement of housing benefit with the housing costs element of universal credit.

152 Article 3(c) of the Scottish Secure Tenancies (Proceedings for Possession) (Pre-Action Requirements) Order 2012 (SSI 2012/127).

153 At para 65.

154 See *Stirling Council v Harrower* 2013 Hous LR 32. In that case, the council argued that that the defender's arrears had an indirect impact on the its resources, such as less money in common good fund; and staff time expended on the pursuer, which could have been used to help other vulnerable tenants. It was also suggested that there was an effect on non-defaulting tenants who may have to pay higher rents and thereby subsidise the defender. The sheriff accepted that, although indirect, these were also effects, for the purpose of s 16(1)(c), which could be taken into account.

worth investigating whether it is actually borne out by the available evidence in relation to the landlord in question.[155]

It may also be argued that rent revenue is lost to the pursuers only when the arrears prescribe or are written off, which happens only after the tenant is evicted. Therefore, the pursuers are more likely to recover existing arrears by allowing the tenant to stay. The counter-argument is that the tenant has demonstrated by his conduct that he is a bad payer, and thus it is in the pursuers' interests to put him out and replace him with someone who will pay, rather than being burdened with a tenant who will probably incur further rent arrears in the future.

Action taken by the landlord before raising proceedings: s 16(3)(d)

In Chapter 4, it was suggested that the imposition of the pre-action requirements may have an impact on the way that the court approaches the issue of whether it is reasonable to grant the order in an arrears case, given that the landlord's compliance with the requirements constitutes action taken by it before raising proceedings, for the purposes of section 16(3)(d).[156]

Payment arrangements and rent arrears direct

In the majority of cases, the landlord will seek an order for recovery of possession, together with a decree for payment of the outstanding arrears. It is submitted that an important consideration in such cases should be whether a decree for payment alone would be an adequate remedy for the landlord. Where the defender is in employment, the arrears could be recovered by way of a wages arrestment. Where the defender is in receipt of income support, income-based jobseeker's allowance, pension credit or income-related employment and support allowance, the arrears may be recovered by way of direct deduction from the defender's benefit, in terms of the "arrears direct" scheme. This ensures regular payment, albeit at small amounts.[157] Similar provision is made for recovering rent arrears from universal credit.[158]

155 The Scottish Government gathers and publishes figures in relation to local authority housing, indicating levels of rent arrears, sums spent on repair and maintenance, the number of properties unlet (resulting in a loss of rental income), and so on. This might indicate, for example, that the authority in question spends comparatively less on repairs than authorities with higher rent arrears.

156 See the discussion in Chapter 4, in particular the first of the three points at pp 92–3.

157 This scheme was set up by sch 9 to the Social Security (Claims and Payments) Regulations 1987 (SI 1987/1968). It allows the tenant to sign a mandate in terms of which a small amount is deducted from his social security benefit, and paid to the landlord. In *Second WRVS Housing Society v Blair* (1987) 19 HLR 104, the Court of Appeal set aside an order for possession on the ground of rent arrears of £1,198, because the judge at first instance had failed adequately to consider: (a) the possibility of arranging direct payment to the landlord of current rent from the housing benefit authority; and (b) the fact that payment towards the arrears could be made by direct deduction from benefits. See also: *Woodspring DC v Taylor* (1981–2) 4 HLR 95; *Brent LBC v Marks* (1999) 31 HLR 343; and *Midlothian Council v Brown* 1991 SLT (Sh Ct) 80, 1990 SCLR 765, in which the sheriff criticised the pursuers' failure to seek payment by arrears direct.

158 See part 9 of the Government's guidance: "Universal Credit and Rented Housing: Guide for Landlords" (n 9). Deductions from universal credit are significantly higher for rent arrears.

This ought to be considered by the landlord before the notice of proceedings is issued: reference is made to the discussion of article 4 of the pre-action requirements order, in Chapter 4.[159] Where that has not been done, or the court does not accept the landlord's view that arrears direct payments are inadequate, it may exercise its judgment in favour of the tenant.

Sequestration cases

A question may arise as to whether there are rent arrears if the tenant has been sequestrated, with the effect that the liability to pay the pre-sequestration rent arrears cannot be enforced.[160] It is submitted that, in this instance, the ground is still established because the rent arrears are "lawfully due",[161] albeit from the trustee rather than the tenant. However, judging whether it would be reasonable to make the order for possession in such a case will be different from the usual run of cases, in that the tenant cannot make proposals for repayment.

The position of tenants subject to sequestration is discussed in the Scottish Government's "Guidance for Social Landlords on Pre-Action Requirements and Seeking Repossession of Social Housing".[162] The salient points made in the Guidance are as follows:

- Under the Bankruptcy (Scotland) Act 1985 a landlord cannot generally recover rent arrears through court action once a tenant has been sequestrated.
- Landlords should be aware that payment of arrears to a landlord by an insolvent debtor may run the risk that the courts would find this an unfair preference to one creditor over all creditors.
- In cases where a tenant is sequestrated before the landlord starts eviction proceedings, the landlord should consider not taking, or threatening, action to evict if the arrears are not paid. Attempting to collect rent arrears in this way could lead to challenge by other creditors; also, a sheriff might not consider eviction reasonable in these circumstances.
- It is recommended that the landlord seeks to recover as much as possible of the arrears through the sequestration process and writes off the remainder at the point of sequestration, treating this as a debt no longer due.
- But if the tenant fails to pay rent that is due for a later period, court action may be taken to evict on the basis of those subsequent arrears. In that

They will typically be deducted at 20% of the applicant's standard allowance, although a request can be made to reduce this to 10%.

159 Or at a later stage, if the possibility of making direct deductions arises then.

160 Sequestration does not have the effect of terminating a Scottish secure tenancy: see p 87.

161 In *Monklands District Council v McAllister* 1992 SCLR 207 the court took the view that where the tenant had been sequestrated, the arrears were still "lawfully due", and the court ought then to consider whether it would be reasonable to grant the order in all the circumstances of the case. This is consistent with the decisions of the Court of Appeal in *Harlow DC v Hall* [2006] 1 WLR 2116, and *Places for People Homes Ltd v Sharples* [2011] HLR 45. However, in *Stirling Council v Harrower* (n 154), the sheriff decided that it would not be reasonable to grant the order sought, particularly given the potential effect on the defender and her husband, who suffered from physical and mental health problems.

162 Paragraphs 15–19. The Guidance is discussed in Chapter 4, in relation to the pre-action requirements under s 14A. The landlord is obliged to "have regard" to the Guidance, under section 14A(8), in "in complying with the pre-action requirements". If it has not been followed, it is arguable that it would not be reasonable to grant an eviction order.

situation, the pre-action requirements should need to be undertaken by the landlord only in relation to the subsequent arrears.
- Where a court sequestrates a tenant after court proceedings to repossess a property have begun, the landlord will have already met the pre-action requirements. If the landlord wishes to continue to pursue eviction action, the decision around whether eviction is reasonable is one for the court to decide.

In practice, the possibility of sequestration may arise after the action is raised, and the tenant seeks money advice. The principal argument advanced for the tenant in such cases is that, on the basis of that advice, he seeks a form of debt relief in order to address his debts, and put him in a position of being able to prioritise payments to the rent, in the future.

Ground 1 (part 2): reasonableness in relation to other breaches of the tenancy contract

It is difficult to give any general guidance in this context, as the decision is likely to turn on the nature of the term in question, and the seriousness of the breach. Generally, the issue is also affected by considerations such as whether the breach is continuing, persistent or repeated; its implications for the landlord and so on.[163] The following particular points may be made:

- Where the tenant decides to persist in the breach, and puts the court to a decision on whether it would be reasonable to grant the order, it would be risky to do so on the sole basis that the breach is arguably trivial. In such a case, the court may well take the view that it is reasonable to evict a tenant who, despite being aware of, for example, an obligation that prohibits the keeping of pets without the landlords' consent, and having been given notice that the landlords intend to enforce that obligation, insists on keeping his pet.[164]
- It is sometimes a feature of "breach of contract" cases that the tenant contends that the landlords are barred from insisting on the obligation because they consented to the conduct that constitutes the breach, either expressly, or impliedly by acquiescence; or, alternatively, that the landlord does not enforce the same obligation against other tenants. The persuasiveness of those contentions will depend on the evidence that the defender is able to lead in support of them. There is perhaps an argument to be had about whether the terms of the ground are established by the breach of an express term of the contract, irrespective of any issue of personal bar; but, in any event, it is to be presumed that the court would not find it reasonable to

163 In *Leeds and Yorkshire Housing Association v Vertigan* [2011] HLR 13 there had been a series of breaches of the tenancy agreement. The tenant offered to give an undertaking to desist, during the course of his evidence. However, the judge decided that, given the history of the case, he was unlikely to comply, and she accordingly decided in favour of the landlords.

164 See, e.g., *Sheffield City Council v Jepson* (1993) 25 HLR 299; *Green v Sheffield City Council* (1993) 26 HLR 349; *Thomas-Ashley v Drum Housing Association Ltd* [2010] 2 P&CR 17, [2010] L&TR 17; *Joseph v Nettleton Road Housing Co-operative* [2010] HLR 30, [2010] 2 P&CR 12.

grant the order in the face of compelling evidence that the landlord had consented to the tenant's conduct.[165]

- There is authority in support of the proposition that it is no part of the court's function in determining reasonableness to investigate whether the landlord's policy of including a particular term in a tenancy contract is a good or valid one.[166] However, as previously discussed, the issue of whether obligations on the tenant are "fair" is open for consideration under part 2 of the Consumer Rights Act 2015.[167]
- Where the breach is the keeping of a pet, there have been cases in which the tenant has led medical or other evidence as to the benefits of his having an "animal companion", or the loss that he would suffer as a result of losing his pet.[168]

Ground 2

In cases in which the landlord establishes ground 2, the new section 16(2)(aa) (introduced by section 14 of the 2014 Act) has the effect that it is no longer required to establish that the eviction is reasonable, provided that it served the notice of proceedings for recovery of possession within twelve months of the conviction for the offence that forms the ground for recovery of possession.[169] Therefore the following comments only apply to those cases in which the notice of proceedings comes later, and the landlord has to proceed under section 16(2)(a).

Ground 2 is most commonly deployed in cases in which the tenant or other person residing in the house has been convicted of an offence under the Misuse of Drugs Act 1971.[170] In the case of more serious offences, one would expect that the landlord would place considerable reliance on section 16(3)(b), being the particular effect of the conduct that constituted the offence. In more general terms, the landlord may argue that it is essential for it to deal with, and to be seen to be dealing with, drug dealing in neighbourhoods. Without a sufficiently robust approach, it is difficult to get prospective tenants to move into the area, and this in turn increases the pressure of demand for the landlord's housing in other areas.

165 In *Solihull Metropolitan Borough Council v Reeman* June 1994 Legal Action 10 (an unreported decision of Birmingham County Court) the local authority sought possession on the ground that the smell of the tenant's dogs had caused a nuisance and annoyance to neighbours. The court decided that it would not be reasonable to grant the order, one of the principal considerations being that the council had not enforced its prohibition on pets against fifteen other tenants in the same block.

166 *Barking and Dagenham London Borough Council v Hyatt* (1992) 24 HLR 406.

167 See p 134 and note 51 and Chapter 3, p 73.

168 *Bell London and Provincial Properties Ltd v Reuben* [1947] KB 157; *Thomas-Ashley v Drum Housing Association Ltd* [2010] 2 P&CR 17, [2010] L&TR 17.

169 Section 16(2)(aa) is is the "Streamlined Eviction Process" for ground 2 cases. It is discussed at p 164 below. With effect from 1 May 2019, s 14(2B) of the 2001 Act now requires that, before raising proceedings under ground 2, the landlord must have regard to guidance published by the Scottish Ministers: *Streamlined Eviction Process – Criminal or Antisocial Behaviour: Statutory Guidance for Social Landlords*. Section 14(2B) applies not only to actions raised under the new s 16(2)(aa), but to any case that relies on ground 2. However, the Guidance refers only to actions under the new procedure.

170 Though some actions have followed on conviction for firearms offences. See, e.g., *Fife Council v Buchan* 2008 SLT (Sh Ct) 79, 2008 Hous LR 74.

Circumstances that might be pled on the defender's behalf are: previous good character; subsequent good character, rehabilitation and the cessation of drug use; the circumstances of non-offending occupiers of the house; the fact that the defender has already been punished by the criminal justice system; increased risk of offending and failure of rehabilitation if the defender is evicted.

In several cases, it is has been said that the court should consider, in particular: the public interest; whether the defender was aware of the consequences of his actions; the gravity of the offence; and the consequences of eviction.[171]

Although each case will depend on its circumstances, it seems reasonable to suggest, on the basis of the reported cases, that where the offence is a serious one, the prospects of successfully defending the action are fairly poor,[172] though not hopeless.[173]

Ground 6

The relevant English authorities suggest that where there has been deliberate lying and deceitfulness, it is to be anticipated that the court will find it reasonable to grant the order. This is perhaps typified by the judgment of Beldam LJ in *Shrewsbury and Atcham Borough Council v Evans*,[174] in which he opined that to refrain from making an order for possession in the circumstances of that case would be "an affront to those who put forward their claims honestly, wait patiently and rely on their local housing authority to deal fairly with their claims".[175]

In *West Lothian Council v Reape*,[176] however, the sheriff found that it was not reasonable to grant the order, taking into account all the relevant circumstances in the case.

171 *Glasgow City Council v Lockhart* 1997 Hous LR 99; *South Lanarkshire Council* v *Nugent* 2008 Hous LR 92; *South Lanarkshire Council* v *Gillespie* (n 115); *Glasgow Housing Association v Lilley* (n 8).

172 See, e.g., the cases cited in the previous note, and *Shetland Islands Council v Hassan* 2012 Hous LR 107.

173 The decisions in *Glasgow Housing Association Ltd v Hetherington* 2009 SLT (Sh Ct) 64, 2009 Hous LR 28, and *Glasgow Housing Association Ltd v O'Neill* (Unreported, decision of Sheriff Mackenzie at Glasgow on 2 November 2012) indicate that there is a willingness on the part of sheriffs (at least at Glasgow Sheriff Court) to entertain disposals that are probationary in nature, by way of an adjournment under s 16(1). In *Glasgow Housing Association Ltd v Stuart* 2015 Hous LR 2, another case at Glasgow Sheriff Court, Sheriff Reid simply assoilzied the defender. In that case the possibility of a probationary adjournment under s 16(1) does not appear to have been considered. In *Hjaltland Housing Association Ltd v Sukhram* 2018 Hous LR 100, the sheriff decided that adjournment would serve no useful purpose, and that in the circumstances in was not reasonable to grant the order. Accordingly the action was dismissed.

174 (1998) 30 HLR 123, 133.

175 See also *Rushcliffe Borough Council v Watson* (1992) 24 HLR 123, and *Lewisham London Borough Council v Akinsola* (2000) 32 HLR 414.

176 2002 Hous LR 58.

Ground 7

It is possible to discern a distinct shift from the more lenient attitude taken in the older cases[177] to the harder line adopted in later decisions, in which the pursuers have almost always been successful.[178]

The same trend can be discerned in the relevant English cases. It is instructive to consider the comments made by the authors in the most recent edition of the Legal Action Group's *Defending Possession Proceedings*:[179]

> "Historically, the Court of Appeal has been unwilling to interfere with the decisions of trial judges on 'reasonableness' issues. But in the context of modern concerns about anti-social behaviour, the Court of Appeal has, in a series of decisions, reversed the decisions of judges who have not been satisfied that it was reasonable to order possession in public sector 'nuisance' cases or who have made only postponed orders rather than outright orders.[180] In practice, where the tenant has been found guilty of anti-social or criminal conduct, unless it was abated some time ago, it will be likely to be difficult to avoid a finding that it would be reasonable to make a possession order."

The authors suggest that the court should be invited to consider the following factors:[181]

- the seriousness and frequency of the conduct;
- whether it is continuing or persistent, or has recently abated;
- the likelihood of the behaviour continuing or recurring;
- warnings issued by the landlord;
- the tenant's remorse;
- the relevant personal circumstances of the tenant;

177 *Kyle and Carrick District Council v Currie* 1996 Hous LR 3 (decided in 1984); *Clackmannanshire District Council v Morgan* 1996 Hous LR 9 (1991); *Falkirk District Council v Townsley* 1996 Hous LR 14 (1985).

178 See, e.g., *City of Edinburgh Council v Allan* 1999 Hous LR 3; *East Dunbartonshire Council v Cameron* 2000 Hous LR 126; *City of Edinburgh Council v Watson* 2002 Hous LR 2; *Aberdeen City Council v Molina* 2002 Hous LR 98; *City of Edinburgh Council v HT* 2003 Hous LR 74; *Cadder Housing Association v McVeigh* 2005 Hous LR 85; *Glasgow Housing Association v Marshall* 2006 Hous LR 56.

179 Luba and others, *Defending Possession Proceedings* (8th edn) para 3.176.

180 For example, see *Birmingham City Council v Ashton* [2013] HLR 8. Under the English legislation (Housing Act 1985, s 85(2)) the court has the power to suspend or postpone the date of possession, subject to certain conditions as to future conduct. The law in relation to these powers is quite complex. However, in general terms the effect of the postponement or suspension is that if the tenant breaches the terms of the order, even once, the tenancy is terminated, and the landlords may apply for a warrant for possession. If the terms of the postponement or suspension are fulfilled, the tenant can then apply for the order to be discharged. Under the Housing (Scotland) Act 1988, s 20(2) the courts in Scotland have the same powers in relation to assured tenancies, though these appear to be very seldom used; however, there is no equivalent power in relation to tenancies under the 2001 Act, and accordingly English cases in relation to secure tenancies must be treated with a degree of caution. It is feasible that a Scottish court could, following a proof, find that the ground is established and adjourn the case on certain conditions, in terms of s 16(1) of the Act: see the cases mentioned at note 173 above. In effect, that would be to postpone consideration as to whether it would be reasonable to grant the order to a later date. This seems the nearest approximation to a suspended or postponed order.

181 At para 3.175.

- any medical condition from which the tenant suffers, particularly any mental health condition, to which the antisocial behaviour may be attributable[182] (see below).

Clearly these considerations are also relevant in cases under the Scottish legislation. Also, one would expect the court to place particular emphasis on the section 16(3) factors described above – in particular, section 16(3)(c): "the effect which that conduct has had, is having and is likely to have on any person other than the tenant".

In antisocial behaviour cases it is common for the pursuers to plead a lengthy history of numerous incidents. Where these are admitted or proved, it is submitted that it will clearly be appropriate for the landlord's agent to draw the court's attention to section 16(3)(a). Conversely, the provision may be to the defender's advantage in circumstances where the nature, frequency and duration of the conduct are not so serious, relative to other cases.

As indicated in the general discussion of section 16(3)(b) above, it may be pled in favour of the tenant, especially where the conduct is on the part of someone who no longer resides at or visits the tenancy, but an issue may arise as to the extent to which the tenant may be said to have acquiesced in the acts or omissions in question.[183]

As regards section 16(3)(d), as well as the more general steps outlined in the analysis of that provision, which might be appropriate in any type of case, the landlord also has particular approaches in relation to antisocial behaviour cases, such as mediation between neighbours, good behaviour contracts, and rehousing, where it appears that it may be appropriate for the tenant or his family to make a new start in alternative accommodation. For the defender's agent, it is accordingly worth investigating whether any such steps have been attempted, and suggesting to the landlord that they might be considered. Consideration should also be given to enquiring of the landlords, at an early stage in the case, whether they would be willing to offer the defender an SSST if he consents to decree for eviction.

If no steps have been taken by the landlord to secure cessation of the conduct, or the steps have been limited, this may usefully be relied upon by the defender at a subsequent hearing of the case. Clearly the extent to which this approach will be successful will depend on the circumstances of each case; after the evidence is led, the suggestion that the tenant's behaviour could be appropriately addressed by mediation or rehousing may be untenable. Moreover, where such approaches have been unsuccessfully attempted by the landlord, the defender's position will be increasingly difficult to sustain.

182 See p 151 above, and the discussion of defences based on the Equality Act 2010, in Chapter 11.

183 There are numerous English authorities on the issues that arise if the antisocial behaviour is on the part of persons other than the tenant, in particular the tenant's children. For example: *Newcastle upon Tyne City Council v Morrison* (2000) 32 HLR 891; *New Charter Housing (North) Limited v Ashcroft* [2004] HLR 36; *Knowsley Housing Trust v McMullen* [2006] HLR 43; *Greenwich RLBC v Tuitt* [2015] HLR 10.

STREAMLINED EVICTION PROCESS FOR GROUND 2 CASES

Section 14 of the 2014 Act made amendments to sections 14 and 16(2) of the 2001 Act, the effect of which is to introduce the "streamlined eviction process" in relation to actions in which the landlord relies on ground 2.[184] The new section 16(2)(aa) provides:

> "(2) Subject to subsection (1), in proceedings under section 14 the court must make an order for recovery of possession if it appears to the court–
>
> . . .
>
> (aa) whether or not paragraph (a)[185] applies, that—
>
> (i) the landlord has a ground for recovery of possession set out in paragraph 2 of that schedule and so specified, and
>
> (ii) the landlord served the notice under section 14(2) before the day which is 12 months after—
>
> (A) the day on which the person was convicted of the offence forming the ground for recovery of possession,[186] or
>
> (B) where that conviction was appealed, the day on which the appeal is dismissed or abandoned . . ."

Where the landlord establishes the ground by proving the relevant conviction, and serves the notice of proceedings within the period set out in s 16(2)(aa)(ii), the court must grant the order for recovery of possession, whether or not it considers it reasonable to do so. The Scottish's Government's Guidance, described below, indicates that the purpose of the new procedure is to enable landlords to obtain an eviction order more quickly, in cases in which the offending behaviour is serious, or antisocial.

The removal of the reasonableness requirement in these cases puts the tenant in a section 16(2)(aa) case in a similar position to the short Scottish secure tenant subject to an action under section 36 of the Act. Section 14(2B) is to the same effect as the new section 34(9)(b)(ii), which also requires the landlord to have regard to the guidance, before taking steps with a view to raising proceedings under section 36.[187] However, in contrast to a short Scottish secure tenant, the tenant facing proceedings under ground 2 has no right to seek a review of the decision to serve the notice of proceedings.[188]

184 As was indicated in Chapter 4 (at p 124), changes have also been made to the prescribed form notice of proceedings, to reflect the coming into force of the new procedure for ground 2 cases. The new procedure applies to cases in which the notice of proceedings is served on or after commencement of the amending provisions, on 1 May 2019. See the Housing (Scotland) Act 2014 (Commencement No. 8, Savings, Transitional and Supplemental Provisions) Order 2018 (SSI 2018/153), para 5(b).

185 "Paragraph (a)": s 16(2)(a) is the existing form of action, under which the landlord must establish (i) one of the grounds 1–7 in sch 2, and (ii) that it is reasonable to grant the order. As regards ground 2 cases, this will continue to apply to those cases in which the s 14 notice is served too late to comply with the condition set out in s 16(2)(aa)(ii). Also, the new procedure is optional; the landlord might chose to proceed under s 16(2)(a) in a ground 2 case, even if the new procedure is available. This is confirmed by para 1.6 of the Guidance, which says, of s 16(2)(aa): "This new provision gives landlords the flexibility to choose whether to use a streamlined process for eviction in certain cases . . .".

186 So, if the conviction was on 1 May 2020, the notice would have to be served on the tenant on or before 30 April 2021, unless the conviction was appealed.

187 As regards SSSTs in the first of the two categories described at p 177.

188 For the short Scottish secure tenant, that right now exists under s 36(4A) and (4B).

Guidance

The potentially draconian effect of section 16(2)(aa) is tempered by section 14(2B), which requires the landlord to have regard[189] to guidance published by the Scottish Ministers, before raising proceedings under ground 2. That guidance is "Streamlined Eviction Process – Criminal Or Antisocial Behaviour Statutory Guidance for Social Landlords".[190]

The Guidance states[191] that the purpose of the streamlined eviction process is "to help to speed up eviction" in cases where:

- "serious" antisocial or criminal behaviour has already been proven in court (i.e. in the criminal proceedings which resulted in the conviction);
- the behaviour that led to the conviction was in the locality of the tenant's house; and
- the landlord considers that eviction action is appropriate, such as to protect neighbours and other people living or working in or near a social housing property from harm.

It is suggested that the effect of the "streamlined" process is that the decision as to whether the tenant ought to be evicted because his offending is taken from court and entrusted to the landlord. It is further suggested that the most important part of the Guidance runs from paragraph 4.8, in which examples are given of the factors that landlords might take into account in arriving at that decision:

- the nature and seriousness of the offence, including any recurring nature of convictions or cumulative effect of several incidents, or the potential seriousness of a one-off offence;
- who has been convicted of the offence, and their connection to the property;
- where the offence was committed, and the connection to the social housing tenancy;
- whether, and to what extent, the offence has affected neighbours or others in the community;
- the impact on neighbours and communities over time, and the impact on the stability of the community;
- what action, if any, the person convicted of the offence is taking to make positive change;
- the impact of eviction on household members;
- other steps taken or that could be taken by the landlord or partner agencies to address the antisocial or criminal behaviour;

The guidance expands upon each of those factors.

189 The duty to "have regard" to Guidance is discussed in Chapter 6, at p 192. Note that although s 14(2B) refers to all actions under ground 2, the Guidance only concerns cases in which the landlord chooses to use the streamlined eviction process.

190 This title is somewhat misleading, in that the new rules apply only to ground 2 cases, and so require a criminal conviction. They do not apply to cases under ground 7 or ground 8. However, as is indicated in the main text, the Guidance appears to envisage that the new rules will be used in cases in which the conviction is for some form of antisocial behaviour.

191 At paras 3.1 and 3.2.

Defences

An action under section 16(2)(aa) may be defended on the basis that ground 2 is not met, or the notice of proceedings was not served within the requisite period.

Otherwise, any defence would have to rely on the arguments discussed in Chapter 11 (public law, human rights and unlawful discrimination). The addition of subsection (3A) to section 16 recognises the possibility of such a defence, as does the Guidance.[192]

In practice, one might envisage that the tenant will argue that the landlord has failed to have regard to the Guidance – for example, in that the offence is not sufficiently serious to warrant the use of the procedure.[193] That would be a public law argument, which might be raised in a judicial review challenging the decision to raise proceedings, or stated as a defence in those proceedings.[194] Notably, the Guidance also states that "Decisions on using the streamlined eviction process should be consistent, balanced and transparent . . .",[195] and stresses the importance of the tenant being clearly notified of certain matters, including: "why this action has been taken, including reference to the legislation and the tenancy agreement".[196] Again, the failure to follow these points might form the basis for an argument that the decision to raise proceedings was unlawful. An apparent failure to take into account one of the factors listed at paragraph 4.8 of the Guidance may also vitiate the decision to raise proceedings; however, an argument that more weight ought to have been given to one of those factors (such as attempts by the convicted person to reform) is unlikely to be successful.[197]

Although the Guidance expressly alludes to the possibility of a defence under the Human Rights Act 1998, it is suggested that such a defence is unlikely to be successful if the landlord has followed the Guidance.[198]

GROUNDS 8–14 ("MANAGEMENT GROUNDS"): s 16(2)(b) AND (c)

Actions for recovery of possession under the "management" grounds are much less common. As well as establishing one of the grounds 8–15, the landlord must again prove that an additional requirement is met: that other suitable accommodation will be available for the tenant when the order takes effect. Accordingly, as with actions under grounds 1–7, the defender may admit the

192 See paras 2.7, 4.20 and 6.5 of the Guidance. There is a clear resemblance between actions under the streamlined process for ground 2, and proceedings under s 36 of the Act, as both in involve statutory tenants of social landlords whose scope for defending eviction proceedings is limited. For that reason, readers are referred to the discussion of public law defences etc. in SSST cases, at pp 178 and 213 of Chapter 6.

193 Paragraphs 4.10 and 4.11.

194 Paragraph 4.20. The argument being that it was unlawful for the landlord to raise the action, because it has failed to comply with s 14(2B).

195 Paragraph 4.18.

196 Paragraph 4.19.

197 Because the weight to be given to those factors is a matter for the landlord, subject to the Guidance.

198 See the discussion of Human Rights Act defences in Chapter 11.

ground but defend the action, contending that the additional requirement has not been met. In terms of section 16(4), part 2 of schedule 2 has effect for the purposes of determining what constitutes suitable alternative accommodation. There is no "reasonableness" requirement in relation to actions under grounds 8–14. An action under ground 15, in terms of section 16(2)(c), requires proof of both additional requirements.[199]

The various issues that might be relevant to the consideration of the "reasonableness" requirement are irrelevant in relation to an action under grounds 8–14, except in so far as they also bear upon the question of whether the relevant ground is established, or whether accommodation to be made available to the tenant is "suitable" for the purposes of the Act. Because grounds 8–15 entail moving the tenant to another tenancy, similar to a management transfer, they are sometimes referred to as the "management grounds".

Ground 8: nuisance, annoyance, harassment

"(1) The tenant (or any one of joint tenants) or any person residing or lodging with, or any subtenant of, the tenant–
  (a) has been guilty of conduct in or in the vicinity of the house which is a nuisance or annoyance, or
  (b) has pursued a course of conduct amounting to harassment of a person residing in, visiting or otherwise engaged in lawful activity in the locality,

  and in the opinion of the landlord it is appropriate in the circumstances to require the tenant to move to other accommodation.

(2) In sub-paragraph (1), 'conduct' and 'harassment' have the same meanings as in paragraph 7."

This ground may be used where the landlords consider that the problem of the conduct in question could be addressed by moving the tenant to a property elsewhere.[200] This might be an attractive approach where it appears, for example, that the conduct is related to a personal dispute between the tenant and one other neighbour. That said, it is open to the landlords to offer to move the tenant at any time, without the necessity of an action under ground 8. In particular, another tenancy may be offered as a means of resolving an action under ground 7. In that situation, in particular, the landlords may consider offering the tenant an SSST under section 34 of and schedule 6 to the Act,[201] so that they can see whether the conduct is going to persist in another location.

Ground 9: overcrowding

"The house is overcrowded, within the meaning of section 135 of the 1987 Act, in such circumstances as to render the occupier guilty of an offence."

199 Section 16(3) does not apply to cases under ground 15, though there is nothing to stop the court considering, e.g., the effect of the order, if that point is put to it by one of the parties.

200 See, e.g.: *Langstane Housing Association v Morrow* 2005 Hous LR 103.

201 See Chapter 6. In practice, this would involve a proposal that the tenant consents to decree for eviction in an action under ground 7, on the condition that the landlord offers an SSST at another location, under sch 6, para 1.

The statutory overcrowding standard is quite complex. The threshold is high[202] and, in most cases where overcrowding occurs, one would anticipate that the occupants would be willing to take up an offer of alternative accommodation, without the necessity of an action being raised to force them to do so. For these reasons, only a summary of the standard is given. For the full details, readers are referred to part VII of the 1987 Act.

Section 135 outlines two separate standards. Contravention of either standard constitutes overcrowding for the purposes of the Act. Contravention of the "room standard" occurs when the number of persons sleeping in the dwelling and the number of rooms available as sleeping accommodation (being a room of a type normally used as a bedroom or a living room) is such that two persons of opposite sexes who are not living together as husband and wife must sleep in the same room. Children under the age of ten are left out of account. Contravention of the "space standard" occurs when the number of persons sleeping in the dwelling is in excess of the permitted number, having regard to the number and floor area of the rooms of the dwelling available as sleeping accommodation. Section 135 provides two tables giving the permitted numbers and floor areas.

Ground 10: demolition[203]

"(1) It is intended within a reasonable period of time to demolish, or carry out substantial work on, the building or a part of the building which comprises or includes the house, and such demolition or work cannot reasonably take place without the landlord obtaining possession of the house.

(2) For the purposes of sub-paragraph (1), 'demolition' is to be construed in accordance with section 338(3) of the 1987 Act."[204]

It is important to appreciate that in this context "possession" means full legal possession. In order to establish this ground, the landlord must be able to show that the termination of the tenancy and full possession of the property are necessary in order to carry out the work in question, and that mere access to, or temporary occupation of, the premises is insufficient.[205] This entails: (a) identifying specifically the proposed works; and (b) showing why it is necessary to recover possession in order for the works to be carried out.[206] If the case is not one which is going to involve complete demolition, the ground will not be established if the tenant is willing to move out and stay elsewhere while the work is in progress, as in that case full recovery of possession is unnecessary. Accordingly, it is arguable that the landlord must show that the tenant has refused to accept an offer of decant accommodation,

202 In comparison with what constitutes overcrowding for the purposes of most local authority and housing association allocation policies.

203 See also the discussion of the equivalent grounds under the 1988 and 2016 Acts, in Chapters 8 and 10.

204 The 1987 Act, s 338(3) states: "In this Act, any reference to the demolition of a building shall be deemed to include a reference to such reconstruction of the building as the local authority may approve; and where a building is so reconstructed any reference to selling, letting or appropriating the land, the building on which has been or will be demolished, shall, unless the context otherwise requires, be construed as a reference to selling, letting or appropriating the land and the reconstructed building."

205 See *Heath v Drown* [1973] AC 498.

206 *Wansbeck District Council v Marley* (1988) 20 HLR 247.

or the landlord has no decant accommodation available, as it is only in these circumstances that an order for repossession is necessary in order for the work to be carried out.

The landlord must also establish that there is an intention to carry out the work. In *City of Edinburgh Council v Middlemiss*,[207] the tenant argued that the work was merely "in contemplation". Finding in favour of the landlords, the sheriff noted that the necessary funding was in place, and that the council had the present means and the ability to carry their plans into effect. That being so, he did not require to look at the *minutiae* of the proposed development or attempt to scrutinise the subsequent process of carrying it out.

Certain provisions in the 2001 Act apply specifically to actions under ground 10. In particular, section 16(6) provides:

> "Where, in proceedings under section 14 on the ground set out in paragraph 10 of schedule 2, it appears to the court that the landlord intends that–
> (a) substantial work will be carried out on the building (or a part of the building) which comprises or includes the house, and
> (b) the tenant should return to the house after the work is completed,
> the court must make an order that the tenant is entitled to return to the house after the work is completed; and subsection (5)(a) does not apply in such a case."[208]

If an order is made under this provision, the accommodation provided to the tenant in the meantime will effectively be decant accommodation, to which section 12(2) and (3) apply.[209]

Grounds 11 and 12: special needs

> "11. The house has been designed or adapted for occupation by a person whose special needs require accommodation of the kind provided by the house and–
> (a) there is no person with such special needs occupying the house, and
> (b) the landlord requires it for occupation (whether alone or with other members of the person's family) by a person who has such special needs.
>
> 12. The house forms part of a group of houses which has been designed, or which has been provided with or located near facilities, for persons with special needs, and–
> (a) there is no person with such a need occupying the house, and
> (b) the landlord requires it for occupation (whether alone or with other members of the person's family) by a person who has such a need."

Both of these grounds were amended by section 15 of the 2014 Act:[210] previously, paragraph (a) in both grounds said "there is no *longer a* person". Apparently, the words "no longer" caused difficulties for a social landlord seeking to recover an adapted property that had never had an occupier that required the adaptations. The Scottish Government has issued (short)

207 2007 Hous LR 70.

208 Subsection (5)(a) provides that an order under s 16(2) terminates the tenancy.

209 Under those provisions, landlord is not entitled to bring the tenant's occupation of the decant accommodation to an end before the house that the tenant normally occupies is available for occupation. This applies not only to accommodation provided under s 16(6), but also to decant accommodation provided by agreement with the tenant.

210 With effect from 1 May 2019: the Housing (Scotland) Act 2014 (Commencement No. 8, Savings, Transitional and Supplemental Provisions) Order 2018 (n 184), para 5(c). The amended grounds apply in respect of any notice of proceedings served on or after that date.

guidance entitled "Recovery of Possession of Properties Designed or Adapted for Special Needs: Guidance for Social Landlords", to which readers are referred.

Both grounds effectively require the landlord to show three things:

(1) that the house, or the group of houses in question, meets the description in the first part of the ground. This would presumably require the landlord to lead evidence as to the nature of the design/adaptation/local facilities for persons with special needs;[211]
(2) that none of the persons currently occupying the house has such special needs. In ground 11, there appears to be a clearer connection between the special needs in question and the nature of the design or adaptation, such that it would be possible for the authority to accept that there is a person occupying the house who has special needs, but that they are not the special needs for which the particular design or adaptation was made. In ground 12, that connection appears less clear, presumably because the design and facilities would probably be more general, being intended for a class of special needs, rather than a particular individual; and
(3) that the landlord requires it for occupation by a person who has such a need. It is not clear whether the landlord must identify the person to whom it intends to allocate the house. This would appear somewhat impractical, as there may be a lengthy delay between commencement of the action and the date on which the tenancy becomes available for a new tenant, if the landlord is successful, during which time other suitable accommodation might have become available for the prospective tenant. There is no requirement in the Act for the landlord ultimately to allocate the tenancy to the particular person referred to in ground 11(b) or ground 12(b), in the event that it obtains an order. Therefore, it is submitted that a reasonable course would be for the court to allow this requirement to be satisfied by the landlord showing that it has a waiting list of persons with the requisite needs, one of whom will be allocated the house once the order is granted.

In ground 12, the term "group" refers to special needs dwellings grouped together in the same location, rather than a group of houses spread throughout the area of the landlords' ordinary housing stock.[212]

Ground 13: landlord as lessee

> "The interest of the landlord in the house is that of a lessee under a lease and that lease either–
> (a) has terminated, or
> (b) will terminate within a period of 6 months from the date of raising of proceedings for recovery of possession."

211 There have been several cases in relation to the issue of adaptations to accommodation in the context of succession or the right to buy: *Dundee District Council v Anderson* 1993 SC 214, 1994 SLT 46; *Forsyth v South Ayrshire Council* 2002 Hous LR 101; *Davidson v Dundee City Council* 2002 Hous LR 104; and *City of Edinburgh Council v Catherick* 2006 Hous LR 62.

212 *Martin v Motherwell District Council* 1991 SLT (Lands Tr) 4.

This ground is self-explanatory. It is difficult to envisage the circumstances in which a landlord would grant a Scottish secure tenancy to a person in respect of a house of which it was merely the lessee.[213]

Ground 14

"The landlord is Orkney Islands Council, Shetland Islands Council or Western Isles Council and–

(a) the house is–
  (i) held by the council for the purposes of its functions as education authority, and
  (ii) required for the accommodation of a person who is or will be employed by the council for those purposes,
(b) the council cannot reasonably provide a suitable alternative house for the accommodation referred to in sub-paragraph (a)(ii), and
(c) the tenant (or any one of joint tenants) is, or at any time during the tenancy has been or, where the tenancy passed to the existing tenant under section 22, the previous tenant at any time during the tenancy was, employed by the council for the purposes of its functions as education authority and such employment has terminated or notice of termination has been given."

As with grounds 11 and 12, this ground deals with tenancies of a particular type that are made available for a particular class of person into which the current tenant does not fall. In this case, the council has to show that parts (a)(i) and (ii) are fulfilled. The effect of (b) appears to be that the council is required to show that it does not have a suitable alternative house for the prospective tenant.

Ground 15

"The landlord wishes to transfer the tenancy of the house to–

(a) the tenant's spouse or civil partner (or former spouse or former civil partner), or
(b) a person with whom the tenant has, for a period of at least 6 months immediately prior to the date of the application for transfer, been living in the house as husband and wife or in a relationship which has the characteristics of the relationship between civil partners,

who has applied to the landlord for such transfer; and the tenant or (as the case may be) the spouse or other person no longer wishes to live together with the other in the house."

In terms of section 16(2)(c), this ground, uniquely, requires that both of the additional requirements are fulfilled.[214] Ground 15 would appear to be appropriate in the case of a relationship breakdown that results in a situation where both parties want to live separately, but neither wishes to leave the tenancy, and where the landlord wishes the person who is not the tenant to remain at the tenancy, and the tenant to be transferred to other accommodation.[215]

213 One would expect that a short SST would be granted under sch 6, para 7.

214 That the order is reasonable, and that suitable alternative accommodation will be available to the tenant.

215 If the tenant *was* willing to leave, then presumably an action of recovery of possession would not be necessary; the tenant could be moved to the alternative accommodation, without the requirement for a court order. In the case of joint tenancies, s 13 of the Act provides that a joint tenant may bring to an end that tenant's interest in the tenancy by four weeks' notice

Clearly this would be a fairly unusual set of circumstances. The reference to an application being made to the landlord for a "transfer" of the tenancy is somewhat odd: the landlord of a Scottish secure tenancy has no power to transfer the tenancy from one person to another.[216]

THE ADDITIONAL REQUIREMENT: "SUITABLE ALTERNATIVE ACCOMMODATION"

As already described, the additional requirement applicable to the "management grounds" under section 16(2)(b) is that "other suitable accommodation will be available for the tenant when the order takes effect". There is no requirement that that order is "reasonable", and accordingly, the court's judgment is more narrowly focused.[217]

Under section 16(4), part 2 of schedule 2 to the Act has effect to determine whether accommodation is suitable for the purposes of the Act. The relevant paragraphs are 16–18 of schedule 2.

> "16. For the purposes of sections 16(4), 19(5), 21(5) and 22(7), accommodation is suitable if–
> (a) it consists of premises which are to be let as a separate dwelling under a Scottish secure tenancy or under a private residential tenancy, and
> (b) it is reasonably suitable to the needs of the tenant and the tenant's family."

Paragraph 16(a) has been amended, with the words "a private residential tenancy" replacing "an assured tenancy" following the coming into force of the 2016 Act. This ought to make it easier for local authorities and RSLs to arrange suitable alternative accommodation in the private rented sector, rather than being restricted to offering accommodation from their own stock.[218]

> "17. In determining whether accommodation is reasonably suitable to the needs of the tenant and the tenant's family, regard is to be had to–
> (a) its proximity to the place of work (including attendance at an educational institution) of the tenant and of members of the tenant's family, compared with the tenant's existing house,
> (b) the extent of the accommodation required by the tenant and the tenant's family,
> (c) the character of the accommodation offered compared to the tenant's existing house,

given to the landlord and each of the other joint tenants under the tenancy. In cases of relationship breakdown, many local authorities are willing to accept a homeless application under pt II of the 1987 Act, on the basis that they accept that it is not reasonable, in terms of s 24(2A), for the applicant to remain in the accommodation with his/her partner.

216 The court has the power to transfer a tenancy by the Matrimonial Homes (Family Protection) (Scotland) Act 1981, s 13. The landlord may consent to an assignation of a Scottish secure tenancy under the 2001 Act, s 32, though this is obviously distinct from effecting a transfer.

217 For example, the court could not take into account the fact that the landlord has, in the past, made other offers of accommodation to the tenant, unless that was relevant to the issue of whether other suitable accommodation will be available for the tenant when the order takes effect.

218 Because it would have been quite difficult to find private landlords willing to offer a tenancy under the 1988 Act that was not a short assured tenancy. Under the 2016 Act, there is only one form of tenancy: the PRT.

(d) the terms on which the accommodation is offered to the tenant compared with the terms of the tenant's existing tenancy,
(e) if any furniture was provided by the landlord for use under the existing tenancy,whether furniture is to be provided for use under the new tenancy which is of a comparable nature in relation to the needs of the tenant and the tenant's family,
(f) any special needs of the tenant or the tenant's family."

The factors indicated in paragraph 17 are not exhaustive.[219] The Act does not exclude other considerations that might be relevant to the issue of whether the accommodation is reasonably suitable.[220] As regards the paragraph 17 factors, the following points may be made:

- The members of the tenant's family[221] for the purposes of factor (a) are presumably those members who are to reside with the tenant at the new tenancy.
- As regards the extent of the accommodation "required" in terms of factor (b), it is thought that landlords would determine this question in accordance with their allocation policy, and that this would be sound *prima facie* evidence, at least, of the adequacy of the size of the accommodation.[222] If that is indeed the case, it would be for the tenant to persuade the court why something more extensive should be offered in his case.
- As regards "extent" and "character", a court should have regard to the particular tenant's housing needs, and not to other ancillary advantages enjoyed by the tenant in respect of his current accommodation.[223]
- As regards factor (d), as indicated above, the amendment of paragraph 16(a) has the effect that "suitable alternative accommodation" could be a private residential tenancy ("PRT") under the 2016 Act. However, a tenant under a PRT has less security of tenure than a tenant under a Scottish secure tenancy.[224] The tenant might argue that, because of her particular circumstances, the lesser form of security of a tenancy under the 2016 Act is not suitable.
- As regards factor (f), there is no definition of "special needs" in the Act. Accordingly, these words are to be given their ordinary meaning, which

219 *Enfield London Borough Council v French* (1985) 17 HLR 211.

220 In this respect, it is interesting to note that the factors as to the reasonable suitability of accommodation are different in sch 2, pt 4 of the Housing Act 1985. In that scheme, factors (c) and (f) in para 17 above do not appear. There are factors which are similar to (a), (b), (d) and (e), together with the following two factors: "the nature of the accommodation which it is the practice of the landlord to allocate to persons with similar needs" and "its distance from the house of any member of the tenant's family if proximity to it is essential to that member's or the tenant's well-being". This second factor, in particular, is often a concern for the tenant in cases where a move to alternative accommodation is being considered. As the para 17 factors are not exhaustive, it would also be possible to put this consideration to the court in relation to its decision as to whether accommodation was reasonably suitable for the purposes of para 16(b).

221 "Family" is defined in s 108 of the Act.

222 All RSLs and local authorities have allocation policies that contain rules as to the minimum size of accommodation suitable for applicants, given the composition of the applicant's family.

223 *Hill v Rochard* [1983] 1 WLR 478.

224 Because the grounds for eviction under sch 3 to the 2016 Act are more favourable to the landlord.

is sufficiently wide to extend beyond, for example, medical or educational needs.

- An issue that often concerns tenants being offered alternative accommodation is the desire not to be moved to what is considered to be a "bad area". This might be encompassed in factor (c), though, as the factors are not exhaustive, it may be put before the court in any event, as long as it has some bearing on the issue of whether the accommodation being offered is "reasonably suitable to the needs of the tenant and the tenant's family". It is clear that the list of factors in respect of "suitability" is intended to allow the sheriff to have regard to matters beyond the mere size of the accommodation.
- On the other hand, the fact that what is required is "*reasonably* suitable" must mean that the court can also consider the extent to which the landlord's options are limited by the availability of stock.[225]

In *Reading BC v Holt*,[226] the Court of Appeal held that there is no requirement either that an offer of accommodation has been made before the date of the hearing or that the accommodation is even available at the date of the hearing. Nothing in the legislation requires the court to be satisfied that a particular property is suitable; if the court is satisfied that accommodation having particular characteristics would be suitable and that such accommodation will become available in due course, it has jurisdiction to make a possession order that will not take effect until such accommodation has in fact become available.

The difficulty in applying this reasoning in the Scottish context is that section 16(5) of the 2001 Act provides that an order for possession under subsection (2) must appoint a date for recovery of possession and has the effect of (a) terminating the tenancy, and (b) giving the landlord the right to recover possession of the house. Therefore, it is suggested that, in a Scottish case, if the court were satisfied that the statutory ground was made out, and that accommodation having particular characteristics would be suitable, and that such accommodation will become available in due course, the case could be sisted or continued. The order under section 16(5) could then be granted, once the date on which accommodation will be available is known. That is consistent with granting decree under section 16(2)(b), which requires that the landlord has: (i) a ground for possession, and that (ii) "other suitable accommodation will be available for the tenant *when the order takes effect*".

> "18. If the landlord has made an offer in writing to the tenant of new accommodation which complies with paragraph 16(a) and which appears to it to be suitable, specifying the date when the accommodation will be available and the date (not being less than 14 days from the date of the offer) by which the offer must be accepted, the accommodation so offered is deemed to be suitable if–

225 For a discussion of the issues that might arise under the last two bullet points, see *Dundee City Council v McPhee* 2005 Hous LR 30.

226 [2013] HLR 40. In this case the council sought possession on ground 16 of sch 2 to the Housing Act 1985, which applies when a tenant who has succeeded to the tenancy underoccupies the subjects. There is no equivalent ground under the Scottish legislation. However, the ordering of possession under ground 16 is subject to the requirement under discussion: "suitable alternative accommodation will be available for the tenant when the order takes effect".

(a) the landlord shows that the tenant accepted the offer within the time duly specified in the offer, or
(b) the landlord shows that the tenant did not so accept the offer, and the tenant does not satisfy the court that the tenant acted reasonably in failing to accept the offer."

The effect of paragraph 18 is that the tenant cannot change his mind once he has accepted the offer, as acceptance means that the accommodation is deemed to be suitable. Where an offer is refused, this appears to have the effect of shifting the onus on to the tenant, who is then required to satisfy the court that he acted reasonably in refusing the offer. The offer must comply with paragraph 16(a), and specify the dates on which the accommodation will be available and by which the offer must be accepted. If the offer does not meet those conditions, paragraph 18 does not apply, and the onus remains with the landlords.

Although the Act does not specifically say so, it seems reasonable to suppose that the court would view the issue of whether the tenant has acted reasonably in failing to accept the offer using the same criteria as would have been applicable to a judgment as to whether the accommodation in question is reasonably suitable, being the criteria in paragraph 17.[227]

In both cases to which paragraph 18 applies, it appears that the landlords are required to keep the accommodation available until the eviction order takes effect; this is a prerequisite of the order being granted under section 16(2)(b)(ii).[228]

227 This was the approach adopted by the sheriff in *Dundee City Council v McPhee* (n 225).
228 This is the requirement that "other suitable accommodation will be available for the tenant when the order takes effect".

Chapter 6

Short Scottish Secure Tenancies

INTRODUCTION

Sections 34–37 of the 2001 Act summarised

Sections 34–37 of and schedule 6 to the 2001 Act set out the arrangements for a form of tenancy that was new to that Act: the short Scottish secure tenancy ("SSST").[1] It is a hybrid of the Scottish secure tenancy and the short assured tenancy under the 1988 Act, intended to be used for tenancies in the social rented sector, in cases where it is considered appropriate to offer the tenant less than full security of tenure.

Sections 7–11 of the 2014 Act made various important amendments to that statutory scheme, and widened the circumstances in which an SSST may be used.[2] The Scottish Government has issued Guidance to coincide with the coming into force of the amendments: "Short Scottish Secure Tenancies for Antisocial Behaviour and Other Miscellaneous Changes to Short Scottish Secure Tenancies – Statutory Guidance for Social Landlords".[3] Landlords are required to have regard to the SSST Guidance before carrying out certain actions under the statutory scheme.[4]

Sections 34 and 35 primarily provide for the two different ways in which an SSST may be created. Section 34 deals with new tenancies that are to be SSSTs. Subsection (1) bears a strong similarity to section 32(1) of the 1988 Act, which sets out the two requirements for creation of a short assured tenancy: it must be for a period of at least six months,[5] and the landlord requires to serve a notice in the prescribed form on the tenant. A new SSST may be created only if one of the paragraphs in schedule 6 to the Act is satisfied.[6]

1 Usually referred to as a "triple ST".
2 The amendments made by ss 7–11 of the 2014 Act came into force on 1 May 2019, subject to certain savings provisions, which are described in the main text, at pp 186 and 215 below. See: Housing (Scotland) Act 2014 (Commencement No. 8, Savings, Transitional and Supplemental Provisions) Order (SSI 2018/153). For a discussion of the legislative scheme as originally enacted, readers are referred to the first edition of this work.
3 Hereinafter referred to, in this chapter, as "the SSST Guidance". The Scottish Government also issued guidance on the use of SSSTs for homeowners: see the discussion of para 7A of sch 6, at p 185 below.
4 Section 34(9). See p 191 below.
5 However, as will be explained below, the minimum six-month requirement has now been superseded in ASB SSSTs, by the imposition of a fixed twelve-month period, which may be increased by a further six months.
6 These are summarised at p 183 below.

One of the principal changes made by the 2014 Act is to add new paragraphs to schedule 6.

Section 35 allows for the creation of an SSST by conversion from an existing Scottish secure tenancy. Conversion is effected by the landlord serving a notice under section 35(2) and (3). Originally that could be done only where the tenant (or any one of joint tenants) or a person residing or lodging with, or sub-tenant of, the tenant was subject to an antisocial behaviour order. As a result of amendments to section 35 made by section 7 of the 2014 Act, conversion is possible without the necessity of such an order being obtained, if the circumstances described in the new section 35(2)(b) exist. This change seems likely to increase the number of conversions under section 35.

Section 36 allows for recovery of possession of the subjects in a manner that is similar to the procedure under section 33 of the 1988 Act: the landlord is required to satisfy the court that it has served the correct notices and followed the procedure in terms of section 36. It does not need to prove any ground for recovery of possession, and it need not satisfy any "additional requirement".[7] This is the means by which the legislation limits security of tenure for the classes of tenants for whom the SSST, rather than a Scottish secure tenancy, is considered appropriate.

Section 37 provides that certain SSSTs may convert to Scottish secure tenancies, after the term of the tenancy has expired.

Two different categories of SSST

The legislation, as amended by the 2014 Act, creates two different types of SSST. In the first category are: new tenancies created under section 34 because paragraph 1, 2 or 2A of schedule 6 applies; and tenancies that have been converted under section 35. This type of tenancy arises because of previous antisocial behaviour on the part of the tenant, or someone associated with him.[8] In the second category are SSSTs created under section 34 because paragraph 3, 4, 5, 6, 7 or 7A of schedule 6 applies. Broadly speaking, those paragraphs describe various circumstances, other than previous antisocial behaviour, in which it is considered appropriate for a social landlord to offer a tenancy in which the tenant does not have security of tenure. In the text that follows, these two categories are referred to as "ASB SSSTs" and "non-ASB SSSTs".

The key differences between these two types of SSST are:

(1) The landlord must have regard to the aforementioned SSST Guidance, before creating an ASB SSST.[9]

7 Such as the requirement to show that the eviction is reasonable, or offer suitable alternative accommodation, as would be the case in an action for recovery of possession of a Scottish secure tenancy: see Chapter 5.

8 In ss 34–37 the first category is denoted by the words "a short Scottish secure tenancy created by virtue of section 35 or paragraph 1, 2 or 2A of schedule 6". In the Guidance, this is referred to as "the Short Scottish Secure Tenancy for Antisocial Behaviour".

9 Section 34(9), which was added by the 2014 Act. The SSST Guidance, and the duty to "have regard" to it, is discussed below, at p 191.

(2) ASB SSSTs have a term of twelve months that is fixed by the Act.[10] That term may be extended by a further six months.[11] Non-ASB SSSTs may be for any period, as long as it is "not less than 6 months".[12] That period may then continue by tacit relocation. Therefore, a non-ASB SSST may continue indefinitely.
(3) Under section 37, ASB SSSTs convert to Scottish secure tenancies on expiry of the twelve-month term (or eighteen-month term, if extended),[13] provided that the landlord has not served a statutory notice of its intention to raise possession proceedings before expiry. Non-ASB SSSTs do not convert to Scottish secure tenancies, under the legislative scheme.[14]
(4) In the case of ASB SSSTs, the landlord must provide, or ensure the provision of, such housing support services as it considers appropriate with a view to enabling conversion under section 37 to take place.[15]
(5) In the case of ASB SSSTs, the statutory notice of proceedings under section 36 cannot be served unless the landlord considers that an obligation of the tenancy has been broken;[16] and the landlord must have regard to the SSST Guidance before taking steps with a view to raising proceedings under section 36.

For these reasons, it is suggested that ASB SSSTs may be regarded as probationary in nature, in that the tenant has a trial period in which to demonstrate that he is capable of adhering to his obligations as tenant.[17] If he succeeds, he is rewarded with a Scottish secure tenancy. If he fails, he is liable to be evicted following proceedings under section 36.

Limited security of tenure: "public law" defences, article 8 cases, Equality Act 2010

The scope for defending eviction proceedings by reference to public law principles, the Human Rights Act 1998 and the Equality Act 2010, is discussed in Chapter 11.

As already described, the SSST is a form of statutory tenancy, granted by a social landlord, which limits security of tenure, with the result that in eviction proceedings under section 36 of the Act, it is not necessary for the landlord to show that there is any particular ground for eviction, or that it would be reasonable to grant the order. This is also the case with two special statutory tenancies under the English legislation, the "demoted tenancy" and the "introductory tenancy".[18] It is a special feature of all of these tenancies

10 Section 34(6A).
11 Section 35A. Only one six-month extension is permitted. Consequently, an ASB SSST has a maximum length of eighteen months.
12 Section 34(1)(b).
13 Thus, a Scottish secure tenancy may convert to an ASB SSST under s 35, and later convert back again to a Scottish secure tenancy under s 37.
14 Though it would be possible for parties to terminate a non-ASB SSST and replace it with a Scottish secure tenancy.
15 Section 34(7).
16 Section 36(2)(aa).
17 The original Scottish Government guidance for social landlords on the use of SSSTs described tenancies liable to conversion under s 37 as "probationary" (SEDD 6/2002, para 142). However, that term is not used in the updated guidance.
18 Neither of these types of tenancy is available under the Scottish legislation, but they have

that they are set up under statutory codes that *require* the court or tribunal to grant an order for eviction, provided that the landlord complies with certain minimal procedural requirements. The relevant provisions, read literally, would exclude any defence except one based on the contention that those requirements had not been met.[19]

Consequently, defenders in eviction proceedings under these statutory codes have resorted to the argument that eviction would amount to a violation of their rights under the European Convention on Human Rights ("ECHR"), and in particular article 8, which includes the right to respect for one's home. The two leading cases on the article 8 defence in eviction proceedings are the decisions of the Supreme Court in *Manchester City Council v Pinnock*,[20] which concerned a demoted tenancy; and *Hounslow LBC v Powell*,[21] which featured an introductory tenancy.[22]

The article 8 defence is discussed in greater detail in Chapter 11. However, for present purposes one may say that:

(a) where statutory provisions require a court or tribunal to grant an order for eviction in favour of a landlord that is a public authority,[23] provided that the landlord has complied with certain minimal procedural requirements, a proportionality test must be "read into" such provisions;
(b) accordingly, even if those procedural requirements have been met, the tenant may nevertheless state a defence that argues that an eviction order would be disproportionate, and therefore contrary to article 8;[24]
(c) however, such a defence will succeed only in exceptional circumstances, given the inherent strength of the landlord's case, and the significant "procedural safeguards" that are given to the tenant, in such statutory schemes.[25]

certain features in common with ASB SSSTs. (1) Under pt 5 of the Housing Act 1996, local authorities in England may elect to offer *all* lettings to new tenants as introductory tenancies. These lets operate on a "probationary" or "trial" basis. If the tenancy endures for twelve months (or eighteen months where the trial period has been extended) it becomes a secure tenancy, unless the authority decide to bring it to an end under pt 5 of the 1996 Act. (2) A local authority may apply to the court for a "demotion order" in respect of a secure tenancy, where a person residing in or visiting the tenancy has engaged or threatened to engage in antisocial behaviour, or where the tenancy has been used for unlawful purposes. If the order is granted, the secure tenancy becomes a "demoted tenancy", in which the tenant is subject to a probationary period of twelve months, after which the tenancy becomes a secure tenancy again, unless the local authority has raised eviction proceedings under ss 143A–143P of the 1996 Act.

19 This is also the case with the short assured tenancy: see s 33 of the 1988 Act, discussed in Chapter 7. As is described above, the SSST is a hybrid of the short assured tenancy and the Scottish secure tenancy. Section 33(1) of the 1988 Act is very similar to s 36(5) of the 2001 Act, which is considered at p 211 below.

20 [2011] 2 AC 104.

21 [2011] 2 AC 186.

22 The judgment in *Powell* examined two cases. One involved an introductory tenancy. The other involved a tenancy granted to a homeless person, which was excepted from statutory security of tenure.

23 The issue of whether a registered social landlord is a public authority is discussed in Chapter 11.

24 These two principles were accepted as being applicable to s 36 of the 2001 Act, in the decision of the Inner House in *South Lanarkshire Council v McKenna* 2013 SC 212.

25 See Lord Phillips' judgment in *Powell* at paras [90]–[93].

In *Powell*,[26] those procedural safeguards, in the statutory scheme for introductory tenancies, were said to be: the requirement that the tenant be given notice of the reasons for the landlord's decision to seek a possession order; and the right to seek a review of that decision, and to be given reasons for confirmation of the decision, if it is confirmed.[27]

Those safeguards did not exist, in the statutory scheme for SSSTs under sections 34–37 of the 2001 Act, as originally enacted. However, certain procedural safeguards have now been inserted into the legislation by amendments in the 2014 Act. As we will see, the landlord now requires to give reasons to the tenant for taking various steps – in particular: serving a conversion notice under section 35; extending the tenancy under section 35A; and raising proceedings under section 36. Where notice of proceedings is served by the landlord under section 36(2), the tenant may now seek a review, under section 36(4A), and where the decision is confirmed by the landlord it must give the tenant the reasons for so confirming, under section 36(4B).[28]

Therefore, in light of the above conclusions drawn from the decisions in *Pinnock* and *Powell*,[29] one may say that although it is possible to argue, in an action under section 36 of the Act, that the court should not grant an eviction order, because it would be a violation of the defender's article 8 rights, such a defence is unlikely to be successful.[30]

Instead, it may be more fruitful for defenders to focus on the argument that decree under section 36 should not be granted in favour of the pursuer, because it has acted *unlawfully* at some stage in the process leading up to its motion for decree. As explained in Chapter 11, that is a "public law" defence that relies on the principle that public bodies must respect the rule of law, and must not act unlawfully, or seek to give effect to their unlawful actions or unlawful decisions.

It is suggested that the scope for such a defence has always existed under sections 34–37 of the Act, and has been increased by the amendments made in terms of the 2014 Act. That is so for several reasons. This part of the Act has certain complexities, and there are various pitfalls for the social landlord. Furthermore, the statutory scheme enjoins the landlord to carry out certain actions, but without spelling out the consequences of failure to do so. A good example is the requirement that the landlord is to "have regard to" the SSST Guidance before raising proceedings under section 36. That appears in section 34,[31] but there is no provision there, or in section 36, which indicates what legal effect follows, if the landlord does not have regard to the Guidance.

That suggests the following defence might be pled in proceedings under section 36:

26 n 21.

27 ibid paras [90] and [93].

28 However, the arrangements for procedure to be adopted in relation to such a review are less robust than those under the English legislation. See the discussion at p 209 below.

29 n 21.

30 Though success is not impossible. See *River Clyde Homes v Woods* 2015 Hous LR 33, and 2015 GWD 33-542.

31 Specifically, s 34(9)(b)(ii). Section 34 requires the landlord to have regard to the SSST Guidance before taking various steps under the statutory scheme.

1) Section 34(9)(b)(ii) requires the pursuers to have regard to the SSST Guidance before raising these proceedings.[32]
2) The pursuers have not have had regard to that Guidance.
3) Accordingly, the decision to raise proceedings under section 36 is unlawful.
4) Therefore, in an application to the supervisory jurisdiction of the Court of Session, by judicial review proceedings, the decision to raise proceedings would be reduced.
5) And, thus, the action ought to be dismissed.[33]

Reference is made to the possibility of this type of argument at various points in the discussion that follows.

The defender may also rely on the defence that eviction would be unlawfully discriminatory, being contrary to the Equality Act 2010. For example, in a case in which action is taken against the tenant because of antisocial behaviour, he may assert that he is a disabled person suffering from a mental health condition that is the cause of the behaviour in question. That could be a basis on which an action under section 36 of the 2001 Act, against a tenant under an ASB SSST, is resisted, by reference to sections 15 and 35 of the Equality Act 2010. For more detail on this type of argument, the reader is again referred to Chapter 11.

SSSTs and homelessness

There is an important relationship between SSSTs and the statutory scheme for the assistance and accommodation of homeless persons under part II of the 1987 Act.[34]

First, under paragraph 5 of schedule 6, a non-ASB SSST may be offered "expressly on a temporary basis" to a homeless applicant requiring accommodation. This would be under section 29 of the 1987 Act, pending a decision in relation to an application, a review of a decision, or pending permanent accommodation becoming available. However, not many SSSTs will be offered on this basis. As accommodation provided on an interim basis for homeless persons is exempted from being a Scottish secure tenancy,[35] it is possible for a local authority to offer a homeless applicant a tenancy for a shorter period than the six-month SSST, which will afford it greater flexibility, when it decides to bring the tenancy to an end.

More significant is the effect of section 31(5)(c) of the 1987 Act. Under section 31(2), a local authority has the duty to secure that "permanent accommodation" becomes available for a homeless person whose application under part II has been successful.[36]

32 As to s 34(9), and the duty to "have regard" to the SSST Guidance, see p 192 below.

33 As to why it is possible (and in many cases necessary) to plead this as a defence in the sheriff court, rather than raising judicial review proceedings, see Chapter 11.

34 That scheme is described in Chapter 5, at p 151.

35 In terms of sch 1 para 5, discussed in Chapter 4, at p 84.

36 Unless, in the case of an applicant who does not have a local connection with authority, it chooses to refer her to another authority under s 33 of the Act.

Section 31(5) states:

"(5) For the purposes of subsection (2), 'permanent accommodation' includes accommodation—
(a) secured by a Scottish secure tenancy,
(b) . . .
(c) where paragraph 1, 2 or 2A of schedule 6 to the Housing (Scotland) Act 2001 is satisfied in relation to the applicant, secured by a short Scottish secure tenancy;[37]
(d) secured by a private residential tenancy."[38]

Accordingly, the authority may discharge its duty to a successful homeless applicant under part II of the 1987 Act by the provision of an SSST, rather than a Scottish secure tenancy, but only if the SSST is an ASB SSST, granted because paragraph 1, 2 or 2A of schedule 6 to the 2001 Act applies.[39]

This has the important consequence that, if the authority offers a successful homeless applicant a *non*-ASB SSST, it has not then discharged its duty to provide permanent accommodation under section 31(2), which still has to be met. Therefore, if the SSST is terminated by proceedings under section 36 of the 2001 Act, the authority will continue to be subject to a duty to secure permanent accommodation and, if necessary, interim accommodation under section 29(1)(c) of the 1987 Act, if permanent accommodation is not yet available. If that duty was not met, the authority might then be subject to judicial review proceedings.

CREATION OF SSSTs

New SSTs under section 34(1)–(4) and schedule 6

"**Short Scottish secure tenancies**
(1) A tenancy of a house is a short Scottish secure tenancy if–
(a) it would have been a Scottish secure tenancy but for this section,
(b) it is for a term of not less than 6 months, and
(c) before its creation, the prospective landlord serves on the prospective tenant a notice under subsection (4).
(2) A prospective landlord may serve a notice under subsection (4) only where any of the paragraphs of schedule 6 is satisfied.
(3) The Scottish Ministers may by order modify that schedule.
(4) A notice under this subsection–
(a) must be in such form as the Scottish Ministers may prescribe by regulations,

37 This provision was amended by s 7(5) of the 2014 Act, with effect from 1 May 2019, to include reference to para 2A. This will probably have the effect of increasing the provision of SSSTs, rather than Scottish secure tenancies, to successful homeless applicants. Note that, in terms of s 31(5)(d), the authority may also discharge its duty by securing a private residential tenancy for the applicant, under the 2016 Act.

38 Note that the requirement to provide permanent accommodation does not arise, if s 32A and the Homeless Persons (Provision of Non-permanent Accommodation) (Scotland) Regulations 2010 (SSI 2010/2) apply. Under reg 3, an SSST on ground 6 of sch 6 could be provided to a person following a housing support services assessment.

39 If the homeless person is aggrieved by the offer of an SSST instead of a Scottish secure tenancy, he may appeal against that offer under s 38(1)(c), by summary application. See p 14 below.

(b) must state that the tenancy to which it relates is to be a short Scottish secure tenancy and specify the paragraph of that schedule which is satisfied in relation to it, and

(c) must specify the term of the tenancy."

Prerequisites for creation of a new SSST: s 34(1)

For a further discussion of various terms used in this provision, the reader is referred to other chapters.[40]

Section 34(1) makes a rather confusing impression, particularly in light of the amendments made to that section by the 2014 Act. It is suggested that section 34(1)(a) means that the tenancy is one in respect of which the requirements of section 11(1) of the Act are met.[41] Section 34(1)(b) now has effect only as regards non-ASB SSSTs: subsection (6A) imposes a fixed term of one year on ASB SSSTs, which may be extended by another six months under section 35A.[42] The requirements in respect of the notice referred to in section 34(1)(c) are set out in subsection (4), which is discussed below. Also, it is necessary to appreciate that section 34(1) is not exhaustive in defining the circumstances in which an SSST may come into being: a SSST may arise by conversion under section 35.

Circumstances in which an SSST may be offered: s 34(2), (3)

In contrast to the short assured tenancy under the 1988 Act, the landlord may serve the section 34(4) notice, making the tenancy an SSST, only in certain specified circumstances, which are listed in schedule 6:

(1) *Previous antisocial behaviour*: An order for recovery of possession has, within the period of three years preceding the date of service of the notice, been made against the prospective tenant (or any one of prospective joint tenants) on ground 2 (illegal or immoral conduct) or ground 7 (antisocial behaviour) of schedule 2 to the 2001 Act, or on antisocial behaviour grounds contained in the 1988 and 2016 Acts, and other housing legislation applicable elsewhere in the UK.[43]

(2) *Antisocial behaviour order*: The prospective tenant (or any one of prospective joint tenants) or a person who it is proposed will reside with the prospective tenant is subject to an antisocial behaviour order.[44]

40 "House": Chapter 1; "Scottish secure tenancy": in the discussion of the 2001 Act, s 11 in Chapter 4; "for a term of not less than six months" and in relation to whether service has been effected before the creation of the tenancy: in the discussion of the 1988 Act, s 32 in Chapter 7. As to "service": service of notices under the 2001 Act is discussed in Chapter 15.

41 See Chapter 4, p 81.

42 See the discussion of the duration of SSSTs at p 196 below.

43 Paragraph 1 of sch 6 lists the various statutory grounds contained in the legislation applicable not only in Scotland, but in England and Wales, and Northern Ireland. Notice that, for the purposes of this paragraph, the "Previous antisocial behaviour" extends beyond the antisocial behaviour ground (7) in sch 2, to include the illegal or immoral conduct ground (2). Those grounds are discussed in Chapter 5.

44 Following an amendment made by the Antisocial Behaviour etc. (Scotland) Act 2004, sch 4, this means an antisocial behaviour order ("ASBO")granted under s 4 of that Act, or under s 234AA of the Criminal Procedure (Scotland) Act 1995. Accordingly, in contrast to para 1, para 2 is not applicable in cases in which an ASBO has been granted elsewhere in the UK.

(2A) *Other antisocial behaviour*: Where: (a) the prospective tenant; or (b) any one of prospective joint tenants; or (c) a person visiting a house occupied by the prospective tenant or by a person who it is proposed will reside with the prospective tenant; or (d) a person who it is proposed will reside with the prospective tenant, is subject to an antisocial behaviour order, has acted in an antisocial manner in relation to another person residing in, visiting or otherwise engaged in lawful activity in the locality of a house occupied by the prospective tenant or by a person who it is proposed will reside with the prospective tenant, or pursued a course of conduct amounting to harassment of such other person, or a course of conduct which is otherwise antisocial conduct in relation to such other person. This is a new ground, added by the 2014 Act. It is further discussed below.

Where the any of these three paragraphs applies, the new tenancy will be an ASB SSST, which will be subject to the fixed term of twelve months,[45] under section 34(6A), and may convert to a Scottish secure tenancy under section 37.

(3) *Temporary letting to person seeking accommodation*: The house is to be let expressly on a temporary basis to a person moving into the area in order to take up employment there, and for the purpose of enabling that person to seek accommodation in the area.

(4) *Temporary letting pending development*: The house is to be let to a person expressly on a temporary basis, pending development[46] affecting the house.

(5) *Accommodation for homeless persons*: The house is to be let to a person expressly on a temporary basis, for a period of not less than six months, in fulfilment of a duty imposed on a local authority by part II (homeless persons) of the 1987 Act.[47]

(6) *Accommodation for a person requiring housing support services*: The house is to be let expressly on a temporary basis to a person: (a) to whom no other paragraph of schedule 6 applies; and (b) who is in receipt of a housing support service.[48]

(7) *Accommodation in property not owned by landlord*: The house to be let is leased by the landlord from another body and the terms of the lease preclude the letting of the house by the landlord under a Scottish secure tenancy.

(7A) *Temporary letting where other property owned*: The house is to be let expressly on a temporary basis to a person who owns heritable property (or where a person who it is proposed will reside with that person owns heritable property) pending the making of arrangements in relation to that property.

45 Which may be extended by a further six months, under the new s 35A.

46 As defined by the Town and Country Planning (Scotland) Act 1997, s 26.

47 See the discussion of SSSTs and homelessness at p 181 above.

48 This paragraph was amended by s 7(4)(b) of the 2014 Act, the significant change being the addition of point (a). That seems intended to preclude an SSST being granted on this ground, where there has been previous antisocial behaviour, such that paras 1, 2 or 2A apply. See part 9 of the SSST Guidance. The term "housing support services" is discussed at p 201 below.

Where any of these paragraphs (3–7A) applies, the tenancy will be a non-ASB SSST, which will be for a term of at least six months, and which may renew indefinitely. These tenancies do not convert to a Scottish secure tenancy, under section 37.

The first new ground for creating an SSST: sch 6 para 2A

Paragraph 2A was added by the 2014 Act. It bears a strong similarity to the new section 35(2)(b), which is discussed below. Both provisions have the effect of significantly lowering the threshold for the creation of a SSST, where that is thought to be justified by previous antisocial behaviour. Under paragraphs (1) and (2) of schedule 6, a repossession order or antisocial behaviour order is necessary, with the effect that the behaviour justifying the offer of an SSST would have been admitted or proved in court proceedings. Given the addition of paragraph (2A), that is no longer required.[49] Moreover, paragraph (2A) casts the net wider than (1) or (2), by including antisocial behaviour on the part of persons other than the prospective tenant or joint tenants.

The second new ground for creating an SSST: schedule 6 paragraph 7A

Paragraph 7A was also added by the 2014 Act. The Government has issued specific guidance in relation to SSSTs granted on this basis: "The Short Scottish Secure Tenancy for Homeowners". This indicates that an SSST under paragraph 7A may be granted where, for example, the tenant needs accommodation temporarily, if she intends: to sell her own property and secure alternative accommodation that meets her needs; make the necessary arrangements for building on, extending or installing adaptations to her own property; or carry out repairs needed to make that property habitable.

The prescribed notice: s 34(4)

The form for the section 34(4) notice is prescribed by the Short Scottish Secure Tenancies (Notice) Regulations 2018.[50] It is analogous to the form AT5 served on the tenant in relation to a short assured tenancy under the 1988 Act. The notice informs the tenant that the tenancy being offered by the landlord is to be an SSST. It requires the landlord to specify the ground, under schedule 6, on which an SSST is offered. This is followed by six notes providing information to the tenant as to the purpose of the notice, the term of the tenancy, the right of the landlord to repossess under section 36, and the right of appeal under section 38 (see below), and sources of advice.

In Chapter 7, it is submitted that an omission or mistake in the AT5 notice will not render it invalid if the error is minor, such that a reasonably minded recipient would be in no doubt as to the necessary terms of the notice. Given

49 Paragraph 1.9 of the SSST Guidance summarises the change thus: "Allowing a landlord, *without going to court*, to give a short SST to a new tenant where that person, or other specified person, has demonstrated the specified antisocial behaviour within the previous 3 years." [emphasis added].

50 SSI 2018/154.

the similarity between the notices, it is suggested that the same principle would apply to the notice under section 34(4).[51]

The section 34(1)(c) requirement to issue the prescribed notice does not apply to SSSTs created by conversion in terms of section 35; in those cases, a different notice is required, under section 35(2) and (3).

Creation of an SSST under section 34: savings provisions

Under paragraph 5 of the relevant commencement order,[52] commencement of certain of the amending provisions of the 2014 Act[53] has no effect in relation to an SSST "where a notice under section 34(4) . . . is served prior to 1 May 2019".[54] In that case, the grounds for granting an SSST are those applicable prior to that date. Also, for ASB SSSTs, the change to the term of the tenancy to a fixed period of twelve months, and the right to extend the tenancy by another six months, under section 35A, do not apply.

Conversion: section 35

Creation of an SSST by conversion

> "**35. Conversion to a short Scottish secure tenancy**
> (1) A Scottish secure tenancy of a house becomes a short Scottish secure tenancy by virtue of this section immediately on the landlord serving on the tenant a notice under subsection (3).
> (2) The landlord may serve a notice under subsection (3) only where—
> (a) the tenant (or any one of joint tenants) or a person residing or lodging with, or subtenant of, the tenant is subject to an antisocial behaviour order under
> (i) section 234AA of the Criminal Procedure (Scotland) Act 1995 (c 46); or
> (ii) under section 4 of the Antisocial Behaviour etc (Scotland) Act 2004 (asp 8), or
> (b) the tenant (or any one of joint tenants) or a person residing or lodging with, or subtenant of, the tenant or a person visiting the house has, within the period of 3 years preceding the date of service of the notice–
> (i) acted in an antisocial manner in relation to another person residing in, visiting or otherwise engaged in lawful activity in the locality of a house occupied by the person, or
> (ii) pursued a course of conduct amounting to harassment of such other person, or a course of conduct which is otherwise antisocial conduct in relation to such other person.
> (3) A notice under this subsection must–

51 Furthermore, a defect in a s 34(4) may not be fatal to its validity, given the terms of s 21 of the Interpretation and Legislative Reform (Scotland) Act 2010, which is briefly discussed in Chapter 4, at p 108.

52 Housing (Scotland) Act 2014 (Commencement No. 8, Savings, Transitional and Supplemental Provisions) Order 2018 (SSI 2018/153).

53 In particular: ss 7(4)(b), 9(1) and (2), 10 and 11(d) of the 2014 Act.

54 However, that seems to overlook the fact that SSSTs are also created under s 35. This leaves a doubt as to whether the 2014 changes (particularly the changes as to the duration of ASB SSSTs, and the exclusion of tacit relocation, effected by s 9 of the 2014 Act) apply to tenancies converted under s 35, prior to 1 May 2019.

(a) state that the Scottish secure tenancy to which it relates becomes a short Scottish secure tenancy by virtue of service of the notice,
(b) specify the tenant or other person who is subject to the anti-social behaviour order or, as the case may be, has behaved as described in subsection (2)(b),
(c) if the notice is served under subsection (2)(b), specify–
 (i) the actions of the tenant or other person which the landlord has taken into account, and
 (ii) the landlord's reasons for serving the notice, and
(d) explain the right of appeal conferred by subsection (5).

. . .

(7) In this section
'anti-social', in relation to an action or course of conduct, means causing or likely to cause alarm, distress, nuisance or annoyance,
'conduct' includes speech, and a course of conduct must involve conduct on at least two occasions,
'harassment' is to be construed in accordance with section 8 of the Protection from Harassment Act 1997 (c 40)."

Important changes have been made to section 35 by the 2014 Act – in particular, the insertion of subsection (2)(b), which expands the basis on which an SSST may be created by conversion, in a similar way to the extension of the grounds for creating a new SSST, by the addition of paragraph 2A to schedule 6. As is indicated in the SSST Guidance, the point of these changes is to enable the landlord to create ASB SSSTs without the necessity of going to court to prove that there has been antisocial behaviour.[55] In the event of a conversion notice being served under section 35(2)(b), the landlord's basis for converting the tenancy will be considered by the court only if the tenant appeals under section 35(5).[56]

The date of conversion: s 35(1)

Given the terms of section 35(1), the tenancy becomes an SSST on the day when service of the conversion notice is effected. The exact date of conversion is significant in working out the date from which the twelve-month term of the SSST runs.[57] Service of the conversion notice, like other notices under the Act, is effected under section 40, which is discussed in Chapter 15.[58] It is suggested that a Scottish secure tenancy will become an SSST under section 35(1) on the day on which the conversion notice is delivered to the tenant (under section 40(1)(a)) or left at the tenant's last known address (under section 40(1)(b)).

Where service of the conversion notice is effected by recorded delivery letter under section 40(1)(c), service is deemed to have been effected at the time at which the letter would be delivered in the ordinary course of post, "unless the contrary is proved". This could be as early as the day after sending, or it could

55 See para 1.9 of the Guidance, quoted at n 49.

56 This may be contrasted with the position as regards demoted tenancies in England, in respect of which the landlord must apply to the court for a demotion order.

57 Under s 34(6A), SSSTs created by conversion are subject to a twelve-month term, which may be extended by six months under s 35A. See the discussion of the duration, below. The exact date of expiry of that term is significant: that is the date on which the tenancy may convert back to a Scottish secure tenancy under s 37.

58 At p 500.

be several days later. It is suggested that the landlord ought to ascertain the date on which the notice was signed for, in order that the date of conversion, and the expiry of the twelve-month term, may be determined.

The basis for conversion: s 35(2)(a) and (b), (7)

Under section 35 as originally enacted, conversion could take place only where an antisocial behaviour order had been granted against the tenant or a person residing or lodging with, or sub-tenant of, the tenant. Following the amendments made by the 2014 Act, the existence of such an order is preserved as a basis for conversion under subsection (2)(a), though given the insertion of subsections (2)(b) and (7), it is no longer necessary for an antisocial behaviour order to be obtained.

In order to understand section 35(2)(b) (read with subsection (7)), it is helpful to recognise its similarity to ground 7 of schedule 2 to the Act.[59] It is suggested that readers will benefit from reading the analysis of ground 7, and the application of the "reasonableness" requirement in relation to that ground,[60] in understanding the scope of section 35(2)(b).

The conversion notice: s 35(3)

This provision has also been amended by the 2014 Act.[61] In terms of section 35(1), it is the service of the notice under subsection (3) that effects conversion. Given the importance of the notice, it is surprising that there is no prescribed form. The landlord need include only the four points set out in subsection (3)(a)–(d).[62] It is under no obligation to provide any other information to the tenant; in particular, it is under no obligation to provide all the information that is given to new SSST tenants, in the notice under section 34(4).[63] That, it is suggested, is regrettable. If the point of conversion is to encourage the tenant to address antisocial behaviour at the tenancy, it is important that she is informed of the effect of conversion, and its implications.

It is suggested that the following points may usefully be made in the notice, or in material that accompanies it:

- That conversion is effective immediately, and that the term of the SSST will be twelve months, which may be extended to eighteen months, under section 35A.
- That the effect of conversion is that the tenancy is less secure. The landlord now has special rights to recover possession under section 36 of the Act.

59 The only significant difference is that, in relation to ground 7, the landlord has to show that it is not reasonable in all the circumstances that it should be required to make other accommodation available to the tenant.

60 In Chapter 5, at pp 142, and 182.

61 By the addition of paras (c) and (d), and the words "or, as the case may be, has behaved as described in subsection (2)(b)" in para (b).

62 As to notices for which there is no prescribed form, but which are required by the legislation to contain certain information, see: *Islington LBC v Dyer* [2017] EWCA Civ 150, [2017] HLR 20, in which the Court of Appeal decided that it was permissible for part of the information to be provided in an "information leaflet" that was attached to the relevant notice.

63 In terms of the Short Scottish Secure Tenancies (Notice) Regulations 2018 (n 50).

- That the tenancy will convert back to a Scottish secure tenancy at the end of the twelve- (or eighteen-) month term.
- That the landlord must provide, or ensure the provision of, such housing support services as it considers appropriate with a view to enabling the conversion of the tenancy back to a Scottish secure tenancy to take place, at the end of the twelve- (eighteen-) month term, and that it is in the interests of the tenant to co-operate with that support.
- If the tenant breaches any of their obligations under the tenancy, the landlord may take possession of the property, following court proceedings under section 36 of the Act.
- That if in doubt about the effect of the notice, he/she ought to seek advice as soon as possible.

Most of these points reflect what is said in the notice under section 34(4), in the case of new SSSTs. It is suggested that it is in the interests of the landlord to include this information in order that the tenant is advised of the implications of conversion.[64]

It is also suggested that, in complying with the duty under subsection (3)(d) to "explain the right of appeal conferred by subsection (5)", the notice ought to advise the tenant that any appeal must be made by summary application, within twenty-one days of service of the notice (see below).[65]

Obligation to give reasons: s 35(3)(c)(ii)

Section 35(3)(c)(ii) is the first of three provisions, all introduced in the 2014 Act amendments, that require the landlord to give reasons to the tenant for deciding to adopt a course of action that adversely affects the tenant's security of tenure, or threatens her right to remain in the property.[66]

Generally, a statutory duty to give reasons is construed to mean that the reasons must be "proper, intelligible and adequate".[67] In considering the adequacy of the reasons given it will also be necessary to take account the nature of the decision in question, the context in which it has been made, the purpose for which the reasons are provided and the context in which they are given. These considerations will be informed by the court's view of the intention of

64 This is not to say that the notice will be invalid if these points are not included. To be valid, the notice need only cover the points in s 35(3)(a)–(d). However, it is not impossible that a lack of information as to the effect of conversion could be a factor in an appeal under s 35(5) and (6), or an action under s 36(5).

65 Apart from being fair with the tenant, it is in the landlords' interests to include this information. If the tenant makes an application under r 2.6(3) of the Summary Application Rules (Act of Sederunt (Summary Applications, Statutory Applications and Appeals etc Rules) 1999 (SI 1999/929)) (see note 82 below), to allow an appeal to be received although late, that is less likely to succeed, if she was advised, in the s 35 notice, of the date by which the appeal should be lodged.

66 The other provisions are: s 35A(2)(b)(ii), under which the landlord must give reasons for extending the fixed term of an ASB SSST to eighteen months, thereby preventing the tenancy from converting to a Scottish secure tenancy at the end of the twelve-month term; and s 36(3)(aa) which requires the landlord to state the reason why it is seeking possession of the property.

67 This test was originally formulated by Megaw J in *Re Poyser and Mills Arbitration* [1964] 2 QB 467 at 478. It has been restated in subsequent authorities, in particular *Uprichard v Scottish Ministers* 2013 SC (UKSC) 219, [47] (Lord Reed).

the particular statute in which the duty is stated.[68] Where there is a statutory duty to provide reasons as part of the notification of the decision to the parties, the court will normally interpret the legislation as having made the provision of adequate reasons with the decision a condition of the validity of the decision.[69]

It may also be necessary to recognise that the reasons are addressed to a person who is "informed", in the sense of already being aware of the background to the decision. It is important to maintain a sense of proportion when considering the duty to give reasons, and not to impose on decision makers a burden that is unreasonable having regard to the purpose intended to be served.[70]

Other provisions in section 35 inform the context in which the reasons are given. The obligation to give reasons, under section 35(3)(c)(ii), is imposed only in cases in which the notice is served under subsection (2)(b). The notice must also set out "the actions of the tenant or other person which the landlord has taken into account".[71] Complying with that obligation may go a considerable way to explaining the reason for the conversion notice being served. Under subsection (5), a tenant "aggrieved" by the conversion may raise proceedings by summary application.

It is suggested that the reasons should explain why the landlord considers that the specified actions of the tenant or other person amount to acting "in an antisocial manner" or to "harassment" under subsection (2)(b)(i) or (ii), having regard to the definition of those terms in subsection (7), unless that is self-evident. Given that the landlord's decision to convert the tenancy is discretionary, it is also arguable that the landlord ought to say why it has chosen to adopt that measure, rather than address the antisocial behaviour in some other way.[72] This will enable the tenant to decide whether she is "aggrieved" by the conversion, and whether she wishes to challenge it, under subsection (5).

Failure to comply with s 35(3)(a)–(d)

A failure to comply with the requirements of section 35(3)(a) to (d) calls the validity of the conversion notice into question. This is a ground on which the tenant may seek a declarator that the notice is of no effect. See the discussion of section 35(5) and (6), below.

68 In *Chief Constable of Lothian and Borders Police v Lothian and Borders Police Board* 2005 SLT 315 Lord Reed comprehensively analysed the duty to give reasons, and articulated certain general propositions regarding the duty, the first of which is: "the stringency with which the court requires a statutory duty to give reasons to be complied with will depend on the court's view of the intention of the particular statute . . .".

69 ibid; this is the second of the general propositions.

70 *Uprichard v Scottish Ministers* (n 67) paras [44]–[48].

71 Under s 35(3)(c)(i).

72 Though more arguable, perhaps, in cases in which the antisocial behaviour is at the less serious end of the scale, or in cases in which other approaches have not been attempted by the landlord.

The pros and cons of conversion

What are the pros and cons of converting the tenancy under section 35(2)(b), as opposed to raising an action under section 16(2)(a) of the Act, on the ground of antisocial behaviour?[73]

Converting the tenancy to an ASB SSST may enable the landlord to adopt a more proactive approach to antisocial behaviour. In gathering evidence for section 16 proceedings, the landlord usually has to wait for incidents of sufficient frequency or seriousness to enable it to form the view that an action is likely to be successful. By conversion, the landlord is able to intervene at an earlier stage. Conversion also triggers the requirement to provide such housing support services to the tenant as the landlord considers appropriate under section 34(7), which may address the problem, and which again enables the landlord to play a more active role.

On the other hand, conversion locks the landlord into a fixed term tenancy of at least twelve months. Therefore, it may be inappropriate for cases in which antisocial behaviour is of a serious or an extreme nature, or where it is unlikely that it will stop, even with the provision of support. In that situation, proceedings under section 16 will probably be successful, and will be the quickest route to recovery of possession.[74] Also, as is suggested in the discussion of section 35(5) and (6) below, conversions under the new section 35(2)(b) are more likely to be challenged than was previously the case. If conversion is successfully challenged, the landlord will find itself back at square one. Even if it is successful in resisting the challenge, the landlord may find itself drawn into two actions (being the tenant's challenge to conversion and the landlord's action under section 36) instead of one.

Creating an ASB SSST: Guidance

Section 34(9) and (10) state:

> "(9) A landlord must have regard to any guidance published by the Scottish Ministers—
> (a) before creating a tenancy which is a short Scottish secure tenancy by virtue of section 35 or paragraph 1, 2 or 2A of schedule 6, and
> (b) when taking any steps in relation to such a tenancy with a view to—
> (i) extending the term of the tenancy under section 35A, or
> (ii) raising proceedings for the recovery of possession of the house under section 36.
>
> (10) Before publishing any guidance mentioned in subsection (9), the Scottish Ministers must consult such persons as they consider appropriate."

As indicated at the beginning of this chapter, the Guidance to which these subsections refer is the "Short Scottish Secure Tenancies for Antisocial Behaviour and Other Miscellaneous Changes to Short Scottish Secure Tenancies – Statutory Guidance for Social Landlords".

73 This would be usually be ground 7 in sch 2 or, less commonly, ground 8. See the discussion of those grounds in Chapter 5.

74 Admittedly, under s 36(7), the landlord could still raise an action under s 16, after conversion has taken place. However, that would tend to indicate that the attempt to address the issue by conversion to an SSST has been unsuccessful.

"Have regard"

Under section 34(9)(a), a landlord must "have regard" to the SSST Guidance before creating an ASB SSST under section 34, or by conversion under section 35. A requirement to "have regard" to Guidance does not mean that the landlord is bound by it, or bound to apply it.[75] It is not a source of law.[76] However, it does mean that, in making a decision to create a SSST, or use the conversion power under section 35, the Guidance is a relevant consideration to which regard must be had.[77] Accordingly, if it is evident that regard has not been had to the Guidance, the decision may be regarded as unlawful. However, as with any relevant consideration, where it has been taken into account, it is for the decision maker to decide what weight to place on it.[78]

The landlord may decide to depart from the Guidance, but if it does so, the onus lies on the landlord to justify that departure.[79] In essence, then, the landlord must: (a) take the content of the Guidance into account; and (b) if they decide to depart from it, be able to give clear reasons for doing so.[80]

The relevant parts of the Guidance

The relevant sections of the Guidance are part 2 ("Purpose and use of Short SST for antisocial behaviour") and part 4, which is headed: "Steps to be taken before offering a Short SSST/converting an existing Scottish secure tenancy to a Short SST on 'Other Antisocial Behaviour' Grounds". It is suggested that these parts will have to be carefully considered, by any landlord wishing to create an ASB SSST, or by any tenant wishing to challenge the creation of such a tenancy, and by their respective advisers.

Key points from part 2 include:

- "For landlords [giving a tenant a short SST] means ensuring that any housing support identified by the landlord as being required to help make the tenancy sustainable, is made available. If the landlord identifies the need for support but the support cannot be provided, they should instead consider alternative measures to address the antisocial behaviour." (para 2.7)
- "Landlords will not routinely want to use a short SST for low-level breaches of tenancy agreements, such as not cleaning stairs, or maintaining gardens and will want to ensure that it is appropriate and proportionate in all the circumstances." (para 2.9)

75 *De Falco v Crawley BC* [1980] QB 460.

76 R (*Khatun) v Newham LBC* [2005] QB 37, [2004] HLR 29, [47] (Laws LJ).

77 Though, in giving reasons for a decision under s 35(3)(c)(ii), the landlord is not obliged to spell out the paragraphs of the Guidance to which it has had regard. See *Birmingham City Council v Balog* [2014] HLR 14.

78 "If the decision maker wrongly takes the view that some consideration is not relevant, and therefore has no regard to it, his decision cannot stand and he must be required to think again. But it is entirely for the decision maker to attribute to the relevant considerations such weight as he thinks fit, and the courts will not interfere unless he has acted unreasonably in the *Wednesbury* sense." (*Tesco Stores Ltd. v Secretary of State for the Environment* [1995] 1 WLR 759, 764G–H, (Lord Keith of Kinkel)).

79 It has also been said that a failure to comply with guidance is not unlawful; the issue is whether the authority acted reasonably having regard to the guidance: *R. v Brent LBC, ex p Macwan* (1994) 26 HLR 528, 534–535 (Leggatt LJ).

80 *R (Khatun) v Newham LBC* (n 76), [47].

- "The use of a short SST when any of the antisocial behaviour grounds are met is not mandatory. Landlords wishing to use this power will wish to ensure that they have clear, well-documented evidence which sets out their reasons for giving a short SST." (para 2.10)

Part 4 of the Guidance specifically relates to the creation of an ASB SSST on the "other antisocial behaviour grounds", where there is no previous antisocial behaviour order, or eviction order on antisocial behaviour grounds, i.e. where a new SSST is created under paragraph 2A of schedule 6, or conversion takes place under section 35(2)(b). In such cases, the Guidance states (at paragraph 4.2) that landlords "will need to consider all of the circumstances of the individual case" when deciding whether it is appropriate to create an ASB SSST; "Landlords will have to balance the need to support the tenant, household member or visitor to change their behaviour and sustain the tenancy, with the impact the antisocial behaviour has had, or continues to have, on neighbours and others in the community".

At paragraphs 4.7–4.8 the Guidance states that the landlord should have:

- reliable evidence of the antisocial behaviour;
- evidence of the steps taken to manage or resolve the antisocial behaviour (such as communication and engagement with the tenant; issuing written warnings; provision of acceptable behaviour contracts; and consideration of support needs in consultation with the tenant);
- considered what support may be required to manage or resolve the antisocial behaviour and assist in sustaining the tenancy.

In making a decision to create an ASB SSST on the "other antisocial behaviour grounds" the landlord should consider the following factors (para 4.10):

- who has behaved antisocially, and what their connection to the property is;
- how long the antisocial behaviour has been going on, and the persistence of the behaviour;
- the person affected by the antisocial behaviour, and their connection to housing;
- whether, and to what extent, the behaviour has affected household members, neighbours or others in the community;
- the impact on neighbours and communities over time, and the impact on the stability of the community;
- what action, if any, the person behaving antisocially is taking to make positive change;
- any issues around the vulnerability of the tenant, members of their household or those directly affected by the antisocial behaviour;
- other steps that have been or could be taken by the landlord or partner agencies to address the antisocial behaviour.

These factors are discussed, in greater detail, at paragraphs 4.11–4.24 of the Guidance.

Challenging the creation of an SSST

Challenging a decision to offer an ASB SSST or a non-ASB SSST under s 34, under s 38(1)(c) and (2)

Under section 38(1)(c) of the Act, a person aggrieved by a decision of a landlord to make a house available to him for occupancy on the basis of an SSST instead of a Scottish secure tenancy may appeal against that decision by raising proceedings by summary application. In such proceedings the court may, if it considers that there are "good grounds" for doing so, order the landlord to let the house to the person under a Scottish secure tenancy.[81]

A summary application under section 38(1)(c) would have to be lodged with the sheriff clerk no later than twenty-one days after the date on which the decision to offer an SSST was intimated to the prospective tenant.[82]

There have been no reported cases under section 38 since that provision came into force in 2002. So, there is no judicial guidance on what would constitute "good grounds" for the purposes of section 38(2). However, it seems more likely that section 38 will be deployed in the future, particularly given the changes made by the 2014 Act (which are intended to increase the number of ASB SSSTs being offered) and the content of the SSST Guidance.

Given section 34(9)(a), an apparent failure on the part of the landlord to "have regard" to the SSST Guidance before offering an ASB SSST may found an appeal under section 38(1)(c).[83] However, the nature of that failure would have to be such as to give good grounds for the sheriff ordering the landlord to let the property on a Scottish secure tenancy, rather than an SSST.

It is also possible that an appeal might rely on the Equality Act 2010, contending that the decision to offer an SSST, rather than a Scottish secure tenancy, amounts to unlawful discrimination.[84]

Challenging conversion: s 35(5) and (6)

Section 35(5) permits the tenant to appeal against conversion:

> "(5) Where a Scottish secure tenancy becomes a short Scottish secure tenancy by virtue of this section, a tenant who is aggrieved by the conversion may raise proceedings by summary application.
>
> (6) In such proceedings the court may, if it considers that there are good grounds for doing so, grant a declarator that the notice under subsection (3) is of no effect."

81 Section 38(2).

82 Under r 2.6 ("Time Limits") of the Summary Applications Rules (n 65), that is the time limit that applies where the application is "an appeal or an application in the nature of an appeal", where the time within which the application may be made is not otherwise prescribed. By r 2.6(3), the sheriff may, on special cause shown, hear an application that has been lodged outwith the time limit.

83 For the duty to "have regard" to guidance, see p 192 above.

84 See Chapter 11.

A summary application under section 35(5) would have to be lodged with the sheriff clerk no later than twenty-one days after the date on which the section 35(3) notice was served upon the tenant.[85]

At the time of writing, there is no reported case of such an application having been made.[86] However, again, this may change, following the amendments made by the 2014 Act. Conversion will be more frequent, given the addition of the new ground under section 35(2)(b); furthermore, the section 35(3) notice is now required to "explain the right of appeal" under s 35(5).[87]

As with a summary application under section 38, an appeal under section 35(5) might found on a failure by the landlord to follow the SSST Guidance, or on the argument that service of the conversion notice unlawfully discriminates against the tenant under the Equality Act 2010.

Other possible grounds for an application under section 35(5) could include:

(a) the person specified in the notice under section 35(3)(b) is no longer resident at the tenancy;
(b) the actions specified in the notice under section 35(3)(c)(i) did not take place;
(c) even if they did take place, there has been a delay between those actions and conversion, during which time there have been no significant problems at the tenancy.

Obviously, this list is not exhaustive.

What happens if the tenant wishes to argue that the conversion notice is invalid, because it does not comply with the four requirements set out in section 35(3)(a)–(d), and therefore conversion has not taken place? The wording of section 35(5) is not particularly helpful here, because it appears to proceed on the assumption that the tenancy has become an SSST, that conversation has taken place, and therefore the notice must have been valid.

Nevertheless, it is suggested that if the validity of the notice is in question, that issue can, and should, be raised in an application under section 35(5), rather than through some other process. The power specifically conferred on the court, in subsection (6), is to grant a declaration that the notice is of no effect, if there are good grounds for so doing. So, if the tenant wishes a court to declare that the notice has been ineffective to achieve conversion, whether by reason of failure to comply with section 35(3)(a)–(d) or otherwise, then his remedy is an application under section 35(5).

If that is correct, it is suggested that the court should not entertain a challenge to the validity of the conversion notice at a later stage, during eviction proceedings under section 36, because the tenant has failed to avail himself of the statutory remedy under section 35(5), and is personally barred from challenging the process of conversion.[88]

85 See n 82. The s 35(5) application is clearly "an appeal or an application in the nature of an appeal"; it is so described in s 35(3)(d).

86 The author is aware of only one application having been made under s 35(5). That case was resolved.

87 Section 35(3)(d).

88 If the local authority has taken steps, such as supporting the tenant under s 34(7) etc., on the basis that conversion has taken place, it would be unfair to allow the process of conversion thereafter to be challenged. For personal bar in relation to the competency of notices, see Chapter 13, p 457.

THE DURATION OF AN SSST: s 34(1)(b), (5), (5A) AND (6A); s 35(1), (3A) and (4)(a); EXTENSION OF DURATION OF AN ASB SSST UNDER s 35A

Duration: s 34

The relevant provisions as to duration in section 34 are:

> "(1) A tenancy of a house is a short Scottish secure tenancy if–
> . . .
> (b) it is for a term of not less than 6 months
> . . .
> (5) At the ish of the tenancy it may continue–
> (a) by tacit relocation, or
> (b) by express agreement,
> and the continued tenancy is a short Scottish secure tenancy despite subsection (1) not being satisfied.
> (5A) Subsection (5) does not apply to a tenancy mentioned in subsection (6A).
> . . .
> (6A) A tenancy which is a short Scottish secure tenancy by virtue of section 35 or paragraph 1, 2 or 2A of schedule 6 has a term of 12 months from the day on which the tenancy was granted."

As explained above, this creates an important distinction between ASB SSSTs and non-ASB SSSTs.

Duration of ASB SSSTs created under s 34

ASB SSSTs have a fixed term of twelve months under section 34(6A), which may be extended to eighteen months under section 35A. No further extension is possible. The SSST cannot continue by tacit relocation or agreement, given subsection (5A).

In the case of ASB SSSTs, created under section 34, the term runs from "the day on which the tenancy is granted".[89] It is submitted that this means the date on which parties execute the tenancy agreement,[90] being the date on which the landlord's grant of the tenancy is effective. That is consistent with section 37(1A), to the effect that conversion under that section takes place on the expiry of the period of twelve months following "the creation of the tenancy", i.e. the date on which the parties' agreement is executed.[91] If that is earlier than the date on which the tenant takes entry, the fixed term runs from the date of the grant.[92]

It also appears to be the effect of section 34(6A) that the term of the tenancy, and the date of commencement of that term, is dictated by the Act, irrespective of any contrary stipulation by the parties. This means that the

89 Section 34(6A). It is suggested that, in this case, "12 months from the day" means that the term expires in the corresponding day in the following year: see Chapter 7, p 249.

90 Or, if they sign on different days, the date on which the last party signs.

91 See the discussion of s 37 at the end of this chapter.

92 If that is correct, it creates a potential pitfall for landlords. If the tenancy is granted on, say, 1 September 2020, but the date of entry is not till 8 September, then conversion takes place on 1 September 2021. If the landlord wishes to avoid conversion to a Scottish secure tenancy, it will have to serve notice under s 36(2) or s 14(2) on or before that date.

tenancy would still be an SSST even if, as a result of some error, the term stated in the agreement was more or less than twelve months.[93]

Duration of non-ASB SSSTs

Under section 34(1)(b) and (5), a non-ASB SSST can be for any term, as long as it is for "not less than six months",[94] and may continue by tacit relocation or express agreement, indefinitely. This means that, as with short assured tenancies, the tenancy agreement may provide for an initial term of six months, followed by a renewing shorter term, such as monthly.

By contrast with ASB SSSTs, the duration of the tenancy is dictated by the parties' agreement, and will commence at the date of entry, as is the case with other forms of tenancy. Non-ASB SSSTs do not convert under section 37. However, ascertaining the commencement date, and ish date, of the tenancy will be important for the purposes of correctly specifying the date not earlier that which the landlord may raise proceedings, under section 36(3)(b).

Duration of ASB SSSTs created by conversion under s 35

In terms of section 34(6A), ASB SSSTs created by conversion have the same duration as ASB SSSTs under section 34: twelve months. This is confirmed by section 35(3A) and (4)(a), which state:

> "(3A) A short Scottish secure tenancy created by virtue of this section has a term of 12 months from the day on which the landlord serves a notice under subsection (3).
>
> (4) Where a tenancy becomes a short Scottish secure tenancy by virtue of this section—
>
> (a) subsection (5) of section 34 does not apply to the tenancy . . ."

As regards "the day on which the landlord serves a notice under subsection (3)", see the discussion of section 35(1), above. It is suggested that the day of service is included in the twelve-month term, because, under section 35(1), conversion takes place "immediately" on service.[95]

Extension of the duration of an ASB SSST by six months: section 35A

> **"35A Extension of term of short Scottish secure tenancy**
>
> (1) The landlord under a tenancy which is a short Scottish secure tenancy by virtue of section 35 or paragraph 1, 2 or 2A of schedule 6 may extend the term of that tenancy by 6 months from the day which would otherwise be the day of expiry of the tenancy.
>
> (2) Such an extension may not be made unless–
>
> (a) the tenant is in receipt of housing support services, and

93 In that case, the term stated in the tenancy agreement would have to be disregarded: the statute would rule.

94 In practice, a term of six months is invariably used. The meaning of the phrase "not less than 6 months" is discussed in Chapter 7, in relation to short assured tenancies.

95 If that is correct, in a case where the conversion notice is served on 1 September 2020, the term of the tenancy expires at midnight ending 31 August 2021, unless the term is extended under s 35A.

(b) the landlord has, on or before the day which is 2 months before the day which would otherwise be the day of expiry of the tenancy, served on the tenant a notice informing the tenant of–
(i) the extension, and
(ii) the reasons for the extension.

(3) A landlord may not give a notice if the landlord has previously given a notice under subsection (2) in relation to that short Scottish secure tenancy."

This section was inserted by the 2014 Act.[96] It allows the landlord unilaterally to extend the twelve-month fixed period for an ASB SSST by a further six months. Given the terms of subsection (3), that may be done on only one occasion. There are three prerequisites for extension.

First, the landlord must have regard to the Guidance, "when taking any steps . . . with a view to . . . extending the term of the tenancy under section 35A".[97]

Secondly, under section 35A(2), the tenant must be in receipt of the "housing support services"[98] that the landlord is required to provide under section 34(7). According to the Guidance, the flexibility to extend the fixed term:

> ". . . could for example, give more time for housing support services to have an effect where the tenant's behaviour has not yet reached the standard required for a permanent tenancy. Where the behaviour has not improved sufficiently, landlords can consider whether to give a 6 month extension to the short SST or seek repossession of the property".[99]

Thirdly, the landlord must serve the notice described in subsection (2)(b) no later than two months before the expiry of the original twelve-month period. There is no prescribed form for the notice under section 35A(2)(b). It is suggested that "informing the tenant of the extension" entails specifying the length of the extension, and the date on which the term of the tenancy, as extended, will expire. Section 35A(2)(b)(ii) also requires the landlord to give reasons for its decision to extend the tenancy term.[100]

It appears to follow from the wording of section 35A that the extension of the term of the tenancy is immediately effective upon the service of the notice under subsection (2)(b). At that point, the term of the tenancy is extended from twelve months to eighteen months. If that is correct, the landlord is committed to the extension on serving the notice, and it cannot be withdrawn, in the event that there is antisocial behaviour at the tenancy following service of the notice, but before the original twelve-month period would have expired.

In contrast to section 35, there is no right of appeal against extension under section 35A.[101] It could be challenged in judicial review proceedings, particularly where it is argued that one or both of the conditions under subsection (2) is not fulfilled. However, it is perhaps more likely that an alleged deficiency in the process of extending the tenancy will come under scrutiny in an action

96 It bears a strong similarity to s 125A of the Housing Act 1996, which forms part of the English statutory code in relation to introductory tenancies.
97 Section 34(9)(b)(i). As to "having regard", see p 192 above.
98 For the meaning of this term, see the commentary to s 34(7).
99 At para 11.1.
100 For the obligation to give reasons, see p 189 above. Presumably the landlord could adopt the reasons suggested at para 11.1 of the Guidance, quoted in the main text.
101 Under the introductory tenancies legislation, the tenant has the right to seek review of decision to extend the twelve-month term: Housing Act 1996, s 125B.

under section 36, at the end of the extended period. In such an action, the tenant may argue that the tenancy was not properly extended under section 35A, and therefore it converted under section 37 at the end of the original twelve-month period. If that is correct, the action under section 36 will be incompetent, as the tenancy will be a Scottish secure tenancy.

For the foregoing reasons, it is suggested that extension under section 35A will require some care in execution. The Guidance states:

> "Landlords will . . . have to review the existing provision of housing support services well in advance of the expiry of the 12 month tenancy in cases where they are considering applying a 6 month extension. This is to allow sufficient time for housing support services to be in place if this is not already the case. It is also to give sufficient time to provide the tenant with the 2 months' notice of the extension and the reasons for this, to prevent the tenancy automatically converting to an SST at the end of the 12 months."[102]

DIFFERENCES BETWEEN SCOTTISH SECURE TENANCIES AND SSSTs: s 34(6) AND 35(4)(b)

Section 34(6) states:

> "(6) The provisions of this Chapter, except sections 11(2) and (4), 12 and 22 and schedules 1 and 3, apply to a short Scottish secure tenancy as they do to a Scottish secure tenancy."

Section 35(4)(b) confirms that this provision also applies to SSSTs created by conversion.

Section 34(6) is of particular significance, as it outlines certain important ways in which the short version of the tenancy under the 2001 Act differs from the main Scottish secure tenancy.

The effect of excluding section 11(4) and schedule 1 is that there are certain tenancies that can be short Scottish secure tenancies, but cannot be Scottish secure tenancies, such as tenancies for homeless persons in respect of whom the landlord owes a duty to provide temporary accommodation under part II of the 1987 Act. This is in keeping with the Act's purpose of providing for a form of statutory tenancy in circumstances in which full security of tenure is not appropriate.

The exclusion of section 22 and schedule 3 means that, on the death of an SSST tenant, the tenancy terminates. It does not pass to any other person by succession. Thus, where conversion takes place under section 35, all members of the tenant's family lose any rights of succession that they might have if the tenant were to die, even though the behaviour that prompted conversion may have been on the part of only one member of the household.

How may an SSST be terminated?

The exclusion of section 12 by section 34(6) raises some tricky issues, when read with section 36 of the Act. Section 12(1) states that a Scottish secure tenancy cannot be brought to end, except in the six ways listed from (a) to

102 At para 11.3.

(f).[103] Therefore, the exclusion of that provision suggests that there is no restriction on the termination of an SSST by the parties, and that it might be ended under the terms of the parties' contract and the relevant statutory or common law rules, as described in Chapter 3. One might therefore conclude, for example, that it could be terminated by irritancy or renunciation.[104]

However, section 36 of the Act clearly proceeds on the basis that an SSST continues in existence, at the point when proceedings are raised. Thus section 36(1) talks of the landlord "under a short Scottish secure tenancy" raising proceedings, and section 36(6)(a) provides that an order under subsection (5) "has the effect of terminating the tenancy".[105] On the other hand, section 36(5) seems to proceed on the basis that the parties' contract is at an end, and that there is "no further contractual tenancy . . . in existence".

Accordingly, it seems necessary to make a distinction between the "contractual" aspect of the SSST and its "statutory" aspect, analogous to the difference between a contractual and statutory assured tenancy under the 1988 Act, for the purposes of an action under section 36. The 2001 Act does not expressly make any such distinction but, for the reasons stated, it appears to follow from section 36.

Therefore, the following points may be made, as regards termination of an SSST:

(a) Under section 36(6)(a) an SSST is terminated by an order under section 36(5). Accordingly, even if the tenancy contract has been terminated, say by a notice to quit, or where the fixed term of twelve months has expired, the tenant is entitled to remain in possession.
(b) An SSST may also be terminated by an order under section 16(2). This follows from section 34(6), and from section 36(7), under which the right of action under section 36 is without prejudice to the right of action under sections 14 and 16.
(c) Any other form of action for recovery of possession of an SSST appears to be impliedly excluded by the Act.
(d) An SSST may be terminated by the abandonment procedure under sections 17–19. That follows from section 34(6).
(e) The legislation does not provide that an order under section 36(5) is the *only* way to terminate an SSST. Under section 12, a Scottish secure tenancy will be terminated in the event of "written agreement between the landlord and the tenant, or . . . by 4 weeks' notice given by the tenant to the landlord". Although that section is excluded by section 34(6), there appears to be no reason why an SSST could not also be terminated on the

103 See the discussion of s 12(1) in Chapter 4, at p 87.
104 For the common law position in relation to termination at, or prior to, the ish date, see Chapter 3.
105 See the discussion of the provision as originally enacted in 2001 *Current Law Statutes*, by Dr Simon Halliday and Professor Peter Robson, and the comments at para 23-103 in Rennie and others, *Leases* (SULI 2015). The core provision in ss 34–37 is s 36(5), which enables the landlord to recover possession on the same basis as a landlord under the 1988 Act can recover possession of a short assured tenancy, under s 33(1) of that Act. However, the 2001 Act does not replicate the distinction made in the 1988 Act between a contractual tenancy, and the statutory tenancy that arises under s 16 of that Act, when the contract is terminated. Instead, the 2001 Act treats the SSST as arising from the point of creation of tenancy, or conversion under s 35.

tenant leaving, following agreement between the parties, or notice given by the tenant. However, if the tenant does not leave, following agreement or giving notice, proceedings would have to be raised under section 16 or section 36 of the Act, if the landlord wishes to recover possession.[106]

ASB SSSTs: SUPPORTING THE TENANT UNDER s 34(7)

The landlord under an ASB SSST is subject to a particular obligation, under section 34(7):

> "**34 Short Scottish secure tenancies**
>
> . . .
>
> (7) Where a tenancy is a short Scottish secure tenancy by virtue of section 35 or paragraph 1, 2 or 2A of schedule 6 the landlord must provide, or ensure the provision of, such housing support services as it considers appropriate with a view to enabling the conversion of the tenancy to a Scottish secure tenancy by virtue of section 37.
>
> (8) The Scottish Ministers may issue guidance as to the housing support services which are appropriate for the purposes of subsection (7)."

The term "housing support services" is defined in section 91(8) of the Act, as "includes any service which provides support, assistance, advice or counselling to an individual with particular needs with a view to enabling that individual to occupy, or to continue to occupy, as the person's sole or main residence, residential accommodation other than excepted accommodation".[107]

As regards section 34(8): the SSST Guidance has a specific part (7), which is headed "Housing Support Services", but it is not particularly informative "as to the housing support services which are appropriate for the purposes of subsection (7)."[108] Paragraph 7.2 simply states that: "This is to encourage and support a positive change in behaviour to help the tenant to sustain their tenancy and have their tenancy converted to an SST at the end of the 12 month term. Landlords will need to decide what support is required in consultation with other agencies and support services."

It is suggested that the landlord will have to carry out some form of assessment so as to form a view, for the purposes of section 34(7), as to which housing support services are appropriate. That would appear to be the case even if the tenant refuses to engage in the process of assessment.[109]

106 Whereas, if a Scottish secure tenancy is terminated under s 12 by agreement or notice by the tenant, the landlord could simply raise proceedings on the basis that the tenant no longer has any right or title to remain: see p 87 above.

107 Paragraph 7.3 and footnote 29 in the SSST Guidance confirm that this definition of "housing support services" is applicable to s 34(7). Note that this is distinct from the definition of "*prescribed* housing support services" in s 91(8), which means housing support services prescribed in regulations, being the Housing (Scotland) Act 2001 (Housing Support Services) Regulations 2002 (SSI 2002/444). It is also distinct from the housing support services provided to homeless persons, under the Housing Support Services (Homelessness) (Scotland) Regulations 2012 (SSI 2012/331).

108 Apart from part 7 of the SSST Guidance, no other guidance has been issued by the Scottish Ministers under s 34(8).

109 Paragraph 7.5 of the SSST Guidance suggests that the landlord may make acceptance of the support a condition of the offer a new SSST. A refusal to engage in assessment is more likely to be an issue in conversion cases.

Although the duty under section 34(7) relates to ASB SSSTs, it is suggested that the assessment should encompass the possible need for support in relation to all the tenant's obligations under the tenancy, not just those related to illegal or antisocial behaviour.[110]

Once that is done, it must offer those services to the tenant, or in some way try to make those services available to him, "from the outset" of the ASB SSST.[111] This follows from the requirement to ensure the provision of the services in terms of section 34(7).

If the tenant refuses to engage in the provision of the services, the social landlord may well take the view that it has discharged its duty under section 34(7), on the basis that the tenant cannot be forced to accept the services provided. Where, despite the provision of services, there are persisting problems at the tenancy, it is to be anticipated that the landlords will raise proceedings under section 14 or section 36, at the earliest opportunity.

There is no requirement, in section 36 of the Act, that the landlord must comply with the duty to provide support under section 34(7), before raising proceedings. However, failure to provide support, or follow the relevant guidance, may give rise to a ground for judicial review. See the discussion of possible defences to an action under section 36, below.

ACTIONS FOR RECOVERY OF POSSESSION OF SSSTs: s 36

Introduction

Section 36 is a long and complex provision, which is a mixture of elements from sections 14 and 16 of the 2001 Act and section 33 of the 1988 Act, to which amendments have been made by the Homelessness etc. (Scotland) Act 2003, and the 2014 Act. In particular, the form of subsections (1), (2), (3), (4), (6A) and (6B) of section 36 is lifted directly from the equivalent provisions of section 14, which are, respectively, subsections (1), (2), (4), (5), (5A) and (5B).[112] Section 36(5) is taken from section 33(1) of the 1988 Act, and section 36(6) is effectively identical to section 16(5) of the 2001 Act, as it was originally enacted. Readers are accordingly referred to the analysis of those provisions.[113] The only provisions wholly particular to section 36 are subsections (7) and (8), the purpose of which is clearly to allow the landlord the possibility of initiating an action under section 14, rather than waiting for the ish date of the tenancy before proceeding under section 36. They are discussed below.

The crux of the whole statutory scheme for SSSTs is section 36(5). In contrast to an action under section 16, to succeed in an action for recovery of

110 Because the purpose of the support is to facilitate conversion under s 37. Conversion may be prevented by action under s 36, which may be taken if the tenant fails to perform any obligation under the tenancy, not only those relating to antisocial behaviour. See p 205.

111 See para 7.6 of the SSST Guidance.

112 Subsections (6A) and (6B) of s 36 were, like subsections (5A) and (5B) of s 14, inserted by the 2003 Act.

113 In Chapter 4 for s 14; at Chapter 7 for s 33 of the 1988 Act. Section 16(5) of the 2001 Act is considered in Chapters 5 and 15; the issue of what happens if the landlord does not enforce the eviction decree in terms of that section is considered at the end of Chapter 15.

possession under section 36 the landlord need not show that it has a ground for recovery of possession, or satisfy any other test, such as a requirement that it would be reasonable to grant the order. As we will see, that does not mean that an action under section 36 can never be resisted. However, it does mean that the scope for a stateable defence is much more limited.

Raising proceedings: s 36(1)–(4), (6A), (6B)

"Recovery of possession

(1) The landlord under a short Scottish secure tenancy may raise proceedings by way of summary cause for recovery of possession of the house which is the subject of the tenancy.

(2) Such proceedings may not be raised unless–

(a) the landlord has served on the tenant a notice complying with subsection (3),

(aa) in the case of a short Scottish secure tenancy created by virtue of section 35 or paragraph 1, 2 or 2A of schedule 6, the landlord considers that any obligation of the tenancy has been broken,

(b) the proceedings are raised on or after the date specified in the notice, and

(c) the notice is in force at the time when the proceedings are raised.

(3) A notice under subsection (2) must be in such form as the Scottish Ministers may prescribe by regulations, and must–

(a) state that the landlord requires possession of the house,

(aa) state the reason why the landlord is seeking recovery of possession (including, in a case where subsection (2)(aa) applies, the obligations which the landlord considers to have been broken),

(b) specify a date, not earlier than–

(i) 2 months, or such longer period as the tenancy agreement may provide, from the date of service of the notice, or

(ii) the date on which the tenancy could have been brought to an end by a notice to quit had it not been a short Scottish secure tenancy,

whichever is later, on or after which the landlord may raise proceedings for recovery of possession.

(4) A notice under subsection (2) ceases to be in force 6 months after the date specified in it in accordance with subsection (3)(b) or when it is withdrawn by the landlord, whichever is earlier.

. . .

(6A) Where a landlord raises proceedings under this section, the landlord must give notice of the raising of the proceedings to the local authority in whose area the house in question is situated, unless the landlord is that local authority.

(6B) Notice under subsection (6A) is to be given in the form and manner prescribed under section 11(3) of the Homelessness etc. (Scotland) Act 2003 (asp 10)."

The landlord may raise proceedings by way of summary cause: s 36(1)

As with section 14(1), it is submitted that section 36(1) is correctly interpreted as meaning that the proceedings must be raised as a summary cause, rather than in any other form of process. However, there is authority to the effect that an action may be raised as an ordinary cause. This issue is discussed in Chapter 13.

Prerequisites to raising proceedings: s 36(2)

As is the case under section 14(2) of the Act: an action under section 36 must be preceded by service of statutory notice in the prescribed form;[114] the notice states a date, on or after the proceedings may be raised;[115] and the notice must be "in force" at the time when the proceedings are raised.[116] These three requirements are further specified in subsections (3) and (4). The stipulation in section 36(2)(aa), which was introduced by the 2014 Act, is discussed next.

In contrast to the section 14 notice, there is no requirement to serve the section 36 notice on any qualifying occupier at the tenancy.

The landlord considers that an obligation of the tenancy has been broken: s 36(2)(aa)

As originally enacted, section 36 did not require the landlord to give any reason in the statutory notice for seeking recovery of possession. That was consistent with subsection (5), under which the landlord need not demonstrate any ground for seeking eviction in the subsequent proceedings. Instead, the landlord was simply to state that it required possession, as does the equivalent notice in relation to short assured tenancies in terms of section 33(1)(d) of the 1988 Act. That is still necessary, under section 36(3)(a).

However, where the action under section 36 relates to an ASB SSST, the 2014 Act now requires landlords to identify an obligation of the tenancy that has been broken. It is suggested that subsection (2)(aa) reflects a passage of the judgment of Lord Phillips in *Hounslow London Borough Council v Powell*:[117]

> "The policy behind the introductory tenancy scheme[118] is not in doubt . . . Introductory tenancies place the tenant on probation. They require the tenant to demonstrate that he is a good tenant, both as regards his behaviour towards his neighbours and as regards his contractual obligations to his landlord, before he is granted a tenancy that is secure for life.
>
> When deciding whether to dispossess a tenant who has been granted an introductory tenancy, a local authority must have regard to this policy. The authority cannot simply rely upon the fact that it owns the property and that the tenant has no security of tenure. The decision to dispossess the tenant must be a reasoned decision . . .
>
> It is implicit in this scheme that the reasons for terminating the introductory tenancy before it becomes secure will be that, in one way or another, the tenant has proved unsatisfactory . . ."

The effect of the insertion of subsection (2)(aa) is that these principles are applied to ASB SSSTs. The reason for terminating the tenancy before it becomes secure is that "in one way or another" the tenant has proved to be

114 Sections 14(2)(a) and 36(2)(a).
115 Sections 14(2)(b) and 36(2)(b).
116 Sections 14(2)(c) and 36(2)(c).
117 [2011] 2 AC 186, paras 89–91. See the discussion under the heading, "Limited security of tenure", and the paragraph that precedes that heading, with the relative footnotes earlier in this chapter. It is suggested that s 36(2)(aa) is an amendment that arises from the art 8 jurisprudence, which is also discussed in Chapter 11.
118 Introductory tenancies are granted under the English legislation. See n 18 . They are essentially probationary in nature, and thus bear some similarity to ASB SSSTs. The statutory scheme is described in *Powell* (n 21).

unsatisfactory. The authority cannot simply rely on the fact that it owns the property and that the tenant has no security of tenure, as would be the case in an action by a private landlord under section 33 of the 1988 Act. Under section 35(2)(aa), it must consider that an obligation of the tenancy has been broken.

This is not restricted to further antisocial behaviour: to adopt the words of Lord Phillips, the tenant must demonstrate that he is a good tenant, both as regards his behaviour towards his neighbours and as regards his contractual obligations to his landlord. Therefore, any the breach of a contractual obligation, such as the failure to pay rent, could give rise to the service of the notice of proceedings under section 36.

The stipulation imposed by subsection (2)(aa) is expressly linked, in section 36, to subsection (3)(aa), discussed below: when stating its reasons for seeking possession of a property let under an ASB SSST, the landlord must include the obligations of the tenancy that it considers to have been broken.

The form and content of the statutory notice

The form of notice is now found in two schedules to the Short Scottish Secure Tenancies (Proceedings for Possession) Regulations 2018.[119] The schedule 1 form is used in ASB SSSTs; the schedule 2 form is for non-ASB SSSTs.[120]

The schedule 1 form is in five parts:

1) the name of the tenant, and the address of the house of which the landlord seeks to recover possession;
2) the name, address and telephone number of the landlord, followed by the statement required for the purposes of section 36(3)(a): “we require possession of the house at the address in part 1”;
3) the reason(s) for seeking recovery of possession, as required by section 36(3)(aa);
4) the obligation(s) that the landlord considers to have been broken, as required by section 36(2)(aa) and (3)(aa);
5) a statement that proceedings will not be raised before a certain date, as required by section 36(2)(b) and (3)(b).

This is followed by seven notes to the tenant, providing information concerning sources of advice, explaining the procedure under section 36, and advising of the right to seek a review (see below).

The schedule 2 notice has the same parts, but with the omission of part 4 above, which is not applicable to non-ASB SSSTs. The notice also has seven notes, containing information similar to that stated in the schedule 1 notice.

119 SSI 2018/155.

120 Where it is argued by the defender that the notice departs from the prescribed form, the landlord may rely on s 21 of the Interpretation and Legislative Reform (Scotland) 2010. See Chapter 4, p 108.

Stating that the landlord requires possession: s 36(3)(a)

Compliance with this requirement will be achieved by using the statutory form of notice, part 2 of which contains the requisite statement (in both the schedule 1 and schedule 2 forms).

Stating the reasons why the landlord is seeking recovery of possession: s 36(3)(aa)

Again, this requirement seems to follow from the article 8 jurisprudence – in particular, the decision in *South Lanarkshire Council v McKenna,*[121] in which the Inner House held that an obligation to give reasons for seeking eviction must be read into section 36, standing the decisions of the Supreme Court.[122] With the insertion of subsection (3)(aa), "reading in" is no longer necessary, as the obligation is now explicit.[123]

In contrast to section 36(2)(aa), the requirement to give reasons for seeking possession applies in all section 36 cases, and not only in relation to ASB SSSTs.[124] However, in the case of an ASB SSST, the landlord must include, in the reasons, the obligations that it considers to have been broken.

The general principles applicable to a statutory obligation to give reasons are described at p 189 above. In the case of ASB SSSTs, it is suggested that the landlord ought to say why it considers that the tenant has proved unsatisfactory, and that it would not be appropriate to allow the tenancy to convert to a Scottish secure tenancy under section 37.[125]

The date specified in the notice: s 36(2)(b) and (3)(b)

Subsection (3)(b) is similar to section 14(4)(b), and unfortunately no less convoluted. Again, the landlord is required to hypothesise that the tenancy is not an SSST, and then work out the date on which the tenancy could be brought to an end, in that case by a notice to quit. The words "whichever is later" envisage that the application of section 14(4)(b)(i) and (ii) may lead to two different dates, in which case the landlord must apply the later of those two dates.

This requirement has an important effect, which is not immediately obvious: the landlord cannot raise an action under section 36 until the term of the SSST has expired. That is the case, whether the term is the fixed twelve (or eighteen) months under the ASB SSST, or the term of at least six months in a non-ASB SSST. That is because "the date on which the tenancy could have

121 2013 SC 212, [11].

122 In particular, para 115 in *Powell* (n 21), (Lord Phillips): "I do not believe that the Strasbourg court would tolerate a regime under which a person can be deprived of his home by a public authority without being told the reason for this. Nor would I, for it is fundamentally unfair . . .".

123 Paragraph 96 of the Policy Memorandum to the Bill that became the 2014 Act confirms that this provision was inserted, in light of the decision of the Inner House.

124 Again, this reflects Lord Phillips' judgment in *Powell* (n 21). The passage quoted at p 204 concerns the obligation, in relation to an introductory tenancy that is "probationary" in nature, to specify the obligation of the tenancy that has been broken. The requirement to give reasons is discussed later in his judgment, and applies to actions for recovery of possession by public authorities, in general.

125 See the quotation from *Powell* (n 21).

been brought to an end by a notice to quit" is the date falling at the end of the tenancy's term. Therefore, in the case of an ASB SSST that has been ongoing for, say, two months, a notice served under section 36 would have to state the date at the end of the fixed term, ten months later. It could not state the date two months later, under section 36(3)(b)(i), because that would not be the later of the two dates.

Accordingly, if the landlord wishes to begin possession proceedings as soon as possible, it must do so under sections 14 and 16 of the Act, as is permitted by section 36(7), discussed below. It is for this reason that the SSST Guidance states, at paragraph 13.1:

> "13.1 . . . landlords will wish to note that different processes . . . apply depending on whether recovery of possession action is being taken at the end of the term of a short SST (section 36 of the 2001 Act) or during the term of the short Scottish secure tenancy (section 14 of the 2001 Act)."[126]

The effect of section 36(3)(b) is perhaps best explained by examples.

Section 36(3)(b): ASB SSSTs

Example 1. Say that a tenancy is converted to an SSST under section 35, on 22 April 2022. The tenancy is then for a fixed term of twelve months, and the date on which the tenancy could have been brought to an end by a notice to quit is 21 April 2023.[127] If the landlord is serving the notice at any time before 21 February 2023, then 21 April 2023 is the later of the two dates in section 36(3)(b). In that case, the notice should specify a date that is not earlier than 21 April 2023.[128] If the notice is being served after 21 February and before 21 April 2023, the later of the two dates is the date two months after service of the notice.[129] Therefore, if the notice is served on 8 April, the date specified should be no earlier than 8 June. After 21 April 2023, it is too late to serve the notice, as the tenancy converts to a Scottish secure tenancy under section 37(1A)(a) on the expiry of that day.[130]

This example is applicable to an ASB SSST, which is subject to the fixed term of one year. Where the tenancy has been extended by six months under section 35A, the same reasoning applies. To adapt the above example, the duration of the tenancy would be eighteen months, and the date on which the tenancy could have been brought to an end by a notice to quit, had it not been an SSST, would be 21 October 2021. That would then be the later of the two dates for the purposes of section 36(3)(b), if the notice is served before 21 August. In the case of service after 21 August but before 21 October, the later of the two dates is two months after service of the notice.

126 See also para 7.6. This is example of the SSST being modelled on the short assured tenancy under the 1988 Act. The landlord of such a tenancy cannot raise proceedings under s 33 until the term of the tenancy has run. If he wishes to seek possession earlier, he must proceed under s 18, on one of the eviction grounds in sch 5.

127 See the discussion of the duration of ASB SSSTs, at p 196.

128 The notice does not require to specify the date which is the later of s 36(3)(b)(i) or (ii). It requires to specify a date which is "not earlier than" that date.

129 Assuming that the tenancy agreement does not provide for a longer notice period, which would be unlikely in practice.

130 See p 216.

Section 36(3)(b): non-ASB SSSTs

The application of section 36(3)(b) to non-ASB SSSTs is unfortunately more complicated. This is because non-ASB SSSTs may continue by tacit relocation, under section 34(5)(a),[131] and because the landlord must also serve a notice to quit on the tenant, so as to prevent tacit relocation occurring.[132] Before savouring the complexities of the next example, readers may care to note that the easiest approach (which is usually adopted in practice) is to state the next ish date of the tenancy on both the statutory notice and the notice to quit, and to serve both notices at least two months before that date.[133]

Example 2. Parties enter into a non-ASB SSST that runs for six months, from 11 February to 11 August 2022. On 15 June that year, the landlord decides that it wishes to terminate the tenancy as soon as possible. If the notice under section 36(2) is served on the tenant on 16 June, the date for the purposes of section 36(3)(b)(i) is 16 August, whereas the date for the purposes of section 36(3)(b)(ii) is 11 August, the next ish date, which is earlier. In that case, the landlord could serve the section 36 notice warning the tenant that proceedings are going to be raised on or after 16 August, and at the same time serve a notice to quit, terminating the tenancy contract on 11 August, thereby meeting the requirements of section 36(5).

In this example, 11 August would remain the earlier of the two dates for the purposes of the s 36(3)(b) up to service being effected on 1 July, if the correct period for the notice to quit was forty days. If the period of notice had been reduced by the contract to four weeks, 11 August would remain the earlier date for the purposes of s 36(3)(b) until service on 13 July. After 1 or 13 July (as the case may be), 11 February 2023 becomes the later of the two dates in terms of s 36(3)(b), and the date stated on the section 36 notice could not be earlier.

On the basis of the analysis of periods of notice in Chapter 3, it is submitted that the landlord should assume that forty clear days' notice is required for a notice to quit, unless there is a contractual provision that reduces or extends that period.[134]

The notice is effective for six months: s 36(4)

This provision is identical to section 14(5), discussed at p 112. Where the section 36 notice is served in respect of a tenancy that is capable of converting under section 37, the effect of expiry of the six-month period is that the notice falls, and conversion then takes place, under section 37(2)(a).

131 ASB SSSTs are not subject to tacit relocation, given the terms of s 34(5A) and (6A).

132 Because "tacit relocation is not operating" is one of the requirements of s 36(5), in respect of non-ASB SSSTs. See the discussion of s 36(5) below. It is does not seem to make much sense to hypothesise "the date on which the tenancy could have been brought to an end by a notice to quit" where the landlord is actually serving a notice to quit. This is an example of the difficulties caused by amalgamation, in ss 34–37, of provisions from the secured and assured tenancy regimes.

133 In Example 2, that would entail stating 11 August 2022 on both the s 36 notice and the notice to quit, and serving them both before 11 June.

134 Noting, however, that the period could not be reduced to less than four weeks, given the terms of the 1984 Act, s 112.

Notice to the local authority: s 36(6A) and (6B)

As with the notice under section 14(5A), this is the same as the notice under section 19A of the 1988 Act. All these provisions arise from section 11 of the Homelessness etc. (Scotland) Act 2003. The reader is therefore referred to the discussion of section 19A of the 1988 Act in Chapter 7.

The right to seek a review: s 36(4A), (4B) and (4C)

The following subsections were added to section 36 by section 11(c) of the 2014 Act:[135]

> "(4A) A tenant may, before the end of the period of 14 days beginning with the day of service of a notice under subsection (2), apply to the landlord for a review of a decision to seek recovery of possession of the house which is the subject of the tenancy.
>
> (4B) If an application for review under subsection (4A) is made, the landlord must, before the day specified in the notice by virtue of subsection (3)(b)–
>
> (a) confirm its decision to seek recovery of possession or withdraw its notice under subsection (2),
>
> (b) notify the tenant of its decision on the review, and
>
> (c) where its decision on the review is to confirm the decision to seek recovery of possession, notify the tenant of the reasons.
>
> (4C) The Scottish Ministers may by regulations make further provision about the procedure to be followed in connection with a review following an application under subsection (4A)."

Under the English legislation, the forms of statutory tenancy that have features in common with the SSST (being the introductory tenancy and the demoted tenancy under the Housing Act 1996)[136] have always contained a procedure under which the tenant may seek a review of the decision to raise eviction proceedings.[137] The existence of that procedure was an important reason for the Supreme Court's considering the relevant statutory schemes to be compliant with article 8 of the ECHR and, further, why it would be difficult for the tenant to mount a successful defence to such proceedings under article 8.[138] As part of the 2014 Act's revisal of the statutory scheme, a right to seek review of the landlord's decision has now been enacted. The prescribed form for the statutory notice of proceedings informs the tenant of that right.[139]

Under section 36(4B), the landlord is required, following an application for review, either to confirm its decision or to withdraw the section 36 notice. It must notify the tenant of the decision, and of its reasons,[140] if it chooses to confirm the decision. Confirmation will presumably be followed by an action being raised. In ASB SSSTs, withdrawal of the notice will amount, in effect, to the landlord accepting that the tenancy will convert to a Scottish secure

135 Though, like the other changes made to ss 34–37 of the 2001 Act, the 2014 Act amendments did not come into force until 1 May 2019.

136 See the discussion of the art 8 jurisprudence at p 179 above.

137 See ss 129 and 143F of the 1996 Act.

138 See, in particular, *Powell* (n 21) para 45, (Lord Hope), and paras 90 and 92, (Lord Phillips).

139 At note 5, in both the forms given in sch 1 and sch 2 to the Short Scottish Secure Tenancies (Proceedings for Possession) Regulations 2018 (n 119).

140 As to the requirement to give reasons, see p 189 above.

tenancy.[141] It is stipulated that these steps must be taken before the date specified in the notice of proceedings, under section 36(3)(b) (on or after which the proceedings may be raised).[142]

At the time when the 2014 Act was passed, one could reasonably have anticipated, from subsection (4C), that regulations would be made setting out the procedure for reviews, perhaps along similar lines to the regulations in relation to reviews in introductory and demoted tenancies in England.[143] That has not happened. Instead, the matter is addressed in the SSST Guidance, in such a way as to leave the review procedure (including the manner in which the review is to be sought by the tenant) entirely to the discretion of the landlord.[144]

Paragraph 13.14 of the SSST Guidance states:

> "Landlords should set out clearly in their tenancy information:
>
> - which methods of application for a review they will accept, for example, telephone, email or in writing;
> - who the application should be made to;
> - what information should be provided, for example the reasons why the tenant thinks the decision to take action to recover possession of the property is wrong, and any evidence for the landlord to consider;
> - their timescale for carrying out the review;
> - how the review will be carried out;
> - who will carry out the review (this should be carried out by a member of staff who was not involved in making the original decision to take repossession action);
> - how the landlord will advise the tenant of their decision; and
> - whether or not they will consider a request for a review received outwith the 14 day timescale and if so, how it will be dealt with."

Where the right to seek a review under section 36(4A)-(4C) has not been exercised by the tenant, that may prevent her from subsequently defending an action under section 36 on public law grounds.[145] As is described in Chapter 11, a public law defence will succeed only if, had the same point been taken in judicial review proceedings in the Court of Session, the occupier would have succeeded in having the relevant decision reduced. Rule 58.3(1) of the Rules of the Court of Session (RCS)[146] provides that a petition for judicial review "may

141 Under s 37(2)(a)(ii).

142 This is reiterated at para 13.16 of the Guidance. Paragraph 13.17 then states: "As the tenant's home is at risk, wherever possible, landlords should aim to carry out the review and let the tenant know the outcome within 14 days of receiving the request." Neither s 36 nor the Guidance indicates what is to happen if the landlord fails to comply with s 36(4B) before the date in the statutory notice.

143 Being the Introductory Tenants (Review) Regulations 1997 (SI 1997/72) and the Demoted Tenancies (Review of Decisions) (England) Regulations 2004 (SI 2004/1679). Under both, the tenant is entitled to insist on a hearing at which he has the right to be heard or represented, to call persons in evidence, and to put questions to any person who gives evidence. He also has the right to make written submissions. The review must be carried out by a person who was not involved in the decision to apply for an order for possession.

144 At paras 13.13 and 13.15, the SSST Guidance quotes subss (4A) and (4B), but makes no mention of subs (4C). Arguably, this calls into question whether the review procedure provides a "significant procedural safeguard" in the same way as the English regulations. See *Powell* (n 21) para 90.

145 That type of defence is discussed at p 178 and 213 in this chapter, and in more detail in Chapter 11.

146 Act of Sederunt (Rules of the Court of Session 1994) 1994 (SI 1994/1443) (RCS)). Chapter

not be lodged in respect of an application, if that application could have been made by appeal or review under or by virtue of any enactment". However, this rule is not absolute, and the court has been prepared to entertain applications in special or exceptional circumstances, even though an alternative statutory remedy has not been used.[147]

Making the order for recovery of possession: s 36(5) and (6)

> "(5) The court must make an order for recovery of possession if it appears to the court that–
> (a) the tenancy has reached the ish referred to in section 34(5), or in a case where subsection (2)(aa) applies, the end of the term applicable to the tenancy in accordance with section 34(6A), 35(3A) or 35A(1).
> (b) tacit relocation is not operating,
> (c) no further contractual tenancy (whether or not a short Scottish secure tenancy) is in existence, and
> (d) subsection (2) has been complied with.
> (6) An order under subsection (5) must appoint a date for recovery of possession and has the effect of–
> (a) terminating the tenancy, and
> (b) giving the landlord the right to recover possession of the house,
> at that date.
> (7) This section is without prejudice to sections 14 and 16, but subject to the modification mentioned in subsection (8).
> (8) In relation to the recovery of possession of the house which is the subject of a short Scottish secure tenancy, section 14(4) is to be read as if for paragraph (b) there were to be substituted–
> (b) a date, not earlier than 4 weeks from the date of service of the notice on or after which the landlord may raise proceedings for recovery of possession,
> . . ."

As was originally the case with section 33(1) of the 1988 Act, on which section 36(5) is based, the legislation sets out four conditions that must be fulfilled before the landlord may insist on an order under section 36(5). In discussing those conditions, it is again appropriate to make a distinction between the two different categories of SSST.

In the case of ASB SSSTs, the effect of the amendments made by the 2014 Act, in particular the amendment to section 36(5)(a), is that section 36(5)(b) ("tacit relocation is not operating") no longer applies. The Act now excludes tacit relocation in such cases, under sections 34(5A) and 35(4)(a): the tenancy is for a fixed term of twelve months, which may be extended under section 35A. This change is significant, as it relieves the landlord of the burden of having to serve a notice to quit on the tenant, in order to avoid the tenancy

58 of the RCS deals with applications to the supervisory jurisdiction of the Court of Session by judicial review.

147 See the discussion in Drummond, McCartney and Poole, *A Practical Guide to Public Law Litigation in Scotland* paras 1-023 to 1-027 and 3-051(6), and the authorities to which the authors refer. This issue was recently discussed in two homelessness judicial reviews, in which the petitioner had not exercised the statutory right of review of a decision, under s 35A of the 1987 Act: *Zungunde v Glasgow City Integration Joint Board* 2019 SLT 37; and *Makombo-Eboma v Glasgow City Council* 2019 SLT 1137.

relocating. Thus, in tenancies in this category, the only pre-action notice that is necessary is the statutory notice under section 36(2) and (3).

By contrast, in the case of a non-ASB SSST, tacit relocation has to be prevented. This may be done by the service of a notice to quit, bringing the tenancy to an end at the ish date, or some subsequent ish date, if the tenancy has previously continued by tacit relocation.[148]

In either category of SSST, the landlord will have to proceed under sections 14 and 16, if it wishes to initiate a court action before the term of the tenancy has expired.[149]

Possible defences to a section 36 action

Procedural issues

As section 36(5) requires the court to grant an order for possession if the procedural requirements set out in paragraphs (a)–(d) thereof, it is clear that the landlord's action may be opposed by the contention that one or more of those requirements has not been met. If that is established, the action will fall to be dismissed.[150]

It is unlikely that section 36(5)(a) will be in issue: for the reasons already explained,[151] the action cannot be raised until the term of the tenancy has expired.

A question as to whether section 36(5)(b) is fulfilled is likely to concern the validity of the notice to quit served by the landlord, for which see Chapter 3.[152] Likewise, the action may be opposed on the basis that the statutory notice fails to fulfil the requirements of section 36(2)–(4), and is therefore invalid, and thus the requirement in section 26(5)(d) is not met.

Section 36(5)(c) featured in *City of Edinburgh Council v Smith.*[153] In that case the council raised proceedings seeking recovery of possession under section 36, and decree for payment of rent arrears. It had served a notice to quit and the statutory notice under section 36. However, when the case called before the sheriff, she was advised that an agreement had been reached between the parties, whereby the defender would remain in occupation of the property upon payment of an agreed sum. The pursuers did not seek decree but moved to adjourn the case to a later date. Having heard submissions from counsel for the pursuers, the sheriff concluded that the agreement reached between the parties amounted to the creation of another contractual tenancy and, accordingly, the requirement in section 36(5)(c) was not met. The action was dismissed.

148 Tacit relocation is considered in Chapter 3, at p 51. In *Aberdeenshire Council v Shaw* 2012 SLT (Sh Ct) 144, the pursuers argued that a separate notice to quit was unnecessary, as service of the s 36(2) notice had the effect of preventing tacit relocation. That argument was rejected by the sheriff, and the action was dismissed.

149 See p 214.

150 As happened in *Aberdeenshire Council v Shaw*, and *City of Edinburgh Council v Smith* 2016 SLT (Sh Ct) 343, 2016 Hous LR 30, discussed below.

151 At p 206 above.

152 In *City of Edinburgh Council v Smith* (n 150), the sheriff noted, in passing at para [22], that the pursuers' notice to quit appeared to be invalid, because it stated a date that was not an ish of the tenancy, and therefore it did not prevent tacit relocation.

153 n 150.

Section 36(6) is in the same terms as section 16(5): the recovery of possession order appoints a date on which the tenancy ends, on or after which the landlord may recover possession.

Tenancy is a Scottish secure tenancy, rather than an SSST

As has already been explained, the SSST is, in certain respects, like a short assured tenancy under the 1988 Act, and section 36(5) of the 2001 Act bears a strong similarity to section 33(1) to the 1988 Act. Actions under section 33(1) are often defended on the basis that the landlord has failed to comply with the statutory requirements for setting up a short assured tenancy, and therefore the tenancy is not short assured, and section 33 does not apply. Therefore, it is possible that an action under section 36 might be defended on the same basis.

For example, the defender might argue that the term of the tenancy is less than six months,[154] or that the notice under section 34(4) is invalid, For that reason, it is submitted that, in an action under section 36, the landlord not only has to produce, and if necessary prove service of, the documents that establish that it has complied with section 36(5); it must also do the same as regards the notice under section 34(4), or section 35(3), which establishes that the tenancy is an SSST, rather than a Scottish secure tenancy.[155]

Public law, human rights and Equality Act

As described earlier in this chapter, defences of this type[156] have been pled in actions under section 36, and in cases in relation to similar forms of statutory tenancy under the English legislation. In cases under that section, public law issues, in particular, may arise.

The statutory scheme under sections 34–37 places certain obligations on the landlord, particularly as regards ASB SSSTs. These are:

- in the case of an ASB SSST, to provide, or ensure the provision of, such housing support services as the landlord considers appropriate with a view to enabling the conversion of the tenancy to a Scottish secure tenancy by virtue of section 37 (section 34(7));
- in the case of an ASB SSST, to have regard to guidance published by the Scottish Ministers before creating the tenancy under section 34 or 35, or extending the fixed term from twelve to eighteen months under section 35A, and before raising proceedings under section 36 (section 34(9));
- in respect of all SSSTs, to carry out a review, if requested, under section 34(4A)–(4C).

None of these obligations is mentioned in section 36(5) as being a prerequisite for granting an order for recovery of possession. However, as was discussed earlier in the chapter, and in more detail in Chapter 11, the failure by a social

154 In relation to a non-ASB SSST. In the case of an ASB SSST, the twelve-month term is dictated by the Act, in s 34(6A), rather than by the parties' agreement.

155 By analogy, production of the AT5 notice (equivalent to the s 34(4) notice) is necessary in relation to an application to the First-tier Tribunal for an order under s 33 of the 1988 Act: see r 66(b)(ii) of sch 1 to the First-tier Tribunal for Scotland Housing and Property Chamber (Procedure) Regulations 2017 (SSI 2017/328).

156 Which are discussed in Chapter 11.

landlord to comply with obligations under a statutory scheme could be the subject of judicial review proceedings. Alternatively, proceedings may be met with a "public law" defence to the effect that, given its failure to comply with the statutory scheme, actions on the part of the landlord, such as the decision to raise proceedings, are unlawful, or the notice under section 36(2) ought to be considered invalid.[157]

It is suggested that where there is a recognised ground for judicial review, and the issue is one of law, which can be decided by reference to acts or decisions on the part of the authority that are agreed to have taken place, an action for judicial review may well be the preferable course. In contrast to the sheriff in an action under section 36(5), a judge hearing judicial review proceedings in the Court of Session is not under a direction, made in primary legislation, to grant a decree for recovery of possession.

In sheriff court proceedings it is possible to attack, say, the validity of a notice served under section 36(2), because the landlord is said to have acted unlawfully in issuing the notice. However, in practice, it may be difficult, in such proceedings, to persuade the court to grapple with the sorts of arguments that are normally conducted elsewhere, especially in the face of statutory provision requiring the court to grant decree in favour of the landlord. That said, arguing the issue in the sheriff court may be necessary where: (a) judicial review proceedings are not possible;[158] or (b) where the dispute between the parties is so fact sensitive as to render judicial review proceedings inappropriate.

As was indicated at p 211 above, a public law defence may be more difficult to run if the tenant has not sought a review of the landlord's decision to raise proceedings, under section 36(4A)–(4C).

Proceedings under sections 14 and 16: s 36(7) and (8)

Subsection (7) preserves the right of the landlord to proceed under sections 14 and 16, rather than section 36. As is explained at paragraph 13.1 of the SSST Guidance,[159] the landlord should proceed under sections 14 and 16 where it wishes to take action to recover possession during the term of the tenancy.[160] The option of raising proceedings under s 14 is discussed at paras 13.21–13.29 of the SSST Guidance, which also provides a helpful table,

157 It is interesting to note that the Scottish Government's Guidance on the use of the "streamlined eviction process" for ground 2 cases (discussed in Chapter 5, at p 165) states, at para 4.20: "A tenant who is disagrees with a decision taken by the landlord to raise court proceedings could seek judicial review of the landlord's decision to seek a court order, and/or defend the repossession action." That, it is submitted, is also the case with an action under s 36, if there are grounds on which to attack the decision as unlawful.

158 For example, where judicial review would be time barred. See the discussion of *Wandsworth London Borough Council v Winder* [1985] AC 461 in Chapter 11, p 371.

159 Quoted at p 207 above.

160 For example, in a case in which the tenancy is converted under s 35, but shortly thereafter the behaviour of the tenant deteriorates, such that it is considered appropriate to raise eviction proceedings as soon as possible, rather than waiting for the twelve-month period under s 34(6A) to expire. As the SSST Guidance points out (at para 13.25) an action under ss 14 and 16 may also be preferable, where the landlord is proceeding under ground 2, using the "streamlined" process introduced by the 2014 Act.

setting out the differences between an action under sections 14 and 16 and an action under section 36.[161]

Proceedings under section 16 of the Act are discussed in Chapter 5.

Subsection (8) simplifies the rule in section 14(4)(b) by removing one of the two alternatives in that provision, where the landlord of an SSST wishes to proceed under sections 14 and 16. It is not necessary to hypothesise the date on which the tenancy could be ended by a notice to quit. The tenant is simply given a minimum four weeks' notice.[162]

Actions under section 36: savings provisions

Under paragraph 4 of the relevant commencement order,[163] the introduction of section 36(2)(aa) and (3)(aa) does not affect statutory notices served before 1 May 2019.[164] However, where the SSST was created before that date, and the section 36 notice was served after that date, those provisions will apply.

As is described at p 186 above, the changes made to the duration of ASB SSSTs by the 2014 Act do not apply to ASB SSSTs created before 1 May 2019. In particular, such a tenancy will still be subject to section 34(5), in terms of which an SSST may continue by tacit relocation or express agreement.[165] Therefore, it is suggested that where an ASB SSST is created before, but proceedings are being raised after, that date, the landlord still requires to show that tacit relocation is not operating, under section 36(5)(b), in proceedings under that section.

CONVERSION OF AN SSST TO A SCOTTISH SECURE TENANCY

Section 37 provides:

> **"Conversion to Scottish secure tenancy**
> (1) Where–
> (a) a tenancy is a short Scottish secure tenancy by virtue of section 35 or paragraph 1, 2 or 2A of schedule 6, and
> (b) the landlord has not served on the tenant a notice under section 14(2) or 36(2) before the expiry of the relevant period

161 Note, however, that the Guidance relates to ASB SSSTs, and this is reflected in the table, for example where it states that a notice to quit is not required prior to a s 36 action.

162 This means that s 36(8) effectively deletes s 14(4)(b)(ii) where the tenancy is an SSST. If such simplification was considered desirable (which it clearly is), it is difficult to understand why the 2014 Act did not go further, by amending ss 14(4)(b) and 36(3)(b) by deleting the second of the two alternatives in those provisions, and providing for a straightforward notice period of four weeks (in s 14) and two months (in s 36).

163 Housing (Scotland) Act 2014 (Commencement No. 8, Savings, Transitional and Supplemental Provisions) Order 2018 (SSI 2018/153).

164 This is reflected the Short Scottish Secure Tenancies (Proceedings for Possession) Regulations 2018 (SSI 2018/155), which sets out the prescribed forms for the notice under s 36. Regulation 4, entitled "Saving provision", states: "Nothing in these Regulations affects the validity of a notice under section 36(3) of the Act served prior to 1st May 2019".

165 The exclusion of s 34(5) in the case of ASB SSSTs is effected by s 9(1)(a) of the 2014 Act, which inserts s 34(5A). Under para 3 of the relevant commencement order, that does not affect SSSTs in relation to which the notice under s 34(4) was served before 1 May 2019. However, as mentioned at note 54 above, this transitional provision does not mention ASB SSSTs created by conversion under s 35.

the tenancy becomes, by virtue of this section, a Scottish secure tenancy with effect from the expiry of the relevant period.

(1A) In this section, the 'relevant period' is–

(a) the period of 12 months following the creation of the tenancy, or

(b) if an extension notice has been served under section 35A, the period of 18 months following the creation of the tenancy.

(2) Where subsection (1)(a) applies and the landlord has, in the relevant period, served a notice referred to in subsection (1)(b), then–

(a) if the notice–

(i) has ceased to be in force in accordance with section 14(5) or, as the case may be, 36(4), or

(ii) has been withdrawn by the landlord without proceedings for recovery of possession having been raised,

the tenancy becomes, by virtue of this section, a Scottish secure tenancy with effect from the date on which the notice ceased to be in force or was withdrawn or the expiry of the relevant period, whichever is the later,

(b) if proceedings for recovery of possession have been raised and have been finally determined in favour of the tenant, the tenancy becomes, by virtue of this section, a Scottish secure tenancy with effect from the date on which the proceedings were finally determined or the expiry of the relevant period, whichever is the later.

(3) For the purposes of subsection (2)(b) proceedings are finally determined when–

(a) the period for appealing against the interlocutor disposing of the proceedings has expired without an appeal being lodged, or

(b) where an appeal has been lodged, the appeal is withdrawn or finally determined.

(4) Where a tenancy becomes a Scottish secure tenancy by virtue of this section, the landlord must notify the tenant of that fact and of the date on which the tenancy became a Scottish secure tenancy.

(5) Subsection (6) applies to a tenancy which –

(a) became a short Scottish secure tenancy by virtue of section 35, and

(b) becomes a Scottish secure tenancy by virtue of this section.

(6) The term of the tenancy is the term which applied immediately before the tenancy became a short Scottish secure tenancy."

Conversion to a Scottish secure tenancy under section 37 is only possible for tenancies mentioned in subsection (1)(a), being ASB SSSTs.[166] It takes place when the twelve- (or eighteen-) month term of the tenancy expires, unless the landlord has served a notice of proceedings under section 14 or section 36. That can be done at any time up to the expiry of the term, and has the effect of suspending the operation of section 37. If the proceedings following upon the notice are successful, the tenancy will be terminated, under section 16(5)[167] or section 36(6). If that does not happen, because the landlord does

166 There is no provision for conversion of short Scottish secure tenancies under sch 6 paras 3–7. Therefore, tenants in that category may be stuck indefinitely with the lesser form of tenancy under the 2001 Act. This is a particular issue in relation to sch 6 para 6, which concerns houses "let expressly on a temporary basis to a person requiring or in receipt of housing support services", because there may come a point when the tenant contends that he is no longer in need of such services, and therefore ought to be allocated a Scottish secure tenancy, with full security of tenure. It is submitted that it may be possible to address this problem by way of an application under s 38 of the Act, which is discussed at p 194 above.

167 It is not clear what would happen if the landlord raised proceedings under s 16, on the ground of rent arrears, and the court granted a decree that was subject to s 16(5A) (which

not raise proceedings, or because the proceedings are determined in favour of the tenant, the tenancy converts under section 37(2). That has the effect of considerably raising the stakes in any action under section 16 or 36.

As is indicated in the discussion of the duration of ASB SSSTs, the twelve- or eighteen-month term runs from the date on which the tenancy is granted, in the case of creation under section 34, and from the date of service of the conversion notice, in the case of conversion.

Where conversion takes place under section 37, there is no bar, under the legislation, to the landlord converting the tenancy back to an SSST, under section 35. However, the tenant might object to such conversion by an appeal to the sheriff under section 35(5).

is discussed at p 519). That would not be a final determination in favour of the tenant, in terms of s 37(2), so conversion would appear to be excluded. But the tenancy would not be terminated if the landlord did not enforce the decree.

Chapter 7

Assured and Short Assured Tenancies

INTRODUCTION

This is the first of four chapters concerning statutory tenancies in the "private rented sector". This chapter looks at the creation of assured and short assured tenancies under the Housing (Scotland) Act 1988, and the steps that must be taken by a landlord before eviction proceedings are raised. Chapter 8 discusses the statutory grounds for eviction under that Act. Chapters 9 and 10 deal with the same issues in relation to private residential tenancies ("PRTs") under the Private Housing (Tenancies) (Scotland) Act 2016. The general scheme of security of tenure under those Acts is described in Chapter 1.

Part II of the 1988 Act sets out the statutory regime for private-sector tenancies[1] created between 2 January 1989 and 30 November 2017. For tenancies created prior to 2 January 1989, the regulated tenancy regime under the Rent (Scotland) Act 1984 applies. For tenancies created on or after 1 December 2017, the 2016 Act applies. It is no longer possible to create new assured tenancies from that date.[2]

1 December 2017 also saw another significant change: section 16 of the Housing (Scotland) Act 2014 came into force:

> "**16 Regulated and assured tenancies etc.**
> (1) The functions and jurisdiction of the sheriff in relation to actions arising from the following tenancies and occupancy agreements are transferred to the First-tier Tribunal—
> . . .[3]

1 Between 1989 and 30 September 2002, housing association tenancies were also covered by the 1988 Act. However, these were transferred to the Scottish secure tenancy regime by the 2001 Act, pt 2 of which is headed "Tenants of social landlords". Given the terms of s 11(1)(b) of the 2001 Act, a "social landlord" is a local authority, a registered social landlord (an "RSL") or Scottish Water. Tenancies of dwellinghouses entered into by other public bodies prior to 1 December 2017 may still be tenancies under the 1988 Act. However, sch 4 to that Act, discussed below, excepts tenancies granted by certain bodies, such as educational institutions, with the result that no statutory regime applies to them.

2 Section 12(1A) of the 1988 Act. See the discussion of the transitional arrangements in the legislation, at the end of this chapter. Naturally, people are still entering into agreements that are described as "assured" or "short assured" tenancies. However, these designations are of no effect. The tenancy is subject to the 2016 Act, if created on or after 1 December 2017.

3 In terms of s 16(1)(a) and (b), actions arising from regulated tenancies or pt VII contracts under the 1984 Act are also transferred to the First-tier Tribunal ("FTT"). It was not necessary to include PRTs in s 16 because, under the 2016 Act, proceedings in relation to PRTs are raised in the FTT. There has been no transfer of jurisdiction in relation to tenancies under the 2001 Act.

(c) an assured tenancy (within the meaning of section 12 of the Housing (Scotland) Act 1988 . . .[4]

. . .

(3) Part 1 of schedule 1 makes minor and consequential amendments."

Consequently, actions arising from tenancies under the 1988 Act, including eviction actions, are transferred to the First-tier Tribunal ("FTT"). By section 16(3) of and part 1 of schedule 1 to the 2014 Act, the various references to "court", "sheriff" etc. in part II of the 1988 Act were replaced by references to "First-tier Tribunal" etc.[5] As will be described later in this chapter, the FTT's Procedure Rules have particular provisions which apply to eviction actions raised under the 1988 Act.[6] After 1 December 2017, an action raised in the sheriff court that arises from an assured tenancy, including an eviction action, is incompetent, and ought to be dismissed.[7]

It is important to appreciate that section 16 of the 2014 Act does not effect a transfer of jurisdiction in relation to private-sector tenancies in general. The transfer is in respect of "actions arising from" the particular statutory tenancies specified in subsection (1), which include tenancies under the 1988 Act. Jurisdiction for private-sector tenancies not covered by the 1984, 1988 and 2016 Acts remains with the sheriff court. Accordingly, where a tenancy was created on, say, 1 November 2017, but is excepted from assured tenancy status by schedule 4 to the Act,[8] eviction proceedings in respect of that tenancy should be raised in the sheriff court.[9]

Because three different statutory schemes are now in place in relation to tenancies in the private sector, certain issues arise as to the transition from one regime to another, and the conditions under which tenancies under the older Act may be renewed, or continued, after the later Act came into force. Savings and transitional provisions were made in legislation, consequent upon the coming into force of the 1988 and 2016 Acts, and on the transfer of jurisdiction to the FTT. These are described at the end of this chapter.

Structure of this chapter

The purpose of this chapter is to examine certain issues in relation to the 1988 Act:

- What is an assured tenancy?
- Security of tenure under section 16.
- Recovery of possession under section 18.
- The notice of proceedings (AT6).
- Prerequisites for an application to the FTT under section 18.
- What is a short assured tenancy?

4 This includes short assured tenancies; under s 32 of the 1988 Act, a short assured tenancy is an assured tenancy. See n 12 and p 247.

5 Otherwise, part 1 of sch 1 to the 2014 Act does not make any substantive change to the 1988 Act.

6 Rules 65 and 66 of sch 1 to the First-tier Tribunal for Scotland Housing and Property Chamber (Procedure) Regulations 2017 (SSI 2017/328) (hereinafter: "the Procedure Rules").

7 *Parker v Inkersall Investments* 2019 SLT (Sh Ct) 41, 2019 Hous LR 14.

8 For example, because the landlord is a resident landlord. See the discussion of sch 4 below.

9 For further detail on the transfer of jurisdiction, see Chapter 2, p 36, and Chapter 14, p 477.

- Recovery of possession under section 33.
- Savings and transitional provisions.

Particular consideration will be given to the following sections of the 1988 Act.

Section 12

Section 12 outlines the conditions under which a tenancy became an assured tenancy. The question of whether a given tenancy is an assured tenancy can be critical for the resolution of an action for recovery of possession. Many cases are determined around the issue of whether the tenant has security of tenure under the relevant legislation and, if so, which type of statutory tenancy applies. A tenancy is excepted from statutory control if it falls under any of the categories set out in schedule 4 to the Act. In relation to such tenancies, the landlord need not follow any of the requirements of the Act, such as the requirement to serve a form AT6 in terms of section 19 of the 1988 Act.[10]

Section 16

Section 16 outlines the basis on which security of tenure is conferred on the tenant. An assured tenant is entitled to remain in the tenancy after his lease has been terminated. At the point of termination of the lease, he ceases to occupy by virtue of his rights under that contract, and thereafter occupies under a "statutory assured tenancy", the terms of which are, subject to a few exceptions, the same as the parties' original contract. In order to recover possession of the property, the landlord must raise proceedings under one or both of the two sections of the Act that empower the FTT to grant an order for the tenant's eviction: sections 18 and 33.

Sections 18 and 19

Section 18 outlines the conditions under which the FTT can make an order for possession of a house let under an assured tenancy. In particular, the tribunal must be satisfied that one of the grounds for recovery of possession listed in schedule 5 is established. In addition, in relation to some of those grounds the landlord must also establish that it would be reasonable to grant the order. The various grounds under schedule 5 are considered in Chapter 8.[11] Section 19 provides that, before proceedings are raised, the landlord must serve a notice of proceedings on the tenant in the prescribed form (the "AT6").

Sections 32 and 33

Section 32 provides for a special type of assured tenancy, called a "short assured tenancy", in respect of which the tribunal must order recovery of possession after termination of the tenancy at the ish date, on being satisfied that the landlord has met certain procedural requirements outlined in section 33. It

10 However, the landlord must terminate the parties' contract before raising recovery of possession proceedings on the basis that the former tenant then no longer has any right or title to remain in occupation. Termination of tenancy contracts is covered in Chapter 3.

11 The "reasonableness" test is considered in Chapter 5.

is easier to obtain an order for possession under section 33 than under section 18, because the landlord is not required to establish that he has any particular ground for recovery of possession, or that it would be reasonable to grant the order. For that reason, the short assured tenancy was definitely the preferred option for landlords in the private sector prior to the coming into force of the 2016 Act. Most assured tenancies that are not short assured tenancies[12] arose because the landlord failed to take legal advice before the creation of the tenancy or where, due to some error on the part of the landlord or his agents, the requirements for creation of a short assured tenancy under section 32 were not met. For that reason, the issue of whether a tenancy is a short assured tenancy under section 32 of the Act has commonly arisen in actions for recovery of possession under section 33.

The landlord of a short assured tenancy may make an application to the tribunal, seeking an order under section 18 of the Act. This may be done where, due to some conduct on the part of the tenant, the landlord decides that he cannot wait until the ish of the tenancy before taking action. In such proceedings, however, the landlord derives no benefit from the fact that the tenancy is short assured.[13]

Section 19A

Under section 19A, the landlord must also give notice of the raising of the proceedings to the local authority in whose area the house is situated. This requirement is applicable to actions under both section 18 and 33.

Comparison with assured tenancies in England and Wales

Readers will note that, in the discussion that follows, many of the authorities cited are English cases. The Housing Act 1988 created the assured tenancy and the "assured shorthold tenancy" (which is the equivalent of the short assured tenancy under the Scottish Act). Broadly speaking, private sector tenancies in England and Wales granted between 15 January 1989 and 27 February 1997 are assured tenancies, unless the tenancy was for not less than 6 months, and a notice (equivalent to the AT5[14] under the Scottish legislation) was served, in which case an assured shorthold tenancy was created. This system was changed by section 96 of the Housing Act 1996; subject to limited exceptions, all tenancies in the private sector in England and Wales, created after 28 February 1997, are assured shorthold tenancies.[15]

12 A short assured tenancy is an assured tenancy in respect of which the additional requirements of s 32(1) are fulfilled. Thus, all short assured tenancies are assured tenancies, but not all assured tenancies are short assured tenancies. This can lead to some confusion in terminology: housing law practitioners generally use the term "assured tenancy" when, strictly speaking, what is meant is "assured tenancy which is not a short assured tenancy", as in "the AT5 notice has not been served, so this is an assured tenancy".

13 There seems to be no reason why the landlord could not make applications (under rr 65 and 66) to the FTT, seeking orders under ss 18 and 33 at the same time; presumably this would be done only where there was some doubt, on the part of the landlord's agents, as to whether it was going to be possible to obtain an order under s 33.

14 See p 251 below.

15 Assured shorthold tenancies created after that date have no minimum period, and there is no requirement to serve any notice in advance of creating the tenancy. This has had the effect,

WHAT IS AN ASSURED TENANCY?

An assured tenancy is a tenancy that meets the conditions of section 12 of the 1988 Act:

> "(1) A tenancy under which a house is let as a separate dwelling is for the purposes of this Act an assured tenancy if and so long as—
> (a) the tenant or, as the case may be, at least one of the joint tenants is an individual; and
> (b) the tenant or, as the case may be, at least one of the joint tenants occupies the house as his only or principal home; and
> (c) the tenancy is not one which, by virtue of subsection (2) below, cannot be an assured tenancy.
> (1A) A tenancy cannot be an assured tenancy if it is granted on or after 1 December 2017.[16]
> (2) If and so long as a tenancy falls within any paragraph of Schedule 4 to this Act, it cannot be an assured tenancy; and in that Schedule 'tenancy' means a tenancy under which a house is let as a separate dwelling.
> (3) Subsection (1) is subject to section 46A."[17]

"Tenancy"

This term is discussed in Chapter 1. If occupation is by virtue of a contract that is not a tenancy but merely a licence, or a service occupancy, or some other contract that falls short of being a tenancy, the occupier has no security of tenure under the 1988 Act. For that reason, the owner of the subjects may have tried to avoid statutory security of tenure by seeking to create a licence, or some other form of occupancy agreement, rather than a tenancy. This status of a person occupying under a licence is discussed in Chapter 12. For the purposes of part II of the 1988 Act, "tenancy" includes sub-tenancy.[18]

"House let as a separate dwelling"

This term is discussed in Chapter 1. Further guidance as to its meaning, in the context of assured tenancies, is also given in the Act.

(1) Section 55 of the Act defines "house" as "includes part of a house".
(2) Section 14 applies to bedsit and other flat-sharing arrangements in which the tenant has exclusive occupation of part of a house or flat, such as a single room, but shares the use of other rooms such as the bathroom, kitchen and hall with other single-room tenants. In such cases the separate accommodation of which the tenant has exclusive occupation is deemed to be a house let on an assured tenancy.[19] Accommodation of

in England, "that there are many informal, oral, tenancy agreements": Webber and Dovar, *Residential Possession Proceedings* (10th edn, 2017) para 7.012.

16 This subsection was added by sch 5 para 1 to the 2016 Act. Apart from certain limited exceptions, discussed at the end of this chapter, there are to be no new assured or short assured tenancies after the 2016 Act comes into force.

17 Section 46A allows the parties, by agreement, to convert an assured tenancy into a PRT under the 2016 Act.

18 Section 55(1). Sub-tenancies under the 1988 Act are also discussed in Chapter 12.

19 Absent s 14, a question would arise as to whether the room let to the tenant could be regarded

this type may be subject to the statutory regulation of "houses in multiple occupation".[20]

(3) Section 13 provides that where a house is let together with other land, the land is to be treated as being part of the house "if and so long as the main purpose of the letting is the provision of a home for the tenant or, as the case may be, one of the joint tenants". However, if and so long as that is not the main purpose of the letting, section 13(1)(b) provides that the tenancy shall be treated as not being let as a "separate" dwelling, and will thus not be an assured tenancy in terms of section 12. Section 13 does not affect any exclusion of the tenancy from the protection of the Act by section 12(2) and schedule 4. The words "if and so long as" are discussed below.

(4) Section 15 makes provision in relation to sub-tenancies, which are considered in Chapter 12.

"If and so long as"

As was explained in Chapter 4,[21] a question may arise as to the status of a tenancy, if circumstances change, at some point after it commences. If the tenancy does not fulfil the conditions for coverage by the Act at the outset, but fulfils those conditions at some later date, does it then become protected under the legislation? Conversely, if it is initially protected, can it lose that status if circumstances change?

The phrase "if and so long as" appears in sections 12 and 13. Its effect is that the tenancy may have been assured at its commencement, but ceased to be assured at some later stage where, for example, the tenant was no longer occupying it as his only or principal home.[22] Thereafter, it would have become assured again if occupation as his only or principal home had resumed. Similarly, a tenancy that was assured at its inception would cease to be assured if circumstances changed such that it became a tenancy to which one of the categories listed in schedule 4 applied.[23] Conversely, a tenancy that

as a "separate dwelling" for the purposes of s 12 given the shared use of other rooms. See the discussion of this issue in Chapter 1, p 21. Section 21 of the Act makes certain special provisions for recovery of possession actions in relation to subjects let under s 14, to the effect that, *inter alia*, no possession order can be made for the whole accommodation unless there is a specific order made for the separate accommodation; the FTT may make an order ending the tenant's right to occupy all or part of the shared accommodation which is not living accommodation, or varying the people or number of people who can occupy the shared accommodation.

20 Under pt 5 of the Housing (Scotland) Act 2006.

21 At p 85.

22 Or in the case of a joint tenancy, where none of the joint tenants occupies the tenancy as their only or principal home.

23 E.g. in *Bankway Properties Ltd v Penfold-Dunsford* [2001] 1 WLR 1369, (2002) 34 HLR 42, the landlords sought to remove a tenancy's assured status by utilising a rent review clause to increase the rent so that it would exceed the level referred to in the "tenancies at high rateable values/high rents" exception in sch 1 to the Housing Act 1988 (there is no equivalent exception in the Scottish legislation). The arguments in this case concerned the issue of whether the rent review clause could be used in this manner. However, there appeared to be no question that a tenancy would lose its assured status if, at some point after its commencement, one of the excepted categories applied. It should be noted, however, that this could not happen in relation to the excepted categories, such as lettings to students, or tenancies with a resident

was not assured at its commencement may have become assured at some point thereafter if the requirements of section 12 were fulfilled.[24]

"The tenant, or at least one of the joint tenants, is an individual"

The important effect of these words is to preclude a limited company or a partnership from holding an assured tenancy.[25] This means that a landlord of residential property could seek to avoid security of tenure by insisting on letting only to companies. In a number of cases the English courts have considered whether a company let is a mere sham arrangement, in which the true tenant is the individual who purchased an "off-the-shelf" company and used it as a nominee or agent, in order to obtain the let.[26] As with the various elaborate attempts to create licences instead of leases, this type of avoidance measure does not appear to have caught on in Scotland.

"Occupies the house as his only or principal home"

The terms "occupies", "house" and "only or principal home" are discussed in Chapter 1.

Tenancies excepted under schedule 4: s 12(2)

The categories listed in schedule 4 are:

(1) tenancies entered into before commencement of the 1988 Act (on 2 January 1989);
(2) tenancies at a low rent, or in which no rent is payable (see below);
(3) tenancies of shops;[27]

landlord, which require that certain circumstances existed at the point when the tenancy was granted. See also the discussion of para 2 of sch 4, below.

24 This is subject to the proviso that the subjects must have been let "as" a separate dwelling in the first place. In *Russell v Booker* (1981–82) 5 HLR 10, a property had been let as an agricultural holding, but over the years the agricultural use had been abandoned. The court decided that the Rent Acts did not apply; where the terms of the tenancy provide for or contemplate the use of the premises for some particular purpose, that is the essential factor in deciding whether the property has been let "as" a dwelling. See also *Tan and Anr v Sitkowski* [2007] 1 WLR 1628.

25 This is in contrast to the position under the Rent Acts, in terms of which it is possible for a company to be the *protected* tenant of a house, provided that it is used as a separate dwelling, normally by an employee or a sub-tenant of the company. This means that the company can apply for the rent to be registered: *Ronson Nominees v Mitchell* 1982 SLT (Sh Ct) 18. However, it cannot become the *statutory* tenant, as the security of tenure provisions of the legislation extend only to individuals who can be in physical occupation of the subjects: *Hiller Ltd v United Dairies (London)* [1934] 1 KB 57; *Ronson Nominees v Mitchell*.

26 See, e.g., *Eaton Square Properties Ltd v O'Higgins* (2001) 33 HLR 771; *Estavest Investments Ltd v Commercial Express Travel Ltd* (1989) 21 HLR 106; *Hilton v Plustitle Ltd* [1989] 1 WLR 149, (1989) 21 HLR 72; *Kaye v Massbetter Ltd and Kanter* (1992) 24 HLR 28. The leading definition of a "sham" transaction is that given by Diplock LJ in *Snook v London and West Riding Investments Ltd* [1967] 2 QB 786, 802, namely "acts done or documents executed by the parties . . . which are intended by them to give to third parties or to the court the appearance of creating between the parties legal rights and obligations different from the actual legal rights and obligations (if any) which the parties intend to create".

27 Being a tenancy to which the Tenancy of Shops (Scotland) Act 1949 applies.

(4) a tenancy under which the house consists of or comprises premises licensed for the sale of alcoholic liquor for consumption on the premises;
(5) a tenancy under which agricultural land, exceeding two acres, is let together with the house;[28]
(6) a tenancy under which the house is on or comprised in a lease constituting a tenancy under the Agricultural Holdings (Scotland) Act 1991[29] and is occupied by the person responsible for the control (whether as tenant or as servant or agent of the tenant) of the farming of the holding;
(7) a tenancy that is granted to a person who is pursuing, or intends to pursue, a course of study provided by a specified educational institution and is so granted either by that institution or by another specified institution or body of persons;[30]
(8) a tenancy the purpose of which is to confer on the tenant the right to occupy the house for a holiday (see below);
(9) resident landlords (see below);
(10) a tenancy under which the interest of the landlord belongs to Her Majesty in right of the Crown or to a government department or is held in trust for Her Majesty for the purposes of a government department but not including such a tenancy if it is under the management of the Crown Estate Commissioners (see below);
(11) a tenancy under which the interest of the landlord belongs to: (i) a council constituted under section 2 of the Local Government etc. (Scotland) Act 1994, or a joint board or joint committee of two or more such councils, or the common good of such a council or any trust under the control of such a council; (ii) Scottish Water; (iii) a co-operative housing association within the meaning of section 1 of the Housing Associations Act 1985; (iv) a registered social landlord within the meaning of the Housing (Scotland) Act 2010;
(11A) a tenancy granted expressly on a temporary basis in the fulfilment of a duty imposed on a local authority by part II of the Housing (Scotland) Act 1987;
(11A)[31] accommodation for offenders, being a tenancy for a term of less than six months, to a person under supervision, in terms of section 27 of the Social Work (Scotland) Act 1968;
(11B) accommodation for asylum seekers under section 4 or part VI of the Immigration and Asylum Act 1999;

28 In this paragraph "agricultural land" has the same meaning as in the Rent (Scotland) Act 1984, s 115(1).

29 As amended by the Agricultural Holdings (Scotland) Act 2003. This includes a lease constituting a short limited duration tenancy or a limited duration tenancy, within the meaning of those Acts.

30 The institutions are specified by the Assured Tenancies (Exceptions) (Scotland) Regulations 1988 (SI 1988/2068), as amended by the Assured Tenancies (Exceptions) (Scotland) Amendment Regulations 1993 (SI 1993/995).

31 There are two paras 11A, due to a drafting error in amending legislation. The first para 11A was inserted by the Housing Act 1988, s 140(1) and sch 17, pt 1, para 90. The second was inserted by the 2001 Act, sch 10, para 14(2)(b).

(11C) a tenancy granted under arrangements for the provision of accommodation for persons with temporary protection made under the Displaced Persons (Temporary Protection) Regulations 2005;

(12) shared ownership agreements;[32] and

(13) transitional cases.[33]

Most of the schedule 4 exceptions are self-explanatory and require no further comment. However, the following points might usefully be made:

Tenancies at a low rent, or in which no rent is payable

Paragraph 2 applies in two different types of tenancy: (a) where no rent is payable; or (b) where the rent payable is less than that specified by order made by the Secretary of State.

It is submitted that (a) refers to a tenancy in which the "rent" takes the form of services, rather than a pecuniary rent that is "payable".[34] Therefore, a tenancy in which the tenant performs services in lieu of rent cannot be an assured tenancy.[35]

As regards (b), the level set by the Assured Tenancies (Tenancies at a Low Rent) (Scotland) Order 1988[36] is £6 per week, or equivalent. In determining whether the rent under a tenancy falls under either of these descriptions, sums payable by the tenant in respect of services, repairs, maintenance or insurance are disregarded.

Paragraph 2 also provides that "no tenancy which is or, at any time, was an assured tenancy shall cease to be an assured tenancy by virtue only of this paragraph". Thus the tenant cannot be deprived of his status as an assured tenant, by an agreement to amend the parties' tenancy such that no rent, or a rent below the level set in the order, is payable. However, it appears that where a tenancy is initially excepted by paragraph 2, it may become an assured tenancy if parties subsequently agree that rent above the requisite level is to be paid.[37]

Holiday lettings[38]

Paragraph 8 of schedule 4 applies to a tenancy "the purpose of which is to confer on the tenant the right to occupy the house for a holiday". There was a similar exception for holiday lettings under the Rent Acts, and there are several English cases on this point: the designation of tenancies as "holiday lets" has

32 Within the meaning of s 83(3) of the Housing (Scotland) Act 2001.

33 Which includes protected tenancies under 1984 Act. It is still possible to create new protected tenancies under that Act in certain limited circumstances. By virtue of this paragraph, these will not be assured tenancies. See the discussion of at the end of this chapter.

34 There has to be some form of rent, otherwise the parties' contract would not be a tenancy: *Mann v Houston* 1957 SLT 89. At common law, rent may be "money, the fruit of the grounds, or services " (Erskine, *Principles of the Law of Scotland*, II, vi,8; Paton and Cameron, *Landlord and Tenant* 6) "Fruits of the grounds", is applicable to agricultural tenancies, not tenancies of residential property.

35 That is consistent with the position under the Rent Acts: see *Barnes v Barratt* [1970] 2 QB 657.

36 (SI 1988/2069). This has never been updated.

37 This seems to follow from the words "if and so long as" in s 12(2). See also *Bankway Properties Ltd v Penfold-Dunsford* (described at note 23 above) and *P v O* 2014 GWD 26-528.

38 See also the equivalent exception under the 2016 Act, which is discussed at p 299.

been employed as an avoidance measure. For cases with contrasting outcomes, see: *Buchmann v May*[39] and *R v Rent Officer for Camden London Borough Council, ex p Plant.*[40] In *Buchmann* the Court of Appeal accepted the dictionary definition of a holiday as "a period of cessation of work, or period of recreation", but in *McHale v Daneham*[41] took the view that there was no reason why the "holiday" for the purposes of the Act could not include a working holiday.

In *St Andrews Forest Lodges Ltd. v Grieve,*[42] Sheriff Collins confirmed that a tenancy does not become a holiday let just because one or both of the parties wish it so or describe it as such in a written agreement. In that case, the defenders had occupied the property as their only or principal home for years, and at no time agreed that their occupancy was for the purpose of a holiday. Nor could they have so agreed, given that it manifestly was not. Accordingly, on the facts, paragraph 8 did not apply.

Resident landlords

Paragraph 9 of schedule 4, relating to resident landlords, is longer than all the other paragraphs put together. In essence, the tenancy is excepted under paragraph 9 if:

(a) the house let to the tenant is part of a building;
(b) the tenancy was granted by a person, who at the time of granting the tenancy, occupied as his only or principal home another house which also forms part of the building;
(c) when the tenancy was granted, there was an ordinary means of access from one house to the other; and
(d) at all times since the tenancy was granted the interest of the landlord has belonged to a person who occupied another house in the building as his only or principal home.

In terms of paragraph 9(6), the tenancy is not excepted where, immediately before the inception of the tenancy, the tenant was the assured tenant of that house, or any other house in the building. Most of the detail in paragraph 9 relates to requirements (b) and (d) above, particularly in relation to periods following the sale of the landlord's interest, or the death of the landlord. For those issues, readers are referred to the detailed terms of the Act.

In the author's experience, an argument as to whether a tenancy is excepted under paragraph 9 has always revolved around requirement (c), and the issue of whether there is an "ordinary means of access from one house to the other". The term "ordinary means of access" is not defined in the Act. It is submitted that the wording of the provision appears to envisage a means of access the use of which entails going directly from one house to another, such as an internal door in a wall that is common to both houses. Where the access from one house to another entails going outside, or through an area such as a common close, the use and possession of which is shared between the houses

39 [1978] 2 All ER 993, (1976) 7 HLR 1.
40 (1983) 7 HLR 15.
41 (1979) 249 EG 969.
42 [2017] SC DUN 25, 2017 GWD 14-224, [49]–[53]. The case is discussed in more detail in Chapter 1, p 24, in relation to the lease/licence distinction.

(and perhaps other houses in the building), the access is not "from one house to another".

It is also submitted that the word "ordinary" is capable of referring to two features of the means of access in question. In a general sense, a door may be described as an "ordinary" means of access, in contrast to a window, which might be capable of serving as a means of access, but not ordinarily so. However, in a particular situation the door in question may not ordinarily be in use. It might be permanently locked, blocked by items of furniture, with access from one house to another always being achieved by some other means. In that case, it is submitted, the door would not be an "ordinary" means of access. This is not be confused, however, with a situation in which the use of the door in question is very infrequent, simply because access from one house to another rarely occurs, or only occurs in terms of a tenancy agreement that places restrictions on the landlord obtaining access. The door in question can still be described as the ordinary means of access on the rare occasions when access takes place.

Crown tenancies

Following the decision of the European Court of Human Rights ("ECtHR") in *Larkos v Cyprus*,[43] the excepting of Crown tenancies from security of tenure is open to challenge under articles 14 and 8 of the European Convention on Human Rights ("ECHR") if it does not pursue a legitimate aim and there is no reasonable or objective justification for excluding the tenant from the protection afforded to private tenants. That said, "the protection afforded to private tenants" under the 1988 Act is limited in the case of short assured tenancies, which most landlords chose to create. Thus, the appropriate "comparator" for the purposes of article 14 may be a tenant in the private sector who would not have had security of tenure, or a tenant in the social rented sector whose tenancy would have been excluded from the 2001 Act as a "service occupancy".[44] In eviction proceedings concerning a case to which schedule 4 paragraph 10 applies, the landlord may meet a defence based on articles 14 and 8 with the argument that, had the 1988 Act applied, it would have chosen to create a short assured tenancy; or, had the 2001 Act applied, the tenancy would have been excepted under schedule 1 to that Act.[45]

Originally, a tenancy in which the landlord was a health service body was excepted from assured tenancy status by virtue of schedule 4 paragraph 10. That exception was removed with effect from 1 April 1991 by the National Health Service and Community Care Act 1990.[46] This change was not retro-

43 (2000) 30 EHRR 597.

44 2001 Act, s 11(4) and sch 1, para 1.

45 See *Nicholas v Secretary of State for Defence* [2015] 1 WLR 2116, in which the art 14 argument based on *Larkos v Cyprus* (n 43) was unsuccessful. It is suggested that the comparison with a short assured tenant in the private sector will be more convincing if there are features of the tenancy that are similar to the requirements of s 32: the tenancy was for an initial period of at least six months, and notice was given that the tenant had no security beyond that point.

46 Nowadays, the property of health service bodies is owned by the Scottish Ministers. As regards tenancies held by employees of health service bodies, see also the discussion of ground 17 in Chapter 8.

spective: only tenancies created after that date can be assured or short assured tenancies.[47]

SECURITY OF TENURE

Section 16 of the Act provides:

"(1) After the termination of a contractual tenancy which was an assured tenancy the person who, immediately before that termination, was the tenant, so long as he retains possession of the house without being entitled to do so under a contractual tenancy shall, subject to section 12 above and sections 18 and 32 to 35 below—

(a) continue to have the assured tenancy of the house; and

(b) observe and be entitled to the benefits of all the terms and conditions of the original contract of tenancy so far as they are consistent with this Act but excluding any—

(i) which makes provision for the termination of the tenancy by the landlord or the tenant;

. . .

and references in this Part of this Act to a 'statutory assured tenancy' are references to an assured tenancy which a person is continuing to have by virtue of this subsection, subsection (1) of section 31 below, or section 3A of the Rent (Scotland) Act 1984.{48}

. . .

(2) A statutory assured tenancy cannot be brought to an end by the landlord except by obtaining an order of the First-tier Tribunal in accordance with the following provisions of this Part of this Act.

(3) Notwithstanding anything in the terms and conditions of tenancy of a house being a statutory assured tenancy, a landlord who obtains an order for possession of the house as against the tenant shall not be required to give him any notice to quit."

As was the case under the Rent Acts, there is a critical distinction in the 1988 Act between the tenancies in relation to which the parties' contract is still ongoing, and the statutory tenancy that arises once the contract has been terminated. Under the 1984 Act, the last of the Rent Acts in force in Scotland, the term "protected tenancy" denotes the former and "statutory tenancy" the latter; "regulated tenancy" refers to both. The 1988 Act equivalent of

47 By virtue of the transitional provision contained in para 20 of sch 8 to the 1990 Act. Tenancies created by health service bodies after 1 April 1991 will be assured tenancies. This appears to be one of the few instances in which a 1988 Act tenancy is not held by a private landlord, but a public authority for the purposes of s 6 of the Human Rights Act 1998. In the case of a short assured tenancy, an action under s 33 of the Act (see below) might be defended on the basis that eviction would be contrary to the art 8 rights of the defender. See Chapter 11.

48 Section 31 is the provision in terms of which the spouse or civil partner of an assured tenant may succeed to the tenancy on his death. Prior to 1 December 2017, if the tenancy was still a contractual assured tenancy on death, the successor became the statutory assured tenant. Where the tenant dies after that date, the tenancy to which the spouse or civil partner succeeds becomes a PRT, in terms of s 31A. See Chapter 12, p 425. In terms of s 3A of and sch 1A to the 1984 Act, where a regulated tenant died after 2 January 1989, but before 1 December 2017, the tenancy became a statutory assured tenancy, held by the person entitled to succeed in terms of sch 1A to the 1984 Act. Under s 3B of the 1984 Act, where a regulated tenant dies on or after 1 December 2017, the person entitled to succeed become the tenant under a PRT.

the "statutory tenancy" is the "statutory assured tenancy", which in terms of section 16 comes into being once the parties' contract is terminated. For the ongoing contractual tenancy prior to termination, the Act employs several different terms, for reasons that are by no means clear. Sections 16(1), 18(7), 19(6) and 33(1) all employ the straightforward "contractual tenancy", whereas section 18(6) refers to "assured tenancy, not being a statutory assured tenancy", while section 17 alone uses the term "the former tenancy" which means, in terms of subsection (1), "the tenancy on the termination of which the statutory assured tenancy arises". All these terms appear to mean the same thing. The term "assured tenancy", as it appears in section 18(1), for example, refers to both the contractual tenancy and the statutory assured tenancy.

All assured tenancies begin as contractual tenancies, and may become statutory assured tenancies if the parties' contract is terminated and section 16 of the Act comes into operation. That is also the case if the tenancy is a short assured tenancy.[49]

On the termination of the parties' contract, the tenant has a statutory assured tenancy "so long as he retains possession of the house",[50] which is his "only or principal home".[51] If, at that time, or at some point thereafter, it becomes clear that the tenant has not retained possession, or the property is no longer his only or principal home, the landlord may make an application to the FTT,[52] which would not require to be "in accordance with the following provisions of this Part of this Act" in terms of section 16(2), on the basis that there is no longer any contractual or statutory assured tenancy in existence.[53]

Thus, from the date when a contractual tenancy ends (usually on expiry of a valid notice to quit) the former tenant is either a person with no right to occupy the premises or he is the statutory assured tenant.[54] If the tenant fails to achieve or retain statutory assured tenancy status, it is no longer necessary for the landlord to meet the requirements of the Act in order to recover possession.

49 This is made clear by s 33(4), which provides that, following an order in terms of s 33(1), any statutory assured tenancy that has arisen at the ish date referred to in s 33(1)(a) shall end (without further notice) on the day when the order takes effect.

50 The words "retains possession" are discussed in Chapter 1. There it is suggested that this test requires occupation.

51 See Chapter 1 for a discussion of this test. It applies because, under s 12, the tenancy is assured only "if and so long as" the house is the only or principal home of the tenant, or at least one of the joint tenants.

52 It is suggested that the FTT would have jurisdiction under s 16 of the Housing (Scotland) Act 2014, because the proceedings would be "arising from" an assured tenancy. See the discussion of the transfer of jurisdiction at the beginning of Chapter 14.

53 As the landlords did in *Ujima Housing Association v Ansah* (1998) 30 HLR 831, a case which is discussed in Chapter 1. This procedure may be particularly useful in cases in which the tenant appears to have abandoned the subjects, as the 1988 Act has no equivalent to the abandonment procedure under the 2001 Act. Note also that this is why, in contrast to a Scottish secure tenancy, there is no ground for recovery of possession in relation to assured tenancies to the effect that the tenant is no longer residing in the property. That would be superfluous: if the tenant does not reside at the tenancy, to the extent that it is no longer his "only or principal home", there is no assured tenancy, and therefore no requirement to establish any ground for recovery of possession. In that case the landlord may simply terminate the parties' lease and make an application on the basis that he is entitled to possession at common law.

54 This was also the case with the statutory tenancy under the Rents Acts. See: Paton and Cameron (n 34) 515, citing *Alex Cowan & Sons v Acton* 1952 SC 73, 80, (Lord Patrick).

The effect of the words "without being entitled to do so under a contractual tenancy" is that the parties may end the statutory assured tenancy by entering into a new tenancy contract, without the necessity of an order being sought under the provisions of the Act, as would otherwise be required by section 16(2). In other words, the parties may impliedly renounce the existing tenancy in favour of a new contract.[55]

As well as preserving the tenant's rights under the contract, section 16 also preserves his obligations. In particular, he is obliged to continue paying the rent, and acceptance of rental payments by the landlord does not constitute a new tenancy agreement.[56]

In section 16(2) the "following provisions of this Part of this Act" are, in particular, sections 18 and 33, which empower the FTT to grant an order for recovery of possession. These are considered in detail below.

Section 16(3) should not be read as indicating that it is not necessary for the landlord to serve a notice to quit under any circumstances. A valid notice to quit terminating the tenancy and bringing about a statutory assured tenancy under section 16 *may* be a necessary preliminary to an action under section 18 or 33.[57] However, once the tenancy is terminated and the landlord obtains an order under one of those sections, no further notice to quit is required.

RECOVERY OF POSSESSION OF ASSURED TENANCIES

Orders for possession: s 18

Section 18 provides:

"(1) The First-tier Tribunal shall not make an order for possession of a house let on an assured tenancy except on one or more of the grounds set out in Schedule 5 to this Act.

(2) The following provisions of this section have effect, subject to section 19 below, in relation to proceedings for the recovery of possession of a house let on an assured tenancy.

(3) If the First-tier Tribunal is satisfied that any of the grounds in Part I of Schedule 5 to this Act is established then, subject to subsections (3A) and (6) below, the Tribunal shall make an order for possession.

55 This would be either an assured or a short assured tenancy, if the new contract was created before 1 December 2017, or a PRT, if created after that date.

56 *Morrison v Jacobs* [1945] KB 577; *Davies v Bristow* [1920] 3 KB 428. There appears to be a fairly widespread misconception that the landlord should not accept rental payments after terminating a contractual assured tenancy, as this might enable the tenant to argue that the acceptance of rent implies an obligation to pay rent, and therefore the existence of a tenancy agreement. This might be a concern in relation to common law tenancies, but no such implication is possible in relation to assured tenancies, because the tenant's obligation to pay rent is attributable to the statutory assured tenancy, not to any new agreement. Even if the landlord accepts rent after termination of the contractual tenancy in circumstances where he is not sure whether the person in occupation is entitled to the protection of the Act, and is considering his position, acceptance of the monies will not be treated as creating a new tenancy: *Marcroft Wagons Ltd v Smith* [1951] 2 KB 496. On the other hand, accepting rent after an order for possession has been granted may give rise to the implication of a new tenancy because, in terms of s 18(7) or s 33(4), the order terminates the statutory assured tenancy. Acceptance of rent post decree is discussed in Chapter 15.

57 For a discussion of notices to quit, see Chapter 3.

(3A) If the First-tier Tribunal is satisfied–
(a) that Ground 8 in Part I of Schedule 5 to this Act is established; and
(b) that rent is in arrears as mentioned in that Ground as a consequence of a delay or failure in the payment of relevant housing benefit or relevant universal credit,

the Tribunal shall not make an order for possession unless the Tribunal considers it reasonable to do so.

(4) If the First-tier Tribunal is satisfied that any of the grounds in Part II of Schedule 5 to this Act is established, the Tribunal shall not make an order for possession unless the Tribunal considers it reasonable to do so.

(4A) In considering for the purposes of subsection (4) above whether it is reasonable to make an order for possession on Ground 11 or 12 in Part II of Schedule 5 to this Act, the First-tier Tribunal shall have regard, in particular, to the extent to which any delay or failure to pay rent taken into account by the Tribunal in determining that the Ground is established is or was a consequence of a delay or failure in the payment of relevant housing benefit or relevant universal credit.

(5) Part III of Schedule 5 to this Act shall have effect for supplementing Ground 9 in that Schedule and Part IV of that Schedule shall have effect in relation to notices given as mentioned in Grounds 1 to 5 of that Schedule.

(6) The First-tier Tribunal shall not make an order for possession of a house which is for the time being let on an assured tenancy, not being a statutory assured tenancy, unless—
(a) the ground for possession is Ground 2 or Ground 8 in Part I of Schedule 5 to this Act or any of the grounds in Part II of that Schedule, other than Ground 9, Ground 10, Ground 15 or Ground 17; and
(b) the terms of the tenancy make provision for it to be brought to an end on the ground in question.

(6A) Nothing in subsection (6) above affects the First-tier Tribunal's power to make an order for possession of a house which is for the time being let on an assured tenancy, not being a statutory assured tenancy, where the ground for possession is Ground 15 in Part II of Schedule 5 to this Act.

(7) Subject to the preceding provisions of this section, the First-tier Tribunal may make an order for possession of a house on grounds relating to a contractual tenancy which has been terminated; and where an order is made in such circumstances, any statutory assured tenancy which has arisen on that termination shall, without any notice, end on the day on which the order takes effect.

(8) In subsections (3A) and (4A) above–
(a) 'relevant housing benefit' means–
(i) any rent allowance or rent rebate to which the tenant was entitled in respect of the rent under the Housing Benefit (General) Regulations 1987 (SI 1987/1971); or
(ii) any payment on account of any such entitlement awarded under Regulation 91 of those Regulations;
(aa) *'relevant universal credit'* means universal credit to which the tenant was entitled which includes an amount under section 11 of the Welfare Reform Act 2012 in respect of the rent
(b) references to delay or failure in the payment of relevant housing benefit do not include such delay or failure so far as referable to any act or omission of the tenant."

Section 18: general

Section 18 is the "second leg" of security of tenure. As well as being allowed to retain his tenancy rights following termination of the contract, the tenant may be evicted under section 18 only if the landlord establishes one or more of the grounds for recovery of possession in schedule 5.

Under the 1988 Act there are two different types of statutory ground, set out in parts I and II of schedule 5. The part I grounds are "mandatory grounds",[58] as the tribunal is *bound* to make an order for possession under section 18(3) if the ground is established. The part II grounds are "discretionary grounds", as the tribunal *may not* grant decree on those grounds under section 18(4) unless it considers that it would be reasonable to do so. The various statutory grounds for recovery of possession under the 1988 Act are discussed in Chapter 8.

Section 18(6) is discussed below.

Under section 18(7), any statutory assured tenancy that has arisen under section 16 is terminated on the date when the order for possession granted under section 18 takes effect. Section 33(4) makes similar provision in relation to short assured tenancies.[59]

Subsections (3A), (4A) and (8) were added to section 18 by the Homelessness etc. (Scotland) Act 2003, section 12. These provisions allow the tribunal discretion not to make an order for possession under the mandatory ground 8 of schedule 5 to the 1988 Act[60] in circumstances where the rent arrears are a consequence of a delay or failure in the payment of housing benefit or universal credit. They also direct the tribunal to have regard to delay or failure in payment of those benefits, when considering whether it is reasonable to make an order for possession under ground 11 or ground 12.[61] References to delay or failure in payment do not include circumstances where this is a result of any act or omission of the tenant.[62]

Section 18(6)

Section 18(6) is an important provision. In short, it allows the FTT to grant an order for recovery of possession of a house let on an assured tenancy in cases where the parties' contract has never been terminated.[63] Therefore, the landlord is not required to serve a notice to quit, or otherwise terminate the contract before raising proceedings. Moreover, in cases where the landlord *has* served a notice to quit, but the notice is invalid, the FTT may nevertheless grant an order for possession if section 18(6) applies.

58 Part I of sch 5 is headed "Grounds on which First-tier Tribunal must order Possession"; pt II is headed "Grounds on which First-tier Tribunal may order Possession". The Act itself does not use the terms: "mandatory" and "discretionary".

59 Section 33(4) is considered at p 256 below.

60 Ground 8: at least three months' rent lawfully due from the tenant is in arrears.

61 Ground 11: persistent delay in paying rent; ground 12: rent lawfully due is unpaid.

62 Grounds 8, 11 and 12, and subsection (3A) are further considered in Chapter 8. For further information on the transition from housing benefit to universal credit, see Chapter 5, p 124.

63 The rather cumbersome wording "let on an assured tenancy, not being a statutory assured tenancy" denotes an assured tenancy in which the parties' contract has not yet been terminated; a statutory tenancy arises, in terms of s 16 of the Act, when the tenancy contract is terminated. See the note on terminology in the 1988 Act, in the discussion of s 16 above.

The leading case in relation to section 18(6) is *Royal Bank of Scotland v Boyle*.[64] This case is worth considering in some detail, because it sets out the correct approach to a problem that commonly arises in cases under section 18 of the Act.

The landlord of a property let on a short assured tenancy served on the tenant a notice to quit and an AT6 notice in terms of section 19 of the Act. The grounds for recovery of possession specified in the AT6 notice were 8 and 11. The notice to quit did not contain the information prescribed by the relevant statutory instrument.[65] The landlord raised eviction proceedings by way of summary cause. Defences were lodged and the matter proceeded to proof. The sheriff found it established on the evidence that, at the date of service of the AT6 and at the date of proof, at least three months' rent lawfully due from the defender to the pursuer was in arrears. However, counsel for the defender sought to persuade the sheriff that the action was incompetent, because the pursuers' notice to quit was invalid. That argument was rejected by the sheriff, on the basis that the invalidity of the notice to quit was irrelevant. In particular, he noted that sections 18 and 19 of the Act do not require a notice to quit to be served. Further, the purpose of a notice to quit is to prevent tacit relocation operating, by terminating the tenancy at its ish; it is not appropriate to the situation where the landlord is seeking to terminate the tenancy on the ground of breach of contract by the tenant, which was the situation in the case before him. He further found that ground 8 was established, and granted decree for recovery of possession in terms of section 18(3) of the Act.[66]

The defender appealed to the sheriff principal. There, he argued that the sheriff had not been entitled to grant decree in terms of section 18(6), because the terms of the parties' tenancy did not make provision for it to be brought to an end on the grounds in question, being grounds 8 and 11 in terms of schedule 5.[67]

In his judgment, Sheriff Principal Wheatley outlined the factual and legal issues in the case, and noted that the sheriff had correctly found that the notice to quit served by the landlord was invalid, but had then found that this was irrelevant, for the reasons that he had stated. He then observed:

> "However, this of course means that the subject agreement in the present action continues to be in force both at the time of the hearing and at the appeal by virtue of tacit relocation, and remains a contractual assured tenancy. . . . Accordingly, the agreed position in this tenancy agreement is that it is such a contractual assured

64 1999 Hous LR 43 and 63.

65 See p 55.

66 He also found that it would have been reasonable to grant decree for recovery of possession under ground 11, in terms of s 18(4), given the level of rent arrears and the other relevant factors in the case.

67 There appears to be some doubt about the extent to which this was a new point which was only raised at the appeal. At para 12-14, the sheriff principal expresses the view that it was unfortunate that the arguments in the appeal was not put before the sheriff in the first instance, but the editor's note to the sheriff's judgment (1999 Hous LR at 47) indicates that reference to s 18(6) was made in arguments before the sheriff. In any event, the sheriff principal was certainly of the view that he was considering a new point at appeal; his judgment does not suggest any criticism of the sheriff's reasoning and conclusions on the arguments that were originally put before him.

> tenancy, and that the landlord is attempting to irritate the lease by reference to section 18(6) of the Act."[68]

Given that the grounds relied on by the landlord, being grounds 8 and 11, were both included in section 18(6)(a), the question that fell to be determined in the case was whether the parties' contract made provision for it to be brought to an end on those grounds.

The relevant clause in the tenancy agreement was clause 15, the key part of which read:

> "If the rent or any instalment or part thereof is in arrears and the tenant has failed to make payment of such arrears for a period of fourteen days after he has been required by notice from the landlord to do so the landlord may terminate the Lease and resume possession of the Premises."

The sheriff principal heard argument on the issue of whether this clause complied with section 18(6)(b). He found that it did not. In his judgment, that provision meant that the essential ingredients of the ground in question must be referred to in the tenancy agreement.[69] In the case of both ground 8 and ground 11, clause 15 of the parties' contract failed to refer to the essential ingredients. In particular, in relation to ground 8, it was clear that the contract allowed for a much shorter period of default than the ground. However, the sheriff principal also pointed out that it was a key element of ground 8 that the tenant must be in arrears both at the date of service of the AT6 and at the date of the court hearing, which clearly envisages that the tenant may "purge the irritancy" at any point between those two dates. Accordingly, he allowed the appeal.

In conclusion, therefore, the landlord may do without termination of the lease, if it has an irritancy clause that reproduces the essential ingredients of the ground of eviction on which the landlord seeks to rely. For that reason, there have been numerous decisions of the FTT in which it considers two questions:

- Is the notice to quit, produced with an application under rule 65, valid?[70]
- If the notice to quit is not valid,[71] does section 18(6), as interpreted in *Royal Bank of Scotland v Boyle*, apply?

68 At paras 12-07 and 12-08.

69 The same conclusion was reached by Sheriff Jamieson in *Eastmoor LLP v Bulman* 2014 GWD 26-529. In that case the landlord sought to rely on the provision of the tenant information pack under s 30A of the Act, as providing the necessary information to the tenant of the content of the statutory grounds. That argument was rejected by the sheriff. The giving of the information by the landlord to the tenant did not have the effect that the terms of their tenancy agreement made provision for it to be brought to an end on the ground in question. In any event, the pack did not contain the essential ingredients of the grounds.

70 As is described below, r 65 applies to applications for an order for possession under s 18 of the 1988 and, under r 65(b)(iii), such an application must be accompanied by "a copy of the notice to quit served by the landlord on the tenant (if applicable)". As was explained in Chapter 3, a notice to quit is not necessary if the landlord is able to show that the tenancy contract has been terminated in some other way.

71 Or if no notice to quit has been served, or if there is inadequate evidence of service. The requirements for a valid notice to quit are set out in Chapter 3. As is described there, many applications to the FTT are rejected at the sift because those requirements are not met, particularly the requirement that the date specified by the notice is an ish date.

If the answer to both of these questions is "no", the application falls to be rejected at the sift, or refused at a case management discussion ("CMD") or hearing.[72]

Section 18(6A): antisocial behaviour

Section 18(6) has been subject to amendment. Section 100 of the Antisocial Behaviour etc. (Scotland) Act 2004 added ground 15, the antisocial behaviour ground, to the list of grounds in part II of schedule 5, listed in section 18(6)(a), to which section 18(6) does not apply. In other words, it disapplied section 18(6) to ground 15. Paragraph 222 of the explanatory notes to the Act states:

> Section 100 ensures that landlords can seek possession of houses let under assured tenancies on the grounds of antisocial behaviour whether or not the terms of the tenancy allow for it to be brought to an end on that ground.

Unfortunately, this was not the effect of the amendment. The effect of disapplying section 18(6) to ground 15 cases was that the process of evicting an antisocial tenant became more difficult for the landlord, because he would require to terminate the tenancy contract before raising the action under section 18. If there is no clause in the lease allowing for termination in the event of antisocial behaviour by the tenant, and reproducing the essential ingredients of ground 15, the position is the same as before: the landlord will have to terminate at the next ish date, or possibly seek to rescind the contract.[73]

This problem appears to have been apprehended at some point, as a result of which a further amendment was made by section 180 of the Housing (Scotland) Act 2006, inserting a new subsection (6A) that states that nothing in subsection (6) affects the tribunal's power to make an order for possession of a house that is for the time being let on an assured tenancy, not being a statutory assured tenancy, where the ground for possession is ground 15.

The difficulty is that the tribunal has no such power. Without section 18(6), the tribunal cannot order recovery of possession of a house in respect of which the tenancy has not been terminated, because the tenant has a contractual right to remain in occupation.

It is arguable that, by adopting a purposive interpretation of this provision,[74] it can be read as conferring a power on the tribunal to order recovery of possession in ground 15 cases, even though the tenancy is ongoing, albeit that, read literally, section 18(6A) presupposes that this power already exists. It remains to be seen whether the FTT would be willing to adopt such an interpretation.

72 A very frequent occurrence. A paradigm example of an application failing on this basis is *Sandhu v Barclay* EV/19/2551, 7/10/19.

73 In order to achieve the effect indicated in para 222, the amendment ought to have disapplied s 18(6)(b) to ground 15, not the whole subsection.

74 The purpose of the amendment is made clear by para 202 of the explanatory notes to the Act, which states: "Section 180 amends the Housing (Scotland) Act 1988 to allow a landlord to seek possession, on grounds of antisocial behaviour, of a house let under a contractual assured tenancy, even though the tenancy agreement does not provide that possession could be sought on those grounds." The explanatory notes to an Act may be used as an aid to its construction: *R v Chief Constable of South Yorkshire* [2004] 1 WLR 2196 (Lord Steyn).

NOTICE OF PROCEEDINGS FOR POSSESSION: s 19 (AT6)

Section 19 provides:

"(1) The First-tier Tribunal shall not entertain proceedings for possession of a house let on an assured tenancy unless—
(a) the landlord (or, where there are joint landlords, any of them) has served on the tenant a notice in accordance with this section; or
(b) the Tribunal considers it reasonable to dispense with the requirement of such a notice.

(2) The First-tier Tribunal shall not make an order for possession on any of the grounds in Schedule 5 to this Act unless that ground and particulars of it are specified in the notice under this section; but the grounds specified in such a notice may be altered or added to with the leave of the Tribunal.

(3) A notice under this section is one in the prescribed form informing the tenant that—
(a) the landlord intends to raise proceedings for possession of the house on one or more of the grounds specified in the notice; and
(b) those proceedings will not be raised earlier than the expiry of the period of two weeks or two months (whichever is appropriate under subsection (4) below) from the date of service of the notice.

(4) The minimum period to be specified in a notice as mentioned in subsection (3)(b) above is—
(a) two months if the notice specifies any of Grounds 1, 2, 5, 6, 7, 9 and 17 in Schedule 5 to this Act (whether with or without other grounds); and
(b) in any other case, two weeks.

(5) The First-tier Tribunal may not exercise the power conferred by subsection (1)(b) above if the landlord seeks to recover possession on Ground 8 in Schedule 5 to this Act.

(6) Where a notice under this section relating to a contractual tenancy—
(a) is served during the tenancy; or
(b) is served after the tenancy has been terminated but relates (in whole or in part) to events occurring during the tenancy,

the notice shall have effect notwithstanding that the tenant becomes or has become tenant under a statutory assured tenancy arising on the termination of the contractual tenancy.

(7) A notice under this section shall cease to have effect 6 months after the date on or after which the proceedings for possession to which it relates could have been raised."

Requirement to serve notice in the prescribed form: s 19(1)(a) and (3)

The notice under section 19 is the AT6, the form of which is now prescribed by the Rent Regulation and Assured Tenancies (Forms) (Scotland) Regulations 2017.[75]

The AT6 is in four parts:

(1) the name and address of the tenant;
(2) the name and address of the landlord, and a statement to the effect that the landlord intends to raise proceedings for possession of the house

75 SSI 2017/349. Originally the forms for assured tenancies were found in SI 1988/2109. The forms in the 2017 regulations refer to application being made to the FTT, rather than the court.

under certain grounds set out in schedule 5 to the Act. This part must fully state the grounds to be relied on;

(3) a statement of the particulars of how the landlord believes that the ground(s) have arisen; and

(4) specification of the date on or after which proceedings may be raised by the landlord.

The prescribed form AT6 also contains seven numbered notes to the tenant, in bold capitals, which give certain advice as to the effect of the notice, the tenant's rights under the Act, and what action he might take in order to protect his position.

Dispensing with the AT6: s 19(1)(b) and (5)

The tribunal may dispense with the requirement to serve the AT6 notice if it considers it reasonable[76] to do so, but not where the ground for recovery of possession is ground 8.[77] Several points arise. First, it is probably the case that the landlord can rely on section 19(1)(b) when he *has* served notice, but has failed to do so in the prescribed form.[78] This is an important point to bear in mind: if the AT6 is defective, that is not necessarily fatal to an application to the FTT, because the tribunal may dispense with the requirement for the AT6.

Secondly, where the landlord seeks possession on more than one ground, one of which is ground 8, and the AT6 notice has not been served, or is not in the prescribed form, the effect of dispensing with the requirement for the notice under subsection (5) is that the action proceeds on the remaining grounds, apart from ground 8.

Thirdly, it is submitted that a decision on an application by the landlord under section 19(1)(b) should normally be postponed to the CMD,[79] so that the tenant has the opportunity to object to the application being allowed to proceed, and to explain the basis for that objection.[80] The Act requires that the tribunal consider whether it is reasonable to dispense with notice; it is therefore obliged to take into account all matters that are relevant to the disposal of that application from the points of view of both the landlord and the tenant.[81]

The purpose of the notice is to give information to the tenant to enable him to consider what should be done, in the period before proceedings are raised,

76 In terms of the equivalent provision in the Housing Act 1988, the judge may dispense with the notice if it is "just and equitable" to do so. This difference also appears in relation to the power to dispense with the notices required in terms of grounds 1 and 2 of sch 5. In commentary to the Scottish legislation, Professor Peter Robson indicates that the "just and equitable" test was thought to be inappropriate for Scotland, because a sheriff is bound by "the duty of his office always to be just and equitable" (HC First Scottish Standing Committee, col 662 (11 February 1988)). It is suggested that nothing hangs on the difference between the English and Scottish legislation; the purpose of the two provisions is the same. Accordingly, the relevant English cases may be regarded as persuasive.

77 This is because ground 8 is established by three months' rent being lawfully due both at the date of the hearing, and the date when the AT6 notice is served.

78 See, e.g., *North British Housing Association v Sheridan* [2000] L&TR 115, (2000) 32 HLR 346.

79 The case management discussion under r 17 of the Procedure Rules (n 6).

80 The same point is made in relation to an application to amend or alter the grounds stated in the AT6. See p 244 below.

81 *Knowsley Housing Trust v Revell* (2003) 35 HLR 958, in which the importance of assessing each individual case was stressed.

which is in his power and which will best protect him against the loss of his home.[82] However, there may be factors that weigh more heavily than any prejudice that is suffered by the tenant if he does not receive the notice. For example, if some form of notice has been given to the tenant, albeit not in the statutory form, any prejudice suffered by him may be limited. Alternatively, the circumstances of the case may be such as to indicate, for example, that the tenant has abandoned the tenancy, or may disclose an unusually strong need on the part of the landlord to recover possession as soon as possible, such that the prejudice suffered by the landlord in serving the notice, with the attendant delay, would outweigh the prejudice suffered by the tenant in not receiving the notice. Other matters may be taken into consideration, depending on the facts and circumstances of each case. The tribunal may take into account circumstances that have occurred since the case commenced.[83]

Specifying the grounds: s 19(2) and (3)(a)

The effect of failing to specify the ground is that the tribunal cannot grant decree under that ground. If another ground is specified, the action may proceed on that ground.

The ground may validly be specified in words different from those used in schedule 5 to the Act, provided that the words used set out fully the substance of the ground so that the notice is adequate to achieve the legislative purpose of the provision. That purpose is to give to the tenant the information that the provision requires, to enable the tenant to consider what she should do and, with or without advice, to do that which is in her power and which will best protect her against the loss of her home.[84]

Given the terms of the second clause of section 19(2), the tribunal may grant leave to add other grounds, or presumably to reinstate grounds that otherwise could not be considered, because they were not properly stated in the notice.[85] However, there must be a valid notice before this power may be exercised. It is solely directed to the possibility of adding to or deleting grounds and cannot be used to cure a notice that is invalid because the only ground indicated in the notice has not been properly set out.[86]

Particulars of the ground: s 19(2)

Section 19(2) also requires that the landlord state the particulars of the ground.[87] At part 3 of the prescribed form AT6, where the landlord is given

82 This was the purpose identified by Ralph Gibson LJ for the equivalent notice under the Housing Act 1988 in *Mountain v Hastings* (1993) 25 HLR 427, [1993] 29 EG 96.

83 *Kelsey Housing Association v King* (1996) 28 HLR 270, in which the defendants did not raise the issue of the landlords' failure to serve the notice until some time after their defence to the action had been stated. The requirement for notice was dispensed with.

84 *Mountain v Hastings*. In that case, the notice was held to be defective because the words "at least three months rent is unpaid" did not specify ground 8; it omitted the requirement that "both at the date of the service of the notice . . . and the date of the hearing . . . at least . . . three months rent is unpaid and . . . 'rent' means rent lawfully due from the tenant".

85 For an example of an FTT decision under s 19(2), see *McLaren v Potts* EV/19/3269, 7/1/20.

86 *Mountain v Hastings*.

87 As originally enacted, s 19 did not contain this requirement, which was subsequently added shortly afterwards by the Housing Act 1988, sch 17, para 85.

space to state grounds additional to those stated in part 2, there appears the direction:

> "(state particulars of how you believe the ground(s) have arisen: continue on additional sheets of paper if required)"

In order to fulfil this requirement, the notice must give the tenant sufficient details of the circumstances that the landlord relies upon in asserting that a ground is made out. See the discussion in Chapter 4, at p 108.

Most applications for orders under section 18 are made on one or more of the rent arrears grounds.[88] In such a case, it is not sufficient simply to state that there are arrears of rent.[89] As a bare minimum, it will be sufficient for the particulars to state the amount of the arrears as at the date of the notice.[90]

If insufficient particulars are given, the tribunal cannot entertain the proceedings, unless it is persuaded to dispense with the notice, or to allow it to be altered or amended in terms of section 19(2). It has been held that extensive amendment of particulars at a late stage in proceedings should not be permitted.[91] That said, amendment of the grounds in the AT6 may be allowed at a late stage in proceedings.[92]

A minor error in the particulars does not invalidate the notice.[93]

The period of notice: s 19(3)(b), (4) and (7)

If the only ground, or one of the grounds, is 1, 2, 5, 6, 7, 9 or 17 of schedule 5, the period of notice after which proceedings may be raised by the landlord is two months; otherwise, the period is two weeks. This does not mean that proceedings cannot be raised by the landlord within the notice period. It means that the notice would be invalid for the purposes of such proceedings. In that case, the landlord would have to ask the tribunal to dispense with the requirement to serve the notice in terms of section 19(1)(b).[94]

Although section 19(3) requires that the AT6 inform the tenant that the proceedings: "will not be raised earlier than the expiry of the period of two weeks or two months . . . from the date of service of the notice", it also requires that the notice is in the prescribed form. Part 4 of that form[95] comprises the statement:

88 Being grounds 8, 11 and 12 of sch 5, discussed in Chapter 8.

89 *Torridge District Council v. Jones* (1986) 18 HLR 107, [1985] 2 EGLR 54.

90 *Dudley Metropolitan Borough Council v Bailey* (1990) 22 HLR 424, [1991] 1 EGLR 53. In that case, the Court of Appeal also decided that the notice was not invalid if the amount stated was wrong due to some error. The FTT decision in *Gaul v Gilchrist* EV/18/2964 27/6/19 also contains a discussion of the authorities in relation to particulars, in the context of an arrears case.

91 *South Buckinghamshire District Council v Francis* [1985] CLY 1900.

92 See *P v O* 2014 Hous LR 44, in which the sheriff allowed amendment following a motion made by the pursuers' agent, during the course of the proof.

93 *Dudley Metropolitan Borough Council v Bailey*. See also *Pease v Carter* [2020] 1 WLR 1459, which is summarised at p 242 below.

94 This may be contrasted with notices under s 14 of the 2001 Act, in respect of which s 14(2) specifically provides that proceedings may not be raised except after the date specified in the notice of proceedings for recovery of possession.

95 Now in the Rent Regulation and Assured Tenancies (Forms) (Scotland) Regulations 2017 (SSI 2017/349).

> "Proceedings will not be raised before .... (date) (which is the earliest date at which proceedings can be raised under section 19 of the Housing (Scotland) Act 1988)."

Thus, the notice has to state that date, rather than the relevant period. Two clear weeks, or months, should be given, in accordance with the usual rule that the date of service and the date on which the notice is to take effect are not included in the notice period.[96] If two weeks' notice is required, and notice is served on 1 April, the notice period is constituted by the 2nd to the 15th, being fourteen whole days, and the action may be raised on 16 April. Therefore, 16 April, may be entered in part 4 of the AT6. If two months' notice is required, a date on or after 2 June may be entered. It is suggested that if an earlier date is stated, that invalidates the notice.[97] If a later date is stated, that does not invalidate the notice, because it still fulfils its purpose, under section 19(3)(b), of informing the tenant that proceedings will not be raised before expiry of the relevant period of two weeks or two months.

Under section 19(7) the notice ceases to have effect six months after the date on or after which the proceedings could have been raised. This is the date stated in the notice, which is included in the six-month period.[98] Once the notice has ceased to have effect, it can no longer count as an AT6, for the purposes of an application to the FTT.

In practice, it has been quite common for applications to the FTT to be refused because the AT6 states the wrong date, or because the application was made before the date stated in the notice, or after the six-month period had expired.

The AT6 has no effect on termination of the tenancy: s 19(6)

This provision confirms that the service of the AT6 is not related to the process by which the parties' contract is terminated and the tenancy becomes a statutory assured tenancy in terms of section 16. This means that the landlord may serve the AT6 during the currency of the tenancy. Say that the landlord wishes to recover possession of the tenancy under ground 1 of schedule 5. The ish date of the tenancy is 27 August. The landlord could effect service of the AT6 and the notice to quit at the same time, on or before 26 June, and raise proceedings after the ish.

AT6 notices: final points

In terms of section 54 of the Act service of any notice on a person for the purposes of part II of the Act, including an AT6, may be effected by: (a) delivering it to him; (b) leaving it at his last known address; or (c) sending it by recorded delivery to him at that address. This provision is further considered in Chapter 15, in the section on proof of service of notices.

96 See Chapter 3, p 57. As to service of notices, see Chapter 15.

97 In that case, the landlord could ask the tribunal to dispense with the requirement for the notice, under s 19(1)(b).

98 Because proceedings could have been raised on that day. So, if the date stated in the notice was 16 April, the effective life of the notice is 16 April to 15 October, inclusive.

In *Pease v Carter,*[99] the Court of Appeal considered the effect of an error in a notice of proceedings given under section 8 of the Housing Act 1988.[100] Statutory notices are to subject to the "reasonable recipient" test, set out in *Mannai Investment Co Ltd v Eagle Star Life Assurance Co Ltd.*[101] An error does not necessarily invalidate the notice, where the "reasonable recipient" would understand what the notice meant to say.[102] However, the notice must still meet statutory requirements, when the purposes of those requirements are considered. A failure to meet the precise requirements of statute may be excusable if the notice is substantially to the same effect as stipulated by the legislation and fulfils the statutory purpose.

APPLICATIONS TO THE FIRST-TIER TRIBUNAL UNDER SECTION 18 OF THE 1988 ACT

Rule 65 of the Procedure Rules states:

> "**65. Application for order for possession in relation to assured tenancies**
> Where a landlord makes an application under section 18(1) (orders for possession) of the 1988 Act, the application must—
> (a) state—
> (i) the name, address and registration number (if any) of the landlord;
> (ii) the name, address and profession of any representative of the landlord;
> (iii) the name and address of the tenant; and
> (iv) the possession grounds which apply as set out in Schedule 5 of the 1988 Act;
> (b) be accompanied by—
> (i) a copy of the tenancy agreement (if available) or, if this is not available, as much information about the tenancy as the landlord can give;
> (ii) a copy of the notice served on the tenant by the landlord of intention to raise proceedings for possession of a house let on an assured tenancy;
> (iii) a copy of the notice to quit served by the landlord on the tenant (if applicable); and
> (iv) evidence as the applicant has that the possession ground or grounds has been met;
> (v) a copy of the notice given to the local authority by the landlord under section 11 of the Homelessness (Scotland) Act 2003 (if applicable); and
> (vi) a copy of Form BB (notice to the occupier) under schedule 6 of the Conveyancing and Feudal Reform (Scotland) Act 1970 (if applicable);[103] and
> (c) be signed and dated by the landlord or a representative of the landlord."

As well as rule 65, it is also necessary to be aware of rules 4, 5 and 8 of the Procedure Rules. However, those rules are general to all the applications made

99 n 93. The court sets out the applicable principles at para 39.

100 Which is the equivalent of an AT6 under s 19.

101 Discussed in Chapter 3, p 62.

102 As to whether that is the case, the court requires to take the context into account, which may include an covering letter that was sent along with the notice.

103 This applies to an application made by a heritable creditor in possession. The lender is required to include, with the application to the FTT, a copy of the form BB that was given to the occupier of the subjects when the security was called up. The same requirement is imposed in r 66, and in r 109, in relation to applications made under s 51 of the 2016 Act. This point is discussed in Chapter 8, at p 274.

to the Housing and Property Chamber, and are considered in Chapter 14. Suffice it to say at this point that applications to the Chamber are subject to a "sift", and those made under rule 65 are apt to be rejected, under rule 8, if the requirements of the Act, or rule 65, have not been met.[104] Even if the application makes it through the sift, it may still be refused, at a later stage, due to some failure to follow the requirements for a valid application under the Act.

Under rule 4, "An application to the First-tier Tribunal must be in writing and may be made using a form obtained from the First-tier Tribunal". The form used for applications for an eviction or possession order, whether under the 1984, 1988 or 2016 Act, is form E. Both the form and the guidance notes on its completion can be downloaded from the Chamber website.[105] Rule 65(c) also stipulates that the application must be signed and dated, either by the applicant or by his representative. This requirement appears throughout the Procedure Rules, in relation to applications to the tribunal. Applications that are not signed or dated are rejected.[106]

Apart from these general provisions, the particular requirements of rule 65, in relation to an application for an eviction order under section 18 of the 1988 Act, may be stated as follows.

1. The application must provide names, addresses and other details required by rule 65(a)(i)–(iii)

Where there are joint tenants, or joint landlords, it is suggested that the names and addresses of all the joint landlords, and all the joint tenants, ought to be stated. Likewise, where there is a sub-tenancy, the name and address of the sub-tenant ought to be stated. This would appear to follow from sections 55 of the 1988 Act, and rules 46, 9 and 71 of the Procedure Rules.[107]

In terms of section 55(1), "tenant" includes a sub-tenant.[108] In terms of section 55(3): "Where two or more persons jointly constitute either the landlord or the tenant in relation to a tenancy, then, except where otherwise provided, any reference in this Part of this Act to the landlord or to the tenant is a reference to all the persons who jointly constitute the landlord or the tenant, as the case may require . . .". The same interpretation of "landlord" and "tenant" applies to rule 65(a)(i), by virtue of rule 46(2)(g): "(b) in Chapters 5 and 6, where terms are used which are defined terms in the 1988 Act, the definitions in that Act in respect of those terms apply to those Chapters." Under rule 9: the Tribunal must give notice of the acceptance of application to "each party" and, in terms of rule 71(a), in relation to an application under section 18 of the 1988 Act, the parties to be notified under rule 9(1) are "the landlord" and "the tenant". Again, both of these terms are interpreted in accordance with section 55 of the Act, given the terms of rule 46(2)(g). Therefore, the tribunal

104 Examples are given below. Figures obtained from the Housing and Property Chamber indicate that, for the two years from 1 December 2017 to 30 November 2019, almost 22% of applications under r 65 were rejected at the sift.

105 See the discussion of form E in Chapter 14.

106 Though usually after the applicant/representative has been given the opportunity to sign and date the application. See, e.g., *McCallum v Paterson* EV/19/1767, 28/6/19.

107 Applications in the cases of joint landlords are discussed in Chapter 15.

108 Sub-tenancies under the 1988 Act are discussed in Chapter 12.

is entitled to insist on being informed, in the application, of the names and addresses of all the joint landlords and joint tenants.

If the landlord is registered, rule 65(a)(i) requires that his registration number is entered in the application. However, registration is not a prerequisite for seeking an order.[109]

The requirement, in rule 65(a)(iii), to give the name and address of the tenant, is subject to rule 6(6), which states:

> "(6) Where an action for removing is against a tenant or occupier in possession of heritable property and the name of the tenant in possession or occupier is not known and cannot reasonably be ascertained, the requirement for the tenant's or occupier's name set out in rule 65(a)(iii), 66(a)(iii), 77(a)(iii), 79(a)(iii) or 109(a)(iii) is waived and any formal communication may be served on 'the Occupier'."

2. The application must state the possession grounds which apply as set out in schedule 5 of the Act

In the vast majority of cases, the ground(s) stated in the application, as required by rule 65(a)(iv), will be the same as that stated in the AT6, a copy of which is to be produced with the application, in terms of rule 65(b)(iii). Where the application relies on different grounds, this amounts to a request for the tribunal's leave to alter or add to the grounds stated in the AT6, in terms of section 19(2). It is suggested that the tribunal should normally postpone a decision to exercise the power in section 19(2) to the CMD,[110] so that the tenant has the opportunity to object to the grounds being altered or added to, and to explain the basis for that objection.[111]

3. The application must be accompanied by: a copy of the tenancy agreement (if available) or, if this is not available, as much information about the tenancy as the landlord can give; and a copy of the notice to quit served by the landlord on the tenant (if applicable)

It is suggested that the requirements in rule 65(b)(i) and (iii) are inextricably linked. As already explained, for the tribunal to grant an order under section 18, the parties' contractual tenancy must have been terminated, by notice to quit or otherwise, unless section 18(6) applies. In order to determine whether the notice to quit is valid,[112] the tribunal has to see the tenancy agreement. This is necessary, in particular, to determine whether: the date stated in the notice coincides with an ish date;[113] and the period and mode of notice complies with any stipulation as to notice in the parties' agreement. Where the validity of the notice is in doubt, the tribunal must consider whether section 18(6) applies, which necessarily entails an examination of the tenancy agreement.[114]

109 See Chapter 10, p 366.
110 The case management discussion under r 17.
111 See the discussion of s 19(1)(b) at p 238 above.
112 Or any notice that purports to terminate the contract under its own terms, such as an irritancy notice (see Chapter 3).
113 Or, in the case of an irritancy clause, or a break clause, the notice is given in accordance with that clause.
114 Because one of the two requirements of s 18(6) is that "the terms of the tenancy make provision for it to be brought to an end on the ground in question".

Where there is no tenancy agreement, the information about the tenancy, given in terms of rule 65(b)(i), should include, in particular, some indication of when it commenced, and whether the parties reached any consensus as to duration.[115] That is in order for the tribunal to determine the tenancy's ish, and whether that coincides with the date stated in the notice to quit.

4. The application must be accompanied by a copy of the notice served on the tenant by the landlord of intention to raise proceedings for possession of a house let on an assured tenancy

This follows from section 19(1)(a): the tribunal cannot entertain proceedings for possession of a house let on an assured tenancy unless the landlord (or one of the joint landlords) has served an AT6 on the tenant. As described above, the tribunal has the power to dispense with the requirement for an AT6; where the applicant makes such a request, that ought normally to be considered at the CMD, in order that the tenant has the opportunity to oppose it.

5. The application must be accompanied such evidence as the applicant has, showing that the possession ground has been met

Rule 65(b)(iv) is worded slightly differently to the equivalent rule 109(b)(i), in relation to PRTs.[116]

The vast majority of applications under rule 65 rely on one or more of the rent arrears grounds 8, 11 and 12. In practice, eviction orders granted on those grounds, at a CMD or hearing, are based on the evidence of a rent account or other statement showing that the ground is established. The applicant, or her representative, speaks to the accuracy of the account, before the tribunal. Accordingly, it seems reasonable to suggest that a rent account, or some other statement tending to show the current balance, and the history of non-payment, ought to accompany the application, in order to comply with rule 65(b)(iv).[117]

The evidence tending to show some of the other grounds should be self-evident, for example:

- Grounds 1–5: evidence of any notice given to the tenant, at the creation or commencement of the tenancy, that possession might be recovered on this ground.[118]
- Ground 2: (Property to be sold by lender) – a copy of the extract decree in terms of which the lender is entitled to sell the property.
- Ground 6: planning permission for the relevant works, if applicable.
- Ground 10: the tenant's notice to quit.

115 If there is no consensus as to duration, a period of one year may be implied. See Chapter 3, note 15.

116 Rule 65(b)(iv) includes the words "as the applicant has". See the discussion of r 109(b)(i) in Chapter 9.

117 In the brief decision in *Baird v Bochenek and Comar*, 19/1184, 11 June 2019, the tribunal rejected an application under ground 12, for various reasons, including the lack of "evidence of unpaid rent in the form of a statement".

118 See Chapter 8, p 266.

- Grounds 15 (Antisocial behaviour): an extract conviction, if applicable, or copies of complaints, reports of police attendance, statements etc.

6. *The application must be accompanied by a copy of notice given to the local authority – rule 65(b)(v)*

Section 11 of the Homelessness etc. (Scotland) Act 2003 is headed "Notice to local authorities of proceedings for possession and enforcement of standard securities". Its effect is to require notice to be given of eviction proceedings to the local authority for the area in which the house is situated, unless the person seeking possession is the local authority itself. As a result, a series of similar amendments were made to various Acts.[119] Section 19A is the amendment to the 1988 Act. It provides:

> **"19A Requirement to notify local authority of proceedings for possession**
> (1) Where a landlord raises proceedings for possession of a house let on an assured tenancy, the landlord shall give notice of the raising of the proceedings to the local authority in whose area the house is situated, unless the landlord is that local authority.
> (2) Notice under subsection (1) above shall be given in the form and manner prescribed under section 11(3) of the Homelessness etc. (Scotland) Act 2003 (asp 10)."

This requirement also applies to actions under section 33, given that a short assured tenancy is a form of assured tenancy.[120]

The form of notice for section 19A is provided in schedule 1 to the Notice to Local Authorities (Scotland) Regulations 2008.[121] The form asks the local authority to "Take note that proceedings have been raised as detailed below", and then requires the landlord to give certain information.[122] Under regulation 3, the "manner of giving notice" is "by post or transmitted electronically".

It seems from the drafting of the sections, and the statutory form, that the notice is to be given at the same time as, or shortly after, the proceedings are raised. It is therefore doubtful that failure to serve the notice could be a basis on which to hold that the action is incompetent: the wording of the provisions is not such as to indicate that service of the notice is a prerequisite to an action.[123] In practice, however, the lack of a section 11 notice is picked up

119 Including the 2001 Act (s 14(5A) and (5B)) and the Conveyancing and Feudal Reform (Scotland) Act 1970 (mortgage repossession proceedings). The requirement to serve the notice also applies to proceedings under the 2016 Act, in terms of s 56 and 52(2)(b).

120 This also follows from the generality of the words used in s 11(1) of the 2003 Act: "Where a landlord raises proceedings for possession of a dwellinghouse, the landlord must give notice of the raising of the proceedings to the local authority . . .".

121 SSI 2008/324. Note that this has been amended on several occasions, by SSIs 2010/251, 2017/295 and 2017/421.

122 Being: (a) the name and address of the landlord who has raised proceedings; (b) the name and address of the landlord's legal representatives; (c) the contact telephone number of the landlord; (d) the landlord's registration reference; (e) the name of the tenant/s against whom proceedings have been raised; (f) the full postal address of the property that is the subject of proceedings; (g) the start date of the tenancy; (h) the date of raising of proceedings; (i) the court in which proceedings were raised (or the FTT). The landlord is then required to tick one of a series of boxes indicating the legislation under which notice is given (e.g. section 19A, in cases under the 1988 Act).

123 However, this is not the case with the notice to be given to the local authority, under s 56 of

when an application is sifted by the FTT, and the landlord is asked to provide a copy of the notice. At that point, the landlord may give notice to the local authority, and provide a copy of the notice to the tribunal, failing which the application is liable to rejected.

SHORT ASSURED TENANCIES

Introduction

Under section 32(1) of the 1988 Act, a short assured tenancy is an assured tenancy that is for not less than six months, and in relation to which a prescribed notice was served. That notice is an AT5,[124] which must have been served by the landlord on the tenant "before the creation of the assured tenancy". The advantage of the short assured tenancy, from the landlord's point of view, was that he could utilise section 33 of the Act to recover possession at the end of the tenancy term subject to certain formalities which could be easily met.

In an action under section 33, the landlord does not have to establish that there is ground for recovery of possession in terms of schedule 5; nor is he required to satisfy the tribunal that it is reasonable to grant the order. It is notable that this is "without prejudice to any right of the landlord . . . to recover possession . . . in accordance with section 12 to 31". This stipulation is necessary because the section 33 action can be deployed only at, or after, the ish, and is therefore of no use to the landlord wishing to recover possession during the currency of the lease, on the basis of a breach of contract by the tenant. In that case, the landlord must proceed under section 18.

It is inaccurate to say that the short assured tenant has *no* security of tenure. Had it been the intention of the legislature to remove security of tenure entirely from short assured tenants, it could have done so by a provision to the effect that service of the prescribed notice had the effect of excluding the tenancy from the statutory scheme, along with the tenancy categories in schedule 4 to the Act. In that case, the tenant would have no substantive defence to any action raised after termination of the parties' contract, whether the tenancy was terminated at the ish date, or prior to the term of the tenancy, following, for example, an irritancy. However, the effect of sections 32 and 33 is that the short assured tenant has more security than a mere contractual tenant, because he cannot be evicted prior to the ish unless the requirements of sections 16–19 of the Act are met, by which the landlord must establish one of the grounds for eviction under schedule 5 and, in relation to certain of those grounds, that it is reasonable to grant the order.

the 2016 Act, when an application is made for an eviction order in relation to a PRT. See Chapter 9. In an action under the 2001 Act, it is suggested that, where the landlord has failed to serve the notice required by s 14(5A), the court might be asked to continue the case, to allow service to be effected.

124 Prescribed by the Assured Tenancies (Forms) (Scotland) Regulations 1988 (SI 1988/2109), which has now been repealed. The current regulations for assured tenancy forms (see note 95 above) do not include a form AT5, because it is no longer possible to create new short assured tenancies.

What is a short assured tenancy? s 32

Section 32 provides:

> "(1) A short assured tenancy is an assured tenancy—
> (a) which is for a term of not less than six months; and
> (b) in respect of which a notice is served as mentioned in subsection (2) below.
>
> (2) The notice referred to in subsection (1)(b) above is one which—
> (a) is in such form as may be prescribed;
> (b) is served before the creation of the assured tenancy;
> (c) is served by the person who is to be the landlord under the assured tenancy (or, where there are to be joint landlords under the tenancy, is served by a person who is to be one of them) on the person who is to be the tenant under that tenancy; and
> (d) states that the assured tenancy to which it relates is to be a short assured tenancy. . . ."[125]

"A term not less than six months": s 32(1)(a)

Section 32(1)(a) gives rise to a question that has often arisen in practice: if the tenancy runs from, say, 18 March to 17 September, is it "for a term of not less than six months"? It is submitted that the following principles apply:

(1) The words "not less than" indicate nothing less than a full period of six months. Therefore, where a tenancy begins on 18 March and ends on 17 September, the whole of both of those days would have to be included, such that the tenancy would have to be taken to commence at midnight at the beginning of 18 March and terminate at midnight at the end of 17 September.

(2) In order to ascertain the duration of the tenancy, one must look first to the terms of the lease. In the example given above, an express indication that the whole of 18 March and 17 September were to be included in the term, or the use of words that imply such inclusion, would be sufficient to constitute a term of six months in accordance with the Act.

(3) If the terms of the lease are such that the inclusion of the whole of these days is not express or implied, the general rules as to calculation of time in Scots law apply. These are as follows. A period of time that is to be counted in units of a day or more, such as a month, is to be calculated *civilis computatio*, whereas a period counted in units of less than a day, i.e. an hour or less, is calculated *naturalis computatio*. Calculation *civilis computatio* entails two elements: (a) fractions of a day are not reckoned, and (b) the whole of the first day is excluded and the whole of the last day is included.[126] In the example under discussion, calculation *civilis*

125 Section 32(3), which provides for the continuation of a short assured tenancy by tacit relocation, is discussed at p 259.

126 *Stair Memorial Encyclopedia*, vol 22 para 819 onwards. These two elements are interrelated. The scheme of calculation *civilis computatio* exists for periods calculated in intervals of a day or longer, because a question may arise as to the extent to which the first and last days of a period are to be included, or when the period ends, if it is expressed to begin on a certain day. The reason why such a problem might arise is because fractions of a day present a difficulty

computatio would entail that the tenancy would be taken to commence at midnight at the end of 18 March (not the beginning) and terminate at midnight at the end of 17 September, which would be a day less than six months. However, it must be emphasised that this is a general rule. The starting point in any case is the wording of the contractual provision or the enactment under consideration which, together with the circumstances of the case,[127] may be such as to indicate that the whole of the first day is to be included.[128]

(4) The effect of excluding the first day and including the last day is that where an interval of time is expressed in terms of division of the calendar such as a month or a year, the interval is to be reckoned from the day when the interval begins to the corresponding day in the next division of the calendar. This "corresponding day" rule was articulated, in particular, by the Inner House in *Parish Council of Cavers v Parish Council of Smailholm and Parish Council of Urr*,[129] in which the court held that a period from 29 May 1900 to 28 May 1903 was one day less than three years.[130]

In the context of short assured tenancies, these various principles are illustrated by the case of *McCabe v Wilson*.[131] The parties entered into a lease, the duration of which was agreed in the following terms:

> "2. The lease shall be for a period of six months commencing on the 7th of April 2005 and terminating on the 6th of October 2005."

It was a matter of agreement that the tenant signed the lease at the office of the landlord's agents at some point during normal office hours on 7 April. She also paid the deposit at that time, and was given the keys to the tenancy.

where the action/activity/right/obligation in question subsists for 24 hours per day, for every day during the period in question, but the period commences at some point during the course of the first day. That gives rise to the question: what is to happen to the fraction of one day that elapses after the moment of commencement? The *civilis computatio* method disposes of this problem by disregarding any fraction of the first and last days, which is justifiable because the whole of the first day is excluded, and the whole of the last day is included.

127 For example, *civilis computatio* did not apply in the cases of *Pacitti Jones v O'Brien* 2005 SLT 793 and *Fowler v Falkirk Council* 2005 SLT 404, because the commencement of the period in question did not raise any problem as regards fractions of a day. In those cases, the moment of commencement was at the beginning of an event that was to take place at a set time, for part of the day (respectively a council meeting, and a working day) rather than at an indeterminate time during the course of an entire day. Therefore, there was no question of the initial "day" being split or fractioned, and it was not necessary to employ calculation *civilis computatio*. In those cases, it was clear that the first day had to be included.

128 In the *Stair Memorial Encyclopedia*, vol 22 para 826 there is a discussion of the meaning of certain words and phrases in relation to the calculation of time. 1909 SC 195

129 1909 SC 195 (1908) 16 SLT 627.

130 This suggests that a lease that has no specified termination date, but is expressed to run for, say, one year from 1 March 2005, would therefore end on 1 March 2006. It must be pointed out that this contention is open to question. It conflicts with the decision in *Morrison's Exrs v Rendall* 1989 SLT (Land Ct) 89, in which the court held that the correct date for termination of such a lease was 28 February, though it seems fair to say that this view was reached with some hesitation. This case is further discussed at note 50 in Chapter 3. *Parish Council of Cavers v Parish Council of Smailholm and Parish Council of Urr* was not referred to in *Morrison's Exrs*. For a discussion of the problems raised by that case, see D J Coull, "Termination Date in a Notice to Quit" 1989 SLT (News) 431.

131 2006 Hous LR 86.

Accordingly, as a matter of fact, the tenancy agreement was created at some point after midnight beginning 7 April.[132]

The sheriff accepted that if one took the lease to run from the precise moment that it was signed to midnight ending 6 October, its duration fell short of six months by a fraction of a day. However, he went on to observe:

> "Read as a whole therefore condition 2 only makes sense if the parties intended all of the first day, 7th April, to be treated as part of the lease as well as all of the last day. Only then could the lease be said to be, as parties stated, for a period of six months. It seems to me clear in these circumstances that parties intended the lease to have commenced at the first moment of 7th April."

The sheriff further noted that, in contracting on the basis that the whole of the first day of the period was to be included, the parties were using a method of calculating the passage of time that was known to the law of Scotland as well. On that basis he concluded:

> "In all the circumstances there is in my view no bar in principle to parties to a lease contracting on the basis that the lease is to be deemed to have commenced on the first moment of the first day and it was open to the parties to this case to contract on that basis. . . .
>
> The provision in section 32 that a short assured tenancy must be for a term of six months has to be construed in the context of what, in the law of contract, is properly regarded as a term of six months."

However, the sheriff concluded by stating that his decision turned on the view that the parties had made a clear agreement to use "a particular legitimate method of calculating time". Had this not been the case, the general rule, which entails the first day of the period being excluded, would have applied. In that case the pursuer would have failed.[133]

Therefore, to return to the original example, if the relevant clauses in the contract indicated that the parties intended the whole of 18 March to be included, the tenancy was for a period of "not less than six months". This could have been done where the tenancy agreement was created on 18 March. However, it could not have been done if the tenancy was created on or after 19 March, because in that case the parties would not be using "a particular legitimate method of calculating time".[134]

In *Calmac Developments Ltd v Murdoch*,[135] the relevant clause in the parties' lease stated: "The Date of Entry will be 29th April 2011. The Let will run from that date until 28th October 2011 . . .". As in *McCabe v Wilson*, the lease was executed during the course of the first day. The sheriff decided that the

132 The circumstances in *McCabe v Wilson* are very similar to the English case *Bedding v McCarthy* (1995) 27 HLR 103, in which the Court of Appeal also decided that the tenancy was for a term of not less than six months.

133 Note that the sheriff – it is submitted, correctly – did not place any particular significance on the fact that the parties' agreement stated that the tenancy was to be a short assured tenancy. Any such agreement is of no effect. It is the Act that confers short assured tenancy status, not the parties.

134 I.e. parties can legitimately agree that a period that commences on 7 April is to include the whole of that day; they could not legitimately agree that it also includes 6 April, or 5 April, etc. However, this is not to say that the parties cannot formalise in writing a verbal tenancy that commenced at some earlier date – though a tenancy in that case would not be a short assured tenancy unless an AT5 had been served before the creation of the tenancy.

135 2012 GWD 27-565.

specific use of the words "date of entry" in a lease must mean that the tenant was contemplated to take entry on the first date, and therefore it would not be correct to exclude that day. If one then applied the normal rule that days are indivisible in accordance with computation of time *civilis computatio* then the whole of the first day (and not part of it) had to be included. Therefore, the lease was for a period of not less than six months.

"not less than six months": break clauses

The operation of break clauses in short assured tenancies was considered by the Inner House in *Wishaw and District Housing Association Ltd v Neary*.[136] In that case the break clause was in favour of the tenant only. It was argued on his behalf that the existence of the break clause had the effect of preventing the tenancy from being a short assured tenancy, because it was not for a guaranteed minimum period of six months. That argument was rejected by the court: the break clause had no effect on the period that was to be regarded as the term of the lease. The court expressly reserved its opinion on the effect of any break clause in favour of the landlord which could be utilised before the initial six-month period of the lease expired. Such a clause would arguably be contrary to the protection afforded to the tenant under the legislation. It was suggested in *Neary* that such a clause would be of limited assistance to the landlord in any event, given that decree could not be granted under section 33 until the ish was reached.

AT5 notice: s 32(1)(b) and (2)

Notice must have been given to the tenant before the creation of the tenancy in the prescribed form AT5. The form has three parts:

(1) the name of the prospective tenant;
(2) notice by the landlord, or his agent, to the tenant that the prospective tenancy is to be a short assured tenancy. This part contains a section in which the landlord or agent is to write his name, address and telephone number; and
(3) an optional section in which the parties may enter the names and addresses of their agents.

The form contains six notes to the prospective tenant. As with the form AT6, these are in bold capital letters. They give certain advice to the prospective tenant about his rights under the tenancy, should he choose to enter into it. In addition there is, at the end of the form, a three-paragraph section headed "Special notes for existing tenants".[137]

The omission of the necessary details in the form, or the inclusion of incorrect details, may render the notice invalid. However, there is English authority to the effect that the notice will be valid if the omission or error is minor, such that it accomplishes its statutory purpose of informing the proposed tenant of

136 2004 SC 463.
137 See note 188 below.

the special nature of the short assured tenancy and is substantially to the same effect as the prescribed form.[138]

The notice must have been served before the creation of the assured tenancy. It seems that, in practice, service of the AT5 notice was most often effected by simply handing it to the tenant at the point when the lease was signed. Although this method was certainly convenient, and would constitute delivery for the purposes of section 54 of the Act, it held certain pitfalls for the landlord.

First, the landlord may have difficulties in proving service. As a result, it was not unusual for the tenant to be asked to sign a separate form or letter, acknowledging that he had received the AT5 prior to the creation of the tenancy; alternatively, a clause may have been included in the contract to the effect that the parties acknowledged that they were entering into a short assured tenancy, and that the tenant accepted that he had received the AT5. The former precaution seems preferable. As short assured tenancy status is conferred by the Act, the designation of the lease as a short assured tenancy by the parties is of no consequence if the requirements of section 32 were not met. If the tenant maintains that delivery of the AT5 never took place, his position will be more difficult to argue if the acknowledgement of delivery is in a separate document that he has signed, rather than lurking somewhere in the lease. That said, the outcome of such a dispute would depend on the circumstances of each case.[139]

Secondly, some care should have been taken to ensure that the landlord or his agents are in a position to prove that the notice was delivered to the prospective tenant before the parties, by their signature on the tenancy agreement, created the lease. Furthermore, there should have been a "gap in time" between the service of the notice and entering into the tenancy agreement, so that the tenant was given an opportunity to consider fully the consequences of what is proposed in the notice and to be able to resile if he had a change of mind.[140]

It appears to have been fairly common practice simply to hand the tenant a bundle of documents, including the lease, any schedule to the lease, the AT5, the acknowledgement of the AT5, and any other documents that might be appropriate. If the tenant had no prior warning that the lease was going to be short assured, and he might reasonably argue that he thought the papers being handed to him were simply the lease documentation, there must be some doubt, in that case, as to the exact moment at which delivery takes place. If the prospective tenant signed the lease, and then came upon the AT5, it may be arguable that service of the AT5 was not effected before the tenancy was

138 The relevant authorities are discussed in *Pease v Carter* (n 93), which is summarised at p 242.

139 The contractual term acknowledging receipt of the notice by the tenant appears to have settled the issue in the landlord's favour in *Key Housing Association v Cameron* 1999 Hous LR 47. However, as the sheriff notes in that case (at para 9-16), it was the tenant's position in evidence that "she did not recall whether or not the Form AT5 had been served on her prior to parties signing the tenancy agreement". In *Express Investment Co Ltd v Brown*, EV/19/2335, 17/1/20, the tribunal found, on a balance of probabilities, that, having signed a tenancy agreement acknowledging receipt of the AT5, the tenant had received it (see para 30 of the decision).

140 *Kahlon v Isherwood* [2011] EWCA Civ 602; [2011] HLR 38, paras 27 and 28 (Patten LJ).

created.[141] By this practice the landlord also left himself open to the argument that the purpose of the notice had been defeated, because the tenant had insufficient opportunity to consider it properly, and decide whether he wished to enter into the lease, in any event.

Therefore, the prudent course of action, at least from the landlord's point of view, was to give the tenant the AT5 first, and afford him time to read the notice and consider whether he wished to proceed. The tenant could then be asked to sign a separate document confirming that he had received, read and understood the terms of the AT5, before the lease was signed.[142]

RECOVERY OF POSSESSION ON TERMINATION: s 33

Section 33 provides:

> "(1) Without prejudice to any right of the landlord under a short assured tenancy to recover possession of the house let on the tenancy in accordance with sections 12 to 31 of this Act, the First-tier Tribunal shall make an order for possession of the house if the Tribunal is satisfied—
> (a) that the short assured tenancy has reached its ish;
> (b) that tacit relocation is not operating; and
> [(c) that no further contractual tenancy (whether a short assured tenancy or not) is for the time being in existence; and][143]
> (d) that the landlord (or, where there are joint landlords, any of them) has given to the tenant notice stating that he requires possession of the house.
> (2) The period of notice to be given under subsection (1)(d) above shall be—
> (i) if the terms of the tenancy provide, in relation to such notice, for a period of more than two months, that period;
> (ii) in any other case, two months.
> (3) A notice under paragraph (d) of subsection (1) above may be served before, at or after the termination of the tenancy to which it relates.
> (4) Where the First-tier Tribunal makes an order for possession of a house by virtue of subsection (1) above, any statutory assured tenancy which has arisen as at that ish shall end (without further notice) on the day on which the order takes effect.
> (5) For the avoidance of doubt, sections 18 and 19 do not apply for the purpose of a landlord seeking to recover possession of the house under this section."

Ending the tenancy at the ish date: s 33(1)(a)–(b)

An application to the FTT under rule 66 of the Procedure Rules, seeking an order for possession under section 33, may be made by the landlord once he has served a notice to quit, bringing the tenancy to an end at the ish date, such that tacit relocation is not operating, as is required by section 33(1)(b).[144] In

141 If the landlord or his agent had already signed the lease, creation of the lease would have been effected, when the tenant signed.

142 Some letting agents instead chose to print an acknowledgement of receipt on the AT5 itself, with space for the tenant to sign.

143 Section 33(1)(c) has been repealed by sch 5, para 2(3)(b) to the 2016 Act. See p 254.

144 The requirements for a valid notice to quit are set out in Chapter 3. As is explained there, applications to the FTT under rr 65 and 66 are very often refused because the notice is invalid.

theory, this could have happened some time before the section 33(1)(d) notice is served, and proceedings are raised, by application to the FTT.[145]

It is suggested that if the tenancy has a straightforward term of, say, one year, then, after continuation by tacit relocation, it has not "reached its ish", until the continued term has run.[146] If that is correct, the landlord cannot terminate the contract during its term by irritancy or otherwise, after the first ish, and then raise an action under section 33, unless the tenancy has reached the ish at the end of the continued term.[147]

Many short assured tenancies have an initial term of six months, followed by a shorter term, usually of one or two months, which renews until such time as one of the parties gives notice terminating the lease. Such an agreement contracts out of tacit relocation, which is permissible at common law.[148] In that case section 33(1)(b) is fulfilled, because tacit relocation never operates; the lease continues under the terms of the parties' express agreement. However, the landlord would still have to serve a notice that properly terminates the tenancy at an ish. Otherwise, as is suggested above, the agreement continues to renew, and will not have "reached its ish" under section 33(1)(a).

Repeal of s 33(1)(c)

As originally enacted, section 33(1) also required that "no further contractual tenancy (whether a short assured tenancy or not) is for the time being in existence". This was repealed by the 2016 Act,[149] presumably on the view that, after 1 December 2017, any further contractual tenancy would be a PRT, and an action under section 33 of the 1988 Act would therefore be incompetent, in any event. It is suggested that section 33(1)(c) lives on, given the scope of the saving provision discussed at p 262 below. In cases where it is preserved by the saving provision, a new contractual tenancy will continue to be fatal to an action under section 33.[150] In cases not covered by the saving provision, a new tenancy will presumably be a PRT, which will also be fatal to an action under section 33.

145 Let us say that the tenancy ran for six months from 1 April 2015, and the landlord served a valid notice to quit, with the effect that the parties' contract terminated on 1 October 2015. In that case, the tenancy became a statutory assured tenancy under s 16, given the terms of s 33(4) (see p 256). At that point it had reached its ish, and tacit relocation was not operating. The only remaining requirement is the service of s 33(1)(d) notice, which could happen some time later.

146 Section 33(1)(a) simply refers to "its ish", rather than specifying the initial ish. The ish of the lease is determined by the agreement between the parties. Tacit relocation is an implied agreement between them that the lease is prolonged. In that case, the ish becomes the date at the end of that prolonged period.

147 So, if the tenancy renews for a year and, shortly thereafter, the tenant stops paying the rent, the landlord could raise an action under s 18, and the applicable rent arrears grounds in sch 5. If he wished to raise an action under s 33, he would have to wait till the renewed term expires.

148 See the discussion of the relevant authorities in the Scottish Law Commission Discussion Paper: *Aspects of Leases: Termination* (Scot Law Com No 165, 2018) paras 2.13–2.17, and Rennie and others, *Leases* (SULI 2015) para 11-08.

149 Section 75 and sch 5, para 2(3)(b).

150 For a case in which a new contractual tenancy was fatal to eviction proceedings (albeit under section 36(5) of the 2001 Act, rather than s 33 of the 1988 Act), see *City of Edinburgh Council v Smith* 2016 SLT (Sh Ct) 343; 2016 Hous LR 30.

The "section 33 notice": s 33(1)(d), (2) and (3)

As well as serving a valid notice to quit, the landlord[151] must also give notice "stating that he requires possession of the house". The period of notice is two months, unless the contract between the parties provides for a longer period. There is no prescribed form for the notice. It is not entirely clear from the terms of the Act that the notice requires to be in writing, though this seems implicit.[152] It is submitted that the notice must indicate the date on which it is to take effect, otherwise the tenant will not be aware of the date on which the landlord requires possession. Although the Act stipulates a statement that the landlord "requires possession" of the house, it is suggested that words to that effect, such that a reasonably minded recipient would be in no doubt as to the meaning of the notice, will suffice.[153]

In *Beattie v Rogers*,[154] the landlord had served a single notice that bore to be given under section 33(1)(d), and also contained the prescribed information for a notice to quit.[155] The sheriff held that the notice operated only as a section 33(1)(d) notice and not as a notice to quit. Therefore, it did not terminate the lease, which continued by tacit relocation, and the pursuer was not entitled to an order for possession under section 33. There ought to have been two separate notices.[156]

It is clear from section 33(3) that the notice does not require to take effect at the ish date of the tenancy or at any other particular date. It can be served by the landlord at any time, provided that it takes effect after the tenancy is terminated. This means that a defective notice under section 33(1)(d) is not so much of an inconvenience for the landlord as a defective notice to quit. In the former case, another notice can be served, and the action raised after the two-month period expires. In the latter case, the tenancy will relocate, which may entail a longer delay.

Finally, it might be argued that section 33(1) does not preclude the landlord from raising proceedings during the notice period, or even serving the notice after the proceedings are raised, provided that the notice has been given, and the period of notice has expired, before the tribunal decides whether to grant

151 Or one of the joint landlords. A notice given by a person not having the interest of "landlord", in respect of the tenancy in question, is invalid. For example, where the tenancy is a sub-let, notice could not be given by the landlord of the head tenancy: *Barrow v Kazim* [2019] 1 WLR 3168.

152 This was the view taken by Jonathan Mitchell in *Eviction and Rent Arrears*, notwithstanding that, in relation to the equivalent provision under the Housing Act 1988, it has been suggested that the notice need not be in writing. As he comments: "it is difficult to believe that Parliament can have contemplated a notice of this kind being given by word of mouth alone". In any event, s 33(3) refers to the notice being "served", which in turn means service in terms of s 54 (see Chapter 15). That presupposes that the notice will be in writing.

153 See the summary of the decision in *Pease v Carter*, at p 242 above.

154 2016 Hous LR 107.

155 Under the Assured Tenancies (Notices to Quit Prescribed Information) (Scotland) Regulations 1988 (SI 1988/2067). See Chapter 3, p 55.

156 That was contrary to the decision in *Key Housing Association v Cameron* 1999 Hous LR 47, in which Sheriff McKenzie rejected a submission that a "hybrid" notice was incompetent. However, that appears to have proceed on the view (stated at para 9-19) that formal notice to quit is not necessary in relation to a short assured tenancy. In *Beattie*, Sheriff Jamieson (at para [8]) described that view as incorrect, noting that that it was not adopted by the landlord's agent.

an order for possession. However, there is authority against that argument, as regards the equivalent notice under the English legislation.[157]

Effect of termination: s 33(4)

Section 33(4) confirms that a short assured tenancy, like any other assured tenancy, becomes a statutory assured tenancy under section 16 of the Act on termination of the tenancy contract. As already indicated, following termination of the contract, the landlord may, at any time, serve a section 33 notice, and thereafter raise proceedings seeking an order under that section once the period of notice has expired.[158]

Sections 18 and 19 do not apply: s 33(5)

Subsection (5) was added by section 34 of the Private Rented Housing (Scotland) Act 2011. Its purpose was to resolve a long-standing doubt as to whether it is necessary to serve a notice under section 19, in relation to an action that proceeds under section 33.[159] It is now clear that this is not necessary.

Applications to the First-tier Tribunal under section 33 of the 1988 Act

> **"66. Application for order for possession upon termination of a short assured tenancy**
> Where a landlord makes an application under section 33 (recovery of possession on termination of a short assured tenancy) of the 1988 Act, the application must—
> (a) state—
> (i) the name, address and registration number (if any) of the landlord;
> (ii) the name, address and profession of any representative of the landlord; and
> (iii) the name and address of the tenant;
> (b) be accompanied by a copy of—
> (i) the tenancy agreement (if available) or, if this is not available, as much information about the tenancy as the landlord can give;
> (ii) the notice by landlord that the tenancy is a short assured tenancy;
> (iii) the notice given to the tenant under section 33(1)(d) of the 1988 Act;
> (iv) the notice to quit served by the landlord on the tenant;
> (v) a copy of the notice by the landlord given to the local authority under section 11 of the Homelessness (Scotland) Act 2003 (if applicable); and
> (vi) a copy of Form BB (notice to the occupier) under schedule 6 of the Conveyancing and Feudal Reform (Scotland) Act 1970 (if applicable);[160] and

157 *Lower Street Properties v Jones* (1996) 28 HLR 877, a decision of the Court of Appeal.

158 In *Craig v Taylor* [2019] UT 27, the Upper Tribunal decided that s 33(4) does not provide a basis for an order that postpones the date upon which the order for possession will take effect. However, the FTT does have a specific power, under r 16A(d), to "order a delay in execution of an order by the First-tier Tribunal at any time before it is executed". See Chapter 15, p 512.

159 This doubt was caused by the wording of s 19(1), which is not expressly restricted to actions under s 18.

160 This applies to an application made by a heritable creditor in possession. The lender is

(c) be signed and dated by the landlord or a representative of the landlord."

The requirements of rule 66 are very similar to those imposed by rule 65. Reference is made to the discussion of that rule, above.

The difference is in rule 66(b)(ii) and (iii). The application must be accompanied by the notice by the landlord that the tenancy is a short assured tenancy (the AT5), and the notice given to the tenant under section 33(1)(d) of the 1988 Act.[161] If that is not done, the application is apt to be rejected at the sift.[162]

1984, 1988, 2014 AND 2016 ACTS: SAVING AND TRANSITIONAL PROVISIONS

As was explained in the introduction to this chapter, because different statutory schemes are now in place, issues may arise as to the transition from one regime to another – in particular, the conditions under which tenancies under the older Act may be renewed, or prolonged, after the new Act came into force.

The first point to appreciate is that (subject to limited exceptions) the 1988 Act applies to tenancies created between 2 January 1989 and the coming into force of the 2016 Act on 1 December 2017. From that date, the 2016 regime operates. Neither the 1988 Act nor the 2016 Act is retrospective; neither applies to tenancies created before the relevant date.[163] This means that regulated tenancies created before 2 January 1989, though now rare, are still in existence and still governed by the 1984 Act. The same applies to assured and short assured tenancies created before 1 December 2017, to which the 1988 Act continues to apply. Conversely, where parties enter into a tenancy on or after 1 December 2017 that meets the conditions of the 2016 Act, in particular section 1, that will be a PRT,[164] even if the lease calls itself an "assured" or a "short assured" tenancy. The statutory status of the tenancy is governed by the statutes, not by the parties' agreement.[165]

To these basic principles, the following supplementary points are added.

required to include, with the application to the FTT, a copy of the form BB that was given to the occupier of the subjects when the security was called up. The same requirement is imposed in r 65, and in r 109, in relation to applications made under s 51 of the 2016 Act. This point is discussed in Chapter 8, at p 274.

161 Whereas, under r 65, the landlord is required to provide a copy of the AT6.

162 Figures obtained from the Housing and Property Chamber indicate that, for the two years from 1 December 2017 to 30 November 2019, around 16% of applications under r 66 were rejected at the sift.

163 Subject to s 46A of the 2016 Act: see p 263 below.

164 Subject to the saving provision set out at p 262 below.

165 Obviously the same applies to a new tenancy created in, say, 1990, to which the 1988 Act, and in particular s 12, applies; this will be an assured tenancy, even if the parties described it as a regulated tenancy under the 1984 Act.

Regulated tenancies

It is still possible to create new protected tenancies[166] under section 42 of the 1988 Act, which is headed: "New protected tenancies restricted to special cases". Section 42 is fairly complex but, for practical purposes, the key provision is section 42(1)(b), under which a tenancy that begins on or after 2 January 1989 will be a protected tenancy under the 1984 Act, if:

> "it is granted to a person (alone or jointly with others) who, immediately before the tenancy was granted, was the protected tenant (or one of the protected tenants) or a statutory tenant of the same landlord".

The point of this provision is to ensure that protected or statutory tenants under the 1984 Act cannot be deprived of their status by the creation of a new tenancy agreement.[167] Accordingly, it was not possible for the landlord to end a regulated tenancy and replace it with an assured or a short assured tenancy, even if the new tenancy was the lease of a different property.[168] That is also the position under the 2016 Act. If section 42 of the 1988 Act applies, a new tenancy created after 1 December 2017 will be a protected tenancy under the 1984 Act.[169]

Assured tenancies

Under section 12(1A) of the 1988 Act, a tenancy created on or after 1 December 2017 cannot be an assured tenancy.[170] Conversely, a tenancy created before that date which is an assured tenancy (including a short assured tenancy) under the 1988 Act, cannot be a PRT.[171]

In terms of section 75 of the 2016 Act, schedule 5 makes transitional provisions for the purposes of bringing the new PRT regime into force. Schedule 5 is in two parts.

The first part is headed "No new assured or short assured tenancies". It comprises two paragraphs. Before the 2016 Act came into force, paragraph 2, in particular, caused concern that it would have the effect of preventing short assured tenancies from continuing by tacit relocation or express agreement, after 1 December 2017. An attempt was made to clarify the position by a saving provision being made in the commencement order that brought the Act into force. Unfortunately, this seems to have had the opposite effect, and the overall scheme for transition, particularly as regards short assured tenancies, is confused.

166 I.e. a contractual tenancy regulated by the 1984 Act.

167 This is reinforced by sch 4, para 13(1) to the 1988 Act,: a tenancy cannot be an assured tenancy if it is a protected tenancy within the meaning of the 1984 Act.

168 As was pointed out by note 1 of the "Special Notes for Existing Tenants" at the end of the prescribed form AT5, which states: "1. If you already have a regulated tenancy, other than a short tenancy, should you give it up and take a new tenancy in the same house or another house owned by the same landlord, that tenancy **cannot** be an assured or a short assured tenancy. Your tenancy will continue to be a regulated tenancy."

169 Under sch 1, para 21(a) to the 2016 Act, a tenancy cannot be a PRT if it is a protected tenancy under the 1984 Act. It is a protected tenancy if s 42 of the 1988 Act applies.

170 Subject to the saving provision discussed below, which applies only to short assured tenancies.

171 Schedule 1 para 21(d) to the 2016 Act.

Part 2 of schedule 5 allows parties to an assured tenancy to convert it to a PRT; it also makes provision as regards succession.

Schedule 5 part 1 – No new assured or short assured tenancies; saving provision

Paragraph 1 of schedule 5 is headed "No new assured tenancies". It makes several changes to section 12 of and schedule 4 to the 1988 – in particular, the insertion of section 12(1A) to the effect that a tenancy cannot be an assured tenancy if it is granted after the 2016 Act comes into force.

Paragraph 2 is headed "No new short assured tenancies". The significant part of this paragraph is the repeal of various parts of subsection (3) of section 32 to the 1988 Act.[172] For explanatory purposes, this subsection is shown with repealed parts in italics:

> "**32. Short assured tenancies**
>
> . . .
>
> (3) Subject to subsection (4) below, if, at the ish of a short assured tenancy—
>
> (a) it continues by tacit relocation; *or*
>
> *(b) a new contractual tenancy of the same or substantially the same premises comes into being under which the landlord and the tenant are the same as at that ish,*
>
> the continued tenancy *or, as the case may be, the new contractual tenancy* shall be a short assured tenancy, whether or not it fulfils the conditions in paragraphs (a) and (b) of subsection (1) above."

Before discussing the effect of the repeals, and the subsequent saving provision, it is convenient to say something about the effect of section 32(3), as originally enacted.

Section 32(3)

Even before it was amended by the 2016 Act, the application of section 32(3) was not straightforward. The apparent aim of the provision was that the parties could prolong a short assured tenancy by tacit relocation, or enter into a new agreement for the same property, and the continued (or new) agreement would still be a short assured tenancy, even if it was for less than six months, and without the necessity of the landlord serving another AT5. This is what is meant by the words "whether or not it fulfils the conditions in paragraphs (a) and (b) of subsection (1) above".

That made sense in relation to the new tenancies described by section 32(3)(b). However, one might question whether it was necessary in relation to a tenancy that is continued by tacit relocation. If the term of a short assured tenancy was, say, from 1 March to 1 September 2016, the effect of tacit relocation would be to extend it for another six months, from 1 September 2016

172 Paragraph 2 of sch 2 also repeals references to new tenancies in s 32(4) of the 1988 Act; however, the savings provision discussed in the main text also applies to this repeal. Section 32(4) is a rarely used provision that states that subs (3) does not apply if the landlord serves a notice (AT7) on the tenant that the new or continued tenancy is not be a short assured tenancy. It is suggested (tentatively) that, in light of the saving provision, where the short assured tenancy is continuing by tacit relocation, the effect of serving the notice is that the continued tenancy is an assured tenancy. Where a new tenancy is being created, the effect of serving the notice is that the new tenancy will be a PRT. Paragraph 2(3) of sch 5 repeals s 33(1)(c). This change is discussed at p 254 above.

to 1 March 2017.[173] Therefore, on any view, it would still be a tenancy for a term of "not less than six months". Also, no new tenancy would be created,[174] so there was no need to serve another AT5, in any event: under section 32(2)(b), an AT5 is served before the "creation of the assured tenancy", which in this case would have been before 1 March 2016.

For that reason, it is suggested that section 32(3)(a) was (and still is) superfluous. Even without it, a short assured tenancy of the type described above would still have remained a short assured tenancy, if it continued on 1 September 2016. Service of another AT5 would be inapt in any event, because that would suggest the creation of a new tenancy.

By contrast, section 32(3)(b) is a significant provision, because it enables the parties to make a new agreement, which would also be a short assured tenancy, without observing the requirements of section 32(1).

Short assured tenancies continuing by express agreement

Section 32(3) refers to two situations (tacit relocation and new tenancy) in which the same parties may continue their status as landlord and tenant under a short assured tenancy. However, it does not refer to the fairly common practice of including in a lease, which was to be a short assured tenancy, a provision by which the parties contract out of tacit relocation, by a stipulation that following the initial term (which was invariably for the statutory minimum of six months) the tenancy would thereafter continue on a monthly or bi-monthly term.[175] What was the status of such agreements, under section 32 of the Act?

Let us say that parties entered into an agreement for a term from 1 March to 1 September 2016, and monthly thereafter. When it was continuing, on 1 September, 1 October etc., it was still, it is submitted, a short assured tenancy, in relation to which the requirements of section 32(1) had been met. That is the case for two reasons.

First, the original tenancy was still ongoing. It was not the case that a new tenancy was being created on the first day of every month after 1 September

173 Because the effect of tacit relocation, in the case of a tenancy for a period of less than one year, is to prolong the tenancy for the same period.

174 See the discussion of the historical development of tacit relocation in the SLC's recent discussion paper (n 148), from para 2.4 onwards, in which the authors summarise the effect of tacit relocation thus: "It appears now to be accepted practice that tacit relocation is a prolongation, or a continuation or extension of the original lease. Under the doctrine of tacit relocation, the lease then continues on the same terms as before, except for duration. If the original lease is for more than one year it continues for a further year and then from year to year until appropriate notice of termination is given. Regardless of the length of its original duration, the extension by tacit relocation is for only a year. If the lease is for less than one year, it continues for the same period as the original lease and so on successively until appropriate notice is given."

175 As is indicated at p 254 above, that sort of continuation does not amount to "tacit relocation". The point of the agreement is that parties contract out of tacit relocation, by providing for a shorter term than the original six months. The term "tacit relocation" is not defined in the 1988 Act. It therefore requires to be accorded its technical meaning, in Scots law. See the previous note. If the author is wrong in that view and, in the case of an initial six-month term, the monthly prolongations thereafter are instances of "tacit relocation", the lease relocates and will continue to be subject to s 32(3)(a), which is not repealed by sch 5 to the 2016 Act.

2016. Therefore, the requirement for service of an AT5, before the creation of the tenancy, was met before 1 March 2016.

Secondly, the requirement, under section 32(1)(a), that the tenancy "is for a term of not less than six months" is met by an agreed term from 1 March to 1 September 2016, and monthly thereafter. That is in accord with the decision of the sheriff in *Cavriani v Robinson*,[176] and the decision of the Court of Appeal in *Goodman v Evely*.[177] It is also consistent with *Wishaw and District Housing Association Ltd v Neary*,[178] the only case in which section 32 has been considered by the Inner House.[179]

Section 32(3) as amended, and the saving provision

As a result of schedule 5 paragraph 2 to the 2016 Act, section 32(3) is now subject to the repeals indicated at page 259 above. It was apparently thought appropriate to remove the references to new tenancies from subsection (3), because new agreements (after 1 December 2017) were to be PRTs under the 2016 Act.

However, the scope of the repeal, and the insertion of section 12(1A), seem to have caused concern as to the status of short assured tenancies as at the date of commencement of the 2016 Act, and whether they would still be able to continue. This prompted the Scottish Ministers to include, in a commencement order bringing the Act into force, a saving provision that sought to limit the effect of paragraph 2 of schedule 5 ("No new short assured tenancies"). That, however, was apparently thought to be insufficient, and a new commencement order was prepared, which attempted to clarify the position.[180]

176 2002 Hous LR 67.

177 [2002] HLR 53. The requirement in the English legislation is that the tenancy be "a fixed term tenancy granted for a term certain of not less than six months". In *Goodman v Evely*, that was met by a tenancy that was for one year and thereafter from month to month.

178 2004 SC 463; described at p 251 above.

179 In that case, the tenant argued that the existence of a break clause had the effect of preventing the tenancy from being a short assured tenancy, because it was not for a guaranteed minimum period of six months. That argument was rejected by the court. For present purposes, note that the term of the tenancy as to duration stated: "The Association will let and the Tenant take possession of the house under a short assured tenancy commencing 15th day of September on 2001 (the date of entry) until 20th day of March on 2002 *and monthly thereafter*." There was no suggestion, in the decision, that the words "and monthly thereafter" had the effect of removing the tenancy's short assured status.

180 There were three commencement orders in relation to the 2016 Act: No. 1 (SSI 2016/298) brought in a small number of provisions, but only for the purposes of making regulations; and No. 2 (SSI 2017/293) was intended to bring the rest of the Act into force. However, that order was entirely repealed by the Private Housing (Tenancies) (Scotland) Act 2016 (Commencement No. 3, Amendment, Saving Provision and Revocation) Regulations 2017 (SSI 2017/346), which included the saving provision quoted in the main text. This order was accompanied by a policy note, which is quoted below. Order No. 2 contained a very similar saving provision, but it was restricted to the effect of para 2 of sch 5 on ss 32 and 33 of the Act. The provision quoted in the main text is wider in scope, covering the effect of paras 1, 2 and 3 of sch 5, not only on s 32 and 33, but also on s 12.

The saving provision

The Private Housing (Tenancies) (Scotland) Act 2016 (Commencement No. 3, Amendment, Saving Provision and Revocation) Regulations 2017[181] include the following regulation:

> **"6. Saving provision**
> Despite the amendments made by section 75 and paragraphs 1, 2 and 3 of schedule 5 of the 2016 Act, sections 12, 32 and 33 of the 1988 Act have effect on and after 1st December 2017 as they had effect immediately before that date but only in relation to—
> (a) a short assured tenancy (within the meaning given in section 32(1) of the 1988 Act) which was created before 1st December 2017 and continues in existence on that date;
> (b) a new contractual tenancy (within the meaning given in section 32(3)(b) of the 1988 Act) which came into being before 1st December 2017 and continues in existence on that date; and
> (c) a new contractual tenancy (within the meaning given in section 32(3)(b) of the 1988 Act) which comes into being on or after 1st December 2017 at the ish of a short assured tenancy which is a short assured tenancy in a case mentioned in paragraph (a) or (b)."

Note that the saving provision applies to all of section 32, and also to sections 12 and 33.

A "saving" provision is "a provision the intention of which is to narrow the effect of the enactment to which it refers so as to preserve some existing legal rule or right from its operation".[182] However, savings provisions are often included in legislation "by way of reassurance, for avoidance of doubt or from abundance of caution".[183]

In attempting to make sense of regulation 6 (which is not easy), it is also necessary to note the following statement, which appeared in the policy note that accompanied the commencement order:

> "The saving provision provides that any short assured tenancy which began before 1st December 2017 can continue to operate after that date, regardless of whether or not that short assured tenancy is continuing by tacit relocation or renewing at regular intervals (under section 32(3)(a) or (b) of the Housing (Scotland) Act 1988, respectively). This saving provision is required in order to meet the Scottish Government's stated aim of introducing a new private residential tenancy for future lets. It was not the Scottish Government's intention that the new tenancy would affect those short assured tenancies which are already in operation on the date of commencement."

In light of this statement, it is suggested that, in any case of doubt as to the interpretation of the transitional and savings provisions, one would have to favour the interpretation that results in existing short assured tenancies retaining their status.

181 n 180.

182 Bennion, *Statutory Interpretation* (7th edn) s 17.6. The authors point out that savings are an unreliable guide to the interpretation of the provisions to which they relate, because they are often expressed in wider terms. The drafter will sometimes express a saving in general terms so as to keep it simple, on the view that a saving that incidentally catches things that are not covered by the provision to which it relates does no harm, because a saving cannot confer any right that did not exist already.

183 *Ealing LBC v Race Relations Board* [1972] AC 342, at 363E (Lord Simon of Glaisdale).

The effect of the saving provision

It is necessary to emphasise that, absent the saving provision, the deletions made to section 32(3) by schedule 5 to the Act only affect new agreements made after 1 December 2017. They do not affect tenancies continuing by tacit relocation, or cases in which the tenancy continues for a shorter period, under some express provision of the parties' contract. Therefore, if the 2016 Act had come into force on 1 December 2017, without any saving provision, then the status of these continuing agreements would not have been affected. They would still continue, and would still be short assured tenancies, which is a form of assured tenancy, which cannot therefore be PRTs, given schedule 1 paragraph 21(d) to the 2016 Act. Therefore, as regards those tenancies, it is suggested that the saving provision is simply "by way of reassurance".

What is the effect of the saving provision on new tenancies created after 1 December 2017?

The parties enter into a new agreement after 1 December 2017

It is suggested that the effect of the saving provision is that a new contractual tenancy created after 1 December 2017 will be a short assured tenancy under the 1988 Act, subject to the following conditions:

- it must "come into being" at the ish of an existing short assured tenancy;[184]
- it must be "of the same or substantially the same premises";[185]
- the new tenancy must have the same landlord and tenant.[186]

In these circumstances, the effect of the saving provision is that section 12 would apply as it did before the 2016 Act came into force (i.e. without subsection (1A)). So, the new tenancy would be an assured tenancy. Because the effect of section 32(3)(b) of the 1988 Act on such a tenancy is also preserved by the saving provision, it would also be a short assured tenancy; it not be necessary for the new tenancy to be for a period of not less than six months, nor would it be necessary for the landlord to serve an AT5.

Schedule 5 part 2: conversion and succession

Paragraph 3 of schedule 5 inserts a new section 46A into the 1988 Act, which enables parties, by agreement, to convert an assured tenancy into a PRT.

Paragraphs 4 and 5 provide that, on the death of a regulated tenant under the 1984 Act, or an assured tenant under the 1988 Act, on or after 1 December

184 Presumably the words "at the ish" in reg 6(c), the saving provision, mean that the new tenancy must begin when the old tenancy ends. This would happen where the old tenancy ends and the new tenancy begins on the same day. It could also happen where the old tenancy ends on, say, the last minute of 1 September, and the new tenancy begins on the first minute of 2 September. Otherwise, a new tenancy which comes into being on a later date is not covered by the saving provision. In that case, the amendment to s 12 by the addition of subs (1A) would operate, and the tenancy could not be an assured tenancy or a short assured tenancy.

185 Because in the saving provision, reg 6(c) applies only to "a new contractual tenancy (*within the meaning given in section 32(3)(b) of the 1988 Act*)".

186 ibid.

2017, where an individual has a right to succeed to the tenancy, under the relevant provisions of those Acts, the tenancy is converted to a PRT.[187]

"Winkling"

"Winkling" is evicting a tenant from rented property by underhand or dubious means, usually to enable the property to be sold. This can sometimes be achieved by the landlord inviting an unsuspecting tenant to enter into a new tenancy agreement, in the knowledge that the tenant will have reduced security of tenure under the statutory provisions applicable to the new tenancy.

Section 42(1)(b) of the 1988 Act, mentioned above, precludes this activity, in relation to regulated tenants under the 1984 Act. Entering into a new agreement with the same landlord (even in relation to a different property) does not deprive the tenant of his statutory status.

By contrast, it was possible, under the 1988 Act, for the parties to an assured tenancy to replace it with a short assured tenancy, thereby depriving the tenant of his security of tenure. Section 16(1) of the 1988 Act provides that following termination of the parties' contractual tenancy, a statutory assured tenancy arises if the tenant "retains possession of the house *without being entitled to do so under a contractual tenancy*". Subsection (2) states that "a statutory assured tenancy cannot be brought to an end *by the landlord* except by obtaining an order of the First-tier Tribunal". Thus, it was clear that an assured tenancy could be ended by both parties entering into a new contractual tenancy, which could, of course, be a short assured tenancy.[188]

It is thought that the vast majority of assured tenancies that existed as at 30 November 2017 were short assured tenancies. Where the parties to those tenancies enter into a new contract after that date, unless the saving provision applies (see above), the new tenancy will be a PRT. This is not something from which the short assured tenant needs to be protected, because her security of tenure will be improved under the 2016 Act. Presumably that is why there is no equivalent to section 42 of the 1988 Act in the 2016 Act. However, that still leaves assured tenants (who are not in short assured tenancies) open to being "winkled", because they would have less security of tenure under the 2016 Act.[189]

187 See the discussion of succession to tenancies, in Chapter 12.

188 *Johnstone v Finneran* 2003 SCLR 157. Accordingly, the Special Notes for Existing Tenants in the form AT5 warned: "3. If you are an existing tenant and are uncertain about accepting the proposed short assured tenancy you are strongly advised to consult a solicitor or any organisation which gives advice on housing matters."

189 Because the landlord can only obtain an order for eviction of an assured tenant under one of the grounds in sch 5 to the 1988 Act. The grounds for eviction under sch 3 to the 2016 Act are more favourable to the landlord. In particular, there is no "landlord intends to sell" ground under sch 5 to the 1988 Act and the mandatory ground for eviction for rent arrears is more favourable to the landlord under the 2016 Act.

Chapter 8

Grounds for Possession of Assured Tenancies

The purpose of this chapter is to consider the grounds for recovery of possession in schedule 5 to the 1988 Act. In order for the First-tier Tribunal ("FTT") to grant an order for possession under section 18, the landlord must establish that one or more of the grounds exists.[1] As indicated in Chapter 7, grounds 1–8 are grounds on which the FTT must order possession, and are therefore generally referred to as "mandatory grounds". Grounds 9–17 are grounds on which the tribunal may order possession, and are generally referred to as "discretionary grounds".

Applications to the FTT for an eviction order under section 18 are made under rule 65 of the tribunal's Procedure Rules.[2] A significant number of these applications are rejected when the tribunal sifts applications.[3] If the application passes the sift, it is then invariably appointed to a case management discussion ("CMD"), before a single legal member,[4] unless it is withdrawn.[5] Where a CMD takes place, the application is usually determined there. At most CMDs, the respondent does not appear, and is not represented.

Where an application is determined at the sift or the CMD, it is the practice of the Tribunal to issue a written decision,[6] which is then published on the Housing and Property Chamber's website. There, it is possible to search for decisions in the "Evictions and Civil Proceedings Decisions Database", by rule. Looking at the rule 65 decisions, it is possible then to assess the frequency with which different grounds have been used, and the degree of success enjoyed by landlords in pursuing those grounds, since the transfer of jurisdiction on 1 December 2017.

1 Whereas, in an application for an order under s 33, the landlord may need satisfy the tribunal that the requirements of that section are met. These are discussed in Chapter 7.

2 In the schedule to the First-tier Tribunal for Scotland Housing and Property Chamber (Procedure) Regulations 2017 (SSI 2017/328). Applications for an order under s 33 are made in terms of r 66. Both of those rules are considered in Chapter 7.

3 For the application of the sift, see Chapter 14. In terms of r 8(2), the FTT must notify the applicant of the decision to reject an application at the sift, and state the reasons for that decision.

4 Again, see Chapter 14 for a discussion of r 17, which concerns CMDs. Although r 17(1) states that the FTT "may" order a CMD to be held, it is the practice of the tribunal always to fix CMDs in cases in which an order for possession is sought. Under r 17(4), the FTT may do anything at a CMD that it may do at a hearing, including making a decision.

5 No written decision is issued if the application is withdrawn by the landlord. That might happen if, for example, arrears of rent were cleared prior to the CMD.

6 Where an application is decided at a CMD (under r 17(4)), a statement of reasons *may* be prepared, in terms of r 26(6), though in practice this is invariably done.

A key point that then emerges is that, in the vast majority of cases in which an order for possession was granted under section 18, the ground for eviction was one or more of the rent arrears grounds (8, 11 and 12). Of the remaining grounds, orders under ground 2 (application by heritable creditor in possession) have been the most common.[7] The order was granted on ground 13[8] or ground 15[9] in several cases. A handful of cases featured grounds 1, 5, 6, 10, 14 and 17. The remaining grounds (3, 4, 7, 9 and 16) do not feature in any of the published decisions.[10]

MANDATORY GROUNDS: ACTIONS UNDER 1988 ACT, s 18(3)

Under section 18(3) of the Act, if the tribunal is satisfied that any of grounds 1–8 is established, it "shall make an order for possession".[11] There is no additional requirement and, in particular, no obligation on the landlord to show that it would be reasonable to grant the order.

Before going on to consider the individual grounds, the following points, which apply to more than one ground, may usefully be made:

- In relation to grounds 1, 2, 5, 6 and 7, the form AT6 served on the tenant, in terms of section 19 of the Act, requires to give two months' notice. In relation to grounds 3, 4 and 8, only two weeks' notice is required.[12]
- As was discussed in Chapter 7, section 18(6) allows the landlord to seek recovery of possession on certain grounds without terminating the parties' contract by notice to quit or otherwise, provided that the terms of the parties' tenancy make provision for it to be brought to an end on the ground in question. This does not apply to mandatory grounds 1, 3, 4, 5, 6 and 7. Therefore, decree cannot be granted on these grounds unless the parties' contract has been terminated, and the tenancy has become a statutory assured tenancy under section 16 of the Act.
- It is to be anticipated that the landlord will seek, and obtain, an order for possession when the case comes before the tribunal for consideration for the first time,[13] unless the tenant has some statable basis for maintaining either that (a) the relevant ground is not established or (b) the landlord has failed to serve the requisite notices.[14]
- Grounds 1–5 all require that written notice is given to the tenant, not later than the beginning/commencement/creation of the tenancy, to the effect that

7 In ten cases as at 7 February 2020.

8 In six cases at that date, although in three of those, the order was also granted on one of the rent arrears grounds.

9 In four cases, although in two of those, the order was also granted on one of the rent arrears grounds.

10 As at 7 February 2020.

11 "Subject to subsections (3A) and (6)". Subsection (3A) relates the ground 8, and concerns delay in payment of housing benefit or universal credit. See p 280 below. As to s 18(6), see the second bullet point in the main text, above.

12 See Chapter 7, p 240.

13 Which would be at the CMD held under r 17 of the FTT's Procedure Rules. See the discussion of that rule in Chapter 14.

14 Being the AT6, and, in relation to a case to which s 18(6) does not apply, notice that terminates the tenancy and converts it to a statutory assured tenancy for the purposes of s 16.

possession may ultimately be sought on that ground. There is no prescribed form for any of these notices.[15] In relation to grounds 1 and 2, the tribunal may dispense with the requirement for the notice if it was not served. Somewhat confusingly, grounds 1 and 5 refer to a notice being served before "the beginning of the tenancy"; ground 2 to a notice served before "the creation of the tenancy"; and grounds 3 and 4 to a notice served before "the commencement of the tenancy".[16] Although three different terms are used, there are, it is suggested, only two dates to which those terms could refer: the date on which the parties entered into the agreement, which would seem to be aptly described by the term "creation of the tenancy"; and the date of entry in terms of the lease, which is presumably the date to which the term "commencement of the tenancy" or "beginning of the tenancy" refers. If that is correct, it would appear to mean that the notices required by grounds 1, 3, 4 and 5 could have been served on the tenant after he has entered into a tenancy agreement, but before he takes entry in terms of that agreement.

- Under section 18(5) and part IV of schedule 5, where a notice is given as mentioned in grounds 1–5, it has effect as if it was also given before the beginning of any later tenancy that: (a) takes effect immediately on termination of the earlier tenancy; (b) is granted (or deemed to be granted) to the person who was the tenant under the earlier tenancy; and (c) is of substantially the same house as the earlier tenancy.

Ground 1: landlord wants property for own home

> "Not later than the beginning of the tenancy the landlord (or, where there are joint landlords, any of them) gave notice in writing to the tenant that possession might be recovered on this Ground or the First-tier Tribunal is of the opinion that it is reasonable to dispense with the requirement of notice and (in either case)—
> (a) at any time before the beginning of the tenancy, the landlord who is seeking possession or, in the case of joint landlords seeking possession, at least one of them occupied the house as his only or principal home; or
> (b) the landlord who is seeking possession or, in the case of joint landlords seeking possession, at least one of them requires the house as his or his spouse's or civil partner's only or principal home, and neither the landlord (or, in the case of joint landlords, any one of them) nor any other person who, as landlord, derived title from the landlord who gave the notice mentioned above acquired the landlord's interest in the tenancy for value."

The importance of this ground is underappreciated. In creating tenancies under the 1988 Act, landlords and their agents tended to focus on ensuring that a short assured tenancy was created, thereby avoiding security of tenure. As was pointed out at the beginning of Chapter 7, most assured tenancies that are not short assured tenancies arose because the landlord failed to take legal advice before the creation of the tenancy or where, due to some error on the part of the landlord or his agents, the requirements for creation of a short assured tenancy under section 32 were not met.

15 In Luba and others, *Defending Possession Proceedings* (8th edn) para 11.7, the authors suggest that the notice may be included as a recital in any tenancy agreement, provided that the agreement does not operate retrospectively.

16 The equivalent legislation applicable to England and Wales (being grounds 1–5 of sch 2 to the Housing Act 1988) uses only one term: "the beginning of the tenancy".

However, in a case in which the landlord (or one of the joint landlords) previously occupied the house as his only or principal home, and notice was given that possession may be recovered on ground 1, the landlord's position is better than it would be under a short assured tenancy. The tenant has no defence to an action in which ground 1(a) is established,[17] and therefore no security of tenure. Moreover, an assured tenancy subject to ground 1(a) does not have to have a minimum period of six months.

Even in cases in which notice has not been given under ground 1, it may be possible to persuade the tribunal to dispense with that notice. Thus, where the landlord previously resided in the tenancy, resort may be had to ground 1 where there was a failure to create a short assured tenancy, and no other ground for recovery of possession under schedule 5.

The notice could be appended to the tenancy agreement, though, in that case, the landlord would have to ensure that the agreement was given to the tenant before the date of entry.

In an action for possession, the question of whether to dispense with the notice may be the only issue between the parties; if the tribunal decides in favour of the landlord, and he thereby establishes ground 1, it is obliged to grant decree for recovery of possession in terms of section 18(3).

There have been several English cases on how to approach the issue of whether to dispense with the notice.[18] The principle that may be derived from these authorities is that the tribunal should take into account all the circumstances, including the issue of whether the tenant or the landlord would suffer greater hardship by the tribunal granting, or refusing to grant, decree, not just the circumstances that surround the failure to give notice.[19] Therefore, the tenant's persistent late payment of rent may be taken into consideration.[20] As with the tribunal's power, under section 19(1)(b) of the Act, to dispense with the requirement for service of an AT6 notice,[21] one of the most important considerations will be whether any form of notice has been given at all. If the tribunal is satisfied that oral notice has been given that the landlord intends to return to the subjects, it is more likely that it will be inclined to grant the dispensation.[22] However, if it is apparent that no notice was given because, at the time when the tenancy was granted, the landlord had no intention of returning to the subjects, his position will be more difficult.[23]

17 In theory, the tenant could dispute whether the landlord had ever occupied the subjects as his only or principal home. However, in practice this is unlikely to be a matter that is within the tenant's knowledge.

18 *Bradshaw v Baldwin-Wiseman* (1985) 17 HLR 260; *Fernandez v Parvardin* (1982) 264 EG 49; *Boyle v Verrall* (1997) 29 HLR 436, [1997] 1 EGLR 25; *Wynne v Egan* June 1997 Legal Action 15. These are all decisions of the Court of Appeal.

19 It is suggested that this principle would also be applicable in Scottish cases, notwithstanding the fact that the equivalent ground 1 of sch 2 under the Housing Act 1988 uses the words "just and equitable" instead of "reasonable". Of course, this means that the landlord's failure to serve the notice has, more or less, negated the advantage of relying on a mandatory ground, in that the tribunal's decision will depend on a judgment made in all the relevant circumstances.

20 *Boyle v Verrall* (n 18).

21 Discussed at p 238.

22 *Fernandez v Parvardin* (n 18); *White v Jones* (1994) 26 HLR 477.

23 *Bradshaw v Baldwin-Wiseman* (n 18). *P v O* 2014 Hous LR 44 is a Scottish case in which the sheriff considered (and refused) an application to dispense with the notice under ground 1.

In order to establish the ground, the landlord must then satisfy the tribunal that either condition (a) or condition (b) is fulfilled. As regards (a), the landlord's previous occupation may suffice even if it was only temporary or intermittent.[24] Note that, in contrast to (b), the landlord does not have to give any reason for requiring possession of the subjects.

Condition (b) is somewhat more complicated, and may be divided into two parts. The first part is that the landlord or one of the joint landlords requires the dwellinghouse as his, or his spouse's or civil partner's, only or principal home.[25] The landlord does not have to show that this requirement is reasonable, but he does have to satisfy the tribunal that he "bona fide wants", or "genuinely has the immediate intention" of occupying the premises.[26] He does not have to show that the residence is to be permanent.[27] The second part is that the ground is not available to a person who has purchased the landlord's interest. It is available to a person who acquires that interest by succession,[28] or by a transfer for "love, favour and affection".[29]

Ground 2: mortgage default

"The house is subject to a heritable security granted before the creation of the tenancy and—

(a) as a result of a default by the debtor the creditor is entitled to sell the house and requires it for the purpose of disposing of it with vacant possession in exercise of that entitlement; and

(b) either notice was given in writing to the tenant not later than the date of commencement of the tenancy that possession might be recovered on this Ground or the First-tier Tribunal is satisfied that it is reasonable to dispense with the requirement of notice."

The purpose of this ground is to enable a heritable creditor who has, following a default by its debtor, obtained decree for possession in terms of the relevant provisions of the Conveyancing and Feudal Reform (Scotland) Act 1970, to seek the eviction of any tenant to whom the borrower let the subjects under an assured tenancy.

The letting of residential property that is subject to a mortgage is commonplace. In some cases, the consent of the creditor to let is obtained. In the case of a "buy-to-let" mortgage, it may be obtained before the property is purchased by the landlord. In other cases, the creditor's consent is not sought, and it may be unaware of the existence of the lease until it initiates repossession proceedings against the landlord/debtor under the 1970 Act. In any case, where the subjects have been let by the debtor under an assured tenancy, the creditor must initiate separate proceedings against the tenant (unless the

24 *Naish v Curzon* (1985) 17 HLR 220; *Mistry v Isidore* (1990) 22 HLR 281, [1990] 2 EGLR 97; *Ibie v Trubshaw* (1990) 22 HLR 191.

25 As regards the term "only or principal home" as it appears in conditions (a) and (b), see Chapter 1. In *P v O*, (n 23) the sheriff was not satisfied as to the pursuers' intention to occupy the house as a home, and therefore found that ground 1(b) was not established.

26 *Kennealy v Dunne* [1977] QB 837.

27 *Naish v Curzon* (n 24); *Davies v Peterson* (1989) 21 HLR 63, [1989] 06 EG 130.

28 *Baker v Lewis* [1947] KB 186; *Amaddio v Dalton* (1991) 23 HLR 332.

29 *Mansukhani v Stanley* The Times, 17 April 1992.

tenant agrees to leave). A decree under the 1970 Act against the debtor is not a warrant for the ejection of the tenant.[30]

Where consent to the lease was not obtained, that will almost certainly be a breach of the conditions of the mortgage.[31] In that case, the creditor may seek reduction of the lease.[32] However, there are problems with that course of action, in relation to an assured tenancy of residential property. First, the lease is only voidable at the instance of the creditor, rather than void.[33] Consequently, reduction of the lease simply has the effect of terminating the tenancy, such that it then becomes a statutory assured tenancy, under section 16 of the 1988 Act.[34] In that case, the lender is still required to raise proceedings under the 1988 Act. Secondly, a reduction action might have to be raised in the Court of Session,[35] with the attendant expense and delay, in comparison with proceedings in the FTT.

Consequently, in practice, lenders prefer to proceed under the 1988 Act because that is cheaper and quicker than an action for reduction. In any event, where the lender has consented to the lease, as part of a buy-to-let mortgage or otherwise, there is no ground for reduction, and an application under the 1988 Act will be the only option available to the lender, if it wishes to eject the tenant and sell the subjects with vacant possession.

Terminating the tenancy contract (first stage)

In theory,[36] the process of evicting the tenant usually runs in two stages. First, the contractual tenancy must be terminated, unless such termination has already taken place,[37] or the terms of the tenancy contract are such as to

30 1970 Act s 24(10); Heritable Securities (Scotland) Act 1894 s 5A(8); Bankruptcy and Diligence etc. (Scotland) Act 2007 s 216(2A). These provisions were inserted by Housing (Scotland) Act 2010 s 152. This effectively codifies the decision in *Tamroui v Clydesdale Bank plc* 1997 SLT (Sh Ct) 20.

31 Consent for letting the subjects is required under standard condition 6 of sch 3 to the 1970 Act. The standard conditions may be varied; but it is highly unlikely that a commercial lender would vary standard condition 6 to allow letting without consent.

32 *Trade Development Bank v Warriner & Mason (Scotland) Ltd* 1980 SC 74, 1980 SLT 223 and *Trade Development Bank v David W Haig (Bellshill) Ltd* 1983 SLT 510.

33 *Trade Development Bank v Warriner and Mason (Scotland) Ltd* (n 32), 101 (Lord Cameron).

34 *Govanhill Housing Association Ltd v Palmer* 1998 SLT 887. Section 16 is discussed in Chapter 7. If the lender could demonstrate that the lease was void, there would be no tenancy at all, and therefore no assured tenancy. A declarator to that effect would mean that the lender could simply enforce its decree under the 1970 Act, without the necessity for further proceedings.

35 Since 1 April 2015, the sheriff court has had competence to entertain proceedings for reduction, under s 38 of the Courts Reform (Scotland) Act 2014. However, under s 16 of the 2014 Act, the jurisdiction and functions of sheriff in relation to actions arising from assured tenancies were transferred to the FTT. It is questionable whether the FTT has jurisdiction to reduce a lease. The decision of the Upper Tribunal in *Watt v Chesnutt Skeoch Ltd* UTS/AP/19/0032 28/11/19 appears to indicate that the FTT has jurisdiction to reduce leases, but leaves open the question of how that might be done. There is currently no indication in the Procedure Rules (n 2) that reduction is possible.

36 "In theory" because, in practice, in the ground 2 cases decided by the tribunal so far, the potential difficulty faced by lenders in terminating a contractual tenancy has not arisen for discussion, perhaps because the applications are not opposed, or because the decision in *GE Money Home Lending Ltd v Bianchet*, an unreported decision of Sheriff Principal Kerr at Dumbarton, dated 17 July 2014, is not widely known.

37 It may be the case that, for whatever reason, the debtor/landlord has already terminated the lease contract, such that the tenant occupies under a statutory assured tenancy, in terms of

enable the creditor to utilise section 18(6) of the Act.[38] However, the termination of the tenancy is potentially problematic for the creditor, though, until quite recently, that does not seem to have been appreciated. The difficulty lies with section 20(5) of the 1970 Act, which states:

> "(5) There shall be deemed to be assigned to a creditor who is in lawful possession of the security subjects all rights and obligations of the proprietor relating to—
> (a) leases, or any permission or right of occupancy, granted in respect of those subjects or any part thereof".[39]

It is under this provision that the creditor can acquire the landlord's right to serve a notice to quit,[40] thereby terminating the tenancy contract. The problem is this: where there is a sitting tenant in occupation, how does the creditor achieve the status of being "in lawful possession"?

Under the common law, possession is a question of fact, and may be actual[41] (as in the physical detention or occupation of the thing possessed), or civil (where a person possesses through those who hold actual or natural possession). A landlord has civil possession though the actual possession of his tenants.[42] A heritable creditor repossessing and selling subjects under the 1970 Act would not normally have possession in either of those senses. Most creditors will be corporate entities, and therefore incapable of actual possession of heritable property. Civil possession is possible through the actual possession of a person such as an employee. However, in the vast majority of cases, the creditor does not arrange for such possession to take place. In any event, it would not normally be appropriate for the creditor to take natural possession (if he was a natural person) or to take civil possession, through a natural person such as an employee, given the nature of the rights of the creditor.[43]

That was presumably known to the drafters of the 1970 Act, and it is suggested that, by "possession" in section 20(5)(a), the legislature meant something other than actual possession or civil possession. What it did mean, however, is not clear.[44] This issue came to a head in *GE Money Home Lending*

s 16 of the Act. In that case, termination of the contract by the lender, by service of a notice to quit or otherwise, is unnecessary. The lender can proceed to the second stage.

38 Considered in Chapter 7. In cases in which the let has taken place without the lender's consent, the agreement does not usually contain the necessary term to enable s 18(6) to be utilised.

39 Similar provision is made in standard condition 10(5) of sch 3: "Where [the creditor] has *entered into possession* . . . there shall be transferred to him all the rights of the debtor in relation to the granting of leases or rights of occupancy over the security subjects and to the management and maintenance of those subjects." As with s 20(5)(a), there is an issue as to how the creditor achieves "possession", given that there is a tenant in occupation.

40 Or a notice terminating the tenancy under an irritancy or break clause, for example. For the various ways in which the landlord might terminate the lease as a precursor to eviction proceedings, see Chapter 3.

41 Sometimes referred to as "natural" possession.

42 Gloag and Henderson, *The Law of Scotland* (14th edn) para 34.34. See also the discussion of possession in Johnston, *Prescription and Limitation* (2nd edn) ch 18.

43 See Gloag and Irvine, *Rights in Security* (1897) 100. In essence, the right of the creditor is to obtain payment of the debt out of the proceeds of the subjects. It is not entitled to use the subjects for its own convenience or enjoyment in any manner that has no effect in reducing the debt.

44 See the discussion of this issue in Cusine and Rennie, *Standard Securities* paras 8.66 to 8.72, and in Higgins, *The Enforcement of Heritable Securities* (2nd edn) para 13.4. There is some

Ltd v Bianchet.[45] In that case the pursuers obtained a decree against the debtor under the 1970 Act in relation to subjects that he had let to the defender under an assured tenancy. It then sought to enter into "possession" of the subjects under section 20(5)(a), so far as that was possible, by first intimating on the tenant its intention to exercise the rights of the landlord under that provision, and secondly changing the locks (while giving a set of keys to the tenant) so as to secure the property against entry by the debtor, or any person other than the creditor and the tenant. Thereafter, it purported to serve a notice to quit on the tenant terminating the tenancy and, following service of an AT6, it raised proceedings under the 1988 Act. The pursuers succeeded before the sheriff, but lost on appeal before Sheriff Principal Kerr, who said:

> "[4] It was submitted . . . for the respondents that a changing of the locks was enough and that section 20(5)(a) clearly by its wording envisaged the possibility of a creditor being in lawful possession of the security subjects at the same time as a tenant within them was in actual possession and the two possessions were not mutually exclusive. A creditor in other words might not be able to enter into actual possession/occupation but he could nevertheless still have lawful possession even if someone else enjoyed natural possession. That in my opinion can only happen if the tenant within the subjects becomes by some means the tenant or representative in the subjects of the heritable creditor (such as by virtue of some agreement reached between them). Otherwise, if the tenant within remains a person whose right to be there derives from another source such as the defaulting debtor, the natural possession of the tenant indeed precludes the possibility of the creditor assuming lawful possession as required by section 20(5)(a) of the 1970 Act."

Accordingly, the Sheriff Principal held that the pursuers were not entitled to serve a notice to quit, and their action fell to be dismissed.

Clearly this decision poses a substantial problem for any heritable creditor seeking to eject an assured tenant of the debtor,[46] so as to realise its security by selling the subjects with vacant possession. If the decision in *Bianchet*[47] is correct, it may be difficult for the lender to proceed under the 1988 Act, if the tenancy contract between the landlord/debtor and the tenant is still ongoing, at the point when lender wishes to enforce its security.

consensus in these works that there is a distinction to be drawn between (a) simply changing the locks of a property vacated by the debtor and proceeding to sell the subjects, and (b) entering "into possession", which requires at least some degree of management of the subjects. That would appear to be consistent with standard condition 10, in which the powers of the creditor to "(2) . . . proceed to sell the security subjects . . . (3) . . . enter into possession of the security subjects and may receive or recover the rents of those subjects or any part thereof" seem to be alternatives.

45 (n 36).

46 If the decision is correct. In an application under s 38 of the Sheriff Courts (Scotland) Act 1971, the pursuers were able to persuade the sheriff principal that the case was suitable for appeal to the Court of Session, by reference to proposed grounds for appeal. However, the appeal was not pursued. It is possible that Sheriff Principal Kerr's decision may be critically examined in future cases.

47 n 36.

An action under section 18(3) (second stage)

The second stage in the process of the lender securing the eviction of the tenant is an action under section 18(3) of the 1988 Act, which relies upon ground 2 or any other applicable ground. Here, the problem posed by section 20(5)(a), and the decision in *Bianchet*,[48] is overcome by the extended definition of "landlord" in section 55 of the 1988 Act, which:

> "includes any person from time to time deriving title from the original landlord and also includes, in relation to a house, any person other than a tenant who is, or but for the existence of an assured tenancy would be, entitled to possession of the house".

Under this definition, a heritable creditor holding a decree under the 1970 Act, entitling it to enter into possession, is a "landlord" for the purposes of sections 18 and 19 of the Act. It may accordingly serve an AT6, and raise proceedings seeking an order under ground 2 and section 18(3). If other grounds apply, there is no reason why the creditor could not also include those in the AT6, and seek decree on those grounds as well, under s 18(3) and (4).

If the creditor is not the assignee of the borrower's rights as landlord, then, as already described, it may not be able to get past stage 1: termination of the tenancy contract. However, that would not be an issue if the borrower had already terminated the tenancy, giving rise to a statutory assured tenancy under section 16, or where section 18(6) applies.[49]

Establishing ground 2

As is the case in relation to ground 1, notice must have been given to the tenant that this was to be a ground under which possession might be recovered, but the tribunal may also dispense with the requirement for this notice if it considers it reasonable to do so. It is again suggested (as with ground 1) that this would allow the tribunal to consider all the circumstances in the case, not simply those surrounding the issue of why notice was not given. In cases in which the heritable creditor was never notified of the lease being granted by its borrower,[50] and therefore had no control over whether notice was given to the tenant by the borrower/landlord that possession might be sought under ground 2, there must be a fairly strong argument in favour of dispensing with the notice, as failure to serve it was not due to any fault on the part of the heritable creditor.

Ground 2 applies only where the house is subject to a heritable security granted before the creation of the tenancy. Where the security is granted after creation of the tenancy, the creditor will have to rely on other grounds in schedule 5, or perhaps an action under section 33.[51]

48 ibid.

49 In which case, a decree may be granted under s 18, notwithstanding the fact that the contractual tenancy is still ongoing. See the discussion of s 18(6) in Chapter 7.

50 Which would have been a breach of standard condition 6 of sch 3 to the 1970 Act.

51 In any case, however, the heritable creditor would still have get through the first stage, by terminating the tenancy contract, unless it had already been terminated, or the terms of the tenancy contract are such as to enable the creditor to utilise s 18(6).

Importance of continuing in occupation

The lender already has a decree entitling it to take possession under the 1970 Act. It is only if the house is let on an assured tenancy that it is prevented from enforcing that decree. Therefore, it is as well to bear in mind that, under section 12 of the 1988 Act, "A tenancy under which a house is let . . . is for the purposes of this Act an assured tenancy if and so long as . . . the tenant or, as the case may be, at least one of the joint tenants occupies the house as his only or principal home".

The effect of the words "if and so long as" is that the tenancy may be assured at its commencement, but cease to be assured at some later stage where the tenant is no longer occupying it as his only or principal home. Similarly, a statutory assured tenancy under section 16 continues only as long as the tenant "retains possession".[52]

It follows that if the property has been abandoned by the tenant, the lender may simply enforce its decree under the 1970 Act.

Requirement to include calling-up notice to occupier

As a result of amendments made to the Procedure Rules,[53] rules 65, 66 and 109 now impose a requirement that an application for an order for possession under section 18 or section 33 of the 1988 Act, or an eviction order under section 51 of the 2016 Act, should "be accompanied by . . . a copy of Form BB (notice to the occupier) under schedule 6 of the Conveyancing and Feudal Reform (Scotland) Act 1970 (if applicable)".[54]

Ground 3: holiday letting

> "The house is let under a tenancy for a specified period not exceeding eight months and—
> (a) not later than the date of commencement of the tenancy the landlord (or, where there are joint landlords, any of them) gave notice in writing to the tenant that possession might be recovered under this Ground; and
> (b) the house was, at some time within the period of 12 months ending on that date, occupied under a right to occupy it for a holiday;
>
> and for the purposes of this Ground a tenancy shall be treated as being for a specified period—
> (i) not exceeding eight months, if it is determinable at the option of the landlord (other than in the event of an irritancy being incurred) before the

52 For "only or principal home" and "retains possession", see Chapter 1.

53 By r 2 of the First-tier Tribunal for Scotland Housing and Property Chamber (Procedure) Amendment Regulations 2018 (SSI 2018/378).

54 Rules 65(b)(vi), 66(b)(vi) and 109(b)(iv). It is not clear why these amendments were made. Service of a form BB is a requirement of s 19A of the 1970 Act. It is a notice addressed to "the occupier" of residential subjects, when the lender is calling up. If it is not served, the calling-up notice is of no effect: s 19A(3). In that case, there is no default under standard condition 9(1)(a), and the lender's application to the sheriff, under s 24 of the 1970 Act, is liable to be refused. Thus, the proper service of the form BB is a matter for the sheriff. If she has granted a decree under s 24, it is to be assumed that the process of calling up has been carried out as required by the 1970 Act. Where an application is made by a lender for an order r 65, r 66 or r 109, which includes a copy of the decree granted in its favour under the 1970 Act, it is not clear why the tribunal has any interest in seeing the form BB.

expiration of eight months from the commencement of the period of the tenancy; and

(ii) exceeding eight months, if it confers on the tenant an option for renewal of the tenancy for a period which, together with the original period, exceeds eight months, and it is not determinable as mentioned in paragraph (i) above."

The purpose of ground 3 is to enable landlords to let, "off season", premises that are used for holiday letting during a particular period of the year.[55] In contrast to grounds 1 and 2, the tribunal has no power to dispense with the requirement to serve a notice in terms of condition (a) of the ground.

Clause (b) of the ground requires that the landlord is able to demonstrate that the property has been used for holiday letting within the period of twelve months before commencement of the current tenancy. That would normally be done by the production of a holiday letting agreement.

Under clause (b)(i), the tenancy will be treated as not exceeding the maximum period (eight months) if there is a break clause in favour of the landlord, in terms of which he may terminate the tenancy before expiry of the eight-month period since the beginning of the tenancy. However, under clause (b)(ii), the lease will be taken to exceed the eight-month period if the tenant has an option of renewal, such that the original term, together with the extra period resulting from the tenant's exercising the option of renewal, exceeds eight months. Neither of these clauses makes any reference to the possibility of tacit relocation. Therefore, it is to be assumed that where conditions (a) and (b) are met, and the tenancy for, say, four months relocates on a number of occasions, the mandatory ground 3 will still be available to the landlord.

Ground 4

"Where the house is let under a tenancy for a specified period not exceeding 12 months and—

(a) not later than the date of commencement of the tenancy the landlord (or, where there are joint landlords, any of them) gave notice in writing to the tenant that possession might be recovered on this Ground; and

(b) at some time within the period of 12 months ending on that date the house was subject to such a tenancy as is referred to in paragraph 7(1) of Schedule 4 to this Act;

and for the purposes of this Ground a tenancy shall be treated as being for a specified period—

(i) not exceeding 12 months, if it is determinable at the option of the landlord (other than in the event of an irritancy being incurred) before the expiration of 12 months from the commencement of the period of the tenancy; and

(ii) exceeding 12 months, if it confers on the tenant an option for renewal of the tenancy for a period which, together with the original period, exceeds 12 months, and it is not determinable as mentioned in paragraph (i) above."

Ground 4 is very similar to ground 3. A tenancy "as is referred to in paragraph 7(1) of schedule 4" is a tenancy let by a specified educational institution. That type of tenancy is excepted from assured tenancy status. Ground 4 applies to a

55 So, ground 3 would normally apply to a property let over the winter, which is subject to holiday letting during the summer season. A holiday let during the season would be excepted from assured tenancy status in terms of sch 4 para 8 to the Act: see p 226.

tenancy of a house that was, within the last twelve months, let under a tenancy to which paragraph 7 of schedule 4 applies. Again, the tribunal has no power to dispense with the requirement for notice.

Ground 5: minister or lay missionary property

"The house is held for the purpose of being available for occupation by a minister or a full-time lay missionary of any religious denomination as a residence from which to perform the duties of his office and—

(a) not later than the beginning of the tenancy the landlord (or, where there are joint landlords, any of them) gave notice in writing to the tenant that possession might be recovered on this ground; and

(b) the First-tier Tribunal is satisfied that the house is required for occupation by such a minister or missionary as such a residence."

This ground is self-explanatory. As with grounds 3 and 4, the tribunal has no power to dispense with the requirement for the notice, which the landlord requires to serve before the commencement of the tenancy.[56]

Ground 6: demolition or reconstruction work

"The landlord who is seeking possession or, where the immediate landlord is a registered housing association within the meaning of the Housing Associations Act 1985,[57] a superior landlord intends to demolish or reconstruct the whole or a substantial part of the house or to carry out substantial works on the house or any part thereof or any building of which it forms part and the following conditions are fulfilled (and in those conditions the landlord who is intending to carry out the demolition, reconstruction or substantial works is referred to as 'the relevant landlord')—

(a) either—

(i) the relevant landlord (or, in the case of joint relevant landlords, any one of them) acquired his interest in the house before the creation of the tenancy; or

(ii) none of the following persons acquired his interest in the house for value—

(A) the relevant landlord (or, in the case of joint relevant landlords, any one of them);

(B) the immediate landlord (or, in the case of joint immediate landlords, any one of them), where he acquired his interest after the creation of the tenancy;

(C) any person from whom the relevant landlord (or any one of joint relevant landlords) derives title and who acquired his interest in the house after the creation of the tenancy; and

(b) the relevant landlord cannot reasonably carry out the intended work without the tenant giving up possession of the house because—

(i) the work can otherwise be carried out only if the tenant accepts a variation in the terms of the tenancy and the tenant refuses to do so;

(ii) the work can otherwise be carried out only if the tenant accepts an assured tenancy of part of the house and the tenant refuses to do so; or

56 For a rare example of an order for possession granted under ground 5, see *Church of Scotland General Trustees v Kearns* EV/18/2040, 16/10/18.

57 The application of this ground to registered housing associations has been superseded by the 2001 Act s 11 in terms of which their assured tenancies under the 1988 Act become Scottish secure tenancies at the date when that section came into force: 30 September 2002.

(iii) the work can otherwise be carried out only if the tenant accepts either a variation in the terms of the tenancy or an assured tenancy of part of the house or both, and the tenant refuses to do so; or

(iv) the work cannot otherwise be carried out even if the tenant accepts a variation in the terms of the tenancy or an assured tenancy of only part of the house or both."

The landlord must show that he *intends* to demolish, reconstruct[58] or carry out substantial work. The landlord must also be in a position to satisfy the tribunal that the intention will be fulfilled shortly after the date of the hearing.[59] This in turn entails both a genuine desire to carry out the work, and a reasonable prospect of actually bringing about that result, such that the landlord has an intention rather than a mere aspiration.[60] Thus, where the landlord had failed to show that she had the means and ability to carry out the development that she proposed, the court took the view that she had not established intention for the purposes of the statutory ground.[61] Accordingly, evidence as to the existence of planning permission, the necessary financial backing, arrangements regarding contractors, architectural drawings and so on, will tend to bolster the landlord's case.[62]

Ground 6 bears some similarity to ground 1, in that it is not available to a person who has purchased the landlord's interest after the creation of the tenancy. However, in this case the prohibition is more extensive: ground 6 is not available where the immediate landlord or the landlord from whom the relevant landlord derived his title purchased the landlord's interest for value. If the ground were not so extended, the prohibition could be avoided by the landlord transferring title, say, to a limited company, for no consideration. The "immediate landlord" is presumably the landlord at the present time, as opposed to the "relevant landlord", who is the person proposing to carry out the work, and to whom the landlord's interest will be transferred, in the event that the action is successful.[63]

58 "Reconstruction" – a substantial interference with the structure of the premises and then a rebuilding, in probably a different form, of such part of the premises as has been demolished by reason of the interference with the structure: *Joel v Swaddle* [1957] 1 WLR 1094. See also *Barth v Pritchard* [1990] 20 EG 65 and *Cook v Mott* (1961) 178 EG 637.

59 *Betty's Cafés Ltd v Phillips Furnishing Stores Ltd (No 1)* [1959] AC 20.

60 The concept of "intention" in statutory grounds for eviction is more fully discussed in Chapter 10. The phrase, "the landlord intends" has particular significance under the 2016 Act, because it occurs in several of the grounds in sch 3 pt 1.

61 *Edwards v Thompson* [1990] 29 EG 41. See also *Capocci v Goble* (1987) 284 EG 230. On the difference between intention and mere contemplation (though in the social rented sector), see *City of Edinburgh Council v Middlemiss* 2007 Hous LR 70, a case under the 2001 Act, in which the sheriff placed particular reliance on being satisfied that the funding for the work was available.

62 In *Josephine Marshall Trust v Charlton* [2019] UT 40 the Upper Tribunal decided that the landlord was not precluded from having an intention to demolish the property, by the existence of a repairing standard enforcement order, requiring certain repairs to be carried out at the property, under s 24 of the Housing (Scotland) Act 2006. This decision was affirmed on appeal by the Inner House: 2020 SLT 409. Another example of a successful application under ground 6 is *Cowie v Nicol* EV/18/1796, 11/10/18.

63 Thus the "relevant landlord" might be more accurately termed the "relevant prospective landlord".

In order to establish ground 6, the landlord must also satisfy the tribunal that condition (b) is met. As with ground 10[64] under schedule 2 to the 2001 Act, "possession" means full legal possession. The landlord must be able to show that the termination of the tenancy and full possession of the property are necessary in order to carry out the work in question, and that mere access to, or temporary occupation of, the premises is insufficient.[65] Thus, as with ground 10, the landlord must be able to show that decanting the tenant until such time as the work is complete is not feasible. Moreover, subparagraphs (b)(i)–(iv) of ground 6 provide that the landlord must also establish that the work could not be carried out even if the tenant's rights were reduced by way of variation of the tenancy contract, or by the grant of an assured tenancy for part of the subjects in question, or that he has offered such a variation or grant, which has been refused.

Under section 22 of the Act, where the tribunal makes an order for possession on ground 6 the landlord must pay to the tenant a sum equal to the reasonable expenses likely to be incurred by the tenant in removing from the house. Any question as to the amount payable is to be determined by agreement between the landlord and the tenant or, in default of agreement, by the tribunal.[66]

Ground 7: inherited property

> "The tenancy has devolved under the will or intestacy of the former tenant and the proceedings for the recovery of possession are begun not later than twelve months after the death of the former tenant or, if the First-tier Tribunal so directs, after the date on which, in its opinion, the landlord (or, where there are joint landlords, any of them) became aware of the former tenant's death. For the purposes of this Ground, the acceptance by the landlord of rent from a new tenant after the death of the former tenant shall not be regarded as creating a new tenancy, unless the landlord agrees in writing to a change (as compared with the tenancy before the death) in the amount of the rent, the period of the tenancy, the premises which are let or any other term of the tenancy."

Ground 7 requires to be considered along with sections 31 and 31A of the Act, which are discussed in Chapter 12. In terms of section 31 ("right of succession of spouse or civil partner") the tenant's spouse, cohabitee or civil partner became the statutory assured tenant on the death of the tenant, subject to certain conditions. Under section 31A, the right of succession is to a private residential tenancy ("PRT") under the 2016 Act (rather than a statutory assured tenancy), if the tenant died on or after 1 December 2017.

Under section 31(3), ground 7 cannot be used where: (a) the tenant's spouse, cohabitee or civil partner succeeds under section 31(1); or (b) the ten-

64 The "demolition or substantial works" ground in relation to Scottish secure tenancies. Reference is made to the commentary in relation to that ground.

65 See, e.g., *Heath v Drown* [1973] AC 498, a case under the Landlord and Tenant Act 1954, s 30(1)(f), which allows landlords of business tenants (in England and Wales) to oppose the grant of a new tenancy on a ground that is relevantly similar to ground 6. In that case, the tenant was successful even though the front wall of the premises had to be entirely rebuilt and it was not possible to occupy the subjects while the work was being carried out.

66 Under r 67 of the Procedure Rules (n 2), either the landlord or the tenant may make an application to the tribunal to determine the amount, where the parties cannot agree.

ant's spouse or civil partner succeeds to the tenancy under the will or intestacy of the tenant.[67] In any other case, where the tenancy has devolved under the will or intestacy of the tenant, the landlord may seek an order under ground 7 within twelve months of the date of death, or the date on which, in the opinion of the tribunal, the landlord became aware that the tenant had died. The landlord can continue to accept rent during this period without prejudicing his position, but any change in the tenancy conditions during that period, such as an increase in rent, precludes the use of ground 7. Presumably this is because a change in the essential terms of the agreement as to rent, subjects or duration is to be regarded as, in effect, constituting a new agreement between the landlord and the successor, rather than a continuation of the previous tenancy.

Ground 8: rent arrears

> "Both at the date of the service of the notice under section 19 of this Act relating to the proceedings for possession and at the date of the hearing or the date of the case management discussion, whichever is the earlier, at least three months rent lawfully due from the tenant is in arrears."[68]

This ground, one of three distinct grounds for recovery of possession on the basis of rent arrears, is the most commonly used of all the grounds in schedule 5.[69] The landlord must be able to show that the arrears of the required amount were outstanding both on the date when the section 19 notice was served and at the date of the hearing at which the decree is sought. This is why the tribunal has no power to dispense with the requirement for an AT6 notice in relation to ground 8.[70]

As with the other mandatory grounds, there is no requirement to show that it is reasonable to grant decree for possession and one would expect that the order will be sought and obtained, at the first hearing of the case before the FTT. This will be the CMD: it is the practice of the Housing and Property Chamber to fix CMDs in eviction cases.[71] There was previously some doubt as to whether a CMD was a "hearing" for the purposes of ground 8. That doubt was removed by the amendment of the ground to include the words "or the date of the case management discussion, whichever is the earlier".[72]

Although ground 8 is mandatory, there are possible defences open to the tenant.[73] Because three months' rent arrears must be due both at the date of

67 Section 31(3)(b) could apply where the conditions of s 31(1) were not met – say, where the deceased tenant was himself a successor.

68 The terms "rent" and "lawfully due" are considered in Chapter 5.

69 See the discussion of the frequency of use of the grounds, at the beginning of this chapter.

70 Section 19(5). This is one reason why it is prudent to rely on grounds 11 and 12, in combination with ground 8. If there is a problem with the AT6, the landlord can ask the tribunal to dispense with the requirement for the notice and consider the case on grounds 11 and 12.

71 CMDs are subject to r 17 of the Procedure Rules (n 2); by r 17(4), the tribunal may do anything at a CMD that it may do at a hearing, including making a decision. See Chapter 14.

72 By reg 4 of the First-tier Tribunal for Scotland Housing and Property Chamber (Incidental Provisions) Regulations 2019 (SSI 2019/51).

73 In addition to the possible defences outlined, the tenant may contend that the landlord has failed to serve the requisite notices prior to the commencement of proceedings. Ground 8 is a ground to which s 18(6) does apply. For a case in which the landlord sought decree under ground 8, but failed because the notice to quit was invalid, and s 18(6) did not apply, see *Royal Bank of Scotland v Boyle* 1999 Hous LR 43 and 63, which is discussed in detail in Chapter 7.

service of the AT6 notice and at the date of the CMD or hearing, the tenant may avoid ground 8 by paying a sum of money to the landlord that is sufficient to reduce the outstanding balance to a sum less than three months' arrears. In that case, the application to the tribunal would fail, unless the landlord has sought decree for possession on some other ground. This is the reason why the prudent landlord seeks possession on grounds 11 and 12, as well as ground 8; those grounds will still be available if the tenant makes a payment to reduce the balance to an amount at which ground 8 is no longer available.[74]

Due to amendments made to sections 18 and 20 of the 1988 Act by section 12 of the Homelessness etc. (Scotland) Act 2003, the tribunal has discretion not to make an order for possession under ground 8 in circumstances where the rent arrears are a consequence of a delay or failure in the payment of housing benefit or universal credit. However, for the purposes of the amended provisions, references to delay or failure in payment of benefit do not include such delay or failure so far as referable to any act or omission of the tenant. The various causes of delay or non-payment of housing benefit or universal credit are discussed in Chapter 5.[75] Clearly these provisions could, in theory, lead to situations in which there may be a dispute between the parties as to the cause of the delay or non-payment of benefits, which may require to be resolved by a further hearing at which the tribunal would hear evidence.[76] Also, the terms of section 20(6) of the 1988 Act are amended with the effect that the tribunal may adjourn or suspend ground 8 cases in which the rent arrears are due to non-payment of housing benefit or universal credit. It is suggested that this may be appropriate where the tenant has appealed against a decision in terms of which benefit has been refused, and his appeal has not yet been determined.

Certain of the foregoing points are illustrated by the decision of the Court of Appeal in *North British Housing Association Ltd v Matthews*.[77] In each of the four appeals before the court, the tenant had owed at least eight weeks' rent at the date on which the proceedings came before the district judge, so that, on the face of it, the judge was obliged to make an order for possession. Each tenant made an application for an adjournment in order to give them time to obtain the money to pay the arrears or bring them below the eight-week threshold and thereby defeat the claim for possession. Each tenant contended that the inability to pay their rent had been caused by maladministration or other

74 Of course, the tenant may also dispute whether she owed as much as three months' rent, at the date of service of the AT6, or the CMD. If the tribunal agrees, the application will fall to be dismissed if only ground 8 has been relied upon. For an example, see *Lumsden v Fraser* EV/18/3162, 7/8/19.

75 At p 155.

76 Although, to the author's knowledge, this has not happened. There appears to be no published decision, whether of the sheriff court (prior to the transfer of jurisdiction), or the FTT, in which a tenant has successfully relied upon the argument that arrears are a consequence of a delay or failure in the payment of housing benefit or universal credit. In fact, it is unusual for applications under ground 8 to be defended at all.

77 [2005] 1 WLR 3133, [2005] HLR 17. This was a decision in which the court considered four separate appeals by tenants of housing associations, in actions raised under ground 8 (of sch 2 to the Housing Act 1988). Note that, under the English legislation: housing associations still operate under the assured tenancies regime; the Housing Act 1996 amended ground 8 such that "three months" became "two months" (or eight weeks, if the rent was payable weekly); and there is no equivalent to s 18(3A) in the Scottish Act, which allows the tribunal to refuse to grant an order, if the arrears are due to delay in the payment of housing benefit or universal credit.

unjustified failures by the housing benefit authorities to pay housing benefit. In each case the district judge refused to grant the adjournment and made an order for possession. Dismissing the appeals, the Court of Appeal held that the court's discretion to grant an adjournment should be exercised justly and not for the purpose of defeating the policy of the 1988 Act or the rights that it conferred on landlords. The court had power, to be exercised in exceptional circumstances only, to adjourn possession proceedings for the purpose of enabling the tenant to reduce his arrears to below the threshold provided by ground 8, but the fact that the arrears were attributable to maladministration on the part of the housing benefit authorities was not an exceptional circumstance.[78] Examples of exceptional circumstances given by the court were: (a) where the tenant was on his way to court with the cash to pay the arrears, but was robbed; or (b) the housing benefit authority had promised to pay all the arrears of housing benefit, but a computer failure prevented it from being able to do so until the day after the hearing date. These are circumstances in which the refusal of an adjournment "would be considered to be outrageously unjust by any fair-minded person".

In *Coltrane v Day*,[79] the Court of Appeal considered the procedure that would be appropriate should the tenant attend court on the day of the hearing with a cheque for payment of the arrears. The court decided that an uncleared cheque delivered to the landlord at or before the hearing, which is accepted by him, or which he is bound by earlier agreement to accept, is to be treated as payment at the date of delivery provided that the cheque is subsequently paid on first presentation. In that case, a short adjournment may well be appropriate, in order to establish whether the cheque will clear. If the cheque is not paid on first presentation, decree should be granted at the adjourned hearing. That said, however, the judge at first instance is not bound to adjourn the case if he has reason to conclude that the cheque will not be paid. Therefore, the tenant should be in a position to produce evidence to confirm that there are funds to meet the cheque, and that it will be honoured on presentation.

Withholding rent, abatement, damages

Reference is made to the discussion, in Chapter 5, of cases in which the tenant maintains that rent is not lawfully due, and seeks to withhold the rent, and/or an abatement of the rent, or damages for losses he has suffered, which he proposes to set off against a liability for rent.[80] The authorities indicate that retention of rent is an equitable remedy, "controlled by the Court and regulated by reference to equitable considerations in the light of the circumstances of each case". That function may also be exercised by the tribunal.[81] However, the extent to which the remedy is available to a tenant under the 1988 Act, in the context of tribunal proceedings, is a difficult issue.

78 The court accepted that the statutory scheme was therefore "potentially draconian in its application". However, as indicated above, this is alleviated somewhat, in the Scottish legislation, by s 18(3A).

79 [2003] EWCA Civ 342, [2003] 1 WLR 1379.

80 See pp 128–132.

81 Because, under s 16 of the 2014 Act, "the functions and jurisdiction of the sheriff in relation to actions arising from [assured tenancies] are transferred to the First-tier Tribunal".

As will be explained in Chapter 14, the Housing and Property Chamber treats applications for an eviction order under section 18 of the 1988 Act, and for a payment order for rent arrears, as separate applications, under rules 65 and 70 respectively. These applications will normally be considered together at a CMD, at which the landlord is seeking an order under ground 8 and also grounds 11 and 12.

In order to avoid an order for possession being granted under ground 8 in the rule 65 application, the tenant will have to be in a position to assert that he is exercising an equitable right of retention in respect of the rental payments that would otherwise have been due,[82] until such time as repairs are effected by the landlord. This would have to be in respect of repairs that are more than trivial. Also, the tribunal would have to be satisfied that, in refusing to pay the rent, the tenant is acting in good faith and genuinely exercising the remedy of retention.[83] If the repairs have been effected, the tenant would need to assert that his right to an abatement of the rent, and/or damages, is such that the rent lawfully due is less than three months' rent. Otherwise, the tribunal may grant the order for possession.

Furthermore, in *Stobbs & Son v Hislop*,[84] the court decided that the right to withhold rent does not apply to a statutory tenancy under the Rent Acts, which is broadly equivalent to a statutory assured tenancy under section 16 of the 1988 Act. That is because the equitable remedy of retention of rent is not a "term" or "condition" of the tenancy, and so is not one of the rights available to a statutory tenant once the contractual tenancy has ended.[85] Therefore, the landlord may deprive the tenant of that remedy by termination of the lease. Where the lease is ongoing, the tenant will still be able to withhold rent.[86]

Where the tenant's complaint is that the landlord has failed to comply with the statutory repairing obligations set out in sections 13 and 14 of the Housing (Scotland) Act 2006, it is suggested that the common law remedies of withholding rent, abatement and damages have no application. That is because the 2006 Act provides its own remedy for breach of the repairing standard: an application by the tenant to the FTT under section 22. Under section 27, a "rent relief order" may be made (for up to 90 per cent) of the rent, where it is determined by the tribunal that the landlord has failed to comply with the repairing standard. That would appear to supersede the right to seek an abatement.[87]

82 Or, at least, enough of the rental payments to enable him to say that the amount left, apart from the sum lawfully retained, is less than three months' rent.

83 As is explained in Chapter 5, that may be difficult, if there is no evidence that the tenant has ever asserted a right to withhold rent, or that the unpaid rent has actually been retained, say in a bank account.

84 1948 SC 216.

85 Under s 16(1)(b) of the 1988 Act, following termination of the contractual tenancy the tenant remaining in possession "entitled to the benefits of all the terms and conditions of the original contract of tenancy". The same wording was used in the statutory provision under consideration in *Stobbs v Hislop* (n 84); the court decided that the statutory tenant had no right of retention. Both Rennie, *Leases* (para 17-56) and Robson (para 4-23) question whether *Stobbs v Hislop* is applicable to tenancies under the more recent legislation. But, it is suggested that this part of the judgment is applicable to the interpretation of s 16(1)(b).

86 Hence the decision in *MacLeod v Alexander* 2000 Hous LR 136, in which the parties' contract was apparently still continuing.

87 Of course, the tenant may seek also seek an abatement if she is relying on the repairing obliga-

However, the 2006 Act does not displace the contractual repairing obligations that are implied at common law,[88] or any such obligations that are expressly set out in the parties' contract.[89] Where the landlord is in breach of those obligations, there seems to be no reason why the tenant cannot insist on the right to withhold rent, and thereafter to claim an abatement and damages, as described in Chapter 5, subject to the tribunal's equitable jurisdiction, already described.[90]

The tribunal has accordingly allowed applications under the rent arrears grounds to be defended, on the basis that the rent is being withheld or should be abated due to disrepair. It has fixed hearings in order for that defence to be heard. However, in practice the defence has not been successful, because the respondent has not led evidence in support of that defence, at the hearing.[91]

Consumer Protection from Unfair Trading Regulations 2008 pt 4A

The tenant under an assured or a short assured tenancy may have a right to seek a discount, or damages, in terms of part 4A of the Consumer Protection from Unfair Trading Regulations 2008.[92] "Consumers' Rights to Redress" under part 4A are likely to have application where the tenant is a consumer who, when entering into the lease, dealt with a landlord or letting agent acting in the course of a business,[93] this being an example of a "business to consumer

tions implied by common law, or which are contained in the parties' contract. However, that would seem to be a less effective remedy than an application to the FTT under the 2006 Act, which is much more likely to compel the landlord to carry out repairs. Where an application *has* been made to the FTT under the 2006 Act, and no abatement of rent has been ordered, that may also adversely affect the tenant's ability to insist on the common law remedies. See, for example: *Hunt v Hocking* EV/18/0612, 24/8/18.

88 Statutory repairing obligations (which have existed since the late nineteenth century) have always supplemented, rather than displaced, the common law and contractual obligations. See the author's article "*Todd v Clapperton*: the evolving law on repairing obligations and claims against landlords of residential property" 2010 SLT (News) 31.

89 However, the parties may contract out of the common law obligations, leaving only the statutory repairing obligations under the 2006 Act. Where, however, there is no written contract, or the contract is silent as regards repairs, the common law obligations are implied.

90 In *Stobbs v Hislop* (n 84), the court decided that retention was not available to a statutory tenant having security of tenure under the Rent Acts, as those Acts provided a particular remedy for disrepair, being a suspension of otherwise permitted rent increases. That remedy would be futile if the tenant could exercise a common law right to withhold all the rent. That is quite different from the remedy under the 2006 Act, which exists under a separate statutory code, for the enforcement of the repairing standard under s 13 of that Act.

91 Examples: *Walker v Wilson* EV/18/0550, 29/8/18; *Kingdom Properties* EV/18/3196, 16/4/19; *Shaw v Keogh* EV/18/3459, 26/4/19.

92 Inserted by the Consumer Protection (Amendment) Regulations 2014 (SI 2014/870), with effect from 1 October 2014. Part 4 applies only to contracts created on or after that date. Regulation 27C(4) specifically provides that pt 4A applies to assured tenancies under the 1988 Act, and any lease under which accommodation is let as holiday accommodation. However, that provision does not appear to have been amended to include PRTs under the 2016 Act. For useful guidance on pt 4A, and on the application of consumer protection law to residential lettings in general, see the "Guidance for lettings professionals on consumer protection law" issued by the Competition and Markets Authority ("CMA") in June 2014. Note that, as well as the right to a discount or damages, the consumer also has the right to "unwind" the contract, though this is unlikely to be invoked in eviction proceedings.

93 As was indicated in Chapter 3, it would appear that pt 2 of the Consumer Rights Act 2015 does not apply to an individual landlord who rents, for example, the house in which he

contract". In essence, the right to a discount or damages arises where the "trader" engaged in a "prohibited practice" for the purposes of regulation 27B, being (a) a misleading action under regulation 5; or (b) a practice that is "aggressive" under regulation 7. A key aspect of a "prohibited practice" is that it causes, or is likely to cause, the tenant consumer to enter into the lease.[94]

For the detail as to what constitutes a "misleading action", or an "aggressive" practice, the reader is referred to the regulations.[95] Suffice it to say that the definition of "misleading action" is comprehensive, and includes not only false information, but "overall presentation in any way [that] deceives or is likely to deceive the average consumer . . . even if the information is factually correct". A commercial practice is aggressive if, through the use of harassment, coercion or undue influence, it significantly impairs, or is likely significantly to impair, the average consumer's freedom of choice or conduct in relation to the product.

The right to a discount is described in regulation 27I. It applies both to payments that have been made and those that have not yet been made. The applicable discount depends on the seriousness of the prohibited practice, as follows: (a) if it is "more than minor", 25 per cent; (b) if it is "significant", 50 per cent; (c) if it is "serious", 75 per cent, and (d) if it is "very serious", 100 per cent. Seriousness is to be assessed by reference to the behaviour of the person who engaged in the practice, the impact of the practice on the consumer, and the time that has elapsed since the prohibited practice took place.

Under regulation 27K a consumer has the right to damages if he has incurred financial loss or has suffered alarm, distress or physical inconvenience or discomfort as a result of a prohibited practice.

How might these regulations apply in eviction proceedings? Regulation 27K(1) provides that a consumer with a right to redress under part 4A "may bring a claim in civil proceedings to enforce that right". It is submitted that this permits a claim for a discount or damages to be made by way of counterclaim, or in the form of a defence "in" civil proceedings raised against the consumer. That would appear to follow from the right to claim a discount in relation to payments that have not yet been made by the consumer: that claim is likely to be made in the context of an action for payment at the instance of the trader.[96]

If that is correct, it will be possible to resist a claim, in eviction proceedings brought under grounds 8, 11 or 12, that unpaid rent is "lawfully due" by a defence to the effect that the tenant, as a consumer under the regulations, has exercised her right under regulation 27I(3) to reduce rental payments by the appropriate percentage under regulation 27I(4). On the other hand, if the tenant makes a claim for damages under regulation 27K, that does not amount to a case that the outstanding rent is not lawfully due, and would not serve as a defence to an action under ground 8.

previously resided. That would also seem to be the case as regards the 2008 regulations. See the CMA Guidance, at paras 3.6–3.11.

94 That, it is suggested, would be the effect of regs 5, 7 and 27B(2), as regards residential leases.

95 And the aforementioned CMA Guidance (n 93).

96 It also appears to follow from the words "a claim in". If it was intended that the right to redress could only be sought in proceedings raised by the consumer, it would have been appropriate to omit those words, and simply to allow the bringing of civil proceedings. To allow a claim to be brought "*in* civil proceedings . . ." suggests otherwise.

Landlord registration; tenancy deposits

The failure of a landlord to apply for registration under part 8 of the Antisocial Behaviour etc. (Scotland) Act 2004 may result in a notice being served by the local authority under section 94 of the Act, as a result of which the tenant's liability to pay rent may be suspended. However, the landlord's failure to apply for registration does not have any bearing on his right to initiate or pursue eviction proceedings.[97]

Failure to comply with the statutory provisions in relation to tenancy deposits does not have any bearing on the liability of the tenant to pay rent, and it does not appear that the tenant's application for the landlord to be sanctioned by payment of a financial penalty, under the relevant regulations, could be set off against the rental liability. In the case of both of these statutory schemes, the failure of the landlord to comply with the statutory provision might feasibly be considered relevant to the exercise of the tribunal's discretion, as regards the discretionary grounds in schedule 5.

DISCRETIONARY GROUNDS: ACTIONS UNDER 1988 ACT, s 18(4)

Under section 18(4) of the 1988 Act, the tribunal cannot grant decree under any of the discretionary grounds unless it is satisfied that it is reasonable to do so. Thus, the discretionary grounds are analogous to grounds 1–7 of schedule 2 to the 2001 Act, discussed in Chapter 5. In respect of the matters that might be put before the tribunal in relation to the "reasonableness" requirement, the reader is referred to that chapter[98] Where particular issues arise as to whether it is reasonable to grant an order under the 1988 Act ground, this is commented upon.

Ground 9: suitable alternative accommodation

> "Suitable alternative accommodation is available for the tenant or will be available for him when the order for possession takes effect."

The suitable alternative accommodation must be available to the tenant. Accommodation that was previously available is irrelevant.[99] This highlights a practical problem for the landlord seeking to rely on ground 9. If he offers alternative accommodation to the tenant, which is refused, he may face a considerable delay between the date of the offer and the date when the tribunal ultimately decides in his favour, during which time it may be difficult for him

97 *B v D* [2017] SAC (Civ) 32, 2018 SLT (Sh Ct) 70. "Landlord has ceased to be registered" is a ground for eviction under the 2016 Act. See Chapter 10, p 364. Under r 26(12)(a) of the Procedure Rules (n 2), where the FTT learns, during the course of proceedings, that the landlord is not registered, it may report that fact to the relevant local authority.

98 Although there is no equivalent in the 1988 Act to s 16(3) of the 2001 Act, in terms of which guidance is given to the sheriff on the matters to which he is to have regard, in deciding whether it is reasonable to grant the order, it is suggested that all the matters outlined in the commentary in relation to s 16(3), in so far as they arise in any case, will also be relevant to the issue of whether decree should be granted under s 18(4).

99 *Kimpson v Markham* [1921] 2 KB 157.

to rent the subjects to another person, because they have to be available for the tenant who has previously refused them. That said, there is no requirement in ground 9 that the accommodation is actually available to the tenant at the point when the form AT6 is served, or even when the proceedings are initiated.

Under section 18(5), ground 9 is supplemented by the seven paragraphs of part III of schedule 5. These set out stipulations that are fairly demanding of the landlord. Consequently, actions under this ground are extremely rare.

If the local authority for the area in which the tenancy is situated certifies that suitable alternative accommodation will be provided for the tenant, this is conclusive proof that such accommodation will be available. This will be a fairly rare occurrence. There is no requirement that the certificate provide details of the accommodation, such as its location or size, although, under paragraph 6 of part III, the authority may furnish particulars as to the availability, extent and character of alternative accommodation. If that is not acceptable to the tenant, he may seek to persuade the tribunal that although the ground is established, it would not be reasonable to grant the order for eviction.

If the proposed accommodation is being provided other than by a local authority, the landlord must meet two requirements in order to establish the ground. First, the tenancy must be offered on a basis that, in respect of security of tenure, is equivalent to an assured tenancy, such as a PRT, or a Scottish secure tenancy with a housing association. Secondly, the accommodation must meet the conditions of paragraph 3.

Paragraph 3 contains four conditions. First, the accommodation must be reasonably suitable to the needs of the tenant and his family as regards proximity to place of work. The tribunal should also consider the time it would take to travel to work, the means of transport available and any inconvenience that would be caused.[100]

Secondly, it must be similar as regards rental and extent to the accommodation afforded by houses provided in the neighbourhood by any local authority for persons whose needs as regards extent are, in the opinion of the tribunal, similar to those of the tenant and his family.[101] Information on this point would presumably have to be gathered from the local authority directly.

Thirdly, it must be reasonably suitable to the means and needs of the tenant and his family as regards extent and character. Accommodation may be suitable if it is inferior[102] or considerably smaller,[103] or where it comprises only part of the accommodation currently offered to the tenant.[104] It may be unsuitable if it does not meet the tenant's professional needs, such as an artist using a room as a studio,[105] though this does not appear to extend to the tenant's

100 *Yewbright Properties Ltd v Stone* (1980) 40 P&CR 402, (1980) 254 EG 863; *Minchburn Ltd v Fernandez* (1987) 19 HLR 29, where accommodation was held to be unsuitable because it would have doubled the tenant's thirty-minute walk to work to one hour.

101 In this context, "family" is to be given its ordinary meaning: *Standingford v Probert* [1950] 1 KB 377; *Scrace v Windust* [1955] 1 WLR 475; *Fitzpatrick v Sterling Housing Association* [2001] 1 AC 27.

102 *Warren v Austen* [1947] 2 All ER 185 (Lord Asquith).

103 *Quick v Fifield* (1982) 132 NLJ 140; *Hill v Rochard* [1983] 1 WLR 478. Presumably the accommodation would not be suitable if it was too large.

104 Where, e.g., the tenant is not occupying all of the accommodation let, or because it is larger than he requires: *Parmee v Mitchell* [1950] 2 KB 199; *Thompson v Rolls* [1926] All ER 257; *Yoland v Reddington* (1981–82) 5 HLR 41.

105 *MacDonnell v Daly* [1969] 1 WLR 1482.

ability to earn money by taking in lodgers;[106] it is a shared house for a person currently living alone;[107] or it does not have a garden.[108]

In relation to the "character" of accommodation, *Redspring Ltd v Francis* is of interest.[109] The tenant's current accommodation was in a quiet residential road, and she had the use of a garden. The alternative accommodation was more spacious, but had no garden and was next to a chip shop, and a hospital, cinema and public house were nearby. The Court of Appeal held that these "environmental" factors ought to be taken into account as affecting the suitability of the accommodation as regards its character, or as affecting the issue of whether it was reasonable to grant the order.

The proximity of the tenant's friends and cultural interests are not relevant to the "character" of the alternative accommodation, though they may be taken into consideration in relation to the issue of whether it is reasonable to grant the order.[110]

Fourthly, where furniture is part of the tenancy contract, the alternative furniture must be similar to the furniture provided in the initial premises or be reasonably suitable to the needs of the tenant and his family.

Section 22, in relation to payment of removal expenses, which has already been discussed in relation to ground 6, also applies to orders for possession under ground 9.

Finally, it must be emphasised that even if the tribunal is satisfied that the alternative accommodation is suitable, the landlord must still establish that it would be reasonable to grant the order.[111]

Ground 10: tenant's notice to quit

"The following conditions are fulfilled—

(a) the tenant has given a notice to quit which has expired; and

(b) the tenant has remained in possession of the whole or any part of the house; and

(c) proceedings for the recovery of possession have been begun not more than six months after the expiry of the notice to quit; and

(d) the tenant is not entitled to possession of the house by virtue of a new tenancy."

This ground is self-explanatory. It is more favourable to the landlord than the equivalent ground under the Rent Acts.[112] It is submitted that the ground can be relied upon only if the notice is valid.[113] It follows from the fact that this is

106 *Stewart v Mackay* 1947 SC 287.

107 *Barnard v Towers* [1953] 2 All ER 877.

108 See *Enfield London Borough Council v French* (1985) 17 HLR 211.

109 [1973] 1 WLR 134. See also *Christie v Macfarlane* 1930 SLT (Sh Ct) 5.

110 *Siddiqui v Rashid* [1980] 1 WLR 1018.

111 For a case in which the landlords failed to do so, see *Trustees of Kinrara Estate v Campbell* 1999 Hous LR 55.

112 Ground 5 of sch 2 to the 1984 Act: "Where the tenant has given notice to quit and, in consequence of that notice, the landlord has contracted to sell or let the dwellinghouse or has taken any other steps as the result of which he would, in the opinion of the court, be seriously prejudiced if he could not obtain possession."

113 The requirements for a valid notice to quit are discussed in Chapter 3. If the notice was invalid, the parties' contract would not end, and it would not be possible for the court to grant an order under the 1988 Act, s 18, as the facility allowed by s 18(6) is not available in relation to ground 10.

a discretionary ground[114] that the tenant's having given notice is not sufficient, in itself, to enable the tribunal to determine the issue in favour of the landlord. It will require to weigh the relevant factors; in particular, the reason why the tenant changed his mind, and the extent to which the landlord has been prejudiced by the tenant refusing to leave. Where, for example, the landlord has made arrangements to sell or relet the subjects on the strength of the tenant's notice to quit, that will obviously weigh in his favour.

Grounds 11 and 12: rent arrears

> "11. Whether or not any rent is in arrears on the date on which proceedings for possession are begun, the tenant has persistently delayed paying rent which has become lawfully due.
>
> 12. Some rent lawfully due from the tenant—
>
> (a) is unpaid on the date on which the proceedings for possession are begun; and
>
> (b) except where subsection (1)(b) of section 19 of this Act applies, was in arrears at the date of the service of the notice under that section relating to those proceedings."

These grounds are commonly relied on together, and often with ground 8. The reader is referred to the discussion of that ground, some of which is equally relevant to cases under grounds 11 and 12.[115] In particular, ground 12 is the same as ground 8, except that it does not provide for any particular amount of arrears, and thus will only be relied on by the landlord where the arrears amount to less than three months' rent.[116]

As regards ground 11, there is no need for the landlord to show that there are any arrears outstanding. It is sufficient that the tenant has persistently delayed paying rent. Accordingly, this ground might be relied on where the tenant persistently allows arrears to build up, and then clears the balance at the point when proceedings have been raised, or are about to be raised, by the landlord. It is suggested that the words "persistently delayed" could refer to one instalment of rent that has been outstanding for a lengthy period, or a number of instalments that have been paid late, or both.

Under the FTT's Procedure Rules,[117] applications for an eviction order, and for a payment order in respect of rent arrears, are treated as separate applications, but are usually heard at the same time.[118] Where there is a dispute between the parties as to the level of rent payable, it is suggested that

114 Ground 10 was a mandatory ground in the original Bill, but was changed to a discretionary ground in recognition of the fact that there may be circumstances in which the tenant gave notice to quit, but had a good reason for changing his plans.

115 In particular, all the arrears grounds presuppose that the rent is "lawfully due", which the tenant may dispute, and problems with payment of housing benefit or universal credit often arise in arrears cases under all these grounds.

116 Grounds 11 and 12 may also have to be relied upon, where the tribunal decides that the AT6 is invalid. Under s 19(1)(b), the tribunal can dispense with the requirement for an AT6, but not in relation to ground 8 (s 19(5)).

117 n 2.

118 This means that the application under s 18 may be refused (say, for lack of a valid AT6), but the application for a payment order continues. See Chapter 14.

the landlord ought to quantify the level of arrears said to be due, and demand payment, before an application is made to the tribunal.[119]

Ground 13: breach of tenancy obligations

> "Any obligation of the tenancy (other than one related to the payment of rent) has been broken or not performed."

This ground is the same as part 2 of ground 1 under the 2001 Act. The reader is therefore referred to the coverage of that ground in Chapter 5.[120] There are several cases in which the tribunal has granted an order for possession on ground 13, the breaches including: unauthorised sub-letting;[121] antisocial behaviour;[122] refusing to allow the landlord entry to the property;[123] and tenant not residing in the property as his principal home.[124]

Ground 14: condition of property

> "The condition of the house or of any of the common parts has deteriorated owing to acts of waste by, or the neglect or default of, the tenant or any one of joint tenants or any person residing or lodging with him or any sub-tenant of his; and, in the case of acts of waste by, **or** the neglect or default of, a person lodging with a tenant or a sub-tenant of his, the tenant has not, before the making of the order in question, taken such steps as he ought reasonably to have taken for the removal of the lodger or sub-tenant.
>
> In this ground, 'the common parts' means any part of a building containing the house and any other premises which the tenant is entitled under the terms of the tenancy to use in common with the occupiers of other houses."

Grounds 14 and 16 are in the same terms as grounds 3 and 4 under the 2001 Act, which are discussed in Chapter 5.

Ground 15: antisocial behaviour

> "The tenant, a person residing or lodging in the house with the tenant or a person visiting the house has–
> (a) been convicted of–
> (i) using or allowing the house to be used for immoral or illegal purposes; or
> (ii) an offence punishable by imprisonment committed in, or in the locality of, the house; or
> (b) acted in an anti-social manner in relation to a person residing in, visiting or otherwise engaged in lawful activity in the locality; or
> (c) pursued a course of conduct in relation to such a person as is mentioned in head (b) above.
>
> In this Ground 'anti-social', in relation to an action or course of conduct, means causing or likely to cause alarm, distress, nuisance or annoyance, 'conduct' includes speech and a course of conduct must involve conduct on at least two occasions; and 'tenant' includes any one of joint tenants."

119 See *P v O* (n 23).
120 At p 133 for the ground, and at p 159 for the application of the "reasonableness" test.
121 *Watt v Friel* EV/19/1411, 25/7/19.
122 *Williamson v Bertie* EV/19/1563, 25/7/19 also granted on ground 15.
123 *McLaughlin v Wilson* EV/19/0215, 25/4/19, 25/7/19, also granted on ground 11.
124 *Norris v Paton* EV/18/0670, 11/6/18, also granted on ground 8.

This ground has been significantly amended since the 1988 Act came into force.[125] It is now an amalgamation of grounds 2 and 7 in relation to Scottish secure tenancies. Those grounds are discussed in Chapter 5.

As a result of amendments made by the Antisocial Behaviour etc. (Scotland) Act 2004, and the Housing (Scotland) Act 2006, there is some doubt as to whether this ground is subject to section 18(6) of the Act. This point is discussed in the analysis of that provision in Chapter 7.

Ground 16: deterioration of furniture

> "The condition of any furniture provided for use under the tenancy has deteriorated owing to ill-treatment by the tenant or any other person residing or lodging with him in the house and, in the case of ill-treatment by a person lodging with the tenant or by a sub-tenant of his, the tenant has not taken such steps as he ought reasonably to have taken for the removal of the lodger or sub-tenant."

Reference is made to the comments on ground 4 at Chapter 5.

Ground 17: former employee tenant

> "The house was let to the tenant in consequence of his employment by the landlord seeking possession or a previous landlord under the tenancy and the tenant has ceased to be in that employment.
>
> For the purposes of this ground, at a time when the landlord is or was the [Scottish Ministers][126], employment by a health service body, as defined in section 60(7) of the National Health Service and Community Care Act 1990, shall be regarded as employment by the [Scottish Ministers]."[127]

Again, this ground differs from the equivalent ground under the Rent Acts,[128] in terms of which it was necessary for the landlord to show that the accommodation was reasonably required for occupation by another employee. Ground 17 applies in cases where the tenant has a tenancy in consequence of his

125 Originally the ground read: "The tenant or any other person residing or lodging with him in the house has been guilty of conduct in or *in the vicinity* of the house which is a nuisance or annoyance, or has been convicted of using the house or allowing the house to be used for immoral or illegal purposes." This was the same as ground 2 under the 1984 Act, except that the older ground referred to conduct "which is a nuisance or annoyance to adjoining occupiers", a formulation that is clearly more restricted as to the range of potential victims. Thus it can be seen that the scope of the grounds relating to illegal conduct and nuisance/antisocial behaviour has gradually increased, as is further discussed in the commentary to grounds 2 and 7 under the 2001 Act in Chapter 5.

126 The ground actually reads "Secretary of State"; however, in consequence of the Scotland Act 1998 (in particular s 117) "Scottish Ministers" may be read in place of those words.

127 This paragraph was added to ground 17 by the National Health Service and Community Care Act 1990, sch 8 para 11. Under the 1990 Act, crown immunity for health service bodies was removed. As a result, tenancies created by such bodies (where the tenant is invariably one of their employees) will be assured (or short assured) tenancies, because para 10 of sch 4 to the 1988 Act is no longer applicable. This change was offset by the amendment to ground 17. That amendment is necessary in order for ground 17 to apply to the tenancies of health service employees, in which the employer is, say, a health board, but the landlord (being the owner of the subjects) is the Scottish Ministers. For further consideration of tenancies of health bodies, see the discussion of para 10 of sch 4 to the 1988 Act, in Chapter 7.

128 Ground 7 of sch 2 to the 1984 Act.

employment. It does not apply to service occupancies, which are not tenancies and therefore do not attract the protection of the Act.[129]

Suspended orders under the 1988 Act s 20

Under section 20(2) of the 1988 Act, the FTT has the power, on making an order for possession, to: (a) sist or suspend execution of the order, or (b) postpone the date of possession; both may be done for such period or periods as the tribunal thinks fit. A similar power exists under section 12 of the 1984 Act, in relation to regulated tenancies, but there is no power to make suspended orders under the 2001 or 2016 Acts.

On any such sist, suspension or postponement, the tribunal, unless it considers that to do so would cause exceptional hardship to the tenant or would otherwise be unreasonable, must impose conditions with regard to payment by the tenant of arrears of rent (if any) and rent or payments in respect of occupation after the termination of the tenancy. In addition, it may impose such other conditions as it thinks fit.[130] If any such conditions are complied with, the tribunal may, if it thinks fit, recall any such order.[131] It is for the tribunal to decide the extent to which compliance with the strict terms of the conditions will be required, in order for the order to be recalled.[132]

These powers are not available if the tribunal is satisfied that the landlord is entitled to possession of the house under section 33(1) of the Act[133] or if an eviction order is sought on the basis of any of the mandatory grounds 1–8, set out in part I of schedule 5 to the Act.[134]

Suspended and postponed orders are extensively used in England, where they are also available in relation to secure tenancies in the social rented sector. Because that is not the case in Scotland, the number of actions in which suspension and postponement might be deployed is very much lower. Perhaps for that reason there appears to be less awareness of the fact that such orders are available in Scotland, in cases under the 1988 Act, and section 20(2) is rarely used.[135]

129 Service occupancies (or tied tenancies, as they are sometimes called) are discussed in Chapter 12.

130 Section 20(3). In *Bow Farm Housing Association v Kelly* 1998 Hous LR 98, it was said that it was for the tenant to advance proposals for terms on which the order would be suspended, and the reasons why a suspended order ought to be made.

131 Section 20(4). The Act does not indicate what procedure is to follow after the previous order has been recalled. If it is the position that the tenant has paid off all the rent arrears, one would expect that the action will simply be dismissed. A suspended order under s 12 of the 1984 Act was discharged in *Lorimer v Griffiths* 2013 Hous LR 63.

132 *Knowsley Housing Trust v White* [2009] 1 AC 636, paras 67, 68 and 94–110 (Lord Neuberger of Abbotsbury). See also *Lorimer v Griffiths* (n 131).

133 I.e. where the tenancy is a short assured tenancy and the landlord seeks recovery of possession on the basis that the conditions under s 33(1) of the Act have been met.

134 Section 20(6).

135 The use of suspension and postponement orders in England in discussed in n 180 in Chapter 5.

Chapter 9

Private Residential Tenancies

INTRODUCTION

The Private Housing (Tenancies) (Scotland) Act 2016 is in nine parts, and has five schedules. This chapter is particularly concerned with part 1 (the prerequisites for creation of a private residential tenancy ("PRT")) and part 5 (termination of a PRT), and in particular the requirements for making an application to the First-tier Tribunal ("FTT") for an eviction order under section 51. Chapter 10 examines schedule 3 to the Act, which sets out the statutory grounds under which the tribunal may grant an eviction order.[1]

In Chapter 1, the overall scheme of the Act was described in a historical context. For present purposes, it is convenient to reiterate that, in contrast to tenancies under the 1984, 1988 and 2001 Acts, the PRT is singular. There is no "short" PRT,[2] and no distinction between a "contractual" PRT and a "statutory" one. Once a PRT is created, it cannot be terminated by either party, or by any agreement between them, except in accordance with part 5 of the Act.[3]

Having no short form, the PRT is like an assured tenancy that is not a short assured tenancy: in order for the FTT to grant an "eviction order", under section 51(1), it must find "that one of the eviction grounds in schedule 3 applies". The PRT is also like a Scottish secure tenancy, in that there is no distinction between a "contractual" tenancy and a "statutory" tenancy, as regards termination.[4] There is simply a PRT, which can only be terminated under the terms of the Act. This has the important consequence that it is not necessary for either party to terminate the tenancy contract by a notice to quit,[5] or otherwise, before making an application for an eviction order under section 51. Therefore, the landlord need serve only a single notice (the notice

1 Part 6 of the Act, which concerns succession to a PRT on the death of the tenant, is considered in Chapter 12. Section 75 (in pt 8) and sch 5, which make transitional and savings provision for assured tenancies existing as at the date when the 2016 Act came into force, are discussed at the end of Chapter 7. In this chapter, reference is also made to ss 78 (Interpretation) and 73 (Minor errors in documents).

2 In the 2016 Act there is no equivalent to ss 32 and 33 of the 1988 Act. As was described in Chapter 1, one of the main policy aims of the 2016 Act was to abolish the "short" form of tenure in the private sector.

3 Section 44, which is quoted in this chapter at p 303.

4 Accordingly, there is also no equivalent, in the 2016 Act, to s 16 or s 18(6) of the 1988 Act, which concern the relationship between the "contractual" and the "statutory" assured tenancy (see the discussion of these provisions in Chapter 7).

5 As described in Chapter 1, notice to quit is inept in any event, because most PRTs will not have a specified duration, and cannot tacitly relocate.

to leave under sections 54 and 62 of the Act) as a preliminary to eviction proceedings.[6]

The discussion in this chapter breaks down as follows:

- What is a private residential tenancy? (part 1 of and schedule 1 to the Act).
- Agreements and terms.
- Sections 44–50: security of tenure; termination by tenant; consensual termination.
- Making an application to the FTT for an eviction order under section 51.
- Notice to leave under section 62.

As is often the case with modern legislation, the 2016 Act has given rise to a plethora of material issued by the Scottish Government, which is intended to support the operation of the new regime. This includes, for example, the secondary legislation, the Model Private Residential Tenancy Agreement, the "Easy Read Notes", the "Statutory Terms Supporting Notes"[7] and the guidance "Private Residential Tenancy – Information for Landlords", and "Guidance Notes for Landlords" in relation to the statutory notice to leave. These documents may be used as aids to construction of the Act,[8] and reference is made to them in this chapter where appropriate.

WHAT IS A "PRIVATE RESIDENTIAL TENANCY"?

A private residential tenancy is a tenancy created on or after 1 December 2017,[9] which meets the conditions of section 1 of the 2016 Act:

> "1 **Meaning of private residential tenancy**
> (1) A tenancy is a private residential tenancy where—
> (a) the tenancy is one under which a property is let to an individual ('the tenant') as a separate dwelling,
> (b) the tenant occupies the property (or any part of it) as the tenant's only or principal home, and
> (c) the tenancy is not one which schedule 1 states cannot be a private residential tenancy.
> (2) A tenancy which is a private residential tenancy does not cease to be one by reason only of the fact that subsection (1)(b) is no longer satisfied."

Section 1 is similar to section 12 of the 1988 Act, which defines the term "assured tenancy", but there are several significant differences.

6 The reader is referred to the discussion at the beginning of Chapter 3 as to the different types of notice that the landlord may have to serve, before raising proceedings to recover possession of a residential property from the tenant. The PRT is like the Scottish secure tenancy, in that proceedings under s 16 of the 2001 Act, and s 52 of the 2016 Act, need only be preceded by service of the relevant statutory notice; in the case of a PRT, this is the notice to leave, under s 62.

7 See the discussion of tenancy terms at p 302 below.

8 In general, official statements by government departments administering an Act, or by any other authority concerned with the Act, may be helpful in the interpretation of legislation, and can be taken into account: *Ellis v Bristol City Council* [2007] EWCA Civ 685[2007] 7 WLUK 109, [27] (Lloyd Jones LJ). See also Bennion, *Statutory Interpretation* (7th edn) 635.

9 Subject to the transitional provisions described at the end of Chapter 7.

"Tenancy"; tenancy duration

As with the 1988 Act, the term "tenancy" is not defined, except that the interpretation section states that "tenancy . . . includes a sub-tenancy".[10] Therefore, one might think that (as with the 1988 Act), "tenancy" must mean a tenancy at common law, and only such an agreement can be a PRT under section 1. If that is correct, then, in the case of occupation by virtue of a contract that is not a tenancy but merely a licence, or a service occupancy, or some other contract that falls short of being a tenancy at common law, the occupier has no security of tenure under the 2016 Act.

However, in the 2016 Act, the meaning of "tenancy" is extended by section 4:

> "4 **Extended meaning of tenancy in this Act**
> For the purposes of this Act—
> (a) if an agreement would give rise to a tenancy but for the fact that it does not specify an ish, it is to be regarded as giving rise to a tenancy,
> (b) once an agreement has given rise to a private residential tenancy, it is to continue to be regarded as giving rise to a tenancy despite the term of the agreement requiring the tenant to pay rent subsequently being removed from the agreement or otherwise ceasing to have effect."[11]

An agreed duration is often said to be one of the four cardinal elements of a lease in Scots law: an agreement lacking an ish might merely be a "licence". Or, it might be a tenancy that creates only a personal right for the tenant, but not a right valid against singular successors, under the Leases Act 1449.[12] The effect of section 4(a) is that a specified duration, ending in an ish, is not necessary in order to create a PRT.

At first sight, that may not seem particularly significant. However, it is necessary to appreciate that the Act not only extends its coverage to agreements without durations; it also renders any agreement as to duration ineffective, at least as regards important aspects of the parties' relationship as landlord and tenant. If they *have* agreed a duration, that does not stop either of them serving notice to leave, under part 5 of the Act ("Termination") before the duration expires. Termination of the PRT is governed by the Act, not the parties' agreement.[13]

This aspect of the 2016 Act is perhaps most clearly evident in the Model Private Residential Tenancy Agreement produced by the Scottish Government. Clause 6 is:

> "6. Start Date Of The Tenancy
> The private residential tenancy will start on: ('the start date of the tenancy')."

10 Section 78(1); s 55(1) in the 1988 Act. Thus a sub-tenancy of a PRT is also a PRT. Sub-tenancies under the 2016 Act are discussed in Chapter 12.

11 Section 4(b) is a "change of circumstances" provision that is related to the exception in para 1 of sch 1 to the Act. See p 298 below.

12 See: Rennie and others, *Leases* (SULI 2015) ch 5, and Lord Hope's judgment in *Mexfield Housing Co-operative v Berrisford* [2012] 1 AC 955, in which he explains that a contract lacking an ish could nevertheless be a lease, but not one which was covered by the 1449 Act. At common law, where agreement as to duration is lacking, a term of a year may be implied. See Chapter 3, p 51.

13 Similarly, any agreement as to duration does not prevent the landlord from serving a rent-increase notice under section 22, before the agreed term has expired.

Thus, under the Model Agreement, a PRT has a "start date", but no "end date", presumably because, in the view of the Scottish Government, there would be no point in agreeing an "end date", given the terms of the Act. It is understood that although the Model Agreement is not compulsory, it is extensively used by landlords and letting agents when creating PRTs. Therefore, it seems reasonable to suggest that, in practice, most PRTs will have no agreed duration.[14]

Section 4(b) is a "change of circumstances" provision. See the discussion of that issue below.

"Property"

Another significant difference between section 1 of the 2016 Act and section 12 of the 1988 Act is that the latter uses the term "house", whereas the former uses the term "property". As is suggested in Chapter 1, to describe a building as a "house" normally connotes that it has been designed, built or adapted for use as a residence. The term "property" carries no such connotation. Accordingly, under the 2016 Act the statutory protection extends to persons using any property, "or any part of" a property,[15] which is "let as a separate dwelling", and is occupied as a "home" even if it is not a property that one would normally describe as a "house". In other words, the mode of occupation is the determinative factor, rather than, say, the physical features of the structure in which the tenant dwells.[16]

"Individual"

The use of this term in section 1(1)(a) is subject to section 2(2), which provides that a tenancy is to be regarded as one under which a property is let to an individual notwithstanding that it is let jointly to an individual, or individuals, and another person. The possibility of joint tenancies is also recognised by section 78(3), which provides that where two or more persons jointly are the tenant under a tenancy, references in the Act to the "tenant" are to all of those persons, unless stated otherwise.[17]

As with section 12(1)(a) of the 1988 Act, the effect of the reference to an "individual" in section 1(1)(a) is to preclude a limited company or a partnership from holding a PRT as the sole tenant. However, given the reference to "another person" under section 2(2), it may hold a PRT as a joint tenant, provided at least one of the other joint tenants is an individual.

14 All that said, however, the Act does not proscribe agreements as to duration. So, one might ask whether there are circumstances in which an agreed duration could have some legal effect. Say that L and T enter into a tenancy that is a PRT, but they do not use the Model Agreement. Their lease specifies a duration of two years, and a rent of £1,000 per month. After six months, T gives notice terminating the tenancy under ss 48 and 49 (see p 304 below). Due to a decline in the local rental market, L is unable to re-let the property for several months, and then only at a rent of £800 per month. L cannot prevent T from terminating the tenancy under ss 48 and 49, but does he have a claim for damages against T?

15 Section 1(1)(b).

16 Note, however, that various specific types of "property", such as shops, are excepted from the coverage of the Act by s 1(1)(c) and sch 1.

17 As we will see, this has implications for the right of the joint tenants to terminate the tenancy under ss 48 and 49.

"Let as a separate dwelling"

This term is discussed in Chapter 1. Further guidance as to its meaning, in the 2016 Act, is given in section 2(3) and (4):

> "(3) A tenancy is to be regarded as one under which a property is let as a separate dwelling, despite the let property including other land, where the main purpose for letting the property is to provide the tenant with a home.
> (4) A tenancy is to be regarded as one under which a property is let as a separate dwelling if, despite the let property lacking certain features or facilities—
> (a) the terms of the tenancy entitle the tenant to use property in common with another person ('shared accommodation'), and
> (b) the let property would be regarded as a separate dwelling were it to include some or all of the shared accommodation."

Subsection (3) requires to be read with paragraph 4 of schedule 1, under which a tenancy is excepted from the Act if the let property includes two acres or more of agricultural land, or if it is a "relevant agricultural tenancy".

Subsection (4) should be read along with section 9 ("Protection of terms allowing use of shared living accommodation"). Together, these provisions are similar to section 14 of the 1988 Act. They apply, in particular, to bedsit and other flat-sharing arrangements in which the tenant has exclusive occupation of part of a house or flat, such as a single room, but shares the use of other rooms such as the bathroom, kitchen and hall with other single-room tenants. Where, absent section 2(4), that would not be a "separate dwelling",[18] the shared accommodation is to be regarded as part of the property let to the tenant, such that the "let as a separate dwelling" test is then met.[19] Under section 9, a term of the PRT that entitles the tenant to use the shared accommodation cannot be terminated or modified so as to reduce that entitlement, unless the tenant agrees, after the tenancy commences.

Occupies; only or principal home

These terms are discussed in Chapter 1.

Tenancies excepted under schedule 1: section 1(1)(c)

The equivalent provision in the 1988 Act is section 12(2), by which tenancies listed in schedule 4 fall outside the scope of the 1988 Act.[20] The list of excepted tenancies under schedule 1 to the 2016 Act is similar, and many of the exceptions are effectively the same. However, some of the exceptions, such as "resident landlord", are significantly different.

Given the abolition of the short assured tenancy form of tenure, there may be an increase in the use of measures by property owners, the purpose of which is to allow occupation under a contract, but in such a way as to avoid the application of the 2016 Act. There are two principal ways to do that: (a)

18 See the discussion in Chapter 1.

19 Section 2(4) appears to have been overlooked in the Upper Tribunal's decision in *Affleck v Bronsdon* [2019] UT 49, specifically at [18]. That decision was subsequently quashed by the Inner House on an appeal that was not opposed.

20 The equivalent exceptions in sch 4 to the 1988 Act are covered in Chapter 7, from p 224.

by seeking to create a contract that is a "licence" rather than a tenancy;[21] (b) by creating a tenancy that is covered by one of the exceptions in schedule 1 (such as a holiday let).

The categories listed in schedule 1 are:

(1) tenancies at a low rent (see below);
(2) tenancies of shops;[22]
(3) tenancies under which the let property consists of or comprises premises licensed for the sale of alcohol for consumption on the premises;
(4) tenancies under which the let property includes two acres or more of agricultural land;[23] or one that is a "relevant agricultural tenancy",[24] and the let property is occupied by the person responsible for the control (whether as tenant or as the tenant's agent or employee) of the farming of the let property;
(5) student lets (see below);
(6) holiday lets (see below);
(7)–(11) resident landlords (see below);
(12) police housing, being a tenancy in which the landlord is the Scottish Police Authority;
(13) military housing, being a tenancy in which the landlord is the Secretary of State for Defence.
(14) social housing, being a tenancy in which the landlord is: (a) a local authority landlord within the definition given in section 11 of the Housing (Scotland) Act 2001, (b) a registered social landlord within the definition given in section 165 of the Housing (Scotland) Act 2010, (c) a co-operative housing association within the definition given in section 1 of the Housing Associations Act 1985, or (d) Scottish Water;
(15) any tenancy that arises as a result of a Scottish secure tenancy or a short Scottish secure tenancy (under the 2001 Act) being assigned, sub-let or otherwise given up;[25]
(16) accommodation for homeless persons, being granted on a temporary basis and the purpose of which is the fulfilment of a duty imposed on a local authority by part II of the Housing (Scotland) Act 1987;[26]
(17) accommodation for persons on probation or released from prison, being a tenancy granted for a term of less than six months to a tenant who:

21 The term "licence" is generally used to denote a contract in which a right of occupation of heritable subjects is conferred, but where the contract is not a lease. See Chapter 12.

22 Being a tenancy to which the Tenancy of Shops (Scotland) Act 1949 is capable of applying.

23 In this paragraph "agricultural land" has the same meaning as in the Rent (Scotland) Act 1984, s 115(1).

24 Being a tenancy that falls within the definition given in the Agricultural Holdings (Scotland) Act 2003 of: (i) a 1991 Act tenancy (i.e. a tenancy under the Agricultural Holdings (Scotland) Act 1991); (ii) a short limited duration tenancy; (iii) a limited duration tenancy; (iv) a modern limited duration tenancy; or (v) a repairing tenancy.

25 See the discussion of sub-tenancies under the 2001 Act, in Chapter 12.

26 Note that this exception applies only in the case of temporary accommodation. This would be accommodation secured for the homeless person under s 29(1) of the 1987 Act, pending: (a) a determination of her application for assistance as a homeless person; (b) review of a determination; (c) the authority securing "permanent accommodation" for a successful applicant, under s 31(2). The exception does not apply where, under s 31(5)(d), the local authority discharges its duty to secure "permanent accommodation" for a successful applicant, by securing the provision of a PRT. See Chapter 6, p 181.

(a) is under the supervision provided by a local authority under paragraph (b)(i), (ii) or (vi) of section 27(1) of the Social Work (Scotland) Act 1968, or (b) has requested advice, guidance or assistance from a local authority in fulfilment of its functions under paragraph (c) of that section;

(18) accommodation for asylum seekers or their dependents under section 4 or part VI of the Immigration and Asylum Act 1999;

(19) a tenancy the purpose of which is to provide accommodation under the Displaced Persons (Temporary Protection) Regulations 2005;

(20) shared ownership agreements;[27]

(21) tenancies under previous legislation, being: (a) a protected tenancy under the 1984 Act (b) a tenancy to which part VI of that Act applies, (c) a part VII contract under that Act, or (d) an assured tenancy (including a statutory assured tenancy) under the 1988 Act;[28] and

(22) accommodation provided by a charity for veterans and care leavers.[29] From 1 July 2019, a tenancy cannot be a PRT if the landlord is: (a) a charity providing accommodation to veterans, or (b) a charity providing temporary accommodation to a care leaver. The terms "veteran", "care leaver" and "charity" are defined in paragraph 22.

Most of the schedule 1 exceptions are self-explanatory, and require no further comment. However, the following points may usefully be made.

Tenancies at low rent

Paragraph 1 of schedule 1 states:

> "1(1) A tenancy cannot be a private residential tenancy if—
> (a) it is a tenancy under which rent of, or equivalent to, less than £6 a week is payable, and
> (b) it has not previously acquired the status of a private residential tenancy or been an assured tenancy (including a statutory assured tenancy) within the meaning of the Housing (Scotland) Act 1988.
> (2) In determining the rent payable for the purpose of sub-paragraph (1), no account is to be taken of any amount paid by the tenant in respect of services, repairs, maintenance or insurance."

Reference is made to the discussion of the equivalent exception, under paragraph 2 of schedule 4 to the 1988 Act.[30] In relation to that provision, the relevant amount was specified in a statutory instrument as £6 per week.[31] This was not increased after 1988. The same amount is now stated in the primary legislation, indicating an intention that paragraph 1 should apply in very few cases, and that the set amount will remain at £6 per week.

In one sense, the words "equivalent to" mean the equivalent of £6 per week, if the rent is payable in respect of a different period, such as a month. A ques-

27 Within the meaning of s 83(3) of the Housing (Scotland) Act 2001.

28 Which includes protected tenancies under 1984 Act. See the discussion at the end of Chapter 7.

29 This paragraph was added by the Private Housing (Tenancies) (Scotland) Act 2016 (Modification of Schedule 1) Regulations 2019 (SSI 2019/216), with effect from 1 July 2019.

30 In Chapter 7, at p 226.

31 Assured Tenancies (Tenancies at a Low Rent) (Scotland) Order 1988 (SI 1988/2069).

tion raised by paragraph 1(1)(a) is as to the status of tenancies in which the tenant provides services in lieu of rent. As indicated in Chapter 7, the words "no rent" in the 1988 Act exception appear to mean "no monetary rent", such that tenancies in which rent is in the form of services are not covered by the Act. That was also the case under the older Rent Acts. However, there is no similar wording in paragraph 1 of schedule 1 to the 2016 Act. That notwithstanding, it is suggested that the word "payable" indicates a monetary rent, such that, where services are performed in lieu of rent, the exception under paragraph 1 applies. This is consistent with the position under the previous legislation.

As with the 1988 Act exception, money paid under the lease for services, repairs, maintenance or insurance is not included in the rent, for the purposes of paragraph 1.

The exception does not apply if the tenancy has previously acquired the status of an assured tenancy or a PRT. Under section 4(b),[32] a PRT continues to have that status, even if the term requiring payment of rent is removed, or becomes ineffective.

Student lets

The exception for student lets in paragraph 5 of schedule 1 is much longer than the equivalent provision in the 1988 Act.[33] Paragraph 5 applies if the purpose of the tenancy is to confer on the tenant "the right to occupy the let property while the tenant is a student", provided that paragraph 5(2) or (3) applies. Paragraph 5(2) applies if the landlord is one of the entities listed therein, which includes "a university or constituent college, school or hall of a university". Paragraph 5(3) applies if "planning permission for the construction, conversion or change of use of the building (or part of the building) of which the let property forms part was given on the basis that the let property would be used predominantly for housing students", and the landlord is an "institutional provider"[34] of student accommodation.

Holiday lettings

This exception is effectively the same as the equivalent paragraph 8 of schedule 4 to the 1988 Act.[35] Short-term lets for holiday purposes have become increasingly common, due to the popularity of "Airbnb" and other "home-sharing" websites.[36] Such short-term lets are unlikely to attract the coverage of the 2016 Act because of the requirement, under section 1(1)(b), that the tenant occupies the property (or any part of it) as her "only or principal

32 Quoted at p 294 above.

33 1988 Act, sch 4 para 7.

34 This term, and the term "student", are defined in subparas 5(4) and (5). Note that, under subpara 5(4), a landlord is an institutional provider of student accommodation if it lets, or is entitled to let, other properties in the same building or complex, and the let property and other properties together include at least thirty bedrooms.

35 See Chapter 7, p 226, in particular the reference to the decision in *St Andrews Forest Lodges Ltd. v Grieve* [2017] SC DUN 25, 2017 GWD 14-224.

36 For a discussion of the legal implications of such lets, see: Hunter, "Airbnb – issues for housing lawyers" 2017(2) Journal of Housing Law 39–46.

home". Accordingly, even if the parties' contract is a tenancy, which is not a holiday letting,[37] it is unlikely to be covered by the Act in any event.[38]

Resident landlords

As was the case for assured tenancies, the exception for resident landlords is the most complex and lengthy, taking up paragraphs 7–11 of schedule 1. There are two situations in which the resident landlord exception applies. The first is covered by paragraph 8 of schedule 1, which applies where the tenancy is only a "separate dwelling" because of the right to use "shared accommodation". Where the landlord also has, "from the time the tenancy was granted", the right to use the shared accommodation, in the course of occupying his home, the tenancy will be excepted. This exception will apply, for example, in the case of a bedsit or a house in multiple occupation (an "HMO"), where the landlord and the tenant each occupy a single bedroom, and share the use of the kitchen and bathroom.

Paragraph 9 of schedule 1 is similar to paragraph 9 of schedule 4 to the 1988 Act. It applies if, from the time that it was granted, a dwelling within the same building as the let property has been occupied as the landlord's "only or principal home",[39] and there is an "ordinary means of access"[40] (a) through the let property to the dwelling occupied by the landlord, or (b) through the dwelling occupied by the landlord to the let property, whether or not that access was available to the tenant as of right.

Under paragraph 10, if at any time the landlord holds the landlord's interest as a trustee under a trust, a reference in paragraph 8 or 9 to a landlord or the person having the interest of the landlord includes a person who is a beneficiary under the trust. Under paragraph 11, in a case where two or more persons jointly are the landlord under a tenancy, references to the landlord in paragraphs 8 –10 are to any one of those persons.

Changes in circumstances

Reference is made to the discussion of changes of circumstances in relation to Scottish secure tenancies,[41] and assured tenancies.[42] There is a significant difference between the 2016 Act and the 1988 Act in the way in which each deals with this issue. Section 12(1) and (2) of the 1988 Act both deploy the phrase "if and so long as". As was explained in Chapter 7, the effect of these words is that the tenancy may have been assured at its commencement, but ceases to be assured at some later stage.[43] With section 1 of the 2016 Act,

37 Say, because the tenant wants accommodation near to a place of short-term employment.

38 Coverage by the Act may also be excluded if the contract is for occupation of a single room without exclusive possession (which would not be a "let . . . as a separate dwelling"), or if the "host" is in occupation of another part of the house (resident landlord exception).

39 See Chapter 1.

40 The meaning of this term is discussed in relation to the 1988 Act exception, at p 228.

41 See Chapter 4, p 85.

42 Chapter 7, p 223.

43 For example, if circumstances changed such that it became a tenancy to which one of the categories listed in sch 4 applied. As indicated at the end of Chapter 7, parties to an assured tenancy could agree to convert it to a PRT under s 46A of the 1988 Act.

the effect of subsection (2) appears to be that, whereas "A tenancy which is a private residential tenancy does not cease to be one by reason only of the fact that subsection (1)(b) is no longer satisfied", it *does* cease to be one where subsection (1)(a) or subsection (1)(c) is no longer satisfied. So, for example, if the premises let to the tenant came to consist of, or comprise, "premises licensed for the sale of alcohol for consumption on the premises", subsection (1)(c) would no longer be satisfied[44] and the tenancy would lose its PRT status.

Conversely, it appears that where a tenancy starts off as an arrangement *not* covered by the Act (say, because it is excepted under schedule 1), and then that ceases to be the case, a PRT would be created if all the conditions of section 1 were fulfilled. There is nothing in section 1 that indicates that a tenancy can be a PRT only if it holds that status at its commencement. Moreover, section 10 of the Act, in particular, envisages that a tenancy can become a PRT "after the day on which the tenancy commenced".[45]

However, these general comments are subject to particular provisions in the Act that preserve the status of the tenancy, in the event of a change, such as section 4(b),[46] paragraph 1(1)(b) of schedule 1,[47] and section 45.[48] Note also that the "resident landlord" exception under paragraphs 8 and 9 of schedule 1 applies only if the landlord has the requisite occupation "from the time [the tenancy] was granted".

AGREEMENTS AND TERMS

Section 3: oral agreements

There is no requirement, in section 1 of the 2016 Act, that a tenancy be in writing, in order for it to be a PRT. However, section 3 states:

> "**3 Writing not required to constitute private residential tenancy**
> (1) A purported contract becomes lawfully constituted, despite not being constituted in a written document as required by section 1(2) of the Requirements of Writing (Scotland) Act 1995, when—
> (a) a person occupies a property as the person's only or principal home in pursuance of the purported contract's terms, and
> (b) the tenancy which the purported contract would create, were it lawfully constituted, would satisfy the conditions in paragraphs (a) and (c) of section 1(1).
> . . ."

44 Because para 3 of sch 1 would apply.

45 Section 10 is the "duty to provide written terms of tenancy". Under s 10(1) and (2), the landlord must provide the tenant with a document setting out the terms of the tenancy on: (a) the day on which the tenancy commences, if the tenancy is a private residential tenancy on that day; or (b) the day falling twenty-eight days after the day on which the tenancy became a private residential tenancy, if it became one after the day on which the tenancy commenced.

46 Once a tenancy is a PRT, it remains a PRT even if the term in the lease that requires the tenant to pay rent is removed, or becomes ineffective.

47 A tenancy cannot come under the "low rent" exception if it has previously acquired the status of a PRT.

48 Which preserves the PRT if the ownership of the property is transferred. See p 303.

The drafting of the section raises some issues. Given its heading, and the relative explanatory note,[49] the term "oral contract" (or something similar) would seem more appropriate than "purported contract". Also, section 1 of the 1995 Act does not require that a tenancy agreement be in writing if the tenancy is not for a period of more than one year.[50] However, the point of section 3 appears to be that an oral tenancy will be a PRT from the date when the tenant takes up occupation, in circumstances where the requirements of section 1(1) are met, and not the date when the oral agreement is made. Once the tenancy becomes a PRT, section 10 is triggered, and the landlord comes under an obligation to "provide the tenant with a document which sets out all of the terms of the tenancy". However, if that is not done it has no bearing on the tenancy's PRT status; it will still be a PRT.[51]

Terms of tenancy – parts 2 and 3 of the Act

In contrast to previous legislation, the 2016 Act sets out a comprehensive set of rules in relation to tenancy agreements and the written terms of tenancies.

Section 7 envisages that the Scottish Ministers are to make regulations, under which certain clauses are to be terms of every PRT, known as the "statutory terms". Under section 8, these regulations are to include the terms set out in schedule 2. The regulations are the Private Residential Tenancies (Statutory Terms) (Scotland) Regulations 2017,[52] in which the statutory terms are set out in schedule 1. For present purposes, paragraph 9 has importance:

> "9. The tenancy may not be brought to an end by the landlord, the tenant, nor any agreement between them except in accordance with Part 5 of the Act."

This effectively incorporates section 44 of the Act into the parties' agreement, and prevents them from contracting out of part 5 of the Act ("Termination").

By section 10, the landlord is required to "provide the tenant with a document which sets out all of the terms of the tenancy". Under the Private Residential Tenancies (Information for Tenants) (Scotland) Regulations 2017 ("the Information Regulations"),[53] this may be in the form of the Model Private Residential Tenancy Agreement, or a document drafted by the landlord.[54] It is understood that the Model Agreement is widely used.[55] At pages 18–21 of the Model Agreement, the key provisions of the Act as regards termination, including the statutory grounds for eviction under schedule 3, are summarised as mandatory clauses.[56]

49 Paragraph 10 of the explanatory notes says that the effect of s 3 is that "a private residential tenancy can arise from an oral agreement to create a tenancy".

50 This would appear to be the case for most PRTs, which do not have any duration at all. See p 294 above.

51 The effect of the landlord's failure to comply with s 10 is that the tenant may make an application to the FTT to draw up the terms of the tenancy (s 14), and for a sanction to be imposed under s 16.

52 SSI 2017/408.

53 SSI 2017/407.

54 Regulation 2(2). Under reg 2(1), the document setting out the terms of the tenancy may be provided on paper or electronically.

55 It can be found on the Scottish Government's website.

56 The Model Agreement has various mandatory clauses in bold text. These are the core rights and obligations that follow from the terms of the Act.

The Model Agreement includes the "statutory terms".[57] Where the tenancy agreement has been drafted by the landlord, the statutory terms are read into that agreement, even if they have not been included.[58] Where the landlord has not complied with section 10, or where the terms of the tenancy drafted by the landlord "purport to displace" one or more of the statutory terms, the tenant may apply to the FTT, under sections 14 and 15, to draw up the terms of the tenancy.

Under section 11, the landlord is also under a duty to provide certain specified information to the tenant, the nature of which is specified in regulation 3 of the Information Regulations.[59] These are the Easy Read Notes (where the Model Agreement has been used) or the Statutory Terms Supporting Notes (where the agreement has been drafted by the landlord).[60] Both of these documents provide further information on the rules for termination of PRTs, under part 5 of the Act.

The obligations under sections 10 and 11 are enforced by means of civil sanctions, under section 16 of the Act ("First-tier Tribunal's power to sanction failure to provide information").[61]

TERMINATION OF PRTS: SECURITY OF TENURE, TERMINATION BY THE TENANT, CONSENSUAL TERMINATION

Part 5 chapter 1: Security of tenure

Sections 44 and 45

Sections 44 and 45 are succinct:

> "44 **No termination by parties except in accordance with this Part**
> A tenancy which is a private residential tenancy may not be brought to an end by the landlord, the tenant, nor by any agreement between them, except in accordance with this Part.
>
> **45 Landlord's interest transfers with ownership of property**
> When ownership of a property let under a private residential tenancy is transferred, the landlord's interest under the tenancy transfers with it."

The effect of section 44 has already been discussed in Chapter 1, and in the introduction to this chapter. It is a sweeping provision. Its seems to rule out certain ways in which a tenancy may terminate at common law – say, by

57 Although there are slight differences in the wording as between the Model Agreement and the Statutory Terms Regulations.

58 This follows from s 7(2).

59 n 53. Regulation 3(2) also specifies the time by which this has to be done, being: (a) before the end of the day on which the tenancy commences, if the tenancy is a private residential tenancy; or (b) before the end of the day falling twenty-eight days after the day on which the tenancy became a private residential tenancy, if it became one after the day on which the tenancy commenced. This provision mirrors s 10(1) and (2): see note 45 above.

60 Again, these can be found on the Scottish Government's website.

61 Subject to rules set out in s 16, the tenant may apply for an order requiring the landlord to pay her up to three months' rent, for a breach of either s 10 or s 11, or six months' rent in the case of a breach of both sections.

express or implied renunciation,[62] total or partial destruction of the subjects – because termination is only possible under part 5 of the Act. Parties might achieve the same effect as, say, a renunciation, by agreeing that the tenant gives notice under section 48, terminating the PRT, and then, if so desired, replacing it with another PRT.[63] However, that is effectively turning one mode of termination (renunciation), into another (notice by the tenant), which seems artificial.

As to section 45: the transfer of ownership cannot, in itself, have the effect of terminating the tenancy, given the terms of section 44. Therefore, in the event of such a transfer, the new owner, being the transferee of the "landlord's interest" becomes the landlord under a PRT and, like the transferor, can only terminate the tenancy in accordance with part 5 of the Act. If the transferee is a registered social landlord (an "RSL"), the transfer would appear to have the effect of denuding the tenancy of its status under the 2016 Act, because paragraph 14 of schedule 1 would apply,[64] and the tenancy would then fail to fulfil section 1(1)(c).[65]

Security of tenure (1): sections 46 and 47 – sub-tenancies

Within chapter 1, sections 46 and 47 form part of the Act's treatment of sub-tenancies, which is discussed in Chapter 12.

Part 5 chapter 2: termination by the tenant

As termination by the tenant is unlikely to lead to eviction proceedings by the landlord, sections 48 and 49 of the Act are not analysed in detail. The following points are, however, made.

Under section 48(1), a "tenant" may bring to an end a tenancy that is a PRT by giving the landlord[66] a notice that fulfils the requirements described in section 49. In the case of a joint tenancy, notice would have to be given by all the joint tenants. This is due to section 78(3), which provides that, in a case where two or more persons jointly are the tenant, "references in this Act to the tenant are to all of those persons unless stated otherwise".[67] Therefore, the security of one of the joint tenants is not taken away by the service of a

62 Implied renunciation of an existing tenancy could occur by parties entering into a new tenancy agreement without formally terminating the old agreement. That is possible under Scottish secure tenancy, because it would be an instance of termination by a "written agreement" by s12(1)(e). See Chapter 4, p 88.

63 Also, where it is intended to replace one of the joint tenants with another joint tenant, assignation of a joint tenant's interest would appear to be possible, with the landlord's consent, under para 3(c) of the schedule to the Private Residential Tenancies (Statutory Terms) (Scotland) Regulations 2017 (n 52).

64 "14. A tenancy cannot be a private residential tenancy if the landlord is . . . a registered social landlord . . .".

65 See the discussion of changes in circumstances, above. Note that in this scenario, the tenancy would not become a Scottish secure tenancy under the 2001 Act. See Chapter 4, p 86. In order for the tenant to regain statutory security of tenure, it would be necessary for the RSL to grant a new tenancy, which would be a Scottish secure tenancy under the 2001 Act.

66 Or in the case of joint landlords, any one of them: s 48(4).

67 The Model Agreement (p 18), Easy Read Notes (p 32) and the Statutory Terms Supporting Notes (p 6) all expressly state that the agreement of all the joint tenants is needed to end the tenancy.

termination notice by one of the others. Such a notice is invalid, and does not terminate the tenancy.[68]

If the tenant serves the notice, and then changes his mind, he can effectively withdraw the notice if he "makes a request" under section 48(3),[69] provided that the landlord "agrees to the request". Where the Model Agreement is used, it is suggested that the "request" would be subject to clause 4, under which the parties agree that "all communications which may or must be made under the Act" must be made in writing, using "hard copy by personal delivery or recorded delivery; or the email addresses set out in clauses [2 or 3] and 1". Where the Model Agreement is not used, there may be an equivalent clause in the parties' agreement. In either case, it will be prudent for the tenant to insist on the landlord confirming her agreement to the request, under section 48(3)(b), in writing.

If the landlord refuses a request under section 48(3), or the tenant fails to make the request on time, or at all, the tenancy terminates on the date stated in the tenant's notice. In that case, if the tenant does not leave, there is no eviction ground.[70] An order under section 51 would be inept, in any event: the effect of such an order is to bring the tenancy to an end on a specified date in terms of section 51(4). In this case, the tenancy has already been terminated, under section 48(2). The landlord would have to initiate eviction proceedings,[71] on the basis that the tenant no longer has any right or title to be in occupation of the property. It is suggested that those proceedings would be raised in the FTT, under section 71 of the Act.[72]

There is no prescribed form for the tenant's notice under section 49. It is valid if it is given freely and without coercion of any kind, after the tenant begins occupying the let property; it is in writing; and it states as the day on which the tenancy is to end a day that is after the last day of the minimum notice period. That period is twenty-eight days. The parties may agree a longer period,[73] but only if the agreement is made in writing, and was entered after the tenancy became a private residential tenancy.[74]

68 Note that, for the same reason, the security of tenure of one of the joint tenants is not threatened by one of the other joint tenants ceasing occupation, as non-occupation by all the joint tenants is required for ground 10 to operate. The rent arrears ground may arise, however, if the non-occupying tenant stops paying his share, and the other joint tenants cannot afford to cover it.

69 Again, in the case of joint tenants, the request would have to be made by all of them.

70 In contrast to the 1988 Act, under which ground 10 in sch 5 is "tenant's notice to quit". See Chapter 8, p 287.

71 Proceedings are necessary, given s 23 of the 1984 Act, which is discussed in Chapter 2.

72 Which confers on the FTT, "In relation to civil proceedings arising from a private residential tenancy", "whatever competence and jurisdiction a sheriff would have". It is suggested that in this instance, the application could be made under r 79 of the Procedure Rules ("Application to evict an occupier upon termination of a tenancy"), which is apt "Where an owner makes an application under section 23 (prohibition of eviction without due process of law) of the 1984 Act".

73 Under s 49(3)(b)(i) and (4).

74 The Government's Guidance "Private Residential Tenancy – Information for Landlords" states, at p 10: "You and your tenant can agree a different notice period. But this must be in writing and can only be done once the tenant has started to live in the let property."

Section 50: consensual termination

At first sight, section 50 appears straightforward, but it raises some tricky issues:

> "**50 Termination by notice to leave and tenant leaving**
> (1) A tenancy which is a private residential tenancy comes to an end if—
> (a) the tenant has received a notice to leave from the landlord, and
> (b) the tenant has ceased to occupy the let property.
> (2) A tenancy comes to an end under subsection (1) on the later of—
> (a) the day specified in the notice to leave in accordance with section 62(1)(b), or
> (b) the day on which the tenant ceases to occupy the let property.
> (3) For the avoidance of doubt, a tenancy which is to come to an end under subsection (1) may be brought to an end earlier in accordance with section 48."

This is the first section in chapter 3 of part 5: "Termination at the landlord's instigation". Section 50 itself has a distinct heading: "Consensual termination". Section 50(1)(a) is where the term "notice to leave" makes its first appearance in the Act.[75] For the purposes of understanding section 50, it is necessary to appreciate that, in terms of section 62(1)(b), the notice to leave must state a date, after the end of the notice period calculated in accordance with section 54, on or after which the landlord may make an application to the tribunal.

Consensual termination and abandonment

In order for the PRT to come to an end under section 50, two things must happen. First, the tenant must have *received* the notice to leave from the landlord. Where service of the notice has been effected in accordance with section 26(2)(b) or (c) of the Interpretation and Legislative Reform (Scotland) Act 2010,[76] there is a presumption that it will have been received by the tenant forty-eight hours after it is sent, "unless the contrary is shown".[77] Secondly, the tenant must have "ceased to occupy the let property".

It is suggested that section 50 is intended to deal with a situation in which the landlord serves a notice to leave, which is "received" by the tenant, as required by section 50(1)(a), and the tenant then decides to leave voluntarily, thereby avoiding the need for proceedings in the FTT to be pursued. That is why, in the Act, section 50 has the heading: "Consensual termination".

Section 50 is not an abandonment procedure.[78] It does not grant the landlord a warrant to take possession; its effect is simply to terminate the tenancy. There is a risk in taking possession of subjects on the basis that the tenancy has

75 Under the 2016 Act, the "notice to leave" is the statutory notice informing the tenant that the landlord intends to seek recovery of possession. See the discussion of s 62 at p 321.

76 Section 26 of the 2010 Act is discussed in Chapter 15. It applies where ". . . an Act of the Scottish Parliament or a Scottish instrument authorises or requires a document to be served on a person (whether the expression 'serve', 'give', 'send' or any other expression is used)". Section 26(2)(b) deals with service by recorded delivery or registered post and s 26(3) with service by email. The other option is "by being personally delivered to the person", under s 26(a). In that case, receipt would occur at the same time as delivery.

77 Section 26(5) and (6).

78 I.e. it is not the equivalent of ss 17 and 18 of the 2001 Act, discussed at the end of Chapter

ended under section 50, without obtaining an order from the tribunal.[79] The existence of both prerequisites under section 50(1)(a) and (b) are potentially open to dispute.[80] Therefore, it is suggested that, where the tenant elects to leave, the landlord should seek written confirmation from the tenant that: (a) he has received the notice to leave; (b) the date on which he intends to cease occupation; and (c) an acknowledgement that the tenancy will end on the date stated in the notice, or the date of the tenancy ceasing occupation, if that is later. In absence of that confirmation, it may be prudent for the landlord to seek an order under section 51, on ground 10 ("Not occupying let property") and any other ground which is applicable,[81] unless it is clear that the tenant has ceased occupation. An order under section 51 grants the landlord legal warrant to take possession of the subjects, and eject the tenant, and anyone else residing at the property.

Options for the tenant

It follows from section 50(2) that termination of the tenancy could take place at any time between the date specified in the notice, and the date when the tenant chooses to leave.[82] This is confirmed by the Easy Read Notes, which indicate[83] that, on receipt of the notice to leave, the tenant has four options:

> "1. The tenant could choose to leave on the date in the Notice to Leave.[84]
> 2. Despite the date stated in the notice, the tenant may ask the landlord to agree to a later date for ending the tenancy.[85]
> 3. If the tenant believes that the ground(s) for ending the Agreement given in the notice do not apply, then they should discuss this with the landlord and seek advice.
> 4. Wait for the landlord to apply to the Tribunal for an Eviction Order."

In describing option 4, the Easy Read Notes state: "You don't need to move out until an Eviction Order is granted by the Tribunal." It would be more accurate to say: "You don't need to move out until the date specified in the Order granted by the Tribunal, when the tenancy will end."[86] In any case, it is

4. The point of that procedure is that, if it is correctly carried out, the landlord is "entitled to take possession of the house without any further proceedings", under s 18(3).

79 The risk being that the landlord is accused of unlawfully evicting the tenant: see Chapter 2.

80 As is explained later in this chapter, it is not unusual for the landlord to make a mistake in the completion of the prescribed form notice to leave that renders it invalid. Also, in the absence of confirmation from the tenant, the fact that "the tenant has ceased to occupy the let property" will usually be a matter of inference, which may be disputed.

81 In practice, apparent non-occupation often coincides with rent arrears. Also, as is explained in the discussion of ground 10 in Chapter 10, non-occupation is likely to be a breach of the tenancy agreement, as a result of which ground 11 may be invoked.

82 If the tenant does not leave in response to the notice, the tenancy terminates when the tribunal's order takes effect, under s 51(4).

83 At pp 33–34.

84 In the relevant passage of the Easy Read Notes, this is referred to as the "tenancy end date", but that would be the case only if the tenant chooses option 1, leaving on the date specified in the notice.

85 Though, given the terms of option 4, it is not clear why the agreement of the landlord is necessary. The tenant could leave at any time up to the order under s 51 taking effect, thereby ending the tenancy under s 50. Agreeing the date of termination may, however, be advisable for the tenant, in order to make clear the date on which her liability to pay rent ends.

86 In terms of s 51(4).

clear that the tenant is under no compulsion to take the option of consensual termination under section 50.[87] Given that she is unlikely to be subject to an award of expenses of the tribunal proceedings,[88] it may well be in the tenant's interests to take option 4, unless she has somewhere else to go.

Occupation by other persons

Where the property has been sub-let, both the tenant and the sub-tenant must have ceased occupation in order to establish section 50(1)(b): under section 78(2) "tenant" includes a sub-tenant.

Where the tenancy is a matrimonial home, and one of the spouses, being the sole tenant, leaves, but the other spouse remains in occupation, the tenancy is not terminated under section 50. That follows from section 2(8) of the Matrimonial Homes (Family Protection) (Scotland) Act 1981.[89]

Where it appears that the tenant has ceased occupation on receipt of the notice, but another person (such as a friend or relative of the tenant) remains in occupation, the landlord ought to obtain an order for recovery of possession from the tribunal,[90] given the terms of section 23(2A) of the 1984 Act.[91] This may be sought under ground 10 in schedule 3.[92]

APPLICATIONS FOR EVICTION ORDERS UNDER s 51

Section 51: FTT's power to issue an eviction order

Section 51 provides that the FTT is to issue an eviction order if, on an application by the landlord, it finds that one of the schedule 3 grounds applies. In that case, the order must state the ground(s) on the basis which it is granted, and it will also state a date on which the PRT will end. It is understood that the practice of the FTT is to state a date that is at least thirty-one days after date of the order being granted, given the thirty-day time limit for applications for

87 It is suggested that this has significant implications for the practice of local authorities in relation to applications by persons seeking assistance under the homelessness legislation (pt II of the Housing (Scotland) Act 1987). Prior to 1 December 2017, most authorities in Scotland were willing to deal with applications made by tenants in receipt of a valid notices terminating an assured or a short assured tenancy, even if they were still in occupation; i.e. they did not withhold assistance until such time as an eviction order had actually been granted in the sheriff court. That approach was based on the view that it was no longer reasonable for the tenant to continue to occupy the accommodation, under s 24(2A) of the 1987 Act, because: (a) the tenant no longer had a right to remain in occupation; (b) he should not be forced to face eviction proceedings in court, followed by order for expenses. However, neither of these factors applies, in relation to PRTs, because the tenancy continues until the date stated in the eviction order, and expenses are not awarded by the FTT, save in exceptional cases.

88 See the discussion of expenses in FTT applications, in Chapter 14.

89 Section 2(8): "(8) Where (a) the entitled spouse is a tenant of a matrimonial home; and (b) possession thereof is necessary in order to continue the tenancy; and (c) the entitled spouse abandons such possession, the tenancy shall be continued by such possession by the non-entitled spouse."

90 Because, as previously stated, s 50 does not grant a warrant to eject any person in occupation.

91 See Chapter 2, p 37.

92 Alternatively, an order might be sought under s 71 of the Act, on the basis that there is no need to terminate the PRT by an order under s 51, as it has already been ended under s 50.

permission to appeal.[93] Section 51 and the grounds for eviction are discussed in Chapter 10.

Section 52 of the Act and Procedure Rules, r 109

Procedural requirements for applications for eviction orders

The procedural requirements for an application to the FTT for an eviction order under section 51 of the 2016 Act are set out principally in section 52 of the Act:

> "**52 Applications for eviction orders and consideration of them**
> (1) In a case where two or more persons jointly are the landlord under a tenancy, an application for an eviction order may be made by any one of those persons.
> (2) The Tribunal is not to entertain an application for an eviction order if it is made in breach of—
> (a) subsection (3), or
> (b) any of sections 54 to 56 (but see subsection (4)).
> (3) An application for an eviction order against a tenant must be accompanied by a copy of a notice to leave which has been given to the tenant.
> (4) Despite subsection (2)(b), the Tribunal may entertain an application made in breach of section 54 if the Tribunal considers that it is reasonable to do so.
> (5) The Tribunal may not consider whether an eviction ground applies unless it is a ground which—
> (a) is stated in the notice to leave accompanying the landlord's application in accordance with subsection (3), or
> (b) has been included with the Tribunal's permission in the landlord's application as a stated basis on which an eviction order is sought."[94]

In order fully to understand the requirements for making an application to the FTT, section 52 has to be read along with sections 54–56 and 62–64. These are reinforced, and extended, by rule 109 ("Application for an Eviction Order") of the Procedure Rules:[95]

> "**109. Application for an eviction order**
> Where a landlord makes an application under section 51(1) (for an eviction order) of the 2016 Act,[96] the application must—
> (a) state—
> (i) the name, address and registration number (if any) of the landlord;
> (ii) the name, address and profession of any representative of the landlord;
> (iii) the name and address of the tenant; and
> (iv) the ground or grounds for eviction;

93 In terms of reg 2 of the Scottish Tribunals (Time Limits) Regulations 2016 (SSI 2016/231). See Chapter 15, p 511.

94 Section 52(5) provides that is considered in relation to s 51.

95 Which are set out in sch 1 to the First-tier Tribunal for Scotland Housing and Property Chamber (Procedure) Regulations 2017 (SSI 2017/328), as amended, in particular, by the First-tier Tribunal for Scotland Housing and Property Chamber (Procedure) Amendment Regulations (SSI 2018/378). In this chapter and the next, references to any rule or rules are to the Procedure Rules.

96 Rule 109 is particular to applications made under the 2016 Act. Applications for an order for possession under the 1988 Act are under rr 65 and 66, as discussed in Chapter 7.

(b) be accompanied by—
  (i) evidence showing that the eviction ground or grounds has been met;
  (ii) a copy of the notice to leave given to the tenant as required under section 52(3) of the 2016 Act; and
  (iii) a copy of the notice given to the local authority as required under section 56(1) of the 2016 Act; and
  (iv) a copy of Form BB (notice to the occupier) under schedule 6 of the Conveyancing and Feudal Reform (Scotland) Act 1970 (if applicable);[97] and
(c) be signed and dated by the landlord or a representative of the landlord."

As well as rule 109, it is also necessary to be aware of rules 4, 5 and 8. However, those are general to all the applications made to the Housing and Property Chamber, and are considered in Chapter 14. Suffice it to say at this point that applications to the Chamber are subject to a "sift", and those made under rule 109 are apt to be rejected, under rule 8, if the requirements of the Act, or rule 109, have not been met.[98] Even if the application makes it through the sift, it may still be refused at a later stage due to some failure to follow the requirements for a valid application under the Act.

In terms of rule 4, "An application to the First-tier Tribunal must be in writing and may be made using a form obtained from the First-tier Tribunal". The form used for applications for an eviction or possession order, whether under the 1984 Act, the 1988 Act or the 2016 Act, is form E. Both the form, and guidance notes on its completion, can be downloaded from the Chamber's website.[99] Rule 109(c) also stipulates that the application must be signed and dated, either by the applicant or by his representative. This requirement appears throughout the Procedure Rules, in relation to applications to the tribunal. Applications that are not signed or dated are rejected.[100]

Apart from these general provisions, the particular requirements of the 2016 Act, and rule 109, in relation to an application for an eviction order under that Act may be stated as follows. The application must:

1. be made by the landlord, or one of the joint landlords;
2. provide names, addresses and other details required by rule 109(a)(i)–(iii);
3. state the ground(s) on the basis of which an eviction order is sought, which must be the same as the ground(s) stated in the notice to leave;
4. be accompanied by evidence showing that the eviction ground or grounds has or have been met;
5. be accompanied by a copy of a valid notice to leave, which has been served on the tenant;
6. be made after the relevant notice period has expired;
7. be made within six months of the expiry of the notice period;

97 This applies to an application made by a heritable creditor in possession. The lender is required to include, with the application to the FTT, a copy of the form BB that was given to the occupier of the subjects when the security was called up. The same requirement is imposed, in rr 65 and 66, in relation to applications made under ss 18 and 33 of the 1988 Act. See the discussion of applications by lenders, in Chapter 8, at p 274, and Chapter 10, p 342.

98 Examples are given below.

99 See the discussion of form E, in Chapter 14.

100 Though usually after the applicant/representative has been given the opportunity to sign and date the application. See, for example, *McCallum v Paterson* EV/19/1767, 28/6/19.

8. be accompanied by a copy of notice given to the local authority of the landlord's intention to seek an eviction order.

These rules are explained in more detail below.

1. Application must be made by landlord or one of joint landlords (s 52(1))

This follows from section 51(1) ("on an application by the *landlord*") and section 52(1) (any of the joint landlords may apply).

Under section 63, references to the "landlord" include "a creditor in a heritable security over the let property who is entitled to sell the property". Applications for eviction orders may be made by heritable creditors under ground 2 of schedule 3, which is discussed in Chapter 10.

2. Application must provide names, addresses and other details required by r 109(a)(i)–(iii)

Where there are joint tenants, or joint landlords, it is suggested that the names and addresses of all the joint landlords, and all the joint tenants, ought to be stated. Likewise, where there is a sub-tenancy, the name and address of the sub-tenant ought to be stated. This would appear to follow from section 78 of the Act, and rules 46, 9 and 112 of the Procedure Rules.[101]

In terms of section 78(1), "tenant" includes a sub-tenant.[102] Under section 78(2) and (3):

> "(2) In a case where two or more persons jointly are the landlord under a tenancy, references . . . to the landlord are to all of those persons unless stated otherwise;
>
> (3) In a case where two or more persons jointly are the tenant under a tenancy, references . . . to the tenant are to all of those persons unless stated otherwise."

It is suggested that the same interpretation of "landlord" and "tenant" applies to rule 109(a)(i) and (iii), by virtue of rule 46(2)(g):

> "(g) in Chapter 12, where terms are used which are defined terms in the 2016 Act, the definitions in that Act in respect of those terms apply to that Chapter."

Against that, one could argue that, in rule 109(a)(i), the term "landlord" has to take its sense from the opening words of the rule ("Where a landlord makes an application"), which might be only one of the joint landlords, given the terms of section 52(1). However, under rule 9, the tribunal must give notice of the acceptance of application to "each party"; and, in terms of rule 112, in relation to an application under the 2016 Act, the parties to be notified under rule 9(1) are "the landlord" and "the tenant". Again, both of these terms are interpreted in accordance with section 78 of the Act, given the terms of rule 46(2)(g). This means that where one of the joint landlords applies, the others will have to be notified by the tribunal. Therefore, it is logical to regard rule 109(a)(i) as requiring the names and addresses of the all the joint landlords to be stated in the application.

101 n 95.

102 Sub-tenancies under the 2016 Act are discussed in Chapter 12.

If the landlord is registered, rule 109(a)(i) requires that his registration number is entered in the application. Registration is not a prerequisite for seeking an order.[103] However, under section 72 of the Act, the tribunal has a duty to report unregistered landlords to the relevant local authority.

The requirement, in rule 109(a)(iii), to give the name and address of the tenant, is subject to rule 6(6), which is set out in Chapter 7, at p 244.

3. Application must state ground(s) on which order is sought: r 109(a)(iv) and s 52(5)

In the vast majority of cases, the ground(s) stated in the application, as required by rule 109(a)(iv), is/are the same as that stated in the copy of the notice to leave: that follows from section 52(5)(a).

However, this is not, strictly speaking, a requirement for lodging because, under section 52(5)(b), the tribunal may give permission for an eviction ground to be included in the application, even though it was not stated in the notice to leave.[104]

It is suggested that, normally, the tribunal should be slow to allow the applicant to pursue an application that replaces the ground stated in the notice to leave with a different ground, as that would tend to defeat one of the main purposes of the notice.[105] In that situation it is also submitted that permission should be sought under section 52(5)(b), when the application is made. Otherwise, given the terms of section 52(2)(a), the application is liable to be rejected under rule 8.

Where the application seeks to add to the ground stated in the notice (rather than replacing it), it is again suggested that permission ought to be sought on lodging the application, or as soon as possible in the process.

In either case (adding additional grounds, or replacing the ground in the notice), the tribunal should consider whether it is appropriate to postpone a decision to exercise the power in section 52(5)(b) to the case management discussion ("CMD"),[106] so that the tenant has the opportunity to object to new grounds being added, and to explain the basis for that objection.[107]

4. Application must be accompanied by evidence that eviction ground(s) met: r 109(b)(i)

Rule 109(b)(i) seems somewhat pre-emptive: it is for the tribunal to decide, after a hearing,[108] whether the evidence presented by the landlord shows that the eviction ground has been established.

That view is consistent with the wording used in grounds 1, 3, 4, 5 and 6. These are all "intention" grounds, contained within part 1 of schedule 3 to the

103 See Chapter 10, p 365.
104 Consequently, r 109(a)(iv) requires the ground to be stated in the application, but does not stipulate that this must be same ground as is stated in the notice to leave.
105 On this point, see also the discussion under the heading "Grounds 11 and 12: a case for use of section 73?" at p 331 below.
106 Under r 17.
107 The same view is expressed in the relation to the corresponding power in s 19(2) of the 1988 Act, for the reasons discussed in Chapter 7, at p 244.
108 Or at the CMD, if the tribunal decides to make decision then, under r 17(4).

Act. As is explained in Chapter 10, each of those grounds includes a provision that begins: "Evidence *tending* to show [the relevant intention] . . . includes (for example) . . .". There then follows reference to some piece of evidence, such as a letter, an affidavit, planning permission, a contract, and so on.

The relationship between rule 109(b)(i) and those statutory grounds featured in the decision of the Tribunal President in the application of *Davis*.[109] In that case, the application relied on grounds 1 and 6.[110] However, no supporting evidence, whether of the type described in the grounds or otherwise, was submitted with the application. The President said:

> "The applicant's representative gives an explanation as to why the types of evidence referred to in grounds 1 and 6 have not been lodged but that explanation is insufficient for the purpose of complying with rule 109(b)(i) when making an application. Rule 109(b)(i) provides that evidence showing that the eviction ground or grounds has been met must be lodged. The statutory provisions in schedule 3 part 1 at ground 1 (3) and ground 6(3) refer to 'Evidence tending to show that the landlord has the intention mentioned'. It is insufficient merely to rely on a statement of intent that the house will be sold in the future or, failing such sale, used for non-residential purposes, and some form of independent evidence to support that intention must be produced."

On that basis, the application was rejected under rule 8(1)(c).[111] It appears to follow that, at least as regards the "intention" grounds 1, 3, 4, 5 and 6 in part 1 of schedule 3, the evidence mentioned in those grounds, or something similar, ought to be submitted with the application, failing which it is liable to be rejected.

What about the other grounds? In the vast majority of applications under rule 109, the sole ground, or at least one of them, is ground 12 (rent arrears). That ground makes no reference to evidence "tending to show" that the arrears exist. In practice, eviction orders granted in ground 12 cases, at a CMD or a hearing, are based on the evidence of a rent account or other statement showing that the various elements of the ground are established. The applicant, or her representative, speaks to the accuracy of the account, before the tribunal. Accordingly, it seems reasonable to suggest that a rent account, or some other statement tending to show the current balance, and the history of non-payment, ought to accompany the application, in order to comply with rule 109(b)(i).[112]

The evidence tending to show some of the other grounds should be self-evident, such as:

- Ground 2: (Property to be sold by lender) – a copy of the extract decree in terms of which the lender is entitled to sell the property.

109 *Davis v Skelton and Ashan*, EV/19/0191, 14/3/19.

110 1.Landlord intends to sell, and 6. Landlord intends to use for non-residential purpose.

111 Rule 8(1)(c): "The Chamber President . . . must reject an application if— (c) they have good reason to believe that it would not be appropriate to accept the application". See the discussion of r 8(1)(a) and (c) in Chapter 14.

112 In the brief decision in *Baird v Bochenek and Comar*, EV/19/1184, 11/6/19, the tribunal rejected an application under ground 12 for various reasons, including the lack of "evidence of unpaid rent in the form of a statement".

- Ground 9: (No longer in need of supported accommodation) – written confirmation that the tenant has been assessed as no longer having a need for community care.
- Ground 13 (Criminal behaviour): an extract conviction.
- Grounds 14–15 (Antisocial behaviour): evidence of "relevant antisocial behaviour" in the form of complaints, reports of police attendance, statements etc.
- Grounds 16–18: written confirmation from the local authority that the landlord has ceased to be registered, an HMO licence has been revoked, or an overcrowding statutory notice has been served on the landlord.

In other cases, the evidence might take the form of an affidavit from the landlord, to the effect that the requirements of the ground are met.[113]

5. Application must be accompanied by copy of "Notice to leave", "given" to tenant: s 52(2)(a) and (3); r 109(b)(ii)

It is suggested that section 52(3) imposes three distinct requirements on the landlord making the application. First, a valid "notice to leave" must have been prepared. Secondly, it must have been "given" to the tenant. Thirdly, a copy of the notice must accompany the application to the tribunal. If any one of those is not met, the tribunal "is not to entertain" the application, in terms of section 52(2)(a). The application is then liable to be rejected at the sift stage, under rule 8, or refused at a CMD or a subsequent hearing.[114]

The term "notice to leave" is defined in section 62, which is discussed in detail below. The form of notice is set out in schedule 5 to the Private Residential Tenancies (Prescribed Notices and Forms) (Scotland) Regulations 2017 ("the Notices and Forms Regulations").[115] A notice that does not comply with the requirements of section 62 is not a "notice to leave".[116] It is therefore invalid for the purposes of section 52(3).[117] As is apparent from the tribunal decisions, the most common reason for the notice being invalid is that it fails to specify the correct date, for the purposes of section 62(1)(b) and (4).[118]

The requirement that the notice be "given" to the tenant entails that it must have been served, in accordance with section 26 of the Interpretation and

113 Grounds 4(4) and 5(7) expressly state that evidence tending to show that the ground is met could include an affidavit, so there seems no reason why such evidence could not accompany an application made on other grounds.

114 *Panpher v McDonald* [2019] UT 18. At para [4] Sheriff Deutsch said: "a further feature of section 52 which deserves attention is the fact that subsection (4) confers a discretion on the Tribunal to waive an application made in breach of section 54 (restriction on applying during the notice period), which raises the clearest implication possible that no such discretion exists for a breach of subsection (3)".

115 SSI 2017/297.

116 Subject to s 21 of the Interpretation and Legislative Reform (Scotland) Act 2010, and s 73 of the 2016 Act (minor errors in documents). See the discussion below, at p 326.

117 *Panpher v McDonald* (n 114). There are numerous examples of applications being rejected at the sift, or refused at the CMD, because the notice to leave is invalid. A sample: *Mughal v Bernard* (19/1556, 11/6/19); *Crawford Property v Murray and Sturgeon* (19/1286, 23/5/19); *Ross v Lafferty* (19/0866, 16/5/19); *Holleran v McAlister* (19/3231, 2/5/19); *Thyme Property Developments v Mitchell* (18/0496, 25/4/18).

118 This issue is discussed from p 323 below onwards.

Legislative Reform (Scotland) Act 2010, which is discussed in Chapter 15.[119] Given the terms of section 78(3), service must have been effected on all the joint tenants.[120]

A copy of the notice to leave must be attached to the application. This is confirmed by rule 109(b)(ii).[121]

6. Application must be made after relevant notice period has expired: ss 54 and 52(2)(b)

In terms of section 54(1), the landlord cannot make an application until the "relevant period" has expired:

> "54 **Restriction on applying during the notice period**
> (1) A landlord may not make an application to the First-tier Tribunal for an eviction order against a tenant using a copy of a notice to leave[122] until the expiry of the relevant period in relation to that notice."

It is therefore necessary to work out the "relevant period".

Subsection (2) goes on to say:

> "(2) The relevant period in relation to a notice to leave—
> (a) begins on the day the tenant receives the notice to leave from the landlord, and
> (b) expires on the day falling—
> (i) 28 days after it begins if subsection (3) applies,
> (ii) 84 days after it begins if subsection (3) does not apply."

Therefore, calculation of the "relevant period" is a two-part exercise, establishing: (i) when the period begins; and (ii) whether it expires twenty-eight or eighty-four days later.

The beginning of the relevant period will depend on the mode of service that is chosen, from the available alternatives in section 26 of the 2010 Act.[123] If the notice is personally delivered to the tenant,[124] the period begins on the day of delivery, being "the day the tenant receives the notice to leave from

119 In contrast to the 1988 and 2001 Acts, there is no specific provision in the 2016 Act dealing with the mode of service of notices given under the Act. Therefore, s 26 of the Interpretation and Legislative Reform (Scotland) Act 2010 has effect, subs (1) of which states: "This section applies where an Act of the Scottish Parliament or a Scottish instrument authorises or requires a document to be served on a person (whether the expression 'serve', 'give', 'send' or any other expression is used." In *Ahuja v Peck and McHugh* (18/2446, 27/2/19) the application was refused at the CMD, because the tribunal was not satisfied that the notice to leave had been served.

120 In part 1 of the prescribed form, the notice is addressed to the "tenant(s)". It is suggested that the names of all the joint tenants should be entered. It appears possible to serve a single notice on all the joint tenants, or separate notices (in identical terms) on each of them: see para 10 of the Guidance Notes for Landlords on the Notice to Leave.

121 Examples of applications rejected at the sift, because no notice to leave accompanied the application: *Nelson v McCourt* (19/1202, 5/6/19); *Ridley v Maxwell* (19/1349, 28/5/19)

122 Both ss 54(1) and 55(1) begin with these words. In terms of ss 54(4) and 55(3), "using a copy of a notice to leave" means submitting it to the tribunal along with the application, in order to satisfy the requirement in s 52(3).

123 As discussed above, the notice to leave must be "given" to the tenant, which entails that it must have been served under s 26 of the Interpretation and Legislative Reform (Scotland) Act 2010, which is discussed in Chapter 15.

124 In terms of s 26(2)(a).

the landlord", under section 54(2)(a). If the notice is "sent" by registered post or recorded delivery,[125] or by email,[126] the notice is "taken to have been received 48 hours after it is sent *unless the contrary is shown*".[127] The effect of the italicised words is that the date of receipt may not be forty-eight hours after sending.

Let us say that the landlord effects service of the notice by email and, five minutes later, the tenant sends an email that acknowledges receipt of the notice. In that case, receipt on the same day is shown, and the relevant date, for the purposes of calculating the relevant period under section 54(1), should be taken to be the day of sending. Likewise, if the notice is sent by recorded delivery, and the landlord receives a record that the tenant signed for the notice three days after sending, then the date of receipt is three days later.[128]

Expiry of the relevant period is worked out by reference to section 54(3):

> "(3) This subsection applies if—
> (a) on the day the tenant receives the notice to leave, the tenant has been entitled to occupy the let property for not more than six months, or
> (b) the only eviction ground, or grounds, stated in the notice to leave is, or are, one or more of the following—
> (i) that the tenant is not occupying the let property as the tenant's home,
> (ii) that the tenant has failed to comply with an obligation under the tenancy,
> (iii) that the tenant has been in rent arrears for three or more consecutive months,
> (iv) that the tenant has a relevant conviction,
> (v) that the tenant has engaged in relevant anti-social behaviour,
> (vi) that the tenant associates in the let property with a person who has a relevant conviction or has engaged in relevant anti-social behaviour."

If section 54(3) (a) or (b) applies, expiry of the relevant period is twenty-eight days after receipt of the notice.[129] If neither applies, expiry of the relevant period is eighty-four days after receipt of the notice. In practice, the twenty-eight-day period will be applicable in most cases.[130]

For the purposes of section 54(3)(a), the six months' occupation would normally begin on the "start date" of the tenancy:[131] on that day the tenant will be "entitled to occupy" the let property. Note, however, that section 54(3)(a)

125 In terms of s 26(2)(b)(i) or (ii).
126 In terms of s 26(2)(c).
127 Respectively under s 26(5) and (6) of the 2010 Act.
128 However, for the purposes of preparing the notice to leave, and specifying the date in part 4, the effect of s 62(5) is that receipt forty-eight hours after sending should be assumed. See point (1) at p 323 below, and the FTT decision in *Talon Alba Ltd v Lane* EV/19/3052, 6/2/20.
129 On this point, see the discussion of the example from the Scottish Government's Guidance Notes for Landlords, discussed at p 325 below.
130 Because the vast majority of applications are made on the ground of rent arrears, or one of the other "conduct" grounds in pt 3 of sch 3; these are the grounds that are listed in s 54(3)(b). Where other grounds are used, the tribunal decisions indicate that the landlord tends to serve the notice to leave before the six months have expired under s 54(3)(a). That might lead one to question the value of having an eighty-four-day period if, in practice, its main effect is to incentivise landlords to serve the notice to leave within six months of the start of the tenancy.
131 See the discussion of cl 6 of the Model Agreement, at p 294.

does not stipulate that the entitlement is under the current PRT.[132] Also, the fact that the parties agree a specific duration for the tenancy has no bearing on the issue of how long the tenant "has been" entitled to occupy.[133]

The reference to "six months" in section 54(3)(a) must be understood in light of section 64(1):

> "64 **Six month periods**
> (1) A reference in this Part to a period of six months (however expressed) is to a period which ends in the month which falls six months after the month in which it began, either—
> (a) on the same day of the month as it began, or
> (b) if the month in which the period ends has no such day, on the final day of that month."

Say, then, that the entitlement to occupy begins on 15 August. In that case, given the terms of section 64(1)(a), the six months end on 15 February the following year. If the tenant receives the notice on 16 February, section 54(3)(a) does not apply.[134] If the entitlement to occupy begins on 31 August, then, given the terms of section 64(1)(b), the six months end on 28 February in the following year, or 29 February in the case of a leap year.

Section 54(3)(b) is a list of the "tenant's conduct" grounds in part 3 of schedule 3. Where any of the other grounds is relied upon, and the tenant has been entitled to occupy the let property for more than six months, the relevant period is eighty-four days.[135] This means that where the landlord has a ground for eviction under part 3 (say, rent arrears), but also wants to rely on, say, ground 1 (in part 1 of schedule 3), he will have to make a decision between (1) relying on both grounds, but waiting for eighty-four days for expiry of the notice; or (2) restricting the notice to ground 12 (rent arrears), so as to limit the period of notice to twenty-eight days.

Where the tenant takes up occupation under a PRT and, shortly thereafter, an eviction ground arises under part 1, part 2 or part 4 of schedule 3, it may be in the landlord's interest to ensure that he serves the notice sooner rather than later. Where the application is rejected or refused by the tribunal, say because the notice to leave is invalid, the six months may have passed by the time the landlord is able to serve another notice. In that case, any new notice will be subject to the eighty-four-day period, resulting in a substantial delay.

Further examples of the operation of section 54, in conjunction with requirements for a valid notice to leave under section 62, are discussed below.[136]

132 If the tenant previously occupied on some other basis, it is suggested that that occupation would be taken into account in calculating the six month period. That is consistent the Act's recognising that the tenant may have occupied before the current tenancy commenced. See s 10(2)(b), for example.

133 So, if parties were to agree a tenancy that ran for a year from 1 May, on which date the tenant took up occupation, it is not the case, for the purposes of s 54(3)(a), that the tenant is entitled to occupy for more than six months, from the beginning. The tenant "has been entitled to occupy" for more than six months, as at 2 November that year.

134 In that case, the period of notice would have to be eighty-four days, unless the ground(s) for eviction were stated in s 54(3)(b).

135 For a case in which the landlord fell foul of this rule, see *Andreccetti v Sinclair* 19/1720, 1/7/19.

136 At p 324.

Section 52(4)

Given the terms of section 54(1), an application for an eviction order under section 51 is likely to be rejected by the tribunal, if made during the applicable notice period in terms of section 54; under section 52(2)(b), the tribunal is "not to entertain" such an application. Applications have been rejected on this basis.[137]

Section 52(4) provides that the tribunal may entertain an application "made in breach of section 54" if it considers that it is reasonable to do so. Accordingly, the tribunal has the power to allow an application to be made during the notice period. This might be appropriate where, for example, the landlord seeks an order as a matter of urgency, due to antisocial behaviour, or has a reasonable apprehension of the tenant causing damage to the property.

It is suggested that the tribunal's exercise of the power in section 52(4) is subject to considerations similar to those discussed in relation to section 52(5)(b).[138] The landlord should ask for the power to be exercised, in the application, otherwise it is liable to be rejected under rule 8.[139] Again, it is also suggested that a decision to exercise the power in section 52(5)(b) ought not to be made until the tenant has had the opportunity, at the CMD, to object to the application being made during the notice period, and to explain the basis for that objection.[140]

7. Application must be made within six months of expiry of notice period: ss 55 and 52(2)(b)

Section 55(1) provides:

> "**55 Restriction on applying 6 months after the notice period expires**
> (1) A landlord may not make an application to the First-tier Tribunal for an eviction order against a tenant using a copy of a notice to leave more than six months after the day on which the relevant period in relation to that notice expired."

It may be best to illustrate the application of this rule with an example. L serves a notice to leave on T by email sent on 11 May 2022. This is taken to have been received by T on 13 May.[141] The notice specifies ground 12 as the ground on which eviction will be sought. Therefore, the relevant period of notice is twenty-eight days, and expires on 10 June. In terms of section 64 (discussed above) six months after that day is 10 December.[142] Therefore, the

137 For example: *McCauley v Cambridge* (19/1158, 20/5/19); *Pearson v Martin* (18/1302, 18/6/18); *McTeague Trust v McComb* (19/1892, 1/7/19).

138 Section 52(5)(b) confers on the tribunal discretion to allow the landlord to include grounds for eviction in the application that were not stated in the notice to leave. See p 312 above.

139 In the decisions mentioned at note 137, there was no reference to the power under s 52(4), presumably because the tribunal was not asked to exercise it.

140 Unless, for some reason, the tribunal considers that the application under s 52(5)(b) can simply be rejected.

141 In terms of s 26(6) of the Interpretation and Legislative Reform (Scotland) Act 2010 (discussed in Chapter 15).

142 Note that, as discussed below, the date stated at part 4 of the notice to leave would be 11 June, being the day after the expiry of the notice period, as required by s 62(4). However, the six-month period for the purposes of s 55(1) would run from 10 June, being "the day on which the relevant period in relation to that notice expired" to 10 December.

application must be made (i.e. received by the tribunal), no later than that date.[143] In contrast to section 54, the tribunal has no discretionary power to allow an application to be made in breach of section 55.[144] Given the terms of section 52(2)(b), such an application cannot be entertained.

8. Application must be accompanied by a copy of notice given to local authority: ss 56 and 52(2)(b) and r 109(b)(ii)

Reference is made to the discussion of the equivalent rule 65(b)(v) in relation to applications made under section 18 of the 1988 Act.[145] Section 56 is the provision, in the 2016 Act, which implements section 11 of the Homelessness etc. (Scotland) Act 2003 in relation to PRTs:

> "**56 Restriction on applying without notifying local authority**
> (1) A landlord may not make an application to the First-tier Tribunal for an eviction order against a tenant unless the landlord has given notice of the landlord's intention to do so to the local authority in whose area the let property is situated.
> (2) Notice under subsection (1) is to be given in the manner and form prescribed under section 11(3) of the Homelessness etc. (Scotland) Act 2003.
> (3) In a case where two or more persons jointly are the landlord under a tenancy, references in subsection (1) to the landlord are to any one of those persons."

The requirement in section 56 is mandatory, there being no power conferred on the tribunal to allow an application without notice in terms of section 11 of the 2003 Act being given to the local authority.[146] Under rule 109(b)(iii), a copy of the notice must be attached to the application. In practice, the lack of a section 11 notice is picked up when an application is sifted by the FTT, and the landlord is asked to provide a copy of the notice. At that point, the landlord may give notice to the local authority, and provide a copy of the notice to the tribunal, failing which the application is liable to rejected.[147]

Joint landlords and joint tenants

Applications in the case of joint landlords

At common law, all the co-proprietors must concur in the granting of a lease and in removings.[148] However, in terms of section 52(1), in a case where two

143 I.e. lodged in the manner required by the Act, and the Procedure Rules, in particular r 109. If, in this example, the application was received by the tribunal on 10 December, but was not lodged in the prescribed manner, it would not be "made" in terms of r 5, until the "mandatory requirements for lodgement have been met". See the discussion of r 5, in Chapter 14.

144 In *Watt v Cooke* (19/0799, 30/5/19), the tribunal made a decision at the CMD to dismiss an application made in breach of s 55. In that case, the notice period expired on 7 August. The application was dated 25 October, but was not actually submitted to the tribunal until 9 March in the following year.

145 See Chapter 7, p 246.

146 Thus s 56, in combination with s 52(2)(b), is more stringent than the equivalent s 19A of the 1988 Act.

147 In *Clarke v Chatham* EV/19/1202, 5/6/19, this was one of the reasons for rejection of the application. It also appears to have been the principal reason for rejection in *Felt Properties v Crowhurst* EV/19/0912, 1/7/19.

148 "Thus a removing could not go on without the consent of all the proprietors . . ." (Rankine, *Law of Leases in Scotland* (3rd edn) 82). By contrast, an action of ejection, to recover

or more persons jointly are the landlord under a tenancy, an application for an eviction order may be made by any one of those persons.[149] Thus section 52(1) is an exception to the general rule in section 78(2) that, in the case of joint landlords, reference in the Act to "landlord" means all of them.

Let us say that L1 and L2 jointly let subjects to T under a PRT. Some time later, T falls into arrears. L1 serves a valid notice to leave, and makes an application to the tribunal. In the application, he gives the name and address of L2.[150] The tribunal clerk intimates the application to L2, who does not respond. In that case, it is suggested that, if L1 establishes ground 12, he is entitled to an eviction order under section 51(1), even if L2 has never indicated her consent to the application being made or the order being sought. That is because, under section 51(1), the FTT "is to issue an eviction order against the tenant" under a PRT if, "on an application by the landlord, it finds that one of the eviction grounds named in schedule 3 applies", and, under s 52(1), such an application may be made by any one of the joint landlords. Thus, it is suggested that, in contrast to the common law position, any one of the joint landlords is entitled to make the application, establish the statutory ground and insist on an order being granted.[151]

This reading of the Act is subject to two provisos. First, where the ground is discretionary, the tribunal would be entitled to take into account the fact that that the other joint landlord does not concur in the proceedings, in deciding whether it is reasonable to grant the order. Secondly, as is explained in Chapter 10, in the case of grounds 1, 3 and 6, which entail the landlord establishing that it "intends" to do something, all the joint landlords would have to have the requisite intention.[152]

Applications in the case of joint tenants

As has already been explained, the effect of section 48 is to require that termination by the tenant has the agreement of all the joint tenants. This is an instance of the general rule, in section 78(3), that, in the case of joint tenants, reference in the Act to "tenant" means all of them. This rule also applies to notices to leave and applications for an eviction order. In sections 51(1) and

possession from a squatter or trespasser, could be raised by any one of the co-proprietors. See the discussion of the common law rules in *Morris v Eason* [2012] CSOH 125, 2012 GWD 27-564.

149 Likewise, a notice to leave may be given by only one of the joint landlords, given the terms of s 62(2).

150 As required by r 109(a)(i): see p 311 above.

151 It is further suggested that that is the case, even if the other joint landlord opposes the application. If that is correct, then whereas the common law requires all joint landlords to consent in taking proceedings, in the case of a PRT in which a ground for eviction apparently exists under sch 3, it is a decision *not* to seek an eviction order that effectively requires the agreement of all the joint landlords. Where there is no such agreement any one of the joint landlords may unilaterally seek an order. If this reading of ss 51(1) and 52(1) is correct, it provides another example of the way in which the 2016 Act displaces the common law, and the agreement of the parties, with a scheme in which eviction orders are granted solely on basis set out in the Act.

152 Because, in accordance with s 78(2), "the landlord intends", in those grounds, means "all of the joint landlords intend". By contrast, ground 4 ("Landlord intends to live in property"), contains an express provision to the effect that only one of the joint landlords need have the requisite intention.

52(3) the words "an eviction order against the tenant" and "notice to leave . . . given to the tenant" mean all the joint tenants: there is no provision under the Act in terms of which the landlord may select those joint tenants he wishes to put out.[153]

This creates a potential pitfall for the landlord. Let us say that L lets to T1 and T2. During the course of the tenancy, T1 sends an email to the landlord, stating that he is leaving and that, henceforth, the rent will be paid entirely by T2. Several months later, the landlord decides to serve a notice under ground 1, because he intends to sell the property. In this case, it is suggested that the notice to leave must be given to both T1 and T2, and the application must proceed against both of them: given the terms of sections 44 and 48, the joint tenancy has never been terminated.[154]

NOTICE TO LEAVE: s 62

A "notice to leave" is a notice under section 62 of the Act, the form of which is set out in schedule 5 to the Notices and Forms Regulations.[155] As has already been discussed, section 52(3) requires that a valid notice to leave must have been prepared and served on the tenant, and a copy of that notice must accompany the application to the tribunal. If that is not done, the tribunal "is not to entertain" the application, in terms of section 52(2)(a), and it is liable to rejected at the sift stage, under rule 8, or refused at a CMD or a subsequent hearing.

Here, the requirements for valid notice to leave are considered. Section 62 states:

> "**62 Meaning of notice to leave and stated eviction ground**
>
> (1) References in this Part to a notice to leave are to a notice which—
>
> (a) is in writing,
>
> (b) specifies the day on which the landlord under the tenancy in question expects to become entitled to make an application for an eviction order to the First-tier Tribunal,
>
> (c) states the eviction ground, or grounds, on the basis of which the landlord proposes to seek an eviction order in the event that the tenant does not vacate the let property before the end of the day specified in accordance with paragraph (b), and
>
> (d) fulfils any other requirements prescribed by the Scottish Ministers in regulations.
>
> (2) In a case where two or more persons jointly are the landlord under a tenancy, references in this Part to the tenant receiving a notice to leave from the landlord are to the tenant receiving one from any of those persons.

153 As indicated in note 120 above, it appears that a single notice to leave may be served on all the joint tenants, or a separate notice may be served on each of them.

154 Also bear in mind that, under s 1(2), a tenancy continues to be a PRT, even if the tenant ceases to occupy it as his only or principal home. See the decision of the FTT in *Tadakamalla v Jardine*, EV/19/3532, 15/1/20. If the current whereabouts of T1 were unknown, the notice could perhaps be sent to his last known address, under s 26(2)(b) and (4)(c) of the 2010 Act, or by email, if that was permissible under the tenancy agreement. See the discussion of service under s 26, in Chapter 15.

155 n 115.

(3) References in this Part to the eviction ground, or grounds, stated in a notice to leave are to the ground, or grounds, stated in it in accordance with subsection (1)(c).
(4) The day to be specified in accordance with subsection (1)(b) is the day falling after the day on which the notice period defined in section 54(2) will expire.
(5) For the purpose of subsection (4), it is to be assumed that the tenant will receive the notice to leave 48 hours after it is sent."

Section 62(1) sets out four necessary elements of a valid notice to leave, which are considered below.[156]

The Scottish Government has issued "Guidance Notes for Landlords on the Notice to Leave".[157] These are useful in clarifying some aspects of the legislation, and reference is made to them where appropriate.[158]

Written notice in the prescribed form: section 62(1)(a) and (d)

The notice to leave must in writing, and "must [fulfil] any other requirements prescribed by the Scottish Ministers in regulations". The regulations are the Notices and Forms Regulations.[159]

Regulation 6 is:

> **"6. Notice to leave**
> A notice to leave given by the landlord to the tenant under section 50(1)(a) (termination by notice to leave and tenant leaving) of the Act must be in the form set out in schedule 5."

It is not clear why this provision refers to section 50 (consensual termination), and not section 62, which defines the meaning of "notice to leave".[160] The preamble to the Regulations: states: "The Scottish Ministers make the following Regulations in exercise of the powers conferred by sections . . . *62(1) (d)* . . .". Therefore, it is suggested that notice to leave in schedule 5 is that prescribed for the purposes of section 62(1)(d).[161]

156 Effectively three, because in complying with s 62(1)(d) the landlord complies with s 62(1)(a).
157 These were published on the Scottish Government's website on 29 November 2017, along with the prescribed form notice to leave. There are also Guidance Notes for Tenants. However, the Guidance for Landlords are of greater interest in understanding what the legislation requires, as regards completion of the notice to leave.
158 However, as will be explained below, the Guidance for Landlords contains an error in relation to the calculation of the date to be stated at part 4 of the notice.
159 n 115.
160 The reference to s 50 is repeated in the prescribed form in sch 5 to the Regulations, which is headed, in bold capitals: "Landlord's notice to a tenant to leave under section 50(1)(a) of the Private Housing (Tenancies) (Scotland) Act 2016". It also appears in the explanatory note to the Regulations. It is respectfully suggested that this is an instance of careless drafting. The term "notice to leave" appears for the first time in the Act in s 50, but it is defined in s 62. A notice to leave is not necessarily a "notice under section 50(1)(a)", because that provision only has application if s 50(1)(b) is also fulfilled, by the tenant ceasing occupation. If that does not happen, the notice served by the landlord in the prescribed form will still be a notice to leave for the purposes of fulfilling the requirements of s 52(3), in respect of an application for an eviction order.
161 Where the prescribed form is not used, that does not necessarily invalidate the notice "unless the difference materially affects the effect of the form or is misleading": under s 21 of the Interpretation and Legislative Reform (Scotland) Act 2010. See also the discussion of s 73 of the 2016 Act below.

Specifies the day: section 62(1)(d), (4) and (5), and section 54

Part 4 of the prescribed form notice to leave is set out as follows:

> "**Part 4 THE END OF THE NOTICE PERIOD**
> An application will not be submitted to the Tribunal for an eviction order before (insert date). This is the earliest date that the Tribunal proceedings can start and will be at least the day after the end date of the relevant notice period (28 days or 84 days depending on the eviction ground or how long you have occupied the Let Property).
>
> Signed:
> (Landlord(s) or Agent):
> Dated: "

In *Panpher v McDonald*,[162] no date had been entered in the blank space before "(insert date)". The application was rejected at the sift, and the applicant appealed to the Upper Tribunal. Refusing the appeal, Sheriff Deutsch said:

> "[1] The appellant ... advances a number of cogent reasons why, if it had a discretion to do so, the tribunal might allow the application for an eviction order to proceed, notwithstanding the defect identified in the notice to leave upon which the appellant relies. Unfortunately no such discretion exists. The tribunal can only operate within the terms of the ... 2016 Act and subordinate legislation in the form of regulations made by the Scottish Ministers. In terms of that legislation the tribunal is prohibited from entertaining an application for an eviction which is not accompanied by a valid notice.
>
> [8] ... If no date is inserted then there has not been compliance with regulation 6. If regulation 6 has not been complied with then the notice is not compliant with section 62(1)(d) and accordingly it is not a notice to leave within the meaning of the 2016 Act. The Tribunal cannot overlook that fact ... It is not for the Tribunal to pass comment on whether the form is well-designed or otherwise."

On a reading of the decisions issued by the FTT, the failure to insert the correct date in part 4 of the notice appears to be the single most common basis on which applications to the tribunal under rule 109 are rejected under rule 8, or refused at a subsequent CMD or hearing. This is not surprising, as the applicable statutory provisions are disjointed and confusing, and the prescribed form itself is somewhat misleading.[163] Therefore, it is worth considering this matter in some detail.

Calculation of the correct date is a three-stage exercise:

(1) *Working out when the notice period begins.* The notice period begins when the tenant receives the notice.[164] This will depend on the manner in which it is served, under section 26 of the 2010 Act.[165] In the case of personal delivery, the tenant will receive the notice on the day of service.

162 A decision of the Upper Tribunal: [2019] UT 18.

163 The author delivered numerous seminars on the 2016 Act, for various bodies, around the time when the Act came into force. The seminar papers included a case study that posed the problem in the worked example in the main text below. About 5% of the delegates answered the problem correctly.

164 Section 54(2)(a).

165 Service by personal delivery, registered post, recorded delivery, or email are all permitted

If service is effected by sending the notice to the tenant by registered post, recorded delivery, or email, section 62(5) provides that, for the purposes of stating the date in the notice to leave, "it is to be assumed that the tenant will receive the notice 48 hours after it is sent".[166] The same period is stated, as regards these modes of service, in section 26(5) and (6) of the 2010 Act. However, under those provisions, the relevant document is "taken to have been received 48 hours after it is sent *unless the contrary is shown*". The italicised words do not appear in section 62(5). Therefore, in calculating the date to be entered in part 4 of the notice to leave, the person preparing the notice need not be concerned that it might arrive twenty-four hours later, or seventy-two hours later. He is to assume that it will arrive forty-eight hours later. If, in fact, it arrives seventy-two hours later, that has no bearing on the validity of the notice, if it was correctly prepared.

(2) *Ascertaining the date on which the notice period expires.* The notice period ends either twenty-eight days or eighty-four days after the assumed date on which it begins.[167] As to which of those periods applies, see the discussion of section 54.

(3) *Adding a further day.* The date to be specified in the notice is the day falling after the day on which the notice period expires.[168]

A worked example

L decides to move out of her flat (which she owns), to live with her boyfriend. She lets the flat to T under a PRT with a start date of 2 March 2022. By May, things are not working out between L and her boyfriend, and she wants to move back into her flat. If she sends a notice to leave to T by recorded delivery post on 10 May, relying on ground 4 in schedule 3,[169] what date should be stated in the notice to leave?

Given the terms of section 62(5), it is to be assumed that T receives the notice on 12 May. The applicable period of notice is twenty-eight days, under section 54(3)(a), because T has been entitled to occupy the let property for not more than six months. The period of notice expires on 9 June. Therefore, the date to be stated in the notice is 10 June 2022.

by s 26 of the Interpretation and Legislative Reform (Scotland) Act 2010, discussed in Chapter 15.

166 Section 62(5). Note that part 4 of the prescribed form, set out in the main text, makes no reference to the rule stated in s 62(5). It refers to the notice period, and the rule in s 62(4) (the date stated should be the day after expiry of the notice period), but not the rule as to the presumed date of service.

167 Section 54(2)(b). In *Andreccetti v Sinclair* EV/19/1720, 1/7/19, the notice relied on grounds 1 and 12, and the eighty-four-day period applied. The landlord gave only eighty-three days' notice. His agent sought to argue that the notice was sufficient for an application under ground 12, given that more than twenty-eight days' notice had been provided. That argument was rejected, on the basis that the notice had failed to give the requisite period required by the Act.

168 Section 62(4). This is often overlooked. A good example is *Crawford Property v Murray and Sturgeon* EV/19/1286, 23/5/19, in which the applicant sought a review (under r 38) of the decision to reject the application, on the basis that the date stated in the notice to leave was too early. As the review decision explains, the applicant had apparently overlooked the effect of s 62(4).

169 Ground 4: "Landlord intends to live in property".

Thus, where the notice is sent by recorded delivery, registered post, or email, and the period of notice is twenty-eight days, the date stated in the notice will be thirty-one days after the date of sending.

If the notice had been delivered personally,[170] on 10 May, the notice period would begin on that day, and expire on 7 June. In that case, the date stated should be 8 June.

If L had waited until, say, 7 September 2022 before sending the notice by recorded delivery, the assumed date of receipt would be 9 September, and the period of notice would be eighty-four days.[171] In that case, the notice period would expire on 2 December, and the date to be stated in the notice would be 3 December 2022, eighty-seven days after sending the notice.

The example given in the "Guidance notes for Landlords"

Under the heading "How to give this notice", the Guidance notes originally stated, at paragraph 9:

> "For example, if you are required to give your Tenant 28 days' notice and you send the notice to leave by recorded delivery post on 23 January, your Tenant will be expected to receive the notice on 25 January. The 28 days' notice period will start on 25 January and end on 21 February. If your Tenant chooses not to leave the Let Property following the expiry of the notice period, the earliest date that you can submit an application to the Tribunal for an eviction order is 22 February."

This is wrong, because it takes the twenty-eight-day notice period to run from the very beginning of 25 January to the end of 21 February, which would indeed be twenty-eight days. However, section 54(2) provides that the notice period "begins on the day the tenant receives the notice", and "expires on the day falling 28 days after it begins". Accordingly, if the tenant is taken to have received the notice on 25 January, the notice period expires on 22 February, not 21 February. Therefore, the earliest date on which an application could be submitted is 23 February. This error was subsequently corrected.[172]

Errors: section 73

As has already been mentioned, a notice that states the wrong date is apt to lead to an application to the tribunal under section 52 being rejected. That is because the notice fails to comply with 62(1)(d) and (4), and is therefore not a "notice to leave" as defined in that section.[173] The landlord will therefore fail to comply with section 52(3), because the application will not "be accompanied by a copy of a notice to leave which has been given to the tenant". In

170 Under s 26(2)(a) of the 2010 Act.

171 Because by the time the notice is served, T has been entitled to occupy for more than six months. Therefore, neither s 54(3)(a) nor (b) would apply, and the longer period of notice would be required.

172 It is believed around October 2019. However, the same example was used in the document: "Private residential tenancy: information for landlords", which was published by the Scottish Government on 26 April 2017. As at 12 February 2020, that example had not been corrected, and still stated that the twenty-eight days' notice would end on 21 February.

173 *Panpher v McDonald* (n 114).

that case, the tribunal "is not to entertain" the application, given the terms of section 52(3)(a).[174]

Consequently, a number of applications have been rejected at the sift stage, or at the CMD, solely for the reason that the notice states the wrong date. Usually the date stated is too early,[175] but applications have also been rejected where the date stated is too late.[176]

In other cases, the tribunal's decision has explored the issue of whether entering the wrong date at part 4 of the prescribed form is necessarily fatal to the application.

In *Holleran v McAlister*,[177] the tribunal considered whether section 73 might rescue the landlord, in a case in which the date stated in the notice (29 August) was three days earlier than the correct date (1 September). Section 73 states:

> "**73 Minor errors in documents**
> (1) An error in the completion of a document to which this section applies does not make the document invalid unless the error materially affects the effect of the document.
> (2) This section applies to—
> . . .
> (d) a notice to leave (as defined by section 62(1))."[178]

The explanatory note to section 73 of the 2016 Act states:

> "105. Section 73 provides that any errors in specified documents do not invalidate the document if they are sufficiently minor that they do not materially alter the effect of the document. Of necessity, there are a number of documents which the Act requires the use of at certain times. This section ensures that a common sense approach can be taken to meeting these requirements, and a party is not penalised for an obviously minor error. The protection applies equally to landlords and tenants."

Thus, section 73 confers on the tribunal a specific power to treat a notice to leave as being valid, notwithstanding the fact that it contains an error, provided that the requirements of that section are met.[179] It is suggested that this rules out any other approach by which errors in notices may be treated as not having the effect of invalidating the notice, such as the "reasonable recipient" test.[180] If that is correct, section 73 is the only route to salvation.

174 Under s 19(1)(b) of the 1988 Act, the tribunal has the power to dispense with the AT6 notice of proceedings: see the discussion in Chapter 7, at p 238. Therefore an error in an AT6 is not fatal to an application under s 18 of that Act. There is no equivalent power under the 2016 Act.

175 This is a frequent occurrence. To take just three examples: *Choudrey v Ellison* EV/19/2154, 5/8/19; *Kyle v Andrew* EV/19/2820, 11/11/19; and *Cathcart v Dall* EV/19/3720, 7/1/20.

176 For example: *Lewis-Flannigan v Mill* EV/19/0726, 25/3/19; *Speers v Lindsay* EV/19/0958.

177 EV/18/3231, a decision made by the author on 2 May 2019.

178 Note that the words "materially affects the effect" also appear in s 21 of the Interpretation and Legislative Reform (Scotland) Act 2010, see note 161 above, and Chapter 4, p 108.

179 Where the prescribed form is not used, s 21 may apply. Where the prescribed form is used, but is incorrectly completed, s 73 of the 2016 Act may apply.

180 As described in Chapter 7, the Court of Appeal confirmed, in *Pease v Carter* [2020] 1 WLR 1459, that the "reasonable recipient" approach applies to statutory notices given under the Housing Act 1988. It is doubtful, in any event, that that approach would assist in relation to an error in a notice to leave. In *Pease v Carter,* the landlord had sent a notice on 7 November 2018, informing the tenant that proceedings would not be raised before "26 November 2017". This is a paradigm example of when the "reasonable recipient" test is appropriate to

In *Holleran*, the landlord's agent argued that the error did not "materially affect the effect of the form", because the application for an eviction order was not made till near the end of October. Therefore, it was submitted, the error was not prejudicial to the respondent, as the application had not been made until after the correct date. The "effect" of the notice to leave (if correct) would have been to warn the tenant that an application would be made on or after 1 September. That was, in fact, what had happened.

That argument was rejected by the tribunal, for the following reasons:

(1) As a general proposition, the validity of a notice to leave cannot be determined by reference to circumstances that occur after it was served.[181] If that were the case, it might not be possible for the FTT to judge whether a notice was valid, and whether an application ought to be entertained, without first determining what had happened after service.
(2) The word "effect" in section 73 (and in the explanatory note) denotes the effect that the notice is intended to have, if it is completed without error. It follows from section 62(1)(b) and (4) that a notice to leave completed correctly will inform the tenant of the day on which the landlord under the tenancy in question expects to become entitled to make an application for an eviction order to the FTT, being the day after the notice period expires.
(3) If the notice does not give the correct date, that accordingly "affects the effect" of the notice.
(4) Furthermore, it "materially" affects the effect of the notice. To state an earlier date than that required by the legislation is not an "obviously minor error" of the type indicated in the explanatory note. The correct date is part of the information that is expressly required by the primary legislation. It is an error that causes the notice to fail to achieve one of its fundamental purposes.

It may be added that in part 2 of the form, discussed below, the tenant is expressly advised that, unless he leaves at the stated date, the landlord will make the application to the tribunal. If the date stated in part 4 is too early, the tenant is in danger of being misled, and leaving the property earlier than he needs to. Given that one of the purposes of the notice is also to give him a chance to put things right,[182] an error of this type may appear to give him less time than he ought to be given. These considerations also suggest that the "affect" on the "effect" is material.

If that reasoning is correct, it follows that if part 4 of the notice to leave states a date that is earlier than the correct date, the notice cannot be rescued under section 73, and is invalid. That is consistent with the approach taken

apply: the error is obvious, as is the fact that the landlord meant to say "26 November 2018". Given the complexity of the 2016 Act provisions, it would not be obvious to the tenant, in a case like *Holleran*, that there was an error, or what the landlord meant to say.

181 In *Pease v Carter* (n 180), at para 53, Arnold LJ indicated that the date on which the proceedings were actually raised is an irrelevant consideration.

182 It is suggested that, as with the AT6 under the 1988 Act, the purpose of the notice to leave is to give information to the tenant to enable him to consider what should be done, in the period before proceedings are raised, which is in his power and which will best protect him against the loss of his home. See: *Mountain v Hastings* (1993) 25 HLR 427, [1993] 29 EG 96.

to notices at common law, and under previous legislation: if the period of notice given to the tenant is less than that to which he is entitled, the notice is invalid.[183]

What if the date stated in the notice is later than the correct date? In answering this question, it is necessary first to point out that, in contrast with the equivalent provisions under the 1988 Act and 2001 Act, section 62 does not expressly allow a later date to be stated. Section 14(4) of the 2001 requires a date to be stated in the notice of proceedings but says: "(4) A notice under subsection (2) must . . . specify— . . . (b) a date, *not earlier than*—". Section 19(4) of the 1988 Act requires the notice to state a "minimum" period, rather than an exact date. Consequently, if in doubt, the landlord may err on the side of caution by stating a date that is probably a few days later than the correct date, but is certainly not too early, and therefore avoids the notice being invalid. There is no equivalent wording in section 62, which seems a strange omission.

It is suggested that, where date stated in the notice is later than the correct date, that is more apt to be regarded as a minor error for the purposes of section 73, which does not "affect the effect" of the form. In that case, the notice still has the effect of warning the tenant that proceedings will be raised, and gives him more than the relevant statutory period to decide whether he wants to leave, and a longer period in which to put matters right, if he is able to do so. Strictly speaking, the notice is misleading. The landlord's error does not affect the calculation of the notice period under section 54. So, were the notice to state "8 May" when the correct date is 1 May, the landlord might raise proceedings between those two dates, arguing that he was entitled to do so under section 54. In that case, however, the FTT would have the option of rejecting the application at the sift, under rule 8(1)(c) of the Procedure Rules,[184] on the basis that it would not be appropriate for the tribunal to accept an application from the landlord, earlier that the date stated on the notice.[185]

However, at the time of writing, the relationship between section 73 and notices that state the wrong date has not yet been considered by the Upper Tribunal. It is understood that the legal members of the FTT have differing views on whether an error of, say, one day, invalidates the notice. Also, there have been numerous decisions of the tribunal in which an apparent error in stating the date, which might have formed a basis on which to oppose the application, has not been recognised.[186]

183 See, in particular, the quotations from *Signet Group v C J Clark Retail Properties* 1996 SC 444, 1996 SLT 1325 and *Rae v Davidson* 1954 SC 361 at 366, 1955 SLT 25 at p 62 in Chapter 3. Also note that this type of error is less likely to occur in relation to an AT6 under the 1988 Act, because the statutory provisions are more straightforward. Also, where the AT6 is wrong, the tribunal can dispense with the notice under s 19(1)(b), except if the order is sought under ground 8 of sch 5.

184 n 95.

185 In *Lower Street Properties Ltd v Jones* (1996) 28 HLR 877, the Court of Appeal held that it was objectionable that legal proceedings should be instituted against an assured shorthold tenant before the stated period in the notice requiring possession had come to an end. That principle seems applicable to the scenario under consideration.

186 As explained in Chapter 10, the majority of eviction orders made by the tribunal under s 51 Act are granted under ground 12 (rent arrears) in applications that are not opposed. It is

Error in stating date: section 52(4) again

In several cases, the tribunal has entertained (and granted) applications, notwithstanding the fact that the wrong date was stated in the notice. In all these cases, the tribunal expressly noted that the wrong date had been stated, but considered that it nevertheless had discretion to entertain the application under s 52(4).[187] With respect to the legal members who made those decisions, it is submitted that this approach is dubious.

Section 52(4) allows the tribunal to entertain an application made "in breach of" section 54, if the tribunal considers it reasonable to do so. However, a failure to state the correct date in the notice to leave is a breach of section 62(1)(b) and (4), not section 54. It is suggested that section 54, which bears the title "Restriction on applying during the notice period", is breached by making an application before the expiry of that period, as correctly calculated in accordance with subsections (2) and (3) of that section. It is this breach that the tribunal has the power to excuse under section 52(4).[188] There is no discretionary power to entertain applications made in breach of section 62.[189] There is only the power, under section 73, already described.

Notice states the eviction ground, and particulars (and evidence) of it: s 62(1)(c) and (d)

Section 62(1)(c) requires that the landlord's notice to leave "states the eviction ground". This is done at part 2 of the prescribed form, which lists all eighteen grounds in schedule 3, next to boxes that the landlord ticks or crosses. However, the grounds are summarised in single sentences, which are similar to the headings that the grounds bear, in schedule 3.[190] This represents a significant departure from the requirement, under the 1988 and 2001 Acts, to set out the ground as it appears in the Act.[191] The desirability of that change seems open to question, given that the prescribed form expressly states that it

believed that errors in stating the date in the notice are now more likely to be picked up at the sift.

187 These are: *Andrzejczak v McGreechin* EV/19/0305, 4/4/19 and *Winter v Robertson* EV/18/1273, 11/9/18, in which the date stated was too early; and *Hendry v Wale* EV/18/2216, 29/11/18, in which the date stated was about two months too late, apparently because the eighty-four-day period was used, rather than the twenty-eight-day period.

188 As discussed at p 318 above, this power might be exercised in circumstances where proceedings have to be expedited for some reason. In all three cases mentioned in the last note, proceedings were raised after the expiry of the notice period. Accordingly, it is suggested that s 52(4) had no application.

189 *Panpher v McDonald* (n 114), paras [3] and [4].

190 As explained in Chapter 10, each of the sch 3 grounds has a heading that may be regarded as summarising the ground, such as "Landlord intends to sell" or "Rent arrears". In part 2 of the prescribed from, most are stated in a way that addresses the tenant, such as "Your landlord intends to sell the property" and "You are in rent arrears over three consecutive months".

191 See the discussion at Chapter 4, p 108 and Chapter 7, p 239. Section 19 of the 1988 Act and the s 14 notice of the 2001 Act require the landlord to specify/state the ground. The prescribed form of notice leaves space in order to do so. It has long been established, in particular by the Court of Appeal's decision in *Mountain v Hastings* (n 182), that this requires the landlord not merely to identify the ground, but to set out the substance of the ground, which is best done by repeating the ground verbatim, as it appears in the relevant schedule to the Act.

"is important that the Tenant fully understands why you are seeking to evict them and that the action you are taking is justified".

Part 3 of the prescribed form is headed "Details and Evidence of the Eviction Ground". This comprises a series of statements, which, confusingly, alternate between addressing the sender of the notice and the recipient:

> "I/We also inform you that we are seeking under the above ground(s) for the following reasons:
>
> [State particulars of how you believe the ground(s) have arisen – continue on additional sheets of paper if required. Please give as much detail as possible including relevant dates, and in cases of rent arrears state the amount of arrears outstanding, and the period over which it has built up.][192]
>
> It is important that the Tenant fully understands why you are seeking to evict them and that the action you are taking is justified. The provision of supporting evidence can help to do that.
>
> I/We attach the following evidence to support the eviction action:"[193]

Under section 62(1)(d), the Scottish Ministers have the power to prescribe additional requirements for the notice to leave, in the Regulations. It appears from the first two of the above statements that the requirement to state the particulars of the ground has been prescribed.[194] As to what this entails, reference is made to the discussion of the equivalent requirement in relation to the notices under section 14 of the 2001 Act,[195] and section 19 of the 1988 Act.[196] However, the Tribunal's decision in *Thyme Property Developments v Mitchell* is an example of an application being rejected at the sift, because the section 62 notice failed to state particulars of the ground.[197]

It is not clear, from the third and fourth statements made in the quotation above, whether the provision of evidence with the notice is to be regarded as compulsory or merely advisable. However, paragraph 5 of the "Guidance Notes for Landlords" states:

> "If your Tenant does not leave the Let Property on the date shown in Part 4 of this notice, you will need to apply to the First-tier Tribunal for Scotland Housing and Property Chamber to obtain an eviction order for their removal. The Tribunal will ask you to provide evidence to support the eviction ground(s) you are using to evict your Tenant. It is advisable to include copies of any evidence along with this notice, in order to satisfy your Tenant that the eviction ground you are using is valid. This may encourage them to move out at the end of the notice period without you having to refer the case to the Tribunal."

192 There follows a space in which particulars can be entered.

193 Again, there follows a space in which the evidence can be described.

194 This is similar to the position in relation to the notice under s 14 of the 2001 Act: the requirement to state the particulars in found in the prescribed form of the notice, rather than the Act; see Chapter 4 p 108. By contrast, the requirement to state the particulars of the ground in an AT6 notice is expressly stated in s 19(2) of the 1988 Act.

195 At Chapter 4, p 108.

196 At Chapter 7, p 239.

197 EV/18/0946, 25/4/18. This was a rent arrears case in which part 3 of the notice contained on the statement: "You have failed to pay rent as and when due and are now in considerable rent arrears", without any information as to the level of arrears or the dates of non-payment. Finding the notice to be deficient, the legal member said: "the purpose of the Notice to Leave is . . . in not simply to initiate eviction and provide the tenant with fair notice of the threat to evict but to provide the tenant with fair notice of steps necessary to avoid eviction through making payment of the arrears". For another example, see: *Ker v Finn* EV/19/1237, 4/6/19.

This indicates that it was not the intention of the Scottish Ministers to prescribe the giving of evidence along with the notice as a "requirement" for the purposes of section 62(1)(d). Therefore, that would appear to be optional, though desirable.

Grounds 11 and 12: a case for use of section 73?

It is a ground for eviction under schedule 3 that the "tenant has failed to comply with an obligation under the tenancy": ground 11. However, that does not apply to the obligation to pay rent,[198] because there is specific ground applicable to rent arrears. Therefore, in a case in which the only basis for service of the notice to leave is rent arrears, the notice should state ground 12, and not ground 11. This has evidently been the source of some confusion: several applications have been rejected at the sift, or at the CMD, because the notice to leave stated ground 11, but the application is made, or the eviction order was ultimately sought, on ground 12.[199] In several of these decisions, reference was made to the possibility of the Tribunal permitting ground 12 to be included in the application, in exercise of the power in section 52(5)(b).[200] However, it was not argued, in any of the cases, that the problem might be remedied by section 73 of the Act.[201]

Let us say that, in part 2 of the prescribed form, the landlord has ticked only the box "You have breached a term of your tenancy agreement", but not the box "You are in rent arrears over three consecutive months". However, in stating the particulars at part 3, and providing evidence to support the eviction action, it is clear that the ground for eviction is rent arrears. In that case, the landlord might make an application to the tribunal under ground 12, arguing: section 73 is engaged, because there has been an error in completion of the form, at part 2; that error does not "materially affect the effect" of the form, because the tenant has been informed, in part 3, that the ground for eviction is rent arrears; therefore the notice should be treated as valid, for the purposes of founding an application on ground 12.[202]

Anticipatory notices (in rent arrears cases)

The most commonly used statutory ground for eviction is ground 12, which is that the tenant "has been in rent arrears for three or more consecutive months". In respect of the mandatory part of the ground, the FTT is to decide whether the rent has been arrears over that period, "at the beginning of the day on which the Tribunal first considers the application". Section 62(1)(c)

198 Ground 11(3).

199 *Ker v Finn* EV/19/1237, 4/6/19; *Kean v Duffy* EV/19/1466, 22/5/19; *Kwai Li v Dempster* EV/19/0496, 3/5/19; *White v Murray* EV/18/3503, 7/3/19; *Houston v Todd* EV/18/2914, 4/1/19. In *Ker*, there were other problems with the application.

200 Discussed at p 312 above. In *Ker*, that possibility was rejected. Mention was made of the discretionary power in *White* and *Houston*, but no request had been made to exercise the power.

201 See p 326.

202 Failing that, the landlord could also ask the tribunal to exercise its discretion under s 52(5)(b). The tribunal might allow the application to proceed, but on the basis that the competency of application would be determined at the CMD.

requires that the notice "(c) states the eviction ground, or grounds, on the basis of which the landlord *proposes to seek* an eviction order".

These provisions arguably support the view that the landlord could serve the notice to leave after the tenant fell into arrears, but before the three-month period had elapsed, on the basis that he proposed to seek an order on ground 12, if the arrears were not cleared. Against that, section 54(3)(b)(iii) refers to the "ground stated in the notice to leave" as "that the tenant *has been* in rent arrears for three or more consecutive months". Likewise, part 3 of the prescribed form for the notice to leave states requires the landlord to "State particulars of how you believe the grounds *have* arisen". It goes on to say: "It is important that the Tenant fully understands why you are seeking to evict them and that the action you are taking is justified."

This question has now been resolved by the decision of the Upper Tribunal in *Majid v Gaffney*.[203] In that case the application to the FTT was accompanied by a notice to leave, dated 1 July 2019, which informed the tenant: "You are in rent arrears of £1525 from rent due 30/4/19, 31/5/19 and 30/6/19. Despite repeated reminders and promises of payment, your account remains in arears." The application had been rejected by the FTT at the sift, on the basis that, if the tenants were first in arrears on 30 April, they could not be in arrears for three months until 30 July. The FTT decision stated that a notice to leave could be valid only if the eviction ground specified therein was satisfied as at the date of the service of the notice. If that were not the case, the result would be that tenants could be threatened with eviction for something they had not yet done on the basis that, if they subsequently did it, an application for eviction could be raised. In refusing the landlord's application for permission to appeal, that view was endorsed by the Upper Tribunal judge, who said: "It . . . could never have been intended by Parliament that a landlord could serve a notice specifying a ground not yet available in the expectation that it may become available prior to the making of an application. Such an approach would be open to significant abuse."

203 A decision of Sheriff Fleming: [2019] UT 59.

Chapter 10

Grounds for Eviction under the 2016 Act

INTRODUCTION

The grounds for eviction under the 2016 Act are set out in eighteen paragraphs in schedule 3. As was explained in Chapters 1 and 9, there is no equivalent to the short assured tenancy in the 2016 Act. Under the new regime, there must be a statutory ground for an eviction order. That change is of benefit to tenants in the private sector, affording them greater security of tenure. In order to redress the balance, however, the schedule 3 grounds are more favourable to the landlord than is the case under schedule 5 to the 1988 Act. There are more grounds, and the threshold for obtaining an order is generally lower.[1]

The eighteen paragraphs of schedule 3 are divided into four groups:

1) let property required for another purpose (1–7);
2) tenant's status (8 and 9);
3) tenant's conduct (10–15); and
4) legal impediment to let continuing (16–18).

The grounds are drafted in a particular style. Each has a number and a heading, such as "1. Landlord intends to sell".[2] This is then followed by a subparagraph (1), which, in every case, is a single sentence that begins with the words "It is an eviction ground that . . .". This sentence may be regarded as summarising the ground.[3]

There follows, in all but two of the grounds,[4] a subparagraph (2), which sets out the requirements for the ground to be established.

In grounds 1, 2, 3, 4, 6, 7, 10 and 13, subparagraph (2) begins with the words: "The First-tier Tribunal *must* find that the ground named by subparagraph (1) applies if . . .". These may accordingly be described as "mandatory" grounds.[5]

1 This lower threshold is particularly evident in relation to the rent arrears ground (para 12 of sch 3), which is, by far, the most commonly used ground.

2 The number and heading appear in bold, like the titles of the sections in the Act.

3 Though in several cases (for example para 3 ("Landlord intends to refurbish") and 17 ("HMO licence has been revoked")), the title to the ground seems to give a more accurate summary than subpara (1).

4 Grounds 8 and 12.

5 The terms "mandatory" and "discretionary" are not used in s 51, or in any of the paragraphs of sch 3, but they are used, to describe the grounds, in the explanatory notes to the Act.

In grounds 5, 9, 11, 14, 15, 16, 17 and 18, subparagraph (2) begins with the words: "The First-tier Tribunal *may* find that the ground named by sub-paragraph (1) applies if . . .". In each case, one of the requirements in subparagraph (2) is that "the Tribunal is satisfied that it is *reasonable* to issue an eviction order . . .".[6] These may accordingly be described as "discretionary" grounds. Reference is made to the discussion of "reasonableness" as a requirement in the context of eviction proceedings, in Chapter 5.[7]

Ground 8 ("Not an employee") and ground 12 ("Rent arrears"), both have a "mandatory" subparagraph (2), and a "discretionary" subparagraph (3), which are alternatives.

In most of the grounds there is then further material in the subparagraphs that follow which expands on the requirements of subparagraph (2).[8]

Section 51

Section 51 sets out the First-tier Tribunal's ("FTT's") power to issue eviction orders, under the 2016 Act:

> "**51 First-tier Tribunal's power to issue an eviction order**
> (1) The First-tier Tribunal is to issue an eviction order against the tenant under a private residential tenancy if, on an application by the landlord, it finds that one of the eviction grounds named in schedule 3 applies.
> (2) The provisions of schedule 3 stating the circumstances in which the Tribunal may or must find that an eviction ground applies are exhaustive of the circumstances in which the Tribunal is entitled to find that the ground in question applies.
> (3) The Tribunal must state in an eviction order the eviction ground, or grounds, on the basis of which it is issuing the order.
> (4) An eviction order brings a tenancy which is a private residential tenancy to an end on the day specified by the Tribunal in the order."

As regard s 51(1), as has already been described, in the case of the mandatory grounds the FTT *must* find that the ground applies if the conditions in subparagraph (2) of the ground are met. In that case, it is required to issue an eviction order. In the case of the discretionary grounds, it *may* find that the ground applies. If it finds that the ground applies, it must issue the order. If it does not find that the ground applies, it does not issue the order.[9]

What does subsection (2) mean? The explanatory note to the Act says, at paragraph 80:

> "The Tribunal can only find that an eviction ground named in schedule 3 applies in the circumstances in which the schedule states that the Tribunal may or must find that the ground applies. The Tribunal cannot find that an eviction ground applies by considering only the name assigned to the ground by the first sub-paragraph of the relevant paragraph of schedule 3."

6 The exception is ground 14 ("Antisocial behaviour"), in which the incorporation of the "reasonableness" requirement is more complex. See p 362.

7 From p 144.

8 Or subparas (2) and (3), in the case of grounds 8 and 12.

9 Therefore, the mandatory/discretionary distinction in the 2016 Act appears within the statutory grounds in the relevant schedule, whereas, in the 1988 Act, the distinction is made in s 18(3) and (4): see p 231 in Chapter 7.

Thus, it appears to be the point of subsection (2) that, in order for the ground to apply, the tribunal must find that all the requirements of subparagraph (2)[10] are met. It cannot find that the ground applies on the basis of the summary in subparagraph (1), or the title.[11]

Under subsections (3) and (4), the eviction order must state the ground or grounds on which the order is granted,[12] and date on which the tenancy ends. In practice, this is one month later, given the time limit for applying for permission to appeal against a decision of the tribunal.[13]

Frequency of the use of grounds; rates of success

As described in Chapter 9, applications to the FTT for an eviction order under section 51 are made in terms of rule 109 of the Procedure Rules.[14] A significant number of these applications are rejected at the sift.[15] If the application passes the sift, it is then appointed to a case management discussion ("CMD"), before a single legal member,[16] unless it is withdrawn.[17] Where a CMD takes place, the application is invariably determined there; hearings in relation to rule 109 applications are unusual. As will be explained below, this is for two reasons: (i) the vast majority of applications feature one or more mandatory grounds for eviction; (ii) at most CMDs, the respondent does not appear and is not represented.

Where an application is determined at the sift or the CMD, it is the practice of the tribunal to issue a written decision,[18] which is then published on the Housing and Property Chamber's website. There, it is possible to search for decisions in the "Evictions and Civil Proceedings Decisions Database", by rule. Looking at the rule 109 decisions, it is possible then to assess the frequency with which different grounds are used, and the degree of success enjoyed by landlords in pursuing those grounds.[19]

A key point that then emerges is that, in around 84 per cent of cases in which an eviction order was granted under section 51, the sole ground for eviction,

10 Or, in the case of grounds 8 and 12, subpara (2) or (3).

11 However, one might ask: what is the significance, if any, of the words used in the title to the ground or in subpara (1)? Could they be used, for example, to resolve a dispute over the interpretation of words used in subpara (2)?

12 Given the terms of s 52(5), this will invariably be same ground, or one or more of the grounds, stated in the notice to leave. See Chapter 9, p 312.

13 Which is thirty days, in terms of r 2 of the Scottish Tribunals (Time Limits) Regulations 2016 (SSI 2016/231). See the discussion of review and appeal of FTT decisions in Chapter 15.

14 First-tier Tribunal for Scotland Housing and Property Chamber (Procedure) Regulations 2017 (SSI 2017/328) (Procedure Rules).

15 See Chapter 14. In terms of r 8(2), the FTT must notify the applicant of the decision to reject an application at the sift, and state the reasons for that decision.

16 Again, see Chapter 14 for a discussion of r 17, which concerns CMDs. Although r 17(1) states that the FTT "may" order a CMD to be held, it is the practice to of the tribunal always to fix CMDs in cases in which an eviction order is sought. Under r 17(4), the FTT may do anything at a CMD that it may do at a hearing, including making a decision.

17 No written decision is issued if the application is withdrawn by the landlord. That might happen if, for example, arrears of rent were cleared prior to the CMD.

18 Given the terms of r 26(6), where an application is decided at a CMD (under r 17(4)), a statement of reasons *may* be prepared, though in practice this is always done.

19 Applications under r 109 were first determined in February 2018. At the time of writing (February 2020), the author had looked at 500 decisions. The figures given in this section of the main text are based on this cohort of decisions.

or one of the grounds,[20] was ground 12(2) (being the mandatory part of the arrears ground). Of the remaining grounds, orders under ground 1 (landlord intends to sell) are by far most common (almost 10 per cent of the decisions in which the application is granted). The application was granted on ground 4 (landlord intends to live in property) in about 2.4 per cent of cases, and on ground 11 (breach of tenancy agreement) in about 1.6 per cent. A handful of cases feature grounds 2, 3, 5, 6, 10, 14 and 15. However, where an application combines one or more of those grounds with ground 12 (as is common), the tribunal will often grant the application on ground 12(2) at a CMD, without considering the other ground.[21] The remaining grounds (7, 8, 9, 16, 17 and 18) do not feature in any of the decisions.[22]

Where applications are rejected at the sift[23] or refused at the CMD, that is invariably due to some "technical" failure, such as, in particular, a defect in the notice to leave. [24] Consequently, decisions to reject at the sift do not always indicate which grounds are relied upon in the application. However, several rejection decisions have been based on a failure by the landlord to provide, with the application, "evidence showing that the eviction ground or grounds has been met", as is required by rule 109(b)(i).[25] Of course, applications under rule 109 may also fail because the tribunal finds that the ground has not been established, but this is much less common.

PART 1: LET PROPERTY REQUIRED FOR ANOTHER PURPOSE

Intention grounds

Requiring and intending

Grounds 1, 3, 4 and 6, which are all mandatory grounds, contain the requirement that the landlord "intends" to do something in relation to the property.[26] Ground 5, which is a discretionary ground, contains a requirement that "a member of the landlord's family *intends* to occupy the let property".

The concept of intention thus assumes some importance in the 2016 Act – more so than in the previous legislation. In the 1988 Act, only ground 6 requires the landlord to show that it "intends" something.[27] None of the grounds for possession in the 1984 Act refers to intention.

20 In a small number of cases, the application was granted on ground 12, and another ground.

21 Particularly when it would require a hearing to determine the other ground.

22 As at February 2020.

23 Figures obtained from the Housing and Property Chamber indicate that, in the two years from 1 December 2017 to 30 November 2019, more than 15% of r 109 applications were rejected at the sift. Given that some applications are also refused at the CMD, it is thought that the total number of applications that have failed on some technical ground is nearer 20%.

24 See Chapter 9, and the discussion of the sift in Chapter 14.

25 See Chapter 9, p 312.

26 Ground 2 ("Property to be sold by lender") refers to the intention of the lender in subpara (1), but not in subpara (2). Given the apparent meaning of s 51(2), as discussed in the main text, it is suggested that the ground is established by the lender demonstrating the three points in subpara (2), without the necessity of the tribunal considering its intention.

27 Ground 6 of sch 5 to the 1988 Act: "The landlord . . . intends to demolish or reconstruct the whole or a substantial part of the house or to carry out substantial works on the house . . .".

It is suggested that the heading to part 1 of schedule 3 "Let property *required* for another purpose" is inaccurate, because it implies a more stringent test than most of the grounds impose. Of the seven grounds in that part, only ground 7 asks the landlord to demonstrate that the property is "required" for some purpose. Intention sets a lower bar: the difference between intending some purpose for a property and requiring the property for that purpose is like the difference between wanting and needing.

Intention jurisprudence

The meaning of "intends" was re-examined by the Supreme Court in *S Franses Ltd v Cavendish Hotel (London) Ltd*.[28] That case concerned the application of the statutory test in section 30(1)(f) of the Landlord and Tenant Act 1954, which relates to the renewal of business tenancies in England and Wales.[29] The courts apply a test to the landlord's "intention" in such cases. This originated in the speech of Lord Justice Asquith in *Cunliffe v Goodman*,[30] and in particular the following passage, which has come to be regarded as the *locus classicus*:[31]

> "The question to be answered is whether . . . the plaintiff . . . 'intended' to pull down the premises on this site. This question is in my view one of fact. If the plaintiff did no more than entertain the idea of this demolition, if she got no further than to contemplate it as a (perhaps attractive) possibility, then one would have to say . . . either that there was *no* evidence of a positive 'intention,' or that the word 'intention' was incapable as a matter of construction of applying to anything so tentative, and so indefinite. An 'intention' to my mind connotes a state of affairs which the party 'intending' – I will call him X – does more than merely contemplate: it connotes a state of affairs which, on the contrary, he decides, so far as in him lies, to bring about, and which, in point of possibility, he has a reasonable prospect of being able to bring about, by his own act of volition.
>
> X cannot, with any due regard to the English language, be said to 'intend' a result which is wholly beyond the control of his will. He cannot 'intend' that it shall be a fine day tomorrow: at most he can hope or desire or pray that it will. Nor, short of this, can X be said to 'intend' a particular result if its occurrence, though it may be not wholly uninfluenced by X's will, is dependent on so many other influences, accidents and cross-currents of circumstance that, not merely is it quite likely not to be achieved at all, but, if it is achieved, X.'s volition will have been no more than

Similarly, ground 10 under sch 2 to the 2001 Act applies where "It is intended . . . to demolish, or carry out substantial work on, the building . . . which comprises or includes the house". None of the other grounds in the 2001 Act refers to an intention on the part of the landlord.

28 [2019] AC 249. Lord Sumption gave the main judgment in the case. A shorter judgment was given by Lord Briggs.

29 Under the 1954 Act, the tenant is entitled to a new tenancy at the end of the original tenancy, unless the landlord establishes one of seven grounds of opposition under s 30(1). One of those is in s 30(1)(f): "that on the termination of the current tenancy the landlord intends to demolish or reconstruct the premises comprised in the holding or a substantial part of those premises or to carry out substantial work of construction on the holding or part thereof and that he could not reasonably do so without obtaining possession of the holding . . .".

30 [1950] 2 KB 237, 253.

31 The approach of Lord Justice Asquith in *Cunliffe* was approved by the House of Lords in *Betty's Cafes Ltd v Phillips Furnishing Stores Ltd (No 1)* [1959] AC 20. At 34, Viscount Simonds said: "In this context your Lordships have the advantage of a judgment delivered by Lord Asquith . . . than whom there have been few greater masters of the English language in judicial interpretation or exposition . . .".

a minor agency collaborating with, or not thwarted by, the factors which predominately determine its occurrence. If there is a sufficiently formidable succession of fences to be surmounted before the result at which X aims can be achieved, it may well be unmeaning to say that X 'intended' that result."

In subsequent cases, it has been established that the landlord has to prove: (i) that it has an intention, which is both "genuine" and "firm and settled", to carry out qualifying works; and (ii) that it would be able to carry out those works.[32]

The reason for the court insisting on an intention that is "genuine" and "firm and settled" was expressed with typical clarity in Lord Denning's judgment in *Fisher v Taylor's Furnishing Stores Ltd*:[33]

> "For this purpose the court must be satisfied that the intention to reconstruct is genuine and not colourable; that it is a firm and settled intention, not likely to be changed; that the reconstruction is of a substantial part of the premises, indeed so substantial that it cannot be thought to be a device to get possession; that the work is so extensive that it is necessary to get possession of the holding in order to do it; and that it is intended to do the work at once and not after a time. Unless the court were to insist strictly on these requirements, tenants might be deprived of the protection which Parliament intended them to have. It must be remembered that if the landlord, having got possession, honestly changes his mind and does not do any work of reconstruction, the tenant has no remedy. Hence the necessity for a firm and settled intention."[34]

The second leg of the "intention" test (whether the landlord is able to carry out the work) is usually considered by reference to the legal and practical restraints upon the landlord, such as planning permission, requisite funding, etc.

The key elements of section 30(1)(f) of the Landlord and Tenant Act 1954 are the same as the statutory ground for repossession of residential property under the housing legislation, on the ground of demolition or substantial works.[35] Thus, in the Scottish case *Charlton v Josephine Marshall Trust*[36] and in the Court of Appeal's decision in *Wansbeck District Council v Marley*,[37] the court recognised the applicability of the approach in *Cunliffe v Goodman*[38] to actions for recovery possession of residential property, on the statutory ground that the landlord "intends" to carry out demolition or substantial works.

S Franses Ltd v Cavendish Hotel (London) Ltd concerns the first part of the "intention" test: whether the landlord has a genuine firm and settled intention to carry out the works. On that matter, the court reiterated and developed the previous case law, articulating the following principles:

32 See the discussion of the case law in Lord Sumption's judgment in *S Franses Ltd v Cavendish Hotel (London) Ltd* (n 28), in particular paras 1, 2, 8 and 9.

33 [1956] 2 QB 78 84.

34 However, in the case of a PRT, as will be explained at the end of Chapter 15, the tenant would have a remedy under ss 57–60 of the Act, in the form of an application for a wrongful termination order, if the landlord has misled the tribunal.

35 I.e. ground 6 in the 1988 Act, and ground 10 in the 2001 Act.

36 2020 SLT 409, summarised below. See also *City of Edinburgh Council v Middlemiss* 2007 Hous LR 70.

37 (1988) 20 HLR 247.

38 n 30.

- There has to be a genuine firm and settled intention on the part of the landlord to carry out the relevant work.
- It does not have to be the landlord's only intention, or even its primary one, provided that it is a firm and settled intention.
- The landlord's motive for carrying out the works is irrelevant, save as material for testing whether such a firm and settled intention exists.
- Since the statutory test assumed that the landlord's intention was being obstructed by the tenant's occupation, that intention could not be conditional on the works being necessary to get the tenant out of the premises. Rather, the test had to be whether the landlord would intend to do the same works if the tenant left voluntarily.

In *S Franses Ltd v Cavendish Hotel (London) Ltd*, the landlord was candid in its position that the sole purpose of proposing the works was to obtain vacant possession. However, the court recognised that, in some cases, ascertaining the landlord's true position might be a matter of inference.[39]

As regards the second part of the test,[40] the main legal constraint has been the planning legislation. The case law indicates that if the landlord has a reasonable prospect of obtaining the relevant planning permission or consent, it should be regarded as having the requisite intention.[41] It may also be necessary to consider private rights that might impede the works, such as servitudes. Generally, it is sufficient for the landlord to show that, if there remain hurdles in his way, he is likely to be able to overcome them.[42]

In *Charlton v Josephine Marshall Trust*,[43] a case under ground 6 of sch 5 to the 1988 Act, the Inner House rejected the argument that the existence of a repairing standard enforcement order under the Housing (Scotland) Act 2006 was a legal constraint on the landlord, such that it could not be regarded as having the intention to demolish the property. Accordingly, the statutory ground (which is mandatory) was established.

Application to the 2016 Act grounds

As already described, the courts have adopted a particular approach to the meaning of the word "intends" in section 30(1)(f) of the 1954 Act, and have extended that approach to statutory grounds for eviction under the housing legislation. However, all those provisions refer to a particular intention: to carry out demolition, reconstruction or substantial works. The question is whether the same approach ought also to be adopted in relation to grounds for eviction that are based on some other intention, such as those described in grounds 1, 3, 4, 5 and 6 of schedule 3 to the 2016 Act.

It is suggested that this question should be answered in the affirmative, for the following reasons.

39 See paras 8, 18 and 21 of Lord Sumption's judgment, and the judgment of Lord Briggs.

40 For which, see Woodfall, *Landlord and Tenant* para 22.109.

41 As we will see, both grounds 3 and 6 in the 2016 Act specifically refer to the existence of planning permission as "Evidence tending to show that the landlord has the intention mentioned in sub-paragraph (2)".

42 Woodfall (n 40) para 22.109.

43 n 36.

(1) Although an intention to carry out demolition, reconstruction or substantial works is not a ground under the 2016 Act, ground 3 (landlord intends to refurbish) and ground 6 (landlord intends to use for non-residential purpose), are similar. In broad terms, the intention is to effect some change to the property, which necessitates the removal of the tenant. Both grounds 3 and 6 make reference to the existence of planning permission as tending to show the intention. That accords with the approach taken in the cases following *Cunliffe*. So, there is a clear basis for applying the principles of those cases to grounds 3 and 6. If that is correct, the application of the same principles to grounds 1, 4 and 5 achieves consistency in the tribunals' approach to the issue of intention.

(2) The relevant passage from Lord Asquith's speech in *Cunliffe v Goodman*,[44] which is the foundation of the approach described, is not restricted to any particular intention. The reason for insisting on a genuine, firm and settled intention, as described in the quotation from *Fisher* above,[45] also applies irrespective of the nature of the intention. Unless the tribunal were to insist strictly on these requirements, tenants might be deprived of the protection that Parliament intended them to have. If the landlord, having got possession, honestly changes his mind, the tenant has no remedy.[46] Hence the necessity for a firm and settled intention, which the landlord is able to carry out.

All that said, however, there may be a limit, in practice, to the extent to which the tribunal can look behind the stated intention of the landlord, to do something that is more straightforward than "demolition, reconstruction or substantial works", and in relation to which there is less scope for critical examination.[47]

Evidence "tending to show" an intention

Each of grounds 1, 3, 4, 5 and 6 includes a subparagraph that begins:

> "Evidence tending to show that the landlord has the intention mentioned in sub-paragraph (2) [. . .] includes (for example) . . ."

There then follows reference to some piece of evidence, such as a letter, an affidavit, planning permission, a contract, and so on. That should be submitted along with the application.[48]

It is suggested that these provisions mean no more than what they say. If, taking ground 1 as an example, the landlord produces "a letter of engagement from a solicitor or estate agent concerning the sale of the let property", the

44 n 30.
45 n 33.
46 There is a remedy, in the form of an application under s 57 of the 2016 Act ("Wrongful termination by eviction order"). But this application is granted where the tribunal is satisfied that "it was misled into granting the eviction order". There is no remedy, if the landlord has honestly changed his mind, after the order is granted.
47 This is well illustrated by the decision of the tribunal in *Lopez v Ortega* EV/19/0967, 23/7/19, a case under ground 4 in which the tenant made submissions based on *Cunliffe v Goodman*, and questioned whether the landlord's intention was genuine. Nevertheless, the tribunal decided in favour of the landlord.
48 In terms of r 109(b)(i): see Chapter 9, p 313.

tribunal is directed by the Act to treat that letter as evidence tending to show the intention to sell the property. However, as this is just "for example", the landlord is not required to produce such evidence, to show the intention, which could be demonstrated in some other way. Nor is it the case, if the letter is produced, that the intention is thereby necessarily established. The tenant could produce evidence that tends to show the contrary.

However, it is to be expected that, if the landlord produces the "evidence tending to show" mentioned in the ground that, in the absence of any evidence to the contrary, the ground will be established.[49] Therefore, it is suggested that, where possible, it will be prudent for the landlord to obtain the evidence described in the relevant ground.

Intention grounds and wrongful termination

Sections 57–60 of the Act are headed "wrongful termination". These provisions are described at the end of Chapter 15, in which it is suggested that wrongful termination orders are most likely to be made in cases in which an "intention ground" has been used.

GROUNDS 1–7

Ground 1

"1 **Landlord intends to sell**

(1) It is an eviction ground that the landlord intends to sell the let property.

(2) The First-tier Tribunal must find that the ground named by sub-paragraph (1) applies if the landlord—

(a) is entitled to sell the let property, and

(b) intends to sell it for market value, or at least put it up for sale, within 3 months of the tenant ceasing to occupy it.

(3) Evidence tending to show that the landlord has the intention mentioned in sub-paragraph (2)(b) includes (for example)—

(a) a letter of engagement from a solicitor or estate agent concerning the sale of the let property,

(b) a recently prepared document that anyone responsible for marketing the let property would be required to possess under section 98 of the Housing (Scotland) Act 2006 were the property already on the market."

In cases in which the tribunal has granted an eviction order, this has been the second most commonly used ground. It is mandatory. In most of the decisions in which ground 1 was relied upon, the order was granted at the CMD, unopposed, on the production of written evidence confirming that a solicitor or estate agent was engaged.

In subparagraph (2)(a), "entitled to sell" presumably entails that the landlord is the owner of the property, which may be established by production of the title sheet from the Land Register.[50] In the case of joint landlords who are

49 That is what has happened in practice. See the discussion of grounds 1 and 4.

50 A title sheet for the property (if is a registered title) is normally obtained by the tribunal and placed with the papers for the application.

joint proprietors, the tribunal would have to be satisfied that they all have the intention to sell.[51]

The question of whether the intention is to sell for "market value"[52] has not arisen in the tribunal decisions; if an estate agent is engaged, this may be assumed. However, if there was evidence that the landlord intended a private sale to a family member or other associated person, the tribunal might question whether that was for market value.

The intention must be to sell, or put the property up for sale, "within 3 months of the tenant ceasing to occupy [the property]". This is consistent with the above quoted passage from Lord Denning's judgment in *Fisher*, to the effect that the landlord must intend to do the relevant act "at once and not after a time . . .".

Subparagraph 3(b) refers to a home report. Under section 98 of the 2006 Act ("Duty to have information about a house which is on the market"): "A person who is responsible for marketing a house which is on the market must possess the prescribed documents in relation to the house." The prescribed documents are the documents listed in regulation 4 of the Housing (Scotland) Act 2006 (Prescribed Documents) Regulations 2008,[53] being: (a) a survey report containing (i) the information in, or as nearly as may be in, the form set out in part 1 of Schedule 1; and (ii) the information on energy efficiency in part 2 of Schedule 1; and (b) a property questionnaire in, or as nearly as may be in, the form set out in Schedule 2. These are collectively referred to as "the home report". The report should be "recently prepared".[54]

Ground 2 and section 63: eviction order sought by lender

There is a lengthy discussion, in Chapter 8, of eviction proceedings by heritable creditors under ground 2 of schedule 5 to the 1988 Act, in cases in which the secured property is let under an assured tenancy. The provisions in the 2016 Act are much more favourable to actions by heritable creditors, in cases in which the secured property is let under a private residential tenancy ("PRT"), and it is suggested that the gradual transition from assured tenancies to PRTs will be of benefit to lenders.

Under the 2016 Act there is a specific provision that confers on lenders the right to raise eviction proceedings. Section 63 of the Act states:

> "**63 Landlord includes lender in some cases**
> In—
> (a) sections 50 to 56, and
> (b) sections 61 and 62,[55]

51 Because s 78(2) provides: "In a case where two or more persons jointly are the landlord under a tenancy, references in this Act to the landlord are to all of those persons unless stated otherwise."

52 In subpara (2)(b).

53 SSI 2008/76.

54 In *Masterson v McLeish* EV/19/2718, 26/10/19, the application was refused, *inter alia* because the home report was three years old.

55 Note that this is effectively the entirety of ch 3 of pt 5 of the Act, which concerns termination of the tenancy at the landlord's instigation, under the exception of ss 57–60, which concern wrongful termination.

references to the landlord under a private residential tenancy include a creditor in a heritable security over the let property who is entitled to sell the property."

In essence, this means that, by virtue of holding a decree under section 24 of the Conveyancing and Feudal Reform (Scotland) Act 1970[56] the lender will have title and interest to make an application for an eviction order under the 2016 Act, without having to assert that it is the assignee of the proprietor of the subjects, under section 20(5) of 1970 Act.[57] The lender is also entitled, in its own right, to serve a notice to leave and take any other steps that are the prerequisites of an application for an eviction order. As section 50 also applies to lenders, they may take possession under that section, in the case of consensual termination.[58]

It is to be assumed that applications by lenders will be made under ground 2, which states:

"2 **Property to be sold by lender**

(1) It is an eviction ground that a lender intends to sell the let property.

(2) The First-tier Tribunal must find that the ground named by sub-paragraph (1) applies if—
   (a) the let property is subject to a heritable security,
   (b) the creditor under that security is entitled to sell the property, and
   (c) the creditor requires the tenant to leave the property for the purpose of disposing of it

with vacant possession."

There are important differences between this ground and the equivalent ground under the 1988 Act. First, there is no requirement for notice to be given to the tenant, prior to the commencement of the tenancy, that possession might be recovered on this ground.[59] Secondly, it is not necessary that the heritable security is granted before the creation of the tenancy. Accordingly, the owner of the house might let it under a PRT, then grant a security over it, and then default on the security, with the result that the tenant is subsequently evicted by the lender.

As regards subparagraph (1), for the reasons stated in the discussion of section 51(2) above, the lender's intention is not subject to the same potential scrutiny as under grounds 1, 3, 4, 5 and 6, because that intention is not one of the requirements of subparagraph (2).[60]

In subparagraph (2), requirements (a) and (b) should be apparent from the extract of the decree in the lender's action under the 1970 Act, which ought to be lodged along with the application.[61] As regards (c), it is suggested that "disposing of it" means "selling it", given the references, elsewhere in the ground,

56 In practice, where a property is residential, and is occupied by a tenant, mortgage repossession proceedings are taken under s 24 of the 1970 Act. In such proceedings, the lenders will always seek a warrant to sell the subjects, in order to apply the sale proceeds to the debt over which the property is secured.

57 See the discussion of s 20(5) of the 1970 Act, in Chapter 8.

58 See Chapter 9, p 306.

59 The landlord is, however, required to provide the tenant with the specified information as required by s 11 of the Act (see p 303 in Chapter 9). That includes information to the effect that "property to be sold by lender" is a ground for eviction.

60 It is difficult to see how one could challenge the lenders' stated intention to sell the property, in order to realise the security.

61 Under r 109(b)(i) of the Procedure Rules (n 14), which is discussed in Chapter 9, at p 313.

to selling the property.[62] That being so, subparagraph (2)(c) will presumably be met, given that the lenders require vacant possession to market and sell the subjects, and comply with section 25 of the 1970 Act, under which "it shall be the duty of the creditor to . . . take all reasonable steps to ensure that the price at which all or any of the subjects are sold is the best that can be reasonably obtained".

It should be noted that rule 109(b)(vi) requires, in an application for an eviction order made by a heritable creditor in possession, that the lender includes a copy of the form BB that was given to the occupier of the subjects when the security was called up. The same requirement is imposed in rules 65 and 66, in relation to applications made under sections 18 and 33 of the 1988 Act.[63]

Ground 3

> "**3 Landlord intends to refurbish**
> (1) It is an eviction ground that the landlord intends to carry out significantly disruptive works to, or in relation to, the let property.
> (2) The First-tier Tribunal must find that the eviction ground named by sub-paragraph (1) applies if—
> (a) the landlord intends to refurbish the let property (or any premises of which the let property forms part),
> (b) the landlord is entitled to do so, and
> (c) it would be impracticable for the tenant to continue to occupy the property given the nature of the refurbishment intended by the landlord.
> (3) Evidence tending to show that the landlord has the intention mentioned in sub-paragraph (2)(a) includes (for example)—
> (a) any planning permission which the intended refurbishment would require,
> (b) a contract between the landlord and an architect or a builder which concerns the intended refurbishment."

This ground is mandatory. The drafting of the ground raises a few issues, the first of which arises from a comparison with ground 6 in the 1988 Act:

> "The landlord . . . intends to demolish or reconstruct . . . or to carry out substantial works on the house or any part thereof . . ."[64]

By contrast, ground 3(2)(a) limits the ground to an intention to "refurbish" the property – a term that is not defined in the Act. Its ordinary meaning[65] is different from "demolish" or "reconstruct", and is more specific than "carry out substantial works". That being so, it appears that, in contrast to the position in relation to the 1988 Act, an intention to demolish the property no longer amounts to a ground for eviction, though it is not clear why that change was thought to be desirable.

62 In the title, and subparas (1) and (2)(b).

63 This point is discussed in Chapter 8, at n 274.

64 Ground 10 in the 2001 Act is similar: "(1) It is intended within a reasonable period of time to demolish, or carry out substantial work on, the building . . .".

65 The *Shorter Oxford English Dictionary* defines "refurbish" as "brighten up, clean up; renovate, restore, redecorate". Thus, it suggested that "refurbish" includes "renovate", which in turn means: "repair; restore by replacing lost or damaged parts; make new again".

To "refurbish" is also not necessarily the same as to "carry out significantly disruptive works", the phrase used in subparagraph (1). Given section 51(2),[66] it is suggested that an intention to carry out such works to (or in relation to) the property would tend to establish subparagraph (2)(c), but not (2)(a), unless those works are reasonably characterised as refurbishment.

At the time of writing, ground 3 has very rarely been used. In one case, the application was accompanied by "estimates in respect of replacing laminate flooring, removal of wallpaper and skim plastering, and a statement from the applicant that the toilet and bath were to be replaced". On the basis of that description it might have been possible to question whether the test in subparagraph (2)(c) was met. However, the respondent did not appear at the hearing, and the tribunal granted the order.[67]

Although the decision in *Josephine Marshall Trust v Charlton*[68] was made in relation to the 1988 Act ground, it indicates that the landlord is not precluded from having the requisite intention, by the existence of a repairing standard enforcement order (an RSEO) made under the 2006 Act.

From the cases on "intention" that have already been discussed, it is implicit in the word "intends" that the landlord is entitled to carry out his intention; however, this is expressly stipulated by subparagraph (2)(a). Likewise, the production of planning permission, and a contract with a builder or architect, in terms of subparagraph (3), may be necessary to establish intention, on the basis of those cases.

Grounds 4 and 5

"4 **Landlord intends to live in property**

(1) It is an eviction ground that the landlord intends to live in the let property.

(2) The First-tier Tribunal must find that the ground named by sub-paragraph (1) applies if the landlord intends to occupy the let property as the landlord's only or principal home for at least 3 months.

(3) References to the landlord in this paragraph—

  (a) in a case where two or more persons jointly are the landlord under a tenancy, are to be read as referring to any one of them,

  (b) in a case where the landlord holds the landlord's interest as a trustee under a trust, are to be read as referring to a person who is a beneficiary under the trust.

(4) Evidence tending to show that the landlord has the intention mentioned in sub-paragraph (2) includes (for example) an affidavit stating that the landlord has that intention."

In cases in which the tribunal has granted an eviction order, ground 4 has been the third most commonly used ground. It is mandatory. Subparagraph (4) allows evidence to be given by affidavit, to confirm that the landlord has the requisite intention. This has commonly been done, with the tribunal granting applications on the basis of one or more affidavits, usually in the absence of opposition from the respondent.

66 See p 334 above.

67 *Guthrie v Brownlee* EV/18/1817, 7/1/19.

68 n 36.

In contrast to the position for ground 1, the reference to the period of "3 months" is not fixed to any particular date.[69] Nevertheless, it is suggested that the tribunal ought not to grant the application unless it is satisfied that the landlord intends to take up occupation when the tenant's occupation ceases.[70] If it is not so satisfied, it may refuse the application, or alternatively consider adjourning the CMD or hearing, thereby delaying the grant of an order so that its effective date will coincide with the date when the applicant hopes to move back to the property.

The application may be opposed, by a tenant questioning whether the landlord has a genuine firm and settled intention to occupy the let property as his "only or principal home"[71] for at least three months. In that event, it may be appropriate to have the applicant appear at the CMD or hearing himself,[72] in order that the tribunal can be satisfied as to the genuineness of intention, if that is in question.[73]

In the case of joint landlords, only one need have the requisite intention. The ground will also apply where the landlord is a trustee under a trust, and it is intended that one of the beneficiaries will occupy the let property.

"5 **Family member intends to live in property**

(1) It is an eviction ground that a member of the landlord's family intends to live in the let property.

(2) The First-tier Tribunal may find that the ground named by sub-paragraph (1) applies if—

(a) a member of the landlord's family intends to occupy the let property as that person's only or principal home for at least 3 months, and

(b) the Tribunal is satisfied that it is reasonable to issue an eviction order on account of that fact.

(3) A member of the landlord's family is to be regarded as having the intention mentioned in sub-paragraph (2) if—

(a) the family member is incapable of having, or expressing, that intention, and

(b) the landlord and (if different) a person entitled to make decisions about where the family member lives, intend that the family member will occupy the let property as the family member's only or principal home for at least 3 months.

(4) For the purposes of this paragraph, a person is a member of the landlord's family if the person is:

(a) in a qualifying relationship with the landlord,

(b) a qualifying relative of the landlord,

(c) a qualifying relative of a person who is in a qualifying relationship with the landlord, or

(d) in a qualifying relationship with a qualifying relative of the landlord.

(5) For the purposes of sub-paragraph (4)—

(a) two people are in a qualifying relationship with one another if they are—

(i) married to each other,

69 Ground 1: "within 3 months of the tenant ceasing to occupy it . . .".

70 See the quotation from Lord Denning's judgment in *Fisher v Taylor's Furnishing Stores Ltd* (n 33): "[The] court must be satisfied that the intention to reconstruct is genuine and not colourable . . . and that it is intended to do the work at once and not after a time."

71 The meaning of this term is discussed in Chapter 1. Where the landlord has another home, the tribunal would have to be satisfied that the let property was intended to be the landlord's principal home, in the event that the application is granted.

72 Rather than relying on the affidavit evidence.

73 See *Lopez v Ortega* EV/19/0967, 23/7/19.

(ii) in a civil partnership with each other, or
(iii) living together as though they were married,
(b) "a qualifying relative" means a parent, grandparent, child, grandchild, brother or sister,
(c) a relationship of the half blood is to be regarded as a relationship of the whole blood,
(d) a person's stepchild is to be regarded as the person's child,
(e) a person ('A') is to be regarded as the child of another person ('B'), if A is being or has been treated by B as B's child.
(6) In a case where two or more persons jointly are the landlord under a tenancy, references to the landlord in this paragraph are to any one of them.
(7) Evidence tending to show that a member of the landlord's family has the intention mentioned in sub-paragraph (2) includes (for example) an affidavit stating that the person has that intention."

This ground is similar to ground 4, but applies where it is a member of the landlord's family who has the intention to occupy the let property as his "only or principal home" for at least three months. Reference is made to the discussion of ground 4, which imposes similar requirements.

Subparagraph (3) anticipates a situation in which the family member is a person incapable of expressing the intention to live at the property, in which case the requisite intention must lie with the landlord and the person entitled to make decisions about where the family member lives.[74]

Subparagraphs (4) and (5) set out a fairly convoluted definition of the term "member of the landlord's family". The definitions of "qualifying relationship" and "qualifying relative" are similar to those used in section 70 of the Act.[75] It follows from subparagraph six that, in the case of joint landlords, the intended occupier need be a member of only one joint landlord's family.

As ground 5 is discretionary, the tribunal may have to weigh the strength of the competing needs of the tenant, and the family member, to occupy the property.[76]

Ground 6

"6 **Landlord intends to use for non-residential purpose**
(1) It is an eviction ground that the landlord intends to use the let property for a purpose other than housing.
(2) The First-tier Tribunal must find that the ground named by sub-paragraph (1) applies if the landlord intends to use the let property for a purpose other than providing a person with a home.
(3) Evidence tending to show that the landlord has the intention mentioned in sub-paragraph (2) includes (for example) any planning permission which would be required if the let property is to be used for the intended purpose."

At the time of writing, there appear to be no cases in which this ground has been successfully used.[77] It is suggested that the tribunal would have to be satisfied as to the nature of the intended use (in order to confirm that it

74 I.e. a person having welfare guardianship in relation to the family member.
75 In relation to the right of certain persons to succeed to the PRT on the death of the tenant.
76 For an interesting example, see the decision in *Koc and Reid v Kazmi* EV/19/2209, 22/11/19.
77 One of the tribunal decisions indicates that the ground was relied upon, along with grounds 14 and 12. However, an order was granted on ground 12 without consideration of the other grounds, with no indication of the basis on which ground 6 was relied upon.

was not residential), and in line with the principles arising from *Cunliffe v Goodman*,[78] that there was a genuine settled intention to put the property to this new purpose, which the landlord has a reasonable prospect of achieving. As with ground 3, evidence tending to show the ground includes a grant of planning permission, presumably for a change of use.

Ground 7

"7 **Property required for religious purpose**

(1) It is an eviction ground that the let property is required for use in connection with the purposes of a religion.

(2) The First-tier Tribunal must find that the ground named by sub-paragraph (1) applies if—

  (a) the let property is held for the purpose of being available for occupation by a person engaged in the work of a religious denomination as a residence from which the duties of such a person are to be performed,

  (b) the property has previously been occupied by a person engaged in the work of a religious denomination as a residence from which that person's duties were performed, and

  (c) the property is required for the purpose mentioned in paragraph (a).

(3) In sub-paragraph (2), reference to a person engaged in the work of a religious denomination includes an imam, a lay missionary, minister, monk, nun, priest and rabbi."

This ground is fairly self-explanatory; it is to be expected that applications on this basis will be fairly unusual. In comparison with the equivalent ground under the 1988 Act,[79] there are more points that have to be established.[80] Also, the scope of persons engaged in the work of a religious denomination has been extended.[81] Subparagraph 2(c) entails a higher test than those for the other grounds in part 1. It is not sufficient that the landlord intends to use the property for the purpose described in 2(a); the property must be required for that purpose.

PART 2: TENANT'S STATUS

Ground 8: Not an employee

"8 **Not an employee**

(1) It is an eviction ground that the tenancy was entered into to provide an employee with a home and the tenant is not a qualifying employee.

(2) The First-tier Tribunal must find that the ground named by sub-paragraph (1) applies if—

  (a) the tenancy was granted to the tenant—

    (i) in consequence of the tenant being an employee of the landlord, or

    (ii) in the expectation that the tenant would become an employee of the landlord,

78 n 30.

79 Ground 5.

80 However, there is no requirement for notice to have been given, prior to the tenancy being created, that possession might be recovered on this ground.

81 The 1988 Act ground applied only to occupation by "a minister or a full-time lay missionary".

(b) the tenant is not employed by the landlord, and
(c) either—
(i) the application for an eviction order that is before the Tribunal was made within 12 months of the tenant ceasing to be an employee of the landlord, or
(ii) if the tenant never became an employee of the landlord, the application for an eviction order that is before the Tribunal was made within 12 months of the tenancy being granted to the tenant.

(3) The First-tier Tribunal may find that the ground named by sub-paragraph (1) applies if—
(a) the conditions set out in sub-paragraph (2)(a) and (b) are met, and
(b) the Tribunal is satisfied that it is reasonable to issue an eviction order, despite the landlord not applying for one within the period of 12 months mentioned in sub-paragraph (2)(c).

(4) In sub-paragraphs (2) and (3), 'landlord' includes any person who has been a landlord under the tenancy."

At the time of writing there have been no decisions of the Housing and Property Chamber in which this ground has been considered. It is rather more complex than the equivalent ground under the 1988 Act (ground 17). In particular, it takes account of the possibility that a tenancy may have been granted in the expectation of the tenant becoming an employee of the landlord, but that never came to pass. Ground 8 does not apply to service occupancies, which are not tenancies and therefore do not attract the protection of the Act.[82]

Both the mandatory and discretionary aspects of the ground require the tribunal to be satisfied that the tenancy was granted either: (i) in consequence of the tenant being an employee of the landlord, or (ii) in the expectation that the tenant would become an employee of the landlord. One would expect that this would be demonstrated by the contract of employment, or correspondence at the time when the offer is made.

Whereas the 1988 ground was discretionary, subparagraph (2) above sets out a mandatory ground. The landlord has twelve months from the date the employment ended to make an application to the tribunal for an eviction order, if it wishes to utilise the mandatory ground.[83] Where the employment never came to pass, the landlord has twelve months from the date of the tenancy being granted.

If the landlord fails to make an application to the tribunal within twelve months, the ground becomes discretionary. Presumably in that case a key issue might be whether the landlord requires the property for use by another employee.

The effect of subparagraph (4) is that, where the interest of the landlord in the tenancy transfers to another person, the ground can still be used by the new landlord.

82 Service occupancies (or tied tenancies, as they are sometimes called) are discussed in Chapter 12.

83 Bear in mind that where the tenant has been in occupation for more than six months, the notice period under s 54 is eighty-four days. In that case, the landlord would have to serve the notice to leave no later than about three months before the twelve-month period expired, in order to make an application to the tribunal relying on the mandatory ground.

Ground 9

"9 No longer in need of supported accommodation

(1) It is an eviction ground that the tenancy was entered into on account of the tenant having an assessed need for community care and the tenant has since been assessed as no longer having that need.

(2) The First-tier Tribunal may find that the ground named by sub-paragraph (1) applies if—

(a) the tenancy was granted in consequence of the tenant being assessed under section 12A of the Social Work (Scotland) Act 1968 to have needs calling for the provision of community care services,

(b) the tenancy would not have been granted to the tenant on the basis of the latest assessment of the tenant's needs under that section, and

(c) the Tribunal considers it reasonable to issue an eviction order on account of that fact.

(3) The condition in sub-paragraph (2)(a) is to be deemed to be met if the tenancy was granted as a result of a local authority taking urgent action by virtue of section 12A(5) of the Social Work (Scotland) Act 1968."

At the time of writing there have been no decisions of the Housing and Property Chamber in which this ground has been considered. It is new, there being no equivalent ground under the 1988 Act.

In Scotland there are institutions (usually charities), which own residential properties that are occupied by persons to whom they are providing support services.[84] Where the institution is not a local authority or a registered social landlord (an RSL), the agreements that it makes with occupiers are not subject to the Scottish secure tenancy regime under the 2001 Act.[85] It is understood that, in such cases prior to the 2016 Act coming into force, the institution might typically grant a short assured tenancy to the person receiving support, in terms of section 32 of the 1988 Act. That arrangement had clear advantages for both parties. It was beneficial for the occupier to be accorded the status of a tenant in his home, rather than a mere "occupier", and to be recognised as such. For the landlord, a short assured tenancy meant that it could enter into an agreement in the knowledge that if, at some point in the future, the tenant no longer required its support services, or chose not to engage with them, it could then recover possession and arrange for the property to be occupied by a person able and willing to utilise its support.

The abolition of the short assured tenancy form of tenure therefore raised a question as to how the 2016 Act would deal with tenancies of this type. Ground 9 is the answer to that question.

In order for the ground to be utilised, it has to have been the case the tenancy was entered into "on account of", or "in consequence of", the tenant being assessed as described in subparagraph (2)(a), or "as a result of"[86] urgent action as described in (3).

84 Typically, because the person requires support due to a mental health condition, learning disability, dementia or addiction issues.

85 As is indicated by subpara (2), a local authority may assess the person as having needs that require the provision of community care services (i.e. support). It will then arrange with the charity for a supported occupancy or tenancy to be provided.

86 It is suggested that these phrases mean the same thing: that the grant of the tenancy resulted from the assessment or the urgent action, and would not have been granted without it.

Therefore, it is suggested that, where the landlord wishes this ground to be available in relation to any tenancy, there be an exchange of letters between the landlord and the relevant local authority confirming that: the tenant has been assessed as described in subparagraph (2)(a) (or that urgent action is being taken under section 12A(5); and the tenancy is being granted in consequence of that assessment (or as a result of that urgent action). Also, it is suggested that the tenancy agreement itself should contain a clause along the following lines:

> "This tenancy is being granted to the tenant by the landlord, either: (a) in consequence of the tenant being assessed by [name the local authority] under section 12A of the Social Work (Scotland) Act 1968 to have needs calling for the provision of community care services, or (b) as a result of [the local authority] taking urgent action by virtue of section 12A(5) of that Act."

If that is done, the landlord should be in a position to establish subparagraph (2)(a).

In satisfying the tribunal as to subparagraph (2)(b), it will presumably be necessary to produce an assessment of the tenant's needs. That may be accompanied by written or oral evidence to the effect that tenancy would not have been granted on the basis of that assessment, i.e. that the tenant's needs have changed. If that is established, the tribunal will make a decision as to whether it is reasonable to grant the order. One might expect that, in support of the application, the landlord will argue that the tenancy ought to be vacated by the tenant, in order that it can be let to a person for whose needs it is appropriate. Against that, the tribunal may have to balance the consequences for the tenant of making the order, particularly if he is a vulnerable person.

As an alternative to the "tenancy" approach, the support provider may seek to avoid creating a tenancy subject to the 2016 Act, by characterising the parties' contract as a licence,[87] under which the occupation of the property is ancillary to, and dependent upon, the provision of support by the provider to the occupier. The success of that approach will depend on various factors, such as the terms of the parties' agreement, the nature of the support, and so on.[88]

PART 3: TENANT'S CONDUCT

There are six grounds in part 3. These may be compared with the grounds in the 1988 Act that could be described as relating to the tenant's conduct,

87 Usually titled an "occupancy agreement". This approach is not possible for RSLs and local authorities because, under the 2001 Act, a "tenancy" is widely defined as an agreement under which a house is made available for human habitation. See Chapter 4, p 82. Instead, a local authority may offer a short Scottish secure tenancy, under ground 6 of sch 6 to the 2001 Act. See Chapter 6.

88 The lease/licence distinction is discussed in Chapter 12. See also the decision of the Court of Appeal in *Watts v Stewart and others (Trustees of the Ashtead United Charity)* [2018] Ch 423. That lends support to the view that a charitable organisation providing accommodation is entitled to exclude security of tenure if that is necessary to ensure that the property is occupied by a person who qualifies for that accommodation, under the charity's own rules. In practice, this usually means a person who still requires the relevant support, and is willing to engage with it.

which are: grounds 8, 11 and 12 (rent arrears); 10 (tenant's notice to quit); 13 (breach of tenancy obligations); 14 and 16 (deterioration of condition of property or furniture); and 15 (antisocial behaviour). Of these, only ground 13 may be regarded as appearing in the same form in the 2016 Act (as ground 11).

Under the 2016 Act there is only one rent arrears ground.[89] There are three distinct grounds (13, 14 and 15), which may be regarded as replacing, and expanding upon, the single antisocial behaviour ground in the 1988 Act. There is no equivalent, in the 2016 Act, of grounds 14 and 16 in the 1988 Act. However, clause 17 of the Scottish Government's PRT Model Agreement obliges the tenant to take reasonable care of the let property, and particularises, in a series of bullet points, what that duty entails. Breach of that clause may give rise to an application for an eviction order under ground 11.

Ground 10

"**10 Not occupying let property**

(1) It is an eviction ground that the tenant is not occupying the let property as the tenant's home.

(2) The First-tier Tribunal must find that the ground named by sub-paragraph (1) applies if—

- (a) the let property is not being occupied as the only or principal home of—
  - (i) the tenant, or
  - (ii) a person to whom a sub-tenancy of the let property has been lawfully granted,

and

- (b) the property's not being so occupied is not attributable to a breach of the landlord's duties under Chapter 4 of Part 1 of the Housing (Scotland) Act 2006.

(3) In sub-paragraph (2), the reference to a sub-tenancy being lawfully granted is to be construed in accordance with section 46(3)."

Mention has already been made of ground 10 in the discussion of "consensual termination" under section 50 of the Act. See Chapter 9, p 307.

The terms "occupy" and "principal home" are discussed in Chapter 1.

In the case of joint tenants: given the terms of section 78(3), the ground is applicable only if all the joint tenants are no longer in occupation. It is also suggested that the ground is not applicable if property is a matrimonial home under the Matrimonial Homes (Family Protection) (Scotland) Act 1981 and is occupied by the non-entitled spouse of the tenant.[90]

Ground 10 speaks in the present tense, which suggests that the test of non-occupation is to be applied as at the date when the tribunal is considering whether to grant an application under section 51. If that is correct, it would mean that the tenant could defeat the application by moving back into the

89 As will be described below, ground 12 comprises distinct mandatory and discretionary bases on which an order can be granted. However, it is evident from the tribunal's decisions that the discretionary ground very rarely applies.

90 Because s 2(1)(b) of the 1981 Act entitles the non-entitled spouse, for the purposes of securing his occupancy rights, to perform any obligation incumbent on the entitled spouse; and s 2(8) states: "Where (a) the entitled spouse is a tenant of a matrimonial home; and (b) possession thereof is necessary in order to continue the tenancy; and (c) the entitled spouse abandons such possession, the tenancy shall be continued by such possession by the non-entitled spouse." See the discussion of the rights of non-entitled spouses in Chapter 12.

property. In this respect, it is interesting to make a comparison between ground 10 and the equivalent "non-occupation" ground in schedule 2 to the 2001 Act (ground 5).[91] That also applies where the tenant[92] has ceased to occupy the house as his principal home. However, that ground may also be established where the tenant: "has been absent from the house without reasonable cause for a continuous period exceeding 6 months" – a circumstance that might be proved, even if the tenant had resumed occupation by the time the case was determined.[93]

In practice it is likely that ground 10 will be combined with other grounds, in particular ground 11 ("breach of tenancy agreement") and ground 12 ("rent arrears"). Ground 11 will be applicable where the Model Tenancy Agreement is used, because clause 7 ("occupation and use of let property") states that "The Tenant agrees to continue to occupy the Let Property as his or her home". Even where the model agreement is not used, non-occupation will be a breach of the tenancy contract if the tenant has parted with, or given up to another person, possession of the let property, without the written agreement of the landlord.[94] In either case, ground 11 may be relied upon, even if the tenant has resumed occupation as at the date when the tribunal is determining the application.[95] Ground 12 may well be applicable, because non-occupation is often accompanied by non-payment of rent.

Under subparagraph (2)(b), ground 10 is not applicable if the tenant's non-occupation is attributable to the landlord's failure to comply with his obligation to ensure that the property meets the repairing standard, under sections 13 and 14 of the 2006 Act.

As to references in ground 10 to sub-tenancies, see the discussion of the rights of sub-tenants in Chapter 12.

Proof of non-occupation

To date, there have been several cases in which the tribunal has considered evidence tending to show non-occupation.

In one case in which the ground was found to be established, the tribunal had regard to the condition of the property as disclosed during visits made by the landlord's agents, which showed: a lack of furniture and personal belongings within the property; the presence of mould on plates that had been left out; the same items within the fridge; and that there appeared to have been no changes to the property and its condition during each visit by the letting agent.[96]

91 There is no equivalent ground in the 1988 Act because, under ss 12 and 16, non-occupation means that the tenancy is no longer an assured tenancy, and does not enjoy the protection of the Act. See Chapter 7, p 230.

92 And, as the case may be, the tenant's spouse or civil partner, or a person who has been living with the tenant as a spouse or civil partner.

93 On the other hand, ground 5 is discretionary, whereas ground 10 in the 2016 Act is mandatory.

94 That would be a breach of statutory term 3, in the schedule to the Private Residential Tenancies (Statutory Terms) (Scotland) Regulations 2017. See the discussion of tenancy terms in Chapter 9, at p 302.

95 Although ground 11 is discretionary, whereas ground 10 is mandatory.

96 *Sepehr v Lockyer and Langfield* EV/19/1209 and 1212; 18/6/19. In the cases *Dollar Property v Turnbull* EV/18/3113, 15/1/19 and *Connor v Eweka* EV/18/1307, 2/11/18, the tribunal did not

Ground 11

"**11 Breach of tenancy agreement**

(1) It is an eviction ground that the tenant has failed to comply with an obligation under the tenancy.

(2) The First-tier Tribunal may find that the ground named by sub-paragraph (1) applies if—

(a) the tenant has failed to comply with a term of the tenancy, and

(b) the Tribunal considers it to be reasonable to issue an eviction order on account of that fact.

(3) The reference in sub-paragraph (2) to a term of the tenancy does not include the term under which the tenant is required to pay rent."

Apart from subparagraph (3), this ground is effectively the same as the equivalent ground 13 under the 1988 Act, and the second part of ground 1 under the 2001 Act. The reader is referred to the discussion of the 2001 Act ground in Chapter 5.

The effect of subparagraph (3) is that ground 11 is not applicable where the breach is failure to pay rent. As was discussed in Chapter 9, this has led to some confusion, with notices to leave, and applications to the tribunal, relying on the wrong ground.[97]

Given the preponderance of applications on mandatory grounds,[98] ground 11 cases may afford the tribunal a rare opportunity to make a judgment as to whether it is reasonable to grant an order. In cases in which that judgment was exercised in favour of the landlord, the tenancy breaches included:

- failure to pay the deposit;[99]
- antisocial behaviour;[100]
- keeping Rottweiler dogs at the tenancy without the landlord's permission;[101]
- letting out the property on Airbnb without the landlord's consent.[102]

The order was refused in cases where:

- the breach (a false declaration in the tenancy agreement) was not serious, and the respondent was otherwise a good tenant;[103]
- the alleged breach (allowing another person to reside at the property) was not established;[104] and

grant the application on ground 10, due to lack of evidence, but granted it on ground 12. In *Burns v Kane* EV/18/1385, 17/8/18, ground 10 would have been applicable, as the respondent accepted at the CMD that he had ceased occupation, but it was not one of the bases on which the order was sought. Again, in this case, an eviction was ordered on ground 12. *Vaughan v Stewart* EV/19/3346, 13/1/20, is a rare example of an application being granted on ground 10 alone. In that case, the landlord had received a letter from the local authority, confirming that the tenant had made an application for housing benefit in relation to another tenancy.

97 See p 331.

98 In particular subpara (2) of ground 12; see the discussion at p 335 above.

99 *Pearson v Martin* EV/18/1752, 18/9/18 and *Miller v Zielinska* EV/19/0801, 24/5/19.

100 *Northwood v Dhami* EV/18/2889, 12/2/19 and *Andrews v Campbell* EV/19/0523, 12/4/19. In these cases, the order was also granted on ground 14.

101 This was one of a number of breaches considered by the tribunal in *Fraserburgh Car Sales v Baff* EV/18/1244 and 2430, 2/5/19.

102 *Wood v Hanscombe* EV/19/1252, 14/6/19 and *Leiper v Hanscombe* EV/19/1948, 5/9/19.

103 *KJB Housing v Rae* EV/18/0737, 2/8/18.

104 *Yan Li v Tonner* EV/18/2542, 4/2/19.

- the tenant had left a sofa on an upper floor landing, in a dangerous position, because the danger had been removed, and the breach was not part of pattern of such behaviour.[105]

In several cases in which on which the application was made on more than one ground, the tribunal has granted the order on a mandatory ground at the CMD, without considering whether ground 11 was established.[106]

Ground 12

"12 **Rent arrears**

(1) It is an eviction ground that the tenant has been in rent arrears for three or more consecutive months.

(2) The First-tier Tribunal must find that the ground named by sub-paragraph (1) applies if—

(a) at the beginning of the day on which the Tribunal first considers the application for an eviction order on its merits, the tenant—

(i) is in arrears of rent by an amount equal to or greater than the amount which would be payable as one month's rent under the tenancy on that day, and

(ii) has been in arrears of rent (by any amount) for a continuous period, up to and including that day, of three or more consecutive months, and

(b) the Tribunal is satisfied that the tenant's being in arrears of rent over that period is not wholly or partly a consequence of a delay or failure in the payment of a relevant benefit.

(3) The First-tier Tribunal may find that the ground named by sub-paragraph (1) applies if—

(a) for three or more consecutive months the tenant has been in arrears of rent, and

(b) the Tribunal is satisfied that it is reasonable on account of that fact to issue an eviction order.

(4) In deciding under sub-paragraph (3) whether it is reasonable to issue an eviction order, the Tribunal is to consider whether the tenant's being in arrears of rent over the period in question is wholly or partly a consequence of a delay or failure in the payment of a relevant benefit.

(5) For the purposes of this paragraph—

(a) references to a relevant benefit are to—

(i) a rent allowance or rent rebate under the Housing Benefit (General) Regulations 1987 (S.I. 1987/1971),

(ii) a payment on account awarded under regulation 91 of those Regulations,

(iii) universal credit, where the payment in question included (or ought to have included) an amount under section 11 of the Welfare Reform Act 2012 in respect of rent,

(iv) sums payable by virtue of section 73 of the Education (Scotland) Act 1980,

(b) references to delay or failure in the payment of a relevant benefit do not include any delay or failure so far as it is referable to an act or omission of the tenant."

105 *Adelphi Scott Ltd v Rushton* EV/19/3476, 6/1/20.

106 For example, *Allardyce v Letham* EV/18/1803, 28/9/18 and *McMahon v Stanners* EV/18/2196, 19/10/18.

As has already been described at p 335 above, ground 12 is, by far, the most commonly used ground.

Subparagraphs (2) and (3) set out two distinct bases on which an order may be granted, the first being mandatory and the second discretionary. In either case, the ground applies only where the tenant has been in arrears for three or more consecutive months. Therefore, as is apparent from subparagraph (1) of the ground, the Act accords primacy to the duration of the arrears, rather than the amount.[107] Where that three-month duration is established, the order will be granted under subparagraph (2) if the arrears are equal to, or more than, one month's rent at the beginning of the day when the tribunal considers the application.[108] If the tenant has been in arrears of rent for three or more consecutive months, but the conditions of 12(2) are not met, or where subparagraph (2)(b) is established, the tribunal must make a judgment as to whether it is reasonable to grant the order. That is rarely necessary, as the one-month threshold is so low.[109]

"Rent arrears"

Reference is made to Chapters 5 and 8 for a discussion of the terms "rent" and "rent arrears".[110] In contrast to ground 8 in schedule 5 to the 1988 Act, ground 12 does not use the term "lawfully due", but there seems no difference in substance between those words and "arrears of rent . . . which would be payable . . . under the tenancy" in ground 12(2)(a)(i).[111]

Eviction orders granted in ground 12 cases, at a CMD or a hearing, are based on the evidence of a rent account or another statement showing that the various elements of the ground are established.[112] The applicant, or his representative, speaks to the accuracy of the account, before the tribunal.

Where there is a dispute as to the exact amount of rent due, that will clearly have a bearing on any application that the landlord has made, under rule 111, for a payment order in respect of the arrears.[113] However, it does not necessarily affect the application for an eviction order. Let us say that parties are agreed that the rent has been in arrears for three or more consecutive months, and that the landlord maintains that the amount due is £1,500 but the tenant insists that it is £1,000. If £1,000 is equal to or more than one month's rent,

107 See examples 2 and 3 below.

108 Subject to the protection allowed to the tenant under subpara (2)(b), where the arrears are due to delay or failure in the payment of a relevant benefit. However, that protection is limited: see example 4 below.

109 For a rare example of the tribunal making a decision under the discretionary part of the ground, see *MacDonald v Galvin* EV/18/2528, 4/1/19.

110 In Chpater 5, from p 125, and in Chapter 8, from p 279.

111 In any event, the ordinary meaning of "arrear" is not just "unpaid", but due. The *Shorter Oxford English Dictionary* (6th edn) defines "arrear" as "behind in time, behind in the discharge of duties or liabilities; behind in payment . . . a duty or liability undischarged".

112 An up-to-date rent account should be lodged with the application. See Chapter 9, p 313.

113 As willl be explained in Chapter 14, where the landlord seeks (a) an eviction order under s 51 of the 2016 Act, and (b) an order for payment of arrears and/or damages (for which the FTT has jurisdiction under s 71 of the Act), these are separate applications, made under rr 109 and 111 respectively. They would be heard together, at the same CMD, but the tribunal would issue separate decisions.

there is no dispute that ground 12(2) is established,[114] and the order can be granted. The dispute over the amount of rent can be determined at a hearing on the rule 111 application. Where the tenant claims to be withholding rent, or seeks an abatement, the position is more complex. See the discussion below.

The mandatory ground

In practice, "the day on which the Tribunal first considers the application for an eviction order on its merits" is invariably the CMD.[115] The majority of decisions made by the FTT, in applications under rule 109 for an eviction order, are decisions to grant an order on ground 12(2), at a CMD at which the respondent did not appear, and was not represented.[116]

What happens if the tenant makes payment during the course of that day, before the CMD or hearing takes place, or attends at the CMD and offers to make payment there and then?[117] That would not make any difference as to the level of arrears for the purposes of paragraph 12(2)(i): it is the amount due at the beginning of the day that is relevant. In that case, the tenant's payment could not be taken into account in deciding whether the rent was in arrears by an amount greater than, or equal to, one month's rent.

However, it appears to be the effect of the words "up to and including that day", in paragraph 12(2)(a)(ii), that the reckoning of the continuous period of three months includes the day on which the tribunal first considers the application for an eviction order on its merits. So, if the hearing takes place on, say, 3 November, the rent must have been in arrears for the period from 4 August to 3 November, inclusive, at least. Accordingly, if the tenant cleared the arrears earlier on 3 November, or pays at the CMD, it is suggested that the continuous period is not established for the purposes of 12(2).

It is also suggested that, if an order is granted under ground 12(2), at a hearing at which the respondent did not appear, it will not avail him to pay the arrears and then seek to recall the order under rule 30 of the Procedure Rules.[118] That is because, in terms of subparagraph 12(2)(a), the Tribunal would still have to proceed on the basis of the duration and level of arrears that existed as at the date on which it first considered the application on its merits, being the date on which the eviction order was granted.

In residential leases in the private sector, rent is usually charged monthly in advance. Where some other period is used, it may be necessary to calculate "the amount which would be payable as one month's rent under the tenancy".

114 Subject to ground 12(2)(b).

115 Under r 17(4) of the Procedure Rules (r 14), the tribunal may do anything at a CMD that it may do at the hearing of the case, "including making a decision".

116 In cases in which the respondent *does* appear at the CMD, it makes no difference to the order being granted if it is accepted that the duration and level of arrears are such as to establish ground 12(2).

117 This could well happen, particularly given that CMDs are often scheduled for 11:30am or 2pm. Where payment is offered by cheque, it is suggested that the approach suggested by the Court of Appeal in *Coltrane v Day* [2003] EWCA Civ 342 would be applicable. See Chapter 8, p 281.

118 n 14.

Examples of the operation of ground 12

In practice, an application under ground 12, which is not rejected at the sift, or refused at the CMD due to some technical issue,[119] is granted at the CMD.

However, the drafting of the ground gives rise to some tricky issues, which are explored in the following examples.

1. L rents a flat to T. It is a PRT under the 2016 Act. The rent is £500 per month, payable in advance, on the 1st of the month. T regularly pays the rent a couple of weeks late. T misses the monthly rental payment due on 1 April 2022, and also fails to make the next payment on 1 May. She is then £1,000 in arrears. T makes a payment of £1,000 on 1 June, and a payment of £500 on 1 July, leaving her £500 in arrears. In this case, L may serve a notice to leave on 2 July as, at that point, the rent has been in arrears for a continuous period of three months, from 2 April to 1 July inclusive.[120]
2. Let us say that T then makes another payment of £500 on 1 August. She is still in arrears by £500 at 10 August, and L makes an application to the tribunal on that date. T then makes a payment of £500 on 29 August, clearing the arrears, and reducing the debit balance on her rent account to nil. However, on 1 September she fails to pay the rent. The tribunal fixes a CMD to take place on 3 November. T also fails to make the rental payments due on 1 October and 1 November, leaving her in arrears by £1,500. However, on 3 November, the tribunal cannot grant the application on ground 12(2) because, as at that date, the rent has not been in arrears for a continuous period of three months.

This example raises several issues. First: it might be argued that the tribunal could still grant the order under ground 12(3) because, in contrast to 12(2), there is no requirement that the rent has been in arrears for three months "at the beginning of the day on which the Tribunal first considers the application". Therefore, provided that the rent "has been" in arrears for three or more consecutive months at any time in the tenancy, the order may be granted. However, that argument was rejected in the tribunal's decision in *Skoll v Humanes and Ors*,[121] in which the legal member observed that, if correct, this would have the drastic effect that the tenant could never purge his default by paying the arrears in full, and would no longer have full security of tenure.

Another issue is whether, in scenario 2 above, the landlord could ask the tribunal: (a) not to "consider the application for an eviction order on its merits"; but (b) to continue the CMD to a further CMD or hearing, after 1 December, in the hope of establishing ground 12(2) at that hearing. The tribunal has a discretionary power under rule 17(4) to decide the application at a CMD, which it can choose not to use. Against that, it could be argued that the tribunal can, and should, dismiss the application on 3 November. Under rule 17(3), "the purpose of a case management discussion is to enable the First-tier Tribunal to explore how the parties' dispute may be *efficiently* resolved": if the

119 See the discussion on the frequency of the use of grounds and rates of success at p 335 above.
120 As was explained at the end of Chapter 9, the decision in *Majid v Gaffney* [2019] UT 59 confirms that it is not possible to serve the notice to leave during the three-month period.
121 EV/19/3012, 29/11/19.

facts are not disputed, and application can be determined at the CMD without any further delay, that is the most efficient resolution.

3. Let us say instead that T made a payment of £490 on 29 August, leaving arrears of £10, and then makes the payments due on 1 September and 1 October, still leaving arrears of £10. She makes payment of the rent for 1 November on the morning of 3 November, and then attends the CMD in the afternoon. In this case, the tribunal must grant the application under the mandatory ground, because T has been in arrears continuously since the beginning of April and, as at the beginning of the day on which the tribunal first considers the application for an eviction order on its merits (i.e. 3 November), those arrears stood at £510, which is more than one month's rent.

Withholding rent, abatement of rent, damages

This issue has already been considered, in the context of Scottish secure tenancies (in Chapter 5), and assured tenancies (in Chapter 8). Where the remedy of retaining rent is asserted by a tenant under a PRT, the following particular issues arise.

Where the parties use the model PRT agreement, that will set out the obligations of the landlord to comply with the repairing standard under sections 13 and 14 of the Housing (Scotland) Act 2006, and the tenant's remedies in respect of a failure to do so.

As indicated in Chapter 8, that does not displace the landlord's common law repairing obligations, or the right of the tenant to exercise the common law remedy of retention of rent.[122] However, as has been described in previous chapters, that remedy is subject to the equitable jurisdiction of the tribunal.

In one case in which it was accepted by the landlord that the property was in disrepair, the tribunal was prepared to continue the CMD to allow repairs to be carried out, and for the withheld rent then to be paid.[123] In another, the tribunal was not satisfied that the tenant had ever notified the landlord that he was withholding rent in respect of outstanding repairs, or that he was actually retaining the rent that he had not paid.[124]

"wholly or partly a consequence of a delay or failure in the payment of a relevant benefit"

Subparagraphs (2)(b) and (4) aim to give protection to the tenant by enjoining the tribunal to take into account delay or failure in the payment of the benefits specified in subparagraph (5), when considering whether to grant an order under the mandatory or discretionary ground.[125] However, it is suggested that

122 Unless the landlord has added a clause to the agreement by which the parties contract out of the common law.

123 *Price v Robertson* EV/18/1863, 28/9/18; however, the respondent nevertheless decided to consent to the eviction order being granted.

124 *McGill v Brebner* EV/18/3471, 10/6/19. This was a decision at a hearing.

125 These provisions are similar to subss (3A), (4A) and (8) of s 18 of the 1988 Act, which were introduced by s 12 of the Homelessness etc. (Scotland) Act 2003. See Chapter 7, p 280.

the words "over that period" in subparagraphs (2)(b) and (4), without reference to the amount of the arrears, has the effect of limiting that protection.[126]

Example:

4. L rents a flat to T. It is a PRT under the 2016 Act. The rent is £500 per month, payable in advance, on the 1st of the month. T fails to make payment on 1 April, but makes the payments of £500 due in May, June, July and August. Having served a notice to leave, L makes an application to the tribunal on 16 August. T makes a payment of £750 on 1 September, paying the rent and reducing the arrears to £250. However, she loses her job during that month, and makes an application for universal credit. She is unable to make any payment on 1 October and 1 November. As at the CMD on 16 November, universal credit has not been paid, and the arrears stand at £1,250. In that case, subparagraph 12(2)(b) does not assist T. It is not the case that her "being in arrears of rent *over that period* [i.e. the three-month period up to 16 November] is . . . wholly or partly a consequence of a delay or failure in the payment of a relevant benefit", because she had arrears, due to the missed payment in April, that pre-existed the benefit claim. The delay in payment of the benefit has increased the amount of the arrears, but it has made no difference to the fact that T has been in arrears since April. Therefore, the application would have to be granted under ground 12(2), if the landlord insisted upon it.

   If the tribunal is satisfied that subparagraph 12(2)(b) *does* apply, even if the tenant being in arrears "over that period" is only "partly" due to the delay or failure in the payment of the benefit, that precludes the application being granted on the mandatory ground. However, the landlord could still ask for the application to be granted on the discretionary ground, with the tribunal taking into account the delay or failure in the payment of the benefit in deciding whether it was reasonable to grant the eviction order.

Grounds 13–15: Criminal and antisocial behaviour

In the 1988 Act, there is a single discretionary ground that is applicable to criminal or antisocial behaviour on the part of "the tenant, a person residing or lodging in the house with the tenant or a person visiting the house".[127] The approach of the 2016 Act is somewhat more involved. There are three separate grounds. Grounds 13 and 14 apply respectively to criminal and antisocial behaviour on the part of the tenant, whereas ground 15 applies to criminal or antisocial behaviour on the part of someone with whom the tenant "associates in the let property".

At the time of writing, these grounds have been relied upon in only a handful of the cases on which the FTT has issued decisions.[128] In most of those cases,

126 This is another example of the period of arrears having primacy, rather than the amount.

127 Ground 15. See Chapter 8.

128 In *Dalglen 1810 Ltd v Watson* EV/19/2777, 18/11/19 and *Executors of Athwal v McClimonds* EV/19/1656, 7/1/20, an order was granted on ground 14 alone. Neither of those applications was opposed. In *Northwood (Glasgow) LTS v Dhami* EV/18/2889, 12/2/19, the tribunal granted an eviction order under grounds 11 and 14 at a CMD, despite the respondent

the ground was combined with ground 12. Consequently, the tribunal has, in several decisions, considered it unnecessary to decide whether the ground has been established, because it has been possible to grant an eviction order under ground 12 at the CMD.[129]

All these grounds end with a provision to the effect that, where there are joint tenants, the ground can be established in relation to the conduct of any one of them.

Ground 13

"**13 Criminal behaviour**

(1) It is an eviction ground that the tenant has a relevant conviction.

(2) The First-tier Tribunal must find that the ground named by sub-paragraph (1) applies if—

(a) after the tenancy is granted, the tenant receives a relevant conviction, and

(b) either—

(i) the application for an eviction order that is before the Tribunal was made within 12 months of the tenant's conviction, or

(ii) the Tribunal is satisfied that the landlord has a reasonable excuse for not making the application within that period.

(3) In sub-paragraph (2), 'a relevant conviction' means a conviction for an offence—

(a) which was committed by using, or allowing the use of, the let property for an immoral or illegal purpose, or

(b) which—

(i) was committed within or in the locality of the let property, and

(ii) is punishable by imprisonment.

(4) In a case where two or more persons jointly are the tenant under a tenancy, the reference in sub-paragraph (2) to the tenant is to any one of those persons."

This ground bears a strong similarity to ground 2 in schedule 2 to the 2001 Act, which, following amendments made by the 2014 Act, is now also mandatory, if proceedings are raised within twelve months of the criminal conviction.[130]

As with that ground, it may be easier to show that the offence is "punishable by imprisonment" than that it entailed "the use of the let property for an immoral or illegal purpose".[131]

However, there are several differences, as between the 2001 and 2016 Act grounds, in the application of the twelve-month time limit. Under the earlier Act, it is the notice of proceedings that must be served within twelve months of the conviction, failing which the landlord must use the old procedure, under which ground 2 is discretionary.[132] By contrast, ground 13 of the 2016 Act

appearing and opposing the application. In several other cases, the order was granted on ground 14, in combination with ground 12. In *Donald v Isles* EV/19/3439, 17/1/20, the order was sought on grounds 14 and 15, but was granted on ground 15 only: the respondent accepted that there had been antisocial behaviour on the part of her ex-partner, and she did not oppose the application. The author is aware of only one decided case in which the landlord relied on ground 13, but the application was not granted on that ground.

129 Whereas it might require a hearing in order properly to consider whether grounds 13, 14 or 15 were established.

130 See the discussion of the "streamlined" procedure for ground 2 cases in Chapter 5. The 2001 Act ground becomes discretionary if the landlord fails to serve the notice of proceedings within twelve months of the conviction.

131 See Chapter 5, p 137 as to that point, and the meaning of "locality".

132 See Chapter 5, pp 135 and 164.

applies the time limit to the period between conviction and application to the tribunal. If the landlord fails to make the application in time, the tribunal must be satisfied that he has a reasonable excuse. That might be the case where, for example, the landlord was ignorant of the conviction until some time after it took place.

If the tribunal is not so satisfied, the ground does not apply.[133] Notably, the 2001 Act ground also allows for the possibility that the conviction might be appealed, in which case the twelve months run from the date on which the appeal is dismissed or abandoned. There is no similar dispensation in ground 13.

Ground 14

"14 **Anti-social behaviour**

(1) It is an eviction ground that the tenant has engaged in relevant anti-social behaviour.

(2) The First-tier Tribunal may find that the ground named by sub-paragraph (1) applies if—

(a) the tenant has behaved in an anti-social manner in relation to another person,

(b) the anti-social behaviour is relevant anti-social behaviour, and

(c) either—

(i) the application for an eviction order that is before the Tribunal was made within 12 months of the anti-social behaviour occurring, or

(ii) the Tribunal is satisfied that the landlord has a reasonable excuse for not making the application within that period.

(3) For the purposes of this paragraph, a person is to be regarded as behaving in an anti-social manner in relation to another person by—

(a) doing something which causes or is likely to cause the other person alarm, distress, nuisance or annoyance,

(b) pursuing in relation to the other person a course of conduct which—

(i) causes or is likely to cause the other person alarm, distress, nuisance or annoyance, or

(ii) amounts to harassment of the other person.

(4) In sub-paragraph (3)—

'conduct' includes speech,

'course of conduct' means conduct on two or more occasions,

'harassment' is to be construed in accordance with section 8 of the Protection from Harassment Act 1997.[134]

(5) Anti-social behaviour is relevant anti-social behaviour for the purpose of sub-paragraph (2)(b) if the Tribunal is satisfied that it is reasonable to issue an eviction order as a consequence of it, given the nature of the anti-social behaviour and—

(a) who it was in relation to, or

(b) where it occurred.

(6) In a case where two or more persons jointly are the tenant under a tenancy, the reference in sub-paragraph (2) to the tenant is to any one of those persons."

133 In contrast to ground 8, under which failure to make the application within twelve months results in the ground being discretionary.

134 Harassment of a person" is not defined by s 8 of the 1997 Act; s 8(3) simply states that it "includes causing the person alarm or distress".

Again, this ground may usefully be compared with the equivalent ground in schedule 2 to the 2001 Act.[135] For reasons that are not clear, ground 14 is more complex, and presents some difficulty in interpretation. Both grounds are discretionary, and the definitions of "conduct", "course of conduct" and "harassment" are the same as those used in the 2001 Act ground. There is also a similar distinction (in paragraph (3)(a) and (b)) between "doing something" and "pursuing . . . a course of conduct".[136]

However, in contrast to the 2001 Act ground, paragraph (2)(c) applies a twelve-month time limit, which is the same as that applied in relation to ground 13. It is not clear why that was thought to be appropriate, given that a criminal conviction is a single event, whereas antisocial behaviour (which may include a course of conduct), can occur over a period of time.

Ground 14 also adopts a curiously atomised approach to the application of the "reasonableness" test. Let us say that L lets a flat to T, which is in a tenement of eight flats. Over a period of time, T does things that cause alarm, distress, nuisance or annoyance to each of her neighbours, on one occasion each. All the neighbours complain to L, who makes an application to the FTT under ground 14. Given the terms of paragraphs (2)(b) and (5), it would seem that, rather than looking at the incidents cumulatively, and then deciding whether it would be reasonable to grant an eviction order, the tribunal has to consider each of the incidents in isolation, and decide whether it would be reasonable to issue an eviction order in respect of each of them.[137]

Ground 15

"**15 Association with person who has relevant conviction or engaged in relevant anti-social behaviour**

(1) It is an eviction ground that the tenant associates in the let property with a person who has a relevant conviction or has engaged in relevant anti-social behaviour.

(2) The First-tier Tribunal may find that the ground named by sub-paragraph (1) applies if—
- (a) a person who falls within sub-paragraph (4)—
  - (i) has received a relevant conviction as defined by paragraph 13(3), or
  - (ii) has engaged in relevant anti-social behaviour,
- (b) the Tribunal is satisfied that it is reasonable to issue an eviction order on account of that fact, and
- (c) either—
  - (i) the application for an eviction order that is before the Tribunal was made within 12 months of the conviction or (as the case may be) the occurrence of the anti-social behaviour, or
  - (ii) the Tribunal is satisfied that the landlord has a reasonable excuse for not making the application within that period.

(3) In sub-paragraph (2)(a)(ii), 'relevant anti-social behaviour' means behaviour which, if engaged in by the tenant, would entitle the Tribunal to issue an

135 Ground 7. See Chapter 5, p 142.

136 Though, as with the 2001 Act, one might think that any conduct that establishes (b) would also establish (a).

137 However, this problem is unlikely to arise in practice. Of course, it would be possible to look at incidents cumulatively if they are in relation to the same person.

eviction order on the basis that the tenant has engaged in relevant anti-social behaviour.

(4) A person falls within this sub-paragraph if the person—
   (a) resides or lodges in the let property,
   (b) has sub-let the let property (or part of it) from the tenant, or
   (c) has been admitted to the let property by the tenant on more than one occasion.

(5) In a case where two or more persons jointly are the tenant under a tenancy, the references in sub-paragraphs (3) and (4) to the tenant are to any one of those persons."

This is a discretionary ground, which is subject to the same twelve-month time limit as grounds 13 and 14.

Under the 2001 Act, the criminal conviction and antisocial grounds apply not only in respect of the tenant, but also to conduct by "a person residing or lodging in the house with, or subtenant of, the tenant, or a person visiting the house".[138] Consequently, antisocial behaviour by the tenant, and by other members of the household, can be considered together in deciding whether it is reasonable to grant an order.

Under the 2016 Act, the criminal or antisocial conduct of an associated person gives rise to a separate ground that applies where that person is covered by subparagraph (a), (b) or (c) of paragraph (4) of ground 15. Where that person has a criminal conviction to which ground 13(3) applies, or has engaged in relevant antisocial behaviour, the tribunal must then decide whether it is reasonable to grant an eviction order. "Relevant anti-social behaviour" means behaviour that, if engaged in by the tenant, would entitle the Tribunal to issue an eviction order under ground 14.

PART 4: LEGAL IMPEDIMENT TO LET CONTINUING

Grounds 16–18 are new grounds, for which there was no equivalent in the 1988 Act. They are all discretionary, and may be said to arise from a decision by the local authority, in whose area the tenancy property is situated, which adversely affects the ability of the landlord to continue letting the property. At the time of writing, none of these grounds has featured in any of the rule 109 decisions published on the Housing and Property Chamber's website. It therefore seems reasonable to suggest that applications on grounds 16–18 will be rare.

Ground 16

"**16 Landlord has ceased to be registered**

(1) It is an eviction ground that the landlord is not registered by the relevant local authority under the Antisocial Behaviour etc. (Scotland) Act 2004 ('the 2004 Act').

(2) The First-tier Tribunal may find that the ground named by sub-paragraph (1) applies if—

138 In ground 15 under the 1988 Act, the equivalent wording is: "a person residing or lodging in the house with the tenant or a person visiting the house".

(a) the landlord is not entered in the register prepared and maintained for the purposes of Part 8 of the 2004 Act by the local authority within whose area the let property is situated because either—
  (i) the local authority has refused to enter the landlord in the register, or
  (ii) the local authority has removed the landlord from the register in accordance with section 88(8) or 89 of the 2004 Act,
(b) by continuing to let the property to the tenant the landlord—
  (i) is committing an offence under subsection (1) of section 93 of the 2004 Act, or
  (ii) would be doing so but for subsection (6) of that section, and
(c) the Tribunal is satisfied that it is reasonable to issue an eviction order on account of those facts."

Landlord registration

The statutory scheme for registration of private landlords is found in part 8 of the Antisocial Behaviour etc. (Scotland) Act 2004.[139] In accordance with sections 82–89, each local authority maintains a register of private landlords, and receives and determines applications for registration.[140] The legislation applies a "fit and proper person" test.[141] The local authority may, in certain circumstances, remove a person from the register.[142] Where a local authority refuses to enter a person in the register, or removes a person from the register, there is a right of appeal to the FTT, under section 92.

Under section 93, where a "relevant person" owns a house within the area of a local authority, which is subject to (i) a lease; or (ii) an occupancy arrangement, by virtue of which an "unconnected person" may use the house as a dwelling, and the relevant person is not registered by that authority, the relevant person shall be guilty of an offence,[143] and the local authority may serve a notice under section 94. Following service of that notice, no rent or other consideration is payable under any lease or occupancy arrangement, from the date on which the notice takes effect (which must not be earlier than the day after the day on which it is served): section 94(3).[144]

Significantly, section 94(8) provides that, apart from subsection (3), "nothing in [part 8 of the 2004 Act] affects the validity of any lease or occupancy arrangement under which an unconnected person has the use as a dwelling of a house during the relevant period." This means that the initiation of criminal proceedings under section 93, or the service of notice under section 94, does

139 Which was significantly amended by pt 1 of the Private Rented Housing (Scotland) Act 2011. The statutory provisions in respect of the registration of private landlords are described in detail in Robson and Combe, *Residential Tenancies* (4th edn) ch 5.

140 In February 2017, the Scottish Landlord Register was launched by the Registers of Scotland, offering a central online access point to each of the thirty-two local authorities' registers.

141 Section 84(3).

142 Under ss 88(8) or 89(1), (3A) or (4).

143 Subject to the possible defences under that section. Under s 93(2), an offence is also committed where a relevant person communicates with another person with a view to entering into a lease or an occupancy arrangement. To date, there have been no reported decisions in relation to prosecutions under this section, though it is understood that prosecutions have taken place. Where a person is convicted under s 93, the court may disqualify him from being registered as a landlord by any local authority for a period of up to five years (s 93A).

144 Provision is made, in s 94(6), for service of the notice in circumstances where the identity, or current address, of the relevant person is unknown to the local authority.

not prejudice the right of a person to remain in occupation under the relevant lease or occupancy agreement, or under the 1988 Act or the 2016 Act, should either of those Acts apply.[145] Furthermore, the landlord's failure to apply for registration does not have any bearing on his right to initiate or pursue eviction proceedings,[146] though where a notice is served under section 94 it will have the effect of suspending rental liability.

All the rules that apply to applications to initiate eviction proceedings in the FTT[147] require that the application states the landlord's registration number. Under section 72 of the 2016 Act, the FTT must notify the relevant local authority if, in the course of proceedings before it, it learns or is given cause to suspect that the landlord under a tenancy is not registered.

Conditions for eviction order under ground 16

Subparagraph (2) sets out three conditions for the granting of an eviction order on ground 16. The first is that the local authority must have either refused to enter the landlord on the register or removed him from the register. Accordingly, ground 16 is not available if the landlord has never applied to be registered, or his application has not been determined.[148]

The second condition is that, by continuing to let the property to the tenant, the landlord is committing an offence under section 93(1) of the 2004 Act – or would be, but for section 93(6).[149] Given the terms of section 93, this would appear to follow as a necessary consequence from the fact that a PRT is in existence, but the landlord is not registered.

Thirdly, the tribunal must be satisfied that it would be reasonable to make an eviction order "on account of *these facts*". This indicates that the tribunal must weigh, on the one side, the fact that the landlord's application has been refused, and that he is committing an offence under section 93,[150] against any factors argued by the tenant, as tending to show that it would not be reasonable to grant the order. There is no mention in ground 16 of the possibility of the local authority having issued a notice under section 94, suspending the rental liability, and no indication of whether that would have a bearing on the tribunal's decision.

145 See also *B v D* [2017] SAC (Civ) 32, 2018 SLT (Sh Ct) 70, a decision of Sheriff Principal Murray that confirms that, where the landlord is not registered, that does not have the effect that the parties' contract is illegal. Nor does it have the effect that the tenant is absolved of the liability to pay rent (absent a notice under s 94).

146 *B v D*. Though, as is the case with a failure to comply with the Tenancy Deposit Schemes (Scotland) Regulations 2011 (SSI 2011/176), in deciding whether it was reasonable to grant an order under any of the discretionary grounds in the 1988 or 2016 Acts, the tribunal might be persuaded to take into account a failure to register.

147 Ruless 65 and 66 for the 1988 Act; r 109 for the 2016 Act.

148 Both the title and subparagraph (1) of the ground are inexact. Ground 16 is not restricted to cases in which the landlord has "ceased to be registered": it applies if the landlord has never been registered, because his application has been refused. Also, the ground does not apply to all cases in which "the landlord is not registered", as is suggested by subpara (1), but only in the case of refusal of the application or removal from the register, as is indicated by subpara (2)(a). It is the conditions of subpara (2), rather than the title of subpara (1), that are determinative. See the discussion of s 51(2), at the beginning of this chapter.

149 Section 93(6): "It shall be a defence for a person charged with an offence under subsection (1) or (2) to show that there was a reasonable excuse for acting in the way charged."

150 Subject to s 93(6).

Ground 17

"17 HMO licence has been revoked

(1) It is an eviction ground that the let property or associated living accommodation is in multiple occupation and not licensed under Part 5 of the Housing (Scotland) Act 2006 ('the 2006 Act').

(2) The First-tier Tribunal may find that the ground named by sub-paragraph (1) applies if—

(a) under section 139(1) or 157(2) of the 2006 Act, the HMO licence for the let property has been revoked, and

(b) the Tribunal is satisfied that it is reasonable to issue an eviction order on account of that fact."

Part 5 of the 2006 Act contains the statutory scheme in respect of "houses in multiple occupation" ("HMOs").[151] Under the old system, the licensing of HMOs was subject to the provisions covering licensing in general, in the Civic Government (Scotland) Act 1982. The effect of part V of the 2006 Act is to create a special statutory scheme for the licensing of HMOs, which it is beyond the scope of this work to examine.[152]

Suffice it to say that, given the terms of subparagraph (2)(a), ground 17 applies only where an HMO licence has been revoked.[153] It does not appear to apply where the let property or associated living accommodation is in multiple occupation, and not licensed because no application has been made for a licence.[154] Again, ground 17 is discretionary; therefore the legislation envisages that the tribunal might decide that, notwithstanding the revocation of the HMO licence, an eviction order should not be granted, with the result that the PRT would continue.

"18 Overcrowding statutory notice

(1) It is an eviction ground that an overcrowding statutory notice has been served on the landlord.

(2) The First-tier Tribunal may find that the ground named by sub-paragraph (1) applies if—

(a) an overcrowding statutory notice in respect of the let property has been served on the landlord under section 17(3) of the Private Rented Housing (Scotland) Act 2011, and

(b) the Tribunal is satisfied that it is reasonable to issue an eviction order on account of that fact."

Part 3 of the 2011 Act (sections 17–31) is entitled "Overcrowding Statutory Notices". Under section 17(1), a local authority may require the landlord of a house to take steps to ensure that it is not overcrowded, by serving an overcrowding statutory notice under section 17(3). This is done following consideration of the matters specified in section 18. At the time of writing, however, part 3 of the Act is not yet in force.

151 Although this did not come into force until 31 August 2011.

152 The statutory scheme, and the some of the history of licensing of HMOs, is described in Robson and Combe (n 139) ch 6.

153 Under s 139(1) of the 2006 Act. Section 157(2) applies where a court convicts a person of an offence relating to an HMO, under s 154, in which case it may, as well as imposing a penalty under s 156, revoke the HMO licence.

154 As with ground 16, it is subpara (2)(a) that sets the scope of the ground, rather than subpara (1). See n 148, and the discussion of s 51 at p 334.

Overcrowding is also an eviction ground under the 2001 Act.[155] The same statutory definition of overcrowding, under section 135 of the 1987 Act, is used for both grounds.[156]

Again, ground 17 is discretionary, therefore the legislation envisages that the tribunal might decide that, notwithstanding the service of an overcrowding statutory notice, an eviction order should not be granted, with the result that the PRT would continue.

155 Paragraph 9 of sch 2 to the 2001 Act.

156 Under s 31(2) of the 2011 Act, references to a house being overcrowded are to be construed according to the definition of overcrowding in s 135 of the 1987 Act. Section 135 is summarised at Chapter 5, p 168.

Chapter 11

Public Law, Human Rights and Equality Act Defences

INTRODUCTION

Three examples

This chapter concerns a special type of defence that may be pled in eviction proceedings.[1] Broadly speaking, the defender[2] may argue that, in terminating his tenancy (or right of occupation), or raising eviction proceedings, or pursuing those proceedings, the pursuer is acting unlawfully. Alternatively, he may argue that it would be an unlawful violation of his rights for the court to grant an eviction order. Here, the defender relies not on his contractual rights, or the common law and statutory rules that are applicable to his occupation. Instead, he deploys an argument such as those described in the following examples:

1. The tenant of a Scottish secure tenancy is convicted of an offence punishable by imprisonment, committed at the tenancy property. His landlord raises proceedings in terms of section 16(2)(aa) of the 2001 Act, using the new "streamlined eviction process" for ground 2 cases,[3] under which it is not necessary to show that it would be reasonable to grant the order. The requirements for granting decree under section 16(2)(aa) are met. However, the tenant lodges a defence arguing that, because the landlord failed, under section 14(2B) of the Act, to have regard to guidance issued by the Scottish Ministers, the decision to raise the proceedings was unlawful, and therefore the action ought to be dismissed.
2. A, the tenant of a Scottish secure tenancy, dies. Prior to his death, his partner B and her two children also lived at the tenancy. A and B were in a relationship for many years. However, they only began living together when B gave up her own tenancy, eleven months before A died. Under the rules applicable to succession to Scottish secure tenancies, B is not entitled to succeed.[4] She asks the landlord to allow her to become the tenant, but it refuses. The landlord raises proceedings, on the basis that

1 This type of defence is now well established in English law, and most of the authorities cited in this chapter are from that jurisdiction. For readers interested in this area, there is a more comprehensive discussion of public law, human rights and Equality Act defences in chs 25–27 of Luba and others, *Defending Possession Proceedings* (8th edn), which work is highly recommended. The author has examined the implications, for eviction proceedings, of the Equality Act 2010, in *Housing and Equality Law in Scotland* (Shelter 2018) ch 3.

2 Or respondent, in proceedings before the First-tier Tribunal.

3 Discussed in Chapter 6.

4 Because she has not occupied the property for long enough. See Chapter 12.

B has no right or title to occupy the property. B defends the proceedings, arguing that the property is her home, and the home of her children, and that eviction would be unnecessary and disproportionate, and therefore contrary to article 8 of the European Convention on Human Rights ("ECHR").

3. The tenant of a private residential tenancy ("PRT") suffers from severe depression. Following a bereavement, her condition deteriorates. She loses her employment, and fails to claim universal credit. She falls into arrears of rent. The landlord demands payment. The tenant explains her condition to him, but still fails to make a claim for universal credit. The landlord makes an application to the First-tier Tribunal ("FTT") for an eviction order under ground 12 of schedule 3 to the 2016 Act. Prior to the case management discussion ("CMD"), the tenant provides a report from a psychiatrist explaining her condition and opining that the failure to pay rent or claim benefits has been caused by that condition. At the CMD, the landlord argues that the tribunal must grant an order for eviction, under the mandatory terms of ground 12(2). The tenant provides evidence of a recent claim for universal credit, which has not yet been determined. She argues that she is a disabled person, for the purposes of section 6 of the Equality Act 2010, and that the landlord's decision to seek her eviction amounts to unlawful discrimination under sections 15 and 35 of the Equality Act 2010.

These examples describe, respectively, public law, human rights and Equality Act defences. These are distinct,[5] but have a common theme. In each, the defender/respondent had no basis on which to defend the proceedings raised by the pursuer/applicant by reference to the contractual rights, common law or statutory rules applicable to his/her occupation. In cases 1 and 3, occupation was under a tenancy covered by legislation but, in terms of the relevant statute, eviction of the tenant was mandatory. In case 2, B's occupation was not under a tenancy protected by legislation, and there was no private law right (whether in terms of a contract or otherwise) to remain in occupation. Nevertheless, it is possible, in each case, to plead a defence to the effect that the conduct of the pursuer/applicant is, in some way, unlawful, or that eviction itself would be unlawful, and therefore, the court or tribunal should not grant an eviction order.

How can eviction proceedings be defended on this basis?

Prior to the introduction of security of tenure by the Tenants' Rights, Etc. (Scotland) Act 1980, a local authority tenant was liable to be evicted following termination of her tenancy by a valid notice to quit.[6] In that case, the tenant would have no defence to eviction proceedings. However, the decision of the

5 And accordingly, could be pled as alternative positions, in a single case. See: *R (JL) v Secretary of State for Defence* [2013] EWCA Civ 449, [2013] HLR 27, [58]-[64] (Arden LJ).

6 See: *City of Aberdeen District Council v Christie* 1983 SLT (Sh Ct) 57, following the decision of the House of Lords in *Shelley v London CC* [1949] AC 56, which determined that local authority tenants did not enjoy the protection of the Rent Acts. In *Shelley,* Lord Porter said (at 66) that local authorities could "pick and choose their tenants at will".

Court of Appeal in *Cannock Chase DC v Kelly*[7] had left open the possibility that a tenant might challenge a notice to quit, on the basis of alleged bad faith, or abuse or excessive use of statutory powers by a local authority, as a defence to eviction proceedings in the county court. That is to say: the tenant might defend herself by reference to "public law" grounds that would normally be regarded as appropriate to judicial review proceedings,[8] but without raising such proceedings.

The scope of this type of argument was further explored in the important decision of the House of Lords in *Wandsworth London Borough Council v Winder*.[9] The defendant Mr Winder was a secure tenant under the English housing legislation. In 1981 and 1982, the council resolved to increase rents, and served him with two notices to that effect. Mr Winder considered the increases to be excessive. He refused to pay the increase, but continued to pay his original rent. In due course, the council took proceedings against him, claiming for arrears of rent, and also seeking recovery of possession on the statutory ground that rent lawfully due had not been paid. Mr Winder defended the action on the basis that the council's decisions to make the increases, and the increases themselves, were *ultra vires* and void as being unreasonable. He counterclaimed for a declaration to that effect. The council argued that the defence and counterclaim should be struck out, as being an abuse of process: the only procedure by which the decision to increase rent could be challenged was judicial review.[10]

Mr Winder had been unable to pursue judicial review proceedings because his application was made too late. He accepted that judicial review would have been an appropriate procedure for the purpose, but he maintained that it was not the only procedure open to him, and that he was entitled to wait until he was sued by the council and then to defend the proceedings.[11] Ultimately his argument succeeded. The House of Lords held that it was a paramount principle that the private citizen's recourse to the courts for the determination of his rights was not to be excluded except by clear words and that there was nothing in the language of relevant legislation, or the rules of court, that could be taken as abolishing a citizen's right to challenge the decision of a local authority in the course of defending an action of the present nature. In this case, the defendant did not select the procedure to be adopted and was merely seeking to defend the proceedings brought against him on the ground that he was not liable for the whole sum claimed. Moreover, he put forward his defence as a

7 [1978] 1 WLR 1.

8 However, Mrs Kelly lost, because the court decided that, in the defence pled, she had not said enough to set out the basis for such a challenge.

9 [1985] AC 461.

10 This argument relied upon the decisions of the House of Lords in *O'Reilly v Mackman* [1983] 2 AC 237 and *Cocks v Thanet District Council* [1983] 2 AC 286. In the first of those cases, the court had decided that as all remedies for infringements of rights protected by public law could now be obtained upon an application for judicial review, it would, as a general rule, be contrary to public policy, and as such an abuse of the process of the court, to permit a person seeking to establish that a decision of a public authority infringed rights, to which he was entitled to protection under public law, to proceed by way of an ordinary action. To do so would, in effect, allow that person to evade the provisions of judicial review procedure which were for the protection of public authorities, such as the three-month time limit for applications, and the requirement for the applicant to obtain leave from the court.

11 He had been refused leave to apply for a judicial review out of time.

matter of right, whereas in an application for judicial review, success would require an exercise of the court's discretion in his favour.

Later in this chapter, there is a discussion of the decisions of the Supreme Court in *Manchester City Council v Pinnock* and *Hounslow LBC v Powell*.[12] At this point, however, it is appropriate to mention that the decision in *Winder* is of importance to those cases. This is made particularly clear by paragraph 88 of the judgment in *Pinnock*, where the court said:

> "88 For these reasons we are satisfied that we should apply the approach of the House of Lords in *Wandsworth London Borough Council v Winder* . . . This permits us to confirm our earlier conclusion that [the relevant legislation] should be read as allowing the county court to exercise the powers which are necessary to consider and, where appropriate, to give effect to, any article 8 defence which the defendant raises in possession proceedings brought in that court."[13]

In other words, to allow an article 8 defence to be pled in eviction proceedings was an extension of the principles already articulated in *Winder*. In the pre-*Pinnock* authorities in which the House of Lords had considered a defence to eviction proceedings based on article 8, it had already been said that the ability of a defendant to challenge the decision of a public authority to recover possession, as in *Winder*, went some way to safeguarding his article 8 right to be protected from eviction proceedings that were arbitrary or unjustified.[14] However, the extent to which the requirements of article 8 could be met by judicial review proceedings, or arguments made in county court proceedings on judicial review grounds (as in *Winder*), was in doubt.[15] Those doubts were removed by the decision in *Pinnock*. For present purposes, it may be noted that the Supreme Court had this to say about the role of judicial review principles in eviction proceedings in the county court:[16]

> "72 Rightly, in our view, it is common ground that a court has jurisdiction, under normal judicial review principles, to satisfy itself that the local authority and panel have indeed acted reasonably and have investigated the relevant facts fairly, when deciding to bring possession proceedings.[17] From this it must

12 Respectively [2011] 2 AC 104 and [2011] 2 AC 186. These were cases in which the court set out the basis on which it is possible to rely on a defence to eviction proceedings based on art 8 of the ECHR.

13 See also paras 27, 81 and 86 of the judgment.

14 See, in particular: *Kay v Lambeth London Borough Council* [2006] 2 AC 465, para 110, quoted below.

15 See the differing views expressed by the judges in *Doherty v Birmingham City Council* [2009] 1 AC 367. The history of the pre-*Pinnock* jurisprudence is summarised in paras 25–29 of the judgment in *Pinnock*. In his estimable book *The Rule of Law* (43–44) Tom Bingham used the pre-*Pinnock* cases as an example of judicial decisions that may be "inaccessible" due to "length, prolixity and elaboration".

16 The passage quoted from paras 72 and 73 appears in a section that begins with a reference (in para 68) to "the county court judge who is asked to make an order for possession". It is clear that in the succeeding paragraphs, "court" refers to the county court hearing eviction proceedings.

17 At [81], the court also said: "where a tenant contends that the decision of a local authority landlord to issue, or indeed to continue, possession proceedings can in some way be impugned, the tenant should be entitled to raise that contention in the possession proceedings themselves, even if they are in the county court".

> follow that any decision by the local authority to continue possession proceedings is similarly susceptible to judicial review . . .
>
> 73 In our judgment, once it is accepted that it is open to a demoted tenant to seek judicial review of a landlord's decision to bring and continue possession proceedings, then it inevitably follows that, as a generality, it is open to a tenant to challenge that decision on the ground that it would be disproportionate and therefore contrary to article 8 . . . ."[18]

Proceedings in Scotland

Clyde and Edwards[19] point out that a question as to whether a decision of a public authority is *ultra vires* may arise in both civil and criminal proceedings, outwith judicial review, and it is competent for a sheriff to rule on the *ultra vires* acts of a public authority in order to dispose of an action before the court. However, in doing so, the sheriff is not exercising a power of review, and in particular, he has no power to quash an act or decision that he finds to be *ultra vires*. After discussing the English authorities, including *Winder*, the authors say:

> "So, too, in Scotland, the exclusivity of the judicial review procedure does not preclude judicial review issues arising outside judicial review. Where the substance of the action is a private right or the issue is raised as a properly pleaded defence, the exclusivity of judicial review is not a ground for insisting that questions as to the legality of a decision maker's decision only be raised in judicial review."

That statement is consistent with the subsequent decision of Lord Clarke in *Vaughan Engineering Ltd v Hinkins & Frewin Ltd*, in which he said:

> "Following the approach of the House of Lords in the case of *Wandsworth London Borough Council v Winder* . . . it does not seem to me that the wording of rule 58.3(1) [of the Rules of the Court of Session] can, or should, be read to have the effect of curtailing, by imposing additional procedural hurdles, well established rights of defenders to defend actions brought against them which rely on decisions or acts, by challenging the validity of the decision or act in question, without the need to resort to having the decision or act reduced by way of judicial review."[20]

Lord Clarke then made reference to *Vaughan Engineering* in delivering the opinion of the Extra Division in *South Lanarkshire Council v McKenna*,[21] which confirmed that the principles articulated in *Pinnock* were also applicable to eviction proceedings in Scotland:

> "In reaching our conclusion regarding the compatibility of the Scottish legislation with Art 8 of ECHR we have adopted the approach of the Supreme Court in Pinnock (para 78–80) by relying on the provisions of secs 6(1) and 7(1) of the Human Rights Act. Moreover . . . we are of the opinion that by virtue of secs 6 and 7(1) of the Human Rights Act any proportionality challenge may be taken by the

18 This is not to say, however, that the court's assessment of proportionality in an art 8 cases is akin to a judicial review. In such cases the court is not reviewing the legality of decision by a public authority; it is deciding whether an eviction order sought by that authority is proportionate: *Aster Communities v Akerman-Livingstone* [2015] AC 1399, para 38 (Baroness Hale). See the discussion of art 8 cases at p 386 below.

19 *Judicial Review* 327–332.

20 2003 SLT 428, at the end of para 33. Rule 58.3(1) requires that applications to the supervisory jurisdiction of the Court of Session shall be made by petition for judicial review.

21 2013 SC 212.

> occupier of the house in question, as a defence to the proceedings brought against him for possession, and need not be taken by way of petition for judicial review. Compare also *Vaughan Engineering Ltd v Hinkins and Frewin Ltd.*"

It is also notable that, in the early part of his speech in *Kay v Lambeth LBC*,[22] Lord Hope makes specific reference to the similarity between eviction actions in Scotland and England, which he clearly takes to proceed on substantially the same basis.[23] He gives no indication that the following conclusion[24] would not be applicable in Scotland:

> "if the defendant wishes to challenge the decision of a public authority to recover possession as an improper exercise of its powers at common law on the ground that it was a decision that no reasonable person would consider justifiable, he should be permitted to do this provided again that the point is seriously arguable: *Wandsworth London Borough Council v Winder* [1985] AC 461."

Turning back to Example 1 at the beginning of this chapter, at the same time as section 16(2)(aa) was inserted into section 16 of the 2001 Act by amendment, creating the "streamlined eviction process" for ground 2 cases,[25] the following subsection was also added:

> "(3A) Subsection (2) does not affect any other rights that the tenant may have by virtue of any other enactment or rule of law."

Section 16(2) is the provision that sets out the requirements to be met, before the court grants an order for recovery of possession. Thus, section 16(3A) explicitly recognises that, in defending eviction proceedings, the tenant may rely not only on an argument that the requirements of section 16(2) are not met, but on the contention that eviction would be unlawful under by virtue of some other enactment or rule of law. The Government's "Guidance on the Streamlined Eviction Process" states:

> "4.20 A tenant who disagrees with a decision taken by the landlord to raise court proceedings could seek judicial review of the landlord's decision to seek a court order, and/or defend the repossession action."[26]

Defences alleging unlawful discrimination

Before the enactment of the Equality Act 2010, the courts in England had already explored the relevance, to possession proceedings, of the contention that eviction of a defendant would amount to unlawful discrimination under the Disability Discrimination Act 1995.[27] In *North Devon Homes Ltd v*

22 [2006] 2 AC 465.
23 At paras 71, 73 and 74.
24 At para 110(b).
25 See Chapter 5, p 164.
26 "*Streamlined Eviction Process – Criminal Or Antisocial Behaviour Statutory Guidance For Social Landlords*". See also paras 2.7 and 6.5.
27 Prohibitions against discrimination in relation to evictions existed in the pre-2010 Act "legacy enactments": s 21(2)(b) of the Race Relations Act 1976; and s 30(2)(b) of the Sex Discrimination Act 1975; s 22(3)(c) of the Disability Discrimination Act 1995. However, *Brazier* appears to have been the first reported case in which reliance was place on one of these provisions, in the context of eviction proceedings.

Brazier[28] the court held that a statutory prohibition of discriminatory evictions could be relied upon as part of a defence in eviction proceedings. That was subsequently confirmed by the Court of Appeal in *Manchester City Council v Romano; Manchester City Council v Samari*.[29] However, in all three of these cases, the tenants had statutory security of tenure,[30] and therefore the unlawfulness of the proceedings under the 1995 Act was considered as an aspect of whether it would be "reasonable" to grant the order.[31] In *Romano/Samari*, the court suggested that it would be preferable, in a case involving a secure or an assured tenancy, for the tenant to assert unlawful discrimination as part of his case that it would be unreasonable for the court to make a possession order, rather than complicating the proceedings by adding a counterclaim seeking a declaration that the landlord's conduct amounts to unlawful discrimination"[32]

That left open the question of whether an allegation of unlawful discrimination could be relied upon in eviction proceedings, where there was no security of tenure, and no other defence available to the occupier. That was answered in the affirmative, by the House of Lords in *Malcolm v Lewisham LBC*,[33] in which Lord Neuberger said:[34]

> "160 . . . If the service of the notice to quit in the present case was unlawful under section 22(3)(c) [of the 1995 Act], then the court could not give effect to it. If, by seeking an order for possession, a landlord is acting in a way the legislature has held to be unlawful, then, again, the court cannot make such an order. In either case, the court would be permitting, indeed facilitating, an unlawful act. The fact that the court will not always enjoin an unlawful act (e.g., a trespass) is nothing to the point: it is one thing to refuse to restrain a common law tort; it is another to make an order enforcing a statutorily unlawful claim . . . ."[35]

28 [2003] EWHC 574(QB), [2003] HLR 59.

29 [2004] EWCA Civ 834, [2005] 1 WLR 2775.

30 In *Brazier*, the defender was an assured tenant under the Housing Act 1988. In *Romano*, both tenants had secure tenancies under the Housing Act 1985.

31 See para [63] in *Romano*. All three of these cases involved tenants with mental health problems, whose eviction was sought on the ground of antisocial behaviour. Each argued that it would not be reasonable for the court to grant an order for her eviction, because it would be unlawful under ss 22 and 24 of DDA 1995. In *Brazier*, the court accepted that argument. In *Romano*, the Court of Appeal decided that action of the council in seeking an eviction order was justified under the 1995 Act; was therefore not unlawful; and was also reasonable, and so the council succeeded.

32 At para [64].

33 [2008] UKHL 43, [2008] 1 AC 1399.

34 See also para [19] (Lord Bingham) and paras [101] and [104] (Baroness Hale). Note that those two judges disagreed as to whether this type of defence would be made out very often.

35 Note, however, that Mr Malcolm was unsuccessful in his defence, as the court decided that the eviction was not "for a reason which related to his disability" for the purposes of the 1995 Act. This decision had important ramifications for disability discrimination law in general, and led to the enactment of s 15 of the Equality Act 2010. See the discussion at p 401 below.

In what types of cases would public law, human rights and Equality Act defences be pled?

Two types of case

In *Pinnock*,[36] the judgment of the Supreme Court includes the following passage:

> "55. The conclusion that, before making an order for possession, the court must be able to decide not only that the order would be justified under domestic law, but also that it would be proportionate under article 8(2) [of ECHR] to make the order, presents no difficulties of principle or practice in relation to secure tenancies. As explained above, no order for possession can be made against a secure tenant unless, inter alia, it is reasonable to make the order. Any factor which has to be taken into account, or any dispute of fact which has to be resolved, for the purpose of assessing proportionality under article 8(2), would have to be taken into account or resolved for the purpose of assessing reasonableness . . .
>
> 56. Moreover, reasonableness involves the trial judge 'taking into account all the relevant circumstances . . . in . . . a broad common-sense way": *Cumming v Danson* [1942] 2 All ER 653, 655, per Lord Greene MR. It therefore seems highly unlikely, as a practical matter, that it could be reasonable for a court to make an order for possession in circumstances in which it would be disproportionate to do so under article 8.
>
> 57. The implications of article 8 being potentially in play are much more significant where a local authority is seeking possession of a person's home in circumstances in which domestic law imposes no requirement of reasonableness and gives an unqualified right to an order for possession. In such a case the court's obligation under article 8(2), to consider the proportionality of making the order sought, does represent a potential new obstacle to the making of an order for possession . . . ."

Here, the court draws a distinction between two different types of eviction proceedings in relation to residential property.

In the *first* type of case, the defender is a tenant who has statutory security of tenure, and cannot be evicted unless: (a) a ground for eviction in the statute is established; and (b) the court considers it reasonable to grant an order for eviction, in all the circumstances of the case. In this type of action, the defender may argue that one or both of these requirements is or are not met. In Scotland, this would be the case for an assured tenant under the Housing (Scotland) Act 1988,[37] or a private residential tenant under the Private Housing (Tenancies) (Scotland) Act 2016, where the landlord relies on a "discretionary" ground for eviction.[38] It would also be the case for a Scottish secure tenant under the Housing (Scotland) Act 2001, where the ground for eviction is in paragraphs 1–7 of sch 2 to that Act.[39]

36 n 12.

37 But not a tenant under a short assured tenancy, if an order is sought under s 33 of the Act.

38 Schedule 5 to the 1988 Act and sch 3 to the 2016 Act set out both mandatory and discretionary grounds. See Chapters 8 and 10.

39 Though, in ground 2 cases, the new "streamlined" procedure is now available, if the notice of proceedings is served within one year of the criminal conviction that gives rise to the ground. In that case, ground 2 is effectively mandatory. See Chapter 5, p 164. In relation to grounds 8–15 in sch 2, there is no overall reasonableness requirement, but the court has to be satisfied,

In the *second* type of case there is no "reasonableness requirement", or in some cases no security of tenure at all, and the scope for defending the eviction proceedings is more limited.

All four of the statutory schemes currently in force (being the Acts of 1984, 1988, 2001 and 2016) contain provisions to the effect that certain types of tenancies are excepted from the scheme of that Act.[40] Consequently the tenant has no rights under the legislation, and her entitlement to remain in occupation ends when the tenancy contract ends. That being the case, she has no common law or statutory defence to proceedings for recovery of possession, provided that the parties' lease has been terminated.

Even where a tenancy is covered by either the 1984 Act, the 1988 Act or the 2016 Act, each of those statutes creates mandatory grounds for eviction, in relation to which the landlord need only establish that the ground applies; there is no "reasonableness" requirement. Again, in these cases, the scope for defending proceedings is more limited.

Also, forms of statutory tenancy have been created by the legislature, which limit security of tenure, with the result that in eviction proceedings it is not necessary for the landlord to show that there is any particular ground for eviction, or that it would be reasonable to grant the order. It is a special feature of these tenancies that they are set up under statutory codes that *require* the court or tribunal to grant an order for eviction, provided that the landlord complies with certain minimal procedural requirements. The relevant provisions, read literally, would exclude any defence except one based on the contention that those minimal requirements had not been met. In Scotland, these are the short assured tenancy under the Housing (Scotland) Act 1988, and the short Scottish secure tenancy under the Housing (Scotland) Act 2001.

From time to time, eviction proceedings are raised against defenders who are not (and never have been) tenants of the subjects, such as persons who took up occupation with the permission of a tenant who is no longer resident.[41] In these cases, there is no right to remain in occupation of subjects under a contract or statutory provision, and no requirement to show that the eviction is reasonable.

Reference is made to the examples given at the beginning of this chapter. The contention that proceedings are unlawful tends to be made in cases in which the defender has no case (or at least a weak case), by reference to the contractual rights, common law, or statutory rules applicable to his/her occupation, i.e. the *second* type of case discussed above.

under s 16(2)(b)(ii) that other suitable accommodation will be available for the tenant when the eviction order takes effect. The vast majority of eviction proceedings raised in the Scottish courts are actions under paras 1–7 of sch 2 to the 2001 Act; most of those cases are on the ground of rent arrears.

40 In the 1988 Act, excepted tenancies are listed in sch 4; in the 2001 Act in sch 1; and in the 2016 Act in sch 1. As described in Chapter 1, these exceptions tend to relate to: (1) the character of what is let, for example agricultural tenancies; (2) the status of tenant, for example asylum seekers; (3) the status of the landlord, for example where the landlord is also resident in the property of which the tenancy subjects form part; or (4) some combination of these factors, such as temporary accommodation for homeless persons, or tenancies granted by educational institutions to students.

41 For example, occupants who would wish to succeed to a Scottish secure tenancy after the tenant's death, or to have such a tenancy assigned to them by the tenant, but who are not entitled, or have been unable, to do so under the 2001 Act.

It is less likely (though not impossible) that arguments based on public law or human rights will have any independent significance in the *first* type of case. That is because the very broad scope of the concept of "reasonableness" is sufficiently wide to allow the court to take into account all the circumstances that it considers to be relevant[42] Thus, the broad judgment on reasonableness can encompass questions such as whether the landlord's conduct is, say, "irrational" (a judicial review ground) or "disproportionate" (contrary to article 8 of the ECHR).[43]

As regards Equality Act arguments: in cases in which the defender occupies under a tenancy that confers security of tenure, the older cases *Brazier*[44] and *Romano*[45] suggested that the unlawfulness of the eviction under anti-discrimination legislation would not be determinative of the issue of reasonableness, but would be a factor in deciding whether eviction was reasonable. It is doubtful that that reasoning holds, standing the decisions in *Malcolm*[46] and *Aster Communities Ltd v Akerman-Livingstone*.[47] The court cannot make a possession order if it is satisfied that an eviction would amount to unlawful discrimination under section 35(1)(b). Therefore, it must follow that the eviction order would not be reasonable.[48] Conversely, if the defence under the 2010 Act is not established, the court may nevertheless find that the eviction was not reasonable, based on other factors.[49]

Public authorities, private landlords

Judicial review grounds are unlikely to have any application in eviction proceedings pursued by private individuals, whether under the 1988 Act or the 2016 Act or at common law.[50] That is because the acts or decisions that bring about such proceedings would not be subject to the supervisory jurisdiction of the Court of Session, and therefore could not be subject to judicial review.[51]

42 In some cases, however, an argument on judicial review grounds *will* have independent significance. For instance, in *Wandsworth London Borough Council v Winder* (n 9), Mr Winder's argument on judicial review grounds, if correct, would have led to the conclusion that he was not in arrears of rent, and therefore, there was no ground for eviction at all. That would be distinct from any argument he might have made as to whether it would be reasonable to grant the order, if he did have a liability to pay rent arrears.

43 See para [56] in *Pinnock* (n 12).

44 n 28.

45 n 29.

46 n 33.

47 [2015] UKSC 15, [2015] AC 1399, discussed at p 402.

48 This point was explicitly recognised in *Teign Housing Association v Lane* [2018] EWHC 40 (QB) at [41].

49 For example, let us say that in an action for eviction on the ground of rent arrears, under para 1 of sch 2 to the 2001 Act, the tenant (a) relies on s 15 of the 2010 Act, saying that the arrears were due to a relapse in a psychiatric condition, and (b) offers to make repayments at a certain rate. The court could reject the first point, but refuse to grant an order, on the basis of the repayment proposal.

50 "The whole premise of a public law defence is that the claimant is a *public* body which has failed to act in accordance with . . . public law principles . . . There is no obligation on a *private* individual or company when carrying out private functions to follow or apply such principles." Luba and others(n 1) para 25.34.

51 For the scope of supervisory jurisdiction, see *West v Secretary of State for Scotland* 1992 SC 385. A helpful discussion of the relevant principles is found in Drummond, McCartney and Poole: *A Practical Guide to Public Law Litigation in Scotland* paras 1-06 to 1-09.

Likewise, defences based on the ECHR have application where possession is sought by a "public authority", for the purposes of section 6 of the Human Rights Act 1998. In terms of section 6(3)(b), "public authority" includes "any person certain of whose functions are functions of a public nature". However, under section 6(5), "in relation to a particular act", such as the decision to terminate a tenancy, "a person is not a public authority by virtue only of subsection (3)(b) if the nature of the act is private".

Local authorities are plainly public bodies subject to the supervisory jurisdiction of the Court of Session, and are also public authorities for the purposes of the 1998 Act. In England, there have been several important decisions on the issue of whether housing associations are "public", such that judicial review and human rights arguments may be pled against them.[52] It is suggested that the "public" status of registered social landlords ("RSLs") in Scotland is clearer, given that they are subject to the same statutory regime for tenancies, under the 2001 Act, as local authorities, and the same regulatory regime, under the Housing (Scotland) Act 2010.[53]

In *Ali v Serco Ltd*,[54] the Inner House held that, when providing accommodation to asylum seekers and former asylum seekers in terms of its contract with the Home Office, Serco Ltd was not exercising a public function. The court observed that there was no single test of universal application to be used in deciding whether a function was a public one such that the body exercising it fell to be classed as a public authority. However, the fundamental distinction was between the entity that was charged with the public law responsibility and a private operator who contracted therewith to provide the service. It was the Home Secretary who was charged with the public law responsibility for providing accommodation to asylum seekers and Serco Ltd, by contrast, was merely subject to a private law contract with the Home Office to provide the necessary services.

There was, for some time, a doubt as to whether the ECHR had any application to eviction proceedings raised by private landlords. On the one hand, section 6(1) of the 1998 states that "It is unlawful for a *public authority* to act in a way which is incompatible with a Convention right". On the other hand, a court or tribunal is a public authority, in terms of section 6(3)(a), and by section 3(1), any legislative scheme set up to regulate the rights of landlords and tenants in the private sector must "so far as it is possible to do so . . . be read and given effect in a way which is compatible with the Convention rights".

This question was answered by the case of *McDonald v McDonald*,[55] in which the Supreme Court held that the provisions of the relevant legislation,

52 In particular: *Poplar HARCA v Donoghue* [2001] EWCA Civ 595, [2002] QB 48; *R (Weaver) v London & Quadrant Housing Trust* [2009] EWCA Civ 587, [2010] 1 WLR 363; *R (McIntyre) v Gentoo Group Ltd* [2010] EWHC 5 (Admin), [2010] 2 P&CR DG6). Following the decision in *Weaver*, RSLs and other providers of social housing are generally regarded as being subject to public law principles in possession claims. An exception is *R (Macleod) v Peabody Trust Governors* [2016] EWHC 737 (Admin), [2016] HLR 27, in which the relevant housing stock was purchased with private funds, the stock offered intermediate rent levels and was thus not pure social housing.

53 The regulatory regime under the 2010 Act applies to all "social landlords", which are defined in s 165 as "a registered social landlord, local authority landlord or a local authority which provides housing services".

54 2020 SC 182, 2019 SLT 1335.

55 [2016] UKSC 28, [2017] AC 273. See, in particular, paras [40]–[46] of the court's decision.

in particular the Housing Act 1988, reflect the state's assessment of where to strike the balance between the article 8 rights of residential tenants and the rights of private-sector landlords to protection of their property, under article 1 of protocol 1 to the Convention. Accordingly, although article 8 might be engaged when a judge made an order for possession of a tenant's home at the suit of a private-sector landlord, the tenant's article 8 rights could not be invoked to justify a different order from that which was mandated by the contractual relationship between the parties,[56] and the relevant legislation.[57] Therefore, where a court or tribunal is asked to make an order for possession against a residential tenant of a private landlord pursuant to domestic statutory provisions it is not required to consider the proportionality of such an order, under article 8.[58]

Thus, as a rule, judicial review and human rights arguments may be pled in eviction proceedings at the instance of local authorities and RSLs, but not private landlords.

The position as regards defences relying on the Equality Act 2010 is different. Under section 35(1)(b), "A person (A) who manages premises must not discriminate against a person (B) who occupies the premises . . . by evicting B (or taking steps for the purpose of securing B's eviction)". This provision applies to landlords in the socially rented sector, and to private landlords.[59]

DEFENCES BASED ON "PUBLIC LAW" GROUNDS

A public law defence is based on the principle that public bodies must respect the rule of law, and must not act unlawfully, or seek to give effect to their unlawful actions or unlawful decisions. A public body must act lawfully throughout the process by which it seeks to gain possession. Accordingly, the defence could be directed against any decision of the pursuer, relevant to its seeking possession, including any decision to continue with proceedings that have been initiated.[60]

Following the Supreme Court's decision, the appellants made an application to the ECtHR. In a judgment dated 29 November 2018 (*FJM v UK* Application No. 76202/16) [2019] HLR 8) that court unanimously found the application to be manifestly ill founded, and rejected it. See in particular paras 41–43 of the judgment. As was the case before the Supreme Court, the claimants did not argue that the legislation itself was incompatible with the Convention. However, para [45] of the Supreme Court's decision was quoted with approval in the ECtHR judgment, and it is clear that the court regarded the balance struck by the 1988 Act as within the state's margin of appreciation.

56 Thus, even where the relationship is ruled by the parties' contractual relationship, rather than the legislation (for example, where the tenancy is excepted under sch 4 to the 1988 Act, or sch 1 to the 2016 Act), art 8 rights cannot be invoked by the tenant.

57 Which, in Scotland, would be the 1984, 1988 and 2016 Acts.

58 As will be explained below, it is possible that other articles under the Convention, particularly art 6, may be invoked in eviction proceedings, though this is a lot less common than reliance on art 8.

59 This point was emphasised in the Supreme Court's decision in *Aster Communities Ltd v Akerman-Livingstone* (n 47), which is discussed below. Note, however, that a defence that relies on s 149 of the 2010 Act (the public sector equality duty), rather than s 35(1)(b), could not be pled in eviction proceedings by a private landlord. See p 408 below.

60 *Central Bedfordshire Council v Housing Action Zone Ltd and Ors* [2009] EWCA Civ 613, [2010] 1 WLR 446.

A public law defence will only succeed if, had the same point been taken in judicial review proceedings in the Court of Session, the occupier would have succeeded in having the relevant decision reduced.[61] Furthermore, a public law defence should be advanced only where it has real substance. Such a defence should be raised at the earliest opportunity, and set out in written defences in time for the first calling of the case, if possible. That will assist in satisfying the court that the point raised has "real substance".[62]

The Court of Appeal has said, in the context of possession proceedings, that it is not appropriate to mount attacks of a "technical and over-theoretical sort" or "to construct intellectual edifices of public law without any proper foundations in reality".[63] The defender may also have difficulty running a public law defence if there is some alternative means by which the decision in question could have been impugned, such as, in particular, a statutory right of appeal or review.[64]

If illegality is established, in the process leading to a decision to seek possession, that does not automatically result in the proceedings being dismissed. That depends on the nature and effect of the illegality.[65]

It is beyond the scope of this work to discuss all the possible judicial review grounds on which a decision of a social landlord might be impugned.[66] Instead, the following examples are given of cases in which public law arguments have been deployed in eviction proceedings.

Ultra vires*; judicial review proceedings as an alternative*

As described earlier in this chapter, in *Wandsworth LBC v Winder*,[67] the tenant defended eviction proceedings, on the ground of rent arrears, on the basis that the council's decisions to make the increases, and the increases themselves, were *ultra vires* and void as being unreasonable.

An important aspect of this case was the fact that Mr Winder had applied for leave to raise judicial review proceedings challenging the increase, but that had been refused, as out of time. That notwithstanding, he was permitted to argue his grounds for judicial review, as a defence to the council's eviction proceedings.

In Scotland, judicial review proceedings have, since 2015, been subject to a three-month time bar, and a requirement to obtain permission from the court,

61 *Barnsley MBC v Norton* [2011] EWCA Civ 834, [2011] HLR 46, paras 36 and 37 (Lloyd LJ). See also the survey of the authorities, and the conclusions drawn, in Luba and others (n 1) para 25.33.

62 The later the point is taken, the more difficult it becomes to persuade the court to hear it. See: *Beech v Birmingham City Council* [2014] EWCA Civ 830, [2014] HLR 38, [77]–[78].

63 *London Borough of Brent v Corcoran* [2010] EWCA Civ 774, [2010] HLR 43, [12] and [26] (Jacob LJ).

64 As described in Chapter 6, at p 211, this is a potential issue in eviction proceedings under s 36 of the 2001 Act, in respect of an SSST because, in terms of s 36(4A)–(4C), the tenant has the right to seek a review of the decision to seek possession under that section.

65 *TM v Metropolitan Housing Trust Ltd* [2020] EWHC 311 (QB), [33].

66 Readers are referred to other works, in particular: Clyde and Edwards *Judicial Review*; Drummond, McCartney and Poole (n 51) ch 3; Fordham, *Judicial Review Handbook* (6th edn); and *De Smith's Judicial Review*.

67 n 9.

before the application may proceed.[68] It is suggested that, given *Winder*, it would possible to challenge a decision to raise eviction proceedings, relying on judicial review grounds, even where an application to the supervisory jurisdiction of the Court of Session would be time barred. This may be important where the particular decision under attack was taken more than three months ago.

Conversely, where such an application would not be time barred, the defender has the option of seeking judicial review. In that case, if eviction proceedings have already been raised, the defender may apply for them to be sisted.

Decision to take proceedings unreasonable

A well-known ground for judicial review of a decision is that it is *Wednesbury* unreasonable, i.e. it is a decision so unreasonable that no public body properly directing itself could have reached it.[69] However, that is a high test, and is rarely likely to be satisfied where the decision is made in good faith.[70]

In *Doherty v Birmingham City Council*,[71] the local authority owned a site that had been used for many years as a travellers' caravan site. The defendants had been resident there for seventeen years, under a licence granted by the authority. In exercise of certain powers, the authority had served notice to quit on them. The defendants relied principally on an argument that eviction violated their right to respect for their home under article 8 of the ECHR. Rather than accepting that such a defence could be made out,[72] the House of Lords remitted the case back to the High Court, to determine the legitimacy of the authority's decision to seek possession. As to the nature of that determination, Lord Hope said:[73]

> "I think that in this situation it would be unduly formalistic to confine the review strictly to traditional *Wednesbury* grounds. The considerations that can be brought into account in this case are wider. An examination of the question whether the council's decision was reasonable, having regard to the aim which it was pursuing and to the length of time that the first defendant and his family have resided on the site, would be appropriate. But the requisite scrutiny would not involve the judge substituting his own judgment for that of the local authority. In my opinion the test of reasonableness should be . . . whether the decision to recover possession was one which no reasonable person would consider justifiable."[74]

68 Respectively, ss 27A and 27B of the Court of Session Act 1988, which were added by the Courts Reform (Scotland) Act 2014.

69 This is derived from *Associated Provincial Picture Houses Ltd v Wednesbury Corporation* [1948] 1 KB 223. To rely on "*Wednesbury* unreasonableness" as ground for judicial review is to ask the court to determine that a decision is so unreasonable that it ought to be quashed. The scope of that ground has been the subject of many judicial formulations, and is a complex subject in itself. See, for example, Fordham (n 66) para 57.

70 *Doran v Liverpool City Council* [2009] EWCA Civ 146, [2009] 1 WLR 2365, [67] (Toulson LJ).

71 n 15.

72 That was not finally accepted until the decision of the Supreme Court in *Manchester City Council v Pinnock* (n 12), discussed below.

73 At [55].

74 This is the same test as Lord Hope articulated in *Kay v Lambeth LBC* (n 14) in the quotation at p 374.

One could question whether this "*Wednesbury*-plus" test is superseded by the decision in *Manchester City Council v Pinnock.*[75] In any event, whether the test is *Wednesbury* or "*Wednesbury* plus", it is clearly not a test of "reasonableness" that the court is applying, to decide for itself whether the occupier/tenant ought to be evicted.[76] Were the court to adopt that approach, in cases such as *Doherty*, that would not only amount to "substituting its own judgment for that of the landlord/owner"; it would effectively collapse the distinction between the first and second types of case, described at pages 376–377.[77]

Breach of natural justice; failure to follow own policies and procedures

In *McGlynn v Welwyn Hatfield DC,*[78] the tenant was a homeless person who had been provided with a temporary tenancy by the council.[79] The council served a notice to quit, following complaints of antisocial behaviour. It had previously stated, in a letter to a charity that was supporting the tenant, that its policy was not to take possession proceedings against a tenant unless it was satisfied that there had been a significant breach of the terms of the tenancy agreement. The tenant argued that the council had not done enough to satisfy itself that there had been a significant breach, and to explain the basis for that decision. Natural justice required that he be told of the nature of the allegations against him, and to have an opportunity to respond to them, before the eviction proceedings were initiated. The Court of Appeal accepted that this defence was seriously arguable, and remitted the case for trial.

In *Barber v Croydon LBC,*[80] the non-secure tenant had been violent towards a resident caretaker. Medical evidence indicated that the defendant had significant mental health problems, and that the violent incident had been due to his condition. The public law defence was that, in pursuing proceedings, the council had failed to have regard to its own policies relating to the management

75 (n 12). Because in *Doherty* (n 15), the test described by Lord Hope, which entails considering whether the council's decision is "justifiable", by reference to "the aim which it was pursuing", was as far as the court was prepared to go, without allowing a proportionality test under article 8. Post *Pinnock*, there is no need for a "*Wednesbury* plus" test. Hence, in *Fareham BC v Miller* [2013] EWCA Civ 159, [2013] HLR 22, 33, a case (post-*Pinnock*) in which the decision of the council to take proceedings was impugned as disproportionate, it was said that "The only real issue therefore is whether the Council's decision to press ahead with the claim for possession is either *Wednesbury* unreasonable or can be subject to a proportionality challenge under art.8" (Patten LJ). One might also question whether, in practice, the application of Lord Hope's test, as opposed to "traditional *Wednesbury* grounds", would lead to substantially different outcomes.

76 Such as it would, in the first type of case described at p 376 above. See the discussion of the "reasonableness" requirement, in Chapter 5.

77 "A *Wednesbury* challenge depends not on whether the decision to continue the possession claim was objectively reasonable but whether it was a decision which no reasonable authority could have taken in the light of all the relevant circumstances." *Fareham BC v Miller*, 34 (Patten LJ).

78 [2009] EWCA Civ 285, [2010] HLR 10.

79 Accordingly, this was not a secure tenancy under the English legislation. See the discussion of interim accommodation for homeless persons, below.

80 [2010] EWCA Civ 51, [2010] HLR 26.

of antisocial behaviour by vulnerable occupiers.[81] The Court of Appeal upheld that defence, and dismissed the possession claim.[82]

More recently, in *Ahern v Southern Housing Group Ltd*,[83] giving the leading judgment in the Court of Appeal, Sir James Munby said:

> "The dispute before us turned on the proper application, in the particular circumstances of this case, of the principle, articulated in a long line of authorities to which we were taken, including at the highest level, that Mr Ahern was entitled in the County Court to challenge the landlord's decision to serve the notice[84] on traditional public law grounds. It was common ground before us, as at the trial, that (i) the landlord was obliged to follow its own policies, save where there was good reason not to, (ii) there was no need for Mr Ahern to establish a legitimate expectation that the landlord would do so, and (iii) if there had been a breach of policy, the question for the court was whether the breach was material to the decision to serve the notice."

This explains the court's view that the case raised "no point of principle":[85] the relevant principles had already been established. Even where eviction is apparently required, in terms of the relevant statutory provision, a decision to serve notice, under that provision, may be challenged on public law grounds, as a defence to eviction proceedings.

Failure to consider exercising a power

In *Leicester City Council v Shearer*,[86] the circumstances bore some similarity to Example 2 in the introduction to this chapter. The defendant, Mrs Shearer, was the widow of the sole tenant of a secure tenant. She wished to take over her late husband's tenancy, and live there with her children, but was not permitted to succeed to the tenancy under the relevant legislation. The council's housing allocation policy contained a provision that gave it a discretionary power to make a "direct offer" of a property to an applicant where, *inter alia*, there were "exceptional circumstances that merit priority rehousing".[87] The council advised Mrs Shearer that she could not succeed to her husband's ten-

81 This case predated the coming into force of the Equality Act 2010. Were similar circumstances to arise now, it could also be argued that the eviction would be contrary to ss 15 and 35 of the 2010 Act. See the discussion of defences under that Act, below.

82 Another case along these lines is the decision of the High Court in *Eastlands Homes Partnership v Whyte* [2010] EWHC 695 (QB), in which it upheld a defence which argued that the council had failed to follow its own policy in relation to rent arrears, and had not adopted a fair procedure in respect of the tenant's appeal against its decision to pursue proceedings, or followed its own rules in relation to such appeals. Holman J said at para 47: "The courts are entitled to expect that RSLs, in the same way as local authorities, will, for the protection of the interests of their tenants, adhere to their procedures."

83 [2017] EWCA Civ 1934. The quoted passage comes from para [4].

84 This was a notice under s 21 of the Housing Act 1988, in relation to an assured shorthold tenancy. In England, there has been no process (such as that achieved in Scotland by the 2001 Act) by which housing association tenancies transferred from the assured to the secure tenancy regime. Accordingly, most housing association tenancies are assured, and some are "assured shorthold" being broadly the equivalent of a short assured tenancy. Mr Ahern had no defence under the 1988 Act to proceedings following on a section 21 notice. He relied, instead, on a "public law" defence.

85 Paragraph [21].

86 [2013] EWCA Civ 1467, [2014] HLR 8.

87 This type of provision is quite common in the allocation policies of local authorities and RSLs. It allows a social landlord to bypass the rules of the policy, in exceptional cases.

ancy and did not, at any time before raising proceedings, advise her that if she made an application under its allocation policy, she might be made an direct offer. The Court of Appeal accepted an argument that the council had acted unlawfully in raising proceedings without giving any proper consideration to the option of making a direct offer.[88]

Homelessness cases

The relationship between judicial review and eviction proceedings is a feature of the provision of accommodation to homeless persons by local authorities, under part II of the 1987 Act.[89] For example, let us say that a homeless person makes an application to a local authority under the Act and, in compliance with its duty under section 29 to provide interim accommodation, the authority lets a property to her, pending its determination of her application.[90] In due course it decides that it has discharged its duties to her under the 1987 Act, and seeks recovery of possession of the tenancy property in an action in the sheriff court. The tenant does not defend that action but, instead, raises judicial review proceedings in the Court of Session. In her petition, she maintains that the authority has not complied with its duties under the 1987 Act, and asks the Court of Session, in exercise of its supervisory jurisdiction, to ordain the authority to comply with those duties; meantime she seeks an interdict to prevent the authority from enforcing any decree obtained in the eviction proceedings. If the court grants interim interdict, pending determination of the petitioner's case, any decree obtained in the sheriff court action cannot be enforced.[91]

However, it is submitted that it would be difficult for the defender to rely on the same judicial review grounds in the sheriff court eviction action, *instead* of raising judicial review proceedings in the Court of Session. There is very clear English authority to the effect that the question of whether or not a local authority has fulfilled its statutory obligations to a homeless person is irrelevant in proceedings to evict that person from interim accommodation provided under the homelessness legislation.[92]

In those cases, the court considered that, in the dispute between the parties, the defendant's rights existed solely in public law terms. It is suggested that this would also be the case in Scotland. A person provided with accommodation under section 29 of the 1987 Act has rights under the homelessness

88 Note, however, that the court considered that the circumstances of Mrs Shearer's case were, indeed, exceptional, and that therefore a direct offer was an option that merited serious consideration.

89 The statutory scheme for the assistance and accommodation of homeless persons is outlined in Chapter 5, from p 151. The relationship between SSSTs and homelessness applications is considered in Chapter 6, at p 181.

90 Such a tenancy would be excepted from Scottish secure tenancy status under para 5 of sch 1 to the 2001 Act: see Chapter 4, p 84.

91 If the interim interdict had been obtained whilst the sheriff court action was still ongoing, an application might be made for that action to be sisted. On occasion, an application is made to sist the sheriff court action, on the basis that judicial review proceedings between the parties are about to be initiated.

92 *Tower Hamlets LBC v Abdi* (1993) 25 HLR 80; *Hackney LBC v Lambourne & Anr* (1993) 25 HLR 172. See also *Ali v Tower Hamlets LBC* [1993] QB 407. These are all decisions of the Court of Appeal.

legislation, but those rights do not include the right to occupy any particular temporary accommodation. It would therefore be open to the local authority, if it so wished, to move an applicant from one place of interim accommodation to another, by serving notice to quit, and providing him with alternative interim accommodation, or permanent accommodation if his application had been successful, without failing in its duties under the 1987 Act. Once that point is recognised, it becomes apparent that the applicant has no right to remain at the interim accommodation that is the subject of the proceedings. His rights under the Act can only be vindicated in judicial review proceedings, in which he would ask the court to ordain the council to comply with its duties under the Act, including the duty to provide accommodation, or meantime to interdict the council from removing him from his existing interim accommodation.[93]

Actions under section 36 (SSSTs) and section 16(2)(aa) (ground 2) of the 2001 Act

Reference is made to the discussion of possible public law defences in section 36 cases, in Chapter 6, at pp 178 and 213. The streamlined eviction process for ground 2 cases features in example 1 at the beginning of this chapter. As described at p 374 above, the addition of subsection (3A), and the Scottish Government's Guidance on the streamlined process, recognise that the tenant may rely on other enactments or rules of law (apart from section 16(2)) in defending proceedings. Accordingly, it is suggested that the defence described in Example 1 would have to be considered by the court.

DEFENCES BASED ON SECTION 6 OF THE HUMAN RIGHTS ACT 1998

Introduction

Section 6(1) of the 1998 Act states that is unlawful for a public authority to act in a way that is incompatible with a Convention right.[94]

Article 8 of the Convention states:

> "**Article 8**
> 1. Everyone has the right to respect for his private and family life, his home and his correspondence.
> 2. There shall be no interference by a public authority with the exercise of this right except such as is in accordance with the law and is necessary in a democratic

93 In the type of action under discussion (for eviction of person from interim accommodation provided under s 29 of the 1987 Act), it is possible for art 8 to be invoked as a defence: see paragraphs 34–43 of the judgment in *Hounslow LBC v Powell* (n 12). However, as is the case with art 8 defences in general, the likelihood of success is low. By contrast, the prospects of success for an argument which relies on the Equality Act 2010 is greater, given the decision in *Aster Communities v Akerman-Livingstone* (n 47). In that case (discussed below), the defendant occupied accommodation on a temporary basis, under the homelessness legislation.

94 Under s 1(1), "Convention rights" means the rights and fundamental freedoms set out in arts 2–12 and 14 of the European Convention on Human Rights, arts 1–3 of the first protocol, and art 1 of the thirteenth protocol, as read with arts 16–18 of the Convention.

> society in the interests of national security, public safety or the economic well-being of the country, for the prevention of disorder or crime, for the protection of health or morals, or for the protection of the rights and freedoms of others."

This sets out certain interests that a person has which are worthy of respect, such as his home, and in which there should be no interference without justification. As to such interference, the Strasbourg Court has said:

> "the loss of one's home is the most extreme form of interference with the right to respect for the home. Any person at risk of an interference of this magnitude should in principle be able to have the proportionality of the measure determined by an independent tribunal in light of the relevant principles under art.8 of the Convention, notwithstanding that, under domestic law, his right to occupation has come to an end."[95]

Let us say that that a person is in occupation of a house owned by a public authority, and that the authority wants to recover possession. The authority raises proceedings against him, asserting that he has no right or title to remain in the house, or that any right of occupation that he had in the past has come to end. The defender argues:

1) The house is my "home".
2) Eviction would constitute an "interference" in my "right to respect" for my "home".
3) Although that "interference" would be "in accordance with law", it would not be "necessary" in any of the "interests" that are set out in article 8(2), because it would not satisfy the test of proportionality outlined in the jurisprudence of the Strasbourg Court.
4) Eviction would therefore be "incompatible with a Convention right", and unlawful under section 6(1) of the 1998 Act.
5) I am entitled to rely on that right in the proceedings that have been raised against me under section 7(1) of the 1998 Act.[96]
6) Consequently, although I have no right to occupy the house under domestic law (whether by virtue of a contract, statutory provision or otherwise), the public authority is not entitled to an order for my eviction.

This argument has a different focus from the public law argument described earlier in this chapter. A public law defence would concern the public authority's decision-making process. By contrast, human rights or "proportionality" defences focus on the outcome of the proceedings, being the eviction that is an interference in the occupier's right to respect for his home, that requires to be justified.[97] In considering such a defence the court is therefore deciding, on

95 *Kay v UK* [2010] ECHR 1322, [2011] HLR 2, [68]. This statement has appeared in numerous cases, such as: *Connors v UK* [2004] ECHR 223, [2004] HLR 52, [83]; *McCann v UK* (2008) 47 EHRR 40, [2008] HLR 40, [49]–[50]; and *Buckland v UK* (2013) 56 EHRR 16, [2013] HLR 2, a[65].

96 Section 7(1)(b) of the 1998 Act: "A person who claims that a public authority has acted (or proposes to act) in a way which is made unlawful by section 6(1) may . . . rely on the Convention right or rights concerned in any legal proceedings, but only if he is (or would be) a victim of the unlawful act."

97 Thus as Lord Bingham said in *R (Begum) v Denbigh High School Governors* [2006] UKHL 15, [2007] 1 AC 100 at [31]: "what matters in any Convention rights case is the practical outcome, not the quality of the decision making process that led to it". See also *Aster Communities v Akerman-Livingstone* (n 47), para 38 (Baroness Hale).

the facts as agreed (or found after proof), whether the making of a possession order would be proportionate.

Following certain decisions made by the House of Lords, it was thought that an argument based on article 8 did not amount to a defence to eviction proceedings. In essence, the court held that the balance of interests arising under article 8(2) had already been struck by the legislature when enacting statutory provisions that accorded security of tenure to some, and not to others. Therefore, in deciding a claim for possession, the court was not required to investigate the individual circumstances of each case in order to decide whether article 8(2) had been satisfied. On that view, the issue was one of law, not of fact, and the order for possession had to be granted if the public authority was legally entitled to that order under the relevant national laws. There was no consistent line of authority from the European Court of Human Rights ("ECtHR") to the contrary.[98]

Manchester City Council v Pinnock

These earlier decisions were effectively overturned by the Supreme Court in *Manchester City Council v Pinnock*.[99]

After a survey of House of Lords cases, and the decisions of the ECtHR, the court found that "it is clear that the following propositions are now well established in the jurisprudence of the European court":[100]

(a) Any person at risk of being dispossessed of his home at the suit of a local authority should in principle have the right to raise the question of the proportionality of the measure, and to have it determined by an independent tribunal in the light of article 8, even if his right of occupation under domestic law has come to an end.
(b) A judicial procedure that is limited to addressing the proportionality of the measure through the medium of traditional judicial review (i.e., one that does not permit the court to make its own assessment of the facts in an appropriate case) is inadequate as it is not appropriate for resolving sensitive factual issues.
(c) Where the measure includes proceedings involving more than one stage, it is the proceedings as a whole that must be considered in order to see whether article 8 has been complied with.
(d) If the court concludes that it would be disproportionate to evict a person from his home notwithstanding the fact that he has no domestic right to remain there, it would be unlawful to evict him so long as the conclusion obtains – for example, for a specified period, or until a specified event occurs, or a particular condition is satisfied.

Therefore, if UK law was to be compatible with article 8, where a court is asked to make an order for possession of a person's home at the suit of a

98 This is a crude summary of the reasoning of the majority in *Harrow LBC v Qazi* [2004] 1 AC 983 and *Kay v Lambeth London Borough Council* (n 14) and of the court in *Doherty v Birmingham City Council* (n 15). It would be impossible to do justice to the complexity of the judgments in those cases in this text, and in any event it is unnecessary, given the decision in *Pinnock* (n 12).

99 (n 12).

100 Paragraph [45].

local authority, the court must have the power to assess the proportionality of making the order, and, in making that assessment, to resolve any relevant dispute of fact.

The legitimate aims of the public authority; the strength of its case

Before discussing the implications of this conclusion in practice, the court interposed a discussion under the seemingly innocuous heading "Exceptionality".[101] This part of the judgment contains certain observations, at paragraph 52–54, which, it is suggested, are of critical importance in understanding the approach that it envisaged for article 8 cases:

1) The question is always whether the eviction is a proportionate means of achieving a legitimate aim.
2) The legitimate aims that may be invoked by a local authority when seeking to justify, under article 8.2 of the Convention, the eviction of an occupier are: (a) the vindication of the authority's rights of ownership; (b) the authority's compliance with its public duties in relation to the management and allocation of housing stock.
3) These "twin aims" may be taken as read by the court, and do not require to be expressly pled.
4) These aims are of real weight, and amount, in themselves, to a very strong case for saying that making an order for possession would be proportionate, and therefore compliant with article 8. Therefore, the threshold for raising an arguable case on proportionality is a high one.
5) The local authority is under no onus to rely on any additional factor as justifying an order for possession, but it may choose to do so if, in the circumstances of the case, that seems appropriate.
6) The administration of public housing under various statutory schemes is entrusted to local housing authorities. It is not for the court to second-guess their allocation decisions.

The significance of these points is apparent from the court's subsequent decision in *Hounslow LBC v Powell*: the judgments of Lord Hope and Lord Phillips refer to paragraphs 52–54 of *Pinnock* on several occasions.[102] These paragraphs are clearly of considerable importance to any public authority seeking to resist an argument that eviction would be contrary to article 8. In particular, points (3) and (4) are fundamental. The "twin aims" are assumed and, of themselves, amount to a very strong case that an eviction is proportionate.[103]

101 This begins by making the point that it is "both unsafe and unhelpful" to proceed on the basis that that it will only be in "very highly exceptional cases" that it will be appropriate for the court to consider a proportionality argument. It is unhelpful because exceptionality is an outcome and not a guide. It is unsafe, because there may be more cases than one might suppose, in which art 8 could reasonably be invoked by a residential tenant. That notwithstanding, in subsequent cases the courts have found it difficult to resist making statements to the effect that a successful art 8 defence will be possible only in exceptional cases. See, for example: *Thurrock BC v West* [2013] HLR 5, para 24 (Etherton LJ).

102 See, in particular: paras 34–37 and 41 (Lord Hope) and paras 80 and 87 (Lord Phillips).

103 Thus in *Powell* (n 12), at [41], Lord Hope said that: "In the ordinary case the relevant facts will be encapsulated entirely in the two legitimate aims that were identified in *Pinnock* . . . para 52." See also Baroness Hale's summary of the decisions in *Pinnock* (n 12) and *Powell* (n 12) at paras 20-22 and 29 in *Aster Communities Ltd v Akerman-Livingstone* (n 47).

The implications, for eviction proceedings, of the conclusion that article 8 may be relied upon as a defence

In *Pinnock*,[104] the court also made certain observations that, although brief, are of importance in understanding the procedural approach that it envisages for eviction proceedings in which article 8 is in issue.

The court expanded upon the point, already made at paragraph 52, that the authority's legitimate aims should be assumed and do not require to be pled. From this it necessarily follows, as a general rule, that any article 8 issue has to be raised by the defender. If it is not raised by the defender, the court need not consider it.[105]

If an article 8 point *is* raised by the defender, the court should initially consider it summarily and if, "as will no doubt often be the case", the court is satisfied that, even if the facts relied on are made out, the point would not succeed, it should be dismissed. Only if the court is satisfied that it could affect the order that the court might make should the point be further entertained.[106] This follows from the premise that the legitimate aims of the authority are of real weight, and amount, in themselves, to a very strong case, and therefore the threshold for raising an arguable case on proportionality is a high one.

From a Scottish perspective, an article 8 defence ought, in any event, to be dealt with summarily under rule 8.3(3)(d) of the Summary Cause Rules,[107] unless it raises a disputed issue of fact that requires to be resolved before the court can make a decision.[108] It is suggested that this part of the court's judgment is important for an authority seeking an order for the eviction of an occupier as soon as possible. If it is met with an argument under article 8, both the judgment in *Pinnock*, and the Summary Cause Rules, indicate that the defence should usually be dealt with at the first calling (or a continuation thereof).

The necessity of "reading in" the article 8 review

Another issue in *Pinnock*[109] was whether the demoted tenancy regime[110] set out in the Housing Act 1996 could be interpreted so as to comply with the requirements of article 8, or whether at least some aspects of that regime were incompatible with the Convention. The court decided that, notwithstanding that the statutory provision made it mandatory for the court to grant a decree for eviction if certain minimum conditions were met, the jurisdiction of the county court to conduct a review of the compatibility of the eviction with article 8 could be "read in" to the legislation. In *Powell*,[111] the court reached the same conclusion as regards the statutory scheme for introductory tenancies in the 1996 Act. The same conclusion was reached as regards the legislative

104 At paras 61 and 62.
105 Again, this point is reiterated in *Powell*, paras 34 and 41 (Lord Hope).
106 ibid.
107 Act of Sederunt (Summary Cause Rules) (SSI 2002/132).
108 See the discussion of r 8.3(3)(d) in Chapter 13.
109 n 12.
110 The demoted tenancy is a particular type of statutory tenancy. It bears some similarity to the short Scottish secure tenancy under ss 34–37 of the 2001 Act. See Chapter 6, note 18.
111 n 12.

regime for short Scottish secure tenancies ("SSSTs") under the 2001 Act, in *McKenna v South Lanarkshire Council.*[112]

Hounslow LBC v Powell[113]

In *Pinnock*[114] the Supreme Court anticipated that its forthcoming consideration of certain pending conjoined appeals, in the judgment that was to be *Hounslow LBC v Powell*, would provide a more appropriate vehicle for the giving of general guidance in article 8 cases, because cases involving the type of tenure applying to Mr Pinnock – the demoted tenancy – were relatively rare.[115] The judgment in *Powell* concerns three different cases, two of which involved introductory tenancies (*Leeds City Council v Hall* and *Birmingham City Council v Frisby*), and one that involved a person provided with temporary accommodation under the homelessness legislation (*Hounslow LBC v Powell*). In contrast to *Pinnock*, in which a single judgment was given by the ourt, two full judgments were given by Lord Hope and Lord Phillips,[116] with whom the other five judges agreed. Much of the judgment reiterates the key points in *Pinnock*,[117] and comes to the same conclusion as regards the statutory regime for introductory tenancies, that the court had reached as regards the demoted regime in the earlier case. Where the defender invokes article 8, the court has the jurisdiction to review the proportionality of the eviction.[118]

What is a "home" for the purposes of article 8?

It is apparent from the jurisprudence of the Strasbourg Court that an individual has to show sufficient and continuing links with a place to establish that it is his home for the purposes of article 8.[119] However, Lord Hope stated that this issue was likely to be of concern only in cases where an order for possession is sought against a defendant who has only recently moved into accommodation on a temporary or precarious basis.[120] Therefore, "In most cases it can be taken for granted that a claim by a person who is in lawful occupation to remain in possession will attract the protection of article 8".

112 n 21.
113 n 12.
114 ibid.
115 See paras 58–59 in *Pinnock* (n 12), and para 4 in *Powell* (n 12).
116 Then respectively the Deputy President and the President of the Court.
117 See, in particular, Lord Hope's comments at paras 34–37, 41 and 43.
118 Paragraphs 50–56 (Lord Hope).
119 See the cases cited by Lord Hope at para 33: *Gillow v United Kingdom* (1989) 11 EHRR 335, para 46; *Buckley v United Kingdom* (1997) 23 EHRR 101, 115, para 54; *Harrow London Borough Council v Qazi* (n 98), paras 9, 61–68. In *Paulic v Croatia* (App. No. 3572/06) judgment, 22 October 2009, para 3.
120 At para 33. Lord Hope gives an example of a case in which art 8 would not be engaged: the Leeds appeal in *Kay v Lambeth London Borough Council* (n 14), where the defendants had been on recreation ground in their caravan for only two days without any authority to be there.

The rejection of a "structured approach" to proportionality

Having indicated in *Pinnock* that the court regarded *Powell* as the more appropriate vehicle for the giving of guidance as to the conduct of an article 8 review, its consideration of that matter was something of an anti-climax, as the court rejected a "structured approach" to the assessment of whether the eviction is proportionate.

A "structured approach" to proportionality, in the context of eviction proceedings, would be one in which the court asks the following questions.[121]

- First, is the objective pursued by the landlord/owner sufficiently important to justify limiting a fundamental right?
- Secondly, is the measure (eviction) rationally connected to the objective?
- Thirdly, are the means chosen (eviction proceedings) no more than is necessary to accomplish the objective?
- Fourthly, does the eviction strike a fair balance between the landlord/owner's need to accomplish its objectives and the disadvantages thereby caused to the defender?

In *Powell*,[122] the court said that such an approach would be wholly inappropriate, "in the context of a statutory regime that has been deliberately designed by Parliament, for sound reasons of social policy, so as not to provide the occupier with a secure tenancy".[123] Given that the "twin aims"[124] are taken for granted, and amount to a very strong case for the public authority, the court would only be considering "any factual objections that may be raised by the defendant and what she has to say about her personal circumstances".[125] However, as the subsequent case law has borne out, it will be a rare case in which the defendant is able to question the applicability of either of the twin aims, as a matter of fact, or rely on the personal circumstances such as to outweigh those aims.

Subsequent cases

Given the very high bar set in *Pinnock*[126] and *Powell*,[127] it is not surprising that article 8 defences have been almost entirely unsuccessful.[128] The reported

121 See: *Aster Communities Ltd v Akerman-Livingstone* (n 47), paras 28, 64 and 73. In that case, the court reiterated that the structured approach is inappropriate for eviction cases in which article 8 is pled, but is required in cases subject to s 15 of the Equality Act 2010. See the discussion of Equality Act defences below.

122 n 12.

123 At [41] (Lord Hope). Lord Phillips agreed, at [87] and [88]. Paragraph [41] is quoted by Baroness Hale at [29] in *Aster Communities Ltd v Akerman-Livingstone* (n 47). It is suggested that a "structured approach" was rejected because it would come too close to collapsing the distinction between the first and second types of case described at p 376.

124 See points (3) and (4) at p 389 above.

125 Paragraphs [37], [41], [87] and [88].

126 n 12.

127 ibid.

128 Luba and others (n 1) para 26.99 describe the circumstances of a "handful" of English county court cases in which the court decided that it would be disproportionate to grant an order.

cases are too numerous to consider. Instead, two decisions of the Court of Appeal may be taken as illustrative.

In *Corby BC v Scott* (which was joined with the case of *West Kent Housing Association Ltd v Haycraft*)[129] the defendant Scott was an introductory tenant. She had a drink problem and had been the subject of a serious assault (her assailant pled guilty to attempted murder). She had rent arrears, and the council had received reports of noise nuisance. They raised proceedings in which the Circuit Judge held that Ms Scott's circumstances were exceptional (particularly given the gravity of the assault), and refused to make the order. *Haycraft* involved an assured shorthold tenancy granted by a private registered provider of social housing. Allegations of antisocial behaviour were made against Mr Haycraft by his neighbours, one of which was of indecent exposure, but these were made some time before the claim was brought. Mr Haycraft suffered from liver and kidney problems. The landlords served the relevant notice on him and then conducted a formal review of its decision to end the tenancy. There were three review hearings. At the third such hearing, it was clear that Mr Haycraft disputed the allegations that had been made against him, but the panel found that he had been guilty of indecent exposure and upheld its decision to seek possession. He defended the proceedings at first instance on article 8 grounds, without success.

Before the Court of Appeal, the landlords succeeded in both cases. What is significant about this decision, it is suggested, is the way in which Lord Neuberger[130] approached certain issues that had been raised by the defendants in advancing their article 8 cases. For him, the issue of the assault sustained by Ms Scott was irrelevant. The judge had been misled by virtue of the circumstances of the case being exceptional. However, there was no suggestion that the attack had resulted in mental or physical injury that would render it particularly harmful to her to be evicted. Although no doubt shocking, it simply had nothing to do with the claim for possession, or the respect for her home to which she was entitled. The case that she advanced as to why it would be disproportionate to require her to give up possession of her flat was hopeless as a matter of law and should have been stopped at a preliminary stage.

In Mr Haycraft's case the judge had been fully entitled to conclude that he had not raised a sufficiently strong proportionality argument to justify a full hearing on the issue. Lord Neuberger was also dismissive of Mr Haycraft's argument that, in the event of the order being granted, he would be treated as intentionally homeless. He observed that article 8 is primarily concerned with respect for a particular home, as opposed to a general right to be provided with a home. Moreover, the right to be re-housed is a factor weighing against the article 8 claim prevailing, rather than the absence of such a right being a factor in favour of such a claim. Lord Neuberger also sought to emphasise that, in cases in which an article 8 defence is raised, the judge at first instance should be rigorous in ensuring that only relevant matters were taken into account on the proportionality issue, and should not let understandable sympathy for a particular tenant have the effect of lowering the threshold identified in

129 [2012] HLR 23.

130 Then the Master of the Rolls, and subsequently President of the Supreme Court. The other two judges agreed.

Powell.[131] Although the court declined to give firm guidance on the procedure to be adopted in article 8 cases, it emphasised the desirability of a judge considering at an early stage whether the tenant had an arguable case on proportionality, before the issue was ordered to be heard. If it was a case that could not succeed, then it should not be allowed to take up further court time and to delay the landlord's right to possession. Clearly those remarks are applicable to summary cause proceedings in Scotland, in so far as the procedure under chapter 8 of the rules entails the sheriff considering whether it is necessary to fix a diet of proof, or whether the case may be disposed of at the first calling or at a continuation thereof.

In *Thurrock BC v West,*[132] the local authority appealed against the dismissal of its claim for possession of a property occupied by the respondent Mr West. It had granted a secure joint tenancy to Mr West's grandparents in 1967. In 2007, Mr West moved in and was subsequently joined by his partner and son. On the grandfather's death in 2008, the tenancy vested automatically in Mr West's grandmother as successor in terms of the relevant statutory provisions. She died in 2010, and under the English legislation there was no further succession.[133] The authority claimed possession and Mr West resisted on human rights grounds, arguing that the family would become homeless and would need to be rehoused by the authority in any event. The judge below dismissed the claim, holding that to evict the family only to re-house them in another property one bedroom smaller would be disproportionate. Allowing the local authority's appeal, the court noted that social landlords held their housing stock for the benefit of the whole community and were better equipped than the courts to make management decisions about its administration. There was nothing exceptional about the housing needs of a couple with limited financial means who were the parents of a young child. Indeed, such a family was entirely typical of those with a need for social housing. The fact that they had occupied the property for some time was also irrelevant, as succession to a secure tenancy was limited, however long a person's association with it. That legislative policy did not infringe article 8. Sympathy for Mr West and his family should not obscure the remarkable effect of the judge's decision, which had precluded the local authority from recovering possession from Mr West, who had no right to occupy, and conferred a right to remain without limitation of time in conflict with the lawful legislative policy limiting succession rights to secure tenancies. The effect of the judge's decision had been to compel the authority to grant Mr West a new tenancy to which he had no legal right.[134]

It may be helpful to draw attention to certain points in these decisions. Firstly, although, in *Powell,*[135] the Supreme Court recognised that an article 8 defence might be based on the defender's "personal circumstances", the decision in the Scott appeal tends to suggest that it will be very difficult to succeed in such a defence because, as Lord Neuberger pointed out, those circumstances, however extreme, do not necessarily bear upon the requirement

131 n 12.
132 n 101.
133 In Scotland, the tenancy would have passed to Mr West under s 22(2) of the 2001 Act: see the discussion of succession cases in Chapter 12.
134 See paras 33 and 36.
135 n 12.

to have respect for the defendant's home. Article 8 requires that respect to be balanced against the public authority's pursuit of the legitimate aims set out in the article. Certain issues, such as the possible homelessness of the occupier (as in *West*) are not relevant to that exercise.

Secondly, it is surprising that, in *Thurrock v West*,[136] it counted against the occupier that he would have an indefinite right of occupation if the court refused to grant the order. That was part of the reasoning of the majority in cases such as *Qazi*,[137] which *Pinnock*[138] was supposed to have overruled. In *Pinnock*, the Supreme Court accepted that, in cases where it is established that eviction would be a violation of article 8, the occupier will effectively have the right to stay put indefinitely. However, that result does not support the conclusion that eviction would not be a violation of article 8.

Thirdly, in cases in which the occupier's argument effectively amounts to saying: "this house should be allocated to me", whether by succession, assignation or otherwise, the prospects of success must be slim to non-existent, if the authority can show that, under its allocation rules, the house would go to someone else. It is not for the court to usurp the local authority's allocation function. Thus, returning to Example 2 at the beginning of this chapter, B's argument would be very unlikely to succeed.

Other issues under the Convention

The requirement to give reasons

The statutory procedure in relation to introductory and demoted tenancies in England[139] requires that the authority give reasons for seeking its decision. There was no stipulation to that effect in section 36 of the 2001 Act, in relation to SSSTs, but that is now addressed by section 36(3)(aa).[140] However, there are other situations[141] in which there is no requirement at common law, or in statute, for the authority to give reasons before raising eviction proceedings against a tenant or occupier.[142] In *Hounslow LBC v Powell*,[143] Lord Phillips said:

> "115 I do not believe that the Strasbourg court would tolerate a regime under which a person can be deprived of his home by a public authority without being told the reason for this. Nor would I, for it is fundamentally unfair . . .

136 n 101.

137 n 98.

138 n 12.

139 These were the types of statutory tenancies, under the English legislation, that were under discussion in *Pinnock* (n 12) and *Powell* (n 12). See note 18 of Chapter 6.

140 Considered in Chapter 6. This was the principal point in issue when the Inner House considered the devolution issue in *McKenna v South Lanarkshire Council* (n 24): it was argued on behalf of Ms McKenna that, as there was no obligation to give reasons in s 36 (as it then was), the procedure was not compatible with art 8. The court decided that a requirement to give reasons could be "read in" to the legislation. However, that "reading in" is no longer necessary, given the amendments made by the 2014 Act.

141 Such as certain instances of the "second type of case" discussed at p 376.

142 For example, as is described in Chapter 3 at p 54, there is no need for a landlord serving a notice to quit to give any reason for terminating a tenancy, other than that it will reach its ish on the day the notice takes effect.

143 n 12.

> 116 I do not suggest that there is any burden on a local authority, in the first instance, to justify to the court its application for a possession order or to plead the reason for seeking this. What I do suggest is that the tenant must be informed of the reason for the authority's action so that he can, if so minded, attempt to raise a proportionality challenge . . . ."

However, the court declined to give any specific direction as to how that conclusion ought to affect the conduct of any case in which it is said that the authority has failed to give reasons, preferring to leave that to be worked out in the lower courts.[144] In particular, it did not express the view that, in a case in the authority raised proceedings without having given notice of its reasons, the action was incompetent, or that it would require to be struck out or dismissed.

Therefore, in cases in which the authority has raised proceedings to evict a person from his home, without any prior indication of its reasons for doing so, and that point is raised by the defender, it is suggested that the authority could propose a short continuation of the case for the purpose of: (a) giving written reasons; and (b) the defender being allowed to consider, in light of those reasons, whether he wishes to raise a proportionality challenge. Perhaps the failure to give reasons before raising the action might have a bearing on the question of expenses.

Tenancies of a "probationary" nature

In the Housing Act 1996, the term "probationary tenancy" is not used. However, near the beginning of his judgment in *Hounslow LBC v Powell*,[145] Lord Phillips characterises introductory tenancies as having the effect of "putting the tenant on probation, with good behaviour likely to earn the reward of a secure tenancy".[146] This point is reiterated at paragraph 89.[147] It is clear that for Lord Phillips this gives the article 8 review in such cases a different character, the nature of which he describes at paragraphs 90–94.[148]

When deciding whether to dispossess the tenant, the authority cannot simply rely upon the facts that it owns the property and that the tenant has no security of tenure. The decision to dispossess the tenant must be a reasoned decision. Accordingly, under the legislation, notice of the reasons must be given, and the tenant is entitled to seek a review.[149] It is implicit in this scheme that the reasons for terminating the tenancy before it becomes secure will be that, in one way or another, the tenant has proved unsatisfactory. Any attack on the proportionality of dispossession is likely to amount to an attack on the reasons given to the tenant for seeking the possession order. Either the tenant

144 See para 4 (Lord Hope) and para 118 (Lord Phillips).

145 n 12.

146 At para 79; see also the preceding paragraph.

147 "Introductory tenancies place the tenant on probation. They require the tenant to demonstrate that he is a good tenant, both as regards his behaviour towards his neighbours and as regards his contractual obligations to his landlord, before he is granted a tenancy that is secure for life."

148 Part of this passage has already been quoted in Chapter 6, at p 204.

149 As explained in Chapter 6, following the coming into force of certain amendments to s 36 of the 2001 Act, made by the 2014 Act, there is now a corresponding requirement in the Scottish legislation to give reasons for seeking an order, and the right to seek a review.

will argue that the facts relied upon by the authority to justify seeking the order do not do so, or he will contend that those facts were not accurate.

However, Lord Phillips also said that it is only in "very highly exceptional cases" that it will be appropriate for the court to consider a proportionality argument. The authority has a relatively low threshold to cross to justify terminating an introductory tenancy. Secondly, significant procedural safeguards are provided to the tenant, being the requirement to give reasons and the right to seek a review.

The authority can properly require a high standard of behaviour by the tenant during the probationary period. It is not the case that the reason for seeking possession must be behaviour on the part of the tenant that has some adverse impact on a third party.[150] Furthermore, if a tenancy has given rise to complaints by neighbours of antisocial behaviour the authority does not have to be in a position to prove that these are well founded in order to justify terminating the tenancy.[151]

Subsequently, in *Southend-on-Sea BC v Armour*,[152] an introductory tenant succeeded in an argument that, because his behaviour had, for some time, been acceptable, eviction would be disproportionate.[153]

As was explained in Chapter 6,[154] introductory tenancies bear some similarity to antisocial behaviour SSSTs ("ASB SSSTs")[155] under the 2001 Act. In *South Lanarkshire Council v McKenna*,[156] it was argued that the defender's SSST was also probationary in nature, and therefore, the principles set out by Lord Phillips in *Powell* in relation to such tenancies applied. As the local authority had not pled any breach by the defender of any of the tenancy conditions, or suggested that she had failed in her probation, therefore eviction was disproportionate. Sheriff Principal Scott nevertheless granted an order under section 36, having rejected the contention that the tenancy was probationary.

150 See para 93. In other words, it is not only antisocial behaviour that will serve as a reason for the landlord to conclude that the tenant has failed in his probation, but any breach of the tenancy agreement, including, for example, the non-payment of rent. This point is reflected in the new s 36(2)(aa) of the 2001 Act: "proceedings may not be raised unless . . . (aa) in the case of a short Scottish secure tenancy created by virtue of section 35 or paragraph 1, 2 or 2A of schedule 6, the landlord considers that *any obligation of the tenancy* has been broken . . .".

151 Paragraph 93, quoting Waller LJ, was remarked on in *R (McLellan) v Bracknell Forest Borough Council* [2002] QB 1129, para 97: "Under the introductory tenancy scheme it is not a requirement that the council should be satisfied that breaches of the tenancy agreement have in fact taken place. The right question under the scheme will be whether in the context of allegation and counter-allegation it was reasonable for the council to take a decision to proceed with termination of the introductory tenancy."

152 [2014] EWCA Civ 231, [2014] HLR 23.

153 In that case, the tenant suffered from Asperger's syndrome and depression. He had been verbally abusive to a neighbour, and members of the council's staff, in the initial months of the tenancy. However, by the time the case was heard by the court, there had been no further incidents for more than a year, during which time Mr Armour had complied with the terms of his tenancy.

154 At note 18 in Chapter 6.

155 I.e. SSSTs where there has been previous antisocial behaviour, which come into being by virtue of conversion under s 35 or in terms of paras 1, 2 or 2A of sch 6, and which are able to be converted (back) to Scottish secure tenancies, under s 37. Such tenancies, it is suggested, have the effect of "putting the tenant on probation, with good behaviour likely to earn the reward of a secure tenancy."

156 2014 SLT (Sh Ct) 51, 2014 Hous LR 2.

Subsequently, however, in *River Clyde Homes v Woods*,[157] the sheriff decided that it would be disproportionate, under article 8, to grant an order under section 36(5), given that the tenant's behaviour had been without criticism since the beginning of the tenancy.

Both of these cases pre-dated the changes made to the SSST regime by the 2014 Act. Whether one accepts that any form of SSST is correctly characterised as being "probationary" in nature, the amended version of section 36 now requires, as regards ASB SSSTs, that the landlord cannot raise an action under section 36 unless it considers that an obligation of the tenancy has been broken. Further, it must state the reason for which it is seeking recovery of possession, including, if applicable, the obligations that it considers to have been broken. If a local authority were to proceed under section 36 without complying with those requirements, its action could be challenged as unlawful, without needing to rely on article 8.

In *Hounslow v Powell*,[158] Lord Phillips thought that, where the authority had terminated an introductory tenancy, grounds for a proportionality argument would arise only rarely. One reason that he gave was that the authority could require a high standard of behaviour from an introductory tenant, and not only as regards abstaining from antisocial behaviour. However, in introductory tenancies, there is no requirement to provide support for the tenant, to enable him to complete the probation successfully. By contrast, under section 34(7) of the 2001 Act, the landlord "must provide, or ensure the provision of, such housing support services as it considers appropriate with a view to enabling the conversion of the tenancy to a Scottish secure tenancy by virtue of section 37". Accordingly, a question might arise as to whether a failure to comply with an obligation of the tenancy is attributable to a failure to provide adequate support.

Also, Lord Phillips referred to the "significant procedural safeguards" provided to the tenant, being the requirement to give reasons, and the right to seek a review. Those safeguards now exist in section 36 of the 2001 Act, though not in the same form, as regards the right to review. As was explained in Chapter 6,[159] the requirements for a review under section 36(4A)–(4C), and the Guidance thereon, are much less rigorous than their equivalents under the English legislation.

Article 3

Thus far, the discussion has concerned cases in which article 8 is relied upon, in actions by social landlords, in which the twin aims have invariably carried decisive weight.

Different considerations may arise in cases involving the withdrawal of support and accommodation from asylum seekers, who face the prospect of destitution if their accommodation is withdrawn. That may give rise to a defence

157 2015 Hous LR 33: this was effectively a debate on whether the pursuers ought to be granted decree, given the decision in *McKenna*, or whether the sheriff should allow a proof. Sheriff McKay allowed a proof, the outcome of which is reported at 2015 GWD 33-542.

158 n 12.

159 At p 210.

under article 3 of the ECHR.[160] In *Ali v Serco Ltd*,[161] article 3 was invoked, but the court noted[162] that, for conduct to constitute a breach of article 3, it must meet a minimum level of severity, which usually means actual bodily injury or intense physical or mental suffering.[163] The court further observed that "there is available to an asylum seeker who maintains that eviction would breach art.3 or art.8, the remedy of a judicial review challenging the notice to quit intimated by the Secretary of State . . ." It follows that, were proceedings to be raised, seeking the eviction of an asylum seeker, a defence invoking article 3 might be pled.[164]

CASES UNDER THE EQUALITY ACT 2010

Introduction

The author has discussed the impact of the 2010 Act on eviction proceedings in another work,[165] to which readers are referred. The main points of that discussion are summarised here.

Under section 35(1)(b) of the 2010 Act, a person who manages premises must not discriminate against a person who occupies those premises, by evicting him or taking steps for the purposes of securing his eviction. "Discrimination" under the Act takes various forms, such as direct or indirect discrimination, failure to make reasonable adjustments, and so on. These forms of "Prohibited Conduct" are set out in chapter 2 of part 2 (sections 13–27) of the Act. The Act also specifies "protected characteristics"[166] in chapter 1 of part 2, in relation to which the aforementioned forms of discrimination are unlawful, in the various contexts described in the Act.[167]

Accordingly, a case of unlawful discrimination has three elements:

- the protected characteristic, such as race or disability;
- the prohibited conduct, such as direct discrimination; and

160 "No one shall be subjected to torture or to inhuman or degrading treatment or punishment."

161 (n 54) Discussed in Chapter 2, at p 39.

162 At [48].

163 In *Pretty v United Kingdom* (2002) 35 EHRR 1, the ECtHR held, at para [52]: "Where treatment humiliates or debases an individual showing lack of respect for, or diminishing, his or her human dignity, or arouses feelings of fear, anguish or inferiority capable of breaking an individual's moral and physical resistance, it may be characterised as degrading and also fall within the prohibition of Article 3."

164 Although the effect of the decision in *Ali v Serco* (n 54) is that Serco could evict asylum seekers without a court order, it did raise a number of summary cause eviction proceedings at Glasgow Sheriff Court in 2019. It is understood that, in some, defences were lodged that invoked art 3. At the time of writing, those cases have not yet been determined.

165 (n 1) ch 3. This book was the result of a commission by Shelter (Scotland), made possible by funding from the EHRC, for the purpose of raising awareness among advisers and legal practitioners of the relevance of the 2010 Act for housing law cases in Scotland. Copies are free, and may be obtained from Shelter Scotland.

166 At s 4: age, disability, gender reassignment, marriage and civil partnership, pregnancy and maternity, race, religion or belief, sex and sexual orientation. These characteristics are further defined in ss 5–12.

167 Such as "Services and Public Functions" (part 3); "Work" (part 5) and "Education" (part 6). Part 4 concerns "Premises" and, in particular, the disposal and management thereof. "Management", under s 35, includes eviction.

- a provision that makes discrimination unlawful in a particular context.[168] In eviction proceedings, that provision is section 35(1)(b).

Where it can be shown that the defender[169] has a protected characteristic, and that, in taking steps for the purpose of securing a person's eviction, there has been unlawful prohibited conduct on the part of the pursuer, such as direct discrimination, that would give rise to a defence to eviction proceedings, even where there is no other defence.[170]

Whereas public law defences are only applicable to decisions that could be challenged in judicial review,[171] and defences under the Human Rights Act 1998 apply in actions by public authorities, the prohibition in section 35 applies to any person, including private individuals.[172]

Section 25 of the 2010 Act provides a useful list of the various types of unlawful discrimination under the Act, which links the protected characteristics, and the various types of prohibited conduct. Thus, for example, under section 25(8), "sex discrimination" is either direct discrimination under section 13 because of sex, or indirect discrimination under section 19 where the relevant protected characteristic is sex. For most of the protected characteristics, the only two forms of unlawful discrimination are direct and indirect discrimination.

For the protected characteristic of disability, there are two additional forms of prohibited conduct, which establish disability discrimination. Those are: discrimination arising from disability under section 15, and failure to make reasonable adjustments under sections 20 and 21.

Apart from the contention that eviction amounts to unlawful discrimination under section 35, eviction proceedings by public authorities have also been resisted on the basis that the authority has failed to comply with the public sector equality duty ("PSED") under section 149 of the 2010 Act. This issue is discussed at the end of the chapter.

Section 15 of the 2015 Act

It would be possible for a defence under section 35(1)(b) of the 2010 to be based on any one of the protected characteristics, or forms of prohibited conduct. However, in practice, by far the most common type of defence relies on section 15 of the Act, which applies only to the protected characteristic of disability. To understand why this is the case, it may be helpful to consider that section:

168 For readers seeking an introduction to those concepts, the EHRC's publications, particularly the Statutory Code of Practice on Services, Public Functions and Associations, which can be found on the EHRC's website, are strongly recommended, in particular for their explanation of the various forms of prohibited conduct. The Services Code seeks to apply legal concepts in the Act to everyday situations, through the use of hypothetical examples.

169 In this part of the chapter, the terms "pursuer" and "defender" are used for brevity. However, as s 35 applies also to private landlords, the 2010 Act could be invoked in proceedings before the FTT, in which the parties would be the "applicant" and the "respondent".

170 Say, in cases in which there is a mandatory ground for eviction, or no security of tenure. See p 377 and, in particular, the quotation from *Malcolm v Lewisham LBC*, at p 375.

171 And are therefore unlikely to arise in cases taken by private landlords or owners.

172 See p 407 below.

> **"15 Discrimination arising from disability**
> (1) A person (A) discriminates against a disabled person (B) if—
> (a) A treats B unfavourably because of something arising in consequence of B's disability, and
> (b) A cannot show that the treatment is a proportionate means of achieving a legitimate aim.
> (2) Subsection (1) does not apply if A shows that A did not know, and could not reasonably have been expected to know, that B had the disability."

This section does not envisage any comparative test between disabled and non-disabled persons. It refers to B being treated "unfavourably", not "less favourably".[173] Nor does it require the disabled person to show that the treatment puts him at a "disadvantage" in comparison with non-disabled persons.[174] In applying section 15, it is not necessary (and would be wrong) to make some comparison between the treatment of the disabled person and that of a non-disabled person (whether real or hypothetical) in the same circumstances.

The purpose of section 15 is to ensure that treatment that is unfavourable because of "something arising in consequence of" a person's disability may amount to discrimination, even where the reason for the treatment is not the disability itself. It does not require a direct causal link between the treatment and the disability. Instead, section 15 is triggered where the unfavourable treatment is caused by some result, effect or outcome of a disabled person's disability.

It may be helpful to explain this with an example. Let us say that a local authority, L, grants a SSST to T, on the ground that he requires housing support services.[175] T suffers from schizophrenia. During a relapse in his condition, he hears voices in his head, and plays loud music to block them out. He does this at various times of the day and night, which disturbs his neighbours, who complain to L. L decides to terminate the tenancy. In this case, section 15 is likely to be engaged, because there is unfavourable treatment (the termination of the tenancy), because of something arising (the playing of loud music), which is a consequence of T's disability (schizophrenia). It would not avail L to say: there is no discrimination, because we would seek to terminate the tenancy of any tenant who disturbs his neighbours with loud music, whether he is disabled or not.[176] That is because T does not have to show that his treatment is less favourable, but simply that it is unfavourable, and is because of something arising in consequence of his disability. That being so, it will be necessary for L to show that T's eviction is a proportionate means of meeting a legitimate aim.

Given that many eviction cases are raised as a response to some unsatisfactory conduct on the part of the defender, and some defenders suffer from mental health problems or other disabilities, it is not difficult to see why section 15 has played a key role in the case law relating to section 35(1)(b) defences.

173 Treating a person "less favourably" because of a protected characteristic is direct discrimination under s 13.

174 This is one of the requirements for demonstrating indirect discrimination, under s 19.

175 Under s 34 of and sch 6 para 6 to the 2001 Act.

176 This, in essence, was the argument with which the council succeeded, under the old legislation, in *Malcolm v Lewisham Council* (n 33). Section 15 was specifically designed to address the concerns raised by that decision.

Aster Communities Ltd v Akerman-Livingstone[177]

Mr Akerman-Livingstone suffered from a severe stress disorder. He was a disabled person in terms of section 6 of the 2010 Act. He had made an application to Mendip District Council for assistance under the homelessness legislation. Aster, a private registered provider of social housing, had an arrangement with the council, under which it provided temporary accommodation to homeless persons while the council determined their applications. It accommodated Mr Akerman-Livingstone in a flat in Glastonbury. He did not have security of tenure in that accommodation.[178]

Subsequently, the council made offers of permanent accommodation to Mr Akerman-Livingstone, in order to discharge its duties to him under the homelessness legislation. He refused the offers, notwithstanding the fact that the accommodation offered was suitable for him. A psychologist provided the court with a report in which he concluded that the defendant's mental health problems had played a major part in his refusing the offers of accommodation. Therefore, section 15 of the 2010 Act applied: the eviction proceedings were unfavourable treatment, caused by something (the refusal of the offers) arising in consequence of Mr Akerman-Livingstone's disability.

At first instance, the county court judge decided that Mr Akerman-Livingstone's case, relying on sections 15 and 35(1)(b) of the Act, was not seriously arguable. In doing so, he adopted the same approach to the proportionality test in section 15(1)(b) as had been adopted in the article 8 cases described above. The twin aims[179] of the local authority (on whose behalf the accommodation was provided) amounted to a compelling case, against which Mr Akerman-Livingstone's defence under the 2010 Act was not seriously arguable. The case was summarily decided in favour of the claimants. The same approach was taken by the High Court and the Court of Appeal.

However, on Mr Akerman-Livingstone's further appeal, the Supreme Court held that, in a claim for possession against a disabled person, the test as to whether a landlord's treatment of the tenant is a proportionate means of achieving a legitimate aim, for the purposes of section 15(1)(b), is significantly different from the test of whether it is proportionate to make a possession order for the purposes of article 8 of ECHR. When a defence under section 15 is raised to a claim for possession by a social landlord, the question is not simply whether the landlord is entitled to recover the property in order to fulfil its public housing functions; it is also whether the landlord has done all that can be reasonably be expected of it to accommodate the consequences of the disabled person's disability, and whether vindication of the landlord's property rights and its need to allocate and manage its housing stock are sufficient to outweigh the effect on the disabled person.[180]

177 n 47.

178 He therefore had a contractual tenancy with no statutory protection. That would also have been the case in Scotland. Accommodation provided on an interim basis, pending the determination of a homeless application, is excepted from Scottish secure tenancy status under para 5 of sch 1 to the 2001 Act (see Chapter 4, p 84). Similar exceptions are made by para 11A of sch 4 to the 1988 Act, and para 16 of sch 1 to the 2016 Act.

179 "Twin aims": see p 389.

180 However, the appeal was unsuccessful, because the court also held that there was no point in

Accordingly, whereas, in *Powell*,[181] the Supreme Court rejected the "structured approach" to the proportionality test in article 8 cases,[182] it accepted the applicability of such a test in section 15 cases. Baroness Hale said:

> "No landlord is allowed to evict a disabled tenant because of something arising in consequence of the disability, unless he can show eviction to be a proportionate means of achieving a legitimate aim. He is thus obliged to be more considerate towards a disabled tenant than he is towards a non-disabled one. The structured approach to proportionality asks whether there is any lesser measure which might achieve the landlord's aims. It also requires a balance to be struck between the seriousness of the impact on the tenant and the importance of the landlord's aims. People with disabilities are entitled to have due allowance made for the consequences of their disability . . . It certainly cannot be taken for granted that the first of the twin aims will almost invariably trump that right. Even where social housing is involved, the general considerations involved in the second of the twin aims may on occasions have to give way to the equality rights of the occupier and in particular to the equality rights of a particular disabled person. The impact of being required to move from this particular place on this particular disabled person may be such that it is not outweighed by the benefits to the local authority or social landlord of being able to regain possession."[183]

"Less intrusive measure"

Of the four questions entailed in the structured proportionality test, the third question is often the most important in practice: is eviction no more than is necessary to achieve the landlord's aim? This entails asking: could a less intrusive measure be used without unacceptably compromising the achievement of that aim?

In *Birmingham City Council v Stephenson*,[184] the court said that since the burden was on the council to show that no less drastic action would be appropriate, it was incumbent on it to at least show that alternatives had been considered and that there were reasons for its rejection. The flaw in the approach of the council was to treat the question of proportionality as a binary choice between eviction, on the one hand, and doing nothing on the other hand. It may well be that intermediate steps could have been taken, short of evicting

remitting the claim back to the county court. In the circumstances that by that time existed, a judge would inevitably conclude that evicting the defendant would strike a fair balance between the landlord's need to accomplish its objectives and the disadvantages thereby caused to the defendant. The appeal was therefore refused.

181 n 12.

182 The "structured approach" is set out at p 392 above.

183 Paragraph [31]. At [25] she said: "Parliament has . . . expressly provided, in sections 15 and 35, for disabled people to have rights in respect of the accommodation which they occupy which are different from and extra to the rights of non-disabled people. Landlords may be required to accommodate, or to continue to accommodate, a disabled person when they would not be required to accommodate, or continue to accommodate, a non-disabled person."

184 [2016] EWCA Civ 1029, [2016] HLR 44. Mr Stephenson had an introductory tenancy under the English legislation. He had a history of mental health problems.

the tenant.[185] By contrast, in *TM v Metropolitan Housing Trust*,[186] the court accepted the landlords' argument that there was no reasonable alternative to eviction.

Other issues in section 15 cases

It is important that a party seeking to advance a disability discrimination defence makes clear the nature of the impairment that is the basis for the defence. That will virtually always require expert medical evidence.[187] That evidence should confirm:

- the nature and degree of the impairment;
- whether that impairment has a substantial and long-term adverse effect on the ability of the individual to carry out normal day-to-day activities;[188]
- that there is "something arising" from that disability, being some result, effect or outcome, which is said to have caused the landlord to take the steps for the purposes of securing his eviction, under section 35(1)(b).

In the case of eviction proceedings on some statutory ground, the "something arising" will be the circumstances that underlie the ground, such as non-payment of rent, breach of tenancy conditions or antisocial behaviour. Alternatively, the landlord's reason for seeking possession may be apparent from its communications with the tenant. In other cases, the court or tribunal may be asked to conclude, under the "Burden of Proof" rule in section 136(2) of the 2010 Act, that there are facts from which it could decide, in the absence of any other explanation, that the landlord has contravened section 15.

The question of whether the unfavourable treatment, being the steps taken by the landlord to secure the tenant's eviction, is because of some result, effect or outcome of the disability will be a matter for the court or tribunal to decide.[189] The "something arising" need not be the sole cause of the decision to seek the disabled person's eviction. Discrimination may be made out if it is "a cause, the activating cause, a substantial and effective cause, a substantial reason, and important factor".[190]

185 At para 22 (Lewison LJ). For example, the tenant could be given support from social services in reminding him of appointments that have been made for him to receive medication. He might be given support from mental health professionals. His medication could be changed or its dosage increased. Sound attenuation measures could be installed in his flat. There could be specific agreement on permitted hours for the playing of music rather than the general prohibition on antisocial behaviour contained in the tenancy conditions. The council might seek an injunction prohibiting the antisocial behaviour under the Anti-social Behaviour, Crime and Policing Act 2014, which would require supervised compliance. Or the council might provide him with more suitable alternative accommodation.

186 n 65. See, in particular, [57]–[60].

187 *McNicol v Balfour Beatty Rail Maintenance Ltd* [2002] EWCA Civ 1074, [2002] ICR 1498, para 16. See also: *Swan Housing Association Ltd v Gill* [2013] EWCA Civ 1566, [2014] HLR 18, in which the court held that, in the absence of medical evidence, the "mere likelihood" that the defendant suffered from a disability was insufficient to establish the existence of the protected characteristic.

188 These first two requirements arise from the definition of "disability" under s 6 of the Act.

189 Though this may be uncontroversial, particularly in antisocial behaviour cases.

190 *Nagarajan v London Regional Transport* [1999] UKHL 36, [2000] 1 AC 501, 513 (Lord Nicholls).

If the requisite evidence is available, the defender may argue that: (a) eviction would be contrary to sections 15 and 35 of the Act; (b) it is incumbent on the landlord to specify what alternatives to eviction have been considered, and to give reasons for their rejection.

In such a case, the provision of alternative accommodation, perhaps with support for the defender, is a key alternative. That is particularly so if the defender is a tenant occupying under a Scottish secure tenancy, whose eviction is sought under the antisocial behaviour ground (ground 7) of schedule 2 to the 2001 Act. In that case, the landlord could have raised proceedings under ground 8 of schedule 2, which applies where, as a result of antisocial behaviour, the landlord considers that it is appropriate in the circumstances to require the tenant to move to other accommodation.[191] To that end, an expert witness might be asked to say whether the provision of support in another tenancy could assist in addressing the behaviour, and to specify the nature of that support.

Knowledge of the disability

One of the issues that was not explored in *Akerman-Livingstone*[192] was the defence under section 15(2), which applies where "A shows that A did not know, and could not reasonably have been expected to know, that B had the disability". It is suggested that there is a particular difficulty in applying this defence to eviction proceedings.

Section 35(1)(b) makes it unlawful for A to discriminate against B "by evicting B *(or taking steps for the purpose of securing B's eviction)* . . .". By this wording, the legislature has explicitly recognised that eviction is not a single event, but is an action preceded by a process. That process will typically entail the service of a notice under statute and/or at common law, the raising of proceedings, the prosecution of those proceedings, and the enforcement of the order, if necessary by officers of the court. It is suggested that all these steps may be regarded as unfavourable treatment for the purposes of section 15(1)(a), for, as Lord Wilson said in *Akerman-Livingstone*:

> "In that the claimant is taking steps for the purpose of securing [the defendant's] eviction from the flat in Glastonbury, it is treating him unfavourably within the meaning of section 15 (1)(a) of [the] Act."[193]

That being so, it is difficult to see how the defence under section 15(2) could apply in an eviction action. Once the proceedings are defended, on the basis that eviction would be contrary to section 15(1), the landlord has knowledge of the disability, as regards any further steps taken for the purpose of securing the defender's eviction, and as regards the eviction itself. If that is correct, and if section 15(1)(a) is established, justification by the proportionality test is the only option.

191 The possibility of alternative accommodation is also referred to in Lord Neuberger's judgment in *Akerman-Livingstone* (n 47) at [56].

192 ibid.

193 ibid [67]. Later in the same paragraph he said: "One may therefore confidently conclude that, at any full trial, the only issue would be whether the claimant can show that the steps *which it is taking* for the purpose of securing the defendant's eviction are a proportionate means of achieving a legitimate aim within the meaning of section 15 (1)(b) of that Act."

Other forms of prohibited conduct

Where it can be shown that, in taking steps for the purpose of securing a person's eviction, the landlord or owner has treated that person less favourably, because of a protected characteristic, this would amount to direct discrimination,[194] and would afford a defence to eviction proceedings. In contrast to indirect discrimination, and discrimination arising from disability, direct discrimination cannot be justified on the basis that it is proportionate.

Where, in relation to the eviction, the landlord or owner has applied to the occupier a provision, criterion or practice that puts persons with whom the occupier shares a protected characteristic at a particular disadvantage, that may found a defence based on indirect discrimination.[195] For example, if a landlord required all tenants in rent arrears to complete a statement showing full details of their financial circumstances before it would entertain an offer of payment, this practice may well discriminate against a tenant who was unable to provide such a statement without assistance, because of a learning disability.[196]

The duty to make reasonable adjustments for disabled persons in relation to "premises", under section 36 of and schedule 4 to the Act, may have relevance in eviction proceedings. In *Defending Possession Proceedings*,[197] the authors point out that the "reasonable adjustments" duty may have a particular bearing on proceedings on the ground of rent arrears, or other cases in which it is argued that steps ought to have been taken (in the past) by the landlord to support or assist the tenant in complying with his duties under the tenancy. It may also found an argument that (now, or in the future) the landlord could address an issue by making a reasonable adjustment, rather than seeking an eviction order. Reasonable adjustments could include: facilitating a care assessment; consulting or seeking support from other specialist agencies; or offering an antisocial behaviour contract. It is not necessary for the disabled person to show that the adjustment would definitely eliminate the disadvantage: it is enough that there is some prospect of removing it.[198]

In rent arrears cases taken by social landlords, the tenant might request an adjustment[199] by the landlord in the way that it carries out the pre-action requirements for rent arrears cases, under section 14A of the Housing (Scotland) Act 2001.[200] It is suggested that these requirements describe ben-

194 Under s 13 of the 2010 Act.

195 Under s 19 of the Act. In that case, the landlord or owner might have to show that the eviction was justified under s 19(1)(d), by reference to the "proportionality" test.

196 This example is taken from Luba and others (n 1) para 27.10.

197 Ibid ch 27 ("Disability Discrimination Defences") discusses many of the same issues as are raised here. Paragraphs 27.43–27.53 consider the duty to make reasonable adjustments in relation to premises, and its relevance to eviction proceedings.

198 Ibid para 27.51.

199 Under s 35 and sch 4 para 2(6), the duty to make reasonable adjustments in relation to premises applies only if the landlord receives a request from or on behalf of the tenant or a person entitled to occupy the premises.

200 As supplemented by the Scottish Secure Tenancies (Proceedings for Possession) (Pre-Action Requirements) Order 2012 (SSI 2012/127) (commonly referred to as "the PAR Order") and the Housing (Scotland) Act 2001 and 2010 Guidance for Social Landlords on Pre-Action Requirements and Seeking Repossession of Social Housing ("the PAR Guidance") issued in June 2012. See Chapter 4.

efits or facilities that the tenant is entitled to receive.[201] That being so, once the duty to make reasonable adjustments is engaged by a request, it is not discharged until the disabled person is no longer at a substantial disadvantage in relation to the use of those benefits or facilities. This could involve, for example, adjusting the landlord's usual practice with regard to meeting the pre-action requirements by providing personal contact or home visits, for persons unable to understand written materials due to a learning disability.[202]

Where there has been a failure to comply with the duty to make reasonable adjustments, that may give rise to the conclusion that it would not be reasonable to grant the order, in the case of eviction proceedings on a discretionary ground. Alternatively, it may also be relevant to the question of proportionality under section 15 or section 19: where an issue could be addressed by a reasonable adjustment, eviction is unlikely to be proportionate.

Private landlords

At the time of writing there have been no reported cases that address the implications of *Akerman-Livingstone*[203] for eviction proceedings raised by private landlords. However, in that case the Supreme Court specifically placed importance on the fact that section 35 of the Act applies to both public and private landlords.[204] Therefore, eviction proceedings in the First-tier Tribunal[205] may be met by a response arguing that it would be unlawful to grant an order under section 35(1)(b), combined with, say, direct discrimination, indirect discrimination or discrimination arising from disability.

It remains to be seen how Equality Act defences would play out in the context of evictions by a private landlord. It is suggested that the application of a proportionality test may raise different issues: the measures envisaged as alternatives to eviction in *Stephenson*[206] may be less feasible for a private landlord with limited means. However, some private landlords have considerable resources, and substantial portfolios of accommodation. In any case, in the application of the proportionality test, it is suggested that the landlord will still

201 Such that the carrying out of pre-action requirements is a "relevant matter" for the purposes of the first and third requirements of s 20 of the 2010 Act, given the terms of sch 4 para 2(5) (b.

202 Neither the PAR Order nor the PAR Guidance (n 200) makes reference to the 2010 Act, or any duty to make reasonable adjustments. However, as to what amounts to "reasonable efforts" under s 14A of the 2001 Act, paras 34–35 of the Guidance state: "Landlords should take account of tenants' preferences on how they wish landlords to contact them. Landlords should consider a range of methods and not rely on a single approach . . . Where landlords know that tenants have support needs they should also consider those needs when preparing for giving help and advice, taking into account the tenant's health and social care needs. If landlords are aware that tenants have difficulty in reading or understanding information, landlords should take reasonable steps to make sure that they have appropriately communicated the information in ways that tenants can understand."

203 n 47.

204 ibid [24]: this was one of reasons for distinguishing between Equality Act defences, and those relying upon art 8 of the ECHR, which applies only to public authorities.

205 Discussed in Chapter 14. Where a private owner or landlord raises eviction proceedings where the occupation does not arise from any form of statutory tenancy, the sheriff court still has jurisdiction.

206 n 184, discussed at p 403.

require to say what alternatives to eviction have been considered, and to give reasons for their rejection, irrespective of his resources.

Counterclaims for damages

In *Defending Possession Proceedings*,[207] the authors suggest that, in eviction proceedings defended under the 2010 Act, the tenant or occupier may counterclaim for damages. Damages may include compensation for injured feelings.[208] However, the sheriff must not make an award of damages unless she first considers whether to make any other disposal.[209] In eviction proceedings, the court may consider that the rights under the Act have been sufficiently enforced by a finding of unlawful discrimination, and the dismissal of the action. As the sheriff court has jurisdiction to hear claims in relation to a contravention of part 4 of the Act,[210] it seems doubtful that such a counterclaim could be made in eviction proceedings raised by a private landlord in the FTT. Compensation would have to be sought in separate proceedings in the sheriff court.

Social landlords and the public sector equality duty

The PSED is set out in section 149 of the 2010 Act.[211] The PSED applies to local authorities.[212] It is suggested that it also applies to RSLs in Scotland. Section 149(2) provides that a person who is not a public authority but who exercises "public functions" is subject to the PSED in the exercise of those functions.[213] RSLs exercise the public function of providing housing services.[214] They are now subject to the same statutory code in relation to their tenancies, and the selection of tenants, as local authorities (under the Housing (Scotland) Act 2001) and the same regulatory regime as "social landlords" (under the Housing (Scotland) Act 2010).[215]

207 Luba and others (n 1) paras 27.19 and 27.38.
208 Under s 119(4) of the 2010 Act.
209 Section 119(6).
210 Section 114(1)(b), though judicial review proceedings may also be raised in respect of a contravention of the 2010 Act, under s 113(3).
211 The EHRC has published extensive guidance on the PSED, which is available on its website, including, in particular: "Essential Guide to the Public Sector Equality Duty: a Guide for Public Authorities (Scotland)" (July 2016); and "Technical guidance on the Public Sector Equality Duty: Scotland" (September 2016). The author has described the PSED, and its application, in particular to homelessness cases, in Stalker (n 1) ch 5.
212 Under s 150, a "public authority" is a person specified in sch 19, pt 1 of which lists public authorities generally, and pt 3 of which specifies relevant Scottish authorities. A council constituted under s 2 of the Local Government etc. (Scotland) Act 1994 is a public authority.
213 Note, however, that there is an important difference between public authorities and persons exercising public functions. Under s 153, additional specific duties may be imposed on public authorities listed by regulations. In Scotland, this has been done by the Equality Act 2010 (Specific Duties) (Scotland) Regulations 2012 (SSI 2012/162), as amended. Particularly notable is reg 5, which imposes a duty to assess the impact of applying a proposed new or revised policy or practice against the needs in s 149(1) of the Act.
214 Section 165 of the Housing (Scotland) Act 2010 defines a "social landlord" as "a registered social landlord, local authority landlord or a local authority which provides housing services".
215 In terms of s 150(5) of the 2010 Act, a "public function" is "a function of a public nature for the purposes of the Human Rights Act 1998". Note that the same provision is made in s 31(4) as regards the definition of "public function" for the purposes of pt 3. Following the

The PSED applies not only to the formulation of policies, but to the exercise of housing functions in individual cases.[216] It requires the social landlord to have due regard to the potentially discriminatory effect of policies or decisions. It specifically requires the social landlord to take account of a disabled person's disabilities, which may involve treating some people more favourably than others.[217] The decision maker must "focus very sharply" on the section 149 criteria. Each stage of a decision-making exercise must be made with the equality duty well in mind.[218]

It is for the decision maker to decide what weight to give to the matters set out in section 149.[219]

The court must be satisfied that there has been a proper consideration of the duty. Normally this would have to be demonstrated in the social landlord's written decisions, or its own records. However, the courts have apprehended a danger that analysing decisions to check for compliance with the PSED "can lead to no more than formulaic and high-minded mantras". Irrespective of the words used, the court has to be satisfied that the equality duty has been exercised in substance, with rigour and with an open mind.[220]

The decision in *London and Quadrant Housing Trust v Patrick*[221] provides a useful summary of the principles applicable to the PSED in eviction cases. When a public-sector landlord is contemplating taking or enforcing possession proceedings affecting a disabled person, it is subject to the PSED. The duty is to have due regard to the need to achieve the results identified in section 149. The landlord has to weigh the factors relevant to promoting the objects of the section against any material countervailing factors. In housing cases, the countervailing factors included the impact of the disabled person's behaviour on others. The landlord is not required in every case to take active steps to inquire into whether the tenant is relevantly disabled. However, where the available information raises a real possibility that that might be the case, a duty to make further enquiries arises.

The duty has to be exercised in substance, with rigour and an open mind, and should not be reduced to a "tick-box" exercise. The duty is a continuing one and is not discharged at any particular stage of the decision-making process. The landlord has to assess the risk and extent of any adverse impact, and the ways in which such risk could be eliminated before seeking and enforcing possession, and not merely as a rear-guard action following a decision. However, the duty to have "due regard" only takes on any substance when the disability is or ought to have been apparent. In such cases, the lateness of the knowledge might impact on the discharge of the duty, and could justify a

decision of the Court of Appeal in *R (Weaver) v London & Quadrant Housing Trust* [2009] EWCA Civ 587, [2010] 1 WLR 363, RSLs in England are invariably regarded as exercising public functions, even in cases concerning particular contractual obligations to tenants (see: *R (McIntyre) v Gentoo Group Ltd* (n 5)).

216 *Pieretti v Enfield LBC* [2011] HLR 3.

217 Section 149(4) and (6).

218 *Hotak v Southwark LBC* [2016] AC 811.

219 This follows from the wording of s 149(1): the duty is to have "due regard" to certain matters, but not to achieve any specified result. This point was discussed and emphasised in the Court of Appeal's decision in *Poshteh v Kensington & Chelsea RLBC* [2015] EWCA Civ 711, [2015] HLR 36. See, in particular, paras 34–41 (McCombe LJ).

220 *Hotak* (n 218), [75].

221 [2020] HLR 3, a decision of Turner J, in the High Court, at para [42].

less formal assessment than would otherwise have been appropriate. Thus, a tenant whose antisocial conduct had adversely affected neighbours for a considerable time, but whose disability was raised at the eleventh hour, might find that the discharge of the duty did not necessarily mandate a postponement of the date or enforcement of a possession order.

In *Forward v Aldwyck Housing Group Ltd*,[222] the landlord accepted that its consideration of the PSED was inadequate, because the officer conducting the assessment had not obtained any medical evidence about the defendant's physical disability and had not performed the assessment with an open mind. However, the Court of Appeal held that where an authority has failed to comply with the PSED, it does not follow that any decision taken after such a breach must necessarily be set aside.[223] In deciding the consequence of the breach, the court should look closely at the facts of the case and, if it is highly likely that the authority's decision would not have been substantially different if the breach had not occurred, there will be no need to quash the decision. In the instant case, compliance with the PSED would have made no difference to the result of the claim.[224]

222 [2020] 1 WLR 584, [2019] HLR 47.

223 Note, however, that is not the case with a breach of s 35(1)(b), which would amount to unlawful discrimination. In that case, dismissal of the action is appropriate. See the quotation from *Malcolm v Lewisham Council* (n 33), at p 375.

224 The same conclusion was reached in *TM v Metropolitan Housing Trust* (n 65).

Chapter 12

Other Occupiers

This chapter discusses the rights of various classes of occupier, apart from tenants:

(1) sub-tenants;
(2) putative successors to tenancies under the 1988, 2001 and 2016 Acts;
(3) non-entitled spouses under the Matrimonial Homes (Family Protection) (Scotland) Act 1981;
(4) qualifying occupiers under the 2001 Act;
(5) occupiers under contracts that are not tenancies, such as occupancy agreements, licences, service occupancies (tied tenancies) and tenancies where services are rendered in lieu of rent;
(6) hostel dwellers.

SUB-TENANTS

Consideration is given here to the position of sub-tenants of Scottish secure tenants, assured tenants, private residential tenants and tenants at common law.

In all cases, there is a relationship between three parties: the landlord, the tenant and the sub-tenant. In practice, the question that usually arises is what rights, if any, are available to the sub-tenant against the landlord once the head tenancy has ended.

It is important to make a distinction between the rights of the parties under a contract, and the rights granted by statute, in particular those associated with security of tenure.

Sub-tenancies at common law

A tenant may sub-let with the consent of the landlord. Without such consent, he may sub-let only as far as he has the power to do so in his lease. Many leases contain express terms prohibiting sub-letting. However, in Scots law, exclusion of sub-letting is implied in most leases in any event. Unauthorised sub-letting is a breach of contract, which may enable the landlord to terminate the lease.[1] Where sub-letting is excluded, either expressly or by implication, the landlord's right to object to a sub-let may be renounced expressly or by

1 Where a lease prohibits sub-letting, one would expect that the irritancy clause would provide that a breach of that prohibition would entitle the landlord to terminate.

acquiescence.[2] On the basis of these rules, a sub-let will thus be either lawful (permitted by the lease or where the landlord has consented) or unlawful.

The lawful sub-tenant has rights against the head tenant under his tenancy contract, including the right to remain in occupation until the termination of the lease. However, the termination of the head tenant's contract also terminates the rights of the sub-tenant. If the effect of that termination is that the sub-tenant is forced to leave before the end of the contractual period of his sub-tenancy, he may have an action in damages against the head tenant. The unlawful sub-tenant's position is less secure, because his sub-tenancy might have to be terminated along with the head tenancy if the landlord learns of the unauthorised sub-let and decides to terminate the head lease.

As regards protection from unlawful eviction, both lawful and unlawful sub-tenants cannot be evicted by the landlord or the head tenant without a court order, either during the course of the sub-tenancy or after it has come to an end. However, where the landlord raises an action for recovery of possession against the head tenant, any decree that he obtains is also enforceable against the sub-tenant; he is not required to raise separate proceedings against the sub-tenant.[3]

Sub-tenants under the 2001 Act

Sub-letting and assignation of Scottish secure tenancies are subject to rules set out in section 32 of the 2001 Act.[4] These were amended by section 12 of the 2014 Act, with effect from 1 November 2019.[5] The effect of the amendments is to make sub-letting and assignation more difficult.[6]

Section 32 of the 2001 Act, as amended, provides:

2 This is a very brief summary of the common law rules in relation to sub-letting. For a full exposition, readers are referred to the standard works, such as Paton and Cameron, *Landlord and Tenant* ch X; *Stair Memorial Encyclopaedia of the Laws of Scotland* vol 13; and Rennie and others, *Leases* (SULI 2015) ch 18.

3 Bankruptcy and Diligence (Scotland) Act 2007, s 216(2), discussed in Chapter 15. There is no conflict between this provision and s 23 of the 1984 Act (discussed in Chapter 2); s 23(1) provides that the landlord cannot recover possession otherwise than by proceedings in court, but it does stipulate that those proceedings must be against the occupier.

4 Note that, at least in theory, a short Scottish secure tenancy (an "SSST") could also be sub-let or assigned, because, under s 34(6) of the 2001 Act (discussed in Chapter 6, p 199), s 32 applies to SSSTs. However, given the reasons for which SSSTs are created, it seems unlikely in practice that the landlord would agree to an assignation or a sub-let.

5 By virtue of the Housing (Scotland) Act 2014 (Commencement No 8, Savings, Transitional and Supplemental Provisions) Order 2018 (SSI 2018/153). In this edition of this work, the provisions as amended are discussed. See the previous edition for the 2001 Act provisions as originally enacted. Note also that the Scottish Government has issued Guidance entitled: "Scottish Secure Tenancies and Short Scottish Secure Tenancies – Assignation, Subletting, Joint Tenancies and Succession: Guidance for Social Landlords" ("the Guidance")

6 In particular, by changing the qualifying period of residence from six months in s 32(1)(b) to twelve months; applying that requirement to both the tenant and the assignee; and introducing the requirement in relation to sub-letting that is now in s 32(1)(c). Subsections (1)(b) and (c) are made subject to further requirements under the new subsections (1A) and (1B), to which readers are referred.

"**Assignation, subletting etc**

(1) It is a term of every Scottish secure tenancy that the tenant may assign, sublet or otherwise give up to another person possession of the house or any part of it or take in a lodger—

(a) only with the consent in writing of the landlord

(b) in the case of an assignation, only where the house has been the tenant's and the assignee's only or principal home throughout the period of 12 months ending with the date of the application for the landlord's consent to the assignation under paragraph 9 of schedule 5, and

(c) in the case of a sublet, only where the house has been the tenant's only or principal home throughout the period of 12 months ending with the date of the application for the landlord's consent to the sublet under paragraph 9 of schedule 5.

. . .[7]

(7) An assignation, subletting or other transaction to which this section applies is not—

(a) a protected tenancy or a statutory tenancy within the meaning of the Rent (Scotland) Act 1984 (c.58), or

(b) an assured tenancy or

(c) a private residential tenancy,

. . .

(8) In this section and schedule 5, 'sub-tenant' means a person entitled to possession of a house or any part of a house under an assignation, subletting or other transaction to which this section applies, and includes a lodger."

Because of section 32(7), a sub-let by a Scottish secure tenant cannot be a tenancy under the 1984, 1988 or 2016 Acts. It also cannot be a Scottish secure tenancy, because the landlord in respect of a sub-tenancy, being the head tenant, will not be one of the bodies specified in section 11(1)(b) of the Act.

On that basis, the position of a sub-tenant of a Scottish secure tenancy is the same as that of a sub-tenant of a common law tenancy, in that termination of the head tenancy under section 12 of the Act also terminates any sub-tenancy. However, that is subject to the following points:

(1) Written consent is required for a sub-let. Most landlords under the 2001 Act provide standard application forms for this purpose. The application can be made only if the requirement in subsection (1)(c) is met.[8] The landlord must intimate its consent or refusal and, in the case of refusal, the reasons for the refusal, to the tenant in writing within one month of receipt of the application. If it fails to do so, it is taken to have consented to the application.[9] Apart from under these rules, acquiescence or implied consent to sub-lets is not possible under the 2001 Act.

7 Subsections (2)–(6) and (9) of s 32, and part 2 of sch 5, set out the rules in terms of which the landlord may consent or refuse to consent to a sub-let.

8 That requirement is subject to subsection (1B): "For the purposes of a sublet mentioned in subsection (1)(c), a period may be considered in relation to a tenant only if— (a) the tenant was the tenant of the house throughout that period, or (b) at any time before that period began, the landlord was notified by— (i) the tenant, or (ii) any other person who was the tenant of the house in question when the notice was given, that the house in question was the tenant's only or principal home". Subsections (1)(c) and (1A) were added by the 2014 Act, as part of a series of amendments that make it more difficult for SSSTs to be sub-let and assigned, and also impose limitations on the right to succeed, as indicated below.

9 Schedule 5 paras 9, 12 and 13.

(2) Given the terms of section 32(1), an unauthorised sub-let is a breach of the terms of the Scottish secure tenancy. The landlord may accordingly seek recovery of possession under ground 1 of schedule 2 to the Act. If the head tenant no longer occupies the subjects as his only or principal home, that is also a breach of the tenancy, under section 11(7).[10] It may also be possible for recovery of possession to be sought on ground 5 (tenant has ceased to occupy).

(3) In practice, where landlords under the 2001 Act allow sub-tenancies, it is often for a specified period. If that period expires, and the tenant does not return to the property, possession may be sought on ground 5.[11]

(4) Where the sub-tenancy has been granted with the tenant's consent, the sub-tenant is a qualifying occupier under sections 14 and 15 of the Act. Qualifying occupiers are considered below.

Sub-tenants under the 1988 Act

The position under the 1988 Act is more complex. Under section 55, the definition of "tenancy" includes "sub-tenancy". So, if a sub-tenancy meets the requirements of section 12 of the 1988 Act, it will also be an assured tenancy.[12] In that case, the sub-tenant and the tenant will have the rights and obligations applicable to a landlord and a tenant under part II of the 1988 Act. In particular, the security of tenure provisions in section 16 of the Act, especially section 16(2), will apply between the sub-tenant and the tenant, as they would apply between a landlord and a tenant. Accordingly, if the tenant wanted to evict the sub-tenant, he would have to make an application to the FTT based on one of the grounds under the legislation. If the tenant had served an AT5 notice on the sub-tenant, and the sub-tenancy was for a period of six months or more, the sub-tenancy would be a short assured tenancy and, therefore, the tenant could make an application under section 33 of the Act.

The 1988 Act contains three sections that address different aspects of sub-tenanting.

> "**23 Limited prohibition on assignation etc without consent**
>
> (1) Subject to subsection (2) below, it shall be an implied term of every assured tenancy that, except with the consent of the landlord, the tenant shall not—
> (a) assign the tenancy (in whole or in part); or
> (b) sublet or part with possession of the whole or any part of the house let on the tenancy.
>
> (2) Subsection (1) above does not apply if, under the terms of the tenancy, there is provision prohibiting or permitting (whether absolutely or conditionally) assignation, subletting or parting with possession by the tenant."

10 Note, however, that, by s 11(8), the tenancy does not cease to be a Scottish secure tenancy by virtue of the tenant's failure to occupy.

11 In *East Lothian Council v Duffy* 2012 SLT (Sh Ct) 113, 2012 Hous LR 73, the sub-let had been permitted by the council for a period of one year. After that period expired, the tenants decided not to return. The sub-tenants remained in occupation and desired, against the landlords' wishes, to become the principal tenants. In due course the landlords raised an action under ground 5, which was defended by the sub-tenants (as qualifying occupiers). The action was successful.

12 Subject to the exception set out in s 32(7) of the 2001 Act (see above): a sub-let of a Scottish secure tenancy cannot be an assured tenancy.

As with Scottish secure tenancies, an unauthorised sub-let is a breach of contract, which may found eviction proceedings under ground 13 of schedule 5. However, if the head tenant no longer occupies the subjects as his only or principal home, it may be possible for the landlord simply to terminate the tenancy on the basis of that breach of contract, and to raise proceedings on the footing that there is no longer any assured tenancy.[13] The Act does not make any further provision in relation to consent. In contrast to the position in relation to secure tenancies, there is no requirement that consent be given in writing.

> **"15 Certain sublettings not to exclude any part of sub-lessor's premises from assured tenancy**
>
> (1) Where the tenant of a house has sublet a part but not the whole of the house, then, as against his landlord or any superior landlord, no part of the house shall be treated as excluded from being a house let on an assured tenancy by reason only that the terms on which any person claiming under the tenant holds any part of the house include the use of accommodation in common with other persons.
>
> (2) Nothing in this section affects the rights against, and liabilities to, each other of the tenant and any person claiming under him, or of any two such persons."

The effect of this provision is that a tenant's sharing living accommodation with his sub-tenants does not remove the protection of the Act. Where part of the property is sub-let, this does not remove it from the assured tenancy regime.

> **"28 Effect of termination of tenancy on sub-tenancies which are or are under assured tenancies**
>
> (1) If the First-tier Tribunal makes an order for possession of a house from a tenant nothing in the order shall affect the right of any sub-tenant to whom the house or any part of it has been lawfully sublet on an assured tenancy before the commencement of the proceedings to retain possession by virtue of this Part of this Act, nor shall the order operate to give a right to possession as against any such sub-let.
>
> (2) Where an assured tenancy of a house is terminated, either as a result of an order for possession or for any other reason, any sub-tenant to whom the house or any part of it has been lawfully sublet shall, subject to the provisions of this Act, be deemed to become the tenant of the landlord on the same terms as he would have held from the tenant if the tenant's assured tenancy had continued.
>
> (3) A tenancy which, but for paragraph 2 of Schedule 4 to this Act, would have been an assured tenancy shall be treated for the purposes of subsection (2) above as an assured tenancy."[14]

It is not easy to make sense of this provision. It is perhaps best to begin by imagining a situation in which the assured tenant of the subjects lawfully sublets, and the sub-let is also an assured tenancy, the conditions under section 12 of the Act being met. In that case, on termination of the head tenancy, the sub-tenant becomes, according to section 28(2), the assured tenant of the landlord on the same terms as he held from the tenant. Section 28(1) then seems to follow as a logical consequence: if the landlord obtains an order for possession against the head tenant, that does not affect the sub-tenant's rights

13 This point is considered in Chapter 7, in the discussion of the 1988 Act, s 16.

14 Schedule 4 para 2 is the exception in respect of tenancies at a low rent.

under the Act. In short, if both the head tenancy and the sub-tenancy are assured tenancies, the effect of section 28 is clear.

The problem is that neither subsection expressly stipulates, as a precondition for its operation, that both the head tenancy and the sub-tenancy are assured tenancies. Section 28(1) requires that the sub-tenancy is an assured tenancy, whereas section 28(2) requires that the head tenancy is an assured tenancy.

Let us say that a landlord let a flat to a limited company, which the company then sub-let to an individual. The let to the company (the head lease) could not have been an assured tenancy because, under section 12, the company was not an individual occupying the house as his only or principal home. However, any sub-let to an individual by the company could have been an assured tenancy, provided that it complied with the requirements of section 12. The landlord terminates the head tenancy. At this point, section 28(2) does not operate, because the head tenancy is not an assured tenancy. However, it might be argued that section 28(1) does operate if the landlord obtains an order for possession against the head tenant. If that were correct, however, it would mean that an assured sub-tenant's right to retain possession would persist by virtue of an order for possession being made against the head tenant, whereas the same sub-tenant would have no tenancy if proceedings were not raised against the head tenant. That seems absurd and, for that reason, it is suggested that section 28(1) must be for the protection of the category of assured sub-tenants described in section 28(2) (being cases in which the head lease is also an assured tenancy).[15]

Sub-tenants of assured tenancies under the tribunal's rules

There is no specific reference to sub-tenants in the Procedure Rules.[16] However, as is explained in Chapter 7,[17] the term "tenant" in part 6 of chapter 3 of the rules includes a sub-tenant.[18] Accordingly, under rules 9 and 71, the sub-tenant is one of the parties to whom notice of acceptance of an application must be given. Given the terms of rule 9, the sub-tenant would then be able to make written representations, perhaps for the purposes of asking the tribunal to make a determination as to the effect of termination of the head-tenancy, in light of section 28 of the 1988 Act.

15 If the sub-tenant were to have a right to "retain possession" under s 28(1), in a case to which s 28(2) was not applicable, the respective positions of the landlord and the sub-tenant would be quite unclear. Would the sub-tenant then pay rent to the landlord? What would be the status of his occupation, given that the sub-tenancy contract is effectively at an end?

16 First-tier Tribunal for Scotland Housing and Property Chamber (Procedure) Regulations 2017 (SSI 2017/328) (Procedure Rules).

17 At p 243.

18 Because under r 46(2)(b) the definition of "tenant" in the 1988 Act, which includes a sub-tenant, applies to the term "tenant" in ch 6 of pt 3 of the Procedure Rules (n 16).

Sub-tenancies under the 2016 Act

Sections 46 and 47

The position in relation to sub-tenancies under the 2016 Act is more complex still. As with the 1988 Act, the definition of "tenancy" in section 78(1) includes "sub-tenancy". So, any sub-tenancy that meets the requirements of section 1 will be a private residential tenancy ("PRT").[19]

The key provisions are sections 46 and 47:

"**46 Protection for sub-tenants**

(1) Subsection (2) applies (subject to section 47) where—

(a) a lawfully granted sub-tenancy is terminated by the termination of the tenancy of the person who was the landlord under the sub-tenancy, and

(b) immediately before it terminated, the sub-tenancy was a private residential tenancy.

(2) On the termination of the sub-tenancy, the person who was the tenant under the sub-tenancy becomes the tenant under a new tenancy which—

(a) has the same terms as the sub-tenancy had immediately before it was terminated, and

(b) is deemed to have been granted at the time that the sub-tenancy terminated by whoever was entitled to grant a tenancy in those terms at that time.

(3) A sub-tenancy is not lawfully granted for the purpose of subsection (1) if—

(a) sub-letting the let property is precluded by a term of—

(i) the tenancy of the person who granted the sub-tenancy ('the mid-landlord'), or

(ii) the tenancy of a tenant from whom the mid-landlord's tenancy is held (directly or indirectly), and

(b) the person entitled to enforce the term mentioned in paragraph (a) has not expressly or impliedly consented to the sub-tenancy being granted or continuing.

47 Qualification of sub-tenant protection

(1) Section 46(2) does not apply where the tenancy of the person who was the landlord under the sub-tenancy was brought to an end by an eviction order and either—

(a) the order was issued (exclusively or not) on the basis of an eviction ground mentioned in subsection (2), or

(b) the order states that section 46(2) does not apply.

(2) The eviction grounds referred to in subsection (1)(a) are—

[There then follows a list of all the grounds contained in parts 1, 2 and 4 of schedule 3,[20] but not the grounds in part 3, which are the 'Tenant's conduct grounds'.]"

These sections are not easy to follow. However, clearly, the core provision is section 46(2), which is the protection for sub-tenants to which reference is made in the titles to both sections. Sub-tenants need protection because, at

19 Subject to the exception set out in s 32(7) of the 2001 Act (see above): a sub-let of a Scottish secure tenancy cannot be a PRT. This is confirmed by para 15 of sch 1 to the 2016 Act. By contrast, a sub-tenancy of an assured or a short assured tenancy will be a PRT if it is granted after 1 December 2017. This means that the landlord of a short assured tenancy would have to give careful consideration to allowing a sub-let after that date, because the sub-tenant would have security of tenure under the 2016 Act.

20 Being the grounds in paras 1–9, and 16–18.

common law, the termination of the head lease has the effect of terminating any sub-tenancy, leaving the sub-tenant with no title to remain in possession.[21] Statutory protection must therefore be conferred on sub-tenants holding PRTs, because a PRT gives "security of tenure".[22]

Broadly speaking, the basic idea of the "sub-tenant protection" is that where a tenant grants a sub-tenancy that he was entitled to grant, the subsequent termination of his tenancy (i.e. the head lease) does not have the effect of defeating the rights of the sub-tenant. Under section 46(2), when the tenancy of the "mid-landlord" is terminated, the sub-tenant's security of tenure is not defeated. He becomes the tenant of the head landlord under a new PRT.

However, the "sub-tenant protection" is subject to two conditions (in section 46(1)(a) and (b), and a qualification (in section 47).

Conditions for "sub-tenant protection": section 46(1) and (3)

In essence, in order for section 46(2) to apply, the sub-tenancy has to: (a) have been "lawfully granted"; and (b) be a PRT at the time when the head lease was terminated. Note, however, that there is no requirement that the head lease itself be a PRT.[23]

The term "lawfully granted sub-tenancy" is understood by reference to section 46(3), which describes the circumstances in which a sub-tenancy is not "lawfully granted". Put simply, this is where the sub-letting is precluded by a term of the head tenancy,[24] and the landlord has not expressly or impliedly consented to the sub-tenancy.

As regards section 46(3)(a), it is suggested that, in the vast majority of cases, sub-letting will be precluded by a term of the tenancy. If the head tenancy is itself a PRT, it will be subject to paragraph 3 of the Statutory Terms Regulations,[25] in terms of which "the tenant may not, without the written agreement of the landlord . . . sublet the let property (or any part of it)". Even if the head tenancy is not a PRT, sub-letting is likely to be excluded. Written leases invariably exclude sub-letting without the landlord's consent. Where the head tenancy is an assured tenancy, there is an implied term that the tenant cannot assign or sub-let without the landlord's consent.[26]

In the case of sub-tenancies that have not been lawfully granted, the landlord will have a ground for eviction under ground 11, on the basis of a breach of the tenancy agreement. However, it is suggested that ground 10 may also apply, and an application to the tribunal under both grounds will have a better chance of success.[27]

21 This rule is presupposed by s 46(1)(a).

22 In pt 5 of the Act, ss 46 and 47 are in ch 1, which is headed "security of tenure".

23 The head lease could be an assured tenancy. See n 19.

24 Or is precluded by a term of the tenancy of a tenant from whom the mid-landlord's tenancy is held (directly or indirectly): s 46(3)(a)(ii). This appears to mean that, where there is chain of sub- and sub-sub-tenancies, all of which have terms precluding sub-letting without consent, the consent of the landlord, the tenant and all the sub-tenants in the chain would have to be obtained.

25 Private Residential Tenancies (Statutory Terms) (Scotland) Regulations 2017 (SSI 2017/408) (Statutory Terms Regulations) and s 7 of the Act.

26 1988 Act, s 23.

27 Ground 10 is mandatory, and applies where the tenant is no longer occupying the let property

Qualification of the "sub-tenant protection": sections 47 and 53

The "sub-tenant protection" does not apply if the head lease is a PRT, and "termination" under section 46(1)(a) is by an order under section 51 of the Act,[28] in which the ground (or one of the grounds) is in part 1, 2 or 4 of schedule 3. Therefore, in the case of termination of the head lease under section 51, the protection applies only if the ground is under part 3 of schedule 3, which contains the "Tenant's conduct grounds". Even in those cases, the tribunal granting the section 51 order is given the power to remove the sub-tenant protection by section 47(1)(b); and section 53, which states:

> "**53 First-tier Tribunal's power to disapply protection for sub-tenants**
> (1) This section applies in a case where a sub-tenant would become a tenant by virtue of section 46(2) were the First-tier Tribunal to issue an eviction order against the sub-tenant's landlord.
> (2) If the First-tier Tribunal considers it is reasonable to do so, it may state in an eviction order that section 46(2) is not to apply when the tenancy of the sub-tenant's landlord is brought to an end by the order."

Presumably the idea of section 47 is that the sub-tenant should have protection where the ground for eviction is due to the conduct of the tenant (mid-landlord), not that of the sub-tenant. A clear example would be where the sub-tenant is paying rent to the mid-landlord, but the mid-landlord falls into arrears of his rent payable to the head landlord, leading to an order under ground 12. However, where the ground for eviction is in part 1 of schedule 3:[29] the tenant is not entitled to protection.

It is suggested that, in certain cases, the disapplication of the sub-tenant protection under section 53(2) may be inevitable. Under ground 10 ("Not occupying let property"), the order would not be granted, in the case of a sub-tenancy, unless there was non-occupation by both both the mid-landlord and the sub-tenant. In such a case, presumably section 46(2) would be disapplied. Under ground 15 ("Association with person who has relevant conviction or engaged in relevant anti-social behaviour"), an order might be granted because a sub-tenant has a relevant conviction, or has engaged in antisocial behaviour. Again, presumably in this case, the sub-tenant protection would be disapplied.

Difficulties

Conferring security of tenure on sub-tenants is a complex exercise. At first sight, it may appear that section 46(2) would apply in only a small minority of cases, given the conditions and the qualification. That appearance may be deceptive.

In order to make sense of section 46(1)(a) (and the other provisions in part 5 of the Act that deal with sub-tenancies), it helps to bear in mind that:

as her home. Occupation by a sub-tenant is no defence to the ground, unless the sub-tenancy was "lawfully granted" under s 46(3).

28 The term "eviction order" in s 47(1) means an eviction order under s 51 of the Act: see s 78(1). Therefore, the qualification in s 47 applies only to cases in which the head lease is a PRT.

29 E.g. ground 1 ("landlord intends to sell") or ground 4 ("landlord intends to live in property").

- in cases in which the head tenancy is not a PRT (say, where it is an assured tenancy),[30] the section 47 qualification does not apply;
- in cases in which the tenancy *is* a PRT, but termination takes place under section 48 or section 49,[31] or section 50[32] (as opposed to section 51), the section 47 qualification does not apply.

Sub-tenancy notice to leave: section 61

> "**61 Sub-tenancy notice to leave**
> (1) In addition to giving a tenant a notice to leave, a landlord ('the superior landlord') may give to anyone who holds a tenancy directly or indirectly from the superior landlord's tenant a sub-tenancy notice to leave.
> (2) In the event that a person to whom a sub-tenancy notice to leave has been given becomes a tenant of the superior landlord by virtue of section 46(2), references in this Part to a notice to leave are to be read as references to the copy of the notice to leave which, in accordance with subsection (3), forms part of the sub-tenancy notice to leave.
> (3) A sub-tenancy notice to leave is a notice which—
> (a) incorporates the notice to leave given to the superior landlord's tenant, and
> (b) fulfils any other requirements prescribed by the Scottish Ministers in regulations.
> (4) In a case where two or more persons jointly are the landlord under a tenancy, a sub-tenancy notice to leave may be given by any one of those persons."

The statutory form for the sub-tenant notice to leave is found in schedule 6 to the Private Residential Tenancies (Prescribed Notices and Forms) (Scotland) Regulations 2017.[33] The form begins with "Important information for sub-tenants", followed by four sections that are similar to those appearing in the notice to leave served on the tenant.

Several parts of the form are confusing. Section 61(3)(a) indicates that the sub-tenant notice to leave is simply to incorporate the notice to leave given to the tenant. However, parts 1–4 of the sub-tenant notice are addressed directly to the sub-tenant. In particular, part 3 of the form requires the landlord to say whether the eviction ground relates directly to the tenant or the sub-tenant. Accordingly, it may be prudent to follow the directions given in the sub-tenant notice when completing it, but to also provide the sub-tenant with a copy of the notice to leave served on the tenant.

Section 61(1) seems to indicate that the landlord may choose whether to serve the sub-tenant notice to leave; however, the form states:

> "The let property you live in is sub-let, so in addition to giving a notice to leave on their tenant, the Head Landlord must also give a notice to any sub-tenant(s) if they wish to evict the sub-tenant(s) on particular grounds."

30 Or where the tenant under the head lease is not an individual.
31 Termination by the tenant.
32 Consensual termination. This may be a *lacuna* in s 47. Note that in any case in which the landlord serves a notice to leave on the tenant (mid-landlord), the tenancy will arguably be terminated under s 50 (not s 51), because the tenant has ceased to occupy the property. Therefore, both of the conditions in s 50(1) will have been met.
33 SSI 2017/297.

The explanatory note to section 61 indicates that the landlord may give notice to any sub-tenant "regardless of what type of tenancy the sub-tenant possesses". However, it then states:

> "95. The point of a sub-tenancy notice to leave is that it puts the sub-tenant on notice that he or she may face eviction proceedings. If the sub-tenant remains a tenant of the let property by virtue of the sub-tenant protection given by section 46, the sub-tenancy notice to leave can be treated as a notice to leave so that the landlord can proceed to eviction proceedings without having to serve another notice to leave and wait for a new notice period to expire before applying to the Tribunal for an eviction order."

If that is the reason for serving the sub-tenant notice, it is difficult to see how that purpose would be applicable if the sub-tenancy is not itself a PRT; in that case, there would be no necessity to serve another notice to leave in any event.

Sub-tenants of PRTs under the tribunal rules

Reference is made to the above discussion of assured tenancy sub-tenancies under the Procedure Rules. The same reasoning applies to PRT sub-tenancies. There is no specific reference to sub-tenants in the Procedure Rules. However, as is explained in Chapter 9,[34] the term "tenant" in part 12 of chapter 3 includes a sub-tenant.[35] Accordingly, under rules 9 and 112, the sub-tenant is one of the parties to whom notice of acceptance of an application must be given. Given the terms of rule 9, the sub-tenant would then be able to make written representations, perhaps for the purposes of asking the tribunal to make a determination as to the effect of termination of the head-tenancy, in light of sections 46 and 47 of the 1988 Act.

That being so, it is tentatively suggested that it may be desirable to serve the sub-tenant notice to leave on any sub-tenant known to the landlord, because any subsequent application will have to be intimated on the sub-tenant in any event. Earlier notice may prompt the sub-tenant to look for other accommodation. Also, in the event that the protection under section 46(2) applies, it will not be necessary to serve another notice to leave, at a later date, as indicated in paragraph 95 of the explanatory note.

Unlawful sub-tenants; sub-tenancy not a PRT

Where the sub-tenancy has not been lawfully granted under section 46, or it is a sub-tenancy that is not a PRT, the "protection for sub-tenants" under section 46 does not apply, and the sub-tenant has no security of tenure. In that case, the common law applies, and the sub-tenant has no right to remain in occupation once the PRT is terminated, whether under section 48, section 50 or section 51.

If the sub-tenant remains in occupation after termination of the tenancy under section 48 or section 50, an application may be made to the First-tier

34 At p 311.

35 Because under r 46(2)(g) the definition of "tenant" in s 78 of the 2016 Act, which includes a sub-tenant, applies to the term "tenant" in ch 12 of pt 3 of the Procedure Rules (n 16). Note that there is no distinction in the s 78 definition between sub-tenancies that are or are not lawfully granted.

Tribunal ("FTT"), under section 71 of the Act, for an order for recovery of possession. See the discussion of the transfer of jurisdiction at the beginning of Chapter 14. If an eviction order has been granted against the tenant under section 51, that is a "decree for removing" under part 15 of the Bankruptcy and Diligence etc. (Scotland) Act 2007 and, once a charge before removing is served, is a warrant for removing any occupant deriving right or having permission from the tenant, under section 216(2).

PUTATIVE SUCCESSORS TO TENANCIES UNDER THE 1988, 2001 AND 2016 ACTS

In all three Acts, provision is made in terms of which certain persons may succeed to the tenancy.[36] In all cases there are qualifying requirements, and a dispute may arise as to whether the person in question has succeeded to the tenancy under the statute or whether he fails to meet those requirements. The appropriate manner in which to resolve such an issue is for the landlord to raise proceedings averring that the putative successor has no right or title to remain in occupation,[37] which can be defended on the basis that the tenancy has passed to the occupier under the relevant statutory provision. In practice, there is usually a factual dispute as to whether the tenancy was the only or principal home of the occupier when the tenant died, or during some stipulated period prior to the tenant's death.

In such cases, an important practical point applies. The occupier (if financially eligible) should make an application for universal credit, to include a housing costs element, in respect of his rental liability. If that is not done, there is a danger that a substantial sum in rent arrears will build up during the course of the proceedings in which his right to succeed to the tenancy is determined, which he might have no means of paying.[38]

2001 Act

Section 22(1) of the Act provides that, on the death of a tenant under a Scottish secure tenancy, the tenancy passes by operation of law to a "qualified person". Under section 22(5) and schedule 3 paragraphs 1–4A, provision is made as to who is a "qualified person". If there is no qualified person, or every qualified person declines the tenancy, it is terminated.[39] Schedule 3 is subject to important amendments, made by section 13 of the 2014 Act, with effect from 1 November 2019.[40] Guidance for social landlords on the effect of

36 The right of succession is excluded in relation to SSSTs by s 34(6) of the 2001 Act.

37 As discussed in Chapter 2, the occupier is protected from eviction *brevi manu* by the 1984 Act s 23(3A).

38 If the application is refused, it is suggested that the applicant could seek mandatory reconsideration or appeal, arguing that his application for payment of the housing costs element should be finally be determined once the eviction proceedings, in which his right to succeed is in issue, are concluded.

39 Section 22(3).

40 By virtue of the Housing (Scotland) Act 2014 (Commencement No 8, Savings, Transitional and Supplemental Provisions) Order 2018 (SSI 2018/153). In this edition, the provisions as amended are discussed. See the previous edition for the 2001 Act provisions as originally enacted.

the amendments is given in the Scottish Government's publication "Scottish Secure Tenancies and Short Scottish Secure Tenancies – Assignation, Subletting, Joint Tenancies and Succession: Guidance for Social Landlords".[41]

In light of the amendments, paragraphs 1–4A read:

"**Schedule 3: Qualified Persons**

1. For the purposes of section 22, a person falling within any of paragraphs 2 to 4 is a qualified person.
2. (1) A person whose only or principal home at the time of the tenant's death was the house and—
   (a) who was at that time—
   (i) the tenant's spouse or civil partner, or
   (ii) living with the tenant as husband and wife or in a relationship which has the characteristics of the relationship between civil partners, or
   (b) who is, where the tenancy was held jointly by two or more individuals, a surviving tenant.
   (2) In the case of a person referred to in sub-paragraph (1)(a)(ii), the house must have been the person's only or principal home throughout the period of 12 months ending with the tenant's death.
3. A member of the tenant's family aged at least 16 years where the house was the person's only or principal home throughout the period of 12 months ending with the tenant's death.
4. A carer providing, or who has provided, care for the tenant or a member of the tenant's family where—
   (a) the carer is aged at least 16 years,
   (b) the house was the carer's only or principal home throughout the period of 12 months ending with the tenant's death, and
   (c) the carer had a previous only or principal home which was given up.

4A. Only or Principal Home

For the purposes of paragraph 2, 3 or 4 a period may be considered in relation to a person only if, at any time before that period began, the landlord was notified by—
(a) the person, or
(b) any other person who was the tenant of the house in question when the notice was given
that the house in question was that person's only or principal home."

As originally enacted, section 22 and schedule 3 made certain modifications to the statutory scheme for succession to secure tenancies that had operated under the 1987 Act. Each of these changes made it more likely that succession would occur. The most important was the introduction, by section 22(2), of a second tier of succession with the effect that, on the death of a qualified person who succeeded to a tenancy under section 22(1), the tenancy passes by operation of law to another qualified person. Once that qualified person dies, the tenancy is then terminated.[42]

41 In this part of the chapter, this is referred to as "the Guidance" (see also n 5).

42 Section 22(4). The Act makes further provision, in s 22(6)–(9), for what is to happen on such termination. The landlord must make available alternative accommodation that is suitable (defined with reference to sch 2 pt 2) to any person who would have been a qualified person had succession been possible. In the meantime, such a person is entitled to continue as a tenant for six months, but the tenancy ceases to be a Scottish secure tenancy. Finally, termination does not occur under s 22(4) if a joint tenancy was in operation, provided that the joint tenant continues to use the house as his only or principal home. Note that, under

In the case of succession by a member of the tenant's family (paragraph 3 of schedule 3), the 2001 Act also removed the requirement that the relevant person had resided in the property as his only or principal home for a period of 12 months prior to the tenant's death, requiring only that the tenancy was the person's only or principal home at the time of death. However, by section 13 of the 2014 Act, that qualifying period has been reinstated.[43] A qualifying period has also been introduced in the case of succession by a carer (paragraph 4 of schedule 3).[44] In a similar vein, the qualifying period under paragraph 2(2) has been increased from six to twelve months.[45]

Paragraph 4A is, however, entirely new.[46] It is a common feature of disputed succession cases that the landlord is able to show that it was never informed, by either the deceased tenant or the putative successor, that the latter had taken up residence at the tenancy. Previously, it would then have been a matter for the court to decide whether the failure to inform the landlord had an adverse impact on the putative successor's case that the tenancy was his only or principal home at the relevant time. Now, under paragraph 4A, the failure to notify the landlord will determine the issue in its favour.[47]

Para 4A has the potential to give rise to an issue as to how notice is given to the landlord. The mode of giving notice under the 2001 Act is specified under section 40. However, that applies to a "notice or other document". One might question whether paragraph 4A expressly or impliedly requires a notice in writing, and whether such notification must specifically advise the landlord that the tenancy is the relevant person's "only or principal home".

Also, paragraph 4A seems apt to deal with a situation in which the putative successor has moved into the property during the course of the tenancy. But, a qualified person under paragraphs 2, 3 and 4 may have been living in the tenancy from its commencement. The composition of the tenant's household would normally be ascertained by the landlord as part of the process of allocating the tenancy. If that is so, it is not clear whether members of that household must notify the landlord of their presence, after the tenancy is granted, in order to preserve their succession rights.[48]

Paragraph 6.8 of the Guidance suggests that:

the equivalent English legislation, succession to a qualified person can take place only once. This was challenged, unsuccessfully, as being contrary to art 14 of the European Convention on Human Rights ("ECHR"), and s 19 of the Equality Act 2010, in *Simawi v Haringey LBC* [2019] EWCA Civ 1770, [2020] HLR 13.

43 The "only or principal home" test is discussed in Chapter 1. For succession cases under the 2001 Act in which that test was applied, see: *City of Edinburgh Council v Johnston* 2005 SLT (Sh Ct) 100, 2005 Hous LR 80; *City of Edinburgh Council v Catherick* 2006 Hous LR 62; and *City of Edinburgh Council v Baillie* 2004 Hous LR 15.

44 Succession by a carer under para 4 was an innovation of the 2001 Act.

45 Note that *R (Turley) v Wandsworth LBC* [2017] HLR 21, an attack on the qualifying periods of occupation for succession, as being contrary to arts 8 and 14 of the ECHR, was unsuccessful.

46 The stipulation made by para 4A was also introduced in relation to the assignation and sub-let of tenancies: s 32(1)(c) and (1A).

47 However, where notification under para 4A *has* been given, that would not necessarily decide the issue in favour of the putative successor, because the landlord might still dispute that he had occupied for the relevant period, irrespective of the notice.

48 Furthermore, let us say that the tenant advises the landlord that the tenancy is his son's only home. Thereafter, the son moves out and, after several years, moves back in again. Is a second notification required under para 4A?

"6.8 Landlords should set out clearly in their tenancy information such as tenants' handbooks, which methods of notification they will accept and who the notification should be made to. For example this could include notification by email or letter or by the tenant updating their household information on web-based tenancy management systems. Where a child in the household reaches the age of 16 landlords will want to take a practical approach to the notification of this information. For example if they were part of the household when the house was allocated and/or it is their long-term and principal home, the landlord will know who is living in the property and that should be considered as notification."

Where a tenant gives up a Scottish secure tenancy in order to occupy another house that is subject to a Scottish secure tenancy, following termination of the first tenancy by an order under section 16(2)(b),[49] those tenancies are, for the purposes of this succession, to be treated as being a single tenancy.[50]

Schedule 3 (in paragraphs 5–12) also makes further provision as to:

- succession to specially adapted houses;
- the order of succession in cases where there is more than one qualified person;
- the procedure where the qualified person declines the right to succeed to the tenancy; and
- succession in the case of co-operative housing associations.

1988 Act

Reference is made to the discussion, in Chapter 8, of ground 7 of schedule 5. Prior to the 2016 Act coming into force, where the sole tenant under an assured tenancy died, a right of succession to a statutory assured tenancy was then conferred, under section 31(1) of the 1988 Act, to the tenant's spouse, cohabitee[51] or civil partner.[52] There were two preconditions:

(1) immediately before the death of the tenant, the putative successor must have been occupying the house as his or her only or principal home;[53] and
(2) the deceased tenant was not himself a "successor" as defined in subsection (2) or (3).

If those conditions were fulfilled, the putative successor became the statutory assured tenant. A spouse, cohabitee or civil partner could also succeed where the tenancy devolved to him or her under the will or intestacy of the deceased. Where, however, the tenancy devolved to another person under the will or intestacy of the deceased, the landlord could raise eviction proceedings under the mandatory ground 7.[54]

Under section 31A of the 1988 Act, if the assured tenant dies on or after 1 December 2017, the assured tenancy to which the tenant's spouse, cohabitee or civil partner succeeds becomes a private residential tenancy under the 2016

49 I.e. under one of the management grounds 8–14 in sch to the Act.
50 Section 22(10).
51 Section 31(4).
52 By amendment of s 31 by the Civil Partnership Act 2004 sch 28 para 56.
53 For the meaning of this term, see Chapter 1.
54 Section 31(3).

Act.[55] As section 31 makes no distinction between a short assured tenancy and an assured tenancy, this would appear to mean that the successor to a short assured tenancy becomes a tenant under the 2016 Act, and thereby enjoys greater security of tenure than the deceased tenant did.

Proceedings under ground 7 of schedule 5 would be raised as an action under section 18(3) of the 1988 Act,[56] by an application to the FTT under rule 65. Let us say, however, that the person in occupation has no right or title to occupy under the will or intestacy of the deceased tenancy or under the Act. In that case, it is suggested that the landlord's application for an eviction order would still be an "action arising from an assured tenancy" under section 16 of the 2014 Act, and accordingly an application to the FTT would be appropriate.[57]

2016 Act

In comparison with the 1988 Act, the 2016 Act grants a right of succession to a wider class of persons. However, there is no specific statutory ground for eviction that applies on the death of the tenant. Also, there is no reference in the 2016 Act to the tenancy devolving to another person on the will or intestacy of the deceased tenant. Succession is regulated entirely by the 2016 Act.[58] The relevant provisions are to be found in p 6 ("Death of the Tenant") between sections 65 and 70, which are quite detailed and to which readers are referred.

In summary, section 65 provides that a PRT ends on the death of a sole tenant, unless someone inherits the tenancy under section 67 ("Partner's entitlement to inherit"), section 68 ("Other family member's entitlement to inherit") or section 69 ("Carer's entitlement to inherit"). If the deceased person was a joint tenant, his interest in the tenancy is terminated by death, under section 66.[59]

The rights to succeed under sections 67–69 are in order of priority.[60] The right applies to three classes ("partner", "family member" and "carer"), which are defined in section 70.[61] Succession to a private residential tenancy under

55 Note that this then triggers an obligation on the part of the landlord to comply with ss 10 and 11 of the 2016 Act, for which see Chapter 9, pp 302–303.

56 Because ground 7 is mandatory. As is described above, and in Chapter 8, ground 7 applies where the tenancy devolves, on the will or intestacy of the deceased, to a person other than the tenant's spouse or civil partner.

57 Because the landlord ceded the right of possession under an assured tenancy, and the occupier, having that right of possession, permitted the occupier to stay at the property. See the discussion of the transfer of jurisdiction at the beginning of Chapter 14.

58 It may be gathered from these points that succession under the 2016 Act is much more like succession under the 2001 Act than that under the 1988 Act.

59 This is consistent with the references to "sole tenant" in ss 65, 67, 68 and 69. The statutory rights of succession under ss 67–69 apply only if the deceased tenant was a sole tenant. So if there are two joint tenants, one of whom dies, the surviving tenant becomes the sole tenant of the PRT under s 66. The deceased's tenant's interest does not pass to another person.

60 I.e. a person cannot succeed under s 68 if another person inherits the tenancy under s 67, and a person cannot succeed under s 69 if another person inherits under s 67 or s 68.

61 In the case of "partner" and "family member", this definition is based on the concepts of a "qualifying relationship" and a "qualifying relative". Note that ss 67 and 68 also provide that the relevant "family member" or "carer" must be at least sixteen years of age when the tenant died.

these provisions can occur only once: on the death of a sole tenant who inherited under sections 67–69, the tenancy terminates.[62] In the case of all putative successors, the property must have been the successor's "only or principal home" at the time of the tenant's death. Apart from successors who are spouses or civil partners, the successor must have had a qualifying period of 12 months' occupancy as the successor's "only or principal home" prior to the death of the tenant.

Furthermore, each of sections 67, 68 and 69 contains the requirement that the tenant told the landlord, in writing, that the let property was being occupied by the person in question as their only or principal home.[63] Until that is done, occupancy does not count towards establishing the requirements of those sections. That is consistent with paragraph 3 of schedule 2 to the Act, in terms of which one of the statutory terms of the tenancy[64] is:

> "if a person aged 16 or over (who is not a joint tenant) occupies the let property with the tenant as that person's only or principal home, the tenant must tell the landlord in writing—
> (a) that person's name, and
> (b) the person's relationship to the tenant."[65]

Failure to comply with this requirement is a breach of the terms of the tenancy, which might lead to the landlord seeking eviction under ground 11 in schedule 3.

Clearly, the obligation to tell the landlord of another person's occupation of the property bears some similarity to paragraph 4A of schedule 3 to the 2001 Act, discussed above. The stipulation is clearer in the 2016 Act, because it is explicitly required that the tenant tells the landlord "in writing". However, one might question whether the 2016 Act leaves room for the "practical approach" described in the Guidance for Scottish secure tenancies, quoted at p 425 above.

As with the death of an assured tenant, where another person remains in occupation following the death of a tenant under a PRT, but has no right or title to succeed under the 2016 Act, it is suggested that the landlord's application for an eviction order would be an "action arising from a private residential tenancy" under section 71 of the 2016 Act, which would be made to the FTT.[66]

62 Because succession can occur only under s 67, s 68 or s 69, and under each of those provisions one of the conditions is that the tenant's interest under the tenancy was not inherited by the tenant.

63 In ss 67(2)(b), 68(3) and 69(3).

64 By ss 7 and 8 of the 2016 Act, statutory terms are terms of every PRT. These are set out in sch 2, and in the Private Residential Tenancies (Statutory Terms) (Scotland) Regulations 2017 (n 25). For good measure, they are repeated in the Government's model PRT agreement, at cl 13.

65 Under para 4 of sch 2, the next statutory term of a PRT is: "If— (a) in accordance with the term specified in paragraph 3, the landlord has been told about a person occupying the let property, and (b) that person has ceased to occupy the let property as that person's only or principal home, the tenant must tell the landlord that."

66 See the discussion of the transfer of jurisdiction at the beginning of Chapter 14.

NON-ENTITLED SPOUSES UNDER THE MATRIMONIAL HOMES (FAMILY PROTECTION) (SCOTLAND) ACT 1981

A non-entitled spouse has three important rights that are of relevance in the context of residential tenancies.[67] First, under section 2(1)(b) of the 1981 Act he is entitled, for the purposes of securing his occupancy rights, with or without the consent of the entitled spouse, to perform any obligation incumbent on the entitled spouse. Clearly this includes paying the rent and attending to the other obligations with a view to avoiding the "conduct" grounds under the 1988, 2001 or 2016 Acts being established. However, it is submitted that in cases in which the entitled spouse no longer resides at the tenancy, section 2(1)(b) also includes any obligation to retain possession of the subjects or remain in occupation of the house as an only or principal home.[68] Therefore, where the tenant (being the entitled spouse) leaves the tenancy, any status that the tenancy might have had, such as that of contractual or statutory assured tenancy or a short assured tenancy, will continue to apply for the purposes of sections 12 and 16 of the 1988 Act where the non-entitled spouse remains in occupation.[69]

Secondly, under section 2(1)(f), the non-entitled spouse is entitled "to take such other steps, for the purpose of protecting the occupancy rights of the entitled spouse, as the entitled spouse may take to protect the occupancy rights of the entitled spouse". This means that where eviction proceedings are raised in the sheriff court against the entitled spouse, the non-entitled spouse may apply, under chapter 14 of the Summary Cause Rules,[70] to enter the process as an additional defender and state a defence to the action, even if the entitled spouse does not enter appearance in the case. In the case of proceedings in the FTT, an application may be made, under rule 32(3) of the tribunal's Procedure Rules,[71] to be added as a party to the proceedings.[72]

Thirdly, the non-entitled spouse has the right, under section 13 of the 1981 Act, to make an application to have the tenancy of the matrimonial home transferred to him, subject to the conditions set out in that section.[73]

67 These rights also extend to non-entitled cohabitees, including cohabitees in same-sex relationships: 1981 Act, s 18; *Armour v Anderson* 1994 SC 488, 1994 SLT 1127; *Souter v McAuley* 2010 SLT (Sh Ct) 121, 2010 Hous LR 73.

68 This is confirmed by s 2(8), which provides that: "Where (a) the entitled spouse is a tenant of a matrimonial home; and (b) possession thereof is necessary in order to continue the tenancy; and (c) the entitled spouse abandons such possession, the tenancy shall be continued by such possession by the non-entitled spouse."

69 Under the 2001 Act (s 11(8)) and the 2016 Act (s 1(2)), non-occupation by the tenant does not have the effect that the tenancy loses its statutory status. However, there are "non-occupation" grounds for eviction in both Acts. Ground 5 in the 2001 Act is not met if the house is occupied by a spouse or civil partner, or a person who was the tenant's cohabitee for at least six months before the tenant ceased to occupy. By contrast, in ground 10 in the 2016 Act, there is no express reference to occupation by anyone other than the tenant. See the discussion of that ground in Chapter 10.

70 Act of Sederunt (Summary Cause Rules) 2002 (SSI 2002/132) (Summary Cause Rules). The summary cause procedure will no longer apply to eviction proceedings, when the new simple procedure for heritable cases comes into force: see Chapter 13. It remains to be seen whether the new procedure will contain some equivalent of ch 14 of the Summary Cause Rules.

71 n 16.

72 Note that, under r 1, "party" is defined as "includes . . . any . . . third party applicant . . . and any other person permitted by the First-tier Tribunal to be a party to proceedings".

73 See, e.g.: *Souter v McAuley* (n 67). The effect of transfer of jurisdiction on s 13 of the 1981 Act is not clear. There has been no amendment to s 13, and there is no reference to the 1981 Act

The effect of these rights in eviction proceedings may be best illustrated by an example.

Example 1

Mr A is the sole tenant of a Scottish secure tenancy. He resides at the tenancy with his wife, Mrs A. Their marriage breaks down, and Mr A leaves. Subsequently, Mrs A discovers that her husband has not been paying the rent. She also learns that the landlords have raised eviction proceedings against Mr A in the local sheriff court. Mrs A makes an application to the court under section 15 of the 2001 Act, and chapter 14 of the Summary Cause Rules, seeking leave to enter the action as an additional defender, as she has title and interest to do so in her capacity as a non-entitled spouse and a qualifying occupier. That application must be granted, given the terms of section 15 of the 2001 Act. Mrs A is then able to state a defence to the effect that although there is a ground for recovery of possession under that Act, it would not be reasonable to grant the order, given the circumstances of the case, and the fact that she is willing and able to pay the rent. She further seeks that the case be continued or sisted to enable her to make a separate application under section 13 of the 1981 Act.

In this example, a question arises as to what happens to the rent arrears. The non-entitled spouse has no obligation to make any payment towards the arrears until such time as her application under section 13 of the 1981 Act is granted and she becomes the tenant. However, under section 2(1)(b) of the Act, she does have the power to make "any payment due by the entitled spouse in respect of rent", which would appear to include rent arrears. It is suggested that, at the very least, the non-entitled spouse should offer to pay the ongoing rent; otherwise, notwithstanding her successful application to enter the process as an additional defender, the sheriff may take the view that it is reasonable to grant the order for recovery of possession. Similarly, where the arrears are high, it may be in the interests of the non-entitled spouse to enter into an agreement in terms of which she makes payments towards the rent arrears or, failing agreement, to make such an offer when the case calls, the better to persuade the sheriff that it would not be reasonable to grant the order. One would expect these payments to have a bearing on any amount that the sheriff chooses to award the entitled spouse by way of compensation for the transfer of the tenancy under section 13 of the 1981 Act.[74]

In cases in which the ground for recovery of possession is antisocial behaviour or illegal or immoral conduct, there may be an issue as to the extent to which the non-entitled spouse has participated or acquiesced in the conduct in question.[75]

in the FTT's Procedure Rules (n 16). It is suggested that, notwithstanding the transfer, the sheriff court would still have the power to grant an application transferring the tenancy of an assured tenancy or a PRT, in divorce proceedings, given s 13(2)(a).

74 Under s 13(1) and (9).

75 E.g., in *Glasgow Housing Association v Gourlay* 2006 Hous LR 52, the pursuers sought to recover possession on ground 2 of sch 2 to the 2001 Act; when the action was raised, the defender tenant was serving a period of imprisonment for offences under the Misuse of Drugs Act 1971. His wife entered the process as a qualifying occupier and sought to defend the action on the basis that she and the defender were now leading separate lives. This argument

Where the entitled spouse voluntarily terminates a Scottish secure tenancy by agreement, or by giving four weeks' notice under section 12(1)(e) or (f) of the 2001 Act, the non-entitled spouse may insist on remaining in the tenancy. In that case, the landlord may raise proceedings by summary application seeking an order under section 7 of the 1981 Act, dispensing with the non-entitled spouse's consent to the termination.[76] In the event that the application is granted, the landlord may then raise proceedings on the basis that the non-entitled spouse no longer has any right or title to remain in occupation.

QUALIFYING OCCUPIERS UNDER THE 2001 ACT

The following discussion applies to qualifying occupiers under section 14 of the 2001 Act who do not have rights under the 1981 Act. Their rights under sections 14 and 15 of the 2001 Act are limited to: (a) having the proceedings intimated upon them; and (b) being sisted as a party to the proceedings. The effect of the qualifying occupier being sisted under section 15 is that she is then entitled to make representations to the court on the matters that it has to determine. In a case under section 16(2)(a) of the Act, those matters are: (i) whether the ground for eviction is established; and (ii) whether it is reasonable to grant an order for recovery of possession.

Therefore, the rights under section 14 and 15 may be useful where, for some reason, the tenant is unwilling or unable to protect his own position. However, where the defender tenant has entered appearance on his own behalf, there will be usually be little point in the qualifying occupier also becoming a party to the case. Apart from sections 14 and 15, no other provision in the Act accords any right or entitlement to a person designated as a qualifying occupier. Any right of occupancy that is held by the qualifying occupier is entirely derivative of the tenant's rights. That is to say: insofar as the qualifying occupier derives a right of occupancy in the subjects from the tenant, by contract, permission or otherwise, the termination of the tenant's rights in the subjects also terminates any right of occupancy vesting in the qualifying occupier.[77] Thus an order under section 16(2) of the Act that has the effect of terminating the tenancy also terminates any right of occupancy that derives from the tenant. Where a charge for removing has been served on the tenant, the qualifying occupier may subsequently be removed.[78]

Accordingly, when the court orders that the qualifying occupier is sisted to the action, there is no change to the substantive rights of the landlord, the tenant and the qualifying occupiers in respect of the Scottish secure tenancy.

failed to convince the sheriff, who further found that the wife must have known about the defender's drug dealing. Decree was granted.

76 For an example, see *East Ayrshire Council v McKnight* 2003 Hous LR 114. This case proceeded on an agreed understanding between the parties that termination of the tenancy by the entitled spouse was a "dealing" for the purposes of s 6 of the 1981 Act, after which the non-entitled spouse was entitled to continue exercising his occupancy rights. That being so, an action under s 7 was necessary.

77 The statement of this view in the first edition of this work was endorsed in *East Lothian Council v Duffy* 2012 SLT (Sh Ct) 113, 2012 Hous LR 73. See also *Glasgow Housing Association Ltd v McNamara* 2008 Hous LR 38, [24] (Sheriff Ross).

78 Under s 216 of the Bankruptcy and Diligence etc. (Scotland) Act 2007, discussed in Chapter 15.

The qualifying occupier's rights are still derivative of those of the defender. What he can seek to argue is that the defender's tenancy should not be brought to an end, but he does not argue for the continuation or protection of any substantive right of his own. The decree for eviction in those proceedings will be against the tenant alone. There is no requirement to grant an additional decree against the qualifying occupier.

Again, it may be best to illustrate this with an example.

Example 2

Mr A is the sole tenant of a Scottish secure tenancy. He resides at the property with his 21-year-old daughter, Ms A. They have an argument, and Mr A decides to leave. Subsequently, Ms A discovers that her father has not been paying the rent. She also learns that the landlords have raised eviction proceedings against Mr A in the local sheriff court. Ms A makes an application to the court under section 15 of the 2001 Act, and chapter 14 of the Summary Cause Rules, seeking leave to enter the action as an additional defender, in her capacity as a qualifying occupier. That application must be granted, given the terms of section 15 of the 2001 Act. However, the question that then arises is: what, if anything, can Ms A do to safeguard the continuing existence of the tenancy? Unlike Mrs A in Example 1, she has no right to make payments towards the rent. The landlord may decline such payments. Ms A also has no right to seek a transfer of the tenancy equivalent to the right of Mrs A under section 13 of the 1981 Act. Accordingly, with the rent arrears rising, it is difficult to see what basis she has for arguing that it would not be reasonable for the order for recovery of possession to be granted.

In a case in which the qualifying occupier wishes to protect her position, it is suggested that consideration should be given to making an application to the landlord for its consent to an assignation of the tenancy to the qualifying occupier, under section 32. If that application is refused, an appeal by summary application may be made, under part 2 of schedule 5 to the Act.[79] Alternatively, the existing tenant and the qualifying occupier may make an application to the landlord, under section 11(5), for the qualifying occupier to be made a joint tenant.[80] The qualifying occupier could then ask the court to

79 For an example, see *Docherty v Tollcross Housing Association Ltd* 2020 GWD 9-135. Such appeals are very rare. Both the assignation application and the appeal by summary application must be made by the tenant, rather than the proposed assignee. Usually it is the proposed assignee who wishes the assignation to go ahead. The tenant wishing to assign does not often have a strong incentive to go to the lengths of raising legal proceedings to challenge a refusal. Moreover, the scope for a landlord to reasonably refuse assignation and sub-let applications has been significantly extended by amendments made to s 32 of the 2001 Act by the 2014 Act. See the discussion of sub-letting and succession under the 2001 Act above.

80 Once again, the 2014 Act makes amendments to the 2001 Act that place obstacles in the path of such applications. Now the tenancy must have been, for the preceding 12 months, the only or principal home of the person who wishes to become a joint tenant with the existing tenant. The notification requirement is also inserted (see the discussion of para 4A of sch 3 to the Act at p 424 above). A landlord must consent to an application under s 11(5) unless it has reasonable grounds for not doing so. There is no procedure under the 2001 Act by which the joint applicants can appeal against refusal. A challenge by judicial review may be possible. In the example under discussion, if the s 11(5) application is granted, in due course the original tenant could terminate his interest under s 13 of the 2001 Act, with the result that the tenancy

continue or sist the case to enable the application to be determined. However, in this case she would still not have the right to make payments towards the rent, and it may be difficult for her to satisfy the court that it would not be reasonable to grant the order where, for example, it may be some time before the assignation appeal is determined.

LICENSEES

As was explained in Chapter 1, the term "licence" is generally used to denote a contract in which a right of occupation of heritable subjects is conferred, where the contract is not a lease. The occupier's right is therefore merely personal and contractual.

In the context of evictions, the particular differences between a lease and a licence are:

(1) the rule of tacit relocation does not apply to licences;[81]
(2) the rights to notice on termination of a lease, as described in Chapter 3, do not apply to licences, though it would appear that a licensee is still entitled to "reasonable notice" of an eviction;[82]
(3) at common law, on the expiry of the contract, the licensee has no further right or title to remain in occupation, and may be ejected without a court order.[83] However, as was outlined in Chapter 2, a court order is required by virtue of section 23(2A) of the 1984 Act, provided that the licence does not fall into any of the categories described in section 23A;
(4) security of tenure under the Rent Acts, the 1988 Act and the 2016 Act extends only to tenancies, not licences.[84]

Service occupancies; tied tenancies; services in lieu of rental payment; agricultural employees; no rental liability

The term "service occupancy" refers to occupation by an employee of a house provided by his employer, where that occupation is ancillary to the contract of service or employment. The house is often referred to as a "tied house". Usually the limited nature of the occupier's rights in respect of the accom-

would have been effectively assigned to the qualifying occupier. Unlike an application under s 11(5), that would not require the consent of the landlord.

81 Paton and Cameron (n 2) 221.

82 *Gloag on Contract*; *Dunlop & Co v Steel Co* (1879) 7 R 283, 288 (Lord Deas); *Conway v Glasgow City Council* 1999 SLT (Sh Ct) 102, 2001 SLT 1472 (Note). That is also the position as regards licensees in English law: "it is clear law that, where the relevant period has not been specified by the licence itself, a licensee is entitled, following revocation of the licence, to whatever in all the circumstances is a reasonable time to remove himself and his possessions" (*Gibson v Douglas* [2017] HLR 11, para 20 (Sir James Munby, citing *Minister of Health v Bellotti* [1944] KB 298)). As to the period of notice, see the quotation at the end of this chapter.

83 Rankine, *Leases*, 597; *MacDonald v Duchess of Leeds* (1860) 22 D 1075; *MacDonald v Watson* (1883) 10 R 1079. This was confirmed by the decision of the Inner House in *Ali v Serco Ltd* 2019 SLT 1335.

84 However, note that s 4 of the 2016 Act extends the meaning of "tenancy". See Chapter 9, p 294. In the 2001 Act, the meaning of "tenancy" is also extended, by the definition of that term, in s 41. See Chapter 4, p 82.

modation is laid down in his contract of employment, including in particular a stipulation to the effect that the right of occupancy ceases on the cessation of the employment. However, such a condition may be implied if the circumstances of the case indicate that the occupation is for the better performance of the employment.

The categorisation of a contract as a lease or a service occupancy is often difficult: the nature of the occupancy should be decided on the particular circumstances of each case, including the effect of any express contractual stipulation that may be applicable.[85] The fact that the tenant pays a nominal rent, or no rent at all, does not of itself indicate a service occupancy: it may instead indicate a lease in which some form of service is given by the tenant to the landlord in lieu of rent. As a general rule, however, a service occupancy will be inferred only if the occupation of the house is necessary for the performance of the employment and, therefore, the occupation is that of an employee, rather than a tenant. The fact that one is eligible to be offered a house if one is in a certain type of employment is insufficient.

The following examples are offered by way of illustration. In *MacGregor v Dunnett*,[86] the occupier paid a small rent for a house that he was told "went with the job"; he was also informed that occupation would cease on the termination of his employment. This was held to be a lease, as the occupancy was in no way related to the better performance of his job as a baker. However, in *Pollock v Assessor for Inverness-shire*[87] in which a teacher occupied a house that was next to a school and was owned by the school board, this was held not to be a lease, notwithstanding the "rent" that was paid.

Even if the circumstances of the case are such as to indicate a lease, as was indicated in Chapter 4, this may nevertheless be excepted from the security of tenure provisions of the 2001 Act, by virtue of paragraph 1 of schedule 1 to the Act. There is no equivalent exception in relation to tenancies under the 1988 Act or the 2016 Act.[88]

In the case of a lease in which no rental payment is made, but services are carried out or work is done by the tenant instead of such a payment, the tenant does not have security of tenure under the Rent Acts, or the 1988 Act.[89] This is probably also the case under the 2016 Act, although the position is less clear.[90]

Where the agreement contains no rental obligation, by way of monetary payment or performance of services in lieu of rent, there is no lease.[91]

85 In particular, contractual provisions that use terms common to tenancies, such as "let" or "notice to quit", may be apt to infer a lease: *British Transport Commission v Assessor for Inverness-shire* 1952 SC 511.

86 1949 SC 510.

87 1923 SC 693.

88 Though, under the 1988 Act, a tenancy in which the interest of the landlord belongs to Her Majesty in right of the Crown, or to a government department, is excepted from assured tenancy status under sch 4 para 10. Under the 2016 Act, "police housing " and "military housing" are both excepted under paras 12 and 13 of sch 1.

89 See the discussion of para 2 of sch 4 to the 1988 Act in Chapter 7.

90 See the discussion of para 1 of sch 1 to the 2016 Act in Chapter 9.

91 *Mann v Houston* 1957 SLT 89. At common law, rent may be "money, the fruit of the grounds, or services " (Erskine, *Principles of the Law of Scotland*, II, vi,8; Paton and Cameron, (n 2) 6). "Fruits of the grounds" is applicable to agricultural tenancies, not tenancies of residential property. Note that, under s 4(b) of the 2016 Act, once an agreement has given rise to a PRT, it is to continue to be regarded as giving rise to a tenancy, despite the term of the agreement

Under section 24 of the 1984 Act, special provisions apply to tenants[92] occupying a former tenancy under the terms of employment as a person employed in agriculture. In eviction proceedings the sheriff has the power to suspend the execution of any order for recovery of possession on such terms and conditions as he thinks fit, including conditions as to the payment of arrears of rent, compensation to the owner for loss of possession or otherwise as the court thinks reasonable. The extent of this power is outlined in the detailed terms of section 24, to which the reader is referred.

HOSTEL DWELLERS

The legal status of hostel dwellers is uncertain. They are excepted from the prohibition of eviction without due process, under section 23 of the 1984 Act, by section 23A(5). Following the decision in *Conway v Glasgow City Council*,[93] which is discussed below, section 7 of the 2001 Act conferred on the Scottish Ministers the power to make regulations to establish minimum rights for homeless people living in hostels and other types of short-term accommodation. It was intended that the regulations would, in particular, specify terms that are to have effect as terms of an occupancy to which that section applied[94] as between the occupier and the person providing the accommodation. However, to date, no regulations have been made under this section.

The most important case in this area is *Conway v Glasgow City Council*. Unfortunately, its outcome was somewhat inconclusive. The occupier of a bed in a hostel for homeless persons was summarily evicted during the night,[95] as a result of an alleged incident earlier in the evening. She raised an action of damages claiming that she had been a tenant[96] or, alternatively, that her occupation of the premises had arisen by virtue of a contractual arrangement that required reasonable notice before she could be evicted. After debate, the sheriff concluded that it was unrealistic and wrong in law to regard the pursuer as a tenant, but he allowed proof before answer on the alternative aspect of the case. The defenders successfully appealed to the sheriff principal, who held that there was no invariable rule that such a contractual arrangement could be terminated only on reasonable notice, that the arrangement in question

requiring the tenant to pay rent subsequently being removed from the agreement or otherwise ceasing to have effect.

92 By virtue of s 24(2A), which mirrors s 23(2A) of the Act (discussed in Chapter 2), the statutory protection is extended to persons occupying a dwelling otherwise than under a tenancy. Clearly this would include service occupancies. Under s 24(2)(a), "occupier" also includes the widow or widower of the tenant.

93 n 82.

94 Under s 7(1), it is also for the Scottish Ministers to specify the forms of residential accommodation to which the regulations apply. However, the heading of s 7 ("Persons living in hostel and other short-term accommodation") gives an indication as to the nature of the accommodation in question.

95 The enforcement of decrees for eviction at night was made unlawful on the coming into force of the Bankruptcy and Diligence etc (Scotland) Act 2007, s 217, which is further discussed in Chapter 15. This provision does not, however, appear to include evictions *brevi manu*, of the type that took place in *Conway*.

96 Had the pursuer been able to establish that she was a tenant, it would have been unlawful, at common law, to evict to evict her without a court order. See the discussion of s 23(5) of the 1984 Act in Chapter 2.

did not contain any implied condition to that effect, and that the defenders' employees had a discretion to remove the pursuer. The pursuer appealed to the Court of Session. Her grounds of appeal were *inter alia* that the sheriff principal had erred, in particular in holding that: (a) the pursuer's averments failed to provide any basis for the importation into the contract of an implied condition that reasonable notice required to be given to terminate it; (b) in the absence of an express contractual term as to reasonable notice of termination, the pursuer's contract for residential occupation of a local authority hostel for homeless persons gave the defenders a discretion to terminate it and eject her without notice or cause; and (c) in the circumstances where it was accepted that there was a contract for residential occupation between the parties, and that the normal rule was that such a contract could be terminated only on reasonable notice, it was incumbent on the pursuer to aver that such a term should be implied where not expressed, rather than for the defender to aver why it should be excluded. When the case ultimately called for before an Extra Division, senior counsel for the respondents indicated that he did not support the decision of the sheriff principal. The appeal was accordingly allowed and the interlocutor of the sheriff restored.

On that basis, it seems reasonable to conclude that the pursuer's alternative case (that the pursuer's occupation in the hostel was by virtue of a contract in which was implied a requirement for reasonable notice before she could be evicted), was well founded. That is also the position in English law.[97] As to what constitutes "reasonable notice", it was said, in *Gibson v Douglas*:[98]

> "At one end of the spectrum, the unwanted visitor who presents himself at the front door, is asked in but then told to go, must leave immediately, taking the quickest route back to the highway and not delaying; so his period of grace may be measured in minutes: see *Robson v Hallett* [1967] 2 QB 939. On the other hand, a period measured in years may in some cases be appropriate: see, for example, *Parker v Parker* [2003] EWHC 1846 (Ch), where the Earl of Macclesfield was held entitled to two years to leave the ancestral home, Shirburn Castle, which he had been occupying as a licensee for some ten years. There was some discussion before us as to what the appropriate period might be in a case such as this. It depends on the circumstances. That said, I very much doubt that it would be a period measured in minutes, hours or even days. On the other hand, I can well imagine that it might typically be a period measured in weeks rather than months or years. Further than that I am not prepared to go."

97 Under which a licensee is entitled, following revocation of the licence, to whatever in all the circumstances is a reasonable time to remove himself and his possessions: *Minister of Health v Bellotti* [1944] KB 298 (n 82).

98 [2017] HLR 11; a decision of the Court of Appeal. The quoted passage comes from the judgment of Sir James Munby at para 21.

Chapter 13

Eviction Actions in the Sheriff Court

Since the 1970s, the majority of actions for recovery of possession of heritable property have been raised as summary causes in the sheriff court. That remains the case at the time of writing. However, since 1 December 2017, proceedings in relation to tenancies under the 1984 and 1988 Acts must be raised by application to the Housing and Property Chamber of the First-tier Tribunal ("FTT"), given the terms of section 16 of the 2014 Act; eviction orders in relation to tenancies under the 2016 Act are also made by the tribunal, under section 51 of that Act.

Under the relevant provisions of the Courts Reform (Scotland) Act 2014, the small claims and summary cause procedures are to be abolished, and replaced by the "simple procedure", for which the rules are drawn up by the Scottish Civil Justice Council.[1] On 28 November 2016, the Simple Procedure Rules[2] replaced the small claims procedure in its entirety and largely replaced summary cause procedure. Since that date, the simple procedure must be used to make a claim that has a monetary value of £5,000 or less, or seeks delivery, the recovery of moveable property or an order for someone to do something specific.

It is intended that the simple procedure will be extended to include other types of claim at a later date. These claims are referred to collectively as "special claims" and will include claims for recovery of possession of heritable property, i.e. eviction proceedings. At the time of writing, it is not known when these rules will come into force, or the extent to which they will be similar to the current summary cause rules.

It may be anticipated that the simple procedure will be less formal.[3] Under section 75 of the Courts Reform (Scotland) Act 2014, the rules will be drafted "so far as possible with a view to ensuring that the sheriff before whom a simple procedure case is conducted: (a) is able to identify the issues in dispute, (b) may facilitate negotiation between or among the parties with a view to securing a settlement, (c) may otherwise assist the parties in reaching a settlement, and (d) can adopt a procedure that is appropriate to and takes account of the particular circumstances of the case".

1 The Scottish Civil Justice Council is created by the Scottish Civil Justice Council and Criminal Legal Assistance Act 2013. The council replaces both the Sheriff Court Rules Council and the Court of Session Rules Council.

2 In sch 1 to the Act of Sederunt (Simple Procedure) 2016 (SSI 2016/200) .

3 For instance, under s 77(1) of the Act, "Any enactment or rule of law that prevents evidence being led on grounds of admissibility before a court of law does not apply in simple procedure cases."

At the time of writing, then, the Summary Cause Rules 2002 ("SCR")[4] remain in force, in relation to eviction proceedings, and cover the vast majority of such actions in the sheriff court. It is beyond the scope of this work to consider the SCR in detail. Most of this chapter is concerned with the application of particular rules in the context of such actions. Chapter 14 concerns the procedure in the FTT. Chapter 15 discusses matters that are apt to arise in the course of eviction proceedings in general, whether in the sheriff court or the tribunal, and, further, the issues that arise after the decree is granted, including the procedure for enforcing decree.

The discussion in this chapter breaks down as follows:

- The requirement to raise eviction actions as summary causes (or under the simple procedure, once it comes into force).
- Commencement of a summary cause and pleading issues.
- Undefended actions: Rule 7.1 of SCR.
- Defenced actions and first callings: Chapter 8 of SCR.
- Minutes for recall: Chapter 24 of SCR.
- The special rules under Chapter 30 of SCR.
- Other summary cause rules.

The discussion of the first issue is unlikely to be significantly affected by the transition to simple procedure, because section 72 of the Courts Reform (Scotland) Act 2014 is very similar to section 35 of the 1971 Act, the interpretation of which is discussed below. The analysis in the rest of the chapter is likely to have less relevance, depending on the extent to which the special procedure for heritable cases is similar to that in the SCR.

REQUIREMENT TO RAISE EVICTION ACTIONS AS SUMMARY CAUSES

Sheriff Courts (Scotland) Act 1971, s 35(1)(c)

"35 Summary Causes

(1) The definition of 'summary cause' contained in paragraph (i) of section 3 of the Sheriff Court (Scotland) Act 1907 shall cease to have effect, and for the purposes of the procedure and practice in civil proceedings in the sheriff court there shall be a form of process, to be known as a 'summary cause', which shall be used for the purposes of all civil proceedings brought in that court, being proceedings of one or other of the following descriptions, namely—

. . .

(c) actions *ad factum praestandum* and actions for the recovery of possession of heritable or moveable property, other than actions in which there is claimed in addition, or as an alternative, to a decree *ad factum praestandum* or for such recovery, as the case may be, a decree for payment of money exceeding £5,000[5] in amount (exclusive of interest and expenses)."[6]

4 Act of Sederunt (Summary Cause Rules) (SSI 2002/132).

5 Previously the figure was £1,500 for many years. The new limit was introduced by the Sheriff Courts (Scotland) Act 1971 (Privative Jurisdiction and Summary Cause) Order 2007 (SSI 2007/507).

6 Under the Courts Reform (Scotland) Act 2014, this section is repealed. The relevant provision will then be s 72(3)(e) of the 2014 Act, which states: "(3) The following types of proceedings

As was outlined in Chapter 1, one of the purposes of this provision was to remove the previous confusion in relation to actions of removing and ejection by creating a single form of summary cause process "for the recovery of possession of heritable property". This is the form of process that must be used. By virtue of section 35(1)(c), an ordinary cause action that is solely for removing or for ejection is incompetent.[7]

It follows from the wording of section 35(1)(c) that it is not possible to evict only one of several *pro indiviso* tenants or occupiers in a summary cause action;[8] in that case the pursuer would not be recovering possession of the subjects.

Because section 35(1)(c) stipulates that all actions for recovery of possession must be raised as summary causes, except where there is an additional crave for a sum of money exceeding £5,000, it appears to exclude the possibility of actions with other additional craves, such as declarator. Such actions cannot be raised under the ordinary cause procedure, because of section 35, and cannot be raised as summary causes because the additional crave (such as one for declarator) may be sought only in an ordinary cause. Thus in *Gerber v Greggs Bakeries Ltd*,[9] Sheriff Principal O'Brien held, in relation to an action for declarator of irritancy and removing, that the removing crave was incompetent; it was observed that the action should have been raised as a summary cause and thereafter remitted to the ordinary roll. In *Disblair Estates Ltd v Jackson*,[10] the sheriff found that an ordinary action for ejection and interdict[11] was incompetent. It was his view that the pursuers ought to raise a summary cause action for recovery of possession, and a separate ordinary action for interdict, with the possibility that the summary cause could be remitted to the ordinary cause roll and conjoined with the interdict action. Subsequently, in *Monklands District Council v Johnstone*,[12] the court considered an ordinary action seeking: (a) declarator that a missive of let was null and void; and (b) a warrant for ejection. The sheriff held that the action was incompetent, albeit "with some reluctance and hesitation".[13]

may only be brought subject to simple procedure . . . (e) proceedings for the recovery of possession of heritable property . . . other than proceedings in which there is claimed, in addition or as an alternative to a decree for such recovery, a decree for payment of a sum of money exceeding £5,000."

7 In *Tennant Caledonian Breweries Ltd v Gearty* 1980 SLT (Sh Ct) 71, objection had been taken to the competency of an action on that basis. The pursuers tried to address the problem by seeking leave to add, by way of amendment, a crave for payment of a sum of money over the requisite limit. This was refused, on the basis that there was, in effect, no process and therefore nothing to amend. By contrast, in *Borthwick v Bank of Scotland* 1985 SLT (Sh Ct) 49 the court allowed a motion by the pursuer's agent to remit an action that had been erroneously raised as an ordinary cause to the summary cause roll.

8 *Prestwick Investment Trust v Jones* 1981 SLT (Sh Ct) 55. However, this may be possible in an ordinary action: see Rankine, *Leases* 520: "Where the lease is held jointly or *pro indiviso* by two or more tenants all must be called if it is intended that all should be removed; but it is quite competent to oust certain *pro indiviso* lessees, while allowing others to sit in."

9 Hamilton Sheriff Court, 18 October 1981 (unreported).

10 Aberdeen Sheriff Court, 24 November 1982 (unreported)

11 An action for the ejection of unauthorised occupiers was traditionally accompanied by a crave for interdict to prevent the defenders from taking entry to the property again.

12 1987 SCLR 480, a decision of Sheriff Boyle at Airdrie.

13 In its report *Recovery of Possession of Heritable Property* the Scottish Law Commission recommended that s 35 be amended, so as to allow a recovery of possession action to be raised as an ordinary cause where it was accompanied by a crave for a decree other than a decree for

Consequently, it might be thought that in any ordinary action a crave for ejection, removing or recovery of possession must be accompanied by a crave for payment of a sum of money for £5,000 or more. However, that conclusion appears to have been refuted by the decision in *Milmor Properties Ltd v W and T Investment Co Ltd.*[14] In that case the parties were owners of contiguous heritable property. The pursuers complained that the defenders had encroached on their property. They raised an action seeking certain declarators, a decree *ad factum praestandum* and interdicts. The defenders pled that the action as laid was incompetent: under section 35(1)(c) of the 1971 Act: a decree *ad factum praestandum* (like a decree for recovery of possession of heritable property) could be pursued only in a summary cause, unless it was accompanied by a crave for payment of money exceeding the relevant limit. The pursuers' argument relied on the use of the phrase "actions *ad factum praestandum*" in section 35(1)(c), which was to be contrasted with "actions containing a crave for decree *ad factum praestandum*". The correct approach was to ask "What kind of action is this?". In the present case, the action was essentially one of declarator and interdict, the crave *ad factum praestandum* being ancillary to those remedies. In accepting the pursuers' argument, Sheriff Principal Risk observed:

> "it is immediately obvious that paras (a), (b) and (c) [of section 35(1)] refer to *actions* of various kinds. It seems to me that the natural reading of those paragraphs supports the sheriff's view that the task of the court is to categorise the action which is before it rather than to categorise the craves seriatim. As the solicitor for the pursuers pointed out, the subsection makes no mention of individual craves. On that approach, an action which was in normal course appropriate to ordinary procedure would not lose that character if it included an ancillary crave for a remedy which, had it been sought on its own, would have required to proceed by way of summary cause".[15]

Thus the sheriff principal suggested that the decision in *Disblair Estates Ltd v Jackson*[16] was correct, because it was an action for the recovery of heritable property to which a crave for interdict, against the defender re-entering the subjects after his eviction, had been appended. However, he disagreed with the decision in *Monklands District Council v Johnstone*.

On the basis of the foregoing authorities, the following guidelines are suggested, in relation to an action in which an order for recovery of possession (or equivalent) is sought.

As Sheriff Principal Risk pointed out in *Milmor Properties*,[17] section 39 of the Sheriff Courts (Scotland) Act 1907 states that, subject to the provisions of any Act of Parliament, the procedure in all civil causes raised in the sheriff court is to be the ordinary cause.[18] It follows that, in any case in which the ordinary cause procedure is used, the onus falls on the defender disputing the competency of the action to persuade the court that the answer to the question

payment of money (Scot Law Com No 118, 1989) paras 8.7–8.13). However, like most of the Commission's other recommendations, this never became law.

14 2000 SLT (Sh Ct) 2.

15 At 4.

16 n 10.

17 n 14.

18 Section 39 of the 1907 Act is due to be repealed by para 4(f) of sch 5 to the Courts Reform (Scotland) Act 2014. At the time of writing, that has not yet happened.

"What kind of action is this?" is "an action for recovery of possession" under section 35(1)(c) of the 1971 Act. It is not enough that one of the craves seeks an order for recovery of possession or some equivalent. It is suggested that the defender will have to show that the other craves are to be regarded as consequent upon, or ancillary to, the crave for removing or ejection, such as the crave for interdict in *Disblair Estates Ltd v Jackson*,[19] or that they are simply unnecessary.

For example, where a declaratory crave is necessary, in order to establish some disputed right or title, and a further crave for removing or ejection may be regarded as following from the declaration sought, the action is not one for recovery of possession. It is correctly categorised as an action for declarator, and therefore ought to be raised as an ordinary cause.[20] Where, however, a declaratory crave is not necessary, the court may take the view that the action is, in substance, an action for recovery of possession to which the declaratory crave is "an unnecessary decoration".[21] Where there is any doubt about the matter, the pursuers may pray in aid the following remarks of Sheriff Principal Risk:

> "The approach of [allowing the action to proceed] has the immediate attraction that it produces a result which is practical and sensible. Solicitor for the defenders did not suggest any benefit which would accrue to either party, or to the interests of justice as a whole, from the upholding of his submission, and I can think of none . . . If the defenders' contention were correct, the pursuers would have to raise an ordinary action for declarator and interdict, and a summary cause for the removal of the offending buildings etc. Thus, immediately, there would be additional procedure making additional demands on court time and laying additional expense on the parties."[22]

When the new simple procedure for heritable cases replaces the summary cause, and section 35 of the 1971 Act is repealed, it is to be expected that the same approach will be adopted to the question of whether an action ought to be raised using the simple procedure under section 72 of the Courts Reform (Scotland) Act 2014, or as an ordinary action.[23]

19 n 10.

20 See *Hart v Kitchen* 1989 SC 391, 1990 SLT 54, in which the parties were neighbours in dispute as the ownership of a strip of ground, on which the defender had built an extension. The pursuer raised a summary cause action for recovery of possession of the ground. Consequently, there was no crave before the court by which it could declare the pursuer to be the owner of the strip. The case eventually went to the Inner House, where it was held, in essence, that it was too late for the defender to argue that the action was incompetent. The court expressed the view (at 394) that if the defender had been intending to raise the issue of competency, it would have expected him to move, in terms of s 37 of the 1971 Act, that the cause should be treated as an ordinary cause, observing: "Indeed it is perhaps surprising that both parties were not agreed upon this course". *Creston v Land and Estates plc v Brown* 2000 SC 320 is an example of a case in which the court upheld the competency of an ordinary action for declarator and ejection. An action for declarator (usually of irritancy) and removing may be raised in the Court of Session; such actions are quite common in relation to commercial leases.

21 A case that is the opposite of *Creston* is *Rutherford v Virtue* 1993 SCLR 886, discussed in *Milmor Properties* (n 14). In *Rutherford v Virtue* the pursuers raised an ordinary action for declarator and an order *ad factum praestandum*. The declarator was said to be unnecessary, since it did little more than to state an obligation in a disposition that is not challenged by any of the other parties. Therefore the case ought to have proceeded as a summary cause.

22 At 3.

23 See the decision of Sheriff Foulis in *Clydesdale Financial Services Ltd v Wojcik* 2019 SLT

Actions under the 2001 Act

Section 14(1) of the 2001 Act states:

> "The landlord under a Scottish secure tenancy may raise proceedings by way of summary cause[24] for recovery of possession of the house."

Section 36(1) is effectively in the same terms, as regards short Scottish secure tenancies ("SSSTs).

Conflicting views have been expressed as to whether these provisions mean that an action for recovery of possession cannot be raised under the ordinary cause procedure, even if it *does* include a crave for payment of money exceeding £5,000, in terms of section 35(1)(c) of the 1971 Act. At paragraph 23.09 of Macphail, the authors simply state: "An action for recovery of possession of a Scottish secure tenancy under section 14 of the Housing (Scotland) Act 2001 is directed by that Act to proceed by way of summary cause. A Scottish short secure tenancy is also repossessed using the summary cause procedure."[25] However, in *City of Edinburgh Council v Burnett*, Sheriff Principal Stephen was persuaded that an action for recovery of possession under section 36 of the 2001 Act could proceed as an ordinary cause, as the pursuers' writ also contained a crave for payment of rent arrears exceeding £7,000.[26] The crux of her judgment appears to lie in the following passage:

> "[31] Section 36 of the 2001 Act states that the landlord may raise proceedings by way of summary cause. The wording of the statute must be given its ordinary meaning. 'May' is an enabling or discretionary power; it does not mean 'must' and furthermore there is no basis upon which it should be construed as such or as being directive.
>
> [32] I can find no reason or basis for construing the word 'may' as 'must'."

It is respectfully submitted that this reasoning is open to question, and the view stated in Macphail's *Sheriff Court Practice* is to be preferred. It is unfortunate that the sheriff principal had to consider this matter in the absence of any contradictor to the pursuers' argument: there was no appearance by the defender at the appeal (or before the sheriff who originally decided that the action was incompetent).[27] It is suggested that the error in the pursuers'

(Sh Ct) 286. At [5], he said of the 2014 Act: "If there is any significance in the replacement of 'actions' in s.35(1)(c) by 'proceedings' in s.72(3)(e) it is lost on me, particularly when 'actions' is used in s.72(3)(b)–(d). In short, what was said in *Milmor Properties Ltd* applies with equal force when considering what types of proceedings require to be raised under simple procedure. The fact that that decision was referred to in the explanatory notes to the preceding bill simply confirms this."

24 This will require to be read as "simple procedure", once the special rules for eviction proceedings come into force: under s 83(1) of the Courts Reform (Scotland) Act 2014, any reference to proceedings being taken by way of summary cause is to be construed as a reference to proceedings being subject to simple procedure.

25 Macphail, *Sheriff Court Practice*. This was also the view taken by Paul Watchman in his commentary to s 47(1) of the 1987 Act (*Annotated Housing (Scotland) Act 1987* (1991)) and in Rennie and others, *Leases* (SULI 2015) para 23-76.

26 2012 SLT (Sh Ct) 137; 2012 Hous LR 52. It should be mentioned that the same conclusion was reached in *Dundee City Council v Bailey* 1998 Hous LR 93, a case that does not appear to have been cited in *Burnett*.

27 It is notable that pursuers and the sheriff principal placed reliance on certain passages in Macphail (n 25), which the sheriff principal describes at [16] as "the authoritative text".

submission, and in the sheriff principal's conclusion, lies in maintaining that the provision under discussion must be interpreted as either permissive or directive. It is both.

In so far as the word "may" is permissive, that relates to the act of raising eviction proceedings, not the procedure under which the action is raised. That is suggested by the order of the words used in section 14(1) and section 36(1). The word "may" is followed by "raise proceedings", which is then modified by the words "by way of summary cause". In this context it is also important to remember that the Scottish secure tenancy and the SSST are creations of the 2001 Act, which strictly prescribes the requirements for termination of occupation under those tenancies. Hence these sections permit the raising of proceedings after service of the relevant notices. In contrast, raising an action for recovery of possession as a summary cause does not require to be permitted by the 2001 Act; it is already stipulated in terms of section 35(1)(c) of the 1971 Act.[28]

Thus, it is submitted, the correct interpretation of section 14(1) and section 36(1) is that the landlord is permitted to raise proceedings to recover possession, but that permission is subject to a direction: that the proceedings must be raised as a summary cause. To illustrate by an analogy, let us say that A says to B: "I understand that there is a meeting at your offices on Monday afternoon. May I attend?". B replies: "You may attend after 4pm." B's reply is analogous to: "The landlord . . . may raise proceedings by way of summary cause"; an action is permitted, but the mode of carrying out the action is restricted.

Moreover, to interpret section 14(1) as meaning that the landlord can also raise proceedings by way of an ordinary action is to render the words "by way of summary cause" superfluous, as the effect of permitting the action to be raised as an ordinary or a summary cause would be achieved by the words "The landlord . . . may raise proceedings for recovery of possession". Such an interpretation contravenes the principle that every word of an enactment is to be given meaning where possible.[29]

Finally on this point, it is interesting to note that, during the passage of the Bill that become the 2001 Act, an MSP sought to amend the provision that became section 36(1), by the addition of the word "only", after "proceedings", so as to "ensure that eviction proceedings raised against tenants could only be by way of summary cause procedure". It appears that the amendment was dropped on the basis of the following assurance given by the Deputy Minister for Social Justice: "I can reassure [the MSP] our clear intention is for the procedure that is set out in section 30 to be that that will be used for

Perhaps a contradictor would have drawn her attention to para 23.09 (quoted in the main text), which is at odds with her conclusion.

28 At paras [30] and [32] the sheriff principal appears to suggest that the sheriff's conclusion entails some contradiction between s 35(1)(c) of the 1971 Act and s 36(1) of the 2001 Act. However, under s 39 of the 1907 Act (see the discussion of *Milmor Properties* (n 14)), all civil causes in the sheriff court must be raised as ordinary actions: "subject to the provisions of *any* Act of Parliament in force". Therefore, although s 35 lists the actions that are to be raised as summary causes, it is possible for the 2001 Act also to specify a class of cases in which actions must be raised as summary causes, thereby effectively modifying the rules set out in s 35.

29 Bennion, *Statutory Interpretation* (7th edn) section 21.2, p 511: "On the presumption that Parliament does nothing in vain, the court must endeavour to give significance to every word of an enactment. It is presumed that if a word or phrase appears, it was put there for a purpose and must not be disregarded."

the recovery of possession. My understanding is that the bill as drafted already provided for that."[30]

If it is indeed the case that actions under section 14 or section 36 of the 2001 Act may be raised only by way of summary cause, it is open to the landlord to raise such an action and thereafter lodge an incidental application seeking to increase the sum sued for and remit the case to the ordinary cause roll.[31]

COMMENCEMENT OF A SUMMARY CAUSE, AND PLEADING ISSUES

A summary cause action is commenced by a summons that is in the form prescribed by the SCR.[32] The form of the order sought by the pursuer is also prescribed.[33]

Before the pursuer may serve a copy of the summons on the defender, it must be authenticated by the sheriff clerk,[34] who inserts on the summons, in the relevant boxes in the prescribed form: (a) the return day, which is the last day on which the defender may return a form of response to the sheriff clerk; and (b) the calling date, which is the date set for the action to call in court. The calling date must be fourteen days after the return day.[35] The pursuer then serves a copy of the summons on the defender.[36]

30 The MSP was Tommy Sheridan; the minister was Margaret Curran. The relevant passage is in the minutes of a meeting of the Social Justice Committee, at stage 2 of the Bill. It can be found at p 270 of vol 2 of SPPB 23 (Scottish Parliament Passage of Bill). Section 30 of the Bill became s 36 of the Act. As is apparent from the minutes, it was recognised that the same issue arose in relation to the provision that became s 14 of the Act. However, Mr Sheridan appears to have missed the deadline for moving an amendment in relation to that section.

31 1971 Act, s 37. There is also no reason why the landlord cannot advise the court, in a summary cause action on the ground of rent arrears, that the true rent arrears figure is in excess of the sum of £5,000 to which he is restricted under s 35 of the 1971 Act, with a view to persuading the sheriff that it would be reasonable to grant decree in terms of the 2001 Act, s 16(2).

32 Rule 4.1(1). The prescribed form is always form 1. This is in contrast with the old Summary Cause Rules, in terms of which different forms of summons were prescribed for different actions.

33 Rule 4.1(2). Form 2 is the form for the claim for payment of money: "The pursuer claims from the defender(s) the sum of £.......... with .... interest on that sum at the rate of ....% annually from the date of service, together with the expenses of bringing the action." Form 3 is the claim for recovery of possession of heritable property: "The pursuer claims that, in the circumstances described in the statement contained on page 2 of this copy summons, he is entitled to recover possession of the property at (*address*), and that you refuse or delay to remove from said property. The pursuer therefore asks the court to grant a decree against you, removing you, and your family, sub-tenants and dependants (if any) with your goods and possessions from the said property. The pursuer also claims from you the expenses of bringing the action."

34 Rule 4.4. In certain circumstances specified in that rule, the summons may instead be authenticated by a sheriff.

35 Rule 4.5(6) and (7).

36 This is required by r 4.3, in terms of which there are four types of defender's copy summons. In eviction actions in relation to dwellinghouses, form 1a must be used if there is also a claim for payment of money. Otherwise, form 1c will be used.

Rule 4.2: statement of claim

> **"The pursuer must insert a statement of his claim in the summons to give the defender fair notice of the claim; and the statement must include—**
> **(a) details of the basis of the claim including relevant dates . . .**

The extent of the requirement to give fair notice in actions for recovery of possession of heritable property has been considered in several cases. The most important authority is *Gordon District Council v Acutt*,[37] which concerned an action for recovery of possession of a secure tenancy under the 1980 Act, in which the landlords had produced a notice relating to arrears of rent but made no averment that, as at the date of the raising of the action, the defender was in arrears of rent, nor any averment that it was reasonable for the court to make the order. Sheriff Stewart held that in the absence of such averments the action was incompetent, and he continued the cause to allow the statement of claim to be amended.

Averment in relation to the pre-action requirement in arrears cases

In an action under section 16 of the 2001 Act, where the ground (or one of the grounds) is rent arrears, "the writ submitted for warranting must include a statement of claim with an averment confirming to the court that the pre-action requirements . . . have been complied with".[38] However, in *Aberdeen City Council v Beattie*,[39] Sheriff Lewis decided that it was possible to add the necessary averment by amendment, during the course of the action.

Rule 4.5: Notice

Under rule 4.5, the pursuer is required to give the appropriate period of notice to the defender prior to the return day, being twenty-one or forty-two days.[40] The sheriff may, on cause shown, shorten or extend the period of notice on such conditions as to the form of service as he may direct, but in any case where the period of notice is reduced at least two days' notice must be given.[41] Incidental applications by landlords to reduce the period of notice to forty-eight hours are quite common, particularly in cases involving antisocial behaviour, or where the tenancy appears to have been abandoned. However, it should be noted that the sheriff's power is limited to reducing the period of notice before the return day. The rules confer no power to reduce the period

37 1991 SLT (Sh Ct) 78, followed in *Midlothian District Council v Brown* 1991 SLT (Sh Ct) 80; *Renfrew District Council v Inglis* 1991 SLT (Sh Ct) 83.

38 Scottish Secure Tenancies (Proceedings for Possession) (Confirmation of Compliance with Pre-Action Requirements) Regulations 2012 (SSI 2012/93), art 2.

39 Unreported decision of Sheriff Lewis, 21 October 2014 (Aberdeen Sheriff Court).

40 21 days where the defender is resident or has a place of business within Europe; or 42 days where the defender is resident or has a place of business outwith Europe. If the appropriate period of notice is not given, the action cannot proceed on the calling date. The pursuer should then seek an order for re-service under r 5.10. Note, however, that, in terms of r 5.11, the defender is barred from objecting to the regularity of service if he appears on the calling date.

41 Rule 4.5(3).

of fourteen days between the return day and the calling date,[42] except in cases to which rule 30.2 applies.[43]

UNDEFENDED ACTIONS: r 7.1

The copy of the summons served on the defender contains a response form, which he must complete and return to the sheriff clerk on or before the return day if he wishes to defend the action, challenge the jurisdiction of the court or the competency of the action, or state a counterclaim.[44]

Rule 7.1 indicates what is to happen if the defender does not lodge a response form. For present purposes, only rules 7.1(4) and 7.1(7) are relevant.[45] The application of rule 7.1(4) is limited to the two types of action specified in that rule, whereas the power to grant decree in the circumstances outlined in rule 7.1(7) applies to all actions in which a response form has not been lodged.

> "(4) Where no form of response has been lodged in an action—
> (a) for recovery of possession of heritable property; or
> (b) of sequestration for rent,
> the action shall call in court on the calling date and the sheriff shall determine the action as he thinks fit.
>
> . . .
>
> (7) If the defender does not lodge a form of response in time or if the sheriff is satisfied that he does not intend to defend the action on the merits or on the amount of the sum due, the sheriff may grant decree with expenses against him."

The important consequence of rule 7.1(4) is that actions for recovery of possession of heritable property, in contrast to actions for payment of money, always call in court on the calling date. In practice, this gives rise to two possible scenarios: (a) the defender does not appear and is not represented; and (b) the defender appears or is represented. Before considering those two possibilities, the following general observations are made.

As well as the powers to dispose of actions as indicated in the SCR, the sheriff also has a statutory power to adjourn certain cases under section 16(1) of the 2001 Act.[46] This power is stated in broad terms, and there appears to be no reason why an undefended action could not be adjourned. It is quite common for cases to be adjourned where no response form has been lodged:[47] this might happen, for example, if the landlord has decided not to seek decree on the basis of payments made by the defender towards rent arrears since the

42 Rule 4.5(7).

43 Rule 30.2 is discussed below.

44 Rule 8.1.

45 Rule 7.1(1), (2) and (3) sets out a procedure in terms of which the pursuer may lodge a minute seeking decree, with the result that the action may not require to call in court on the calling date. This is not possible in relation to actions for recovery of possession of heritable property, given the terms of r 7.1(4). Rule 7.1(5) and (6) respectively deal with actions of multiplepoinding and for count, reckoning and payment.

46 Limited to actions under grounds 1–7 and of sch 2. These grounds are discussed in Chapter 5.

47 An adjournment on this basis is usually referred to as a "continuation", although as is indicated below, the court does not appear to have any power under the Rules to continue cases which are undefended.

action commenced. However, it may lead to a situation in which, as a result of a series of adjournments, an action calls in court on numerous occasions, even though it has never been defended in terms of the rules.[48]

Otherwise, the sheriff has no power to continue or adjourn eviction actions in which no response form is lodged.[49] In relation to an action to which rule 7.1(4) applies, the rule states that the sheriff "shall determine the action" – a phrase that clearly envisages that a final decision will be made on the calling date.

That said, the sheriff would have the power, under rule 3.1,[50] to dispense with the requirement to lodge a response form. This could be done in cases in which the defender does not lodge the form, but appears at the calling date and indicates that he wishes to defend the action. In that case, the sheriff could dispense with the response form and proceed with the cause under chapter 8 of the SCR, in which case he has the power to dispose of the action in terms of that rule, including the power to continue the proceedings under rule 8.2(3).

Rule 7.1(7) gives a discretionary power to the sheriff to grant decree in two separate circumstances. The first of these is where the defender *does not timeously lodge* a response form. If, at the calling date, no response form has been lodged, the sheriff is enjoined, in terms of rule 7.1(4) cases, "to determine the action as he thinks fit" in any event, which would include granting decree. If the response form has been tendered to the sheriff clerk, or produced at the calling date, and the sheriff allows it to be lodged late, one would expect that the action would proceed as defended under chapter 8.

The second circumstance in which the sheriff may grant decree in terms of rule 7.1(7) is where he or she is satisfied that the defender does not intend to defend the action on the merits. The rule is set out in a way that suggests that this power is to be used in cases in which a response form *has* been lodged, but the sheriff nevertheless forms the view that the defender does not intend to defend the action. To that extent it is closely related to powers available to the sheriff under chapter 8, including the power to grant decree against a defender who lodges a response form but fails to appear or be represented on the calling date (rule 8.2(5)), and the power to grant decree where the claim or defence is not soundly based in law (rule 8.3(3)(c)). The issue of whether a sheriff can be satisfied that the defender does not intend to defend the action on the merits, which has caused some difficulty in the past, is considered below.[51]

The defender does not appear

Where the action is undefended, the sheriff has a common law duty to consider only those matters that are *pars judicis*.[52] Those are thought to be limited

48 As a result of continuations under the Rules, adjournments under the legislation, or sists, rent arrears cases, in particular, may be ongoing for lengthy periods, sometimes years. This point is further considered in the discussion of r 8.2(3), below.

49 There is such a power in relation to defended actions in terms of r 8.2(3).

50 The dispensing power: "The sheriff may relieve any party from the consequences of any failure to comply with the provisions of these Rules which is shown to be due to mistake, oversight or other excusable cause, on such conditions as he thinks fit."

51 See, in particular, the discussion of *City of Edinburgh Council v Ure* 2004 SCLR 306, 2004 Hous LR 2 and *Midlothian Council v Roxburgh* 1999 Hous LR 50, below.

52 "*Pars judicis*" means what the judge has the duty to do, which may entail taking notice of

to whether the court has jurisdiction, and questions of competency in respect of either the form of the proceedings or the remedy sought.[53] That would include, for example, whether the cause ought to have been raised in the FTT, under section 16 of the 2014 Act. It would not include a question as to whether the action was incompetent because, for example, the notice of proceedings served on the defender under section 14 of the 2001 Act was in the correct form, or because the pursuers failed to comply with the pre-action requirements.[54]

However, different considerations apply where the court is asked to grant an order for recovery of possession in terms of the provisions of a particular Act. Under the 2001 Act, such an order may be granted under section 16(2), or under section 36(5) (where the tenancy is an SSST).

Section 16(2) requires the court to grant decree "if it appears to the court" that the landlord has a statutory ground for recovery of possession, and the relevant additional requirement is met.[55] There seems to be a wide variation in practice in the way that the courts approach this function, particularly the issue of whether it is reasonable to grant an order under section 16(2)(a)(ii), where that provision applies.

In arrears cases, some sheriffs consider the terms of the statement of claim and make enquiry of the pursuer's agent in relation to such matters as the composition of the defender's household, eligibility for housing benefit, the history of payment, and efforts made by the pursuer to make contact with the defender. If, as a result of these enquiries, the sheriff is reluctant to grant the order, he may adjourn the case in order for more information to be put before the court by the pursuer's agent, or for further attempts to be made by the pursuer to contact the defender.[56]

Other sheriffs rely solely on the information stated at the bar of the court by the pursuer's agent. In arrears cases, this would usually consist of an indication of the level of the arrears and the recent history of repayment. Prior to the 2001 Act, this approach was sanctioned by *City of Glasgow Council v Erhaiganoma*,[57] a decision of the Inner House that confirmed that, once the statutory ground is established and a *prima facie* case for reasonableness is made out, it is for the tenant to put matters before the court to show why the order should not be granted, and thus if the tenant does not appear, decree may be granted.

certain matters, whether or not she has been asked to do so, by either of the parties. See: *Cabot Financial UK Ltd v McGregor, Gardner and Brown* 2018 SLT (Sh Ct) 249, para [33].

53 *Cabot*, para [34]. This distinction is reflected in rr 8.3(1) and 8.3(3)(c), which apply to defended actions. See p 455 below. Where the cause is clearly incompetent or lacking jurisdiction, the sheriff may dismiss the action under r 8.3(1). Questions as to whether the claim "is soundly based in law" require the sheriff to hear the parties on that matter, under r 8.3(3)(c).

54 *Glasgow West Housing Association v Silva* (unreported decision of Appeal Sheriff MacFadyen, GLA-SD422-18, 12 July 2019), paras 33–36. See also: *Hill v Black* 1914 SC 913, 1914 2 SLT 123; *Cabot* (n 52), para [33]. Accordingly, it would be for the defender to raise this point.

55 See Chapter 5.

56 Cases are often adjourned for further attempts to be made to contact the defender, when the arrears are relatively low.

57 1993 SCLR 592.

Given the terms of section 16(3) of the 2001 Act, however, a question arises as to the extent to which the sheriff must be informed, or ought to enquire into, the four factors listed in that provision. It is submitted that section 16(3) has implications for the handling of cases in which no appearance is made by the defender: the sheriff is obliged to "have regard" to the section 16(3) factors, whether the defender appears or not.[58] At this point, reference is made to Chapter 5, where consideration is given to each of the four factors. The conclusion of that analysis was that each factor must always be regarded as relevant to the exercise of the discretion, whenever it arises. Section 16(3)(a) must always arise, because all the grounds 1–7 arise from "conduct", and all conduct has a "nature, frequency and duration". Therefore the court must have regard to that issue in every case in which an order is sought under grounds 1–7, irrespective of whether the defender appears. If there is no appearance by the defender, the necessary information must come from the pursuers. It will presumably be within their knowledge. If it is not available, it is probably appropriate for the court to adjourn the case in terms of section 16(1), to enable the information to be obtained.[59] Given the terms of section 16(3), it is submitted that the court can no longer grant decrees in undefended cases on, for example, a rent arrears figure alone.[60]

Section 16(3)(b) and (c) may or may not have a bearing in the particular circumstances of any given case. For example, it may be that the conduct that establishes the ground is entirely on the part of the tenant, in which case section 16(3)(b) does not arise.

As was suggested in Chapter 5, section 16(3)(b) would generally be relied on by the defender. Where the pursuers seek to establish the statutory ground on the basis of conduct by a person other than the defender, that is usually apparent from the statement of claim. Whether conduct on the part of the tenant occurred "as a consequence of acts or omissions of persons other than the tenant" would probably not be within the knowledge of the pursuers.

58 *Glasgow Housing Association v Fisher* 2008 SLT (Sh Ct) 142; 2008 Hous LR 60, para [6], quoted at p 452 below. See also *Mortgages 1 v Chaudhary* 2014 SLT (Sh Ct) 35. That case concerned a mortgage repossession action under s 24 of the Conveyancing and Feudal Reform (Scotland) Act 1970. Sheriff Principal Lockhart allowed an appeal against a decision of the sheriff granting decree against a defender who failed to appear at a By Order hearing, having lodged written defences earlier in the action. He held that the sheriff had erred in restricting his consideration of whether to grant decree to the appellant's non-appearance and failure to make the contracted payments; the sheriff was obliged to report that he had considered the whether it was reasonable to grant the order under s.24(5)(b), and the matters to which he was to "have regard", under s 24(6) and (7). In that case, the defender had previously lodged defences, which the sheriff ought to have considered. However, even in cases in which no defence has been stated, the court is still required (in an action under s 16 of the 2001 Act) to decide, under s 16(2)(a)(ii) whether it reasonable to grant the order, an exercise which is subject to s 16(3).

59 This suggestion is based on *City of Edinburgh Council v Stirling; City of Edinburgh Council v Lamb* 1993 SCLR 587, in which Sheriff Principal Nicholson held that where matters are raised at a preliminary hearing which cannot be either admitted or contested, the case ought to be adjourned to enable further investigations to be carried out. That said, however, his decision proceeded at least to some extent on the observation that: "it would be going too far to say that a landlord must put himself in a position to deal with all matters . . . at an early hearing of an action . . . and before he knows what sort of defence may be advanced in a particular case." Quite so, but it is submitted that whilst the landlord cannot be prepared to deal with *all* matters, it ought to come prepared to deal with the matters outlined in s 16(3).

60 See para [6] of the quotation from *Glasgow Housing Association Ltd v Fisher* (n 68), below.

Therefore, if the defender is not present to make a case to that effect, the sheriff can proceed on the basis that it is an issue that does not arise.

Conversely, section 16(3)(c) is a factor that will be relied on by the pursuers. In cases under ground 7, for example, one would expect that information as to the effect of antisocial behaviour would be narrated in the statement of claim. If no information is given to the sheriff, he may take it that the issue of the effect of conduct does not arise in the circumstances of the case.

As regards section 16(3)(d), it is submitted that the sheriff ought to make enquiry as to the nature of any action taken by the landlord, before raising the proceedings, with a view to securing the cessation of the conduct that establishes the ground, because it is a matter that is entirely within the knowledge of the pursuers. Again, where the information is not available, the case ought to be adjourned in terms of section 16(1) to enable it to be obtained. In rent arrears cases, the sheriff will be able to consider the pre-action requirements followed by the landlord, which should be described, at least in summary, in the notice of proceedings served on the tenant.[61]

As indicated above, decree for recovery of possession may also be granted under section 36(5) of the 2001 Act, where the tenancy is an SSST. As is explained in Chapter 6, this means that the various requirements of section 36(5) have to be met. It is suggested that the sheriff would have to be satisfied that this was the case before granting decree, irrespective of whether the action was defended.[62]

The defender appears as a party litigant

Very often, the defender does not lodge a response form, but then appears personally at the first calling, without representation. This may give rise to a question as to whether he wishes to defend the action, and on what basis. In particular, the position may not be clear if the action can be resisted on the ground that it would not be reasonable to grant the order[63] because a party litigant defender may not be aware of this possible defence.[64]

Some of the difficulties inherent in this situation may be gathered from the cases of *Midlothian Council v Roxburgh*,[65] and *City of Edinburgh Council v Ure*.[66]

Midlothian Council v Roxburgh, was a case under the old Summary Cause Rules, in which decree had been sought on the grounds of illegal or immoral conduct, the defender having been convicted of two offences of lewd and libidinous behaviour involving young boys, at the tenancy. The defender's wife appeared at the first calling of the case, and made certain representations

61 See Chapter 4, at p 111.

62 This was certainly the approach taken by Sheriff Mackie in the case of *City of Edinburgh Council v Smith* 2016 SLT (Sh Ct) 343, which is considered in Chapter 6, at p 212. That action was not defended, but the sheriff nevertheless dismissed the case, as she was not satisfied that there was "no further contractual tenancy . . . in existence", in terms of s 36(5)(c).

63 It is clear that an action for recovery of possession on one of the "discretionary" grounds under the 1988 Act or the 2001 Act may be defended on this basis alone; see the quotation from *Midlothian Council v Roxburgh* (n 51).

64 Many party litigants in arrears cases are under the mistaken impression that the court is only interested in hearing payment proposals; thus they may not provide other relevant information unless prompted to do so.

65 (n 51).

66 (n 51).

on his behalf. In particular, it was said that he was deaf and housebound, and no longer presented a danger to the public. The sheriff nevertheless granted decree. A minute for recall was then lodged by the defender's agents, which was subsequently refused as incompetent. The defender appealed against the refusal to recall the decree. The issue in this case was whether decree had been granted under the old rule 18(6) or (9). Only decrees granted under rule 18(6) could competently be recalled. Under rule 18(6) the sheriff was entitled to grant decree "If the defender does not appear or is not represented at the first calling . . . *and has not stated a defence or if the court is satisfied that he does not intend to defend the cause on the merits.*" Rule 18(9) allowed the sheriff to decide the case on the merits at the first calling if the facts of the case were sufficiently admitted.[67] In relation to those rules, and in respect of the circumstances in which the case had first called, Sheriff Principal Nicholson stated:[68]

> "It seems to me that the starting point . . . must be that, although the basic facts founded on by the pursuers in this action were not, apparently, denied by Mrs Roxburgh when she spoke on behalf of her husband before the sheriff on 3rd October 1997, she was nonetheless putting forward, albeit not in terms, a defence to the effect that it would not be reasonable for decree to be granted against the defender; and, as I have observed earlier, that is a defence which would have been open to the defender in a case such as this."

On that basis, the sheriff principal decided that the original decree could not have been granted under rule 18(6), and therefore could not be recalled.

In *City of Edinburgh Council v Ure*, the defender appeared at a calling under rule 7.1(4), having failed to lodge a response form. This was an action under section 16 of the 2001 Act, on the ground of rent arrears. Mr Ure advised the court that he no longer wanted to live at the tenancy. However, he also provided reasons for his having had difficulty paying the rent. The sheriff granted decree against Mr Ure, having formed the view that he did not wish to defend the action.

The defender successfully appealed against that decision. Sheriff Principal Macphail took the view that the defender's position had been unclear: although he had said that he did not wish to remain at the tenancy, his other comments were apt to indicate that he might wish to defend the case on the basis that it would not be reasonable to grant the order. Accordingly, further enquiry ought to have been made by the sheriff, given the importance of the decision that he required to make as to whether the order should be granted.

From these cases, it follows that the sheriff must take care to ascertain whether the defender wishes to oppose the granting of decree for recovery of possession. He should be alert to the possibility that the defender is putting forward, albeit not in terms, a defence to the effect that it would not be reasonable to grant an order for eviction, which is a defence available in actions under section 16(2)(a) of the 2001 Act. In an arrears case, for example, it is submitted that an offer to pay the outstanding sum by instalments is enough in itself to amount to a contention that, given the offer, it would not be reasona-

67 This was a recurring problem under the old Rules; decrees were often granted against party litigant defenders without any indication being given by the sheriff as to the rule under which the order was made.

68 At 54.

ble to grant an eviction order. This may not amount to a very strong defence, but it is a defence nevertheless.

The rules give no direction as to what happens if, at a hearing under rule 7.1(4) or (7), the sheriff is satisfied that the defender *does* intend to defend the action on the merits. Clearly, the cause ought then to proceed under chapter 8. It is thought that, in practice, the sheriff is apt to dispense with the requirement to lodge the response form under the dispensing power in terms of chapter 3 of the SCR, and thereafter allow the cause to proceed under chapter 8.

Time to pay directions

In relation to request for time to pay in the context of eviction proceedings, the reader is directed to the discussion of rule 30.9, at p 471 below.

DEFENDED ACTIONS AND FIRST CALLINGS: ch 8

The procedure for first callings and defended actions is outlined in rules 8.2 and 8.3:

Rule 8.2: procedure in defended action

"(1) Where the defender has lodged a form of response in accordance with rule 8.1(1) the action will call in court for a hearing.
(2) The hearing shall be held on the calling date.
(3) The sheriff may continue the hearing to such other date as he considers appropriate.
(4) The defender must either be present or be represented at the hearing.
(5) Where the defender–
(a) does not appear or is not represented; and
(b) the pursuer is present or is represented,
decree may be granted against the defender in terms of the summons.
(6) Where at the hearing–
(a) the pursuer does not appear or is not represented; and
(b) the defender is present or represented,
the sheriff shall dismiss the action and may grant decree in terms of any counterclaim.
(7) If all parties fail to appear at the hearing, the sheriff shall, unless sufficient reason appears to the contrary, dismiss the action and any counterclaim."

Response form: rule 8.2(1)

Although the rules envisage a procedure in terms of which the defender merely lodges a response form, and the sheriff notes disputed issues, written defences are lodged in many cases. It seems that, in some sheriff courts, it is still commonplace for defenders' agents to state a brief defence, ask for a diet of proof to be fixed, and seek a period in which to lodge defences, or "a supplementary note of defence". Such a motion is regularly granted. This arrangement seems to be convenient for all parties. The defenders' agents have more time to prepare defences, the pursuers avoid a continuation in order for defences to be lodged, and the sheriff does not have to "identify and note on the summons the issues of fact and law which are in dispute". But this practice is not sanctioned by the 2002 rules,[69] and it was expressly criticised by Sheriff Principal Taylor in *Glasgow Housing Association v Fisher*:[70]

> "[5] It is bad practice for a defender to only say to the court that the granting of decree would be unreasonable and to request that 14 days be allowed for the lodging of a supplementary note of defence. Such an approach prevents the sheriff from conducting the hearing as required by rule 8.3(2)(a) . . .
>
> If a defender does not put forward at the first calling all the facts upon which the defender wishes to rely, the sheriff is thwarted in accomplishing the tasks which the rules have set him or her. The court is entitled to be fully addressed on the defence when the case first calls. If a party is not in a position so to do without good reason then that party will require to bear the consequences.
>
> [6] Before granting decree a sheriff requires to be satisfied in terms of section 16(3) of the Housing (Scotland) Act 2001 that it is reasonable for decree to be granted. In many cases where the defender/tenant is not present and not represented the information regarding the tenant's personal circumstances and therefore the basis for whether it is reasonable to evict or not is supplied by the landlord. They normally have such information on their file. If the defender wishes to put forward facts to support a proposition that it would be unreasonable to grant decree for possession of recovery of the subjects of let, then it is incumbent upon the tenant, or those representing the tenant, to make that information available to the court at the first hearing."

Continuations: rule 8.2(3)

The power to grant continuations under rule 8.2(3) co-exists with the power, under section 16(1) of the 2001 Act, to grant adjournments. In terms of the rules, the sheriff can allow continuations only at the first calling or a continuation thereof. Where a proof diet has been fixed in terms of rule 8.3(3)(d), it may become apparent, by the time that the date for the proof comes along, that it would be appropriate to adjourn the case, perhaps as a result of an agreement between the parties to that effect.[71] This often happens in arrears cases, where the defender has maintained payments between the first calling and the proof. In that situation, the court may utilise the statutory power to adjourn the proceedings, which can then call again in the heritable court after a suitable period.

The ability to adjourn cases is given to the court in recognition that actions of this type may require to be called on numerous occasions, perhaps for lengthy periods, and in particular for monitoring the payment of rent arrears. Accordingly, causes that are, by definition, supposed to be summary will commonly be ongoing for long periods. To that extent, one might say that summary cause eviction actions in security of tenure cases are something

69 It can be traced back to the old Summary Cause Rules (Act of Sederunt (Summary Cause Rules, Sheriff Court) 1976 (SI 1976/476)) under which a defence could be stated at the bar on the first calling and noted on the summons (r 20). The sheriff then had the power to grant leave to the defender to lodge a supplementary note of defence.

70 (n 58). See also *Glasgow West Housing Association Ltd v Harasimowicz* 2015 Hous LR 77.

71 In cases under ground 2 and ground 7 of sch 2 to the 2001 Act, the court has occasionally been persuaded to adjourn cases to enable the defender to show that he can continue to desist from the conduct that gave rise to the ground; see the discussion of these grounds in Chapter 5.

of a square peg in a round hole. The idea of eviction proceedings being "summary" may have been appropriate in the days before statutory security of tenure, when there was no defence to the action. However, where there *is* a defence to the action on the grounds of reasonableness or otherwise, or where the case has been continued for lengthy periods, the proceedings may be summary only in name.

As a response to the problem of rent arrears, some social landlords have tended to initiate eviction actions on a high-volume basis. In a consultation paper issued shortly prior to the introduction of the pre-action requirements for rent arrears cases,[72] the Scottish Government noted that the number of eviction actions raised in the year 2010/2011 was 14,160. The overwhelming majority of these cases were actions against Scottish secure tenants in which the ground for eviction was rent arrears. Clearly it would be impractical for the landlords to obtain and enforce decrees in the majority of these cases. They are raised in the expectation that most would be continued on payment arrangements. The whole purpose of raising proceedings is not to evict the defender, but to use the threat of eviction to compel the defender to address his arrears. The legitimacy of this approach has been questioned, and it necessarily leads to a large number of actions that call on many occasions.

On this theme, the reader may find it interesting to compare the following two statements:

> "I was told by [counsel] for the GHA, on instructions, that a very large number of cases pass through the Heritable Court daily. Although the crave in each action will include a crave for ejection, in very many of the cases the pursuers will move for decree of ejection only as a last resort. The action will be used primarily to put pressure on the tenant to pay off the arrears".[73]

and

> "[I]n the case of Lamb the sheriff touches in particular on the possibility that landlords may use the recovery procedure not in order to regain possession of let properties but simply in order to acquire a 'sword of Damocles' with which to try to enforce payment of rent arrears. I myself have had great anxiety in this regard for many years and I am in absolutely no doubt that, if a sheriff were to be satisfied on reasonable grounds that that was the true intention of the landlords in a particular case, he would be well entitled to refuse decree for recovery of possession as not being reasonable in the circumstances."[74]

As is described in Chapter 4, one of the aims of imposing pre-action requirements is that eviction actions will be used only as a last resort. The aspiration behind section 14A, the subordinate legislation and the Guidance is that arrears problems will be resolved without the need for proceedings.

The decision to grant a continuation under rule 8.2(3) is obviously separate from the decision as to whether or not to grant decree. However, agents, representatives and sheriffs often seem to lose sight of this distinction. The following sequence of events is unfortunately all too common in rent arrears cases:

72 "Better Dispute Resolution in Housing: Consultation on the Introduction of a New Housing Panel for Scotland" para 3.15.

73 From Lord Glennie's opinion in *Brown v Glasgow Housing Authority Ltd* 2007 Hous LR 2.

74 *City of Edinburgh Council v Stirling, City of Edinburgh Council v Lamb* 1993 SCLR 587.

- The case calls and the pursuers move for decree, narrating the level of arrears and the history of non-payment, broken arrangements and so on.
- The defender's agent moves for a continuation for payments towards arrears to be made, outlining the reasons why payments were not made in the past.
- The sheriff refuses the motion for a continuation, and grants decree for recovery of possession in favour of the pursuers.

The reasons for past non-payment and the defender's proposals to clear the arrears are only two of the factors that the court should consider in deciding whether to grant decree for recovery of possession. Where the relevant statute provides that the decree cannot be granted under a particular ground unless the court considers it reasonable to do so, all the relevant circumstances ought to be considered. As has been seen, the court is directed, in relation to cases under the 2001 Act, to have regard to certain circumstances, in particular in terms of section 16(3).

What *should* happen is that the defender's agent ought to make clear, from the outset of his submission, that the defender wishes to oppose the pursuer's motion for decree on the basis that it would not be reasonable to grant the order; however, he also wishes first to make a motion for a continuation to enable payments to be made towards the arrears.

If that motion is refused, the sheriff should then proceed to deal with the case in terms of rule 8.3, which is considered below.

Finally, as is stressed in the above quotation from *Glasgow Housing Association v Fisher*, it is essential, in any case in which the court must decide whether it is reasonable to grant the order, that the parties put before the court all the matters that are relevant, in order to enable the court to discharge the judicial duty described in *Barclay v Hannah*[75] and the other authorities. Agents for both parties should bear in mind that the court may decide to make a final determination of the case at the first calling, and accordingly give some consideration as to whether all the relevant information is available.

Unfortunately, some tenants have chaotic lifestyles, and may seek advice at a very late stage.[76] If, consequently, the defender's representative is not in position to put all the relevant matters before the court, a continuation should be sought. This motion may be made on the basis that the representative is not in a position, at this calling, to say all that might reasonably be said on behalf of the tenant, and that it is in the interests of justice that certain matters are investigated,[77] in order that the court may be fully appraised of all of the relevant issues at a continued calling, so that it can exercise its judgment on reasonableness properly.[78]

75 1947 SC 245, 1947 SLT 235; discussed in Chapter 5.

76 It is common for defenders in eviction cases to be represented by in-court advice projects, or similar, in which case advice is often sought on the day when the case calls.

77 Such as eligibility for benefits, whether the notice of proceedings is valid, and so on.

78 In rent arrears cases, it may also be necessary to seek a continuation in order to obtain the documentation necessary to confirm whether the landlord has complied with the pre-action requirements, for which see Chapter 4.

Failure to appear: rule 8.2(5)(6) and (7)

Decrees granted under these provisions may be recalled in terms of chapter 24 of the SCR.

Where the defender fails to appear, it is suggested that the same questions arise as to the extent that the sheriff should make enquiries, as have already been discussed in relation to rule 7.1. The only difference will be that the sheriff will be able to consider the terms of the response form lodged by the defender in considering whether, for example, it is reasonable to grant an order in terms of the 1988 Act or the 2001 Act.

Rule 8.3

"(1) If, at the hearing, the sheriff is satisfied that the action is incompetent or that there is a patent defect of jurisdiction, he must grant decree of dismissal in favour of the defender or, if appropriate, transfer the action in terms of rule 16.1(2).

(2) At the hearing, the sheriff shall–

(a) ascertain the factual basis of the action and any defence, and the legal basis on which the action and defence are proceeding; and

(b) seek to negotiate and secure settlement of the action between the parties.

(3) If the sheriff cannot secure settlement of the action between the parties, he shall–

(a) identify and note on the summons the issues of fact and law which are in dispute;

(b) note on the summons any facts which are agreed;

(c) where it appears that the claim as stated or any defence stated in response to it is not soundly based in law in whole or in part, hear parties forthwith on that matter and may grant decree in favour of any party;

(d) if satisfied that the claim and any defence have or may have a sound basis in law and that the dispute between the parties depends upon resolution of disputed issues of fact, fix a diet of proof or, alternatively, if satisfied that the claim and any defence have a sound basis in law and that the facts of the case are sufficiently agreed, hear parties forthwith on the merits of the action and may grant decree in whole or in part in favour of any party; and

(e) enquire whether there is or is likely to be a vulnerable witness within the meaning of section 11(1) of the 2004 Act who is to give evidence at any proof or hearing, consider any child witness notice or vulnerable witness application that has been lodged where no order has been made and consider whether any order under section 12(1) of the 2004 Act requires to be made."

Questions of law: rule 8.3(1) and (3)(c)

Rule 8.3(1) probably reflects the sheriff's common law duty to consider matters that are *pars judicis*, whether or not the parties invite him to do so.[79] Rule 8.3(3)(c) envisages the sheriff hearing parties on the issue of whether the claim and any defence are "soundly based in law" It is common for the competency of eviction actions in the sheriff court to be challenged on the basis that the pursuer has failed to follow the necessary procedural steps prior to raising

79 See p 446.

proceedings. These steps are outlined in Chapters 3 and 4. Suffice it to say at this point that the issues that arise can be quite complex, and may require a legal debate on the competency or relevancy of the action, with reference to authority. However, there is no scope for diets of debate to be fixed under the SCR. In so far as points of law arise at the first calling, rule 8.3(1) and (3)(c) appear to envisage that submissions will be made there and then. However, this may be impractical if the submissions will be lengthy, especially if the sheriff has many other cases to hear on that day; accordingly, issues of law that arise under rule 8.3(1) and (3)(c) may have to be determined at a separate hearing, which has the character of a debate but is, strictly speaking, a continuation of the first calling.[80] If the point has been raised by the defender, but the pursuer is successful, it will then be necessary for the first calling to continue from where it left off, with the sheriff dealing with the case in terms of the remaining parts of chapter 8, perhaps by fixing a proof if there are outstanding factual issues.

If, however, the sheriff takes the view that the legal issues in dispute between the parties cannot be properly considered until evidence is led, it is submitted that it would be appropriate to fix a diet of proof under rule 8.3(3)(c), which is discussed below, on the basis that the term "proof" in that rule includes "proof before answer". This appears to be the only practical approach to cases in which the legal issues cannot be decided before the facts are determined.

The importance of taking competency points at the first calling

Under rule 8.3(3), the sheriff is required to deal with the issue of whether "a claim as stated or any defence stated in response to it is not soundly based in law in whole or in part" at the first calling, or a continuation thereof. He may fix a proof only on the basis that "the claim and any defence have or may have a sound basis in law and that the dispute between the parties depends upon resolution of disputed issues of fact".

For the defender to move for a diet of proof to be fixed, or to consent to the fixing of a proof, is therefore arguably inconsistent with the assertion that the action is incompetent. For example, the argument that an action under the 2001 Act is incompetent for want of service of a valid notice of proceedings under section 14 of the Act is a contention, in effect, that the facts in relation to the merits of the action (establishing the ground, or whether it is reasonable to grant order) do not matter, because the statutory procedure has not been followed.[81]

80 This was the procedure adopted, for example, in *South Lanarkshire Council v McKenna*, in which there were, in effect, two separate debates under r 8.3(3)(c), at which both parties were represented by counsel. These are separately reported at 2010 Hous LR 36 and 2010 Hous LR 82.

81 The position is different, however, as regards an argument that an action on the ground of rent arrears is not competent, because the pre-action requirements have not been met. As explained in Chapter 4, that may involve disputed issues of fact, and an exercise of judgment by the sheriff, probably after hearing evidence. See *Glasgow West Housing Association v Silva* (n 54) para 37. In that case, the competency point was taken in defences lodged after the proof was fixed. However, the proof was discharged on an undertaking by the defender that he would pay the arrears by a certain date. It was at this point, in the view of the Appeal Sheriff, that the defender had abandoned the argument that the action was incompetent.

Therefore once the proof is fixed, allowing such a point to be introduced is arguably problematic. The competency of the action cannot be heard as a preliminary matter at the proof; there is no provision under the rules for the court to separate the proof into different issues in that manner. To have a proof on the merits, with the possibility that the action may be dismissed on a debate point, involves time and expense, the wasting of which would be prejudicial to the pursuers.

There is authority, albeit of some vintage, to the effect that a defender may, by his conduct, be taken to have waived a plea to the competency of an action, and therefore may be personally barred from objecting to proceedings as incompetent, having allowed steps to take place inconsistent such an objection.[82] Therefore, it is suggested that any competency point raised after the proof is fixed is subject to the argument that the defender is barred from taking it.[83] For that reason, it appropriate to emphasise again the importance of defenders' representatives checking statutory notices, notices to quit, pre-action requirements etc. for possible competency issues, in advance of the first calling of the case.

Ascertaining the factual and legal basis of the claim and defence: rule 8.3(2)(a)

The direction given by rule 8.3(2)(a) is independent of the requirement on the parties to lodge a statement of claim or response form. Thus, even though the sheriff has that material in front of him, he is nevertheless directed by the rule to *ascertain* the legal and factual basis of the action and any defence. It may not be possible for him simply to rely on what the response form and the statement of claim tell him. The intention of rule 8.3 is that the sheriff should be interventionist.[84]

In cases in which the parties are represented, it should be straightforward for the sheriff to carry out his duty under rule 8.3(2). However, where the defender or the pursuer is a party litigant, a question may arise as to what sort of intervention is appropriate.

The first point to make is that it is not improper or inappropriate for the sheriff to offer limited assistance to a party litigant in putting matters before the court that would enable the sheriff to exercise its judicial function, so long as that does not result in prejudice to his opponent.[85] To do so is in the interests of justice. It is suggested that the position of the sheriff and a party litigant at the first calling of a summary cause is analogous. The sheriff may make a final disposal of the case at that hearing, on the basis of the information put before him by the parties. A party litigant may be at a disadvantage in relation to that

82 Reid and Blackie, *Personal Bar*, paras 19-41 and 19-42, citing *inter alia*: *North British Railway Co. v Carter* (1870) 8 M 998 and *Lang v Glasgow Court House Commissioners* (1871) 9 M 768. On the other hand, in *McFadyen v McGhee* 2014 GWD 17-308, Sheriff Principal Lockhart said (at para 15 of his judgment): "in my opinion the competency of an action is something which can be noted by either party or by the court at any time during the course of a litigation".

83 Or has, by his conduct, has decided not to insist upon it, as in *Glasgow West Housing Association v Silva* (n 54).

84 Macphail (n 25) para 31.139. This may extend to enquiring into the evidential basis on essential matters of fact are asserted: *Ewen v Smart* 2015 GWD 37-586.

85 Macphail (n 25) para 4.120; *Moore v Secretary of State for Scotland* 1985 SLT 38, 39.

hearing. Where statute provides that an eviction order should be granted only where it is reasonable to do so, it charges the court with a judicial duty to consider the whole of the circumstances in which the application for a decree for recovery of possession is made.[86] Therefore, it may be in the interests of justice for the sheriff to provide some limited assistance to an unrepresented party. He could do so by pointing out the matters that would be relevant to the exercise of his judgment, such as the section 16(3) factors in cases under the 2001 Act, or the defender's personal and family circumstances, the effect that any decree for eviction would be liable to have on him, the reasons why the conduct that establishes the ground occurred, health problems, issues in relation to the payment of state benefits and so on. He could then invite the defender to advise him of any circumstances that are relevant to those matters.

It is reasonable to expect that a party litigant may not be aware that the court may grant decree only if it is reasonable to do so, and also may not be aware that in considering that question, that the court should take into account the whole circumstances in which the motion for decree is made. Further, it is reasonable to expect that, because he is not so aware, there are certain matters that would be relevant to the exercise of the sheriff's judgment that might require to be ascertained from the party litigant by enquiry. Without making such an enquiry, the sheriff will not be in a position properly to discharge his judicial duty to consider the whole circumstances in which the motion for decree for eviction was made.

These contentions might be subject to the objection that the Inner House held, in *City of Glasgow Council v Erhaiganoma*,[87] that once the statutory ground is established and a *prima facie* case for reasonableness is made out, it is for the tenant to put matters before the court to show why the order should not be granted. However, that means that there is something akin to a provisional burden of proof that has shifted to the defender. The question that then arises, in the context of this discussion, is: in so far as it is for the tenant to then put matters before the court, to what extent is it appropriate for the sheriff to assist, facilitate or prompt a party litigant tenant to do so? Thus, it is submitted, the point considered in *Erhaiganoma* is quite separate from the issue discussed in the preceding paragraphs.

Rule 8.3(2)(b)

This requirement, which was an innovation of the 2002 Rules, appears to have received a fairly lukewarm reception from the Bench.[88] It is suggested that, in order to comply with rule 8.3(2)(b), the sheriff might at least enquire whether there has been any dialogue between the parties, and whether further time for discussion might be useful. In practice, in eviction cases, the sheriff invariably proceeds on the basis that such discussions have already taken place, but to no avail. In fairness, this is true in most cases.[89] In addition, there is authority to

86 *Barclay v Hannah* (n 75).

87 (n 57): see p 448 above, in which it is submitted that the decision in *Erhaiganoma* must be considered in light of s 16(3) of the 2001 Act.

88 See, e.g., *Armstrong v Brake Brothers (Frozen Foods) Ltd* 2003 SLT (Sh Ct) 58 and Macphail, (n 25) para 31.139.

89 In arrears cases, the larger local authority and housing association landlords are usually amenable to offers to repay the rent arrears, for the reasons stated at p 453. Also, the pre-

the effect that where the parties are clearly far apart, the sheriff is entitled to conclude that further negotiation would serve little purpose.[90]

Rule 8.3(3)(a) and (b)

The extent to which these rules are followed appears to be variable. It is not uncommon to see cases in which decree has apparently been granted under rule 8.3(3)(d), but in relation to which the disputed issues and the agreed facts have not been noted on the summons. As will be suggested in the next section, this may in itself provide a ground of appeal, it being arguable that the sheriff cannot decide that facts are "sufficiently agreed" in terms of rule 8.3(3)(d) unless he has noted the agreed facts on the summons.

Preliminary considerations: rule 8.3(3)(d)

It is appropriate at this stage to recap on the various steps that the sheriff must go through in order to arrive at this point. First, he may have had to consider (and refuse) any motion that has been made for a continuation or adjournment in the case in terms of rule 8.2(3). Thereafter, he must have:

- ascertained the factual basis of the action and any defence, and the legal basis on which the action and defence are proceeding;[91]
- sought to negotiate and secure settlement of the action;[92]
- identified and noted on the summons the issues of fact and law that are in dispute;[93]
- noted on the summons any (i.e. all) of the facts that are agreed;[94]
- if necessary, heard parties on whether the claim or defence or any part of the claim or defence is not soundly based in law.[95]

It must be emphasised that all these steps are prerequisites to the sheriff fixing a proof, or disposing of the case on the merits, in terms of rule 8.3(3)(d). In particular, where the sheriff grants decree in favour of the defender or the pursuer at the first calling, or a continuation thereof, the sheriff must have identified and noted on the summons the issues of fact and law that are in dispute, and all the facts that were agreed.[96] Two consequences follow. First, it is submitted that, in any case in which these details have *not* been noted, the party against whom decree has been granted under rule 8.3(3)(d) would have

action requirements impose certain obligations on the landlord to try to reach a repayment arrangement with the tenant, as described in Chapter 4. On the other hand, in arrears cases, it is generally not possible to negotiate payment of a sum lower than the outstanding arrears . That is in contrast to the usual run of contractual or delictual actions for payment or damages.

90 *Armstrong v Brake Brothers (Frozen Foods) Ltd* (n 88).

91 Rule 8.2(2)(a).

92 Rule 8.3(2)(b), subject to the somewhat limited sense in which that obligation has been interpreted, as discussed above.

93 Rule 8.3(3)(a).

94 Rule 8.3(3)(b).

95 Rule 8.3(3)(c).

96 Assuming that the decree was granted under r 8.3(3)(d); as seen, the sheriff also has the power to grant decree in terms of other provisions of ch 8.

a stateable ground of appeal.[97] Secondly, any agent advising on the possibility of appealing such a decision should obtain a copy of the summons, in order to ascertain what the sheriff noted.[98]

Further considerations: rule 8.3(3)(d)

In many actions for recovery of possession of heritable property, it will be clear that a diet of proof must be fixed. In particular, where there is a dispute as to whether, as a matter of fact, a statutory ground for recovery of possession is established, it will be apparent that the dispute between the parties does indeed depend upon the resolution of a disputed issue of fact. That may also be the case where there is an argument that an action on the ground of rent arrears is not competent, because the pre-action requirements have not been met. As was explained in Chapter 4, that may involve disputed issues of fact, and an exercise of judgment by the sheriff, probably after hearing evidence.[99]

However, as has been seen, it is also possible for the defender in an action under section 16 of the 2001 Act, on a "discretionary" ground, to admit that the ground is established, but defend the action on the basis that the additional requirement[100] in terms of the Act has not been established.[101]

Consider the nature of the dispute between the parties, and the function of the court in relation to that dispute. Reasonableness is a concept or conclusion determined by an exercise of judgment.[102] The person making such a judgment has "a judicial duty to consider the whole of the circumstances in which the application is made"[103] and must give "such weight as he thinks right to the various factors in the situation".[104] Therefore, what is in issue between the parties is the weight that ought to be attached, individually or cumulatively, to the facts on which they rely. Each party argues, in essence, that the facts on which he founds are more compelling, more persuasive, more convincing,

97 That said, it is open to question whether an appeal on that "technical" ground alone would succeed, irrespective of other factors that might suggest that the sheriff's decision was correct.

98 As well as indicating whether the sheriff followed the requirements of ch 8, the sheriff's notes on the summons may indicate whether he has had regard to the factors listed in s 16(3) of the 2001 Act.

99 *Glasgow West Housing Association v Silva* (n 54) para 37.

100 I.e. that it is reasonable to grant the order, or in the case of an action under grounds 8–15 of sch 2 to the 2001 Act, that other suitable accommodation will be available for the tenant when the order takes effect.

101 The tenant may defend the action on the basis that it would not be reasonable to grant the order: see the discussion of *Barclay v Hannah* (n 75) in Chapter 5. This is also implicit in the remarks made by Sheriff Principal Nicholson in *Midlothian Council v Roxburgh* (n 51), and by Sheriff Principal Macphail in *City of Edinburgh Council v Ure* (n 51), quoted above. Likewise, in a case under grounds 8–15 of sch 2 to the 2001 Act, the defender may admit the ground, but defend the action on the basis of a denial that the accommodation which will be available for him when the order takes effect is not reasonably suitable to his needs and the needs of his family in terms of sch 2 para 16(b).

102 *City of Edinburgh Council v Forbes* 2002 Hous LR 61, 64; *Glasgow Housing Association v Fisher* (n 58). See the discussion of the "reasonableness" requirement in Chapter 5, from p 144. The same can be said of a judgment, in relation to grounds 8–15 under the 2001 Act, as to whether accommodation is reasonably suitable to the needs of the defender and his family, or whether the defender has acted reasonably in refusing an offer of alternative accommodation.

103 *Barclay v Hannah* (n 75).

104 *Cumming v Danson* [1942] 2 All ER 653, 655 (Lord Greene). These words are taken from a passage quoted at 146.

weightier or more important. The sheriff must decide which of these arguments he prefers. This is not a question solely of fact or of law,[105] though it has been described as a mixed question of fact and law.[106]

As regards rule 8.3(3)(d), the question that arises is this: what is to happen if, in relation to the issue of whether the additional requirement is established, the facts founded on by the pursuers are not disputed by the defender, and the facts founded on by the defender are not disputed by the pursuers, but the parties are in dispute as to whether the pursuers have established the additional requirement?

At this point, it may be helpful to consider some specific examples by way of illustration:

Example 1. In an action under ground 1 of the 2001 Act, the case calls before the sheriff on the calling date. The pursuers' agent advises the sheriff that the defender has arrears of £1,143. The arrears have arisen since the action was raised, and have doubled since the notice of proceedings was served on the defender, who has a history of broken payment arrangements. The defender's agent advises that the defender suffered from a period of ill health approximately eighteen months before, when she was diagnosed as suffering from cervical cancer; that her mother had died of that condition at the beginning of 1999 and she had difficulty coping with her loss; that she is a single parent and the sole carer for her eight-year-old daughter; that she is in receipt of incapacity benefit; that she is probably entitled to housing benefit; and that she has recently made a payment of £25 towards the arrears.[107]

Example 2. In an action under ground 2 of the 2001 Act, the case calls before the sheriff on the calling date. The pursuers' agent advises the court that the defender was convicted of two offences under the Misuse of Drugs Act 1971, both involving the supply of a class A drug from her home. The pursuers have a policy of seeking eviction in such cases. That policy is of considerable importance to the pursuers in their efforts to address the effects of drug dealing and drug addiction in their housing estates. The defender's agent advises that the defender served a period of imprisonment for her offences. She underwent a drug rehabilitation programme in prison, and has been drug free since her release. She has the support of the pursuers' social work department in trying to save her tenancy; her social worker considers that her behaviour while on probation after release was exemplary and that she has

105 "[A] question of fact concerns the existence, or some state, at some past time relevant for the inquiry, of some person, or thing, or state of affairs, ascertainable by the senses or by inference from conduct or happenings. Matters of fact thus include e.g. time, place, weather, light, speed, colour, identification of persons, what was said, done, heard and so on, and such inferred facts as a person's intention, sanity, state of mind, knowledge and the like. Matters of fact have to be ascertained, failing admission, by competent and relevant evidence given by witnesses, experts, or provided by deeds, records, reports etc. Matters of law or questions of law on the other hand include what are the rules of law applicable to some issue, what their proper formulations are, and what they require or permit. Matters of law have to be ascertained, failing admission, by interpretation of statutes, cases, and other authoritative sources of the law, aided by the arguments of parties' counsel": D M Walker, *The Oxford Companion to Law* 455.

106 By Jonathan Mitchell in *Eviction and Rent Arrears* para 3.16.

107 These were the facts in *City of Edinburgh Council v Forbes* (n 102), though that case pre-dated the 2001 Act; it was raised under the 1987 Act.

been rehabilitated. There was a considerable delay between the date of her conviction and the pursuers raising proceedings.[108]

Example 3. In an action under ground 10 of the 2001 Act, a local authority seeks to recover possession of subjects from a Scottish secure tenant and his family in order to demolish the building. At the first calling, the tenant accepts that he has received various offers of alternative accommodation, but has refused them on the basis that some were three-apartment properties when he required a four-apartment one, and the two offers made to him of properties that were of a suitable size were situated in unsuitable areas. He states that he is concerned for the health and safety of his family, who have special needs, if they were to move to either of these properties, the first of which is situated in a street where a friend of the defender was murdered. The pursuers contend that the character and nature of the area in which the property is situated are irrelevant. The issue between the parties is whether, in terms of schedule 2 paragraph 18 to the 2001 Act, the tenant has "acted reasonably" in failing to accept the offers.[109]

Under the old SCR, the sheriff was originally obliged, in terms of rule 18(7), to fix a proof in any case in which a defence was stated. Later, rule 18(9) was added, which gave the sheriff a discretionary power to grant decree at the first calling if the facts of the cause were sufficiently admitted.

In *City of Edinburgh Council v Forbes,*[110] in which the facts were as stated in Example 1 above, the sheriff granted decree under rule 18(9). On appeal, Sheriff Principal Nicholson took the view that this decision was within the discretion afforded to the sheriff by that rule. In particular, the sheriff was not obliged to fix a proof on the basis of a contention by the defender that it would not be reasonable to grant the order.

There was clearly a sharp divergence in practice as between different courts in relation to arrears cases, which tended to form the vast majority of the cases that were calling in the "heritable court". To take two examples: at Glasgow Sheriff Court, a proof was invariably allowed if the defender was represented, and a defence was stated to the effect that it would not be reasonable to grant the order; however, at Edinburgh Sheriff Court proofs on reasonableness were rarely fixed. However, in relation to cases under other grounds, such as those described in Examples 2 and 3 above, proofs were always allowed, presumably on the basis that these cases were less usual and presented a greater degree of complexity. It is thought that these differences in approach have not been substantially affected by the 2002 Rules; proofs on the issue of "reasonableness" are the norm in some sheriff courts but not in others.

108 These were the facts in *South Lanarkshire Council v Fraser* Unreported decision of Sheriff Cameron, 26 March 2004 (Hamilton Sheriff Court). In that case, the sheriff granted decree in favour of the pursuers after hearing a proof, at which both the pursuers and defender led evidence. Note that if the action is raised under the new streamlined eviction procedure for ground 2 cases, under s 16(2)(aa) of the 2001 Act, it will no longer be necessary to consider whether it is reasonable to grant the order.

109 This example is based on *Dundee City Council v McPhee* 2005 Hous LR 30. The sheriff's note indicates that "It was agreed by the parties . . . that the only real issue was that of suitability of alternative housing offered by the pursuers to the defender. A joint minute of admission was signed and lodged."

110 (n 102).

To some extent, this is surprising, because it appears to have been the intention of the Sheriff Court Rules Council to effect a change in practice in summary cause cases, with more cases being disposed of at the first calling, and fewer diets of proof being fixed.[111]

That intention is apparent from the wording of rule 8.3(3)(d). A close consideration of the rule indicates that it applies if the sheriff is satisfied that the claim and any defence have or may have a sound basis in law. In that case he *shall*:

- fix a proof, if he is satisfied that *the dispute between the parties depends upon resolution of disputed issues of fact*, or
- hear the parties forthwith on the merits of the action, if he is satisfied that *the facts of the case are sufficiently agreed.*

The use of the term "*sufficiently* agreed" appears to envisage that there will be cases in which the sheriff decides that, even though there is a lack of consensus between the parties on certain matters of fact, this does not prevent him from making a decision on the merits. This may be because the factual issues are not relevant, or because he decides that even if the factual dispute were to be resolved in favour of the pursuer, for example, he would still determine the cause in favour of the defender.

However, the important point is that a case in which the facts are "sufficiently agreed" appears to be one in which any dispute between the parties does not depend upon resolution of any issues of fact which are not agreed. In other words, the two options available to the sheriff in terms of rule 8.3(3)(d) appear to be mutually exclusive. A case falls into one category or the other; it cannot fall into both. Once the sheriff decides whether the dispute between the parties depends upon resolution of disputed issues of fact, his next step, in terms of procedure, is predetermined.

It seems clear that the type of case under discussion, examples of which are given above, is not one in which the dispute between the parties depends upon resolution of disputed issues of fact.[112] Therefore, if one strictly follows the terms of the rules, it appears that in all cases in which the dispute is only as to whether it is reasonable to grant the order,[113] the sheriff is bound "to hear parties forthwith on the merits of the action" and decide the case at the first calling, or a continuation thereof. That appears to be the case irrespective of any constraints of time; the number and complexity of the various factors involved; and whether parties, and indeed the sheriff, consider that it would be desirable for evidence to be led, to enable the sheriff to have a full picture of the relevant issues.

111 I.e. to continue the trend set by the addition of r 18(9) of the old Rules.

112 One could argue that a dispute as to whether it would be reasonable to grant the order is a disputed issue *of* fact, in the sense that the parties' dispute is about the facts, i.e. what weight should be attached to them. However, this would appear to confuse a factual dispute with a disagreement about how agreed facts are to be assessed.

113 Or whether accommodation is reasonably suitable.

A special rule for heritable cases?

As was suggested in the discussion of rule 8.2(3), summary cause eviction cases may be thought of as a square peg in a round hole. Only two types of hearing are available: the first calling, in a busy heritable or summary cause court with all the other business calling; or a proof, which is the appropriate hearing for a resolution of disputed issues of fact. The first calling is inappropriate in many cases because there may be insufficient time to consider the issues properly, and for the sheriff properly to discharge the judicial duty described above. The proof is arguably inappropriate because there is no dispute on the facts between the parties.

It is submitted that, given the number of summary cause cases in which this is the nature of the parties' dispute, and further given the sheriff's judicial duty, as described above, she ought, in terms of the rules, to be able to determine the case at a hearing that, in her view, best enables her to exercise that function. There should not be rigid rules, in terms of which proofs are always fixed or never fixed. Given the volume of actions raised in which this is the nature of the dispute between the parties, and the importance of the matter to the litigants involved, it is submitted that a special rule would be justified. This would be to the effect that, in any case in which the pursuer seeks an order for recovery of possession of heritable property, and where the parties are in dispute as to whether:

(a) in terms of section 16(2)(a)(ii) of the 2001 Act, it would be reasonable to make such an order, or
(b) in terms of section 16(2)(b)(ii) of the 2001 Act, suitable alternative accommodation will be available to the defender once the order takes effect,

the sheriff would have a discretionary power, without prejudice to rule 8.3(3)(d), to fix a hearing (at which evidence may be led) to determine whether the order should be granted. Under section 75 of the Courts Reform (Scotland) Act 2014, the power to make rules for the new simple procedure "is to be exercised so far as possible with a view to ensuring that the sheriff before whom a simple procedure case is conducted . . . can adopt a procedure that is appropriate to and takes account of the particular circumstances of the case". It remains to be seen whether the new rules will allow a degree of flexibility as the form of hearing by the court, in heritable cases in which a judgment of the type under discussion is to be made.

Rule 8.3(3) and defences based on public law, article 8, and unlawful discrimination

Reference is made to the discussion of these defences in Chapter 11. The Supreme Court said in *Manchester City Council v Pinnock*[114] that article 8 defences should be dealt with "summarily": if the court is satisfied that, even if the facts relied on by the defender are made out, the point would not succeed, the defence should not be entertained. Thus, both the judgment of the Supreme Court and rule 8.3(3)(d) suggest that the court should deal with an

114 [2011] 2 AC 104, para 61.

article 8 defence at the first calling (or a continuation thereof), unless it raises a disputed issue of fact that requires to be resolved.

By contrast, defences based on the Equality Act 2010 are more likely to necessitate the leading of evidence, in relation to matters such as: whether the defender is a disabled person under the Act, whether there has been prohibited conduct under chapter 2 of part 2, and so on. Disposal of the case at the first calling is possible, but such cases will be rare.[115]

Where the defence concerns issues as to the legality of the landlord's conduct on other grounds, the appropriate procedure will depend on point raised. Where there are disputed issues of fact, a proof will be appropriate. Otherwise, the court may continue the first calling to a hearing at which to determine, under rule 8.3(3)(c), whether the defence is soundly based in law.[116]

Rule 8.3(3)(e)

This rule effectively enjoins the sheriff to consider whether the case might require any measure under part 2 of the Vulnerable Witnesses (Scotland) Act 2004. That Act may have some application, for example, in actions raised on the ground of antisocial behaviour: under section 11(2)(e) of the Act, the court is required to take into account any behaviour towards a person on the part of any party to the proceedings, or members of the family or associates of any such party, in deciding whether that person is a vulnerable witness.

MINUTES FOR RECALL OF DECREE: ch 24

Recall of decree is of considerable importance in eviction cases; a minute under chapter 24 may be lodged at any time up to the date of ejection, and is the means of preventing eviction for tenants who, for whatever reason, have left it to the last minute before seeking advice. Rule 24.1 has undergone significant amendment.[117] Its importance is such that it is worth setting out in full:

> "**24.1 Recall of decree**
>
> (1) A party may apply for recall of a decree granted under any of the following provisions—
>   (a) rule 7.1; or
>   (b) paragraph (5), (6) or (7) of rule 8.2.
>
> (2) The application is to be by minute in Form 30, which must be lodged with the sheriff clerk.
>
> (3) The application must include where appropriate (and if not already lodged with the sheriff clerk), the proposed defence or the proposed answer to the counterclaim.
>
> (4) A party may apply for recall of a decree in the same action on one occasion only.

115 See *Aster Communities v Ackerman-Livingstone* [2015] AC 1399, paras [35] and [36].

116 See the discussion at p 455.

117 An entirely new version of the rule was inserted by para 16 of the Act of Sederunt (Sheriff Court Rules) (Miscellaneous Amendments) 2011 (SSI 2011/193), with effect from 4 April 2011.

(5) A minute for recall of a decree of dismissal must be lodged within 14 days of the date of decree.
(6) Subject to paragraphs (7) to (9), a minute for recall of any other kind of decree may be lodged at any time before the decree is fully implemented.
(7) Subject to paragraphs (8) and (9), where a charge or arrestment has been executed following the decree, the minute must be lodged within 14 days of that execution (or the first such execution where there has been more than one).
(8) Subject to paragraph (9), in the case of a party seeking recall who was served with the action under rule 5.7, the minute must be lodged—
  (a) within a reasonable time of such party having knowledge of the decree against him or her; but
  (b) in any event, within one year of the date of decree.
(9) Where the decree includes a decree for removing from heritable property to which section 216(1) of the Bankruptcy and Diligence etc. (Scotland) Act 2007 applies, the minute may be lodged at any time before the defender has been removed from the subjects or premises.
(10) On the lodging of a minute for recall of a decree, the sheriff clerk must fix a date, time and place for a hearing of the minute.
(11) Where a hearing has been fixed under paragraph (10), the party seeking recall must, not less than 7 days before the date fixed for the hearing, serve upon the other party—
  (a) a copy of the minute in Form 30a; and
  (b) a note of the date, time and place of the hearing.
(12) At a hearing fixed under paragraph (10), the sheriff must recall the decree so far as not implemented and the hearing must then proceed as a hearing held under rules 8.2(3) to (7) and 8.3.
(13) A minute for recall of a decree, when lodged and served in terms of this rule, will have the effect of preventing any further action being taken by the other party to enforce the decree.
(14) On receipt of the copy minute for recall of a decree, any party in possession of an extract decree must return it forthwith to the sheriff clerk.
(15) If it appears to the sheriff that there has been any failure or irregularity in service of the minute for recall of a decree, the sheriff may order re-service of the minute on such conditions as the sheriff thinks fit."

"A party": rule 24.1(1)

In several cases a person other than a defender has sought to lodge a minute for recall, on the basis that he or she has title and interest, as a non-entitled spouse under the 1981 Act, or as a qualifying occupier under sections 14 and 15 of the 2001 Act, and would be entitled to enter the process by minute in terms of chapter 14. The preponderance of authority now appears to be to the effect that such applications are incompetent, given the terms of rule 24.1(1).[118] Assuming that that is correct, it is notable that the rule on reponing in ordinary causes was amended in 2004, by addition after "defender" of the words "or any party with a statutory title or interest".[119] No equivalent change

118 An application was allowed in *City of Edinburgh Council v Porter* 2004 Hous LR 46, but refused in *North Lanarkshire Council v Kenmure*; 2004 Hous LR 50; and in *Stirling Council v Neil* 2006 SLT (Sh Ct) 51. *North Lanarkshire Council v Cairns* 2012 SLT (Sh Ct) 128, a decision of Sheriff Principal Lockhart against such an application, seems to put the matter to rest.

119 In terms of the Act of Sederunt (Ordinary Cause, Summary Application, Summary Cause and Small Claim Rules) Amendment (Miscellaneous) 2004 (SSI 2004/197), r 2(5)(a)(i).

has been made to the SCR. Similarly, the rules applying to recall of decree in mortgage repossession actions in respect of residential property allow an application to be made by an entitled resident.[120] It follows that the spouse of the defender, resident at the subjects, would have the right to seek recall in a mortgage repossession case, or to be reponed in an eviction action raised as an ordinary cause, but cannot seek recall in an eviction action raised as a summary cause.

Rule 24.1(1): decree granted under rules 7.1 or 8.2(5), (6) or (7)

The effect of this part of the rule is that only decrees granted at the first calling of the case, or a continuation thereof, may be recalled. It is not possible to recall a decree granted by default in terms of rule 22 – for example, after a failure to appear at a proof diet, or a procedural calling fixed in the case, after a proof diet has been discharged[121] though in such a case appeal might be possible.[122] Where a case is sisted at the first calling, the hearing that takes place on recall of the sist may also be be regarded as a first calling.[123] Accordingly, if decree is granted in the absence of one the parties, recall may be sought.[124]

In *City of Edinburgh Council v Ure*,[125] it was held that where a defender attends court at the first calling, and makes representations to the court when the case calls, he has appeared for the purposes of the rules, notwithstanding his failure to lodge a response form. Therefore, he could not seek to recall the decree because, having appeared, he could not state his reason for failure to appear in the minute. Since then, however, the requirement to state in the minute the reason for failure to appear has been removed.[126] Therefore, it is submitted that the defender could appear at a first hearing and subsequently ask for any decree granted against him to be recalled. However, that would be possible only if it could be shown that the decree was granted under rule 7.1. Where the original sheriff has heard representations that amount to a defence to the action, and has then decided in favour of the pursuers, it would seem correct to regard him as dispensing with requirement for a response form and then granting decree under rule 8.3.[127] Were that not so, it would be possible for the defender, by means of the minute for recall, to require the court to consider the same argument twice.

120 Recall may be sought by an "entitled resident", a term defined in s 24C of the Conveyancing and Feudal Reform (Scotland) Act 1970, under s 24D(2)(c). These provisions were inserted into the 1970 Act by amendments in the Home Owner and Debtor Protection (Scotland) Act 2010.

121 *Easthall Park Housing Co-operative Ltd v Martin* 2012 Hous LR 68. See also: *Glasgow West Housing Association v Silva* (n 54). This important point is often overlooked. It is not uncommon for proofs to be discharged on a payment arrangement, and for the case to subsequently call on repeated occasions in the heritable court. However, these are not callings under r 8, and if the defender fails to appear and decree is granted, recall is not possible.

122 For a case in which an appeal was made in such circumstances, see *Aberdeen City Council v Shauri* 2006 Hous LR 40. For an informative discussion of the considerations applicable to appeal against decree by default, see Macphail (n 25) paras 14.14 and 14.15.

123 See the discussion of sists at p 472 below.

124 *BBM Solicitors v Younger* 2014 GWD 34-644.

125 (n 51).

126 See the next section.

127 A decree under r 8.3 cannot be recalled. See also *Midlothian Council v Roxburgh* (n 51).

Rule 24.1(2) and (3): the content of the minute for recall

Under the old Summary Cause Rules (1976), the standard form minute for recall simply required the minuter to state the name and number of the case, and the date on which decree was granted and, if applicable, the date on which a charge was served. The 2002 rules (prior to the amendment in 2011) introduced the requirement to state: (a) an explanation for failure to appear; and (b) the proposed defence.[128] This made the minute for recall more like a reponing note under the Ordinary Cause Rules. In the current version of the rule, the requirement to give an explanation for failure to appear has been discarded.[129]

Given that minutes for recall are often prepared by party litigants or other lay persons, a question can arise as to whether the minute properly states a "defence" to the action. In cases in which this point is in issue, it is suggested that the court ought nevertheless to recall the decree, and consider the adequacy of the defence in the context of the rule 8.3 hearing that then takes place. Rule 24.1(3) requires only that the minute contain a "*proposed* defence". As long as it does, the sheriff has no discretion under rule 24.1(12) to refuse to recall the decree.[130] If the defence is indeed inadequate, decree may be granted anew.

Rule 24.1(4): a party may apply for recall on one occasion only

Simply making an application for recall is enough to preclude a subsequent application. It is not necessary that the previous application was granted.[131]

Rule 24.1(5)-(9): the time limit for lodging the minute

Previously there was some doubt as to the time limit that operated in a case in which a charge had been served.[132] This matter is helpfully clarified by rule

128 In the case of an application for recall by a pursuer, the minute required him to state his response to any counterclaim which had been made. That is still the case, under the amended version of r 24.1.

129 The new form of r 24.1 was inserted by para 16(1) of the Act of Sederunt (Sheriff Court Rules) (Miscellaneous Amendments) (SSI 2011/193). In terms of para 16(2) the words "reason for failure to appear or be represented" are deleted from the form 30 that the minuter requires to use, under r 24.1(2).

130 In *Clydebank Housing Association v McEmerson* 2004 SLT (Sh Ct) 25 the sheriff refused the minute for recall, lodged by the defender as a party litigant, as he was not satisfied that it disclosed a defence to the action; the minute simply referred to ongoing negotiations between the parties. The defender appealed unsuccessfully to the sheriff principal. It is understood that the effect of this decision was that the defender was able to lodge another minute for recall, which was not prohibited in terms of r 24.1(4) because the defender was held not to have made any application in terms of ch 24. That outcome now seems open to question, given the decision in *West of Scotland Housing Association v Daly* 2009 Hous LR 101. However, it is nevertheless submitted that questions as to the adequacy of the defence are best considered in the context of the r 8.3 hearing.

131 *West of Scotland Housing Association v Daly*. For further discussion of this case, see the section on r 24.(12) and (15), below.

132 Say, in an action seeking decree for (a) eviction and (b) payment of a sum of money (e.g. rent arrears). Before the coming into force of pt 15 of the Bankruptcy and Diligence etc. (Scotland) Act 2007, a charge would be served in relation to that part of the decree that was for payment of money, but not the eviction part. This left some doubt as to whether the

24.1(9), which confirms that where the decree includes a decree for removing from heritable property to which section 216(1) of the Bankruptcy and Diligence etc. (Scotland) Act 2007 applies, the minute may be lodged at any time before the defender has been "removed" from the subjects or premises.

Under section 215 of that Act, the procedure for removal is set out in the Act of Sederunt described in Chapter 15.[133] It is submitted that the tenant is "removed" for the purposes of rule 24.1(9) when, under paragraph 7 of the Act of Sederunt, execution of the decree is completed by the certificate of execution being affixed to the main door or other conspicuous part of the property in a sealed envelope. It is also suggested that, in so far as rule 24.1(12) allows a decree to be recalled "so far as not implemented", that implementation of a decree for recovery of possession under the summary cause rules is removal under the 2007 Act and the Act of Sederunt.

Rule 24.1(11) and (13): service and the effect of service

Once the minute for recall has been lodged and served, the decree for ejection can no longer be enforced. That is only the case, however, when proper service is effected. It is thought that this must be done by an officer of the court. It is understood that some citizens advice bureaux and advice organisations have arrangements with local authorities in terms of which the landlord agrees to postpone the eviction if provided with a copy of the minute for recall. This avoids the expense of service by a sheriff officer. The subsequent appearance of a local authority solicitor at the minute for recall hearing cures any defect in service. The difficulty with this approach is that, in the event of some error or breakdown of communication, the tenant may be evicted by the landlord in terms of the decree, leaving the tenant in a position in which his recourse, if any, is unclear, because without proper service under rule 24.1(11) the decree was enforceable. If an eviction occurs by mistake after proper service of the minute, the tenant's position is clear. He has the usual remedies for unlawful eviction described in Chapter 2. In such a case one would expect that he would simply be reinstated, once the error was discovered. It is not so clear that this would be the outcome if the minute for recall had not been properly served.

Rule 24.1(12) and (15): the hearing on the minute

Rule 24.1(12) is a mandatory direction to the sheriff to recall the decree at the hearing fixed by the sheriff clerk in terms of rule 24.1(10). However, there are two grounds on which the sheriff can refuse to recall the decree. First, he may continue the case for reservice of the minute in the circumstances outlined in rule 24.1(15). Secondly, he may refuse to grant the minute if he is satisfied that it is incompetent, given the other provisions of rule 24.1.[134] It may therefore be appropriate for the sheriff to continue the case if the minute has not

defender could seek recall in relation to the eviction part of the decree, after expiry of the charge. For a discussion, see the first edition of this work.

133 Being the Act of Sederunt (Actions for removing from heritable property) 2012 (SSI 2012/136).

134 For example, because the party seeking recall has applied for recall of decree before.

been returned to the court at the point when the case calls, on the basis that he cannot satisfy himself that the requirements of rule 24.1 are met. If, however, the minute has been served and lodged with the papers, but the other party has failed to return the summons and extract decree in terms of rule 24.1(14), it is submitted that the decree should nevertheless be recalled under rule 24.1(12), and the case continued for production of the summons.

On occasion, the party who lodged the minute for recall fails to attend court on the date fixed by the sheriff clerk in terms of rule 24.1(10). In practice, this situation has been dealt with in two ways: either the sheriff has recalled the decree and thereafter disposed of the case under chapter 8, usually by granting decree anew; or the sheriff simply allows the minute to drop. The former approach proceeds on the view that the direction given in rule 24.1(12) is mandatory, irrespective of whether the party lodging the minute for recall appears. The latter approach holds that the sheriff still requires the party formally to move that the minute be granted.

There is authority to the effect that the former approach is preferable.[135] This, it is submitted, is correct. If the sheriff recalls the decree and then disposes of the case under chapter 8, there is no doubt as to the parties' respective positions at the end of that calling. Where the minute is simply dropped, doubt has arisen as to what happens thereafter. In this respect, it must be remembered that rule 24.1(13) states that: "A minute for recall of a decree, when lodged and served in terms of this rule, will have the effect of preventing any further action being taken by the other party to enforce the decree." It is by no means clear that allowing the minute for recall to drop has the effect of enabling the other party to enforce the original decree, given the terms of that rule. It is understood that in certain courts the sheriff clerk has, in this situation, allowed a further minute for recall to be lodged, perhaps on the basis that dropping the minute has an effect as if it were never lodged. That seems a dubious approach, given the terms of rule 24.1(4).

SPECIAL RULES FOR ACTIONS FOR RECOVERY OF POSSESSION OF HERITABLE PROPERTY: ch 30

Although chapter 30 contains special rules that apply only to actions for recovery of possession of heritable property, it plays a role in very few actions of that type. In particular, rules 30.1, 30.3 and 30.5–30.8 largely concern actions under the Sheriff Courts (Scotland) Act 1907, which, for the reasons outlined in Chapter 3, will be unusual.

135 *West of Scotland Housing Association v Daly* (n 130). In that case the sheriff had refused the minute for recall for want of insistence, the defender not having appeared at the hearing. At the appeal before Sheriff Principal Taylor, parties were agreed that the sheriff's interlocutor was incompetent, and this appears to have been accepted by the court. It seems clear, therefore, that in a case such as this, the defender's remedy is to lodge an appeal against the interlocutor allowing the minute for recall to drop, rather than lodging another minute for recall.

Rule 30.2: Action against persons in possession without right or title

Rule 30.2 provides for special rules in relation to "actions for recovery of possession of heritable property against a person or persons in possession of heritable property without right or title to possess the property",[136] the general purpose of which is clearly to expedite such actions. The rule does not, however, apply to any person, such as a former tenant or licensee who has or had a title or other right to occupy the property and who has been in continuous occupation since that title or right is alleged to have come to an end.[137] In actions to which rule 30.2 applies, the sheriff may in his discretion shorten or dispense with any period of time provided anywhere in the rules.[138]

In terms of rule 30.2(3) and (4) there are further special rules in relation to instances in which the name of a person in occupation of a heritable property is not known and cannot reasonably be ascertained. In such cases the pursuer may call that person as a defender by naming him as an "occupier". Rule 30.2(4) makes special provision for the service of the summons in such cases.[139]

In cases to which rule 30.2 applies, it is likely that the pursuer will make an application for immediate extract of the decree, under rule 23.6(1). Extract of decree is discussed in Chapter 15.

Rule 30.4: preservation of the defender's goods and effects

Rule 30.4 originally provided that, in relation to any action for recovery of possession, where decree is pronounced and the defender is neither present nor represented, the sheriff may give such directions as he deems proper for the preservation of the defender's goods and effects. This power was not often used in practice, presumably because there was no one present, on behalf of the defender, to ask for such a direction to be made. The rule has now been amended by deletion of the words: "and the defender is neither present nor represented". Accordingly, it is now possible, in a case in which the sheriff grants decree against him, for the defender to ask for an order for preservation of his good and effects to be made by the court.

Rule 30.9: requests for time to pay

The amended rule 30.9[140] was a welcome addition to the SCR. It states:

> "30.9 Where, in response to a summons for the recovery of heritable property which includes a claim for payment of money, a defender makes a written

136 Rule 30.2(1).

137 Rule 30.2(2).

138 Rule 30.2(5). This power does not apply to the fourteen-day period allowed for appeal specified by r 25.1; see r 25.6(a). In terms of r 30.2(6), an application by a party under r 30.2(5) to shorten or dispense with any period may be made orally – the normal rules in relation to incidental applications under r 9.1 do not apply.

139 These provisions have been used in actions to eject travellers in illegal occupation of unauthorised sites.

140 Inserted by para 8 of the Act of Sederunt (Sheriff Court Rules) (Miscellaneous Amendments) 2008 (SSI 2008/223).

application about payment, he shall not thereby be taken to be admitting the claim for recovery of possession of the heritable property."

The purpose of this rule is to deal with a problem in relation to summary cause actions in which the pursuer seeks: (a) an order for recovery of possession of heritable property; and (b) payment of a sum of money, which is almost always rent arrears. It is very common for the defender, without seeking advice or assistance in relation to the summons, simply to complete the request for a time to pay direction and return it to the court. Invariably in such cases, it is thought that what the defender means to do is to make an offer to pay the arrears in the hope that, if that the offer is accepted by the pursuers or sanctioned by the court, he will be allowed to remain in the tenancy. The difficulty is that in order to complete the time to pay application form in the copy summons, the defender must confirm that he "admits the claim" in its entirety, including the claim for recovery of possession. Presumably, however, the defender's true position is that he admits the claim for rent arrears, but does not admit that it would be reasonable to grant an order for recovery of possession under the relevant statutory provision, standing his offer to repay in instalments.

The new rule 30.9 makes it clear that, in such cases, the application by the defender should not be taken to be an admission of that part of the claim that relates to recovery of possession.

OTHER SUMMARY CAUSE RULES

Chapter 9: sists

It is common for actions on the ground of rent arrears to be sisted for payments to be made in terms of an agreement between the parties. These actions may remain sisted for lengthy periods, sometimes for years, while the defender maintains small payments, perhaps from social security benefits.[141]

If the defender fails in the arrangement, the pursuers will, in due course, lodge an incidental application seeking: (a) recall of the sist; and (b) decree for eviction and the outstanding rent arrears.[142] Given the terms of rule 9.1(2), the defender may receive as little as two days' notice of the incidental application, which gives him limited time to seek assistance to resolve the problems that have caused the arrears to go up again.

Rule 9.2(2) does not indicate what type of hearing is to take place once the sheriff decides to recall the sist. As is indicated above, applications to recall sists generally call in the heritable or summary cause court along with all the other cases. It is submitted that, in the absence of any indication in the rules to the contrary, it is appropriate to proceed on the basis that recalling a sist has the effect that the action restarts from the point at which it left off. Accordingly, if it was sisted at a first calling of the case under chapter 8, or a

141 The rent arrears direct scheme, by which small payments are made to arrears by direct deduction from jobseekers' allowance or income support, is discussed in Chapter 5 at p 157.

142 This can also happen where the defender is continuing to make payments towards the arrears, but the rent is not being paid due to a problem with the defender's claim for benefits.

continuation thereof, the cause should, on recall, resume its progress through the various provisions of chapter 8, as outlined above.[143]

Chapter 11: third party procedure

The introduction of a third party procedure in summary causes was another innovation of the 2002 Rules. The procedure potentially has application in arrears cases in which there is a dispute between the defender and a local authority, or the Department for Work and Pensions (DWP) as to the payment of housing benefit or universal credit. For example, the defender may claim, in terms of rule 11.1(b)(ii), that the local authority is liable to him in respect of his claim for housing benefit, which arises from or in connection with his liability for rent arrears to the pursuer, and may apply by incidental application for an order for service of a third party notice upon the local authority. It is suggested that if the defender wants to avail himself of the procedure, he should lodge defences setting out the basis on which the order for a third party notice is sought, and thereafter apply by incidental application for an order for service of the third party notice upon the local authority.[144]

This procedure appears to be quite effective, at least from the defender's point of view: the service of a third party notice on the local authority usually seems to have the effect of prompting action on the part of the authority to resolve matters. An additional benefit to the defender is that he can ask for the expenses of the process to be awarded against the third party.

Chapter 12: summary decree

Again, the introduction of a summary decree procedure was an innovation of the 2002 Rules. It does not appear to be often used. In a case in which the pursuer wishes to argue that the defences do not disclose a defence to the action, he will presumably seek decree at the first calling under chapter 8.[145] Perhaps summary decree may be utilised where, for some reason, that has not been done. It should be noted that, under rule 12.2(3), a motion for summary decree must be intimated not less than seven days before the date fixed for the hearing of the motion.[146]

Chapter 14: additional defender

In terms of rule 14.1, any person who has not been called as a defender may apply by incidental application to the sheriff for leave to enter an action as a defender, and to state a defence. An application under this rule must specify

143 See, for example, *McFadyen v McGhee* (n 82) and *BBM Solicitors v Younger* (n 124).

144 An incidental application is required in terms of r 11.1(1). An application for service of a third party notice must be made at the time when the defender lodges a form of response, unless the sheriff on cause shown permits a later application: r 11.1(2). Further rules as to procedure are set out in r 11.2.

145 Under r 8.3(3)(c), discussed above.

146 In *Glasgow Housing Association Ltd v Li* 2010 Hous LR 6, the defender successfully appealed against the grant of summary decree against her, on the basis that the motion had not been properly intimated.

the applicant's title and interest to enter the action and the grounds of the defence that he proposes to state.

Two particular classes of persons may have title and interest to enter an action as an additional defender: qualifying occupiers (sections 14 and 15 of the 2001 Act) and non-entitled spouses or cohabitees (Matrimonial Homes (Family Protection) (Scotland) Act 1981). These are both discussed in Chapter 12.

Chapter 22: decree by default

> "**22.1.— Decree by default**
> (1) If, after a proof has been fixed under rule 8.3(3)(d), a party fails to appear at a hearing where required to do so, the sheriff may grant decree by default.
> (2) If all parties fail to appear at a hearing or proof where required to do so, the sheriff must, unless sufficient reason appears to the contrary, dismiss the action and any counterclaim.
> (3) If, after a proof has been fixed under rule 8.3(3)(d), a party fails to implement an order of the court, the sheriff may, after giving him an opportunity to be heard, grant decree by default.
> (4) The sheriff shall not grant decree by default solely on the ground that a party has failed to appear at the hearing of an incidental application."

In most cases in which a proof has been fixed, that proof will be the only hearing at which either party is "required to appear". Where no appearance is made at the proof by one or other of the parties, the sheriff is not bound to grant decree. He may instead fix a peremptory diet at which the non-attending party will be required to attend, to confirm whether he wishes to continue to pursue or defend the action.[147] Although the sheriff is not permitted to grant decree solely on the ground that a party has failed to appear at the hearing of an incidental application, such a failure might lead to a peremptory diet being fixed, at which decree could be granted.

In considering rule 22.1(3) it is appropriate to draw a distinction between two different types of default. The first is a failure to comply with a requirement imposed upon a party by the rules (such as a requirement to lodge defences). The second is a failure to comply with an order of the court. Rule 16 of the Ordinary Cause Rule allows for both types of failure to be a default in respect of which decree might be granted. Rule 22.1 of SCR does not. There is no reference in the latter rule to decree of default being granted in the event of a failure to comply with the rules. That, it is submitted, is because the summary cause procedure is a very much more simple process than that which applies to ordinary causes, and places far fewer requirements on the parties as regards (for example) the lodging of documents. The effect of failing to comply with such rules as there are is that the party simply fails to achieve what would have been achieved, had he complied with the rule. Thus, in the case of the lodging of defences, the way of putting a written defence before the court is by lodging a response form under rule 8.1. Where the defender fails to comply with that

147 See Macphail (n 25) para 14.10, where the authors suggest, in relation to the equivalent ordinary cause rule (r 16.2) "If there is a failure to appear and the sheriff is unaware of the reason for the failure to appear, it will usually be appropriate to fix a peremptory diet."

rule, he is not "in default"; he has simply failed to defend the action, which would then proceed under chapter 7.

Where decree is sought under rule 22.1(3), it may be necessary to consider whether the court had the power to make the "order" that the other party has failed to implement. It is understood that there have been summary cause cases in which the court has ordered written defences to be lodged,[148] and then subsequently granted decree by default where that has not been done. However, the sheriff has no power to order the defender to lodge written defences under the 2002 Rules.[149] Therefore, the failure to comply with such an "order" is not a default.

In *Glasgow West Housing Association v Silva*,[150] a proof was discharged, the defender having given an undertaking to clear the rent arrears by a stated date. He failed to do so. When the case called again, it was continued for seven days, to enable the payment to be made. The defender again failed, and the decree was granted against him, against which he appealed. The Appeal Sheriff accepted the pursuers' argument that the sheriff was entitled to grant decree under rule 22.1(3), there being no distinction in substance between a failure to comply with an order of the court and the failure to comply with an undertaking.

Although decree by default may be granted against the defender in an action for recovery of possession, the sheriff must still observe the statutory requirements in any case under the 1988 Act or the 2001 Act. In particular, he must be satisfied that it would be reasonable to grant the order, in any case to which that additional requirement applies; and in cases under grounds 1–7 of schedule 2 to the 2001 Act, he must have regard to the factors listed in section 16(3).[151] It is therefore submitted that where, for example, the defender fails to appear or be represented at a diet of proof, the sheriff's approach should be similar to that suggested in respect of cases where the defender fails to appear at the first calling – a matter that is considered in the discussion of chapter 7 of the Rules, above.

Appeals

Notwithstanding the Courts Reform (Scotland) Act 2014, appeals in summary causes are still subject to section 38 of the Sheriff Courts (Scotland) Act 1971. The procedure for appeals is found in chapter 25 of the 2002 Rules, and chapter 29 of the Sheriff Appeal Court Rules.[152] Appeals are discussed in Chapter 15 of this work.

148 Perhaps in a case in which the defender's agent has asked the court to allow time for lodging "a supplementary note of defence".
149 See the discussion of r 8.2(1) above.
150 n 54.
151 See *Mortgages 1 v Chaudhary* (n 58).
152 Act of Sederunt (Sheriff Appeal Court Rules) 2015 (SSI 2015/356).

Chapter 14

Tribunal Procedure

INTRODUCTION

The Tribunals (Scotland) Act 2014 created two new tribunals: the First-tier Tribunal for Scotland ("FTT") and the Upper Tribunal for Scotland ("UT"). The FTT is organised into a series of chambers with specialist jurisdictions. One of those is the Housing and Property Chamber ("HPC").[1] By statutory instruments made under the 2014 Act, the functions of several tribunals were transferred to the HPC with effect from 1 December 2016.[2] As regards eviction proceedings, the significant change came one year later, on 1 December 2017, when the functions and jurisdiction of the sheriff in relation to actions arising from tenancies under the 1984 and 1988 Acts, including eviction proceedings, were transferred to the FTT. On the same day, the Private Housing (Tenancies) (Scotland) Act 2016 came into force. Under that Act, eviction orders in relation to private residential tenancies (PRTs) can be granted only by the tribunal.

The HPC is now based at the Glasgow Tribunals Centre,[3] although cases are heard at venues all over Scotland.[4] The Chamber has its own procedural rules, which are set out in the schedule to the First-tier Tribunal for Scotland Housing and Property Chamber (Procedure) Regulations 2017.[5] Specific rules apply to the lodging of applications for an order for possession, which have already been considered in Chapters 7 and 9. Chapter 15 includes a discussion of procedure after an order is granted, including review (rule 39) and permission to appeal (rules 37 and 38). This chapter will discuss certain

1 At the time of writing, the others are the General Regulatory Chamber (Charity Appeals), the Health and Education Chamber (Additional Support Needs), the Social Security Chamber and the Tax Chamber.

2 By SSIs 2016/335–338, the functions of the Homeowner Housing Committees, Homeowner Housing Panel, Private Rented Housing Committees and Private Rented Housing Panel were transferred to the Housing and Property Chamber of the FTT. Thereafter, that chamber initially dealt, in particular, with complaints by homeowners against property factors, under the Property Factors (Scotland) Act 2011, and complaints under s 14(1)(b) and 22 of the Housing (Scotland) Act 2006 (failure of private landlord to ensure that a property meets the repairing standard under s 13 of that Act).

3 20 York Street, Glasgow, G2 8GT.

4 Under s 61(1) of the 2014 Act, "Each of the First-tier Tribunal and the Upper Tribunal may be convened at any time and place in Scotland to hear or decide a case or for any other purpose relating to its functions". As at April 2020, the HPC uses around seventy venues, throughout Scotland.

5 SSI 2017/328, as amended by SSIs 2017/369 and 2018/378. The latter SSI, in particular, made a number of changes to the rules, which came into force on 20 February and 6 March 2019.

other rules, so far as they are relevant to eviction proceedings. First, however, it is appropriate to consider the extent of the FTT's jurisdiction.

TRANSFER OF JURISDICTION

Under section 16 of the Housing (Scotland) Act 2014, the functions and jurisdiction of the sheriff in relation to actions "arising from" an assured tenancy are transferred to the FTT. In the Private Housing (Tenancies) (Scotland) Act 2016, section 71 ("First-tier Tribunal's jurisdiction") provides that the FTT has jurisdiction in relation to civil proceedings "arising from" a PRT.[6]

It is suggested that the words "arising from" might be read in two different ways. On one view, an assured tenancy or a PRT is a contract, and an action that "arises from" that contract is, as a matter of law, an action in which one of the parties seeks a remedy under that contract, such as payment of rent arrears, or damages for failure to comply with one of the contractual terms. On another view, the assured tenancy or PRT is also a circumstance from which, as a matter of fact, other circumstances can arise; there is no reason to take the words "arising from" in the relevant provisions as being restricted to the legal remedies under the contract.

It is the latter view that is now accepted, in particular following the UT's decision in *Anderson v Stark*.[7] Whether an action "arises from" a PRT is a mixed question of fact and law; the tribunal ought to take a wide, inclusive approach, to deal with all PRT-related events, and not just the core lease. It is suggested that the same approach applies to the question of whether an action arises from an assured tenancy, under section 16 of the 2014 Act.

As to how that approach would work in eviction proceedings, it may help to illustrate with an example. Let us say that L lets a flat to T under a PRT. Subsequently, T's friend O comes to live with him at the flat. T informs L of O's occupation, in writing.[8] T then dies. O continues to live at the flat, and offers to pay the rent that would have been payable by T under the PRT. L refuses payment from O. L would like O to leave, but he refuses to go. O has no right of succession under the 2016 Act. Under section 65, the PRT terminated on T's death.

In this case, standing *Anderson v Stark*, the better view is that O's continuing occupation, which is the source of L and O's dispute, "arises from" the PRT, even though that PRT has been terminated under section 65. O occupies the flat because T, the person to whom the flat had been let under a PRT, allowed him to live there. T complied with his obligation, under the legislation applicable to a PRT, to inform L of O's occupation. It is by virtue of those circumstances that O's residence in the flat, immediately prior to L's death, was lawful. Consequently, under section 23 of the 1984 Act, L cannot evict O without due process of law.[9] The necessity of raising proceedings thus arises

6 Section 71(1): "In relation to civil proceedings arising from a private residential tenancy— (a) the First-tier Tribunal has whatever competence and jurisdiction a sheriff would have but for paragraph (b); [and] (b) a sheriff does not have competence or jurisdiction."

7 [2019] UT 48, in particular paras [11]–[16].

8 As is required by para 4 of sch 1 to the Private Residential Tenancies (Statutory Terms) (Scotland) Regulations 2017 (SSI 2017/408).

9 See the discussion of s 23 in Chapter 2.

from a set of circumstances, the first of which is the grant of the PRT, without which none of the other circumstances could have happened. Therefore, the proceedings in which L seeks to recover possession "arise from" the PRT, and an application should be made to the tribunal, under rule 79 of the Procedure Rules.[10]

It is also suggested that, in cases in which it is not clear whether proceedings ought to be raised in court, or in the FTT, an application to the FTT is the better option, because defeat in the sheriff court exposes the pursuer to an award of expenses.[11]

THE PROCEDURE RULES: INTRODUCTION

The schedule to the First-tier Tribunal for Scotland Housing and Property Chamber (Procedure) Regulations 2017 (henceforth in this chapter "the Procedure Rules") is in three parts. Part 1 contains rules that apply to all the applications that are made to the Chamber, including eviction cases. Part 2 makes provision for applications by homeowners under the Property Factors (Scotland) Act 2011. Part 3 comprises twelve chapters, and concerns the "Procedure in respect of private rented applications".

Of the rules in part 3, three are specific to eviction proceedings under the 1988 and 2016 Acts: rules 65 and 66 (in chapter 6), which concern applications for an order for possession under sections 18 and 33 of the 1988 Act; and rule 109 (in chapter 12), which relates to applications for an eviction order under section 51 of the 2016 Act.[12] These rules prescribe the content of such applications and the documents that are required to accompany them, such as the form AT6 under section 19 of the 1988 Act or the notice to leave under section 62 of the 2016 Act. These rules have already been considered, in Chapters 7 and 9.

As is now commonly the case with modern tribunals, the Housing and Property Chamber is subject, under rule 2, to an "overriding objective" to deal with the proceedings justly, which includes:

"(a) dealing with the proceedings in a manner which is proportionate to the complexity of the issues and the resources of the parties;
(b) seeking informality and flexibility in proceedings;
(c) ensuring, so far as practicable, that the parties are on equal footing procedurally and are able to participate fully in the proceedings, including assisting any party in the presentation of the party's case without advocating the course they should take;
(d) using the special expertise of the First-tier Tribunal effectively; and
(e) avoiding delay, so far as compatible with the proper consideration of the issues."

10 Rule 79: "Application to evict an occupier upon termination of a tenancy", which is apt: "Where an owner makes an application under s 23 (prohibition of eviction without due process of law) of the 1984 Act"

11 As happened in *Parker v Inkersall Investments Ltd* 2019 SLT (Sh Ct) 41, 2019 Hous LR 14, when the pursuer's agents wrongly raised an action for damages, for breaches of an assured tenancy, in the sheriff court.

12 Rule 77 concerns applications for possession under s 11 of the 1984 Act.

Under rule 3, "Effect of the overriding objective", the Chamber President and the FTT must seek to give effect to the overriding objective when exercising any power under the Rules; and when interpreting any rule. The parties are also under a duty to assist the Chamber President or the FTT to further the overriding objective.

It has been said that:

> "The overriding objective concerns the tribunal's attitude to the proceedings and parties, both individually and systematically. The essence of the tribunal's procedure is to deal with cases fairly and justly . . . This elevates the rules above being rules for their own sake. It gives them purpose and provides that they must be interpreted and applied to achieve that end."[13]

Applications under rules 70 and 111, and claims by the tenant

An "Application for civil proceedings in relation to an assured tenancy under the 1988 Act" and an "Application for civil proceedings in relation to a private residential tenancy" are made respectively under rules 70 and 111. Where the landlord wishes to make a claim against the tenant for payment of any sum due under the tenancy agreement, such as rent arrears, or for damages for breach of any term of the agreement, an application is made under rule 70 or rule 111, as the case may be. Under the procedure adopted by the Chamber, these are distinct applications, which have separate files and reference numbers.[14] This may be contrasted with proceedings in the sheriff court, in which a single summary cause can be lodged, seeking an order for recovery of possession and a decree for payment.

As was described in Chapters 8 and 10, in applications for orders under section 18 of the 1988 Act, or section 51 of the 2016 Act, the statutory grounds based on rent arrears are by far the most commonly used. Accordingly, applications are often made at the same time under rules 65 and 70,[15] or rules 109 and 111, seeking an eviction order and an order for payment of rent arrears. These applications will commonly be heard together, under rule 12.[16] However, they remain distinct. Consequently, where both applications are determined at the same case management discussion ("CMD")[17] or hearing, as frequently happens, it is the practice of the tribunal to issue two separate decisions. This also means that where the eviction application is refused at the

13 Jacobs, *Tribunal Practice and Procedure* (4th edn, Legal Action Group 2016) 3.23; see also 3.103 onwards. This work deals with tribunals under the English legislation, but it is nevertheless recommended to any reader interested in tribunal practice and procedure.

14 Eviction cases, whether under r 65, r66 or r 109, have an "EV" reference, such as "FTS/HPC/EV/20/0001". Applications under r 70 or r 111 have a "CV" reference, such as "FTS/HPC/CV/20/0001".

15 Where the tenant of a short assured tenancy falls into arrears, the landlord may make an application under r 66 (for a decree under s 33 of the 1988 Act) and r 70. Where the landlord wishes to seek an order under s 33, failing which s 18, two applications (under rr 66 and 65) will have to be made.

16 It is not the practice of the Chamber to conjoin applications. Rather, r 12(1) provides: "The First-tier Tribunal may direct two or more applications to be heard together where they are under consideration by the First-tier Tribunal at the same time and relate to the same—(a) property . . .".

17 Under r 17.

"sift" stage (discussed below), or at a CMD, the application under rule 70 or rule 111 may continue.

There is no equivalent, in the Procedure Rules, to a counterclaim in the sheriff court. However, the tribunal commonly considers applications made by both the tenant and the landlord, at the same hearing. This might happen, for example, where the tenant has applied for an order for payment under rule 103, on the basis that the landlord has failed to carry out duties under the Tenancy Deposit Schemes (Scotland) Regulations 2011,[18] or an application for a sanction to be applied under section 16 of the 2016 Act.[19]

PART 1 OF THE PROCEDURE RULES: PROGRESS OF APPLICATIONS

Application

Under rule 4, "An application to the First-tier Tribunal must be in writing and may be made using a form obtained from the First-tier Tribunal".[20] The form used for applications for an eviction or a possession order, whether under the 1984, 1988 or 2016 Act, is form E.[21] Both the form and guidance notes on its completion can be downloaded from the Chamber's website, and can be submitted electronically. The form expressly refers to the guidance notes, which therefore ought to be consulted.

Form E is four pages long, and has seven sections. The first section requires the applicant to specify the rule under which the application is made,[22] and the statutory provision under which possession is sought. Parts 2 and 3 set out the details of the applicant and, if applicable, the applicant's representative.[23] Part 4 sets out the details of the tenant/occupier.

In part 5 of the form, the applicant enters the grounds for possession and a brief description, for each of these grounds, of the circumstances that led to the application being made.[24] The various statutory grounds for possession, under the 1984, 1988 and 2016 Acts, are set out in the guidance notes. In part 6, the applicant lists the "required documents" that must be submitted along with the application, under the relevant rule. The guidance notes contain a

18 SSI 2011/176.

19 For failure to comply with s 10 or s 11 of the Act.

20 One might wonder whether this is a permissive or directive "may". That question is probably academic, because in practice the form provided by the tribunal is almost always used.

21 In the case of an application under r 70 or r 111, Form F is used.

22 This is done by reference to the date on which the tenancy began, on the basis that this determines whether the tenancy is governed by the 1984 Act (before 2 January 1989), the 2016 Act (on or after 1 December 2017) or the 1988 Act (between those dates).

23 The guidance notes state that where the details of a representative are given, the tribunal will correspond solely with the representative, and any correspondence sent to the representative will be deemed to have been sent to the applicant.

24 The guidance states that if there are multiple grounds, the applicant may continue on a separate sheet headed "Section 5: Possession/Eviction Grounds", writing the address of the property to clearly indicate that it relates to this application. Where the application is made under r 66, it should be sufficient to state, at this part, something like: "Application made under s 33 of the 1988 Act, in relation to a short assured tenancy".

useful checklist of the various required documents applicable to each type of application. Part 7 is where the applicant signs the application.

Rules 5 and 8: the sift

The Housing and Property Chamber sifts applications, for reasons that are apparent from rules 5 and 8. The existence of the sift is one of the most important respects in which the practice of the tribunal differs from that of the sheriff court. Numerous applications under rules 65, 66 and 109 are rejected at the sift stage, either because all the documentation required by the relevant rule has not been submitted, or because there is some respect in which it is inadequate or invalid.

It is difficult to overstate the significance of this process, particularly for eviction proceedings.

The vast majority of applications made to the tribunal for eviction orders under the 1988 and 2016 Acts will, if made in the correct form and with the requisite valid documentation, compel the tribunal to grant an eviction order. That is the case with applications under rule 66 (section 33 of the 1988 Act). It is also the case with applications under rule 65 or rule 109, most of which proceed on the mandatory ground 8 of schedule 5 to the 1988 Act, or the mandatory aspect of ground 12 of schedule 3 to the 2016 Act. It is quite rare for these applications to fail on the basis that the statutory ground is not established. By contrast, applications often fail because of some deficiency in the documentation that accompanies the application.[25]

Rule 5

The relevant parts of rule 5 state:

> "**5.— Requirements for making an application**
> (1) An application is held to have been made on the date that it is lodged if, on that date, it is lodged in the manner as set out in rules . . . 65 to 70 . . . or 105 to 111, as appropriate.
> (2) The Chamber President or another member of the First-tier Tribunal, under the delegated powers of the Chamber President, must determine whether an application has been lodged in the required manner by assessing whether all mandatory requirements for lodgement have been met.
> (3) If it is determined that an application has not been lodged in the prescribed manner, the Chamber President or another member of the First-tier Tribunal, under the delegated powers of the Chamber President, may request further documents and the application is to be held to be made on the date that the First-tier Tribunal receives the last of any outstanding documents necessary to meet the required manner for lodgement.
> . . ."

On receipt of an application, one of the Chamber's caseworkers checks the application form and attachments. Where it is clear that information is missing from the form, or one of the documents required by the relevant rule has

25 Figures obtained from the Housing and Property Chamber indicate that, in the two years from 1 December 2017 to 30 November 2019, the rates of rejection were: 22% of r 65 applications; 16% of r 66 applications; and 15% of r 109 applications.

not been attached to the application,[26] the applicant is asked to remedy the omission.[27]

Where the required documents have not been provided, the application has not been made until the last of the outstanding documents has been submitted. That may have the consequence that an application will not be made within the period required by the legislation. For example, both the form AT6 under the 1988 Act and the notice to leave under the 2016 Act have an effective life of six months,[28] within which the application to the tribunal must be made. Let us say that an application is submitted just before the expiry of the six-month period, but with inadequate documentation. In that case, the statutory period might expire before the application is "made" on submission of the outstanding documents, with the result that it would then be rejected, because the AT6 or notice to leave would no longer be valid.

Rule 8: rejection

Under rule 5(2), a tribunal member[29] is to determine whether an application has been lodged "in the required manner", which means that "all the mandatory requirements" under the relevant rules have been met.[30] If the required documentation is not submitted, or there is an issue with its validity, the application is liable to be rejected under rule 8:

> "**8.— Rejection of application**
>
> (1) The Chamber President or another member of the First-tier Tribunal under the delegated powers of the Chamber President, must reject an application if—
>
> (a) they consider that the application is frivolous or vexatious;
>
> (b) the dispute to which the application relates has been resolved;
>
> (c) they have good reason to believe that it would not be appropriate to accept the application;
>
> (d) they consider that the application is being made for a purpose other than a purpose specified in the application; or
>
> (e) the applicant has previously made an identical or substantially similar application and in the opinion of the Chamber President or another member of the First-tier Tribunal, under the delegated powers of the Chamber President, there has been no significant change in any material considerations since the identical or substantially similar application was determined. [31]
>
> (2) Where the Chamber President, or another member of the First-tier Tribunal, under the delegated powers of the Chamber President, makes a decision under

26 The required attachments are specified in rr 65, 66 and 109, which are discussed in Chapters 7 and 9.

27 It is understood that the practice of the tribunal is to allow fourteen days for a response, after which a seven-day reminder is issued. Failing a reply, the case goes to a legal member for consideration as to whether it should be rejected under r 8(1)(c).

28 Under s 19(7) of the 1988 Act and s 55 of the 2016 Act.

29 Or the Chamber President. In practice, the legal members of the tribunal have "sifting days" at the Glasgow Tribunals Centre, in which they go through a series of applications, considering whether they should be accepted or rejected.

30 Often, the sifting process involves making inquiries of the landlord or his agents. Under r 20(1), the FTT "may make such inquiries as it thinks fit for the purpose of exercising its functions".

31 For an example of an application rejected under r 8(1)(e), see *Dawodu v D&I Scott Property Management* [2019] UT 20.

> paragraph (1) to reject an application the First-tier Tribunal must notify the applicant and the notification must state the reason for the decision."

As is apparent from the decisions available on the Chamber's website, applications have commonly been rejected under rule 8(1)(a) or (c), on the basis that the documentation requested by the tribunal has not been submitted by the applicant, or one or more of the documents submitted is defective or invalid.

To understand why this might give rise to rejection under rule 8(1)(a), it is necessary to appreciate the particular meaning attached to the term "frivolous" by the tribunal. This is derived from a dictum of Lord Bingham in *R v North West Suffolk (Mildenhall) Magistrates' Court, ex p Forest Heath DC*,[32] which appears to be the most commonly cited authority in the decisions of the Housing and Property Chamber. When applications are rejected under rule 8(1)(a), the decision invariably quotes a sentence from Lord Bingham's judgment, in which he says that "frivolous" means: "futile, misconceived, hopeless or academic". However, it is instructive to consider that statement in context:

> "I think it very unfortunate that the expression 'frivolous' ever entered the lexicon of procedural jargon. To the man or woman in the street 'frivolous' is suggestive of light-heartedness or a propensity to humour and these are not qualities associated with most appellants or prospective appellants. What the expression means in this context is, in my view, that the court considers the application to be futile, misconceived, hopeless or academic. That is not a conclusion to which justices to whom an application to state a case is made will often or lightly come . . . But there are cases in which justices can properly form an opinion that an application is frivolous. Where they do, it will be very helpful to indicate, however briefly, why they form that opinion. A blunt and unexplained refusal, as in this case, may well leave an applicant entirely uncertain as to why the justices regard an application futile, misconceived, hopeless or academic. Such uncertainty is liable to lead to unnecessary litigation and expenditure on costs."

Thus, in the context of "procedural jargon" such as rule 8, "frivolous" has a particular meaning ("futile, misconceived, hopeless or academic"), and in numerous cases the tribunal has rejected applications that it has characterised in that way. That rejection is not "a blunt and unexplained refusal". The reasons for refusal are given in a written decision that is issued to the applicant,[33] under rule 8(2), and then published on the tribunal's website.[34]

The following is a sample from rejected applications made under rule 109, for an order under section 51 of the 2016 Act:

- No notice to leave attached to the application.[35]
- The notice to leave was invalid, because the date stated at part 4 was one day earlier than that required by the legislation.[36]

32 [1998] Env LR 9, 16.

33 But not to the respondent named in the application. The respondent only receives notification of the application, under r 9, once it is accepted.

34 Under r 26(10), a decision of the FTT with a statement of reasons must be published. It will appear on the "Decisions" page of the website, under "Eviction and Civil Proceedings Decisions". As is explained in Chapters 7 and 9, those decisions are searchable by the rule under which the application was made, such as r 65, r 66 or r 109. Many of the decisions made in relation to applications under those rules are rejections at the sift. Some of those have the word "reject" in the name of the pdf file of the decision. However, that is not always the case.

35 Application 19/1349, Ridley.

36 Application 19/1150, Perry.

- The notice to leave was invalid, because the date stated at part 4 was significantly later than that required by the legislation.[37]
- The application was submitted during the notice period.[38]
- The landlord had served notices under the 1988 Act, rather than the 2016 Act.[39]

There are also numerous examples from applications made under rule 65 or rule 66, for an order under section 18 or section 33 of the 1988 Act. A large proportion of those rejections relate to defects in notices to quit.[40]

The process of the tribunal sifting applications under rule 8, and refusing applications accompanied by invalid notices, was endorsed by the UT in *Gdula v Rooney*.[41] In that case, the landlord had applied for an order under section 18, serving a notice to quit and an AT6. However, the notice to quit called upon the tenant to leave on a date that was not an ish, and accordingly was invalid. The FTT found that section 18(6) of the Act did not apply, and refused the application as being "frivolous". The UT found no error of law in the FTT's approach.

Where the notices supporting the application are invalid, refusal of the application at the sift, rather than at some later stage, is in the interests of the landlord, because it enables him to take steps to serve the notice in correct form, as soon as possible.[42] That said, other UT decisions have criticised an over-readiness to reject applications at the sift.[43] It is suggested that where the invalidity of notices is an arguable point, the application ought to be accepted, perhaps with notification to parties that the tribunal will expect to be addressed on the issue at the CMD.

From a reading of rule 8 decisions, it is apparent that some legal members treat defective applications or notices as being subject to rule 8(1)(c), on the view that it would not be appropriate to accept an application if the supporting documentation is invalid, or has not been provided at all.[44] In effect, the outcome is the same.

37 Application 19/0726, Lewis-Flannigan.

38 Application 18/1302, Pearson. Under s 52(4), the tribunal has the discretion to allow an application during the notice period. There is no mention of this power in the decision, presumably because the tribunal was not asked to exercise it.

39 Application 19/0920, Harding.

40 Most usually, the problem is that the termination date stated in the notice is not an ish of the tenancy. There are also examples of the notice to quit being invalid because the period of notice given to the tenant was too short. In most of these cases, the tribunal member also considered whether s 18(6) of the 1988 applied, by examining the tenancy agreement. See the discussions of notices to quit in Chapter 3 and of s 18(6) in Chapter 7, at p 233. Examples: Application 19/0749, Matthew; Application 19/0102, Mullberry Homes; Application 19/0335, Cadman. There are many others.

41 [2019] UT 44.

42 Where an application is refused at the CMD because of some difficulty with notices, landlords have been known to complain that they should have been told of the problem at an earlier stage.

43 See, for example, *Timmins v Coyle* [2019] UT 16, and *Anderson v Stark* [2019] UT 48.

44 Some legal members reject such cases under both r 8(1)(a) and (c).

Notification of acceptance; written representations; amendment of application; directions

If the application passes the sift under rule 8, the tribunal then gives notice to "each party", under rule 9, "setting out the detail of the application" and "specifying the day by which any written representations must be made".[45]

In relation to an application under rule 65 or rule 66, the parties to be notified are the landlord and tenant: rule 71(a). In the case of an application under rule 109, the notified parties are the landlord (or former landlord) and the tenant (or former tenant): rule 112. Where there are joint landlords or joint tenants, all will have to be notified.[46]

Notice under rule 9, and any other "formal communication" under the rules, is subject to the provisions in rule 6 as to service, which may be effected by registered post or recorded delivery. Where that fails, the tribunal commonly instructs sheriff officers to effect service.[47] Failing that, service by advertisement may be used, under rule 6A.

Notice to the respondent under rule 9 is usually effected by a letter that: provides a copy of the application; invites the respondent to make written representations by a certain date; notifies the respondent of the date, time and location of the CMD under rule 17(2); and encloses a leaflet explaining the tribunal procedures.[48]

As has been described in previous chapters, many of the respondent tenants in eviction applications do not make written representations, and are not in attendance, or represented, at the CMD. Consequently, most eviction cases in the tribunal proceed without written representations being made, or limited representations from the landlord, which are often for the purposes of updating the application.[49]

Rule 14A allows a party to request to amend the application, including the sum claimed, by intimating the amendment to any other party and the tribunal at least 14 days prior to a CMD or hearing. This is commonly done in respect of an application under rule 70 or rule 111 for payment of rent arrears, in order to update the level outstanding.

Under rule 16, the tribunal may give directions to the parties relating to the conduct or progress of the application. Rule 16(3) gives various examples of the directions that are typically made, which are often for the purposes of focusing issues, lodging evidence and otherwise preparing for a hearing. In the past, directions in advance of a CMD were rare. However, it is becoming more common for directions to be issued at the point when the application has been accepted, for the purposes of identifying issues on which the tribunal wishes to

45 Which must be at least fourteen days after the day on which notice is given: r 9(2)(a).

46 Because the words "landlord" and "tenant" in chs 6 and 12 of pt 3 of the Rules have the same meaning that they bear under the relevant Act: r 46(2). Under s 55(3) of the 1988 Act, and s 78(2) and (3) of the 2016 Act, "landlord" means all the joint landlords, and "tenant" means all the joint tenants. See Chapter 7, p 243, and Chapter 9, p 311.

47 It is understood that the tribunal sometimes proceeds directly to service by sheriff officers, where service is urgent or it is anticipated that recorded delivery service will fail.

48 As indicated in the discussion of r 17 below, it is the practice of the tribunal nearly always to fix CMDs in eviction cases. However, this is not mandatory. Where a hearing is fixed instead, the notice under r 9 would notify the respondent of the date, time and place of the hearing, under r 24.

49 Amendment of written representations is permitted, subject to rr 13 and 14.

be addressed at the CMD. Directions are also sometimes made at a CMD,[50] when the tribunal adjourns the CMD or fixes a hearing.

Case management discussion

Rule 17 has considerable importance in the context of eviction cases:

> "**17.— Case management discussion**
> (1) The First-tier Tribunal may order a case management discussion to be held—
>   (a) in any place where a hearing may be held;
>   (b) by videoconference; or
>   (c) by conference call.
> (2) The First-tier Tribunal must give each party reasonable notice of the date, time and place of a case management discussion and any changes to the date, time and place of a case management discussion.
> (3) The purpose of a case management discussion is to enable the First-tier Tribunal to explore how the parties' dispute may be efficiently resolved, including by—
>   (a) identifying the issues to be resolved;
>   (b) identifying what facts are agreed between the parties;
>   (c) raising with parties any issues it requires to be addressed;
>   (d) discussing what witnesses, documents and other evidence will be required;
>   (e) discussing whether or not a hearing is required; and
>   (f) discussing an application to recall a decision.
> (4) The First-tier Tribunal may do anything at a case management discussion which it may do at a hearing, including making a decision."

Although rule 17(1) is permissive, it is the practice of the tribunal nearly always to fix CMDs in eviction cases.[51] Notice of the CMD is usually given at the same time as notice is given to the parties under rule 9.

A CMD is not a "hearing" for the purposes of the rules,[52] but under rule 17(4) the tribunal may do anything at a CMD that it may do at a hearing, including making a decision.

CMDs are almost always heard by one of the legal members of the tribunal sitting alone, who may be assigned up to three CMDs during the course of day, which are scheduled at 10am, 11:30am and 2pm.[53] The legal member is expected, where possible, to conduct the CMD, and then write a decision, or a note of the CMD, on the same day.[54] This is then issued by the tribunal administration to the parties, shortly thereafter.

Assuming that the application is still being pursued, a CMD will have one of three outcomes:

- The application is decided at the CMD, under rule 17(4), in which case the tribunal issues a decision.

50 Under r 16(2), directions may be given "orally", though it is more common for them to be given in writing, in a separate document.
51 Presumably because most of them are capable of being determined at a CMD.
52 *Dymoke v Best* [2019] UT 50, [15].
53 As is explained above, a CMD may involve more than one application between the same parties, the applications being heard together, under r 12. In that case, it will be necessary to write a note of the CMD, or a decision, in relation to each application.
54 If the application is determined under r 17(4), a decision is issued. Where the application is adjourned to another CMD, or a hearing is fixed, a note of the CMD is issued.

- The tribunal fixes a hearing, and issues a note of the CMD, which should describe what the tribunal did "to explore how the parties' dispute may be efficiently resolved", by reference to steps (a)–(f) in rule 17(3).
- If that process cannot be completed at the first CMD, it may be adjourned to a further CMD. Again, the tribunal will issue a note explaining why the CMD was adjourned and describing what took place, as regards rule 17(3)(a)–(f).

In practice, in eviction cases, the first outcome is the most common. The legal member tends to be engaged in deciding whether the tribunal ought to grant a request from the applicant for an order to be granted at the CMD, under rule 17(4). That usually entails considering whether it is mandatory, under section 18(3) or section 33 of the 1988 Act, or section 51 of the 2016 Act, to grant such an order. Very often, that is done in the absence of the respondent, who has not appeared, and is not represented. Conversely, where it is clear that there is some defect in the process adopted by the landlord, such that the tribunal cannot grant an order, then the application is liable to be rejected at the CMD,[55] irrespective of whether the respondent attends.

As will be explained below, the tribunal has the power to adjourn or postpone hearings (rule 28), or to hear a case in the absence of a party, if he does not appear (rule 29). Because, under rule 17(4), the tribunal may do anything at a CMD that it may do at a hearing, those rules are normally regarded as being applicable to CMDs.[56]

Determining proceedings without a hearing

Rule 18 states that the tribunal may make a decision without a hearing if it considers that, "(i) having regard to such facts as are not disputed by the parties, it is able to make sufficient findings to determine the case; and (ii) to do so will not be contrary to the interests of the parties".[57] It allows the tribunal to decide an application without further procedure, where it is evident from the material before it that there is sufficient agreement on the facts that appropriate findings can be made to determine the application.[58] It is unlikely that this power would be exercised in eviction cases, most of which are determined at the CMD.

55 As already described, problems with notices lead to the rejection of the application at the sift. However, some applications are allowed to proceed, but on the footing that there is some issue with competency of the application, which ought to be considered at the CMD. Also, it is possible that issues with notices etc. may be overlooked at the sift, but noticed by another legal member at the CMD.

56 Hence, where an application is granted in the absence of the respondent, it is customary for the decision to confirm, for the purposes of r 29, that the tribunal is satisfied that notice of the CMD has been given to the respondent.

57 Subject to the requirement, in r 18(2), that, before making a decision under paragraph (1), the FTT must consider any written representations submitted by the parties.

58 *Dymoke v Best* (n 52), [15]. Rule 18 does not apply to a decision made at a CMD, under r 17(4), which determines the proceedings.

Hearings

Most applications under rules 65, 66 and 109 are either rejected at the sift or decided at the CMD. Where a decision cannot be made under rule 17(4), the case proceeds to hearing. Hearings in eviction cases are usually heard by a tribunal of two members.[59]

Where a hearing is fixed, the tribunal has powers, under rules 20 and 21, to make inquiries, and to require the production of documents,[60] or the attendance at the hearing of a person, for the purpose of giving evidence. By rule 22, parties must lodge a list of documents, and copies of the documents, and a list of witnesses, no later than seven days prior to the hearing.[61] Under rule 23, the FTT must take all reasonable steps to provide copies of each document received from a party to the other parties, or at least "sufficient extracts from, or particulars of" those documents.

Rules 24 and 25 concern the notification and conduct of hearings. Each party must be given reasonable notice of the date, time and place of the hearing.[62] The hearing is held in public, unless the FTT, on its own initiative or on an application by a party, decides that it is necessary to do otherwise in the interests of justice.[63] At the outset of the hearing, the chairing member should introduce to the parties the members of the tribunal, explain the purpose of the hearing; and ensure that the parties to the hearing understand, and can participate in, the proceedings.[64] The parties are heard in such order and according to such procedure as the FTT determines.[65] A party or his representative may make representations, call witnesses, give evidence on his or her own behalf and cross-examine any witness called by another party.[66] The tribunal may exclude from the hearing a person who is to appear as a witness until such time as that person gives evidence, if it considers it is fair in all the circumstances to do so.[67]

Rules 27–29: Dismissal, adjournment and hearing a case in the absence of a party

Under rule 27 the tribunal has a specific power to dismiss the whole or a part of the proceedings if it considers that it does not have jurisdiction in relation to

59 One legal member and one ordinary member. The legal member is the chairing member, and has the casting vote: r 26(1). Where the decision is not unanimous, the tribunal's decision must include a brief note of the opinion of the minority: r 26(8). If, at the beginning of the hearing, a member of the FTT other than the chairing member is absent, the hearing may be conducted by the chairing member sitting alone or alongside another member, and in that event the hearing will be deemed to be properly constituted: r 33.

60 Though note that the tribunal's powers under rr 20 and 21 may be exercised at stage at which it is exercising its functions, and not only in advance of a hearing.

61 Under r 22(2), a document may be lodged late if the FTT is satisfied that the party seeking to lodge the document has a reasonable excuse.

62 Rule 24(1). Under r 24(2), the notice period for a hearing must be no less than fourteen days from the date of receipt of the notice, unless the parties consent to a shorter period or there are urgent or exceptional circumstances.

63 Rule 24(3).

64 Rule 25.

65 Rule 24(4)(b).

66 Rule 24(4)(c).

67 Rule 24(5).

the proceedings or that part of them. It may also dismiss the whole or part of the proceedings if the applicant has failed: (a) to comply with an order of the tribunal, if the order stated that failure to comply could lead to the dismissal of the proceedings or part of them; or (b) co-operate with the tribunal to such an extent that it cannot deal with the proceedings justly and fairly. No part of rule 27 specifies any particular point in the proceedings at which this power is capable of being exercised. Accordingly, it appears that the application may be dismissed at the CMD or hearing. Non-attendance by an applicant at a CMD or hearing would not, of itself, be a basis for dismissing the application, because under rule 29 the tribunal has the power to proceed in the absence of one of the parties.

Rule 28 empowers the tribunal to adjourn or postpone hearings, at its own discretion, on its own initiative, or on an application by a party, at any time. CMDs may also be adjourned or postponed.[68] It is quite common for a party to ask for a postponement by email to the tribunal, in advance of a CMD or hearing. This is put to the member(s) of the tribunal hearing the case, or to a legal member sifting applications on that day.

The requirements for an application by a party for an adjournment or postponement are quite onerous, though the extent to which they are rigorously applied seems to vary in practice. The tribunal may only adjourn or postpone a hearing at the request of a party on cause shown.[69] When making the application, the party must: (a) if practicable, notify all other parties; (b) show good reason why an adjournment or postponement is necessary; and (c) at the direction of the tribunal, produce evidence of any fact or matter relied on in support of the application for an adjournment or postponement.[70] Further conditions apply, if the reason for an adjournment or postponement is to allow the party more time to produce evidence.[71]

Under rule 29, where a party is not present or represented at the hearing, the tribunal is empowered to "proceed with the application upon the representations of any party present and all the material before it". However, the tribunal must be satisfied that the requirements of rule 24(1) regarding the giving of notice of a hearing have been duly complied with.

Decisions

As already described, most applications in eviction cases are determined at the sift or decided at the CMD. Where an application is rejected at the sift, rule 8(2) requires that the applicant must be notified of the decision, and the reason for it. A decision made at a CMD or hearing must be recorded in a document signed by the chairing member.[72] The obligation to provide a

68 See the discussion of CMDs above.

69 Rule 28(3).

70 Rule 28(2).

71 Rule 28(4). In that case, the tribunal has to be satisfied that: (a) the evidence relates to a matter in dispute; (b) it would be unjust to determine the case without permitting the party to produce the evidence; and (c) where the party has failed to comply with directions for the production of the evidence, the party has provided a satisfactory explanation for that failure.

72 Rule 26(3). Where a decision is made by more than one member, the legal member is chair, and drafts the written decision. If the absence or incapacity of the chairing member, that may be done by the other member: r 26(9).

statement of reasons does not strictly apply to applications made under rule 65, rule 66 or rule 109[73] but, in practice, reasons are always provided. Those reasons must be: "proper, intelligible and adequate".[74]

Under rule 26(10), decisions of the FTT must be published. These appear in the "Decisions" page of the Chamber's website under "Eviction and Civil Proceedings Decisions". As explained in Chapters 7 and 9, those decisions are searchable by the rule under which the application was made, such as rule 65, rule 66 or rule 109.

Under rule 26(12)(a), where the FTT learns, during the course of proceedings, that the landlord is not registered, it may report that fact to the relevant local authority, by providing a copy of any decision to it.

Recall

Under rule 30(1), a party may apply to the FTT to have a decision recalled where it was made in absence, because that party "did not take part in the proceedings, or failed to appear or be represented at a hearing following which the decision was made".

This rule bears certain similarities to rule 24 of the Summary Cause Rules.[75] As explained in Chapter 13, recall in eviction proceedings under the 2001 Act is commonplace. However, by comparison, recall applications are relatively rare at the tribunal. In eviction cases, this may be largely because orders granted at CMDs under rule 65, rule 66 or rule 109 are usually proceedings in which there is no defence, if the application is properly made.[76] If that is the case, then the tenant applying for recall will have difficulty, under rule 30(2), in stating "why it would be in the interests of justice for the decision to be recalled".

An application for recall must be made within 14 days of the decision, though that period may be extended on cause shown.[77] As with recall in the sheriff court, a party may apply for recall only once.[78] The application cannot be made unless a copy of it has been sent to the other parties, at the same time.[79] Once it is made, enforcement of the order is prevented, until the application is determined.[80] Under rule 30(8), the application may be opposed. After considering the application and any opposition, the tribunal may grant the application and recall the decision; refuse the application; or order the

73 See r 26(4), (6) and (7). Rules 65 and 66 are in ch 6 of pt 3 of the Procedure Rules; r 109 in pt 12.

74 This test was originally formulated in *Re Poyser and Mills Arbitration* [1964] 2 QB 467, 478 (Megaw J). It has been restated in subsequent authorities, in particular *Uprichard v Scottish Ministers* 2013 SC (UKSC) 219, [47] (Lord Reed). See the discussion of the obligation to give reasons in Chapter 6.

75 Act of Sederunt (Summary Cause Rules) 2002 (SSI 2002/132).

76 Because the mandatory rent arrears grounds predominate in applications under rr 65 and 109, and an order must be granted in a r 66 application, if the requirements of s 33 of the 1988 Act are met.

77 Rule 30(4) and (5).

78 Rule 30(6).

79 Rule 30(3).

80 Rule 30(7).

parties to appear at a CMD where the FTT will consider whether to recall the decision.[81]

Expenses

Under section 64 of the 2014 Act, and rule 40, the tribunal may award expenses as taxed by the Auditor of the Court of Session against a party, but only where that party, through unreasonable behaviour in the conduct of a case, has put the other party to unnecessary or unreasonable expense. The amount awarded must be the amount required to cover those unnecessary or unreasonable expenses.

There is a three-stage process in dealing with applications under rule 40. The first stage is to make the finding that there has been unreasonable behaviour in the conduct of the proceedings; the second is to determine whether to exercise the discretion to make an award of expenses; and the third is to determine just what expenses are to be awarded.[82] The tribunal will not readily accept that conduct has been "unreasonable", particularly where it is the conduct of an unrepresented party, or an unqualified representative.[83] Consequently, it is to be expected that expenses will only rarely be awarded.

Post decree

The tribunal rules in relation to review of decisions, appeals and enforcement of eviction orders are discussed in Chapter 15.

81 Rule 30(9). As indicated in Chapter 10, p 357, in an application under ground 12 of sch 3 to the 2006 Act, it is arguable that, at the CMD prompted by the recall application, the tribunal should proceed on the basis of the arrears that were due, on the day on which the tribunal first considered the application for an eviction order on its merits.

82 *Ramirez-Stich v Strachan* [2019] UT 64, [19].

83 *Willow Court Management Co (1985) Ltd v Alexander* [2016] UKUT 290 (LC), [2016] L & TR 34. Paragraphs [24]–[26] of the decision in that case are quoted in *Ramirez-Stich v Strachan*, [17].

Chapter 15

Other Issues in Eviction Proceedings; Post Decree

INTRODUCTION

This chapter considers various issues that commonly arise in eviction proceedings, and also discusses what happens after the decree or order is granted, in particular as regards the law applicable to the enforcement of decrees and orders in eviction cases. The order is as follows:

- title of the pursuer or applicant;
- notices: service;
- notices: proof of content;
- violent profits, payment in respect of occupation, and caution for pecuniary claims;
- after the decree or order is granted;
- enforcing (or not enforcing) the decree or order;
- suspension and reduction of a sheriff court decree;
- wrongful termination orders under the 2016 Act.

TITLE OF THE PURSUER OR APPLICANT

At common law

A lease is usually granted by the proprietor of the subjects,[1] and most eviction actions are raised by the person who is both proprietor and landlord under the lease. There is a well-established common law rule that the title of the landlord under the lease, to prosecute an action for removing, cannot be questioned by the tenant, who derives his right to possess the subjects from the landlord.[2] Where the pursuer is not the landlord under the lease, it will be necessary for him to aver the basis of his title to remove the tenant.

Where two or more persons are *pro indiviso* proprietors, the consent and concurrence of all is required for the granting of a lease, and for any subse-

1 In Rennie and others, *Leases* (SULI 2015) para 8-15, the authors explain: "A landlord should have either a recorded or registered title to the land before the lease is granted. If the landlord does not have a complete title by recording or registration then the lease will remain valid as between the parties, but purely as a matter of personal contract; there can be no question of a real or protected right in favour of the tenant." Note also that a lease might be granted by, for example, a tenant (in which case the tenancy is a sub-let) or by a heritable creditor in possession.

2 *King v Wieland* (1858) 20 D 960; *Dumigan v Kirkpatrick* 1917 2 SLT 241; *Fraser v Sharp* 1957 SLT (Sh Ct) 14.

quent action for removal of the tenant.[3] However, where the action is against a person occupying without right or title, it may be raised by any one of the co-proprietors.[4]

A mandate authorising a joint proprietor to grant a lease on behalf of other proprietors may not imply authority to raise eviction proceedings.[5] Title to sue will be lost by a proprietor divesting himself of the property, but not by the mere assignation of rents.[6]

If the subjects have been sold, the seller retains the right to raise proceedings until the date of entry. Thereafter, the new proprietor must complete title in order to obtain decree.[7] The seller and purchaser may be conjoined in raising an action.[8]

In terms of the Trusts (Scotland) Act 1921,[9] actions may also be raised by trustees, executors, guardians, curators and judicial factors. In other cases, an attorney or agent requires express power in writing, and this may not be implied from a power to grant leases.[10]

Applications to the First-tier Tribunal

An application under rule 65 or rule 66 must be accompanied by a copy of the tenancy agreement.[11] In applications under rules 65, 66 and 109, the First-tier Tribunal ("FTT") also invariably obtains a copy of the title sheet for the property.[12] These documents may give rise to a question as to whether the person making the application has title to do so. If the tribunal is not satisfied that the applicant has title to make the application, it may be rejected at the sift.

Sections 18 and 33 of the 1988 Act do not expressly provide that an application for an order for possession must be made by the landlord, but the statutory notices that precede such applications[13] inform the tenant that the "*landlord* intends to raise proceedings for possession of the house"[14] or that "the *landlord* . . . requires possession of the house".[15] Section 55(1) states

3 "Thus a removing could not go on without the consent of all the proprietors . . ." (Rankine, *Law of Leases in Scotland* (3rd edn) 82). See also Rennie and others (n 1) para 8-18.

4 Rankine (n 3) 82. For a recent discussion of these principles, and the relevant authorities, see *Morris v Eason* [2012] CSOH 125, 2012 GWD 27-564.

5 *Stair Memorial Encyclopaedia*, para 496. Rankine (n 3) 516.

6 *Stair Memorial Encyclopaedia* para 493; *Sinclair v Leslie* (1887) 14 R 792.

7 *Walker v Hendry* 1925 SC 855, 1925 SLT 592; *James Grant & Co Ltd v Moran* 1948 SLT (Sh Ct) 8. Under r 13.1(e) of the Summary Cause Rules (Act of Sederunt (Summary Cause Rules) 2002 (SSI 2002/132)) the purchaser may be sisted as pursuer, in substitution for the original pursuer/seller.

8 *Stair Memorial Encyclopaedia* vol 13, para 495; Rankine (n 3) 515.

9 Sections 2 and 4.

10 *Stair Memorial Encyclopaedia* vol 13, para 498; Rankine (n 3) 518.

11 "or if not available, as much information about the tenancy as the landlord can give": r 65(b)(i) and r 66(b)(i). A copy of the tenancy agreement is not required by r 109, but is often provided anyway.

12 If the title is registered. This is done under r 20, which gives the FTT fairly wide powers of inquiry. By r 20(1) it "may make such inquiries as it thinks fit for the purpose of exercising its functions." This includes, in r 20(3)(c), "consideration of any report instructed by the First-tier Tribunal about any of the matters referred to in the application".

13 Being, in the case of an application under s 18, the AT6 required by s 19 and, in the case of an application under s 33, the s 33(1)(d) notice.

14 Section 19(3)(a).

15 Section 33(1)(d).

that: *"landlord"* "includes any person from time to time deriving title from the original landlord and also includes, in relation to a house, any person other than a tenant who is, or but for the existence of an assured tenancy would be, entitled to possession of the house".[16]

Therefore, it is suggested that the person making the application must be able to show that he is the landlord under the lease, or has derived title to raise the action from the landlord, or that he is entitled to possession. Where there are joint landlords, or co-proprietors, the consent and concurrence of all are required for any action for removal of the tenant.[17]

As regards joint landlords, the position is different under the 2016 Act, because section 52(1) expressly provides that, in a case where two or more persons jointly are the landlord under a tenancy, an application for an eviction order may be made by any one of those persons.[18] This point is discussed in Chapter 9.[19]

SERVICE OF NOTICES

The necessity of serving one or more notices, as a preliminary to raising proceedings, or making an application to the FTT, has been considered in the preceding chapters. As will be apparent from the discussion that follows, the rules as to service of those notices are not entirely clear. Several difficult issues arise,[20] which may be resolved in future decisions of the Upper Tribunal.

Notices to quit

Section 112 of the 1984 Act requires that a notice to quit be in writing, but does not prescribe any mode of service. There is no common law rule that requires service to be effected in any particular way: at common law, notice to quit may be given verbally.[21] Service of documents may be regulated by the parties' contract, although this is more common in commercial leases.

The statutory provisions applicable to service of notices to quit are piecemeal, and do not form a clear or comprehensive code.

16 This would include, for example, a heritable creditor having a decree under s 24 of the Conveyancing and Feudal Reform (Scotland) Act 1970, making an application on ground 2 of sch 5. See Chapter 8, p 273.

17 Under s 55(3), any reference in pt II of the 1988 Act to the landlord is a reference to all the persons who jointly constitute the landlord. However, where there are joint landlords, the statutory notice may be served by any one of them: s 19(1)(a); s 33(1)(d).

18 Likewise, a notice to leave may be given by only one of the joint landlords, given the terms of s 62(2).

19 Also, the 2016 Act expressly provides, in s 63, that the term "landlord" includes a creditor in a heritable security who is entitled to sell. See the discussion of ground 2 in Chapter 10.

20 The author has attended training events for legal members of the FTT at which opposing views have been expressed, in particular as to the mode of service of a notice to quit.

21 Notably, the Scottish Law Commission's *Discussion Paper on Aspects of Leases: Termination* (Scot Law Com No 165, 2018) suggests, at para 3.26, that verbal notice to quit is still competent in commercial leases. See: *Brucefield Estate Trustee Ltd v Computacenter (UK) Ltd* 2017 Hous LR 66.

Removal Terms (Scotland) Act 1886; Interpretation Act 1978, section 7

Section 6 of the Removal Terms (Scotland) Act 1886 allows notice of removal[22] from a house[23] to be given by registered letter, signed "by the person entitled to give such notice" or his law agent or factor. It is suggested that section 6 is an enabling provision. It did not change the common law rule that notice could be given verbally.[24] Its effect was to allow the landlord, where he chose to give notice in writing, to do so by registered letter.

Under section 1 of the Recorded Delivery Service Act 1962, service under section 6 of the 1886 Act may also be effected by registered post or recorded delivery.

As section 6 of the 1886 Act (read along with the 1962 Act) authorises service to be given by registered post, or recorded delivery, section 7 of the Interpretation Act 1978 applies:

> "**7. References to service by post.**
> Where an Act authorises or requires any document to be served by post (whether the expression 'serve' or the expression 'give' or 'send' or any other expression is used) then, unless the contrary intention appears, the service is deemed to be effected by properly addressing, pre-paying and posting a letter containing the document and, unless the contrary is proved, to have been effected at the time at which the letter would be delivered in the ordinary course of post."[25]

Where it is said that service of the notice to quit has been effected by registered post, or recorded delivery, the landlord should produce evidence establishing that a letter containing the notice has been properly addressed, pre-paid and posted, which would usually be in the form of a postal receipt.

If that is done, then it follows that service has been effected in the ordinary course of post, subject to the words "unless the contrary is proved". On one possible reading of section 7, the effect of properly addressing, pre-paying and posting a letter containing the notice is that service is deemed to have been effected, and it is only the *date* of service (not the fact of service) that is open to dispute by the intended recipient. However, the authorities indicate that if it is shown that the document has never been received at all, then it follows that service has not "been effected at the time at which the letter would be

22 Which, for present purposes, is the same as a notice to quit: see Chapter 3, note 19.

23 The 1886 Act relates to removal from "houses". Section 3 defines "house" widely as a dwellinghouse, shop or other building and their appurtenances, and includes a dwellinghouse or building let along with land for agricultural or other purposes.

24 SLC Discussion Paper (n 21) para 3.8. Thus, in *Craighall Cast-Stone Co v Wood Bros* 1931 SC 66, the court was strongly of the view that the provisions of the 1907 Act made no difference to the common law rule that notice could be given verbally, unless the procedures under that Act were being used. There is no mention of the 1886 Act in that case as having altered that rule. A contrasting provision is s 4(4) of the Law Reform (Miscellaneous Provisions) (Scotland) Act 1985, which applies to irritancy notices in commercial leases, and requires that: "Any notice served under subsection (2) above *shall* be sent by recorded delivery . . .". In light of that requirement, service by sheriff officers was held to render the notice invalid, in *Kodak Processing Companies Ltd v Shoredale Ltd* 2010 SC 113.

25 This section came under scrutiny in a series of decisions of the Lands Tribunal in 2019: *K v City of Edinburgh Council* 2019 SLT (Lands Tr) 39; *Boyce v City of Edinburgh Council* 2019 SLT (Lands Tr) 49; and *Thomas v Dumfries & Galloway Housing Partnership Ltd* 2019 SLT (Lands Tr) 59. These cases all arose from applications to exercise the right to buy, just before it was abolished.

delivered in the ordinary course of post", and in that case service has not taken place.[26]

It is reasonable to assume that the date of delivery "in the ordinary course of post" is, in the case of first-class mail, the second working day after posting and, in the case of second-class mail, the fourth working day after posting.[27]

Sheriff Courts (Scotland) Act 1907, sections 34–38

The sheriff court rules, in particular rule 34.8 of the Ordinary Cause Rules ("OCR")[28] and rule 30.7 of the Summary Cause Rules ("SCR")[29] ("Giving Notice of Removal") also provide that a notice under any of sections 34–38 of the 1907 Act may be effected by registered post, first-class recorded delivery, or sheriff officer. No other mode of service is permissible.[30]

Thus, in *Govan Housing Association v Kane*,[31] the defender took exception to a notice to quit, because it was not served in accordance with rule 34.8. The sheriff agreed, and dismissed the case. In the more recent case of *City of Edinburgh Council v Smith*,[32] the sheriff seems to have taken *Govan Housing Association v Kane* as authority for the general proposition that personal service of a notice to quit, by anyone other than a sheriff officer, is inept.[33] However, both of these decisions assume that the pursuers' notice to quit was a "notice of removal", given under one of sections 34–38 of the 1907 Act; but the basis for that assumption is not explained in either case, nor is it clear why the 1907 Act was applicable.

As is explained in Chapter 3, sections 34–38 of the 1907 Act were designed to create a streamlined eviction process enabling the landlord, following service of the requisite "notice of removal", to utilise a form of action in which a decree for removing and a warrant for ejection could be obtained in a single process. The Act allowed for a period of notice of forty days, and provided for a form of notice that both prevented tacit relocation and commenced the removal process.[34] There is a preponderance of authority to the effect that the requirements of sections 34–38 of the 1907 Act[35] are only applicable to the judicial procedures that they set out. They do not apply generally to the type

26 See, in particular, *Boyce v City of Edinburgh Council* (n 25), [40]–[43].

27 Guidance to that effect was given in the English Queen's Bench practice direction [1985] 1 WLR 489, and that guidance has been referred in decisions by English tribunals. See: *St Basil's Centre Ltd v McCrossan* [1991] IRLR 455 and *Richardson v Commissioners for Her Majesty's Revenue & Customs* [2015] 4 WLUK 521.

28 Act of Sederunt (Sheriff Court Ordinary Cause Rules) (SI 1993/1956).

29 n 7.

30 *Department of Agriculture v Goodfellow* 1931 SC 556.

31 2003 Hous LR 125.

32 2016 SLT (Sh Ct) 343, 2016 Hous LR 30.

33 See para 22 of the decision.

34 So, the "notice of removal" under the 1907 Act is an example of a statutory "dual-purpose" notice, which, in addition to preventing tacit relocation, also forms the first step in a process of removing and/or ejection outlined in a particular piece of legislation. This type of notice is served by the landlord, as a necessary preliminary to using the statutory process. This is why a more exacting standard is required as regards the mode of service: the notice of removal forms part of the process set out in the legislation.

35 Sections 34–36 of the 1907 Act apply only to "lands exceeding two acres in extent".

of tenancy mentioned in each section, and do not alter parties' substantive rights.[36]

For that reason, it is arguable that the 1907 Act does not apply to a notice to quit that is served simply for the purposes of preventing tacit relocation, in order that summary cause proceedings for recovery of possession may then be raised; a summary cause is not an application under section 37 or section 38 of the 1907 Act.[37]

Furthermore, there is no provision in the FTT's Procedure Rules[38] that is equivalent to rule 34.8 of the OCR and rule 30.7 of the SCR. Therefore, the 1907 rules for service have no application in tribunal proceedings in any event, particularly as regards actions raised under sections 18 and 33 of the Housing (Scotland) Act 1988.[39]

Rule 14(1)(c) of the Act of Sederunt (Messengers-at-Arms and Sheriff Officers Rules) 1991

Rule 14(1)(c) of the Act of Sederunt (Messengers-at-Arms and Sheriff Officers Rules) 1991 extended the official functions of officers of court to permit them to "execute a citation or serve any document required under any legal process".[40] The term "legal process" is not defined the 1991 Rules. However, on the basis that a lease is a legal instrument, which confers rights and obligations, then termination of the lease, at the ish, is a "legal process". The act of serving the notice has a legal effect.[41] A notice to quit is "required" in order to terminate the lease at the ish, and therefore it is submitted rule 14(1)(c) applies.[42]

If rule 14(1) does apply to service of notice to quit, a sheriff officer serving the notice is acting in his "official capacity", as an officer of court. It follows that the sheriff officer ought to follow the rules relating to citation (service of process), set out in the legislation dating back to 1540 "and which the rules

36 *Craighall Cast-Stone Co Ltd v Wood Bros* (n 24), and *Lormor Ltd v Glasgow City Council* 2015 SC 213, 2014 SLT 1055. See also the SLC Discussion Paper (n 21) paras 3.21–3.26.

37 A contrary view is that a summary cause that is raised under s 35 of the Sheriff Courts (Scotland) Act 1971 *is* a summary application under s 38 of the 1907 Act, because the definition of "summary application" in s 3(p) of the 1907 Act "means and includes all applications of a summary nature . . . brought under any Act of Parliament which provides . . . that the same shall be disposed of in a summary manner, but which does not more particularly define in what form the same shall be heard, tried, and determined".

38 First-tier Tribunal for Scotland Housing and Property Chamber (Procedure) Regulations 2017 (SSI 2017/328).

39 Arguments over the validity of notices to quit tend to be a feature of cases under the 1988 Act. Notices to quit are not necessary in proceedings by social landlords under s 16 of the 2001 Act, and are therefore less likely to be an issue in sheriff court cases, following the transfer of jurisdiction.

40 SI 1991/1397. This Act of Sederunt was enacted under the power given to the Court of Session by the Debtors (Scotland) Act 1987, s 75(1)(d).

41 If is done effectively, in relation to an assured tenancy, it has the effect of triggering the operation of s 16 of the Act, such that a statutory assured tenancy comes into operation.

42 That is consistent with Sheriff Jamieson's interpretation of r 14(1)(c) in *Bank of Scotland v Stevenson*, 2012 SLT (Sh Ct) 155, 2012 Hous LR 60. That case concerned the service of a calling-up notice by a heritable creditor, under s 19(6) of the Conveyancing and Feudal Reform (Scotland) Act 1970. One might question the sheriff's conclusion that service of a calling-up notice by sheriff officers is a mode of service permitted by s 19(6) of the 1970 Act (see note 65 below); but that is a different issue.

of court are but a restatement and refinement."[43] Accordingly, a sheriff officer could effect service in the ways specified in rule 5.4 of the OCR.[44]

Section 114 of the Rent (Scotland) Act 1984

Section 114 of the 1984 Act provides that: "A notice or other document which requires to be served on a person under any provision of this Act may be given to him (a) by delivering it to him; (b) by leaving it at his proper address;[45] or (c) by sending it by recorded delivery post to him at that address." However, it is debatable whether this provision applies to a notice to quit, because that does not "require to be served" under a provision of the 1984 Act; it is given under the common law, the rules of which are modified by section 112.[46] Nevertheless, it is suggested that all the modes of service outlined in section 114(1) are capable of being deployed for service of a common law notice to quit, because there is no rule of law requiring some other mode of service.

Rules 65 and 66 of the Procedure Rules

Rules 65(b)(iii) and 66(b)(iv) require that an application under those rules is accompanied by "a copy of the notice to quit *served* by the landlord on the tenant".[47] It is understood that, for that reason, the landlord is usually required, at the stage of sifting the application, to produce proof that service of the notice has taken place. However, the rules do not prescribe any particular mode of service.

Service of notices to quit: conclusion

If it is correct to say that section 114 of the 1984 Act does not apply to notices to quit, and rule 34.8 of the OCR and rule 30.7 of the SCR only apply to notices served under sections 34–38 of the 1907 Act, there are no statutory rules that prescribe the mode of service of a notice to quit. In particular, there are no rules that require any particular mode of service to be used, in relation to the notice to quit that accompanies an application for an order for possession under sections 18 and 33 of the 1988 Act, made in terms of rule 65 or rule 66 of the Procedure Rules. There are only provisions that allow service to be effected by registered letter/registered post/recorded delivery, or by sheriff officers, but do not preclude any other mode of service.

43 *Bank of Scotland v Stevenson* (n 42, at [93]). In that case, the sheriff officer had deposited a full copy of the notice through the letter box on the door of the defender's dwelling place as, after diligent inquiry, the sheriff officer had been unable to find him personally or any person within his dwelling place to accept service but had established that he resided at the address, and that he could not gain access thereto.

44 See paras [93]–[95] of the sheriff's judgment. Service by the sheriff officer had been in accordance with r 5.4(3) of the OCR.

45 I.e. his last known address: s 114(2).

46 Thus, as was explained in Chapter 3, s 112 does not alter the common law rule that, in the absence of contractual stipulation to the contrary, the minimum period of notice is forty days. The effect of s 112 is that, where there *is* contrary stipulation, the parties cannot reduce the period of notice below twenty-eight days.

47 "if applicable" in the case of r 65 applications.

If that is correct, then under section 112(1) of the 1984 Act, the landlord need only give the notice to the tenant, which might be done in various ways, including delivery personally to the tenant, or leaving at his last known address, or by ordinary post.

However, in that case, the landlord might have difficulty showing that the giving of the notice has taken place, particularly if that is disputed by the tenant. The landlord might also have difficulty satisfying the tribunal that the requirements for lodging an application under rules 65 and 66 have been met, if the fact of service of the notice cannot be shown.

For that reason, it is suggested that, in practice, it is advisable to serve a notice to quit by registered post, recorded delivery or sheriff officer, because those modes provide proof of the fact of service, and the date on which it occurred.

Statutory notices: 1988 and 2001 Acts

Section 54 of the 1988 Act

Section 54 of the 1988 Act states:

> "**54. Notice under Part II.**
> A notice served under this Part of this Act on a person or notice so given to him may be served or given—
> (a) by delivering it to him;
> (b) by leaving it at his last known address; or
> (c) by sending it by recorded delivery letter to him at that address."

This provision allows the same options for service as section 114(1) of the 1984 Act, and section 40(1) of the 2001 Act. On the assumption that the tenant is an individual, it is suggested that "delivering it to him" in section 54(a) means, in effect, personal service; i.e. placing the notice (or an envelope that contains the notice) into the hands of the tenant personally.[48] Alternatively, under section 54(b), the notice may be left at the last known address of the tenant, which will normally be the tenancy property.

The first two options could be effected by the landlord himself, or by an agent.[49] Service under section 54(a) or (b) could also be effected by sheriff officers.[50]

It is suggested that section 7 of the Interpretation Act 1978 applies to section 54(c) of the 1988 Act, which authorises notices under part II of the Act to be served or given by "sending it by recorded delivery letter". No "contrary intention" appears in that section.[51]

48 *Rae v Calor Gas Ltd* 1995 SC 214.

49 Note that where it is shown that a written notice was delivered at the tenant's house, it is presumed that he received it: *Lambert v Smith* (1864) 3 M 43, 46, per Lord Benholme.

50 As to service by sheriff officers effected in other ways, see the discussion at p 502 below.

51 There is extensive authority on the application of s 7 of the 1978 Act. However, see, in particular, the decision of the Court of Appeal in *Freetown Ltd v Assethold Ltd* [2013] 1 WLR 701, which found that s 7 applied to s 15(1) of the Party Walls etc. Act 1996, which is in similar terms to s 54 of the 1988 Act. See also the discussion in *K v City of Edinburgh Council* (n 25), [37]–[39].

It is also submitted that "recorded delivery" in this context means the recorded delivery service provided by Royal Mail. It does not mean any other form of delivery that is recorded.[52]

Section 40 of the 2001 Act

Section 40 of the 2001 Act states:

> "**40 Notices**
> (1) A notice or other document authorised or required by this Chapter to be given to a person (however expressed) may be given—
> (a) by delivering it to that person,
> (b) by leaving it at that person's proper address, or
> (c) by sending it by recorded delivery letter to that person at that address.
> (2) For the purposes of subsection (1) and of paragraph 4 of Schedule 1 to the Scotland Act 1998 (Transitory and Transitional Provisions) (Publication and Interpretation etc. of Acts of the Scottish Parliament) Order 1999 (S.I. 1999/1379), a person's proper address is that person's last known address."

Thus, as with section 54 of the 1988 Act, service may be effected by the landlord's agents or employees, or a sheriff officer, delivering the notice to the tenant, or leaving it at his last known address, which will invariably be the tenancy property.

The Order mentioned in section 40(2) was revoked, and replaced, by the Interpretation and Legislative Reform (Scotland) Act 2010. However, section 55 of the 2010 Act provides that the 1999 Order continues to apply to Acts that received Royal Assent before the 2010 Act came into force. Paragraph 4 of schedule 1 to the Order is in the same terms as section 7 of the Interpretation Act 1978. Accordingly, the same principles apply to service of documents by recorded delivery under section 40(1)(c) of the 2001 Act as apply under section 54(1)(c) of the 1988 Act.

Statutory notices: 2016 Act

Section 26 of the Interpretation and Legislative Reform (Scotland) Act 2010

There are no provisions in the 2016 Act as regards the service of notices under that Act. This means that the rules set out in section 26 of the Interpretation and Legislative Reform (Scotland) Act 2010 apply:

> "**26 Service of documents**
> (1) This section applies where an Act of the Scottish Parliament or a Scottish instrument authorises or requires a document to be served on a person (whether the expression 'serve', 'give', 'send' or any other expression is used).
> (2) The document may be served on the person—
> (a) by being delivered personally to the person,
> (b) by being sent to the proper address of the person—
> (i) by a registered post service (as defined in section 125(1) of the Postal Services Act 2000 (c.26)), or
> (ii) by a postal service which provides for the delivery of the document to be recorded, or

52 *Kodak Processing Companies Ltd v Shoredale Ltd* (n 24).

(c) where subsection (3) applies, by being sent to the person using electronic communications.

(3) This subsection applies where, before the document is served, the person authorised or required to serve the document and the person on whom it is to be served agree in writing that the document may be sent to the person by being transmitted to an electronic address and in an electronic form specified by the person for the purpose.

(4) For the purposes of subsection (2)(b), the proper address of a person is—
(a) in the case of a body corporate, the address of the registered or principal office of the body,
(b) in the case of a partnership, the address of the principal office of the partnership,
(c) in any other case, the last known address of the person.

(5) Where a document is served as mentioned in subsection (2)(b) on an address in the United Kingdom it is to be taken to have been received 48 hours after it is sent unless the contrary is shown.

(6) Where a document is served as mentioned in subsection (2)(c) it is to be taken to have been received 48 hours after it is sent unless the contrary is shown."

In comparison with the particular provisions under the 1988 and 2001 Acts already considered, section 26(2) removes the option of "leaving it at that person's last known address", but adds the option of email service, provided that parties have agreed to allow service in that way, under section 26(3). This means that, apart from postal or email service, the only permissible method is personal service on the intended recipient.[53]

As regards the choice between these modes of service, it is necessary to notice that clause 4 of the Scottish Government's Model Private Residential Tenancy ("PRT") Agreement begins:

"4. COMMUNICATION
The Landlord and Tenant agree that all communications which may or must be made under the Act and in relation to this Agreement, including notices to be served by one party on the other will be made in writing using:

[ ] hard copy by personal delivery or recorded delivery; or
[ ] the email addresses set out in clauses [2 or 3] and 1.

For communication by email it is essential that the Landlord(s) and Tenant(s) consider carefully whether this option is suitable for them. It should be noted that all notices will be sent by email, which includes important documents such as a rent-increase notice and a notice to leave the Let Property."

The drafting of this clause is perhaps misleading, in that it could be read as requiring a choice to be made between hard copy or email. There is no reason why parties could not retain the option of doing either – or both, in which case both boxes should be ticked. Where service of documents by email has been chosen as the sole option under clause 4, that would appear to preclude service being effected by personal delivery or post under section 26(2)(a) or (b). Likewise, choosing only the hard-copy option precludes service by email.[54] If neither option under clause 4 is chosen, or parties use a different form of

53 I.e. placing the notice (or an envelope containing it) into the hands of the tenant personally: *Rae v Calor Gas Ltd* (n 48).

54 Consequently, applications to the FTT have been refused, because the landlord purported to serve the notice to leave in a manner not specified in the tenancy agreement: *Higgins v Riley*

agreement that has no equivalent clause, that also effectively precludes service by email,[55] which requires prior agreement, given the terms of section 26(3).[56]

As with section 7 of the Interpretation Act 1978, on one possible reading of subsections (2) and (5), sending the notice by registered post "or by a postal service which provides for the delivery of the document to be recorded" has the effect that service is deemed to have taken place, with a presumed date of receipt forty-eight hours later.[57] On that view, the intended recipient may, under section 26(5), show that the relevant document was received at a different time. However, he cannot disprove the fact of service itself.[58] Against that one can argue that, as with section 7 of the 1978 Act, showing that receipt never took place at all necessarily shows that it did not take place forty-eight hours later. Therefore, subsection (5) allows the intended recipient to show that receipt never took place. If that is shown, it must follow, as with section 7 of the 1978 Act, that service has not been effected. Otherwise, the intended recipient would be permitted by the section to show that receipt did not take place, but doing so would have no effect.

The same considerations apply where parties have agreed to service by email under section 26(2)(c), (3) and (6), as the rules in subsections (5) and (6) are effectively the same.

Statutory notices: service by sheriff officers

Section 26(2) raises an important question. It states that service "may" be effected in one of three ways. Does that then preclude other modes of service? If it does, is service by sheriff officers invalid, unless that is in one of those three ways, which would then rule out certain modes of service that are typically used by officers of court?

In *Department of Agriculture v Goodfellow*.[59] the Inner House considered rule 113 of the first schedule to the Sheriff Courts (Scotland) Act 1907, which was similar to rule 34.8 of the OCR and rule 30.7 of the SCR, in that it allowed that service "may" be effected in certain ways, which were then specified.[60]

and Harley EV/19/2868, 29/11/19; *Scott v Hards* EV/19/3690, 12/12/19; *Kaur v Milligan*, EV/19/3750, 9/12/19 (see paras 8 and 9).

55 *Selbie v Underhill* EV/19/3005, 28/11/19.

56 Unless parties have otherwise made a written agreement, under s 26(3), that service of the relevant document may be effected by email.

57 Provided that the notice is sent to the "proper address" of the intended recipient, which is an address in the UK: see subss (3) and (5). In eviction proceedings, that will almost always be the tenancy property.

58 On this view, s 26(2)(b) would fall into the category of provisions that irrebuttably deem that service has been effected by the act of sending. Other examples are s 19(6) of the Conveyancing and Feudal Reform (Scotland) Act 1970, and s 23 of the Landlord and Tenant Act 1927, as discussed by the Court of Appeal's decision in *Beanby Estates Ltd v Egg Stores (Stamford Hill) Ltd* [2003] 1 WLR 2064. However, neither of those provisions includes any equivalent to the words "unless the contrary is proved/shown" in s 7 of the 1978 Act and s 26(5) of the 2010 Act. Also, to deem service to have taken place, irrebuttably, by the act of sending may be appropriate for particular notices in particular contexts, where there are reasons for deeming service that outweigh the possible injustice to the intended recipient. But one could question whether it is a desirable rule to impose in a provision that has general application, such as s 26 of the 2010 Act.

59 (n 30).

60 It said: "Removal notices under sections 34, 35, 36, 37, and 38 of the Act may be given by a

The court held that, under rule 113, a landlord was entitled to adopt any one of the three methods of giving notice there set forth, but must adopt one or other of them; and, accordingly, that the notice of intention to bring the tenancy to an end, which had been sent by unregistered letter, was invalid. Lord Justice-Clerk Alness said:[61]

> "I am clearly of opinion that Rule 113 is not enabling in its character, but is exhaustive. In other words, the word 'may' in that rule, in my judgment, imports a choice which is limited to these three methods. There is a choice as between any of the three. There is no choice outside of the three. Neither party is at liberty to invent a new method, and to superadd it to those which are included in the rule. If the pursuers were right in their contention, Rule 113 would run that the notice may be given in any one of the three ways enumerated, or in any other way deemed by the Court to be satisfactory . . . There are no general words in the rule which would admit of the adoption of a reasonable equivalent for the methods which the rule includes. There is no suggestion of that kind within its four corners; and we are not at liberty, in my judgment, to add to the provisions of an Act of Parliament in the way suggested. If the pursuers were right, the whole thing would be thrown loose, and a notice might be served by a taxi-driver or an office boy, or by many other methods which might be conceived, but which receive no sanction whatever from the terms of Rule 113."[62]

In *Kodak Processing Companies Ltd v Shoredale Ltd*,[63] the court held that a notice served by sheriff officers was invalid, because it was given under statutory provisions that required service to be effected by record delivery.[64]

Taking those two authorities together, it arguably follows that service of statutory notices under section 54 of the 1988 Act, section 40 of the 2001 Act and section 26 of the 2010 Act may only be effected by sheriff officers, if it is done in one of the three ways set out in the relevant section.

A contrary view is that whereas, in light of the decision in *Department of Agriculture v Goodfellow*, it is not for parties or the court to superadd modes of services to those set out in the relevant section, that may be done by legislation, and has been done, by rule 14(1)(c) of the Act of Sederunt (Messengers-at-Arms and Sheriff Officers Rules) 1991, already described.[65]

messenger-at-arms or sheriff officer, or by registered letter signed by the person entitled to give such notice. . . .".

61 (n 30) 559.

62 Lord Anderson said, at 560: "The pursuers maintained that the use of the permissive term 'may' in the rule warranted them in employing a manner of giving notice different from any of those prescribed by the rule. In other words, they maintained that the rule was enabling only, and not exclusive. I do not agree. . . . the Act . . . sends an inquirer as to the proper manner of giving notice to Rule 113, and directs him to use one or other of the three modes therein prescribed. The term 'may' of the rule is designed to give a choice, but a choice which is limited to the three categories therein mentioned. These categories, in my opinion, are exhaustive, and it is illegitimate to substitute what may be thought to be adequate equivalents."

63 n 24.

64 The pursuers argued that the notice was valid, because the Act required only that the notice be sent by "recorded delivery". That did not exclude forms of recorded delivery other than by Royal Mail. The notice had been served by a manner in which the delivery had been recorded. That argument was rejected by the Court, holding that "recorded delivery" means the recorded delivery service provided by Royal Mail.

65 At p 497. Essentially, this difference of view also lies at the root of the conflicting decisions in *Bank of Scotland v Stevenson* (n 42) and *Santander UK plc v Gallagher* 2011 SLT (Sh Ct) 203, 2011 Hous LR 26. In those cases, the question was whether a calling-up notice under s 19 of the Conveyancing and Feudal Reform (Scotland) Act 1970 could be served by sheriff officer

PROOF OF THE CONTENT OF NOTICES

Pre-action notices are of some importance in the context of eviction proceedings, as has been discussed in earlier chapters. It is appropriate at this point to draw attention to an important authority in relation to proof of the content of notices.

In *Clydebank District Council v Sweeney*,[66] a dispute arose as to a notice to quit said to have been served by the pursuers. No copy of the notice was produced. The pursuers relied on a letter from the defender to the pursuers, which constituted an extrajudicial admission that a notice to quit had been served upon him. Sheriff Principal Prosser said:

> "I am . . . not satisfied that the 'extrajudicial admission' . . . admits enough to constitute sufficient primary evidence of a valid notice to quit. In the absence of any evidence as to the terms of the notice or of evidence that such notice was in fact prepared and sent in specified (or perhaps standard) terms, it appears to me that the admission is insufficient requiring not only a little formal corroboration, but also substantial supplementary detail."[67]

Accordingly, the onus is on the pursuer to prove not only the service of the notice of a notice to quit, but its content.

It is suggested that this conclusion applies, *a fortiori*, to statutory notices in relation to which the statute requires the notice to be in a certain form, or have a specified content. It is not possible to confirm whether those requirements are met, without sight of the notice. Hence, rules 65, 66 and 109 of the Procedure Rules[68] all require that an application is accompanied by a copy of the relevant statutory notice.[69]

VIOLENT PROFITS, PAYMENT IN RESPECT OF OCCUPATION, AND CAUTION FOR PECUNIARY CLAIMS

Claim for violent profits, damages or recompense

Violent profits may be sought by the proprietor of subjects against any person, including the tenant, who occupies the subjects illegally. They may therefore be payable by a tenant who continues to occupy a property after the lease has been lawfully terminated.[70] In residential tenancies subject to the 1988, 2001 and 2016 Acts, there is no scope for such a claim, because the tenant contin-

(as Sheriff Jamieson decided in *Stevenson*) or could be served only using one of the modes expressly set out in s 19(6) of the Act, as Sheriff Mackie decided in *Gallagher*. A decision is needed at appellate level to determine the relationship between para 14(1)(c) of the Act of Sederunt (Messengers-at-Arms and Sheriff Officers Rules) 1991 and provisions such as s 26(2) of the 2010 Act, s 19(6) of the 1970 Act.

66 Reported at 1998 Hous LR 84, though the decision was made in 1981.

67 At para 16-19. This case was decided before the abolition of the requirement for corroboration in civil proceedings effected by the Civil Evidence (Scotland) Act 1988. However, it is clear that the result would have been the same, even if corroboration had not been required, because there was no primary evidence as to the terms of the notice.

68 n 38.

69 Rule 65(b)(ii); r 66(b)(ii) and (iii); and r 109(b)(ii).

70 Rennie and others (n 1) para 20-28 and the authorities cited therein.

ues to have a right to occupy the property, until the court's order terminating the statutory tenancy has effect.[71] However, it is still possible to seek violent profits in other cases.

At common law, violent profits are double the rent that was payable under the tenancy.[72] However, the pursuer requires to show "bad faith" on the part of the defender, i.e. that he continued in occupation in circumstances in which he clearly had no title to do so.[73] Where possession has been continued during a litigation regarding the title of the possessor, it is sufficient to support the possessor's plea of good faith that he had probable cause in the litigation.[74] Accordingly, where there is a genuine dispute between the parties as to whether the defender is entitled to remain in occupation, a claim for violent profits will not be upheld.[75]

Alternatively, the owner of the property may pursue a claim for unjustified enrichment against a person who occupies and uses the property, without title to do so. The use of another's property attracts the obligation to pay for the use of it.[76] The measure of liability is the "real worth and annual value" of the subjects.[77] It is suggested that, in the case of residential subjects, this will be the amount that the owner could have obtained in rent.

At common law, a landlord who gives notice to quit, but then continues to accept rental payments, is held to have departed from the notice and to have lost his right to regain possession.[78] However, it is suggested that this rule does not apply if payments are expressly accepted on the basis that the landlord does not abandon his right to seek possession, and that the payments are to be treated as being in lieu of violent profits, or in respect of a liability to pay for the use of subjects, where the former tenant continues to occupy them without title.

Caution

In former times, where an action for removing and for payment of violent profits was defended, the defender might be ordered to find caution for violent profits, failing which the court would grant decree against him.

71 Section 16(2) of the 1988 Act; s 16(5) and (5A) of the 2001 Act; and s 51(4) of the 2016 Act.

72 *Jute Industries Ltd v Wilson & Graham Ltd* 1955 SLT (Sh Ct) 46.

73 "Violent profits are profits acquired by violence – by an intruder without any colour of law, who must account on the strictest footing": *Houldsworth v Bain & Ors (Alexander Brand's Trustees)* (1876) 3 R 304, 310.

74 ibid.

75 See *St Andrews Forest Lodges Ltd v Grieve* [2017] 3 WLUK 625, 2017 GWD 14-224, in which a claim for violent profits was made. This failed because the defenders established that they were occupying under an assured tenancy. At [62] the sheriff indicated that, even had he decided that their occupation was precarious, he would still have declined to uphold a claim for violent profits, because the defenders were occupying in good faith, and had probable cause in the litigation.

76 *Earl of Fife v Wilson* (1864) 3 M 323; *Glen v Roy* (1882) 10 R 239; *Rochester Poster Services Ltd v AG Barr plc* 1994 SLT (Sh Ct) 2; *GTW Holdings Ltd v Toet* 1994 SLT (Sh Ct) 16. See also R Evans-Jones: *Unjustified Enrichment: Enrichment Acquired In Any Other Manner,* vol 2, 4.40–4.44.

77 *Glen v Roy*, 240.

78 See, example e.g.: *Coatbridge Town Council v Tamburrino* 1958 SLT (Sh Ct) 4.

Section 219 of the Bankruptcy and Diligence etc. (Scotland) Act 2007 abolished caution for violent profits.[79] Instead, in an action for removing from heritable property[80] the court may, on cause shown, make an "order for caution for pecuniary claims", being an order requiring the defender "to find caution for any payment claimed (other than by way of expenses) by the pursuer for loss arising from the occupation of the subjects or premises by the defender or any other occupant deriving right or having permission from the defender". This includes loss arising from lawful (as well as unlawful) occupation of the subjects or premises by the defender or such other occupant.[81] Thus, the power to order caution seems to extend not only to a claim for unjustified enrichment of the type discussed above, but also to other claims for "loss", such as a claim in respect of damage to the subjects caused by the tenant.[82]

If the order is made, the defender may provide caution by means of a bond of caution or other guarantee; or by consigning an appropriate sum in court.[83] As the "order for caution for pecuniary claims" replaces caution for violent profits, it is to be presumed that the effect of failing to provide caution is the same as under the common law: the court will grant the decree sought by the pursuer. However, in the case of a residential property, that could only happen where the parties' lease was not covered by any of the statutes conferring security of tenure. Under those Acts, an order may be granted only if the legislative requirements are met.

The need to seek an order to find caution, as a means of "flushing out" the defender who is seeking to delay matters, should arise less often in summary causes; if there is no defence to the action decree may be obtained at the first calling of the case, or on a subsequent motion for summary decree.

The power to order the defender to find caution under section 219 does not extend to proceedings in the tribunal.[84]

AFTER DECREE OR ORDER IS GRANTED

This topic may be considered under the following headings:

- appeals and extract decree in the sheriff court;
- eviction order and appeal – proceedings in the tribunal.

79 The right to seek violent profits is not abolished by s 219 – only the right to order caution for violent profits.

80 "Action for removing from heritable property" is defined in s 214. See below.

81 Section 219(4).

82 The types of claim covered by s 219(1) await clarification: although that section came into force in 2011, at the time of writing, there are no reported cases in which an order for caution for pecuniary claims has been sought.

83 Section 219(3).

84 As described below, pt 15 of the 2007 Act was, somewhat belatedly, amended by r 6 of the First-tier Tribunal of Scotland Housing and Property Chamber (Incidental Provisions) Regulations 2019 (SSI 2019/51) to include reference to eviction orders granted by the tribunal. That regulation makes amendments to all of ss 214–218 of the 2007 Act, but not to s 219. Presumably, therefore, the intention is that the power to order caution is not extended to the FTT.

Extract decree and appeal – summary causes

Section 38 of the Sheriff Courts (Scotland) Act 1971

Notwithstanding the Courts Reform (Scotland) Act 2014, appeals in summary causes are still, at the time of writing, subject to section 38 of the Sheriff Courts (Scotland) Act 1971. The procedure for appeals is found in chapter 25 of the SCR, and chapter 29 of the Sheriff Appeal Court Rules.[85] Under rule 25.1 of the SCR, an an appeal is made on form 31, which requests a stated case, and specifies the point of law on which the appeal proceeds. This must be lodged no later than fourteen days after the date of final decree.

The scope for appeal in summary causes is much more limited than in ordinary causes.[86] Under section 38, appeal is made to the sheriff principal "on any point of law from the final judgment of the sheriff". Thus, appeals against incidental orders of the court are not possible. Appeal may be made from the final judgment of the sheriff principal to the Court of Session, but only if he or she "certifies the cause as suitable for appeal".[87]

There is some doubt as to what is meant by the term "final judgment" in section 38. In *W Jack Baillie Associates v Kennedy*, Sheriff Principal Caplan was asked to allow an appeal by the defender against a refusal by the sheriff to grant a minute for recall. This was an action for payment. The recall was too late, having been lodged more than fourteen days after the service of a charge.[88] The defender had asked the sheriff to allow the minute although late, in exercise of the dispensing power. The sheriff principal held that refusal by the sheriff to allow the minute to be lodged late was not a "final judgment", as it could in no way be said to have a direct effect on the issues of the case. However, the sheriff principal left open the wider question of whether a decision to refuse a minute for recall could be appealed at all.[89]

85 Act of Sederunt (Sheriff Appeal Court Rules) 2015 (SSI 2015/356).

86 That scope is also indirectly limited by the fact that, at proof in a summary cause, the evidence is not recorded. It is an established principle of appellate courts in Scotland that the findings in fact of a court at first instance are inviolate if the evidence before that court was not recorded: *Allardice v Wallace* 1957 SLT 225. Also, the outcome of many eviction cases in the sheriff court depends on whether the court considers it reasonable to grant the order. That type of decision is difficult to appeal. See: *City of Edinburgh Council v Forbes* 2002 Hous LR 61; *Glasgow West Housing Association Ltd v Harasimowicz* 2015 Hous LR 77.

87 The procedure for applying for certification is now in r 29.6 of the Sheriff Appeal Court Rules. This is not an appeal in terms of s 113 of the 2014 Act, and therefore the requirements for a second appeal under s 113(2) do not apply. There appears to be no reported authority as to criteria that might be applied by the sheriff principal in deciding whether to certify an appeal under s 38 of the 1971 Act. At para 31.352 of Macphail, *Sheriff Court Practice,* the learned authors suggest that the court would require to be satisfied that there was a "substantial and important question of law raised by the appeal". This seems quite similar to the test in s 113(2)(a): "the appeal would raise an important point of principle or practice".

88 See r 24.1(7) for the current version of the relevant rule. The fourteen-day limit does not apply in eviction proceedings, given the terms of r 24.1(9).

89 1985 SLT (Sh Ct) 53. On the subject of what constitutes a "final judgment", see also: *Napoli v Stone* 2009 SLT (Sh Ct) 125; *Robertson v Robertson's Exr* 1991 SC 21; and *McDermid v D & E Mackay (Contractors) Ltd* 2013 SLT 32. In *North Lanarkshire Council v Kenmure* 2004 Hous LR 50 and *North Lanarkshire Council v Cairns* 2012 SLT (Sh Ct) 128, appeals against the granting and the refusal of a minute for recall were heard by the sheriff principal, without the issue of the competency of the appeal being raised.

Extract

Decree is extracted under rule 23.6 of the SCR, which provides:

> "**23.6.— Extract of decree**
> (1) Extract of a decree signed by the sheriff clerk may be issued only after the lapse of 14 days from the granting of the decree unless the sheriff on application orders earlier extract.
> (2) In an action (other than an action to which rule 30.2 applies) where an appeal has been lodged, the extract may not be issued until the appeal has been disposed of.
> (3) The extract decree—
> (a) may be written on the summons or on a separate paper;
> (b) may be in one of Forms 28 to 28k; and
> (c) shall be warrant for all lawful execution."

There is no requirement for either party to make an application for extract to be granted. It is issued automatically by the sheriff clerk, usually within a few working days of the expiry of fourteen days from the granting of decree.

There is a close relationship between the issuing of extract and the disposal of any possible appeal. As the extract is a warrant for the execution of the decree, it is logical that it should be issued only after appeal is no longer possible. Hence the fourteen-day period in rule 23.6(1) ties in with the period allowed for lodging an appeal under rule 25.1. Under rule 26.1(2), extract of the decree is postponed on the lodging of an appeal, except in relation to an action under rule 30.2.[90]

Rule 30.2(5) is also subject to rule 25.6, which states that, in an action to which rule 30.2 applies: (a) it shall not be competent to shorten or dispense with the period for appeal specified in rule 25.1; (b) it shall be competent to appeal within that period for appeal irrespective of the early issue of an extract decree; and (c) the lodging of a note of appeal shall not operate so as to suspend diligence unless the sheriff directs otherwise.

On occasion, a motion for decree made by the pursuer will be accompanied by a motion for earlier extract, which is competent under rule 23.6(1). This is usually done in actions under rule 30.2, or in cases in which the conduct of the defender at the property is such that his immediate ejection is said to be necessary. In practice "earlier" extract tends to mean immediate extract, the application being made at the hearing at which the court grants decree. As regards applications for earlier or immediate extract, the following points may be usefully made.

- First, if the pursuer's aim is to recover possession as soon as possible, an application for earlier extract should be accompanied by an application, under section 216(4) of the Bankruptcy and Diligence etc. (Scotland) Act 2007, asking the court to dispense with or vary the fourteen-day period of the charge that must be served under that section.[91] The sheriff also has

90 Therefore, in an action under r 30.2, the lodging of an appeal by the defender does not prevent the pursuer from carrying out the eviction, unless the sheriff directs that diligence is suspended, under r 25.6(c). Rule 30.2 is discussed in Chapter 13.

91 Section 216 of the 2007 Act is discussed below.

the power to vary or dispense with the forty-eight-hour period allowed by a notice of the date of removal.[92]

- Secondly, the issuing of an earlier extract does not appear to preclude an appeal being made within the fourteen-day period specified in rule 25.1. The right to appeal to the sheriff principal in a summary cause action is provided by statute, under section 38 of the Sheriff Courts (Scotland) Act 1971. There is no provision elsewhere that suggests that this right is removed by the issue of an early extract.[93] On the contrary, in relation to cases under rule 30.2, the right to appeal is preserved, notwithstanding early extract, by rule 25.6(b). However, the issue of an extract decree *does* preclude the granting of an incidental application to the sheriff principal to allow an appeal to be received although late, after the fourteen days allowed for the lodging of a note of appeal has expired.[94]
- Thirdly, under rule 25.5 the sheriff has the power, notwithstanding an appeal, "(a) to regulate all matters relating to interim possession . . . (d) to make in his discretion any interim order which a due regard for the interests of the parties may require". It is suggested that this power might be used to reinstate a defender who has been evicted following the issue of immediate extract, where he has appealed to the sheriff principal timeously.[95]

Eviction order and appeal – proceedings in the tribunal

Appeal and review of orders made in the Scottish tribunals, including the Housing and Property Chamber, are subject to part 6 of the Tribunals (Scotland) Act 2014. Rules 37 and 38 of the Procedure Rules[96] relate to applications for permission to appeal; rule 39 concerns reviews.[97]

92 The requirement to serve notice of the date of removal is discussed in the next section. The power to vary or dispense with the period of notice is given by para 4(3) of the Act of Sederunt (Actions for removing from heritable property) 2012 (SSI 2012/136, as amended by 2012/273).

93 By contrast, r 31.1 of the OCR specifically provides that "an interlocutor . . . may be appealed within 14 days . . . unless it has been extracted following a motion under r 30.4(2) (early extract)." On 13 August 2015, the author appeared for the petitioner at a pre-service hearing in the Outer House of the Court of Session, on a contested motion for interim orders. The petitioner sought interim suspension of a decree granted at Dumbarton Sheriff Court, which, with the authority of the sheriff, had been immediately extracted, but not yet enforced. The petitioner had then lodged an appeal timeously, under r 25.1 of the SCR (n 7). After hearing submissions, the Lord Ordinary granted the motion and suspended the decree *ad interim*, in order that the appeal could be heard.

94 *City of Edinburgh Council v Swann* 2001 SLT (Sh Ct) 161; 2000 Hous LR 123. Because extract decrees are usually issued very shortly after the fourteen-day period for appeal has expired, the scope for late appeals in summary causes is very limited.

95 In this case, the application would be made by the defender/appellant, following lodging of the appeal. It would be made to the sheriff rather than the sheriff principal. If the application is successful, the defender/appellant would be reinstated pending the outcome of the appeal.

96 n 38.

97 By rr 37(3) and 39(1), there are certain matters in respect of which an application for permission to appeal cannot be made, and which cannot be reviewed. However, none of those relates to eviction proceedings.

Reviews

Under section 43(2)(b) of the 2014 Act, any party to the case can ask the FTT (or the Upper Tribunal ("UT")) to review its decision.[98] Under section 44, the FTT or the UT may, on review: (a) take no action; (b) set the decision aside; or (c) correct a minor or accidental error contained in the decision. Where a decision is set aside by the FTT in a review, it may: (a) re-decide the matter concerned; (b) refer that matter to the Upper Tribunal; or (c) make such other order as it considers appropriate.

Applications to the FTT for a review under section 43 are made under rule 39 of the Procedure Rules.[99] Such an application must be made in writing, within fourteen days of the date on which the decision and reasons are sent to the parties.[100] The application must set out the reasons for which a review of the decision is necessary. Rule 39 prescribes the process by which an application for review is determined, which may include setting a time limit for responses from the other parties, and fixing a hearing on the application.

The 2014 Act does not impose any restriction as to the basis on which a review might be sought, but rule 39(1) indicates that the FTT may review a decision "where it is necessary in the interests of justice to do so". By contrast, appeal may be made on a point of law only.[101]

It is very important to be aware that, under section 43(5): "A right of appeal under section 46 or 48 is not affected by the availability or otherwise of a review". In particular, it is necessary to appreciate that where an application for review has been accepted by the FTT (or the UT), and a decision in relation to that application is pending, that has no effect on the running of the thirty-day time limit for an application to the tribunal for permission to appeal.[102] It also follows from section 43(5) that a party may seek a review, and request permission to appeal, on identical grounds,[103] and both of those applications, if made in proper form, would have to be determined by the tribunal.

Appeals

Under section 46 of the 2014 Act, a decision of the FTT in any matter in a case before the tribunal may be appealed, on a point of law, to the UT.

98 Unless it is an "excluded decision": ss 43(3) and 51–54. Note that, under s 43(2)(a), both the FTT and the UT can review its own decision, at its own instance. As to the procedure in that case, see r 39(7) of the Procedure Rules. By r 36, the FTT also has the power, at any time, to "correct any clerical mistake or other accidental slip or omission contained in a decision, order or any document produced by it".

99 n 38.

100 Rule 39(2)(b) states that the application for review must be: "made within 14 days of the date on which the decision is made or within 14 days of the date that the written reasons (if any) were sent to the parties". As indicated below, the practice of the Housing and Property Chamber is to issue a written decision and a statement of reasons in a single document.

101 Section 46(2)(b) of the 2014 Act.

102 This is explicitly stated in r 39(8). Given that the procedure for reviews under r 39 envisages the possibility of inviting a response from the other parties, and holding a hearing on the review, it is entirely possible that a review application will not be determined within the thirty days allowed for an application for permission to appeal.

103 Though, in that case, the application for review would be on a point of law, rather than on any other basis.

Permission must first be sought from the FTT. If it refuses, permission may be sought from the UT.[104]

In terms of regulation 2(1) of the Scottish Tribunals (Time Limits) Regulations 2016, the period within which an application for permission to appeal may be made is: "the period of 30 days beginning with the relevant date", which may be extended, but not reduced, under regulation 2(2). In eviction cases, the "relevant date" will invariably be the date on which the decision and reasons are sent to the appellant.[105] It may be assumed that this will be the date given in the covering letter attaching the decision. If that is, say, 1 July, then the application must be received by the tribunal no later than 30 July.

An application to the FTT for permission to appeal must be made in writing; identify the decision to which it relates and points of law on which the appeal is to proceed; and state the result that the person making the application is seeking.[106] The FTT must then decide whether to grant permission, and provide parties with a record of its decision.[107] Under section 46(4), permission may be given if the tribunal is satisfied that there are arguable grounds for appeal.

If the tribunal decides to refuse permission, it must also give a statement of reasons for refusal, and notification of the right to seek permission from the UT.[108] In terms of regulation 3(1) and (2) of the Scottish Tribunals (Time Limits) Regulations 2016,[109] the period within which an application for permission to appeal may be made to the UT is the period of thirty days beginning with the date on which notice of the FTT's refusal of permission to appeal was sent to the appellant.[110]

However, under rule 3 of the UT's rules,[111] an application for permission is, in effect, made by lodging a notice of appeal. In particular, rule 3(9) states that:

> "Where the First-tier Tribunal sends a notice of permission or refusal of permission to appeal to a person who has sought permission to appeal, that person, if intending to appeal, must provide a notice of appeal to the Upper Tribunal within 30 days after the day of receipt by that person of the notice of permission or refusal of permission to appeal."[112]

Thereafter, rule 3(6) provides that, where the FTT refused permission to appeal, the UT, on the lodging of the notice of appeal, may refuse permission,

104 Section 46(3) of the 2014 Act.

105 SSI 2016/231 (Time Limits Regulations). Under r 2 of the Time Limits Regulations, the relevant date depends on whether the reasons for the decision are issued later than the decision, and whether a decision is given orally at the hearing. However, as described in Chapter 14, the practice of the Housing and Property Chamber is to issue a written decision and a statement of reasons in a single document. That is done shortly after the case management discussion ("CMD") or the hearing. Therefore, under r 2, the thirty days begin from the date on which the decision and reasons are sent to the appellant.

106 Rule 37(2).

107 Rule 38(1) and (2).

108 Rule 38(3).

109 n 105.

110 Which period may be extended, on cause shown, under r 3(3).

111 Being the the schedule to the Upper Tribunal for Scotland (Rules of Procedure) Regulations 2016 (SSI 2016/232).

112 Thus, the next step, after the FTT makes a decision on the application for permission, is the lodging of the notice of appeal, irrespective of whether the FTT grants or refuses permission.

grant permission, or grant permission on limited grounds, or subject to conditions.[113]

Orders

Rule 41 of the Procedure Rules[114] states:

> "41.—(1) An order in pursuance of a decision of the First-tier Tribunal, or a copy of such an order certified by the First-tier Tribunal, may be enforced as if it were an extract registered decree bearing a warrant for execution issued by the sheriff court.
>
> (2) An order cannot be enforced under paragraph (1) until the expiry of the period within which an application may be made for permission to appeal a decision of the First-tier Tribunal—
>
> (a) under regulation 2(1) of the Scottish Tribunals (Time Limits) Regulations 2016, or
>
> (b) as determined by the First-tier Tribunal under regulation 2(2) of those Regulations."

As already described, the period within which an application to the FTT for permission to appeal must be received by the tribunal is thirty days,[115] beginning with the day on which the decision and reasons are sent to the parties.

Where an eviction order is granted, the legal member of the tribunal signs the order at the same time as making the decision and statement of reasons. However, in practice, the signed order is sent out to the applicant, after the thirty-day period for a permission application has expired.

In contrast to summary cause proceedings, there is no equivalent, under the tribunal's Procedure Rules, to the court's power to grant immediate extract, thereby empowering the landlord to commence measures for the enforcement of a decree, without waiting for the appeal period to expire. However, it has the same power as the court to vary or dispense with the fourteen-day period of a charge for removing under section 216(4) of the 2007 Act,[116] or to vary or dispense with the minimum forty-eight-hour period allowed by a notice of the date of removal.[117] This appears to be the only means by which the enforcement of the eviction order may be accelerated.

The tribunal also has an express power, under rule 16A(d) of the Procedure Rules, to order a delay in the execution of an order made by the FTT, at any time before it is executed. Accordingly, where, due to the circumstances of the case, the tribunal considers it appropriate to delay the period for enforcement

113 Under r 3(7) and (8), where the UT judge, without a hearing, decides to refuse permission, or gives permission on limited grounds, the appellant may make a written application to the UT (within fourteen days) for that decision to be reconsidered at a hearing. That application, in turn, must be heard and decided by a member or members of the UT different from the member or members who refused permission without a hearing. Thus the process of seeking leave to appeal, through the FTT, the UT and by another member of the UT, can become somewhat drawn out.

114 n 38.

115 Unless that period is extended under r 2(2) of the Time Limit Regulations (n 105).

116 For which, see below.

117 Under para 4(3) of the Act of Sederunt (Actions for removing from heritable property) 2012 (n 92); see below.

of an eviction order, this may be done under rule 16A(d), or by extending the fourteen-day period of the charge for removing.[118]

There is also no specific rule stipulating that an appeal, or an application for permission to appeal, has the effect of suspending enforcement of an order made by the FTT. Rather, the UT has a case management power, under rule 7(2) of the Upper Tribunal Rules,[119] to "give an order in relation to the conduct of proceedings before it at any time, including an order amending, suspending or setting aside an earlier order". Under rule 7(3)(m) and (n), this includes a power to: "suspend the effect of its own decision pending an appeal of that decision" and "in an appeal against the decision of the First-tier Tribunal, suspend the effect of that decision pending the determination of any permission to appeal or any appeal". For that reason, it is suggested that, where a decision is made by the FTT to grant an eviction order, and a note of appeal is lodged with the UT, an application should be made, at the same time, for an order under rule 7(3)(n), suspending the effect of the FTT's decision, pending the determination of issue of permission to appeal, and any appeal to be determined by the UT.

If the landlord commences enforcement before an application for permission to appeal has been determined by the FTT, an application may to be made to it, under rule 16A(d), for the execution of the order to be delayed.

ENFORCEMENT

Part 15 of the Bankruptcy and Diligence etc. (Scotland) Act 2007

This area of the law was radically altered by the coming into force of part 15 of the Bankruptcy and Diligence etc. (Scotland) Act 2007. The key provision is section 216, which requires the service of a charge before an eviction may be carried out.

First, however, it is necessary to notice that part 15 applies to any "decree for removing from heritable property", which is defined in section 214(1) and (2) as including any of the following decrees or orders:

"(a) a decree of removing and warrant of ejection obtained in an action of removing;
(b) a decree and warrant of ejection obtained in an action of ejection;
. . .
(d) a warrant for summary ejection obtained by virtue of section 37 of the 1907 Act;
(e) a decree obtained by virtue of a summary application for removing under section 38 of the 1907 Act;
(f) a decree for recovery of possession of heritable property obtained by virtue of a summary cause under section 35(1)(c) of the Sheriff Courts (Scotland) Act 1971 (c.58);

118 As was done by the sheriff in *Reid v Redfern (No 4)* [2019] 4 WLUK 526, 2019 GWD 19-297, where he extended the period of the charge to ten weeks. In theory, the eviction could also be delayed by extending the period for an application for permission to appeal, under r 2(2) of the Time Limits Regulations (n 105), which would delay enforcement, given r 41(2) of the Procedure Rules (n 38). However, that would also have the effect of allowing the respondent more time to seek permission to appeal.

119 n 111.

(g) an order for possession (within the meaning of section 115(1) of the Rent (Scotland) Act 1984 (c.58)) obtained by virtue of the Housing (Scotland) Act 1987 (c.26) or the Housing (Scotland) Act 1988 (c.43);

. . .

(k) an eviction order issued under section 51 of the Private Housing (Tenancies) (Scotland) Act 2016;

. . .

being decrees, orders or warrants which, or extracts of which, authorise the removing or ejection of persons from subjects or premises".[120]

Accordingly, all decrees for eviction granted in the sheriff court, following upon the eviction proceedings discussed in the preceding chapters, are subject to the same enforcement rules under part 15 of the 2007 Act. Those rules are found in the remaining sections in part 15, in particular section 216. The procedure and practice to be followed in the execution of any sheriff court decree for removing from heritable property is also regulated and prescribed by the Act of Sederunt (Actions for removing from heritable property) 2012,[121] made under section 215.

As regards orders granted by the tribunal, the Housing (Scotland) Act 2014 did not make any amendments to part 15 of the 2007 Act, in recognition of the fact that, following the transfer of jurisdiction, eviction orders would be made by the FTT. That has now been remedied by regulation 6 of the First-tier Tribunal of Scotland Housing and Property Chamber (Incidental Provisions) Regulations 2019,[122] which effected various amendments to sections 214–218 so that appropriate reference is made to the FTT. Around the same time, the tribunal's Procedure Rules were also amended.[123] The provisions of the 2012 Act of Sederunt are now repeated, in modified form, in rules 41B–41F of the tribunal's Procedure Rules. Furthermore, rule 41(1) states:

"(1) An order in pursuance of a decision of the First-tier Tribunal, or a copy of such an order certified by the First-tier Tribunal, may be enforced as if it were an extract registered decree bearing a warrant for execution issued by the sheriff court."

Section 216: the power to remove, on service of a charge

"**216 Service of charge before removing**

(1) A defender[124] and any effects of the defender may, by virtue of a decree for removing from heritable property, be removed from subjects or premises but only if—

120 2007 Act, s 214(2). As was pointed out in Chapter 3, the term "decree for removing" has a wider meaning in pt 15 of the 2007 Act than it has at common law.

121 n 92.

122 n 84.

123 By the First-tier Tribunal for Scotland Housing and Property Chamber (Procedure) Amendment Regulations 2018/378, which came into force on 20 February 2019.

124 In eviction orders granted by the FTT, "respondent" would be used. Rule 6 of the First-tier Tribunal of Scotland Housing and Property Chamber (Incidental Provisions) Regulations 2019 (n 84) did not specifically address this point by amending the definition of "defender" in s 214(1). However, it is suggested that, given the other amendments made to ss 214–218, and given that the eviction orders under the 1988 and 2016 Acts are decrees for removing from heritable property under s 214, a respondent against whom such an order is made must be a "defender" for the purposes of ss 216 and 218, and an applicant for such an order is

(a) the defender has been charged to remove from those subjects or premises within the appropriate period after the giving of the charge; and
(b) the period of charge has expired without the defender so removing.

(1A) In subsection (1)(a), *'the appropriate period'* means—
(a) in the case of a decree for removing from heritable property of the type mentioned in paragraph (l) of section 214(2),[125] 28 days,
(b) in the case of a decree for removing from heritable property of the type mentioned in any other paragraph of that section, 14 days.

(2) Where—
(a) the subjects or premises are occupied by an occupant deriving right or having permission from the defender;
(b) the defender has been charged, under subsection (1) above, to remove from those subjects or premises; and
(c) the period of charge has expired without the occupant so removing,
that occupant and any effects of that occupant may be removed from the subjects or premises.

(2A) Subsection (2) does not apply to an occupant with an assured tenancy or private residential tenancy or any effects of that occupant where the decree for removing from heritable property was granted on an application—
(a) to which section 5A of the Heritable Securities (Scotland) Act 1894 (c.44) applies; or
(b) under section 24(1B) of the Conveyancing and Feudal Reform (Scotland) Act 1970 (c.35).

. . .

(3) The officer of court removing the defender, any other occupant and any effects of such a defender or occupant from the subjects or premises—
(a) may, if necessary for the purposes of such removing, open shut and lockfast places; and
(b) must make an inventory of any effects removed.

(4) Where the decree or order for removing from heritable property is granted by a court or the First-tier Tribunal, the court or the First-tier Tribunal may, on cause shown, dispense with or vary the period of charge.

. . .

(6) The Scottish Ministers may, by regulations, prescribe the form of charge under subsection (1) above."

Section 216 is a key provision in the scheme for enforcement set out in part 15 of the 2007 Act. The defender cannot be evicted unless a charge for removing has been served.

Section 216(2): who may be removed?

Once the charge is served on the defender, and has expired, the decree is a warrant for eviction of anyone who occupies the property, "deriving right or having permission from the defender". Let us say that the pursuer has let the property to a tenant, but is aware that the tenant no longer resides there, and also aware that someone else is in occupation. The effect of section 216(2) is that it is not necessary for the pursuer to raise his action against the occupant.

a "pursuer". Otherwise, the current version of s 218 would not make sense. Henceforth, in the discussion of pt 15 that follows, "pursuer" and "defender" include an applicant and a respondent in tribunal proceedings.

125 Section 214(2)(l): a decree of removing and warrant for ejection granted under section 266(8ZA) of the Proceeds of Crime Act 2002.

He should raise his action against the tenant, presuming that any occupant resides with the permission of, or by agreement with, the tenant, and may be evicted under section 216(2), after the charge is served.[126] If the action were raised against the occupant, one might question whether any decree would be effective against the tenant, were he to re-enter before the decree was enforced.

Section 216(2) is subject to the exception in subsection (2A): a decree for removing granted against a defender in mortgage repossession proceedings is not a warrant for the eviction of any person to whom the defender has let the subjects under an assured tenancy or a PRT.[127] However, it is suggested that section 216(2) also does not apply where the right of the occupant derives not merely from the personal obligation of the defender, or permission granted by him, but from a real right in the subjects.[128]

Section 216(4): varying the period of the charge

Under subsection (4), an application may be made to the court or the FTT to dispense with, or vary, the fourteen-day period specified in section 216(1)(a). As is described above, in proceedings in the sheriff court, an application to dispense with the period of the charge might be made at the same time as a motion for immediate extract of the decree.

As well as reducing the period of the charge, the court or tribunal may extend it, in order to delay the eviction, if that is considered appropriate in the circumstances.[129]

Form of charge and service of the charge

The form of charge is in the schedule to the Removing from Heritable Property (Form of Charge) (Scotland) Regulations 2011.[130] That form has been amended by regulation 5 of the First-tier Tribunal of Scotland Housing and Property Chamber (Incidental Provisions) Regulations 2019,[131] to incorporate references to the FTT as well as the sheriff court.

The rules as to the service of the charge, where the decree is granted in court proceedings, are to be found in rule 3 of the Act of Sederunt (Actions for removing from heritable property) 2012, made under section 215 of the Act.[132] In summary, the important points are that the charge must be served by a sheriff officer: (a) on the defender personally; or (b) by being left in the

126 Section 23(1) of the 1984 Act provides that the landlord cannot recover possession otherwise than by proceedings, but it does require that those proceedings must be against the occupant. If the occupant was *not* in occupation deriving right from the tenant, or having permission from him, then he would have no common law protection, and no protection from eviction without due process, under s 23 of the 1984 Act (see Chapter 2), and could therefore be evicted *brevi manu*. In that case, the pursuer would not be required to do anything, in addition to the steps he is taking, to obtain a decree against the tenant and enforce it.

127 Actions by heritable creditors are discussed in Chapter 8, in relation to ground 2 of sch 5 to the 1988 Act, and in Chapter 10, in relation to ground 2 of sch 3 to the 2016 Act.

128 That would be the case, for example, where the occupant had a proper liferent, created and registered in accordance with s 51 of the Land Registration etc. (Scotland) Act 2012.

129 For an example, see: *Reid v Redfern (No 4)* (n 118).

130 SI 2011/158.

131 n 84.

132 SSI 2012/136 (hereinafter “the Act of Sederunt”).

hands of a resident at the defender's dwelling place or an employee at his or her place of business. Where a sheriff officer cannot execute service in that manner he may, after making diligent enquiries, serve the charge: (a) by depositing it in the defender's dwelling place or place of business; or (b) by leaving it at that defender's dwelling place or place of business in such a way that it is likely to come to the attention of the defender.[133]

In the case of eviction orders granted by the tribunal, rule 41B of the Procedure Rules[134] states that, for the purposes of section 216(1)(a) of the 2007 Act, the charge for removing must be served by a sheriff officer on the defender: (a) personally; or (b) by being left in the hands of a resident at the defender's address. Where a sheriff officer has been unsuccessful in executing service in that manner, the officer may, after making diligent enquiries, serve the charge for removing by leaving it at the defender's address.[135]

Notice of the date of removal

Paragraph 4 of the Act of Sederunt provides that, prior to the execution of the decree, notice of the date of removal shall be served by the sheriff officer, in form 4 in schedule 1, by: (a) leaving the notice at the heritable property; and (b) sending a copy of the notice by first-class post to the address at which he thinks it most likely that the defender may be found. The date specified in the notice of the date of removal shall be a period of notice of not less than forty-eight hours after the notice is served. However, as has already been described, the sheriff may, on the application of the pursuer, on cause shown, vary or dispense with the period of notice mentioned in subparagraph (2). Rule 41C of the Procedure Rules imposes the same requirements, in respect of orders granted by the tribunal.[136]

Evidence of service of the charge and notice of removal

Under rule 5 of the Act of Sederunt, a certificate of service signed by the sheriff officer is sufficient evidence of service of the charge, and the notice of removal. That is also the case under rule 41D of the Procedure Rules.

133 Rule 3(2). In that case the sheriff officer must, under r 3(3), as soon as possible after service, send a letter containing a copy of the charge for removing by first-class post "to the address at which he or she thinks it most likely that the defender may be found". Where the address of the defender is not known and cannot be reasonably ascertained, service on the walls of court may be effected, under r 3(5). Rule 3(7) requires the sheriff officer to leave a copy of the charge at the property in a sealed envelope marked "the occupiers" or, in the case of land only, to insert stakes in the ground to which are attached sealed envelopes, addressed to the occupiers, which contain a copy of the charge.

134 n 38.

135 Thus, in contrast to r 3 of the Act of Sederunt (n 132), there is no provision to serve the charge by leaving it at the defender's place of business.

136 Except that, under r 41C, there is no requirement for the sheriff officer to send a copy of the notice by first-class post to the address at which he thinks it most likely that the defender may be found.

Carrying out the eviction

It is appropriate at this point to say something about the process of carrying out the eviction. Under section 216(3)(a) officers of court have the power to "open shut and lockfast places". Accordingly, it is not necessary for that power to be sought in the initiating writ of any of the forms of action listed in section 214(2).

In cases in which the officers of court anticipate resistance to the eviction being carried out, they may bring that to the attention of the police. The police have no locus to become involved in the enforcement of the orders of the civil courts.[137] However, they have the duty, under section 20(1) of the Police and Fire Reform (Scotland) Act 2012, to: "(a) to prevent and detect crime, (b) to maintain order, (c) to protect life and property . . .". Accordingly, they are apt to attend evictions where it is necessary to do so in order to fulfil those duties. For this reason, officers of court may contact the police where they anticipate meeting resistance in enforcing a decree for removing. The police could then attend on the reasonable apprehension that such resistance may lead to the commission of a crime, the disruption of public order, or damage to property. Usually such resistance ends when the police arrive on the scene. If that does not happen, it is suggested that the role of the police officers would be limited to ensuring that the officers of court are able to go about performing the various acts that would be entailed in effecting an ejection, without a criminal offence being committed by any person resisting those acts.

Under section 216(3)(b) the sheriff officer must make an inventory of any effects removed during the course of execution of the decree. That is done in form 6 provided by the Act of Sederunt.[138] The inventory must be witnessed.[139]

Following execution of the decree, the sheriff officer must complete a certificate of execution in form 7, which must also be witnessed. A copy of the certificate must then be: (a) affixed to the main door or other conspicuous part of the heritable property in a sealed envelope; or (b) in the case of land only, attached, in a sealed envelope, to stakes in the ground at conspicuous parts of the land.[140]

Section 217 of the 2007 Act provides that it is not competent to execute a decree for removing from heritable property on a Sunday; a day that is a public holiday in the area in which the decree is to be executed; or such other day as may be prescribed by Act of Sederunt. Furthermore, the execution of such a decree must not begin before 8am or after 8pm, or be continued after 8pm, unless an officer of court has obtained prior authority from the sheriff.

137 *Caldwell v Caldwell* 1983 SC 137, 1983 SLT 610: the function of procurators fiscal and the police is confined to criminal matters; neither sheriffs nor the Court of Session have power to ordain them to perform any tasks in relation to civil causes.

138 There is no form provided in the Procedure Rules (n 38), but presumably form 6 from the Act of Sederunt (n 132) could be used.

139 Rule 6 of the Act of Sederunt; r 41E of the Procedure Rules.

140 Rule 7 of the Act of Sederunt. Rule 41F of the Procedure Rules imposes the same requirements, in respect of orders granted by the tribunal, except that there is no provision for affixing the certificate to stakes, in the case of land only.

Defender's property

Under section 218 the court or tribunal, when granting decree for removing, may direct that the pursuer takes such steps as it considers appropriate for the preservation of any effects removed from the subjects or premises. It may also order that the defender is to be liable for any costs incurred in taking those steps.

Whether or not an order under section 218 is made, it is not uncommon for the landlord to find, on recovering possession, that the tenant has not cleared the property of his own belongings. In that case, it suggested that the landlord take a view as to whether anything left by the tenant is capable of having sentimental or monetary value, or whether it has simply been left behind because it is unwanted rubbish. In the latter case, it may be disposed of. Where it is thought that items might have some value, however small, it is suggested that the statutory rules in relation to lost or abandoned property are applicable, under part VI of the Civic Government (Scotland) Act 1982, to which readers are referred.

Not enforcing the decree or order

It has always been common for landlords in the social rented sector, especially local authorities, not to enforce decrees for eviction granted on the ground of rent arrears. In many cases, discussions will take place, initiated by either the landlord or the tenant, with a view to the eviction being avoided on the basis of a payment of the whole or part of the arrears balance.[141] However, there was a problem with this type of arrangement. Under section 16(5)(a) of the 2001 Act, the decree terminates the Scottish secure tenancy. In cases in which the arrangement with the tenant involved the ongoing payment of rent, as well as the arrears, the parties thereby impliedly created a new tenancy agreement. In that case, it was arguable that the existing decree was no longer a warrant for eviction, because a new tenancy was in existence.[142] This tended to create a situation in which certain tenants were subject to repossession proceedings on numerous occasions, thereby increasing expense for both tenant and landlord.

Section 153 of the Housing (Scotland) Act 2010 addressed this problem by disapplying section 16(5)(a) to cases in which the order has been granted on the ground of rent arrears. In such cases, the new section 16(5A) of the 2001 Act applies:

> "(5A) Where an order is made under subsection (2) in proceedings under section 14 on the ground that rent lawfully due from the tenant has not been paid (as set out in paragraph 1 of schedule 2) or on grounds including that ground—
> (a) subsection (5)(a) does not apply,
> (b) the tenancy is terminated only if the landlord recovers possession of the house in pursuance of the order,

141 See the discussion in Chapter 13, p 453.

142 Therefore, it was possible that a threat to enforce the decree could be met by the tenant raising an action for suspension and interdict in the Court of Session. It should be noted that the scenario could still feasibly occur in relation to eviction decrees granted under s 16(5)(a), i.e. non rent arrears cases, if the actions of the parties after the tenancy is terminated by the Act are such as to infer a new agreement. However, that seems unlikely, as decrees in such cases are much more likely to be enforced, and relatively quickly.

(c) the order must specify the period for which the landlord's right to recover possession of the house is to have effect (being no longer than any maximum period which the Scottish Ministers by order prescribe), and
(d) the landlord must have regard to any guidance issued by the Scottish Ministers about recovery of possession in pursuance of the order."

Under the Scottish Secure Tenancies (Repossession Orders) (Maximum Period) Order 2012,[143] article 2(1), the maximum period for the purposes of (c) above is six months from the date when the decree is extracted. The effect of these provisions is that, when granting a decree in an action in which one of the grounds, or the only ground, is rent arrears, the court is to fix a period during which it is capable of being enforced, which must end no later than six months after extract.[144] When that period has elapsed, the decree cannot then be enforced. If necessary, the landlord will then have to raise further proceedings.

SUSPENSION AND REDUCTION OF A SHERIFF COURT DECREE[145]

As described in Chapter 13, a minute for recall may be lodged by the defender at any time up to execution of the decree for removing. However, recall of decree is possible only if the decree was granted under one of the rules specified in rule 24.1(1) and, in terms of rule 24.1(4), a party may apply for recall on one occasion only. In cases in which recall is not possible, a party may appeal, as already described earlier in this chapter.

Unfortunately, it is quite common for defenders in eviction proceedings to fail to appear or be represented when the case calls, due to personal difficulties, health problems and so on.[146] As a result, a defender who has already used the recall procedure may fail to appear, and find that decree is granted against him again. In that event, an appeal to the sheriff principal may be taken on the basis that there is an explanation for the failure to appear, and a statable defence to the action, and therefore, it would be in the interests of justice to allow the appeal to be granted.[147]

143 SSI 2012/128.
144 In the event that the defender appeals, the note of appeal will normally have to be lodged before the decree is extracted. Once the appeal is determined and the extract is issued, the period (whether six months or shorter) will then run. It is possible that an appeal could be lodged after extract, if the court has allowed immediate extract (see p 508). In that event, art 2(2) of the Order provides that where the decree is upheld (i.e. the defender's appeal is refused) the six months run from the date of the interlocutor disposing of the appeal.
145 Under ch 60 of the Rules of the Court of Session 1994 (Act of Sederunt (Rules of the Court of Session 1994) (SI 1994/1443)) (RCS). As to applications to suspend an order made by a tribunal, see r 60.6 of RCS. Given the decision of the Supreme Court in *R (OWD Ltd) v Revenue and Customs Commissioners* [2019] 1 WLR 4020, it is not clear whether the court can suspend an order made by the FTT.
146 Of course, a failure to appear or be represented may also be due to fault on the part of the defender's agents.
147 The basis for this type of appeal is set out in Macphail (n 87) paras 14.14 and 14.15. In *Grampian Housing Association v Pyper* 2004 Hous LR 22 and *Aberdeen City Council v Shauri* 2006 Hous LR 40 Sheriff Principal Young refused appeals in two eviction cases in which the decree was granted following the defender's failure to appear. However, it is clear from his judgments that he did so because he considered that the defender's argument on "reasonableness" was so poor that it did not amount to a *prima facie* case. In *Pyper* this was due to the

For the tenant facing eviction, in a case in which recall and appeal are not possible, the last-ditch remedy would be an action in the Court of Session for reduction of the decree. In such an action, there is distinction between decrees in absence and decrees *in foro*.[148] It is suggested that if the action for recovery of possession is a summary cause, the decree will be *in foro* in all but exceptional cases.[149]

The general principle is that a decree *in foro* cannot be reduced on the merits. That is to say, it cannot be reduced merely on the basis of averments that the decree should not have been granted on the facts, or that it was granted on an erroneous view of the law. If that were possible, there would effectively be no difference between an action of reduction and an appeal.[150] That said, the court has generally been resistant to categorising the circumstances in which such a decree *can* be reduced.[151] Reduction is an equitable remedy, which lies at the discretion of the court. It may be granted in exceptional circumstances, where it is necessary in order to produce substantial justice between the parties.[152] Thus, it is necessary to examine the circumstances of each case to reach a conclusion as to whether exceptional circumstances exist, and whether reduction is necessary in order to achieve substantial justice.[153]

In *Campbell v Glasgow Housing Association*,[154] GHA had raised summary cause proceedings against Mr Campbell, seeking recovery of possession of subjects let on a Scottish secure tenancy, on the ground of rent arrears. Prior to a calling on 29 September 2009, Mr Campbell had undertaken to make fortnightly payments of £10 towards the arrears.[155] At the hearing on that date, Mr Campbell failed to appear or be represented. The court was advised that he had defaulted on one payment. It granted decree against him. Mr Campbell then raised an action for reduction in the Court of Session. The case then came before Lord Bannatyne on a motion made by Mr Campbell for interim suspension of the decree and interim interdict against ejection.[156]

extent of the arrears and the defender's dreadful payment record. In *Shauri* the arrears were £4,656, which would have taken 18 to 19 years to clear at the repayment rate proposed by the defender. Had it been otherwise, the sheriff principal would have been disposed to grant the appeals. See, in particular, para [32] of his judgment in *Pyper*.

148 A decree *in foro contentioso* is granted against a defender for whom defences or answers have been lodged.

149 That is because reduction of the decree will only be necessary in cases in which recall is impossible. The circumstances in which recall is impossible will invariably be circumstances in which the defender has already stated a defence. That would be the case if the defender had previously lodged a minute for recall stating his defence, or where the court granted decree under r 8.3, or where the court granted decree by default under r 22.1, because the defender had not appeared at a diet of proof.

150 Walker, *Civil Remedies* 176,

151 In *Civil Remedies*, 177–181 Professor Walker discusses various grounds for reduction, such as: no jurisdiction; fraud on the court; *res noviter*; and departure from procedure or practice. However, these may be regarded as examples of grounds on which the court had reduced decrees in the past, rather than being an exhaustive list of grounds on which reduction might be granted.

152 See, e.g., *Bain v Hugh L S McConnell Ltd* 1991 SLT 691.

153 *Johnstone & Clark (Engineers) Ltd v Lockhart* 1995 SLT 440; *McLeod v Prestige Finance Ltd* 2016 Hous LR 43.

154 2011 Hous LR 7.

155 Decree had previously been recalled by Mr Campbell.

156 Such a motion is invariably made in actions of this type, so that eviction cannot take place until the court has determined whether the decree ought to be reduced.

Mr Campbell contended that he had a *prima facie* case for reduction of the decree and that the balance of convenience favoured the grant of interim relief. A significant aspect of his argument was the contention that he had been made a payment on the morning of 29 September 2009, but that had not shown up in GHA's records; as a result, the court had been misinformed as to the payments had made. Granting interim suspension and interim interdict, Lord Bannatyne held that there was a *prima facie* case, in that the decree was apparently granted on the basis of incorrect information. The sheriff had been unintentionally misled by GHA as to whether Mr Campbell was in default in terms of his undertaking. Further, it was premature to have pronounced decree on 29 September as he had until that date to make payment. At the earliest, decree could have been granted on 30 September. The balance of convenience favoured Mr Campbell: he had spent most of his life in care homes and his daughter could not reside with him if he lost his home. These factors outweighed the factors put forward by GHA.[157]

In due course the case proceeded to proof before Lord Woolman.[158] As one would expect, the issue of whether Mr Campbell was in default of his arrangement with GHA was examined in greater detail, with evidence being led, in particular, from the GHA solicitor who had appeared in court at the hearing at which decree was granted. At the proof Mr Campbell argued that there was no agreement that payments had to be made on a particular date; it was enough if the payments were made in the relevant fortnight. Accordingly, it did not matter if a payment was made at the end of the period and did not show up in GHA's records for several days. He had adhered to the arrangement because he had made: (a) a payment on 24 September, which only registered on the GHA system on 26 September (because of two public holidays); and (b) a payment on 29 September itself. Rejecting that argument, Lord Woolman found that, whatever calculation was made, there was a missed payment. The first payment made in accordance with the 28 July agreement was due to be paid on 11 August. No payment was received until 30 August. As the solicitor moving for decree had simply informed the sheriff that Mr Campbell had failed to adhere to the agreement, and did not specify how many payments had been missed, the court had not been misled.

Lord Woolman gave a helpful summary of principles that are applicable in actions for reduction of a decree of this type:

(a) reduction is a question of judicial discretion;
(b) each case turns on its own individual facts and circumstances;
(c) the remedy is applied only in exceptional circumstances;
(d) the test is higher for decrees *in foro*;[159]
(e) reduction should be granted only where it is necessary to ensure that substantial justice is done; and
(f) the existence of, or failure to use, an alternative remedy is not an absolute bar to reduction.[160]

157 The report of this calling of the case can be found at 2010 SLT 274 and 2010 Hous LR 8.

158 His judgment is reported at 2011 Hous LR 7.

159 As opposed to a decree in absence. In the case of the latter, it is not necessary to aver and prove exceptional circumstances: *Robertson's Executor v Robertson* 1995 SC 23. Therefore, reduction of a decree in absence is easier to achieve.

160 However, there is authority to the effect that reduction is not generally available where a

It appears that Mr Campbell's case depended on the argument that, as he was not in default, the court had been inadvertently misled on 29 September 2009, and that this was an exceptional circumstance. That argument failed, because Lord Woolman concluded that the court had not been misled.

It was also argued, on behalf of the pursuer, that it was an exceptional circumstance that the sheriff had not been made aware of all the material factors. In particular, the sheriff had not been told: (i) of the nature and extent of Mr Campbell's mental health problems; and (ii) that GHA was going to retain a £300 disturbance payment to which he was otherwise entitled. The court should also have been informed about the possibility of recovering the arrears direct from Mr Campbell's benefits. That argument was also rejected, on the basis that it was for each party to set out his own position. It is suggested that this must be correct. It is in the nature of these cases that one party has not appeared, and therefore does not have the opportunity to put his position to the court. That cannot be regarded as an exceptional circumstance: were that so, the hurdle set by point (c) above would be easily overcome. Rather, it is suggested that the various arguments that might have been made on behalf of the defender are relevant to point (e): the court's decision as to whether reduction is necessary to ensure that substantial justice is done.

Given the fairly high bar that is set for reduction of decree *in foro*, it is suggested that, in rent arrears cases under the 2001 Act, the tenant should first explore the possibility of making an arrangement with the council, with a view to maintaining payments until the eviction decree is no longer effective, under section 16(5A) of the Act. An action for reduction should be considered only where enforcement of the decree is threatened.

WRONGFUL TERMINATION ORDERS

Sections 57–60 of the 2016 Act are headed "wrongful termination". An application for a wrongful termination order may be made by a former tenant, or a joint tenant, of a PRT, where it has been brought to an end by an eviction order, or by consensual termination under section 50.[161] The tribunal may make the order if it finds that it: "was misled into issuing the eviction order by the person who was, immediately before the tenancy ended, the landlord under the tenancy" or, in the case of consensual termination that the former tenant or joint tenant was "misled into ceasing to occupy the let property by the . . . landlord".[162] The order requires the person who was the landlord under the tenancy to pay the applicant an amount not exceeding six months' rent.[163]

There was no similar provision in the 1988 Act. However, under section 21 of the Rent (Scotland) Act 1984, the court can order a landlord to pay to a former tenant such sum as appears sufficient compensation for damage or loss

party fails, through mistake or otherwise, to pursue other remedies open to him, such as appeal: *Philp v Reid* 1927 SC 224 and *Stewart v Lothians Construction (Edinburgh) Ltd* 1972 SLT (Notes) 75.

161 As to consensual termination, see Chapter 9, p 306. An application for a wrongful termination order is made under r 110 of the Procedure Rules (n 38).

162 Sections 57(3) and 58(3),

163 Section 59(1). Note that in ss 57–59 various provisions deal with cases in which there are joint landlords, joint tenants, or both.

sustained by that tenant as a result of an order for possession being granted, where that order "was obtained by misrepresentation or concealment of material facts". This power only applies to orders obtained under cases 7 and 8 in schedule 2 to the 1984 Act. Case 7 applies where the landlord is reasonably required by the landlord for occupation by his employee. Case 8 applies where the house is reasonably required by the landlord for his own occupation, or for occupation by the family members specified by the Act in relation that case.[164]

Case 8 bears some similarity to grounds 4 ("Landlord intends to live in property") and 5 ("Family member intends to live in property") of schedule 3 to the 2016 Act. Although wrongful termination orders are not restricted to eviction orders made on particular grounds, it is thought that they are most likely to be sought where the landlord used one of the "intention grounds" in part 1 of the Act, as those seem most likely to involve the landlord misrepresenting the true position. This view is supported by the explanatory note to the Act,[165] which states:

> "the test will be whether the landlord genuinely intended to use the property in the way that the eviction ground required (even if, for some reason, that intention has not come to fruition). For example, a landlord might evict his or her tenant because he or she wants to sell the let property. However, after a year on the open market, the property has not sold and the landlord can no longer afford to maintain the mortgage repayments on it, so is forced to withdraw the property from the open market and re-let it to a different tenant. In such a case, if required, it is likely that the landlord could present a strong case to the Tribunal to demonstrate his or her genuine intent to sell".

This example indicates a weakness in sections 57–60. The tenant may find out that the landlord has not acted upon his professed intention. But in most cases, he will not be aware of why that is the case. For all he knows, the intention may have been genuine, but was not acted upon, because of circumstances that occurred after the landlord had secured possession.[166]

That said, the possibility of a wrongful termination order may still be effective in discouraging a landlord who is tempted to obtain possession by professing an intention that is not genuine. Six months' rent could be a significant sum of money. Where the former tenant learns that the property has been re-let,[167] he may consider that he has nothing to lose by making an application under section 57 or section 58. The landlord would then have to oppose the application, and hope that the tribunal will find his position credible.

164 There do not appear to be any reported cases under s 21. In *Clements v Simmonds* [2002] EWHC 1652 (QB), a case taken under the equivalent provision in the Rent Act 1977, the court awarded the tenant £60,000.

165 At para 90.

166 In *Gowling v Wright* PR/19/1867, 9/1/20, the applicant (the former tenant) had moved out of the property in April 2019, having received a notice to leave from the landlord, relying on ground 4. As at the date of the hearing of application in January 2020, it was accepted that the landlord had still not moved into the property. The tribunal nevertheless accepted that the intention had been genuine. The landlord had encountered unexpected difficulties (including health problems), which frustrated her intention.

167 Or has some other basis for believing that the professed intention has not been carried through.

Appendix

Eviction Proceedings and the Coronavirus (Scotland) Act 2020

INTRODUCTION

By section 2 of and schedule 1 to the Coronavirus (Scotland) Act 2020, "temporary modifications" are made to all four of the statutory codes applicable to residential tenancies in Scotland:

- Rent (Scotland) Act 1984 (regulated tenancies);
- Housing (Scotland) Act 1988 (assured and short assured tenancies);
- Housing (Scotland) Act 2001 (Scottish secure tenancies and short Scottish secure tenancies (SSSTs)[1]);
- Private Housing (Tenancies) (Scotland) Act 2016 (private residential tenancies (PRTs)[2]).

Schedule 1, headed: "Eviction from dwelling-houses", "makes adjustments to the law on evictions to protect those renting their homes during the coronavirus outbreak".[3] It comprises ten paragraphs. Each of those paragraphs has an italicised heading that summarises its purpose. However, broadly speaking, schedule 1 makes two major changes to eviction proceedings:

- In the Acts that apply to tenancies in the private sector (being the 1984, 1988 and 2016 Acts), mandatory grounds for eviction are made discretionary (i.e. it is now necessary for the tribunal to be satisfied not only that the ground for eviction applies, but also that it would be reasonable to grant the order). Similarly, the automatic right to obtain an eviction order under section 33 of the 1988 Act (in the case of short assured tenancies) is now subject to a requirement that it is reasonable to grant the order.
- Under all four Acts, the notice periods applicable to the statutory notice of eviction proceedings are lengthened,[4] with the result that landlords will have to wait for a longer period, before raising proceedings. As a consequence, the prescribed statutory forms for certain notices are also amended, to take account of the new notice periods. This has the effect of adding additional complexity to the process of completing statutory notices, and working out the correct notice period. However, that effect is alleviated by a provision,[5] in terms of which notices are not invalidated by reason of a failure to comply with the requirements imposed by the 2020 Act amendments.

1 Henceforth: "SSSTs".
2 Henceforth: "PRTs".
3 Paragraph 10 of the explanatory note to the Bill.
4 Unless the ground for eviction is that the tenant is no longer living in the property.
5 Paragraph 10 of sch 1.

The Act came into force on 7 April 2020. Under section 12, the amendments made by the Act will expire on 30 September 2020. However, the Scottish Ministers may, by regulations, postpone this date to 31 March 2021, and further postpone it to 30 September 2021.[6]

Cases affected by amendments made under schedule 1

The aforementioned changes affect only those notices that are served while the 2020 Act is in force, and the proceedings that follow upon those notices. For example, both paragraphs 1 and 2 of schedule 1, which deal with PRTs under the 2016 Act, begin:

> "(1) The Private Housing (Tenancies) (Scotland) Act 2016 applies, in relation to a notice to leave within the meaning of section 62 of that Act served on a tenant while this paragraph is in force, in accordance with the modifications in this paragraph."

This indicates that the amendments made to the 2016 Act by the 2020 Act do not apply to cases in which the notice to leave was served on the tenant before the Act came into force.[7] Given that the effective life of a notice to leave is six months from the date on which the notice takes effect,[8] it is possible that applications for eviction orders on mandatory grounds, using the existing notice periods, may be made up to the end of 2020.[9]

That is also the case with the changes made to the 1988 Act: paragraphs 3 and 4 of schedule 1 begin:

> "The Housing (Scotland) Act 1988 applies, in relation to a notice served on a tenant under section 19 or 33(1)(d) of that Act while this paragraph is in force, in accordance with the modifications in this paragraph."

The same is true of the changes made to the 1984 Act, and the 2001 Act.[10]

Cases not affected by schedule 1; delay in proceedings and enforcement of orders

The 2020 Act makes no change to the law in relation to tenancies that do not have the protection of the any of the aforementioned Acts. All four of the statutory codes contain provisions to the effect that certain types of tenancy are excepted from the scheme of that Act.[11] Generally speaking, these exceptions relate to:

6 Under s 13, the Scottish Ministers also have the power to bring forward expiry, to a date before 30 September 2020.

7 This confirmed by the revised Guidance, entitled "Ending a tenancy as landlord", on the mygov.scot website, which states: "The new law applies if you are serving notice on your tenant on or after 07 April 2020. If you serve notice on your tenant before 07 April 2020, the changes in the new law do not apply."

8 Under s 55 of the 2016 Act.

9 For example, if a notice to leave is served on ground 1, on 6 April 2020, warning the tenant that proceedings will be taken on or after 30 June (on the eighty-four-day period of notice), an application might still be made up to 29 December 2020.

10 See paras 5 and 6 of sch 1 (1984 Act) and para 7 (2001 Act).

11 In the 1984 Act, excepted tenancies are listed in s 2; in the 1988 Act in sch 4; in the 2001 Act in sch 1; and in the 2016 Act in sch 1.

(1) the character of what is let – for example, agricultural tenancies;
(2) the status of the tenant – for example, an asylum seeker;
(3) the status of the landlord – for example, where the landlord is also resident in the building of which the tenancy subjects form part; or
(4) some combination of these factors, such as temporary accommodation for homeless persons, or tenancies granted by educational institutions to students.

These excepted cases are not affected by the 2020 Act. Likewise, the Act has no effect on eviction proceedings taken against persons occupying a property without right or title to do so.

However, apart from the 2020 Act, one may reasonably anticipate that the coronavirus pandemic itself will affect the progress of eviction proceedings, and the enforcement of eviction decrees and orders. In summary cause proceedings in the sheriff court, requests will no doubt be made for the continuation of first callings, or the discharge of diets of proof, on medical or other grounds related to the coronavirus. Likewise, in the First-tier Tribunal ("FTT"), requests will be made for adjournments of case management discussions ("CMDs") or hearings.

It is also to be expected that, where a decree for recovery of possession or an eviction order is granted, the court or tribunal may be asked to delay enforcement. In the sheriff court, this may be done by superseding extract of the decree. The FTT has an express power, under rule 16A(d) of the Procedure Rules,[12] to delay the execution of an order made by it, at any time before the order is executed.[13]

Note, however, that both the court and the FTT also have the power to delay enforcement by varying the fourteen-day period of the charge for removing required under section 216(4) of the Bankruptcy and Diligence etc (Scotland) Act 2007,[14] or to vary or dispense with the minimum forty-eight-hour period allowed by a notice of the date of removal.[15]

Conversion of mandatory grounds to discretionary, and applications under 1988 Act s 33

There are several notable aspects to the removal of mandatory grounds for eviction in the Acts applying to private-sector tenancies, and the introduction

12 In the schedule to the First-tier Tribunal for Scotland Housing and Property Chamber (Procedure) Regulations 2017 (SSI 2017/328), as amended.

13 The Upper Tribunal also has the power to suspend the effect of an FTT decision pending the determination of any application for permission to appeal, or any appeal: r 7(n) of the Upper Tribunal for Scotland (Rules of Procedure) Regulations 2016 (SSI 2016/232).

14 As was done by the sheriff in *Reid v Redfern (No 4)* [2019] 4 WLUK 526, 2019 GWD 19-297, where he extended the period of the charge to ten weeks under s 216(4) of the 2007 Act, rather than superseding extract. He did so because "this would allow a sheriff officer to serve the charge for removing and the notice of the date of removal on the defender in early course (this would not be possible if I superseded extract to as close to the removal date as possible); she would then have official paperwork to present to the local authority in support of any application she might wish to make to it for homeless accommodation, in the event she could not find suitable private rented accommodation in the area".

15 Under para 4(3) of the Act of Sederunt (Actions for removing from heritable property) 2012 (SSI 2012/136).

of a "reasonableness" test in applications under section 33 of the 1988 Act (short assured tenancies).

First, there is, in the 2020 Act, no express direction to the court or tribunal that it is to have regard to the effect of the coronavirus pandemic on either party, or on the benefits system, or on the availability of housing etc., or to place any particular weight on those factors, in deciding whether it is reasonable to grant an order, whether under the existing discretionary grounds, or the grounds that are now made discretionary.[16] However, in so far as the court or tribunal has to decide whether is reasonable to grant an application for an order for the tenant's eviction, it has a "judicial duty to consider the whole of the circumstances in which the application is made".[17] One would expect that, in the coming months, those circumstances will include the effects of the coronavirus pandemic.

Secondly, some may find it counterintuitive that the 2020 Act imposes a "reasonableness" test in evictions in the private sector, but not in those cases in the social rented sector, under the 2001 Act, in which an eviction order is mandatory. In particular, section 36 of the 2001 Act (proceedings in relation to SSSTs) is based on section 33 of the 1988 Act. However, whereas the tribunal must now be satisfied that an order for possession under section 33 would be reasonable, no such stipulation is made in section 36 cases. Likewise, there is no change to the "streamlined eviction process" in ground 2 cases, under the new section 16(2)(aa).[18]

Thirdly, the imposition of a "reasonableness" requirement in applications under section 33 of the 1988 Act means that the landlord's application to the FTT is one in which he need have no particular ground or reason for seeking an order, but the tribunal must nevertheless be satisfied that it is reasonable to grant the order. This point is discussed below.[19]

Effect of schedule 4 on eviction proceedings

In terms of section 5 ("Justice") and schedule 4, temporary modifications are made to the law in relation to the justice system. Part 1 of schedule 4 is

16 That said, the "Guidance to Scottish Government Stakeholders" issued in connection with the 2020 Act, states (at p 12, under the heading "Eviction grounds being made discretionary"): "This legislation amends all the eviction grounds a private landlord can use to regain possession through to make them all discretionary. This change ensures that the Tribunal – once operational again – will be able to use discretion and take all factors relating to the impact of Covid-19 has had on both the landlord and tenant, into account before deciding whether to issue an eviction order or not."

17 *Barclay v Hannah* 1947 SC 245, 249 (Lord Moncrieff). See also *Cumming v Danson* [1942] 2 All ER 653, in which Lord Greene MR said, in an oft-quoted passage (at 655): "[I]n considering reasonableness . . . it is, in my opinion, perfectly clear that the duty of the Judge is to take into account all relevant circumstances as they exist at the date of the hearing. That he must do in what I venture to call a broad commonsense way as a man of the world, and come to his conclusion giving such weight as he thinks right to the various factors in the situation. Some factors may have little or no weight, others may be decisive, but it is quite wrong for him to exclude from his consideration matters which he ought to take into account."

18 Section 16(2)(aa) was an amendment made by s 14 of the Housing (Scotland) Act 2014, which came into force on 1 May 2019. In essence, it removes the reasonableness requirement in ground 2 cases, where the notice of proceedings is served within twelve months of the relevant criminal conviction.

19 At p 537.

headed "Courts and Tribunals: Conduct of Business by Electronic Means". Paragraph 1 of the schedule states:

> "**1 Electronic signatures and transmission of documents**
>
> (1) An electronic signature fulfils any requirement (however expressed and for whatever purpose) that—
> (a) a document of a type mentioned in sub-paragraph (4), or
> (b) a deletion or correction to such a document,
> be signed, initialled or signetted.
>
> (2) Any requirement (however expressed) that a document of a type mentioned in sub-paragraph (4) be given to a person may be fulfilled by—
> (a) transmitting it to the person electronically, or
> (b) transmitting it (electronically or otherwise) to a solicitor engaged to act on the person's behalf in relation to the proceedings in question.
>
> (3) For the purposes of sub-paragraph (2)—
> (a) electronic transmission of a document by one person ('the sender') to another person ('the recipient') must be effected in a way that the recipient has indicated to the sender that the recipient is willing to receive the document,
> (b) the recipient's indication of willingness to receive a document in a particular way may be—
> (i) specific to the document in question or generally applicable to documents of that kind,
> (ii) expressed specifically to the sender or generally (for example on a website),
> (iii) inferred from the recipient having previously been willing to receive documents from the sender in that way and not having indicated unwillingness to do so again,
> (c) the sender's uploading of a document to an electronic storage system from which the recipient is able to download the document may constitute electronic transmission of the document from the sender to the recipient.
>
> (4) The types of document referred to in sub-paragraphs (1) and (2) are (subject to sub paragraph (5))—
> (a) an order, warrant, sentence, citation, minute or any other document produced by a court or tribunal,
> (b) an extract of any document referred to in paragraph (a),
> (c) any document that an enactment requires be given to a person in connection with, or in order to initiate, proceedings.
>
> (5) A type of document mentioned in sub-paragraph (4) is not to be regarded as being mentioned in that sub-paragraph, for the purposes of sub-paragraph (1) or (2) (or both), if—
> (a) the Lord President of the Court of Session, or
> (b) the Lord Justice General,
> directs that it is not . . .
>
> (6) A direction under sub-paragraph (5) may relate to some or all proceedings.
>
> (7) In this paragraph—
> (a) 'court' includes any office holder of a court,
> (b) 'document' includes a copy of a document,
> (c) 'electronic signature' is to be construed in accordance with section 7(2) of the Electronic Communications Act 2000, but includes a version of an electronic signature which is reproduced on a paper document,
> (d) references to giving a person a document include—
> (i) serving a document on a person,
> (ii) sending a document to a person, and

(iii) lodging a document with, or otherwise applying to or petitioning, a court or tribunal,

(e) 'tribunal' includes any office holder of a tribunal."

Paragraph 1(1)(a) and (4)(a) have the effect, in particular, that orders made by the FTT, including eviction orders, may be signed electronically.

It is suggested that the provisions made in relation to electronic transmission of documents in subparagraphs (2) and (3) apply to the statutory notices in eviction proceedings under the 1988, 2001 and 2016 Acts.[20] That is because, for the purposes of subparagraphs (2), (4)(c) and (7)(d)(i), these are all documents that are subject to a requirement that they be "given" or "served" on a person "in connection with, or in order to initiate, proceedings".[21]

Accordingly, paragraph 1(2) and (3) may be regarded as extending, while the 2020 Act is in force, the existing modes of service specified in the legislation applicable to those notices.[22]

PRIVATE RESIDENTIAL TENANCIES

Paragraph 1 – eviction grounds to be discretionary

As the heading suggests, the purpose of this paragraph is to take all the mandatory eviction grounds in schedule 3 to the 2016 Act, and convert them into discretionary grounds. This is achieved by taking the word "must" where it appears in mandatory grounds, and replacing it with "may", and then adding "and . . . the Tribunal is satisfied that it is reasonable to issue an eviction order on account of those facts", as an additional requirement for the ground to be established.

Consequently, in section 51 of the Act (First-tier Tribunal's power to issue an eviction order), subsection (2) is amended[23] to read:

> "(2) The provisions of schedule 3 stating the circumstances in which the Tribunal may ~~or must~~ find that an eviction ground applies are exhaustive of the circumstances in which the Tribunal is entitled to find that the ground in question applies."

Changes made to the grounds

In terms of schedule 1, paragraph 1(3)(a), ground 1 in schedule 3 is amended as follows:

20 Being: the notice to leave under s 62 of the 2016 Act; the AT6 and s 33(d) notices under the 1988 Act; and the notice of proceedings under s 14(2) or s 36(2) of the 2001 Act.

21 Sections 14(2)(a) and 36(2)(a) of the 2001 Act, and s 19(1)(a) of the 1988 Act, all require that the notice of proceedings is served on the tenant. Section 33(1)(d) of the 1988 Act requires notice to be given to the tenant. Section 52(3) of the 2016 Act provides that an application to the FTT for an eviction order against a tenant "must be accompanied by a copy of a notice to leave which has been *given* to the tenant".

22 Which are the modes of service indicated in: s 54 of the 1988 Act, s 40 of the 2001 Act and, for notices to leave under the 2016 Act, s 26 of the Interpretation and Legislative Reform (Scotland) Act 2010.

23 By sch 1 para 1(2).

"**1 Landlord intends to sell**

(1) It is an eviction ground that the landlord intends to sell the let property.

(2) The First-tier Tribunal ~~must~~ *may* find that the ground named by sub-paragraph (1) applies if the landlord—

(a) is entitled to sell the let property, ~~and~~

(b) intends to sell it for market value, or at least put it up for sale, within 3 months of the tenant ceasing to occupy it, *and*

(c) the Tribunal is satisfied that it is reasonable to issue an eviction order on account of those facts.

(3) Evidence tending to show that the landlord has the intention mentioned in sub-paragraph (2)(b) includes (for example)—

(a) a letter of engagement from a solicitor or estate agent concerning the sale of the let property,

(b) a recently prepared document that anyone responsible for marketing the let property would be required to possess under section 98 of the Housing (Scotland) Act 2006 were the property already on the market."

Amendments to the same effect are made to other mandatory grounds: 2 (Property to be sold by lender); 3 (Landlord intends to refurbish); 6 (Landlord intends to use for non-residential purpose); 7 (Property required for religious purpose); 10 (Not occupying let property); and 13 (Criminal behaviour).

In ground 4 (Landlord intends to live in the let property), the effect of the amendment is that sub-paragraph (2) of that ground now has two requirements rather than one:

"(2) The First-tier Tribunal ~~must~~ *may* find that the ground named by sub-paragraph (1) applies if:

(a) the landlord intends to occupy the let property as the landlord's only or principal home for at least 3 months, *and*

(b) the Tribunal is satisfied that it is reasonable to issue an eviction order on account of those facts."

Under the 2016 Act, two grounds (8 (Not an employee) and 12 (rent arrears)) are either mandatory or discretionary, depending on the circumstances. Under the 2020 Act, ground 8 is converted into a single discretionary ground, as follows:

"**8 Not an employee**

(1) It is an eviction ground that the tenancy was entered into to provide an employee with a home and the tenant is not a qualifying employee.

(2) The First-tier Tribunal ~~must~~ *may* find that the ground named by sub-paragraph (1) applies if—

(a) the tenancy was granted to the tenant—

(i) in consequence of the tenant being an employee of the landlord, or

(ii) in the expectation that the tenant would become an employee of the landlord,

(b) the tenant is not employed by the landlord, and

~~(c) either—~~

~~(i) the application for an eviction order that is before the Tribunal was made within 12 months of the tenant ceasing to be an employee of the landlord, or~~

~~(ii) if the tenant never became an employee of the landlord, the application for an eviction order that is before the Tribunal was made within 12 months of the tenancy being granted to the tenant.~~

> (c) *the Tribunal is satisfied that it is reasonable to issue an eviction order on account of those facts.*
>
> ~~(3) The First-tier Tribunal may find that the ground named by sub-paragraph (1) applies if—~~
>
> ~~(a) the conditions set out in sub-paragraph (2)(a) and (b) are met, and~~
>
> ~~(b) the Tribunal is satisfied that it is reasonable to issue an eviction order, despite the landlord not applying for one within the period of 12 months mentioned in sub-paragraph (2)(c).~~
>
> (4) In sub-paragraph~~s~~ (2) ~~and (3)~~, 'landlord' includes any person who has been a landlord under the tenancy."

In ground 12, the 2020 Act simply deletes sub-paragraph (2), the mandatory part of the ground, such that it then reads:

> "12 **Rent arrears**
>
> (1) It is an eviction ground that the tenant has been in rent arrears for three or more consecutive months.
>
> . . .
>
> (3) The First-tier Tribunal may find that the ground named by sub-paragraph (1) applies if—
>
> (a) for three or more consecutive months the tenant has been in arrears of rent, and
>
> (b) the Tribunal is satisfied that it is reasonable on account of that fact to issue an eviction order.
>
> (4) In deciding under sub-paragraph (3) whether it is reasonable to issue an eviction order, the Tribunal is to consider whether the tenant's being in arrears of rent over the period in question is wholly or partly a consequence of a delay or failure in the payment of a relevant benefit."[24]
>
> . . .

In practice, this is likely to be the most significant amendment to the 2016 Act, given that a very high proportion of eviction orders made under section 51 are granted on the mandatory aspect of ground 12.[25]

None of the discretionary grounds in schedule 3 to the 2016 Act is amended.

Paragraphs 2 and 9(1) – extension of notice periods

The existing section 54 of the 2016 Act lays down two notice periods: twenty-eight days and eighty-four days. The twenty-eight-day period applies if the tenant has been entitled to occupy the let property for not more than six months, or where the sole eviction ground stated in the notice to leave, or all the eviction grounds, are those set out in part 3 of schedule 3 (Tenant's conduct grounds).[26] Otherwise the eighty-four-day period applies. In practice, the twenty-eight-day period applies in the vast majority of cases, because: (a) most applications are made on the conduct grounds, in particular rent arrears; and (b) in cases on other grounds, applications are often made before the tenant has been entitled to occupy for six months.

24 The definition of "Relevant benefit" etc. in subpara (5) is unchanged.

25 On a reading of the tribunal decisions, it is estimated that about 84% of eviction orders are granted in cases where ground 12(2) was the sole ground, or one of the grounds.

26 Such as rent arrears, antisocial behaviour etc.

Under the 2020 Act amendments,[27] subsections (2) and (3) of section 54 are deleted and replaced by new subsections (2), (3) and (3A). As a consequence, there are now three notice periods: twenty-eight days, three months and six months. The amended section 54 reads:

> "**54 Restriction on applying during the notice period**
>
> (1) A landlord may not make an application to the First-tier Tribunal for an eviction order against a tenant using a copy of a notice to leave until the expiry of the relevant period in relation to that notice.
>
> *(2) The relevant period in relation to a notice to leave—*
>
> *(a) begins on the day the tenant receives the notice to leave from the landlord, and*
>
> *(b) expires on the day falling—*
>
> *(i) 28 days after it begins if subsection (3) applies,*
>
> *(ii) three months after it begins if subsection (3A) applies,*
>
> *(iii) six months after it begins if neither subsection (3) nor (3A) applies.*
>
> *(3) This subsection applies if the only eviction ground stated in the notice to leave is that the tenant is not occupying the let property as the tenant's home. [ground 10]*
>
> *(3A) This subsection applies if—*
>
> *(a) the only eviction ground, or grounds, stated in the notice to leave is, or are, one or more of the following—*
>
> *(i) that the landlord intends to live in the let property, [ground 4]*
>
> *(ii) that a member of the landlord's family intends to live in the let property, [ground 5]*
>
> *(iii) that the tenant has a relevant conviction, [ground 13]*
>
> *(iv) that the tenant has engaged in relevant anti-social behaviour, [ground 14]*
>
> *(v) that the tenant associates in the let property with a person who has a relevant conviction or has engaged in relevant anti-social behaviour, [ground 15]*
>
> *(vi) that the landlord is not registered by the relevant local authority under the Antisocial Behaviour etc. (Scotland) Act 2004, [ground 16]*
>
> *(vii) that the let property or associated living accommodation is in multiple occupation and not licensed under Part 5 of the Housing (Scotland) Act 2006, [ground 17] or*
>
> *(b) the only eviction grounds stated in the notice to leave are—*
>
> *(i) the eviction ground mentioned in subsection (3), and*
>
> *(ii) an eviction ground, or grounds, mentioned in paragraph (a).*
>
> (4) The reference in subsection (1) to using a copy of a notice to leave in making an application means using it to satisfy the requirement under section 52(3)."

The effect of these amendments is that:

- There is no equivalent to the existing section 54(3)(a), under which the shorter notice period applies, if the tenant has been entitled to occupy the let property for not more than six months. Accordingly, the notice period now depends entirely on the ground(s) for eviction stated in the notice to leave.
- The eighty-four-day period is repealed.
- The twenty-eight-day period now applies only if the sole ground stated in the notice to leave is ground 10 (Not occupying let property).
- A three-month period is introduced for certain grounds: 4, 5 and 13–17. None of those grounds is commonly used in applications for an eviction order under section 51.[28]

27 Schedule 1 para 2(2).

28 By far the most commonly used ground is ground 12 (rent arrears). Of the other grounds, landlord intends to sell (ground 1) is the most commonly relied upon.

- Where the notice to leave states ground 10 and one or more of grounds 4, 5 and 13–17, the period of notice is three months.[29]
- In any other case, the notice period is six months. Accordingly, that notice period will apply where the sole ground, or any one of the grounds, stated in the notice to leave is ground 1, 2, 3, 6, 7, 8, 9, 11, 12 or 18, the notice period. It is reasonable to expect that this will apply in the vast majority of applications.

The meaning of "six months" was already defined in section 64 of the 2016 Act. That has now been amended[30] so as to cover the new three-month period introduced by the section 54 amendment. Section 64 will now read:

> "**64 Three or six month periods**
> (1) A reference in this Part to a period of three or, as the case may be, six months (however expressed) is to a period which ends in the month which falls three or, as the case may be, six months after the month in which it began, either—
> (a) on the same day of the month as it began, or
> (b) if the month in which the period ends has no such day, on the final day of that month.
> (2) Subsection (1) does not apply in relation to the references to six months in section 59."

This adds a new layer of complexity to the already Byzantine provisions applicable to the exercise of working out the date to be stated in a notice to leave, under section 62 of Act. Note, however, that paragraph 10 of schedule 1 (discussed below) alleviates this effect by making new rules in relation to errors in notices.

A worked example

L and T are the landlord and tenant of a PRT under the 2016 Act. While the 2020 Act is in force, L decides to serve a notice to leave, on the ground of rent arrears (ground 12). The parties' tenancy agreement allows service of notices by email. L serves the notice by email on 27 May 2020. What date should he state, at part 4 of the notice, specifying the day on which he expects to become entitled to make an application for an eviction order to the First-tier Tribunal?
Answer:

- Under section 62(5), for the purposes of stating that date, the landlord is to assume that the notice will be received by the tenant forty-eight hours after it is sent, which in this case is 29 May. This is the day on which the "relevant period" begins, in terms of section 54(2)(a).
- Given the terms of section 64(1)(a) as amended, that period expires on 29 November 2020.
- In terms of section 62(4), the date to be stated in the notice is the day after the notice period expires.
- Therefore, the date to be stated in the notice is 30 November 2020.

29 Under the amended s 54(3A)(b).
30 Schedule 1 para 2(3).

If the sole ground for eviction in the notice was ground 4, the three-month period would apply, and the date to be stated in the notice would be 30 August 2020.

If L had waited until, say, 29 August to serve the notice, relying on ground 12, the assumed date of receipt (for email or recorded delivery service) would be 31 August. In that case, given the terms of the amended section 64(1)(b), the notice period would expire on 28 February 2021, and the date to be stated in the notice would be 1 March 2021.

Increased use of section 52(4)?

In contrast to the AT6 under section 19 of the 1988 Act, no power is conferred on the FTT to dispense with the notice to leave under the 2016 Act. However, under section 52(4), the tribunal may allow the application to be made during the notice period. Given the extension of notice periods under the 2020 Act amendments, applications to exercise that power may become more common in cases in which the landlord has some particularly pressing need to recover possession.

Paragraph 9(1) – consequential modification of prescribed form notice to leave

The prescribed form for the notice to leave is found in schedule 5 to the Private Residential Tenancies (Prescribed Notices and Forms) (Scotland) Regulations 2017.[31] Paragraph 9(1)(a) sets out three distinct amendments that will require to be made to the statutory form in respect of any notice to leave served while the 2020 Act is in force. These reflect the changes to section 54 already described.[32] Paragraph 9(1)(b) sets out equivalent changes, to the prescribed form sub-tenancy notice to leave, in schedule 6 to the 2017 regulations.

ASSURED TENANCIES

Paragraph 3 – eviction grounds to be discretionary

The purpose of this paragraph is to make all the mandatory eviction grounds in schedule 5 to the 1988 Act discretionary, and to provide that, in applications under section 33 of the Act (in relation to short assured tenancies), the FTT will not grant an order unless it is reasonable to do so.

31 SSI 2017/297.

32 The amended version of the notice can be found at: https://www.gov.scot/binaries/content/documents/govscot/publications/form/2017/11/private-residential-tenancy-prescribed-notices-forms/documents/notice-to-leave/7de8561a-c689-463e-b196-bdbe2dee347b/7de8561a-c689-463e-b196-bdbe2dee347b/govscot%3Adocument/3009%2BCOVID-19%2BNotice%2Bto%2BLeave.pdf

Actions under section 18, on schedule 5 grounds

The effect of the 2020 Act amendments[33] is that section 18(1)–(4A) now reads:

> "**18.— Orders for possession.**
> (1) The First-tier Tribunal shall not make an order for possession of a house let on an assured tenancy except on one or more of the grounds set out in Schedule 5 to this Act.
> (2) The following provisions of this section have effect, subject to section 19 below, in relation to proceedings for the recovery of possession of a house let on an assured tenancy.
> ~~(3) If the First-tier Tribunal is satisfied that any of the grounds in Part I of Schedule 5 to this Act is established then, subject to subsections (3A) and (6) below, the Tribunal shall make an order for possession.~~
> ~~(3A) If the First-tier Tribunal is satisfied—~~
> ~~(a) that Ground 8 in Part I of Schedule 5 to this Act is established; and~~
> ~~(b) that rent is in arrears as mentioned in that Ground as a consequence of a delay or failure in the payment of relevant housing benefit or relevant universal credit,~~
> ~~the Tribunal shall not make an order for possession unless the Tribunal considers it reasonable to do so.~~
> (4) If the First-tier Tribunal is satisfied that any of the grounds in *Part 1 or* Part II of Schedule 5 to this Act is established, the Tribunal shall not make an order for possession unless the Tribunal considers it reasonable to do so.
> (4A) In considering for the purposes of subsection (4) above whether it is reasonable to make an order for possession *on Ground 8 in Part I of Schedule 5 to this Act or* on Ground 11 or 12 in Part II of Schedule 5 to this Act, the First-tier Tribunal shall have regard, in particular, to the extent to which any delay or failure to pay rent taken into account by the Tribunal in determining that the Ground is established is or was a consequence of a delay or failure in the payment of relevant housing benefit or relevant universal credit.
> . . ."

In schedule 5, the heading of part 1:

> "Grounds on which First-tier Tribunal must order possession"

is replaced with:

> "Certain grounds on which First-tier Tribunal may order possession in relation to the period of the Coronavirus (Scotland) Act 2020".[34]

The effect of these changes is that the grounds in part 1 of schedule 5 are no longer grounds that, if established, have the effect that the FTT must grant an order for possession under section 18(3). Instead, in respect of all the grounds under schedule 5, the landlord must now establish the ground, and the tribunal must be satisfied, under section 18(4), that it is reasonable to grant the order. Section 18(4A) now applies to all the rent arrears grounds (8, 11 and 12).

33 Schedule 1 para 3(2).
34 ibid para 3(5).

Actions under section 33

The effect of the 2020 Act amendments[35] is that section 33(1) now reads:

> "**33.— Recovery of possession on termination of a short assured tenancy.**
> (1) Without prejudice to any right of the landlord under a short assured tenancy to recover possession of the house let on the tenancy in accordance with sections 12 to 31 of this Act, the First-tier Tribunal ~~shall~~ *may* make an order for possession of the house if the Tribunal is satisfied—
> (a) that the short assured tenancy has reached its ish;
> (b) that tacit relocation is not operating; ~~and~~
> [. . .][36]
> (d) that the landlord (or, where there are joint landlords, any of them) has given to the tenant notice stating that he requires possession of the house; *and*
> *(e) that it is reasonable to make an order for possession.*"

The whole point of an action under section 33 is that the landlord does not require to have a ground for possession, or to show that it is reasonable to grant an order. He merely needs to show that the technical requirements of section 33 have been met.[37]

In light of the amendments made by the 2020 Act, the landlord is still not expressly required to have any particular ground for eviction, but must show that it is reasonable to grant the order. One wonders whether that makes practical sense. If the landlord can offer no particular reason for the order being granted, one would not expect the tribunal to be satisfied that it is reasonable to grant the order. Therefore, in practice, it may be the case that section 33 will apply only to actions in which the landlord has some reason for seeking an order for possession, but which does not amount to a ground contained in schedule 5.[38]

Section 20 – suspended orders

In terms of section 20(2) of the 1988 Act, the sheriff had, and the FTT now has, the power, on making an order for possession, to: (a) sist or suspend execution of the order, or (b) postpone the date of possession. Both may be done for such period or periods as the tribunal thinks fit. A similar power exists under section 12 of the 1984 Act, in relation to regulated tenancies, but there is no power to make suspended orders under the 2001 Act or the 2016 Act.

On any such sist, suspension or postponement, the tribunal, unless it considers that to do so would cause exceptional hardship to the tenant or would otherwise be unreasonable, must impose conditions with regard to payment by the tenant of arrears of rent (if any) and rent or payments in respect of occupation after the termination of the tenancy. In addition, it may impose such other conditions as it thinks fit.[39] If any such conditions are complied

35 ibid para 3(4).
36 Section 33(1)(c) was already repealed.
37 Which, in nearly all cases, means showing that a valid notice to quit, and a valid notice under s 33(1)(d), have been served on the tenant.
38 For example, where the landlord wants to sell the property. This is ground for eviction under the 2016 Act (sch 3 ground 1), but not under the 1988 Act.
39 Section 20(3). Suspended orders usually impose conditions as to the payment of rent arrears. However, they may also be used in other cases. In *Lorimer v Griffiths* 2013 Hous LR 63, the

with, the tribunal may, if it thinks fit, recall any such order.[40] It is for the tribunal to decide the extent to which compliance with the strict terms of the conditions will be required, in order for the order to be recalled.[41]

These powers are seldom used because, under section 20(6), suspended orders are not available if the tribunal is satisfied that the landlord is entitled to possession of the house under section 33(1) of the Act or if an eviction order is sought on the basis of any of the mandatory grounds. The majority of eviction applications under the 1988 Act are made under section 33(1), or under the mandatory ground 8 (three months' rent arrears). However, subsection (6) is repealed by the 2020 Act.[42] This means that suspended orders are now generally available in proceedings under the 1988 Act, and might be used more extensively.

Paragraphs 4 and 9(2) – extension of notice periods

Under the 1988 Act, there are two statutory notices: the AT6 under section 19, and the section 33(1)(d) notice required in actions under that section.

Section 19 – AT6 notice of proceedings for possession

Section 19 is amended[43] in a similar way to the changes made to section 54 of the 2016 Act. The existing periods (two weeks or two months) are replaced by three periods: two months, three months and six months. Section 19(3) and (4) now read:

> "**19.— Notice of proceedings for possession.**
>
> . . .
>
> (3) A notice under this section is one in the prescribed form informing the tenant that—
>
> (a) the landlord intends to raise proceedings for possession of the house on one or more of the grounds specified in the notice; and
>
> (b) those proceedings will not be raised earlier than the expiry of the period of ~~two weeks or two months~~ *two months, three months or, as the case may be, six months* (whichever is appropriate under subsection (4) below) from the date of service of the notice.
>
> ~~(4) The minimum period to be specified in a notice as mentioned in subsection (3) (b) above is—~~
>
> ~~(a) two months if the notice specifies any of Grounds 1, 2, 5, 6, 7, 9 and 17 in Schedule 5 to this Act (whether with or without other grounds); and~~
>
> ~~(b) in any other case, two weeks.~~
>
> *(4) The minimum period to be specified in a notice as mentioned in subsection (3)(b) is—*

order was suspended on the condition that the tenant allowed the landlord to inspect the tenancy property with his contractors. In *Bow Farm Housing Association v Kelly* 1998 Hous LR 98, it was said that it was for the tenant to advance proposals for terms on which the order would be suspended, and the reasons for which a suspended order ought to be made.

40 Section 20(4). The Act does not indicate what procedure is to follow after the previous order has been recalled. A suspended order under s 12 of the 1984 Act was discharged in *Lorimer v Griffiths* (n 39).

41 *Knowsley Housing Trust v White* [2009] 1 AC 636, paras 67, 68 and 94–110 (Lord Neuberger of Abbotsbury). See also *Lorimer v Griffiths* (n 39).

42 Schedule 1 para 3(3).

43 ibid para 4(2).

(a) two months if the notice specifies only Ground 9 in Part II of Schedule 5 to this Act,[44]
(b) three months if the notice specifies any of the following grounds in Schedule 5 to this Act (whether with or without also specifying the ground referred to in paragraph (a))—
(i) Ground 1 in Part I,[45]
(ii) Ground 15 in Part II,[46]
(c) six months if the notice specifies any of the following grounds in Schedule 5 to this Act (whether with or without other grounds)—
(i) Grounds 2 to 8 in Part I,
(ii) Grounds 10 to 14 in Part II,
(iii) Ground 16 or 17 in Part II
. . ."

Accordingly, as with the 2016 Act, the effect of the changes is that, in the vast majority of cases, the notice period will be six months.

The 2020 Act does not affect the power of the tribunal, under section 19(1)(b), to dispense with the AT6. Given the extension of notice periods introduced by the 2020 Act amendments, applications to exercise that power may be more common.

Section 33(1)(d) notice

In section 33(2), the two-month notice period applicable to the section 33(1)(d) notice is amended to six months.[47] In contrast to the AT6, and the notice to leave under the 2016 Act, the FTT has no power to dispense with that notice, or to allow an application to be made to the tribunal, during the notice period. Given the other changes to section 33, described above, this is bound to make section 33 applications less attractive to landlords, and they may become much less common while the 2020 Act is in force.

Paragraph 9(2) – consequential modification of prescribed form AT6

The prescribed form for the AT6 is now found in the Rent Regulation and Assured Tenancies (Forms) (Scotland) Regulations 2017.[48] Paragraph 9(2) sets out a single amendment to note 3 to the tenant in part 3 of the form, which reflects the changes to section 19 already described. There is no consequential modification as regards the section 33(1)(d) notice, because it has no prescribed form.

44 Ground 9: Suitable alternative accommodation is available for the tenant.
45 Ground 1 applies, in summary, where: (a) the landlord previously occupied the tenancy property; or (b) the landlord or his spouse or civil partner intends to occupy the tenancy property as his only or principal home.
46 Ground 15 relates to criminal conviction or antisocial behaviour.
47 Schedule 1 para 4(3).
48 SSI 2017/349.

TENANCIES UNDER THE RENT (SCOTLAND) ACT 1984

Paragraph 5 – eviction grounds to be discretionary

Given that regulated tenancies have been gradually phased out since the coming into force of the 1988 Act, applications for orders for possession under the 1984 Act are now rare.[49] In short, paragraph 5 of schedule 1 makes a series of changes, amending sections 11, 12 and 14, and schedule 2, that are of a similar effect as the amendments made to the 1988 Act.

Paragraph 6 –extension of notice periods

Paragraph 6(3) makes certain amendments to section 112 of the 1984, the scope of which is not entirely clear.

Section 112 is an important provision that originally appeared in section 16 of the Rent Act 1957.[50] The effect of section 112(1) is to modify the common law in relation to notices to quit, by providing that, in a tenancy of a dwellinghouse, such a notice (whether given by the landlord or the tenant) must: (a) be in writing; (b) in certain cases, contain prescribed information; and (c) be given not less than four weeks before the date on which it is to take effect. These requirements apply to any notice to quit, and not just to notices to quit served in respect of tenancies under the 1984 Act. In particular, section 112 applies to notices to quit served in relation to assured or short assured tenancies under the 1988 Act, and to tenancies of dwellinghouses that are not covered by any of the Acts that confer security of tenure.

In consequence of the amendments made by paragraph 6(3) of schedule 1, section 112(1) now reads:

> "**112.— Minimum length of notice to quit.**
>
> (1) No notice by a landlord or a tenant to quit any premises let (whether before or after the commencement of this Act) as a dwelling-house shall be valid unless it is in writing and contains such information as may be prescribed and is ~~given not less than four weeks before the date on which it is to take effect.~~ *given–*
>
> *(a) in the case of a notice by a landlord, not less than the specified amount of time before the date on which it is to take effect,*
>
> *(b) in the case of a notice by a tenant, not less than four weeks before the date on which it is to take effect.*
>
> *(1A) A notice given by a landlord in accordance with subsection (1) must state, in addition to any other information that is prescribed under subsection (1), the basis on which the landlord intends to seek possession of the dwelling-house.*
>
> *(1B) For the purpose of subsection (1)(a), the specified amount of time is—*
>
> *(a) 4 weeks if subsection (1C) applies,*
>
> *(b) 3 months if subsection (1D) applies,*
>
> *(c) 6 months if subsection (1E) applies.*

49 Such applications are now made to the FTT, under r 77 of the Procedure Rules (n 12). The decisions on the Housing and Property Chamber's website indicate that that only two orders for possession have been granted since the transfer of jurisdiction on 1 December 2017.

50 The 1984 Act was a consolidating Act, which brought together the provisions relevant to regulated tenancies, but also those applicable to tenancies of dwellinghouses in general, such as the provisions in pt III, which concern unlawful eviction.

(1C) This subsection applies if the notice under subsection (1) specifies that possession is sought only in accordance with section 11(1)(a) on the basis that suitable alternative accommodation is available, or will be available, for the tenant.

(1D) This subsection applies if the notice under subsection (1) specifies that possession is sought only on the basis that the circumstances are as specified in one or more of the following Cases in Schedule 2—10

(a) Case 2,
(b) Case 6,
(c) Case 8 or 9,
(d) Case 11.

(1E) This subsection applies if the notice under subsection (1) specifies that possession is sought on the basis that the circumstances are as specified in one or more of the following Cases in Schedule 2 (whether with or without specifying any other Cases)—

(a) Case 1,
(b) Cases 3 to 5, 20
(c) Case 7,
(d) Case 10,
(e) Cases 12 to 21."

It is clear that these amendments are very similar to those made under paragraphs 2, 4 and 7 of schedule 1, which amend the notice periods applicable to statutory notices under the 1988, 2001 and 2016 Acts, depending on the ground for eviction that is relied upon by the landlord.

However, section 112 does not have the same function in the 1984 Act as, say, section 19 of the 1988 Act. It does not require a specific statutory notice to be given, warning the tenant that proceedings are to be raised under one or more of the statutory grounds for eviction under the relevant Act. Section 112 applies generally to notices to quit, which have the purpose of terminating the parties' contract.

That being so, it is suggested that the amendments to section 112 by paragraph 6(3) of schedule 1 should be read as applying only in the case of regulated tenancies under the 1984 Act, and not to other tenancies in which a notice to quit is served by a landlord or a tenant. This is for the following reasons:

- The heading of paragraph 6 is: "*Tenancies under the Rent (Scotland) Act 1984: extension of notice periods*".
- In the case of a notice to quit by a landlord, the provisions in the amended subsections (1A)–(1E) are relevant only to regulated tenancies under the 1984 Act.
- If the amendments are not regarded as being restricted to regulated tenancies under the 1984 Act, section 112(1) would no longer specify any minimum period of notice for notices to quit served on other tenants. That would tend to reduce the protection available to them under statute, which would be contrary to the intention of the 2020 Act.

SCOTTISH SECURE TENANCIES

Paragraphs 7 and 9(3) – : extension of notice periods

Notwithstanding the heading of this paragraph, the amendments affect both Scottish secure tenancies and SSSTs. As has already been indicated, the 2020 Act does not introduce any reasonableness requirement, or discretionary element, to eviction proceedings in which, under the 2001 Act, the order is effectively mandatory.

Notice of proceedings under section 14

Paragraph 7(2) of schedule 1 amends section 14 of the 2001 Act, such that the relevant parts of it now read:

> "**Proceedings for possession**
> **14.** (1) The landlord under a Scottish secure tenancy may raise proceedings by way of summary cause for recovery of possession of the house.
> (2) Such proceedings may not be raised unless—
> (a) the landlord has served on the tenant and any qualifying occupier a notice complying with subsection (4),
> (b) the proceedings are raised on or after the date specified in the notice, and
> (c) the notice is in force at the time when the proceedings are raised.
> . . .
> (4) A notice under subsection (2) must be in such form as the Scottish Ministers may prescribe by regulations, and must specify—
> (a) the ground, being a ground set out in Part 1 of schedule 2, on which proceedings for recovery of possession are to be raised,
> (b) a date, not earlier than—
> ~~(i) 4 weeks from the date of service of the notice, or~~
> *(i) the date calculated in accordance with subsection (4A), or*
> (ii) the date on which the tenancy could have been brought to an end by a notice to quit had it not been a Scottish secure tenancy,
> whichever is later, on or after which the landlord may raise proceedings for recovery of possession.
> . . .
> *(4A) For the purpose of subsection (4)(b)(i), the date is the date falling—*
> *(a) 4 weeks after the date of service of the notice if subsection (4B) applies,*
> *(b) 3 months after the date of service of the notice if subsection (4C) applies,*
> *(c) 6 months after the date of service of the notice if subsection (4D) applies. 35.*
> *(4B) This subsection applies if the notice under subsection (2) specifies only the ground set out in paragraph 5 of schedule 2.*[51]
> *(4C) This subsection applies if the notice under subsection (2) specifies a ground set out in any of the following paragraphs of schedule 2 (whether with or without also specifying the ground referred to in subsection (4B))—*
> *(a) paragraph 2,*[52]
> *(b) paragraphs 6 to 8.*[53]

51 Ground 5 – tenant (and tenant's spouse/civil partner/cohabitee) have been absent from the house for six months, or have ceased to occupy the house as only or principal home.

52 Ground 2 – criminal conviction.

53 Ground 6 – landlord was induced to grant the tenancy by a false statement made knowingly or recklessly by the tenant; ground 7 – antisocial behaviour, not reasonable that the landlord

(4D) This subsection applies if the notice under subsection (2) specifies a ground set out in any of the following paragraphs of schedule 2 (whether with or without other grounds)—
(a) paragraph 1,[54]
(b) paragraph 3 or 4,[55]
(c) paragraphs 9 to 15."[56]

Section 14(4)(b) requires the landlord to specify, in the notice of proceedings, a date on or after which proceedings may be raised, thereby giving a period of notice to the tenant. It is already quite an obscure provision and, again, the amendments add another layer of complexity.

The words "whichever is later" in section 14(4)(b) envisage that the application of section 14(4)(b)(i) and (ii) could lead to two different dates, in which case the landlord must apply the later of those two dates. As matters stood (i.e. before the 2020 Act amendments), the later date was almost bound to be the section 14(4)(b)(ii) one. That is because the tenancy could be not be brought to an end, by a notice to quit, earlier than four weeks from the date of service of the notice because, under section 112 of the 1984 Act, a notice to quit cannot give less than twenty-eight days' notice. Therefore, under the pre-amendment provisions, the rule of thumb is that the date stated in the notice of proceedings for the purposes of section 14(4)(b) would be no earlier than the first ish date that occurs more than twenty-eight clear days after the date of service of the notice.[57]

Under section 14, as amended by the 2020 Act, that rule of thumb will now apply only to cases in which the sole ground for eviction stated in the notice of proceedings is ground 5. If the ground is ground 2, 6, 7 or 8,[58] the three-month period will almost certainly apply. That is because the vast majority of Scottish secure tenancies have durations of less than a month.[59] Therefore "the date on which the tenancy could have been brought to an end by a notice to quit had it not been a Scottish secure tenancy" under section 14(4)(b)(ii) will be less than three months. Accordingly, the later of the two dates will be three months from the date of service of the notice, under section 14(4)(b)(i), (4A) and (4C). Therefore, the date to be specified in the notice of proceedings, for the purposes of section 14(4)(b), will be no later than three months after the date of service.

should be required to make other accommodation available to the tenant; ground 8 – antisocial behaviour, other suitable accommodation to be provided to the tenant.

54 Ground 1 – rent lawfully due from the tenant has not been paid, or any other obligation of the tenancy has been broken. This is, by far, the most commonly used ground in sch 2.

55 Grounds 3 and 4 – deterioration of the condition of the house, or of furniture provided for use under the tenancy, due to conduct of tenant or person residing or lodging with him.

56 Grounds 9–15 (along with ground 8) are the various "management" grounds, under which an order cannot be granted unless other suitable accommodation is to be provided to the tenant. These include: overcrowding (ground 9) and demolition or major works (ground 10).

57 The common law rule is forty days, but this does not apply to leases of less than four months' duration: s 5 of the Removal Terms (Scotland) Act 1886. As indicated in the main text, the vast majority of Scottish secure tenancies have a duration of a month or less. Where the duration of the lease is longer than four months, the common law period would apply, in the absence of express stipulation.

58 In cases where more than one ground is stated in the notice, the three-month period under s 14(4C) applies only if the grounds include 2, 5, 6, 7 or 8.

59 Usually the duration is one week or two weeks.

Where the sole ground, or one of the grounds, stated in the notice is ground 1, 3 or 4 or one of grounds 9–15, the six-month period under section 14(4D) will apply, and the date to be specified in the notice of proceedings, for the purposes of section 14(4)(b), will be no later than six months after the date of service.

Notice of proceedings under section 36 (SSSTs)

Paragraph 7(3) of schedule 1 amends section 36 of the 2001 Act, such that the relevant parts of it now read:

> "**Recovery of possession**
>
> **36.** (1) The landlord under a short Scottish secure tenancy may raise proceedings by way of summary cause for recovery of possession of the house which is the subject of the tenancy.
>
> (2) Such proceedings may not be raised unless—
>
> (a) the landlord has served on the tenant a notice complying with subsection (3),
>
> . . .
>
> (3) A notice under subsection (2) must be in such form as the Scottish Ministers may prescribe by regulations, and must—
>
> . . .
>
> (b) specify a date, not earlier than—
>
> ~~(i) 2 months, or such longer period as the tenancy agreement may provide, from the date of service of the notice, or~~
>
> *(i) the date calculated in accordance with subsection (3A), or such longer period from the date of service of the notice as the tenancy agreement may provide, or*
>
> (ii) the date on which the tenancy could have been brought to an end by a notice to quit had it not been a short Scottish secure tenancy,
>
> whichever is later, on or after which the landlord may raise proceedings for recovery of possession.
>
> *(3A) For the purpose of subsection (3)(b)(i), the date is the date falling—*
>
> *(a) 2 months from the date of service of the notice if subsection (3B) applies,*
>
> *(b) 6 months from the date of service of the notice if subsection (3C) applies.*
>
> *(3B) This subsection applies if the tenancy is a short Scottish secure tenancy by virtue of section 35 or paragraph 1, 2 or 2A of schedule 6.*
>
> *(3C) This subsection applies if the tenancy is a short Scottish secure tenancy by virtue of any of paragraphs 3 to 7A of schedule 6.*
>
> . . .
>
> (8) In relation to the recovery of possession of the house which is the subject of a short Scottish secure tenancy, section 14(4) is to be read as if for paragraph (b) there were substituted—
>
> ~~"(b) a date, not earlier than 4 weeks from the date of service of the notice on or after which the landlord may raise proceedings for recovery of possession,".~~
>
> *'(b) a date, not earlier than the date calculated in accordance with subsection (4A), on or after which the landlord may raise proceedings for recovery of possession,'.*"

In order to understand the effect of the amendments to section 36(3), it is necessary to appreciate that the statutory scheme under sections 34–37 of the Act (as amended by the Housing (Scotland) Act 2014) creates two different categories of SSST.

In the first category are: new tenancies created under section 34 because paragraph 1, 2 or 2A of schedule 6 to the 2001 Act applies; and tenancies that have been converted from Scottish secure tenancies, under section 35. This type of tenancy arises because of previous antisocial behaviour on the part of the tenant, or someone associated with him. In the second category are SSSTs created under section 34 because paragraph 3, 4, 5, 6, 7 or 7A of schedule 6 applies. Broadly speaking, those paragraphs describe various circumstances in which it is considered appropriate for a social landlord to offer a tenancy in which the tenant does not have security of tenure. In the text that follows, these two categories are referred to as "ASB SSSTs" and "non-ASB SSSTs".

As regards ASB SSSTs, the amendment makes no difference to the existing position because, under the new subsections (3A)(a) and (3B), the date under section 36(3)(b)(i) will still be two months from the date of service of the notice, or such longer period as the tenancy agreement provides.

For non-ASB SSSTs, the date to be stated in the notice should be no earlier than: six months from the date of service; or the next ish date of the tenancy, if that is later than six months from the date of service.

Section 36(8)

Section 36(7) of the 2001 Act preserves the right of the landlord of a short Scottish secure tenancy to seek an eviction order as it would against a Scottish secure tenant, under sections 14 and 16, rather than section 36.[60] The existing section 36(8) simplifies the rule in section 14(4)(b) by removing one of the two alternatives in that provision, where the landlord of an SSST wishes to proceed under sections 14 and 16.[61] As amended by the 2020 Act,[62] this is still the case, but section 36(8) is amended to reflect the changes made to section 14(4)(b). Now, where the tenancy is an SSST, the date to be stated in the notice of proceedings is not earlier than the date calculated in accordance with subsection 14(4A). If the ground for the eviction proceedings is further antisocial behaviour by the tenant (ground 7 or 8 in schedule 2 to the 2001 Act), the notice period will be three months, under section 14(4C).

Paragraph 9(3) – consequential modification of prescribed form notice of section 36 proceedings

The prescribed form for the notice of proceedings is found in the Short Scottish Secure Tenancies (Proceedings for Possession) Regulations 2018.[63]

60 This would be done where the landlord wishes to recover possession during the term of the tenancy. Note that, because of the amendments made by the 2014 Act, ASB SSSTs now have a fixed term of twelve months, which may be extended to eighteen months under s 35A. Where, for example, antisocial behaviour occurs shortly after the SSST commences, the landlord has the option of raising proceedings under ss 14 and 16, rather than waiting till the end of the fixed term and raising proceedings under s 36. See the Government's "Short Scottish Secure Tenancies for Antisocial Behaviour and Other Miscellaneous Changes to Short Scottish Secure Tenancies – Statutory Guidance for Social Landlords", pt 13.

61 Under the existing s 36(8), it is not necessary to hypothesise the date on which the tenancy could be ended by a notice to quit. The tenant is simply given a minimum four weeks' notice. This means that s 36(8) effectively deletes s 14(4)(b)(ii) where the tenancy is an SSST.

62 Schedule 1 para 7(3)(c).

63 SSI 2018/155.

Paragraph 9(3) sets out a single amendment to note 3 to the tenant in the schedule 2 form, which reflects the changes to section 36(3) already described. There is no change to the prescribed forms for notices of proceedings under section 14.

Paragraph 8 – power to modify notice periods

Under this provision, the Scottish Ministers have the power to modify a reference to any period of time specified in any of paragraphs 2, 4, 6 and 7, and to modify how grounds for possession (however described) are grouped in any of paragraphs 2, 4, 6 and 7 for the purpose of determining which notice period applies.[64] They also have the power to make any consequential modifications to paragraph 9, in order that the relevant statutory forms are also amended.[65] However, those powers may not be exercised so as to result in a period of time being specified that is in excess of six months.[66]

Paragraph 9 – consequential modifications in prescribed forms

The various provisions in paragraph 9 have already been summarised.

ERRORS IN NOTICES

Paragraph 10 – errors in notices

Paragraph 10 applies to the various notices that are affected by paragraphs 2, 4, 6, 7 and 9 of schedule 1.[67]

It provides:

> "**10. Errors in notices**
> (1) Where a notice to which this paragraph applies is completed without taking proper account of paragraphs 1 to 9—
> (a) the notice is not invalid by reason of that error, but
> (b) it may not be relied upon by the landlord for the purpose of seeking an order for possession (however described) until the date on which it could have been relied upon had it been correctly completed."

This is a welcome provision, which ameliorates the effect of schedule 1 in increasing complexity in the calculation of notice periods, and in the completion of the prescribed forms for notices.

Where the notice erroneously states a date that is wrong, given the 2020 Act amendments, the court or tribunal is required, in effect, to substitute the correct date in the notice, and then check whether the action/application has been competently made, if the notice is so read. This point may be illustrated by an example.

Let us say that the landlord of a Scottish secure tenancy serves a notice on the tenant, under section 14 of the Act, on 20 May 2020. The ground for

64 Schedule 1 para 8(1)(a) and (b).
65 ibid para 8(1)(c).
66 ibid para 8(2).
67 ibid para 10(3).

eviction specified in the notice is rent arrears. The date erroneously specified in the notice, for the purposes of section 14(4)(b) of the 2001 Act, is 30 June 2020. It ought to be 20 November 2020.[68] That error does not invalidate the notice, and will not be a problem for the landlord, as long as it raises proceedings on or after 20 November. Proceedings raised before that date will, however, be incompetent.

Paragraph 10(2) of schedule 1 states:

> "(2) Where sub-paragraph (1) applies, the period for which the notice remains in force for the purpose of seeking an order for possession (however described) is to be calculated by reference to the period which would have applied had the notice been correctly completed."

Thus, in the example given, the effective life of the notice will be six months from 20 November 2020, and not six months from the date erroneously stated in the notice.

Paragraph 10 will not assist in rescuing a statutory notice that has some other type of deficiency, such as a failure to specify the ground for eviction. In that case, the usual principles apply.

Adrian Stalker, Advocate
Legal Member of the First-tier Tribunal
(Housing and Property Chamber)
8 April 2020

68 Under the amended s 14(4)(b)(i), (4A) and (4D). See the discussion of para 7 of sch 1 above.

Index

EU Authorised Representative:
Easy Access System Europe Mustamäe tee 50, 10621 Tallinn, Estonia
gpsr.requests@easproject.com

Printed and bound by CPI Group (UK) Ltd, Croydon, CR0 4YY
12/05/2026
02109462-0001